Conservative Christian Beliefs AND Sexual Orientation IN Social Work

Conservative Christian Beliefs and Sexual Orientation in Social Work

Privilege, Oppression, and the Pursuit of Human Rights

Adrienne B. Dessel
Rebecca M. Bolen
EDITORS

Alexandria, Virginia

Library of Congress Cataloging-in-Publication Data

Conservative Christian beliefs and sexual orientation in social work : privilege, oppression, and the pursuit of human rights / Adrienne B. Dessel, Rebecca M. Bolen, editors.

pages cm

Includes bibliographical references and index.

ISBN 978-0-87293-149-7 (alk. paper)

1. Social work education. 2. Social service—Religious aspects—Christianity. 3. Social work—Practice. 4. Social workers—Attitudes. 5. Gay social workers. 6. Social work with sexual minorities. I. Dessel, Adrienne B., 1963– II. Bolen, Rebecca Morris.

HV11.C71834 2014
361.3—dc23

2014017884

Printed in the United States of America on acid-free paper that meets the American National Standards Institute Z39-48 standard.

Council on Social Work Education
1701 Duke Street, Suite 200
Alexandria, VA 22314-3457
www.cswe.org

Contents

SECTION II
Biblical, Methodological, Legal, and Ethical Analyses

SECTION III
Transformation

SECTION IV
Interventions and Approaches to Resolving the Tensions

Dedications

I would like to dedicate this book to Dr. Donna Wright, who was the assistant superintendent of the Knox County, Tennessee, school district in 2007 and who, in a religiously conservative Christian climate, granted me her full support and permission to speak to more than 1,000 teachers in her school district about LGBTQ issues. I also dedicate this book to my children, who should always be free to love who they love, and to the Knoxville women in my life.

ADRIENNE DESSEL

I wish to dedicate this book, with all my love, to my siblings, Melani, Eric, Mike, and Jeff. They are among the most impressive and inspiring people I have ever known.

REBECCA BOLEN

Acknowledgments

This book would not have been possible without the help of many people. First we have the authors of these chapters to thank. We were honored and humbled to work with our authors. The authors in the book represent LGB and heterosexual people, as well as conservative Christians, other Christians, and non-Christians. Several authors developed empirical studies, completed them, analyzed them, and wrote their chapters around their findings. We know that others had to spend large amounts of time researching information for their chapters. By publishing in this book, with its very controversial subject, all authors understood that what they wrote might hurt their professional reputations. Certain authors risked more than others. We deeply appreciate and acknowledge the risks these authors took. We especially want to recognize Dr. Ski Hunter for her contributions to the field over many years. We are also grateful to CSWE Press for inviting us to expand our work to include other perspectives and have a fuller and more complex conversation. Particular thanks goes to Elizabeth Simon at CSWE Press for her guidance and advice along the way. We also want to thank all the reviewers of the chapters for their time and excellent feedback.

Adrienne to Becky: This book would not have been possible without our partnership, and for that I thank Becky Bolen for her initial assignments, which educated me and sparked my thinking, and for her willingness to join with me in this significant, time-consuming, risky, and emotional endeavor. Her excellent editing and conceptual skills have been invaluable, as has her sense of humor. I greatly admire her quantitative mind, and am so appreciative of the thoughtfulness with which she has approached this project, often balancing out my activist tendencies. I am so grateful for her many years of mentorship and for her resolve to stick with me on my very personal as well as professional journey.

Becky to Adrienne: I thank Adrienne Dessel for her heroic efforts on this book. It was primarily because of her knowledge of other professionals that we had such a range of perspectives presented in this book. Furthermore, it was only because of her tenacity that this book was published in a timely manner. Mostly, though, I want to acknowledge Adrienne's deep, passionate, and compassionate sense of social justice that challenges her continuously to work toward human rights for all people. When she learned of this tension between certain conservative Christian beliefs and LGB people in social work, she was driven to understand it better and then to do something about it. I have been lucky to hitch a ride with her ever since.

Preface

Social Work's Uneasy Tension

Social work has a strong historical relationship with religion, and Christianity in particular has undergirded some of the profession's work (Cnaan, Boddie, & Danzig, 2005; Graham & Shier, 2009; Karger & Stoesz, 1998; Magnuson, 1977). Social work practice with lesbian, gay, and bisexual (LGB) people has been less central, falling under the rubric of cultural competence with sexual minorities and social justice education (Hong & Hodge, 2009; van den Bergh & Crisp, 2004). Social work is a profession that avows values in its Code of Ethics. However, the field is at a crossroads with regard to the values of freedom of religious expression and full affirmation of all sexual orientations. At a macro level, religion is a federally protected status, whereas sexual orientation is not. The current political and legal landscape is fraught with conflict around the protection of religious liberty and of human rights for LGB people. At a micro level, faculty and practitioners are challenged as they strive to create safe and welcoming learning environments for all their students and provide services to their clients that support the profession's ethics. This is a critical time for new, innovative thinking and action around these tensions.

For purposes of this book we define conservative Christian beliefs as those reflecting the biblically literalist belief systems of certain Protestant churches, such as many fundamentalist, evangelical, and charismatic churches (Linneman, 2004, p. 61), as well as those that derive from the principle of natural order or law to define moral law, such as that found in the Catholic church (*Catechism,* 1954, 1955).* At the intersection of conservative Christian religious identity and LGB identity in social work, much work remains to be done. Serious accusations that the profession prohibits freedom of speech and promotes ideologies contrary to some Christian moral views have been made (Stoesz & Karger, 2009; Will, 2007), and some conservative Christian social workers are concerned that voicing their views may affect their standing in social work programs (Hodge, 2002; "Missouri School Sued," 2006). Accredited Christian-based schools of social work that exclude gay and lesbian faculty and students have received less media attention (Beless, 2001; Parr & Jones, 1997; Towns, 2006). Absent from much of the literature surrounding this tension is a critical analysis of privilege, power differentials, and human rights issues (Reichert, 2003; Todd, 2010; Todd & Coholic, 2007), as well as "constructive dialogue for mutual understanding" (Canda & Furman, 1999, p. 113).

Social work educational settings have been challenged as being hostile toward students who hold certain conservative Christian beliefs (Hodge, 2002, 2005). Some conservative Christian faculty and students claim discrimination and oppression in social work. They feel silenced and are concerned that if they express their opinions, they will open themselves to criticism and even discriminatory actions (Hodge, 2002). In 2005, Emily Brooker, a BSW student at Missouri State University, refused to participate in a class assignment advocating for gay and lesbian adoption and was later called before the social work ethics board ("Missouri School Sued," 2006). The Alliance Defending Freedom (formerly the Alliance Defense Fund), a Christian legal group, filed a lawsuit on her behalf against the school, cleared her name of ethics concerns, and won damages (Office of University Communications, 2006). Recently, Michigan's House Bill 5040 (the Julea Ward Freedom of Conscience Act) was passed, and Michigan's Senate Bill 518 was proposed to allow social work students to refuse to counsel any client based on "a sincerely held religious belief or moral conviction" (SB 514, 2013) of that student (Dial, 2011; Heflin, 2012; Pines, 2011). These bills were proposed in direct response to a coun-

* The principles of the Catholic church are contained within *The Catechism of the Catholic Church.* The numbers contained within the citation are the paragraphs within the *Catechism* that contain the cited information.

seling student being dismissed from her Eastern Michigan University program because of her refusal to serve LGB clients. The Michigan Psychological Association deemed these bills to be threats to academic freedom, accreditation standards, ethics, and social justice (Kovach, 2011). This bill was not voted on by the full Senate, and did not become law (Senate Bill 0518, 2011).

Christianity is the majority religious perspective in U.S. society (Pew Forum on Religion and Public Life, 2008), thus representing a privileged status. In 2008, 78.4% of U.S. adults affiliated with evangelical Protestant churches, mainline Protestant churches, the Catholic Church, or historically Black churches. Of these groups, evangelical Protestant churches had the greatest membership, representing 26.3% of the American population. This Christian privilege is seldom a part of the discourse in social work, but it is important to examine in the context of social power (Blumenfeld & Jaekel, 2012; Blumenfeld, Joshi, & Fairchild, 2009; Todd, 2010). Case, McMullen, and Hentges (2013) provide important pedagogical tools to help students examine Christian privilege. Some conservative Christians may feel silenced, but it is important to remember that theirs is the predominant rhetoric in society. Whereas some conservative Christian social workers and faculty in the United States are concerned about support for their religious liberties (Ressler & Hodge, 2003), LGB people are concerned about their physical safety, legal equality, and human rights (Dorais, 2004; Elliot & Bonauto, 2005; Harris Interactive and GLSEN, 2005; van Wormer, Wells, & Boes, 2000).

Research has found that social workers who profess a more conservative Christian affiliation or Christian religiosity have more negative attitudes toward lesbians and gay men than social workers with less conservative Christian affiliations, other religious affiliations, or no religious affiliations (Berkman & Zinberg, 1997; Crisp, 2007; Krieglstein, 2003; Newman, Dannenfelser, & Benishek, 2002; Raiz & Saltzburg, 2007; Ryan, 2000). Crisp (2007) found that Catholic and Protestant social workers had more negative attitudes toward lesbians and gay men than those with no affiliation. In another study, Christian social workers had more negative views than non-Christian social workers (Ryan, 2000). Other researchers have determined that greater religiosity (Berkman & Zinberg, 1997; Kreigelstein, 2003), biblical teachings

(Raiz & Saltzburg, 2007), and religious attendance and traditional religious beliefs (Swank & Raiz, 2007, 2010) are related to more negative attitudes of social workers toward lesbians and gay men. Furthermore, one accredited Catholic university social work program includes "homosexuality" in a course on deviant behavior that covers murder, rape, robbery, prostitution, mental illness, and drug use (Brady, 2012). Social work students and faculty have probably been exposed to, and some mirror, the heterosexism, homophobia, and sexual prejudice found in the wider society (Brown & Henriquez, 2008; Hunter, 2010). Although it is a violation of the Code of Ethics to discriminate based on religion or sexual orientation (Kawakami, Young, & Dovidio, 2002; National Association of Social Workers [NASW], 2008), some religious Christian practitioners struggle with this ethic (Hunter, 2010).

Social work institutions, such as NASW and the Council on Social Work Education (CSWE), and policy makers are working diligently to resolve these tensions. A closer exploration of the nature of oppression and an analysis of privilege and power are needed. Some social work faculty view the profession as an open society (Henrickson, 2009; Jimenez, 2006) and express an inherent conflict between certain religious and social work values (Stewart, 2009). Hunter (2010) goes so far as to say social workers should be required to sign an agreement to refrain from discrimination based on sexual orientation. Otherwise, she suggests, the field is colluding in perpetuating heterosexism. A more in-depth and critical discussion of this conflict between religious freedom of expression concerning certain Christian beliefs and LGB orientations from a variety of perspectives is necessary. One purpose of this book is to present different perspectives of these conflicts.

For example, implicating certain conservative Christian religions in the oppression of LGB people must be problematized. Although LGB identity is highly stigmatized in some Latino and Black church communities (Griffin, 2000; Sherkat, de Vries, & Creek, 2010), there are also examples of welcoming Christian communities for sexual minority people (García, Stanley, & Ramirez-Valles, 2008; McQueeney, 2009). The same is true of predominantly Caucasian churches (Levy, 2014; McQueeney, 2009). Some Christian-based social work schools explicitly express nondiscrimination toward sexual minority people (Trinity Christian College, 2011). These and other Christian social work educators and practitioners seek to understand how to integrate their faith with their professional practice (Brandsen & Hugen, 2007; Brice, this book; Chamiec-Case, 2007; Drumm et al., this book) and promote social justice (Donaldson & Belanger, 2012).

There is also wide variation in how Christian social work students interpret their denominational teachings about same-sex sexuality (Woodford, Levy, & Walls, 2013). Woodford, Walls, and Levy (2012) found that syncretism, that is, an individual's endorsement of church teachings, predicts only a small portion of the variance in attitudes about same-sex marriage among social work students, suggesting that students who identify with antigay churches may or may not support same-sex marriage rights. Furthermore, greater right-wing authoritarianism and social dominance orientation, but lower sexual identity development, are related to greater prejudice against lesbians and gay men, whereas religiosity had mixed findings with regard to prejudice against lesbians and gay men, perhaps because of the method of conceptualizing and measuring this construct (Sibley, Robertson, & Wilson, 2006; Worthington, Dillon, & Becker-Schutte, 2005). Frequency of church attendance, a proxy for corresponding social isolation from people with other views, also contributed to sexual orientation prejudice in a study by Wright (2013). Thus, understanding the role of Christian religious beliefs in the oppression of LGB people in society and in social work is more complex than it might appear.

Context of Conservative Christianity in the 20th Century

A certain amount of more recent religious history helps put the intersection of conservative Christian beliefs and sexual orientation prejudice into context. Denominationalism had a "fundamental position . . . in shaping American society and culture" (Swatos, 1981, p. 219). Different Protestant denominations have their own belief systems and administrative bodies (Levy, this book), with parishioners sharing more or less of their denominations' beliefs (Woodford et al., 2012). Denominations range from more conservative to more liberal theological beliefs. Liberal churches are most likely to thrive in states in which most churchgoers are theologically most conservative, such that liberal churches become the midpoint between theologically conservative and secular views (Evans, 2003). Many people choose the church in which they worship because it was the church or denomination of their parents (Caplow, Hicks, & Wattenberg, 2000), although this trend is decreasing (Smith, 2005).

The denomination and church to which one belongs may not only reflect but also affect parishioners' belief systems. To the extent that churches and their denominations affect parishioners' belief systems, the placement of those churches on the continuum from conservative to liberal may have a great effect not only on the parishioners' theological views but also on their political views (Malka, Lelkes, Srivastava, Cohen, & Miller, 2012). In turn, parishioners who belong to Christian churches and denominations on the more conservative end of the continuum are more likely to entertain homophobic beliefs and prejudice toward LGB people (Altemeyer & Hunsberger, 1992; Rowatt et al., 2006).

At the turn of the 20th century, there were already 186 Christian denominations in the United States, increasing to 256 in 1936 (Caplow et al., 2000). Even though Protestant denominations had already proliferated by the 1900s, one of the most difficult issues the churches faced in this era was their attachment to science, for example, how they resolved the different perspectives of Darwin's evolutionary theory and the biblical understanding of the creation of the world (Noll, 2003). With this and other differences between science and theology becoming apparent, Protestant theologies came to be categorized along a continuum from fundamentalism to modernism. Modernists believed God worked within human societies and that the "evolving shape of modern life" was "the realization of God's work in the world" (Noll, 2003, p. 374).

Fundamentalist Movement

Conversely, a breakaway group of Methodists had a heightened concern for the doctrines of the Bible and the practice of holiness. One of the beliefs of this breakaway group was dispensationalism, which stressed biblical prophesy not yet fulfilled, including the belief that secularism and liberalism were signs that society had failed to meet God's tests and that Armageddon, a final battle to be waged on Earth, was near and Christ's return was imminent (Kee, Albu, Lindberg, Frost, & Robert, 1998; Noll, 2003). Perhaps the more influential event in the early 20th century for the new fundamentalist movement was the publication of the 12-volume study *The Fundamentals* (Torrey, 2009), which spelled out belief systems of Christian orthodoxy of the time, including biblical inerrancy (i.e., the original biblical manuscripts are without error) (Noll, 2003). Other beliefs of this movement included the biblical manuscripts as literal (e.g., the creation of the world in 6 days), the virgin birth of Jesus of Nazareth, the crucifixion and death of Jesus as atonement for the sins of others, the resurrection of Jesus, and the battle of Armageddon to herald the return of Christ (Nelkin, 2000; Noll, 2003; Torrey, 2009). As certain denominations began to align with these beliefs, the fundamentalist movement became more active, and by the 1970s the movement had taken full root (Emerson & Hartman, 2006). Perkin (2000) describes fundamentalism as the

> conviction that the adherents have a special knowledge of and relationship to a Diety, based either on a sacred and unquestionable text or direct contact with and experience of God's message. This allows or even enjoins imposing what they take to be God's will upon other people and, if necessary . . . it therefore overrides any appeal to a secular authority, notably to the will of the majority. (p. 79)

Fundamentalist churches are most prevalent in the southern United States (Armstrong, 2000; Shibley, 1991). Fundamentalism is strongly opposed to incorporating modernity into its belief systems (Prandi, 2000). For example, fundamentalists argue that creationism should be taught in science classes (Nelkin, 2000). Not surprisingly, fundamentalist believers also align conservatively on other issues, including gender and family roles, childrearing styles, and sexual orientation (Emerson & Hartman, 2006). The growth of fundamentalism in the second half of the 20th century occurred in part because of these and other social issues that came to the fore in the 1960s (Emerson & Hartman, 2006). The New Christian Right and Moral Majority movements align most closely with fundamentalist views, as does Jerry Falwell (Harding, 2000). Perhaps the hymn that best represents this movement is "Onward Christian Soldiers," by

Baring-Gould, the first verse of which is, "Onward Christian soldiers, marching as to war, with the cross of Jesus going on before. Christ, the royal Master, leads against the foe; forward into battle see his banners go" (Baring-Gould, 1865). One interesting outgrowth of the fundamentalist movement is the exploitation of mass media through televangelism, although other Christian movements took advantage of it, too (Harding, 2000).

Evangelical Movement

The evangelical belief system is not unlike that of the fundamentalist movement, especially the belief that Jesus, as the Son of God, atoned for human sins through his death and resurrection. Those who hold this belief may seek salvation from their sins and rebirth (i.e., being born again) (Hacket & Lindsay, 2008), and most believe that by being reborn, they will have eternal life (Emerson & Smith, 2000). Also associated with the evangelical movement is the belief in the literal interpretation of the Bible, political and social activism, and the active expression and sharing of the gospel (Elisha, 2011; Smith, 2002), most frequently called evangelism or proselytization. Indeed, the word *evangelism* means "sharing the Christian gospel." The desire of evangelical churches to proselytize to nonbelievers has at least two functions. It is seen as a path to spiritual salvation and eternal life for nonbelievers. It is also a method of continuing to build the church by amassing members (Baber, 2000; Hunter, 1983; Langone, 1985). Evangelical denominations and churches can be considered a midpoint between the conservativeness of the fundamentalist movement and the greater liberalness of some mainline denominations. Billy Graham is a well-known evangelical minister (Emerson & Smith, 2000). Another well-known evangelical is James Dobson (Smith, 2002).

Currently, many evangelicals prefer to distance themselves from the more defensive and militant style of fundamentalists (Smith, 2002). The evangelical movement is "like a kaleidoscope" (Marsden, 1991) represented by many traditions, although evangelical churches tend to coalesce around two beliefs: The only source of authority in religion is the Bible, and salvation can come only through faith in Jesus Christ and the Holy Spirit. Many believe the rise in evangelical churches and their increased attendance has been at the expense of mainline denominations, and a sophisticated analysis found that conservative churches have grown primarily because of their higher fertility rate as well as their decreased switching to mainline denominations (Hout, Greeley, & Wilde, 2001). Shibley (1991) refers to the growth of evangelical Protestantism as the "southernization of American religion" (p. 159), suggesting that the more conservative theology of the South has influenced mainstream American churches, in part through outmigration from the South (Berry, 2000).

More recently, evangelicals have inserted themselves into public discussions of social issues, promoting a "narrow set of moral and cultural issues" (Raschke, 2009, p. 147). Raschke further suggests that

> the "evangelical" strain in American politics is the historical key to our long legacy of democratic idealism. . . . The very idea of America itself is founded on the conviction of a higher, transcendent purpose reflected in a shared set of freedoms and a common collective morality. The recent efforts to re-inscribe religious thoughts and value prescriptions within the sphere of political discourse represent a search for a new "moral commons" upon which our identity as a nation can be rebuilt. Because their Biblical faith is rooted in the assurance of a clear calling for certain Christians to play a special or an "exceptional" role in human history they can offer a distinctive perspective on how America's own unique role among the "nations" can be identified and articulated for future generations. (p. 147)

This perspective of exceptionalism of certain citizens, or religions for that matter, and even exceptionalism of certain citizens' or religions' perspectives appears to be anything but a founding principle of America, however. Instead, exceptionalism of certain citizens seems to counter the constitutional belief that all people are created equal. Furthermore, religious pluralism was one of the founding principles of America (Hutchinson, 2003). Golding (1985) also discusses as a myth an evangelical belief that the United States is a second promised land to be led by divine principles and a socially conservative agenda of protecting the traditional family, opposing abortion, and other related views. (Also see Davidson, 2005, for a critique of Manifest Destiny as it relates to religion.)

Charismatic Movement

Another religious movement of the latter half of the 20th century was the charismatic movement, which occurred as mainstream and other types of churches, including some evangelical and Catholic churches, adopted beliefs and methods of worship similar to those of the Pentecostals (Daniel, 2010; Grim, 2009). Pentecostal and charismatic churches believe that gifts of the Holy Spirit are available to believers through baptism in the Holy Spirit. Pentecostals believe that speaking in tongues is an important sign of this baptism within the Holy Spirit, whereas other charismatic parishioners typically believe that this baptism occurs when one is reborn, although they may have the experience of being filled with the Holy Spirit at other times as well (Menzies & Menzies, 2000). Charismatic parishioners also believe that miracles, prophecies, and healing may occur when one is reborn or is filled with the Holy Spirit (Robbins, 2004). Another difference between Pentecostal and charismatic churches is that Pentecostal churches have stronger beliefs in proselytizing and missionary work. The charismatic movement has had a greater impact in urban, rather than rural, environments. Pat Robertson and Oral Roberts are well-known charismatic evangelists (Burgess & Van Der Mass, 2002).

Growth of Nondenominational Christian Churches

A final trend in the latter half of the 20th century and into the 21st was the formation, proliferation, and extraordinary growth of large nondenominational churches (Thumma & Travis, 2007). Somtimes these churches were an outgrowth of divisions within Christian denominations; sometimes these rifts occurred because of the influence of the fundamentalist, evangelical, and charismatic religious movements (Chaves & Sutton, 2004). Some of the deepest divisions were seen in southern Baptist churches, although other denominations experienced these divisions as well (Worthen, 2014). As these movements gained strength, sects often emerged within larger denominations (Sutton & Chaves, 2004). These sects were often more conservative, representing fundamentalism, charismatic renewal, and neo-evangelicalism. These independent churches often become quite large, with thousands of parishioners and organizational structures much like those of other denominations (Smith, Scheitle, & Bader, 2012). Indeed, Watson and Scalen (2008) refer to this proliferation of nondenominational churches as the "McDonaldization" of churches because of their use of corporate business organizational models to consider social, religious, and economic goals (Lindsay, 2006).

Conservative Protestantism

Because of all of these conservative Christian movements—fundamentalism, evangelicalism, and charismatic renewal—certain more recent social and religious trends are noted: an increase in participation in nondenominational churches, a decrease in overall Protestant church attendance, movement from mainline Protestant churches to more conservative churches, and the use of more informal expressions of spirituality and "do-it-yourself" religiosity rather than organized religion (Greeley & Hout, 1998; Hillery, 1982; Smith, 2005, 2006; Swatos, 1981; Varga, 2002). Even in predominantly African American churches, attendance is decreasing in mainline churches along with increasing nonaffiliation of specific religious denominations. Indeed, like Caucasian Christian worshippers, African American worshippers have moved increasingly to more conservative sects, including fundamentalist churches (Sherkat, 2001; Sherkat, 2002; Varga, 2002) and churches that are more racially integrated (Marti, 2009).

The different conservative Christian movements may provide avenues for parishioners to endure an increasingly fragmented, rapidly changing, and relativistic universe (Wald & Colhoun-Brown, 2011). Varga (2002) argues that the increasing movement toward local, conservative churches is a defense against the greater globalization of the world and that there is now more "diffused religion" and "believing without belonging" religiosity, including greater individualization of religion. The explosion in televangelism and other religious media, the marked increase in people attending college, greater affluence in the last half of the 20th century, and the greater secularization of society are also said to be related to greater religious individualization (Stout, 2012).

Catholic Church

A final important religion to be discussed is Catholicism, as it shares certain belief systems with conservative Protestant churches and denominations, although the rationale for these beliefs differs. Whereas conservative Protestant churches tend to explain their more conservative beliefs as based in the inerrancy of the Bible (Noll, 2003), considered the invariant word of God, Catholicism is grounded in a belief in the natural order of the world that God gave humans at creation, or natural law (*Catechism*, 1954, 1955). Like the Protestant belief in the inerrancy of the Bible, however, natural law is considered "immutable, permanent throughout history" (*Catechism,* 1958). It is "the light of understanding placed in us by God; through it we know what we must do and what we must avoid" (*Catechism,* 1955). Thus, natural law "provides the solid foundation on which man can build the structure of moral rules to guide his choices" (*Catechism,* 1959). Natural law is seen as applicable to all people, not just Catholics; "since it is accessible to reason unaided by faith, it directs us all to commit to the goods that are fundamental to our shared human nature" (Campbell, 1997, par. 1).

Moral laws derive from the natural order and "presuppose the rational order, established among creatures for their good and to serve their final end" (*Catechism,* 1951). Therefore, these laws are considered to be similar for all, right for all, and known to all (Budziszewski, 1998). Catholicism believes that because God created humans to be rational beings "who can initiate and control [their] own actions" (*Catechism,* 1730), humans need these laws "to enlighten judgement [sic] and strengthen resolve" (Campbell, 1997, par. 7). Morally good acts "affirm and enlarge our human reality; to do evil is to act, or to fail to act in such a way as to deny and diminish it" (Campbell, 1997, par. 9). Therefore, these laws direct people "to act for, and never against, the goods we must participate in to effect our fulfillment" (Campbell, 1997, par. 9). These guidelines outline "concrete acts that it is always wrong to choose, because their choice entails a disorder of the will, i.e., a moral evil" (*Catechism,* 1761), such as murder and adultery (*Catechism,* 1756). Because of free will, "when we do evil, our conduct is active and direct: we intentionally assail what is good. Our will, in other words, is set against the good we violate" (Campbell, 1997, par. 11).

The *Catechism* discusses sexuality, including same-sex sexuality, stating that all men and women "acknowledge and accept [their] sexual identity, which is to be oriented toward the goods of marriage and the flourishing of family life" (*Catechism,* 2533), and "all human generations proceed from this union" (*Catechism,* 2535). "Sexuality . . . becomes personal and truly human when it is integrated into the relationship of one person to another, in the complete and lifelong mutual gift of a man and a woman" (*Catechism,* 2537). Yet sexual pleasure, when sought for itself, "is morally disordered, isolated from its procreative and unitive purposes" (*Catechism,* 2351). Other morally disordered violations mentioned in the *Catechism* are rape, adultery, fornication (between an unmarried man and woman), pornography, and prostitution (*Catechism,* 2353–2356). Furthermore, "homosexual acts are intrinsically disordered," as indicated in the "Sacred Scripture, which presents homosexual acts as acts of grave depravity" (*Catechism,* 2357) that are thus contrary to natural law. These sexual acts "do not proceed from a genuine affective and sexual complementarity. Under no circumstances can they be approved" (*Catechism,* 2357).

Catholic religious tenets state, "The number of men and women who have deep-seated homosexual tendencies is not negligible. This inclination, which is objectively disordered, constitutes for most of them a trial. They must be accepted with respect, compassion, and sensitivity. Every sign of unjust discrimination in their regard should be avoided" (*Catechism,* 2358). These "persons are called to chastity. By the virtues of self-mastery that teach them inner freedom, at times by the support of disinterested friendship, by prayer and sacramental grace, they can and should gradually and resolutely approach Christian perfection" (*Catechism,* 2359).

Conservative Christian Beliefs

The profound changes in Christianity over the last generation bring certain challenges to the writing of this book. Even though 26% of all U.S. citizens call themselves evangelical (Pew Forum on Religion and Public Life, 2008), they have no central governing body. Therefore, it is problematic to discuss the evangelical Christian institution because so many of these churches belong to no specific denomination. It is also difficult to generalize about evangelical

Christians and other conservative (fundamentalist or charismatic) Christians because, although they may choose to worship at a nondenominational church and share some Christian belief systems considered more conservative, belief systems of evangelical and conservative Christian parishioners may vary from those of the church to which they belong and may also vary from church to church (Smith, 2000). For example, conservative Christians may differentiate their religious views from their attitudes about LGB civil rights (Andersson, Vanderbeck, Sadgrove, Valentine, & Ward, 2013; Linneman, 2004). To avoid the unintentional stereotyping or generalizing that would occur if we were to talk about evangelical, fundamentalist, charismatic, Catholic, or conservative Christians, we have chosen to discuss a belief of the churches to which these Christians belong. To be more specific, our book is about certain negative attitudes shared by many, but not all, conservative Christians about LGB people, centered around the belief that same-sex sexuality is in violation of God's law, as they believe it is described in the Old and New Testaments of the Bible, as well as in the natural order of nature (*Catechism*, 1954, 1955). Social workers who hold these belief systems, and especially students new to the profession, may find it difficult to reconcile their beliefs with certain values of the Code of Ethics (Hunter, 2010; Stewart, 2009).

This book seeks to delve into these areas of scripture, theory, and research in more detail to both understand and contribute to resolving the conflict in social work between conservative Christian beliefs and LGB people. It is our hope that this book provides greater information about this tension, guidance for those with this belief system to reconcile and maintain their strong Christian identity while also becoming practitioners for and advocates of LGB people, and tools for educators and other social workers to use in classes or in the community to resolve this tension.

This book grew out of an invitation by CSWE Press to expand on an article we published in the *Journal of Social Work Education* (JSWE; Dessel, Bolen, & Shepardson, 2011), which represents where we started this journey of critiquing the current state of the profession regarding these tensions. We collaborated to write the first set of articles, published in JSWE, because one of us was teaching a doctoral course that included discussions of various issues in social work, and the other of us was a student. One of the issues addressed in the course was the tension between conservative Christianity and LGB students in social work. Students in the doctoral course were asked to read a variety of articles on this tension and to critically analyze those articles, look for unstated assumptions, consider the validity of theories presented, and discuss the findings. Over the years, students always had many questions about the underlying assumptions and validity of many of the statements made in this literature. Out of the discussions in this class, the authors worked together to more closely analyze some of this literature and to write the articles published in JSWE.

We recognized that we were uncomfortable with the tension as it was framed in the social work literature at that time, and we believed that growth was needed from all perspectives. We start this book with the acknowledgment that we are expressing the tension. Then, in the chapters that follow, we present some of the movement that has been made that has stimulated us, and should encourage others, to move further along in our thinking. We reached out to numerous authors and practitioners to contribute to this book and are deeply grateful for the responses we received, the connections they have made, and their contributions to this book. We hope that as you read through this book, regardless of whether you are LGB or heterosexual, and regardless of your religious belief system, you can find the answers you seek about how to bridge this divide. This is the fundamental purpose of this book.

References

Altemeyer, B., & Hunsberger, B. (1992). Authoritarianism, religious fundamentalism, quest, and prejudice. *International Journal for the Psychology of Religion, 2*(2), 113–133. doi:10.1207/s15327582ijpr0202_5

Andersson, J., Vanderbeck, R., Sadgrove, J., Valentine, G., & Ward, K. (2013). Same sex marriage, civil rights rhetoric, and the ambivalent politics of Christian evangelicalism in New York City. *Sexualities, 16*(3–4), 245–260. doi:10.1177/1363460713481718

Armstrong, K. (2000). *The battle for God.* New York, NY: Ballantine Books.

Baber, H. E. (2000). In defence of proselytizing. *Religious Studies, 36*(3), 333–344.

Baring-Gould, S. (1865). "Onward Christian Soldiers." Retrieved from http://www.lds.org/music/library/hymns/onward-christian-soliders?lang=eng

Beless, D. (2001). Grappling with nondiscrimination and diversity. *Social Work Education Reporter, 49*(2), 3.

Berkman, C. S., & Zinberg, G. (1997). Homophobia and heterosexism in social workers. *Social Work, 42*(4), 319–332. doi:10.1093/sw/42.4.319

Berry, C. (2000). *Southern migrants: Northern exiles.* Chicago, IL: University of Illinois Press.

Blumenfeld, W., & Jaekel, K. (2012). Exploring levels of Christian privilege awareness among preservice teachers. *Journal of Social Issues, 68*(1), 128–144. doi:10.1111/j.1540-4560.2011.01740.x

Blumenfeld, W., Joshi, K., & Fairchild, E. (2009). *Investigating Christian privilege and religious oppression in the United States.* Boston, MA: Sense Publishers.

Brady, J. (2012). *College course lumps homosexuality, rape, murder.* Npr.org. Retrieved from http://www.npr.org/2012/09/10/160763549/college-course-lumps-homosexuality-rape-murder

Brandsen, C., & Hugen, B. (2007). Introduction to special issue: Social work through the lens of Christian faith: Working toward integration. *Social Work & Christianity, 34*(4), 349–355.

Brown, M., & Henriquez, E. (2008). Socio-demographic predictors of attitudes towards gays and lesbians. *Individual Differences Research, 6*(3), 193–202.

Budziszewski, J. (1998, June/July). The revenge of conscience. *First Things,* pp. 21–27. Retrieved from http://catholiceducation.org/articles/religion/re0009.html

Burgess, S. M., & van der Mass, E. M. (2002). *The new international dictionary of Pentecostal and Charismatic movements: Revised and Expanded Edition.* Grand Rapids, MI: Zondervan.

Campbell, J. (1997, September). Sex, natural law, and confusion in high places. *The Canadian Catholic Review,* pp. 16–22. Retrieved from http://catholiceducation.org/articles/sexuality/se0022.html

Canda, E. R., & Furman, L. D. (1999). *Spiritual diversity in social work practice.* New York, NY: The Free Press.

Caplow, C., Hicks, L., & Wattenberg, B. J. (2000). *The first measured century: An illustrated guide to trends in America, 1900–2000.* Washington, DC: AEI Press.

Case, K., McMullen, M., & Hentges, B. (2013). Teaching the taboo: Walking the tightrope of Christian privilege. In K. Case (Ed.), *Deconstructing privilege: Teaching and learning as allies in the classroom* (pp. 188–206). New York, NY: Routledge.

Catechism of the Catholic Church. (1993). Vatican City: Libreria Editrice Vaticana. Retrieved from http://www.vatican.va/archive/ENG0015/_INDEX .HTM#fonte

Chamiec-Case, R. (2007). Exploring the filtering role of Christian beliefs and values in the integration of Christian faith and social work practice. *Social Work & Christianity, 34*(4), 498–513.

Chaves, M., & Sutton, J. R. (2004). Organizational consolidation in American Protestant denominations, 1890–1990. *Journal for the Scientific Study of Religion, 43*(1), 51-66. Retrieved from doi:10.1111/j.1468-5906.2004 .00217.x

Cnaan, R., Boddie, S., & Danzig, R. (2005). Teaching about organized religion in social work. *Journal of Religion & Spirituality in Social Work: Social Thought, 24*(1), 93–110. doi:10.1300/J377v24n01_09

Crisp, C. (2007). Correlates of homophobia and use of gay affirmative practice among social workers. *Journal of Human Behavior in the Social Environment, 14*(4), 119–143. doi:10.1300/J137v14n04_06

Daniel, K. (2010). An assessment of the Catholic charismatic renewal towards peaceful co-existence in the Roman Catholic church. *International Journal of Sociology and Anthropology, 2*(8), 171–177.

Davidson, L. (2005). Christian Zionism as a representation of American manifest destiny. *Critique: Critical Middle Eastern Studies, 14*(2), 157-169.

Dessel, A., Bolen, R., & Shepardson, C. (2011). Can religion expression and sexual orientation affirmation coexist in social work? A critique of Hodge's theoretical, theological and conceptual frameworks. *Journal of Social Work Education, 47*(2), 213–234. doi:10.5175/JSWE.2011.200900074

Dial, K. (2011, October 11). Michigan seeks to protect counselors' rights. *Citizen Link.* Retrieved from http://www.citizenlink.com/2011/10/11/michigan-seeks -to-protect-counselors'-rights

Donaldson, L., & Belanger, K. (2012). Catholic social teaching: Principles for the service and justice dimensions of social work practice and education. *Social Work & Christianity, 39*(2), 119–127.

Dorais, M. (2004). *Dead boys can't dance: Sexual orientation, masculinity and suicide.* Montreal, QC: McGill–Queens University Press.

Elisha, O. (2011). *Moral ambition: Mobilization and social outreach in evangelical megachurches.* Berkeley, CA: University of California Press.

Elliot, R. D., & Bonauto, M. (2005). Sexual orientation and gender identity in North America: Legal trends, legal contrasts. *Journal of Homosexuality, 48*(3/4), 91–106. doi:10.1300/J082v48n03_06

Emerson, M. L., & Smith, C. (2000). *Divided by faith: Evangelical religion and the problem of race in America.* New York, NY: Oxford University Press.

Emerson, M. O., Hartman, D. (2006). The rise of religious fundamentalism. *Annual Review of Sociology, 32,* 127–144. doi:10.1146/annurev.soc.32.061604.123141

Evans, J. (2003). The creation of a distinct subcultural identity and denominational growth. *Journal for the Scientific Study of Religion, 42*(3), 467–477. doi:10.1111/1468-5906.00195

García, D. I., Stanley, J. G., & Ramirez-Valles, J. (2008). "The priest obviously doesn't know that I'm gay": The religious and spiritual journeys of Latino gay men. *Journal of Homosexuality, 55*(3), 411–436. doi:10.1080/00918360802345149

Golding, G. (1985). Evangelism: An American Protestant integrism? *Social Compass, 32*(4), 363–371. doi:10.1177/003776850320040 4

Graham, J., & Shier, M. (2009). Religion and social work: An analysis of faith traditions, themes, and global north/south authorship. *Journal of Religion & Spirituality in Social Work: Social Thought, 28*(1), 215–233. doi:10.1080/15426430802644263

Greeley, A., & Hout, M. (1998). Musical chairs: Patterns of denominational change. *Sociology and Social Research, 72*(2), 75–86.

Griffin, H. (2000). Their own received them not: African American lesbians and gays in Black churches. *Theology & Sexuality, 12,* 88–100. doi:10.1177/135583580000601206

Grim, B. (2009). Pentecostalism's growth in religiously restricted environments. *Society, 46*(6), 484–495. doi:10.1007/s12115-009-9265-y

Hackett, C., & Lindsay, D. M. (2008). *Measuring evangelicalism: Consequences of different operational strategies. Journal for the Scientific Study of Religion, 47*(3), 499–514. doi:10.1111/j.1468-5906.2008.00423.x

Harding, S. F. (2000). *The book of Jerry Fallwell: Fundamentalist language and politics.* Princeton, NJ: Princeton University Press.

Harris Interactive and GLSEN. (2005). *From teasing to torment: School climate in America, a survey of students and teachers.* Retrieved from http://www.glsen.org/cgibin/iowa/all/research/index.html

Heflin, C. (2012, June 14). House passes bill named for student kicked out of EMU program for refusing to counsel gay client. Retrieved from http://www.annarbor.com/news/ypsilanti/house-passes-bill-named-for-student-kicked-out-of-emu-for-refusing-to-counsel-gay-client/

Henrickson, M. (2009). Sexuality, religion, and authority: Toward reframing estrangement. *Journal of Religion & Spirituality in Social Work: Social Thought, 28*(1),48–62. doi:10.1080/15426430802643570

Hillery, G. (1982). Religion in the 1980's: A sociological view. *Quarterly Journal of Ideology, 6*(3), 1–12.

Hodge, D. (2002). Does social work oppress evangelical Christians? A "new class" analysis of society and social work. *Social Work, 47,* 401–414. doi:10.1093/sw/47.4.401

Hodge, D. (2005). Epistemological frameworks, homosexuality, and religion: How people of faith understand the intersection between homosexuality and religion. *Social Work, 50,* 207–218. doi:10.1093/sw/50.3.207

Hong, P., & Hodge, D. (2009). Understanding social justice in social work: A content analysis of course syllabi. *Families in Society: The Journal of Contemporary Human Services, 90*(2), 212–219. doi:10.1606/1044-3894.3874

Hout, M., Greeley, A., & Wilde, M. J. (2001). *The demographic imperative in religious change in the United States. American Journal of Sociology, 107*(2), 468-500. doi:10.1086/324189

Hunter, J. D. (1983). *American evangelicalism: Conservative religion and the quandary of modernity.* New Brunswick, NJ: Rutgers University Press.

Hunter, S. (2010). *Effects of conservative religion on lesbian and gay clients and practitioners: Practice implications*. Washington, DC: NASW Press.

Hutchinson, W. R. (2003). *Religious pluralism in America: The contentious history of a founding ideal.* New Haven, CT: Yale University Press.

Jimenez, J. (2006). Epistemological frameworks, homosexuality, and religion: A response to Hodge. *Social Work, 51,* 185–187. doi:10.1093/sw/51.2.185

Karger, H. J., & Stoesz, D. (1998). *American social welfare policy* (3rd ed.). New York, NY: Longman.

Kawakami, K., Young, H., & Dovidio, J. F. (2002). Automatic stereotyping: Category, trait and behavioral activations. *Personality and Social Psychology Bulletin, 28,* 3–15. Retrieved from http://dx.doiorg/10.1177/0146167202281001

Kee, H. C., Albu, E., Lindberg, C., Frost, J. W., & Robert, D. L. (1998). *Christianity: A social and cultural history.* Upper Saddle River, NJ: Prentice Hall.

Kovach, J. A. (2011). Senate Bill 518/HB. Conscience or unconscionable clause. A threat to academic freedom, accreditation standards, ethics, and social justice. *The Michigan Psychologist.* Retrieved from http://www.michiganpsychologicalassociation.org/docs/3rdQuarter2011.pdf

Krieglstein, M. (2003). Heterosexism and social work: An ethical issue. *Journal of Human Behavior in the Social Environment, 8*(2/3), 75–91. doi:10.1300/J137v08n02_05

Langone, M. D. (1985). Cults, evangelicals, and the ethics of social influence. *Cultic Studies Journal, 2*(2), 371–388.

Lindsay, D. M. (2006). Elite power: Social networks within American evangelicalism. *Sociology of Religion, 67*(3), 207–227. doi:10.1093/socrel/67.3.207

Linneman, T. (2004). Homophobia and hostility: Christian conservative reactions to the political and cultural progress of Lesbians and Gay men. *Sexuality Research & Social Policy, 1*(2), 56–76. doi:10.1525/srsp.2004.1.2.56

Magnuson, N. (1977). *Salvation in the slums: Evangelical social work 1865–1920.* Grand Rapids, MI: Baker Book House.

Malka, A., Lelkes, Y., Srivastava, S., Cohen, A., & Miller, D. (2012). The association of religiosity and political conservatism: The role of political engagement. *Political Psychology, 33*(2), 275–299. doi:10.1111/j.1467-9221.2012.00875.x

Marti, G. (2009). Affinity, identity, and transcendence: The experience of religious racial integration in diverse congregations. *Journal for the Scientific Study of Religion, 48*(1), 53–68. doi:10.1111/j.1468-5906.2009.01429.x

McQueeney, K. (2009). We are God's children, y'all: Race, gender, and sexuality in lesbian- and gay-affirming congregations. *Social Problems, 56*(1), 151–173. doi:10.1525/sp.2009.56.1.151

Menzies, W. W., & Menzies, R. P. (2000). *Spirit and power: Foundations of Pentecostal experience.* Grand Rapids, MI: Zandervan.

Missouri school sued by student who refused to support gay adoptions. (2006, November 2). *USA Today.* Retrieved from http://www.usatoday.com/news/nation/2006-11-02-gay-adoption_x.htm

NASW. (2008). *Code of ethics.* Retrieved from http://www.socialworkers.org/pubs/code/code.asp

Nelkin, D. (2000). *The creation controversy: Science or scripture in the schools* (2nd ed.). Lincoln, NE: W.W. Norton.

Newman, B., Dannenfelser, P., & Benishek, L. (2002). Assessing beginning social work and counseling students' acceptance of lesbian and gay men. *Journal of Social Work Education, 38,* 273–288.

Noll, M. A. (2003). *A history of Christianity in the United States and Canada.* Grand Rapids, MI: Wm. B. Eerdmans Publishing Co.

Office of University Communications. (2006, November 8). *Missouri State settles lawsuit with Emily Brooker.* Retrieved from http://search.gipoco.com/cached/41326/

Parr, R., & Jones, L. (1997). Point/counterpoint: Should CSWE allow social work programs in religious institutions an exemption from the accreditation nondiscrimination standard related to sexual orientation? *Journal of Social Work Education, 33*(3), 297–313.

Perkin, H. (2000). American fundamentalism and the selling of God. *The Political Quarterly, 71*(s1), 79-89. doi:10.1111/1467-923X.71.s1.8

Pew Forum on Religion and Public Life. (2008). *U.S. Religious Landscape Survey. Religious affiliation: Diverse and dynamic.* Retrieved from http://religions.pewforum.org/affiliations

Pines, J. (2011, November 14). Julea Ward Freedom of Conscience Act, like Michigan's amended antibullying bill, should not become law. Retrieved from http://www.mlive.com/opinion/kalamazoo/index.ssf/2011/11/julea_ward_freedom_of_conscien.html

Prandi, C. (2000). The reciprocal relationship of syncretism and fundamentalism from the early history of religion to modernity. *Research in the Social Scientific Study of Religion, 11,* 23–35.

Raiz, L., & Saltzburg, S. (2007). Developing awareness of the subtleties of heterosexism and homophobia among undergraduate, heterosexual social work majors. *The Journal of Baccalaureate Social Work, 12*(2), 53–69.

Raschke, C. (2009). Evangelicals in the public square. *Society, 46*(2), 147–154. doi:10.1007/s12115-008-9176-3

Reichert, E. (2003). *Social work and human rights.* New York, NY: Columbia University Press.

Ressler, L. E., & Hodge, D. R. (2003). Silenced voices: Social work and the oppression of conservative narratives. *Social Thought: Journal of Religion in the Social Services, 22*(1), 125–142.

Robbins, J. (2004). The globalization of Pentecostal and charismatic Christianity. *Annual Review of Anthropology, 33,* 117–143.

Rowatt, W., Tsang, J., Kelly, J., LaMartina, B., McCullers, M., & McKinley, A. (2006). Associations between religious personality dimensions and implicit homosexual prejudice. *Journal for the Scientific Study of Religion, 45*(3), 397–406. doi:10.1111/j.1468-5906.2006.00314.x

Ryan, S. (2000). Examining social workers' placement recommendations of children with gay and lesbian adoptive parents. *Families in Society, 81,* 517–528. doi:10.1606/1044-3894.1053

Senate Bill 0518. (2011). Michigan legislative website. Retrieved from http://www.legislature.mi.gov/(S(mesr2x55xijubl55olowzzrx))/mileg.aspx?page=GetObject&objectname=2011-SB-0518

Sherkat, D. (2001). Investigating the sect–church–sect cycle: Cohort-specific attendance differences across African-American denominations. *Journal for the Scientific Study of Religion, 40*(2), 221–233. doi:10.1111/0021-8294.00052

Sherkat, D. E. (2002). African-American religious affiliation in the late 20th century: Cohort variations and patterns of switching, 1973–1998. *Journal of the Scientific Study of Religion, 41*(3), 485–493. doi:10.1111/1468-5906.000132

Sherkat, D. E., de Vries, K. M., & Creek, S. (2010). Race, religion, and opposition to same-sex marriage. *Social Science Quarterly, 91*(1), 80–98. doi:10.1111/j.1540-6237.2010.00682.x

Shibley, M. (1991). The southernization of American religion: Testing a hypothesis. *Sociological Analysis, 52*(2), 159–174. doi:10.2307/3710961

Sibley, C., Robertson, A., & Wilson, M. (2006). Social dominance orientation and right-wing authoritarianism: Additive and interactive effects. *Political Psychology, 27*(5), 755–768. doi:10.1111/j.1467-9221.2006.00531.x

Smith, B., Scheitle, C. P., & Bader, C. (2012). The ties that bind: Network overlap among independent congregations. *Social Science Computer Review, 30*(3), 259–273. doi:10.1177/0894439311405810

Smith, C. (2002). *Christian America? What evangelicals really want.* Berkeley, CA: University of California Press.

Smith, T. (2005). The vanishing Protestant majority. *Journal for the Scientific Study of Religion, 44*(2), 211–223. doi:10.1111/j.1468-5906.2005.00277.x

Smith, T. (2006). *Religious change in a globalizing world.* Paper presented at the International Sociological Association, Durban, South Africa.

Stewart, C. (2009). The inevitable conflict between religious and social work values. *Journal of Religion & Spirituality in Social Work: Social Thought, 28*(1), 35–47. doi:10.1080/15426430802643315

Stoesz, D., & Karger, H. (2009). Reinventing social work accreditation. *Research on Social Work Practice, 19*(1), 104–111. doi:10.1177/1049731507313976.

Stout, D. A. (2012). *Media and religion: Foundations of an emerging field.* New York, NY: Routledge.

Sutton, J. R., & Chaves, M. (2004). Explaining schism in American Protestand denominations, 1890–1990. *Journal for the Scientific Study of Religion, 43*(2), 171–190. doi:10.1111/j.1468-5906.2004.00226.x

Swank, E., & Raiz, L. (2007). Explaining comfort with homosexuality among social work students: The impact of demographic, contextual, and attitudinal factors. *Journal of Social Work Education, 43*(2), 257–279. doi:10.5175/JSWE.2007.200500560

Swank, E., & Raiz, L. (2010). Attitudes toward gays and lesbians among undergraduate social work students. *Affilia: Journal of Women and Social Work, 25*(1), 19–29. doi:10.1177/0886109909356058

Swatos, W. H. Jr. (1981). Beyond denominationalism: Community and culture in American religion. *Journal for the Scientific Study of Religion, 20*(3), 217–227. doi:10.2307/1385544

Thumma, S., & Travis, D. (2007). *Beyong megachurch myths: What we can learn from America's largest churches*. San Francisco, CA: Jossey-Bass.

Todd, J. (2010). Confessions of a Christian supremacist. *Reflections, 16*(1), 140–146.

Todd, S., & Coholic, D. (2007). Christian fundamentalism and anti-oppressive social work pedagogy. *Journal of Teaching in Social Work, 27*(3/4), 5–25. doi:10.1300/J067v27n03_02

Torrey, E. A. (2009). *The fundamentals a testimony to the truth.* Retrieved January from http://www.webcitation.org/query?url=http://www.geocities.com/Athens/Parthenon/6528/fundcont.htm&date=2009-10-25+06:18:43

Towns, L. (2006). Ethics and oppression of GLBT citizens: CSWE and NASW involvement. *Journal of Progressive Human Services, 17*(1), 1–4. doi:10.1300/J059v17n01_01

Trinity Christian College. (2011). *Social work Trinity catalog.* Retrieved from http://tcc.trnty.edu/depts/PDF/Social_Work_Trinity_Catalog.pdf

van den Bergh, N., & Crisp, C. (2004). Defining culturally competent practice with sexual minorities: Implications for social work education and practice. *Journal of Social Work Education, 40*, 221–238.

van Wormer, K., Wells, J., & Boes, M. (2000). *Social work with lesbians, gays, and bisexuals: A strengths perspective.* Needham Heights, MA: Allyn and Bacon.

Varga, I. (July, 2002). *The postmodern condition, changes in religion and the classics of sociology of religion.* Paper presented at the International Sociological Association, XVth World Congress of Sociology, Brisbane, Australia.

Wald, K. D., & Calhoun-Brown, A. (2011). Religion and politics in the United States (6th ed.). Lanham, MD: Rowman & Littlefield.

Watson, J. B., & Scalen, W. H. (2008). "Dining with the devil": The unique secularization of American evangelical churches. *International Social Science Review, 83*(3–4), 171–180.

Will, G. (2007, October 14). Code of coercion. *Washington Post.* Retrieved from http://www.washingtonpost.com/wpdyn/content/article/2007/10/12/AR2007101202151.html

Woodford, M., Levy, D., & Walls, E. (2013). Sexual prejudice among Christian college students, denominational teachings, and personal religious beliefs. *Review of Religious Research, 55,* 105–130. doi:10.1007/s13644-012-0067-0

Woodford, M., Walls, E., & Levy, D. (2012). Religion and endorsement of same-sex marriage: The role of syncretism between denominational teachings about homosexuality and personal religious beliefs. *Interdisciplinary Journal of Research on Religion, 8*(4), 1–29.

Worthen, M. (2014). *Apostles of reason: The crisis of authority in American evangelicalism.* New York, NY: Oxford University Press.

Worthington, R., Dillon, F., & Becker-Schutte, A. (2005). Development, reliability, and validity of the lesbian, gay, and bisexual knowledge and attitudes scale for heterosexuals (LGB-KASH). *Journal of Counseling Psychology, 52*(1), 104–118. doi:10.1037/0022-0167.52.1.104

Wright, N. (2013). Attendance matters: Religion and ethical affirmation of gay and lesbian sexuality. *Review of Religious Research,* 1–29. Advance online publication. doi:10.1007/s13644-013-0143-0

Introduction

This edited volume seeks to explore the different facets of the debate in social work regarding freedom of expression of conservative Christian religious beliefs and full sexual orientation affirmation, to provide a deeper understanding of topics such as social identity oppression, power and privilege, human rights and social justice, attitudes and prejudice, ethics, policy, and the law. We frame the book around human rights because we believe that gay rights, gay marriage, and related popular terms are less about being lesbian, gay, or bisexual and more about human rights for people who happen to love, be attracted to, and share their lives with others who share their same sexual identity (Chan, 2010; Dworkin & Yi, 2003; Ellis, Kitzinger, & Wilkinson, 2002; Graupner & Tahmindjis, 2005; Swigonski, Mama, & Ward, 2001). It is notable that this framing of oppression of LGB people as a human rights issue is found more often in examinations of international populations than of U.S. communities (Chan, 2010; Fish & Bewley, 2010; Formby, 2011; Graupner & Tahmindjis, 2005; Murrey, 2006). However, President Obama has recently and clearly outlined the inalienable rights of LGBT people (U.S. Department of State, 2011).

The book offers insight into the struggles within some conservative Christian communities around the tensions between certain belief systems and same-sex sexuality. Across a wide range of methodological and theoretical approaches, the authors of these chapters offer opportunities to learn more about the experiences of social work students, social work practitioners, and social work faculty as they engage with the struggles around these issues. Furthermore, this book addresses a significant gap in the literature by discussing multiple ways of addressing and potentially resolving some of the conflicts between the beliefs of some conservative Christian social workers and LGB social workers at both individual and institutional levels. The third section in the book, "Transformation," is a critical contribution that offers theological and practice examples for conservative Christian social workers who hold beliefs with regard to sexual minority people that are in possible conflict with social work values. We also recognize that social workers holding certain liberal values may experience similar dissonance in working with conservative Christian clients, although we do not address that dissonance in this book. Intergroup dialogue, ethical and legal analyses, and a sociodrama approach offer other resources for social work faculty and practitioners. Authors of this edited volume, including Christian and LGB-identified authors, have been brought together to offer a wide range of perspectives as well as theoretical, empirical, and practice-based knowledge related to this conflict. Different terms and definitions are used across chapters as authors have described or defined the terminology they think is relevant for their work.

The book is organized in four sections, each with a unique theme: Section I, "Understanding Conservative Christian Experiences, Perspectives, and Actions"; Section II, "Biblical, Methodological, Legal, and Ethical Analyses"; Section III, "Transformation"; and Section IV "Interventions and Approaches to Resolving the Tensions."

The first section, "Understanding Conservative Christian Experiences, Perspectives, and Actions," includes empirical and policy chapters that examine Christian doctrine, the experiences and attitudes of Christian social work students, and LGB college students from conservative Christian families. Denise Levy reviews a wide range of Christian denominations and their doctrines related to sexual orientation, providing an overview of the policies and an analysis of the intersections with racial identity. A comparative table of 19 denominations outlines views of same-sex sexuality, status of lesbian and gay clergy and same-sex ceremonies, and views on inclusion of sexual orientation in hate crime laws. Then, Jill Chonody, Michael Woodford, Scott Smith, and Perry Silverschanz explore the role of Christian religious teachings about lesbians and gay men in some Christian social work students' antigay bias.

Eric Swank and Breanne Fahs continue the examination of the influence of religiosity, this time on the likelihood of gay and lesbian rights activism of BSW social work students. They examine the role of three variables—religious attendance, biblical literalism, and support of the Christian Coalition—on LGB activism in these students. (In the third section, "Transformation," we return to the discussion of LGB advocacy by conservative Christian social workers in a chapter by Drumm and colleagues.)

N. Eugene Walls and Kristie Seelman examine cultural incongruence, that is, conflict with the perceived values of social work and a graduate social work program's culture, between evangelical Christian first-year MSW students and other Christian and non-Christian first-year MSW students. Their study extends the examination of the role of religiosity by looking at social dominance orientation, right-wing authoritarianism, attitudes toward lesbians and gay men, and modern heterosexism as potential mediators of the relationship between conservative Christian identity and cultural incongruence.

In the next two chapters Warren J. Blumenfeld and Elliott DeVore first develop a literature review on lesbian and gay youth experiences in conservative Christian families. Then they report on a corresponding in-depth qualitative study of five college and graduate students who now identify as lesbian, gay, or bisexual and who grew up in conservative Christian families. They describe themes that emerged, and from this analysis we learn more about the struggles and coping mechanisms of these young adults.

These six chapters offer an in-depth understanding of the range of perspectives within Christian denominations with regard to same-sex orientation. The authors provide recommendations for social work educators and community practitioners, and the chapters are a rich resource for faculty who seek to support students in becoming competent social workers.

The next section of the book contains four chapters on "Biblical, Methodological, Legal, and Ethical Analyses" with regard to religion and sexual orientation. Adrienne Dessel, Christine Shepardson, and Rebecca Bolen critique claims that the profession of social work oppresses conservative Christian people. This is done using a theological analysis of biblical scriptures, religious freedom of expression, and social work ethics. Social work and human rights principles are discussed as a guide for negotiating these issues in the social work educational environment.

Next, Rebecca Bolen and Adrienne Dessel report on a methodological analysis of studies that analyze differences between social workers and the general public and claims that social work discriminates against conservative Christians. External, internal, construct, and statistical validity of these studies are reviewed.

Jay Kaplan describes recent federal litigation involving, among others, Christian graduate social work students who requested exemptions from school nondiscrimination policies protecting LGBT people, and a Christian family who sued a public school system when a teacher discussed LGBT bullying. These unprecedented attempts to carve out religious exceptions to nondiscrimination policies for nonreligious activity have been faced with sustained safeguards from the federal courts applying First Amendment principles.

Frederic Reamer then provides an analysis of the ethical issues, challenges, and moral dilemmas faced by social work faculty with regard to conservative Christian students. He discusses dilemmas of prohibiting discrimination against LGB people and respecting conservative Christian students' free speech and religious beliefs regarding same-sex sexuality within the arenas of admissions, classrooms, and field placements.

These chapters tie together challenges that arise for future practitioners, educators, and researchers with regard to social policy and research methods in the areas of conservative religiosity and sexual minority populations. In some ways Reamer's chapter is the true beginning of the next section, "Transformation," because it provides social workers, and especially social work educators, with guidelines for approaching the tension from the perspective of social work ethics and values, whereas the next section approaches this conflict from the perspective of Christian identity.

The third section of the book illustrates the potential for transformation of some conservative Christian social workers who may move from more polarized views of LGB people toward greater affirmation of LGB people while still retaining their strong Christian identities. This critical section offers role models, guides, and pathways to LGB human rights affirmation. Tanya Brice asks and answers the question of whether homophobia is a Christian value. In this chapter she outlines the biblical scriptures used to justify homophobia and discrimination, the process by which some Christians attend to certain biblical passages and not others, and where biblical mandates align with social work values.

Allison Tan takes this idea further in her empirical study of 127 Christian practitioners regarding their attitudes toward and practice behaviors with LGBT clients. She does so for the purpose of providing a practitioner-focused response to the question of how this type of practice can be done effectively and compassionately.

René Drumm, Kristie Wilder, Evie Nogales Baker, Lauren Souza, Zaire Burgess-Robinson, and Jennifer Adams extend the transformation into the arena of LGBT advocacy. Their qualitative study of 21 social work practitioners, administrators, and educators who self-identify as Christian LGBT advocates seeks to understand the paths these professionals took in understanding sexual orientation, their advocacy role within the faith community, and the barriers for furthering the dialogue among the Christian community and LGBT people.

All of these role models offer a critically important analysis as they integrate sexual orientation knowledge, theological understanding, and social justice action. Across all three of these chapters, the authors tackle difficult questions surrounding the understanding of oppression and affirmation, and they provide direction for social work professionals who struggle with these questions.

The last section, "Interventions and Approaches to Resolving the Tensions," includes chapters that discuss interventions aimed at reducing or resolving this tension in social work. Adrienne Dessel provides an overview of intergroup dialogue pedagogy and practice as an important method to bridge the divide between people who hold certain conservative Christian beliefs and LGB individuals. This chapter highlights the large and growing community of intergroup dialogue researchers and practitioners in the field of social work.

In a later chapter, Dessel, Michael Woodford, robbie routenberg, and Duane Breijak describe a qualitative study of the experiences of 54 heterosexual undergraduate students in a sexual orientation intergroup dialogue course. Religious identity was recognized as salient for some and as an area of conflict in the course, and the results have implications for practitioners who seek to bridge the religion–sexual orientation divide.

Joseph R. Miles, Christy Henrichs-Beck, and Jon R. Bourn describe a mixed-methods analysis of 32 students and facilitators in an intergroup dialogue undergraduate counseling psychology course at a large public southeastern university with a strong conservative Christian culture. Topics included in the course were sexual orientation and religion.

N. Eugene Walls and Julie Todd present a qualitative study of an innovative and important graduate social work course, "Disrupting Privilege Through Anti-Oppressive Practice," which supports students in examining Christian privilege. Through an analysis of weekly blogs for 13 graduate students, the authors describe the themes that emerged and offer insights into how Christian privilege intersects with other forms of privilege to maintain systems of oppression.

Finally, Patti Aldredge used sociodrama and dialogue in a novel social work course designed specifically to address significant conflict between conservative Christian and LGB social work students. This powerful case study describes how the students engaged and joined with each other over concerns about biased curriculum, negative classroom interactions, and dissonance between personal and professional values.

All chapters have in common the purposeful attempt to understand and move beyond the tension in social work between certain conservative Christian beliefs and same-sex sexuality. These chapters do so by reviewing doctrines regarding same-sex sexuality across multiple Christian denominations, illustrating the views of social work students in regard to this tension, the lived experiences of LGB people growing up in conservative Christian environments, and addressing theoretical, methodological, legal, policy, and ethical issues. These chapters also provide methods that can be used in classrooms and that speak to growth and transformation processes available to those social workers holding conservative Christian belief systems regarding LGB individuals. A highlight of the book is the group of chapters by Brice, Tan, and Drumm and colleagues that explore how to move from identifying as a conservative Christian social worker with an anti-LGB bias to one who retains a deeply rooted Christian identity while also avowing the human rights and dignity of LGB people. For some, this transformation includes the capacity to advocate for LGB people.

We offer this book not to further antagonize or incite this tension but to ameliorate the passions elicited by it, not to sever relationships but to bind them together, not to recriminate but to reconcile, and not to find fault but to find hope. We offer this book not with the desire to hurt but to heal. We hope this book finds a place in this process for all those caught in the vexing conflict between certain conservative Christian beliefs and basic human rights for those celebrating their love through same-sex sexuality. Very little has been written about this highly sensitive and controversial topic within social work, and we hope this book is just the beginning of an exploration and extended conversation on these important issues for our field.

References

Chan, P. (Ed.). (2010). *Protection of sexual minorities since Stonewall: Progress and stalemate in developed and developing countries.* New York, NY: Routledge/Taylor & Francis Group.

Dworkin, S., & Yi, H. (2003). LGBT identity, violence, and social justice: The psychological is political. *International Journal for the Advancement of Counselling, 25*(4), 269–279. doi:10.1023/B:ADCO.0000005526.87218.9f

Ellis, S., Kitzinger, C., & Wilkinson, S. (2002). Attitudes towards lesbians and gay men and support for lesbian and gay human rights among psychology students. *Journal of Homosexuality, 44*(1), 121–138. doi:10.1300/J082v44n01_07

Fish, J., & Bewley, S. (2010). Using human rights–based approaches to conceptualise lesbian and bisexual women's health inequalities. *Health & Social Care in the Community, 18*, 355–362.

Formby, E. (2011). Lesbian and bisexual women's human rights, sexual rights and sexual citizenship: Negotiating sexual health in England. *Culture, Health & Sexuality, 13*(10), 1165–1179. doi:10.1080/13691058.2011.610902

Graupner, H., & Tahmindjis, P. (Eds.). (2005). *Sexuality and human rights: A global overview.* Binghamton, NY: Harrington Park Press.

Murrey, D. (2006). Who's right? Human rights, sexual rights and social change in Barbados. *Culture, Health & Sexuality, 8*(3), 267–281. doi:10.1080/13691050600765145

Swigonski, M., Mama, R., & Ward, K. (Eds.). (2001). *From hate crimes to human rights: A tribute to Matthew Shepard.* New York, NY: Haworth Press.

U.S. Department of State. (2011). *The Department of State's accomplishments promoting the human rights of lesbian, gay, bisexual and transgender people.* Retrieved from http://www.state.gov/r/pa/prs/ps/2011/12/178341.htm

SECTION I

Understanding Conservative Christian Experiences, Perspectives, and Actions

Chapter 1

Christian Doctrine Related to Sexual Orientation: Current Climate and Future Implications

Denise Levy, PhD

Religion continues to be important in the lives of many people in the United States, and the majority of Americans identify as Christians. The Pew Forum on Religion & Public Life's (2007) religious landscape survey reports that approximately 27% of U.S. adults identify as evangelical Protestants, 24% as Catholic, 18% as mainline Protestants, and 7% as members of historically Black churches. Christianity provides believers with a framework to understand marriage, sexuality, parenting, and divorce (Hunt, 2012). Many denominations define marriage as between one man and one woman and oppose same sex sexuality through official policies and from the pulpit. Moreover, research confirms that having a Christian identity is positively correlated with homophobia (Plugge-Foust & Strickland, 2000; Finlay & Walther, 2003). Policies and individual congregants vary from supportive to homophobic, and recent studies suggest evangelical Protestants and Black Protestants are less accepting than mainline Protestants and Catholics (Whitehead, 2012). Over time, Christian doctrine related to sexual orientation has become increasingly more accepting (Thomas & Olsen, 2012). Still, a culture war exists between the gay and lesbian community and religious conservatives (Marin, 2011, p. 501).

This chapter presents and analyzes the policies of Christian denominations in the United States regarding sexual orientation. Although these policies certainly do not represent the positions of all individuals or congregations within the organizations, they do provide a context for the current climate in faith groups and a point of reference for social workers, people of faith, researchers, and gay and lesbian people. Therefore, including these policies is essential in a book that addresses tensions in the profession of social work related to Christianity and sexual orientation. Obtained from religious texts, official websites or materials, conference meeting minutes, and news sources, the doctrines are presented in a historical context with changes in policies over time. Additionally, subgroups within each denomination that are welcoming and affirming are noted. Doctrines and policies of all of these groups are compared and analyzed, and analysis attends to the intersections of racial, sexual, and religious identities. Looking to the future, the chapter concludes with suggestions for social workers and advocates to begin or foster continued dialogue with these groups.

Denominational Doctrines and Policies on Sexual Orientation

For decades, Christian denominations in the United States have issued official policy statements on same sex sexuality. Many denominations base their policies in part on their interpretation of six Bible verses: Genesis 19:1–13, Leviticus 18:22, Leviticus 20:13, Romans 1:26–27, 1 Corinthians 6:9–10, and 1 Timothy 1:9–10 (see Levy, 2008, for additional information). However, welcoming groups provide alternative interpretations of biblical texts, often looking to other passages and original language for context. These welcoming groups, though not officially sanctioned by some denominations, continue to advocate for acceptance within their denominations.

Both the official denominational policies (as of August 2012) and welcoming groups are presented here in alphabetical order by denomination. Some denominations are combined under one parent heading, including Baptist, Lutheran, and Methodist denominations. This is just one way to conceptualize and organize denominations, and it can be considered simplistic. In fact, some might call the current state of Christianity postdenominational, citing the growing number of nondenominational affiliates. It is worth noting that, when asked about their religious identification, less than 5% of people in the United States identified as nondenominational in the Pew Forum on Religion & Public Life's (2007) nationally representative survey of more than 35,000 adults. Others might organize the chapter using sociological frameworks, such as Steensland and colleagues' (2000) framework, to categorize religious traditions into mainline Protestant, evangelical Protestant, Black Protestant, Roman Catholic, Jewish, and other. In this chapter, however, it is important to look at the policies of denominations within categories such as mainline Protestant because there is so much variation within traditions. Denominations included in this chapter were chosen primarily based on membership and identification of people in the United States. Christian denominations selected for this chapter include those with the largest U.S. membership and some smaller groups that are particularly known for welcoming gay and lesbian people (Pew Forum on Religion & Public Life, 2007).

Baptist Denominations

According to the Pew Forum on Religion & Public Life (2007), 6.7% of adults in the United States identify as Southern Baptists, 1.8% belong to churches that are part of the National Baptist Convention, and less than 1% identify as Free Will Baptists. The policies of these three denominations, along with a Baptist welcoming group, are presented in this section.

ASSOCIATION OF WELCOMING AND AFFIRMING BAPTISTS (AWAB)

One of the few Baptist welcoming organizations, AWAB includes Baptist churches, organizations, and individuals. Although the group is not specifically tied to any particular Baptist denomination, AWAB's mission is to "create and support a community of churches, organizations and individuals committed to the inclusion of gay, lesbian, bisexual and transgender persons in the full life and mission of Baptist churches" (2010, Article VIII, Section D).

NATIONAL ASSOCIATION OF FREE WILL BAPTISTS (FWB)

The FWB, typically considered more conservative than the other Baptist denominations reviewed here, refer to same-sex sexuality only once in their official doctrine. A portion of the FWB's (2010) *Treatise of the Faith and Practices of the National Association of Free Will Baptists, Inc.* states that same-sex relationships violate the divine plan for marital relationships between one man and one woman and will bring "spiritual despair, guilt, and death to individuals and cultures" (p. 19). Subgroups and individual FWB churches have issued additional statements related to same-sex sexuality.

NATIONAL BAPTIST CONVENTION (NBC)

The NBC, classified by the Pew Forum on Religion & Public Life (2007) as a predominantly African American organization, believes in autonomy of member churches. Therefore, the NBC does not require its constituent churches to take particular positions on issues, including sexuality and same-sex marriage (Scruggs, 2012). The NBC has remained largely silent on these topics. However, in response to President Obama's announcement in support of same-sex marriage in 2012, the NBC's president, Dr. Julius R. Scruggs (2012), affirmed that "marriage is a sacred biblical covenant between a man and a woman" (para. 2).

SOUTHERN BAPTIST CONVENTION (SBC)

The SBC has long been viewed as one of the least supportive denominations, issuing formal resolutions against same sex sexuality in 1977, 1980, 1985, and 1988. The SBC's current policy on sexuality states that "homosexuality is not a 'valid alternative lifestyle.' The Bible condemns it as sin" (SBC, 2012b, para. 1). Accordingly, the SBC does not allow gay or lesbian clergy or support same-sex unions. The SBC's 2003 resolution against same-sex marriage requires Southern Baptist churches to oppose same-sex unions and to perform marriages only between one man and one woman. In 2008 the SBC issued another resolution in response to the California Supreme Court's decision to allow same-sex marriages encouraging "all Christian pastors in California and in every other state to speak strongly, prophetically, and redemptively concerning the sinful nature of same sex sexuality and the urgent need to protect biblical marriage in accordance with God's Word" (para. 10). Three years later the SBC (2011) called on President Obama to legally defend the Defense of Marriage Act, stating that "redefining the concept and legality of marriage to mean anything other than the union between one man and one woman would fundamentally undermine the historic and biblical foundation of a healthy society" (para. 10).

In addition to policies on sexuality, gay clergy, and same-sex unions, the SBC (2012a) also passed resolutions denouncing the use of government funds to encourage "sexually immoral behavior" (in 1991), opposing the inclusion of gay and lesbian people in the U.S. military (in 1993 and in 2010) and in the federal government (in 1998), criticizing President Bill Clinton's proclamation of gay and lesbian pride month (in 1999), and opposing the inclusion of gay and lesbian people in federal hate crime legislation (in 2007).

Church of Christ (CC)

The CC (2012a), not to be confused with the United Church of Christ (presented later) or other Church of Christ organizations, has no creed other than the Bible. Although each individual church maintains autonomy with no central organization, the official CC website does include information about same-sex sexuality. It states that "homosexuality is a lifestyle. It is a choice made by those who desire the unnatural. Can a homosexual person repent and be forgiven by God? The answer is yes" (CC, 2012b, para. 4). The site goes on to say that God condemns homosexuality as sin, and therefore CC cannot support it within the church.

The Church of Jesus Christ of Latter-Day Saints (LDS, also known as Mormons)

The LDS (2012) opposes same-sex sexual acts and, at the same time, attempts to provide outreach to gay and lesbian people. According to the LDS (2012), same-sex attraction is distinct from behavior, and people who do not act on same-sex desires have not sinned. The LDS believe that gay and lesbian people should not be forced into heterosexual relationships, which may result in broken hearts and homes (Holland, 2007). They further state that one cannot be an LDS member and continually engage in same-sex sexual acts (Oaks, 1996).

Regarding same-sex marriage, the LDS president, Gordon B. Hinckley (1999), explained that the church advocates for traditional definitions of marriage and against same-sex marriage. Indeed, the LDS has raised money for this cause in California and other states. Hinckley goes on to say that opposition to same-sex marriage is distinct from homophobia and that the LDS does not endorse violence against gay and lesbian people.

In 2006 the LDS released an official statement on same-gender attraction; it said that people experiencing same-sex attraction, as long as they are celibate and do not act on these desires, are eligible to hold any church office available to people who are single. However, gay and lesbian clergy are not allowed.

AFFIRMATION

A welcoming Mormon group, Affirmation (2012), is not officially affiliated with the LDS. Affirmation supports lesbian, gay, bisexual, and transgender Mormons and strives for equality within the LDS. Their membership includes current and former LDS members as well as nonmembers.

Episcopal Church (EC)

As early as 1979 the EC recommended removal of any barriers to the ordination of celibate gay and lesbian people (Archives of the Episcopal Church, 1979). Almost two decades later, however, at the 1998 Lambeth Conference, EC bishops "overwhelmingly endorsed a resolution declaring homosexual activity to be 'incompatible with Scripture'" (Solheim, 1998, para. 5). Although the resolution acknowledged gay and lesbian people as full members of the church and continued to allow celibate people to be ordained, it advised against allowing noncelibate gay and lesbian people to serve as clergy and condemned same-sex unions. These policies were confirmed several times until 2009, when the EC's new policy endorsed the ordination of gay and lesbian people in monogamous relationships and also allowed same-sex marriage and blessing ceremonies within churches.

In addition to the aforementioned policies related to sexuality, clergy, and same-sex union ceremonies, the EC has passed several resolutions on related topics. In 1976 the EC's 65th General Convention included resolutions supporting equal protection under the law of gay and lesbian people (Archives of the Episcopal Church, 1976). Then, in 1988, the EC denounced the increased violence against gay and lesbian people and encouraged law enforcement to take action (Archives of the Episcopal Church, 1988). The EC has also called on local, state, and federal officials to extend benefits to gay and lesbian couples, including "bereavement and family leave policies; health benefits, pension benefits; real-estate transfer tax benefits, and commitments to mutual support enjoyed by non-gay married couples" (Archives of the Episcopal Church, 1994, para. 1).

INTEGRITY USA

Although the EC's policies are currently very supportive of the gay and lesbian community, this has not always been the case. A welcoming nonprofit group, Integrity USA (2013), has been the "leading grassroots voice for the full inclusion of LGBT persons in the Episcopal Church" (para. 1) since its inception in Georgia in 1974. Integrity USA (2013) acknowledges that the EC has made positive strides since that time but that advocacy and education are still needed in many parishes.

Jehovah's Witnesses (JW)

JW (2012) believe that "the Bible condemns homosexual acts" (p. 232). In addition to describing homosexuality as a sin, JW (2013) believe that marriage is a permanent bond between a woman and a man and that this type of relationship is the only satisfying form of intimacy. JW (2012) have materials designed to help members "avoid homosexuality" (p. 231) by controlling their desires through prayer, reading the Bible, and avoiding pornography and gay materials. Interestingly, even if laws are passed that contradict JW beliefs about same-sex relationships, members are not allowed to protest or advocate for change (JW, 2013).

Lutheran

EVANGELICAL LUTHERAN CHURCH IN AMERICA (ELCA)

In 1991 the ELCA welcomed gay and lesbian people to fully participate in their congregations and encouraged ELCA members to further study and discuss the issue of same-sex sexuality. Eighteen years later, the ELCA (2009a) issued a social statement in which it recognized the disagreement that exists within the ELCA regarding same-sex relationships. Although there is not yet a consensus on this issue, the ELCA (2009a) opposes discrimination, harassment, and assault based on sexual identity and supports civil rights for gay and lesbian people. Individual churches are allowed to bless same-sex relationships if they choose to do so (ELCA, 2009a).

In their first statement about gay and lesbian clergy, the ELCA (n.d.) stated that "people who are homosexual who abstain from homosexual intercourse may therefore serve in the rostered ministries of the ELCA" (p. 7). More recently, however, the Churchwide Assembly voted to recognize and support gay and lesbian clergy who are in committed, monogamous, same-sex relationships, overturning the previous ruling requiring celibacy (ELCA, 2009b).

LUTHERAN CHURCH, MISSOURI SYNOD (LCMS)

Since 1981 the LCMS has issued multiple statements categorizing same sex behavior as sinful (Mahsman, 2003). These include the 1981 report on human sexuality, the 1999 plan for ministry to homosexuals, and a 2001 convention resolution. Likewise, in 2003 the president of the LCMS stated that "homosexual behavior" is contrary to God's will (Mahsman, 2003). As recently as 2011, the LCMS again indicated that same-sex sexuality is unnatural and "intrinsically sinful" (p. 10) and marriage is between one man and one woman. The LCMS (2011) instructs people experiencing same-sex desires to conform to a model of celibacy, to repent and seek forgiveness, and to call on God for help.

RECONCILINGWORKS (RW)

Emerging in the 1970s, RW (2012) was formerly known as Lutherans Concerned. RW "advocates for the full inclusion of lesbian, gay, bisexual and transgender Lutherans in all aspects of the life of their Church" (About ReconcilingWorks section, para. 1).

Methodist

AFRICAN METHODIST EPISCOPAL (AME) CHURCH

The AME is classified by the Pew Forum on Religion & Public Life (2007) as a predominantly African American organization. Although there is little information about their views on same-sex sexuality in general, the AME stands firmly against same-sex marriage and openly gay clergy. In response to an article in *USA Today,* Bishop Richard Franklin Norris issued a statement in 2003 to correct the inconsistencies in the AME doctrine. He explained that the AME does not support ordination of openly gay clergy (Human Rights Campaign, 2012). Additionally, delegates to the AME National Convention in 2004 unanimously voted to prohibit clergy from performing ceremonies blessing same-sex relationships (Human Rights Campaign, 2012).

UNITED METHODIST CHURCH (UMC)

The Book of Discipline, which holds the official teachings of the UMC and was updated at the 2004 General Conference, declares that gay and lesbian individuals are people of sacred worth and should not be rejected. However, it also states that same-sex sexuality is against UMC doctrine and contrary to Christian teaching. Some UMC members attempted to alter these statements 4 years later. After a heated debate at the 2008 General Conference of the UMC, gay rights supporters were dismayed when a resolution failed that would have recognized varied views within the denomination on the issue of same-sex sexuality (Russell, 2008). However, delegates did approve a resolution opposing discrimination and violence based on sexual or gender identity. At the subsequent General Conference in 2012, delegates again voted against altering the *Book of Discipline* (Zaimov, 2012).

Similar to other denominations, the UMC (2011) allows gay and lesbian people to be ordained as clergy as long as they remain celibate. However, the UMC (2010) does not allow clergy to perform ceremonies blessing or honoring same-sex couples, even in states where same-sex marriage is legal.

AFFIRMATION

Affirmation (2011), a welcoming group within the UMC since as early as 1972, is an activist organization that seeks inclusion and equality for lesbian, gay, bisexual, transgender, and queer people worldwide. They continue to advocate within the UMC.

Presbyterian Church of the United States of America (PCUSA)

The PCUSA, though largely supportive, remains divided on the topic of same-sex sexuality. As early as 1978, the PCUSA issued statements about same-sex sexuality, condemning homophobia and welcoming gay and lesbian people as church members. In 2000 the General Assembly Permanent Judicial Commission voted to allow PCUSA clergy to perform ceremonies blessing same-sex couples as long as these unions were not likened to marriage (Pew Forum on Religion & Public Life, 2010). Four years later, commissioners advocated for civil unions (Silverstein, 2004). Then, in 2012, the General Assembly Committee voted to define marriage as between two people rather than one man and one woman (More Light Presbyterians, 2012b).

Regarding gay and lesbian clergy, the PCUSA allowed for celibate gay and lesbian clergy as early as 1978. Although the PCUSA rejected amendments to allow nonmarried, sexually active people (including gay and lesbian people) to serve as clergy in 1997, 2001, and 2008, commissioners later voted to amend their *Book of Order,* allowing gay and lesbian people to be ordained (Van Marter, 2011). The first openly gay man was ordained in the PCUSA in 2011 (Summers, 2011). Still, in a 2008 PCUSA survey, 50% of clergy, 53% of church members, and 59% of elders opposed ordination of noncelibate gay and lesbian people (Marcum, 2009).

MORE LIGHT PRESBYTERIANS

More Light Presbyterians (2012a) is a network of individual members and congregations advocating for full participation of lesbian, gay, bisexual, and transgender people in the PCUSA.

Roman Catholic Church (RCC)

Same-sex sexuality has been discussed in the RCC since as early as 1975, with most statements stressing the sinfulness of same-sex acts (Ratzinger, 1986). According to a letter to the RCC bishops on the pastoral care of "homosexual persons" (Ratzinger, 1986), those engaging in same-sex acts are doing so against God. The RCC posits that same-sex desires in and of themselves are not sinful (although they are viewed as disordered), but acting on them constitutes sin (Grocholewski, 2005). According to the *Catechism of the RCC* (1995), those experiencing same-sex desires should live a life of chastity through the support of friendship, grace, and prayer. People are encouraged to contact Courage (2012), a national Catholic support group.

The RCC has barred gay and lesbian people from ordination since 1961, and more recent Vatican materials clarify this position, stating, "If a candidate practices homosexuality or presents deep-seated homosexual tendencies, his spiritual director as well as his confessor have the duty to dissuade him in conscience from proceeding towards ordination" (Grocholewski, 2005, Section 3, para. 5). Regarding same-sex marriage, the U.S. Conference of Catholic Bishops advocates for laws defining marriage as between one man and one woman (U.S. Catholic Conference, 2003).

DIGNITYUSA

DignityUSA (2011), a welcoming organization that is not endorsed by the RCC, advocates for full participation for gay, lesbian, bisexual, and transgender Catholics. Established in 1969, DignityUSA is also a founding member of an overarching body, Catholic Organizations for Renewal, which includes similar groups advocating for change within the RCC.

Seventh-Day Adventist Church (SDA)

In 1987 the SDA issued a statement on sexual behavior that identified same-sex acts as perversions of God's plan for sexual relationships. The SDA again expressed its opposition in 1999 and has since said that "homosexuality is a manifestation of the disorder and brokenness in human inclinations and relations caused by sin coming into the world" (SDA, 2004, para. 4). They recommend that people repent and accept God's grace (SDA, 1987).

Regarding same-sex marriage, the SDA defined biblical marriage as the monogamous covenant between one man and one woman in 1996. Then, in 1999, they reiterated that "sexual intimacy belongs only within the marital relationship of a man and a woman" (para. 2). Five years later, they again reaffirmed their definition of Christian marriage and opposition to same-sex marriage (SDA, 2004).

GLADVENTIST AND SEVENTH-DAY ADVENTIST KINSHIP

Two main SDA gay-positive organizations, GLAdventist (2012) and Seventh-Day Adventist Kinship (2011), are not endorsed by the SDA. GLAdventist provides a supportive blog and website and Seventh-Day Adventist Kinship promotes affirmation through advocacy.

United Church of Christ (UCC)

The UCC has long been a welcoming community for gay and lesbian people. In 1977, as a result of a study of human sexuality, the UCC encouraged legal recognition of stable relationships (in addition to traditional marriage) and celebrations of committed relationships. Encouraging the participation of gay and lesbian people as full members in the church (1983a), the UCC officially affirmed the ordination of gay and lesbian clergy (1983b), although its first openly gay clergy member was ordained 11 years earlier. Currently, the UCC (n.d.) has a ministry specifically dedicated to lesbian, gay, bisexual, transgender, and same-gender loving people. They declare, "Whoever you are, wherever you are on life's journey, you are welcome here!" (para. 1).

In addition to supporting gay and lesbian people within the church, the UCC (1993) calls on its members to be leaders in advocating for justice for gay and lesbian people, and many have answered this call. In 1969 the UCC opposed laws prohibiting same-sex sexual acts and advocated for civil liberties, including the ability to serve in the military and obtain employment. The UCC issued many more statements to this effect, including one in 1975 that opposed violence against gay and bisexual people. The UCC supports equal marriage rights (1996), inclusion of sexual orientation in hate crime legislation (1998), provision of multicultural education in public schools (2009), and equal adoption rights (2011).

Unitarian Universalist Association of Congregations (UU)

The UU has been advocating for gay and lesbian rights since at least the 1970s. The history of their efforts is available on their website (UU, 2011). Although a 1967 survey of UU members showed that only 0.1% believed in encouraging same sex sexuality, the Reverend James L. Stoll came out as gay in 1969. Over time, opinions changed, and in 1970 the General Assembly called for an end to discrimination against gay, lesbian, and bisexual people. In the early 1970s the UU went on to provide gay-positive materials and develop an Office of Gay Affairs. In the 1980s, the UU affirmed the performance of same-gender commitment ceremonies in its member churches and called for legislation promoting equal rights for gay and lesbian people. They also created the Welcoming Congregation program in 1989, a voluntary program that continues today for UU congregations that want to become more inclusive for gay and lesbian people; more than 650 congregations in the United States have joined the program. UU has also worked for the rights of gay and lesbian people in the military, participated in marches and protests, supported same-sex marriage legislation, and encouraged comprehensive sex education. In sum, the UU (2012) warmly welcomes lesbian, gay, bisexual, and transgender people as full members of the church. They "work to promote acceptance, inclusion, understanding, and equity for LGBT persons of all ages, abilities, colors, and genders, both within our denomination and in society at large" (UU, 2012, para. 2).

Universal Fellowship of Metropolitan Community Churches (MCC)

The MCC (2004) was founded in 1968 by Reverend Troy Perry shortly after the Stonewall Riots in New York. Perry had previously been defrocked as a Pentecostal clergy member because of his sexual orientation, and he decided to create a church that is "loving, affirming, and welcoming" (MCC, 2012, para. 1). Formed as a church in ministry for and with gay and lesbian people, MCC has been known as a welcoming organization since its inception. Gay and lesbian clergy are common. Regarding same-sex unions, MCC (2012) "believes that marriage should be freely available to all people, everywhere" (About MCC for Newcomers Section, para. 4). Therefore, MCC (2012) performs marriage ceremonies for same-sex couples in states where it is legal and Holy Unions in states where same-sex marriage is not legal.

Comparisons and Analysis of Doctrines

The denominations described here vary in their support for same-sex sexuality and related topics. Over time, many denominations have become more welcoming. Table 1 provides a quick summary of each group's current views (as of August 2012) based on official policies. Some groups, such as the MCC, UU, and UCC, have been welcoming and supportive over time, and others, such as the EC, ELCA, and PCUSA, have become supportive in recent years. Finally, denominations such as the SBC, FWB, and LDS remain firmly against same-sex sexuality. Many groups note in their official position statements that disagreement exists between church members, and some, such as the NBC, call for autonomy in order for individual churches and members to decide on these issues for themselves.

Table 1. Summary of Denominations' Doctrines

Denomination	Overall View of Same-Sex Sexuality	Gay or Lesbian Clergy	Same-Sex Ceremonies	Inclusion of Sexual Orientation in Hate Crime or Similar Laws	Welcoming Group (If Applicable)
Baptist—Association of Welcoming and Affirming Baptists	Supportive	Allowed	Allowed	Supportive	
Baptist—National Association of Free Will Baptist	Against	Not allowed	Not allowed	Against	
Baptist—National Baptist Convention	No single view/ autonomous	No single view/ autonomous	Not supported	No single view/ autonomous	
Baptist—Southern Baptist Convention	Against	Not allowed	Not allowed	Against	
Church of Christ	Against	Not allowed	Not allowed/ some autonomy	No information	

(continued)

Table 1 (continued)

Denomination	Overall View of Same-Sex Sexuality	Gay or Lesbian Clergy	Same-Sex Ceremonies	Inclusion of Sexual Orientation in Hate Crime or Similar Laws	Welcoming Group (If Applicable)
The Church of Jesus Christ of Latter-Day Saints	Against/ distinguish attraction from behavior	Not allowed for clergy; those who are celibate may hold any positions open to people who are single	Not allowed	No information	Affirmation http://www.affirmation.org/
Episcopal Church	Supportive	Allowed	Allowed	Supportive	Integrity USA[a] http://www.integrityusa.org/
Jehovah's Witnesses	Against	Not allowed	Not allowed	Against, but members not allowed to protest laws	
Lutheran—Evangelical Lutheran Church in America	Supportive, some disagreement	Allowed	Allowed if member churches choose to do so	Supportive	Reconciling Works[a] http://www.reconcilingworks.org/
Lutheran—Lutheran Church, Missouri Synod	Against	Not allowed	Not allowed	No information	Reconciling Works http://www.reconcilingworks.org/
Methodist—African Methodist Episcopal Church	Against	Not allowed	Not allowed	No information	
Methodist—United Methodist Church	Against, with some disagreement	Allowed if celibate	Not allowed	Supportive	Affirmation[a] http://www.umaffirm.org/
Presbyterian Church of the USA	Supportive, with some disagreement	Allowed	Allowed	Supportive	More Light Presbyterians[a] http://www.mlp.org/

(continued)

Table 1 (continued)

Denomination	Overall View of Same-Sex Sexuality	Gay or Lesbian Clergy	Same-Sex Ceremonies	Inclusion of Sexual Orientation in Hate Crime or Similar Laws	Welcoming Group (If Applicable)
Roman Catholic Church	Against/ distinguish attraction from behavior	Not allowed unless celibate and without deep-seated same-sex desires	Not allowed	No information	DignityUSA https://www.dignityusa.org/
Seventh-Day Adventist Church	Against	Not allowed	Not allowed	No information	GLAdventist http://gladventist.org/ and Seventh-Day Adventist Kinship http://www.sdakinship.org/
United Church of Christ	Supportive	Allowed	Allowed	Supportive	
Unitarian Universalist Association of Congregations	Supportive	Allowed	Allowed	Supportive	
Universal Fellowship of Metropolitan Community Churches	Supportive	Allowed	Allowed	Supportive	

Note: Information in this table was obtained from religious texts, official websites or materials, conference meeting minutes, and news sources. All citations can be found in the narrative text and in the reference list.

[a]These welcoming groups are either sanctioned or acknowledged by the denomination.

Review of Policies

Most denominational policies on same-sex sexuality have changed over time to become more supportive. In fact, most denominations have become more welcoming in recent years. Those with policies against same sex sexuality (such as the SBC and LCMS) have nonaffiliated welcoming organizations.

In a review of denominations' overall views of same-sex sexuality, several themes emerge. First, some denominations, such as the RCC, EC, and

ELCA, have spent considerable time and effort studying sexuality. Findings of their studies cite scientific information, public opinion, views of other denominations, religious texts, and more. Second, two denominations (LDS, RCC) distinguish between sexual attraction and behavior. For these two groups, same-sex sexuality in and of itself is not wrong; acting on these desires, however, is sinful. To manage attractions, celibacy is promoted by official doctrine. However, research shows that celibacy is not a practical solution (Alexander, 2011). Third, several denominations, even those firmly against same sex sexuality such as the LDS, encourage outreach to gay and lesbian people. Finally, one group (the LDS) goes beyond policies in other denominations to state that those engaging in same-sex sexual acts are not allowed to be members of their church.

Regarding ordination of gay and lesbian clergy, most denominations have clear policies. Some allow ordination only if the person is celibate (UMC, RCC). Others allow clergy to be in relationships as long as they are monogamous and lifelong (EC, ELCA). Many do not allow ordination, and as a result groups such as the RCC probably have closeted clergy.

Although same-sex marriage and civil unions are legal in many states, most denominations do not officially allow same-sex ceremonies to be performed in their member churches or by their clergy. For those that do permit such ceremonies, final decisions may be left up to the individual churches or clergy members (such as in the ELCA). Welcoming groups, such as the MCC, perform same-sex marriages in states where it is legal and encourage commitment ceremonies elsewhere.

In addition to church matters such as ordination and commitment ceremonies, some groups (such as the EC, UMC, and PCUSA) have issued official statements opposing discrimination against gay and lesbian people. The SBC is one of the few groups that is adamantly against the inclusion of sexual orientation in discrimination and hate crime legislation.

Intersection of Racial, Religious, and Sexual Identities

Although past scholarship on sexual identity and race has largely remained distinct (Harris, 2009), recent scholars have examined the intersection of racial, religious, and sexual identities (Brown, 2005; Cohen, 2003, Foster, Arnold, Rebchook, & Kegeles, 2011; Garcia, Gray-Stanley, & Ramirez-Valles, 2008; McQueeney, 2009; Parks, 2010; Phillips, 2005; Whitehead, 2012). Two racial groups, in particular, are often mentioned in the literature as less accepting of gay and lesbian people: African Americans and Latinos. These two groups are also recognized as being highly spiritual, with religion permeating all aspects of life.

The Black church often provides a social community, hub for activism, links to spiritual resources, and refuge from a racist society. At the same time, many churches socialize members to conform to traditional family and gender roles (Foster et al., 2011; Harris, 2009; Parks, 2010). Same-sex sexuality has traditionally been equated with sin in Black churches (Cohen, 2003; Foster et al.), often with "harsh criticism" (Foster et al., p. 3) from the pulpit. Indeed, studies show that African Americans tend to be less accepting of same-sex sexuality (Logie, Bridge, & Bridge, 2007; Newman, Dannenfelser, & Benishek, 2002), and this "racial divide is a function of African Americans' ties to sectarian Protestant religious denominations" (Sherkat, de Vries, & Creek, 2010, p. 80).

According to Phillips (2005), "the U.S. Black community has maintained a 'don't ask, don't tell' posture with regard to homosexuality" (p. 11). Race is often the primary identity for lesbian and gay African Americans (Harris, 2009), and homophobia within their families and communities may lead them to conceal their sexual orientation (Brown, 2005), especially within the Black church. Based on the messages that "homosexuality is sinful and immoral" (Griffin, 2000, p. 96), some African American lesbians and gay men also experience guilt and shame. Furthermore, churchgoers may "stay in a place of inferiority to remain in black churches" (Griffin, p. 96).

In the preceding doctrine review, two predominantly African American churches were presented: the NBC and the AME. Though outspoken on other civil rights issues (Guerilus, 2011; Wells, 2007), the AME stands firmly against same-sex sexuality. The NBC, on the other hand, has taken a unique approach, calling for independence of member churches. Although the majority of African American Christians may be opposed to same-sex sexuality, there are notable examples of gay-positive African American groups and churches (Harris, 2009; McQueeney, 2009).

According to Duarte-Velez, Bernal, and Bonilla (2010), several core Latino values, including religion, may conflict with same-sex sexuality. Approximately 60% of Latinos identify as Catholic (Pew Forum on Religion & Public Life, 2007). As in the Black church, being Catholic is often tied to ethnic identity for many Latinos (Ellison, Acevedo, & Ramos-Wada, 2011).

As noted earlier, the RCC focuses on the sinfulness of same-sex sexual acts. However, Catholics tend be more accepting than other Protestant groups (Logie et al., 2007), and this is also the case when we compare Latino Catholics and Latino Protestants (Ellison et al., 2011). However, official doctrine of the RCC still requires gay and lesbian Catholics to remain celibate. This causes conflicts for many gay and lesbian Latinos (Barbosa, Torres, Silva, & Khan, 2010; Garcia et al., 2008). These conflicts may be mediated through affirming groups, and although it is not specifically for Latino Catholics, DignityUSA (2011) is a welcoming organization that encourages people to embrace their Catholic and gay or lesbian identities.

Suggestions for Social Workers

Social workers, community organizers, and advocates may have opportunities to engage with local church leaders on the topic of same-sex sexuality. In doing so, it is important to remember that particular congregations do not necessarily hold the same views as their corresponding denominations, and individual church members do not necessarily agree with their congregations' stances (Woodford, Walls, & Levy, 2012). Several of the suggestions for social workers and others provided here are based on the variety of denominational policies and focus on local-level interventions.

Engaging Clergy

Social workers can begin by engaging in respectful dialogue with clergy. Because most church leaders are uncertain about their own opinions on same-sex sexuality and what they should do about issues that arise in their congregations (Cadge, Girouard, Olson, & Lylerohr, 2012), it is important to assist clergy in clarifying their positions, understanding denominational policies, and addressing issues specific to their congregations. Social workers can take an inquisitive approach, avoiding statements of judgment or condemnation. Rather than changing minds, initial engagement should focus on developing understanding. It is also vital to examine the specific culture and needs of the congregation. For instance, Whitehead (2012) suggests redefining same-sex sexuality as an issue of justice (rather than of morality) for Black Protestant congregations (such as the NBC and the AME).

Initiating Discussions Within Congregations

In addition to working individually with clergy, social workers can reach out to entire congregations. Studies show that many congregations avoid the topic of same-sex sexuality or develop a "don't ask, don't tell" policy (Adler, 2012), and clergy may not know how to address this topic within their churches (Cadge et al., 2012). Social workers can assist clergy by either teaching facilitation skills or leading discussions themselves. Congregations may request that discussion leaders review church and denominational policies. Additionally, congregants may be interested in the policies of similar denominations and how other groups have handled disagreements.

Facilitating Community Dialogue

Some churches embrace ongoing discussions in which they invite community members, researchers, gay and lesbian people, and others to share their experiences. For instance, intergroup dialogue is "a facilitated group experience, often sustained over time, that may incorporate education or experiential material" (Dessel, 2010, p. 561). This type of dialogue, designed to help people appreciate differences, can be effective in changing attitudes related to same-sex sexuality (Dessel, 2010). Some congregations are open to continual "boundary bridging" between their church and gay and lesbian groups in the area (Adler, 2012), and this intergroup contact may lead to further acceptance and understanding (Heinze & Horn, 2009).

Supporting Gay and Lesbian Congregants

Finally, clergy and congregations may have questions about how they can support their gay and lesbian church members. Indeed, many gay and lesbian Christians experience conflict between their sexual and religious identities (Anderton, Pender, & Asner-Self, 2011; Couch, Mulcare, Pitts, Smith, & Mitchell, 2008; Levy & Reeves, 2011; Page, 2011; Rodriguez & Ouellette, 2000; Schuck & Liddle, 2001). Those who attend welcoming churches are typically able to integrate their identities, and integration leads to better psychological health (Lease, Horne, & Noffsinger-Frazier, 2005; Rodriguez & Ouellette, 2000).

Some churches are not welcoming, however, and clergy may support or even facilitate conversion therapy. Proponents of conversion therapy, also known as reorientation or reparative therapy, claim that it eliminates same-sex attraction and helps clients become heterosexual (Blackwell, 2008). Identified as unethical by medical, psychological, psychiatric, and helping professions, this type of therapy does not work and can be harmful to clients (Blackwell; Jenkins & Johnston, 2004; Shidlo & Schroeder, 2002). When working with congregations that support conversion therapy, social workers should educate others on the mental health implications of this approach. Additionally, it is important to encourage collaborations between clergy and supportive mental health practitioners.

Conclusion

Christian denominations, churches, and members have beliefs about same-sex sexuality that range from accepting to opposing. Reflecting this range of views, many denominations have official policies on same-sex sexuality in general, ordination of gay or lesbian clergy, performance of same-gender blessing ceremonies, and inclusion of sexual orientation in hate crimes and other laws. Although official doctrine is not necessarily representative of congregational or individual views, it can provide a frame of reference for social workers and advocates by highlighting structural and institutional oppression within denominations (Adams, Bell, & Griffin, 2007). These helping professionals can engage clergy, initiate discussions within congregations, facilitate community dialogue, and support gay and lesbian congregants.

References

Adams, M., Bell, L. A., & Griffin, P. (Eds.). (2007). *Teaching for diversity and social justice: A sourcebook* (2nd ed.). New York, NY: Routledge.

Adler, G. (2012). An opening in the congregational closet? Boundary-bridging culture and membership privileges for gays and lesbians in Christian religious congregations. *Social Problems, 59*(2), 177–206. doi:10.1525/sp.2012.59.2.177

Affirmation. (2011). About us. Retrieved from http://www.umaffirm.org/um/about-us

Affirmation. (2012). We are Affirmation. Retrieved from http://www.affirmation.org/about/

Alexander, K. (2011). Men of God: Homosexual and Catholic identity negotiation, through Holland's Catholic priests. *ISP Collection.* Paper 1092. Retrieved from http://digitalcollections.sit.edu/isp_collection/1092/

Anderton, C. L., Pender, D. A., & Asner-Self, K. K. (2011). A review of the religious identity/sexual orientation identity conflict literature: Revisiting Festinger's cognitive dissonance theory. *Journal of LGBT Issues in Counseling, 5*(3–4), 259–281. doi:10.1080/15538605.2011.632745

Archives of the Episcopal Church. (1976). Support the right of homosexuals to equal protection of the law. Retrieved from http://www.episcopalarchives.org/cgi-bin/acts/acts_resolution.pl?resolution=1976-A071

Archives of the Episcopal Church. (1979). Recommended guidelines on the ordination of homosexuals. Retrieved from http://www.episcopalarchives.org/cgi-bin/acts/acts_resolution.pl?resolution=1979-A053

Archives of the Episcopal Church. (1988). Decry violence against homosexuals. Retrieved from http://www.episcopalarchives.org/cgi-bin/acts/acts_resolution.pl?resolution=1988-D100

Archives of the Episcopal Church. (1994). Call on US government to extend benefits to gay and lesbian couples. Retrieved from http://www.episcopalarchives.org/cgi-bin/acts/acts_resolution.pl?resolution=1994-D006

Association of Welcoming and Affirming Baptists (AWAB). (2010). The AWAB mission. Retrieved from http://www.awab.org/mission-and-vision.html

Barbosa, P., Torres, H., Silva, M. A., & Khan, N. (2010). Agape Christian reconciliation conversations: Exploring the intersections of culture, religiousness, and homosexual identity in Latino and European Americans. *Journal of Homosexuality, 57*(1), 98–116. doi:10.1080/00918360903445913

Blackwell, C. W. (2008). Nursing implications in the application of conversion therapies on gay, lesbian, bisexual, and transgender clients. *Issues in Mental Health Nursing, 29*(6), 651–665. doi:10.1080/01612840802048915

Brown, E. (2005). We wear the mask: African American contemporary gay male identities. *Journal of African American Studies, 9*(2), 29–38. doi:10.1007/s12111-005-1020-x

Cadge, W., Girouard, J., Olson, L. R., & Lylerohr, M. (2012). Uncertainty in clergy's perspectives on homosexuality: A research note. *Review of Religious Research,* advanced online copy, 1–17. doi:10.1007/s13644-012-0058-1

Church of Christ (CC). (2012a). Internet ministries. Retrieved from http://church-of-christ.org/

Church of Christ (CC). (2012b). What does the word of God say about homosexuality? Retrieved from http://church-of-christ.org/homosexuality.htm

Church of Jesus Christ of Latter-Day Saints (LDS). (2006). Same-gender attraction. Retrieved from http://www.mormonnewsroom.org/official-statement/same-gender-attraction

Church of Jesus Christ of Latter-Day Saints (LDS). (2012, January). To the point. *Liahona.* Retrieved from http://www.lds.org/liahona/2012/01/to-the-point/what-is-the-churchs-position-on-homosexuality-is-it-ok-to-be-friends-with-people-who-have-homosexual-feelings?lang=eng&query=homosexuality

Cohen, C. J. (2003). Contested membership: Black gay identities and the politics of AIDS. In R. J. Corber & S. Valocchi (Eds.), *Queer studies: An interdisciplinary reader* (pp. 46–60). Malden, MA: Blackwell.

Couch, M., Mulcare, H., Pitts, M., Smith, A., & Mitchell, A. (2008). The religious affiliation of gay, lesbian, bisexual, transgender and intersex Australians: A report from the private lives survey. *People and Place, 16*(1), 1–11.

Courage. (2012). The Courage apostolate home page. Retrieved from http://couragerc.net/

Dessel, A. B. (2010). Effects of intergroup dialogue: Public school teachers and sexual orientation prejudice. *Small Group Research, 41*(5), 556–592. doi:10.1177/1046496410369560

DignityUSA. (2011). What is Dignity? Retrieved from http://www.dignityusa.org/content/what-dignity

Duarte-Velez, Y., Bernal, G., & Bonilla, K. (2010). Culturally adapted cognitive–behavioral therapy: Integrating sexual, spiritual, and family identities in an evidence-based treatment of a depressed Latino adolescent. *Journal of Clinical Psychology, 66*(8), 895–906. doi:10.1002/jclp.20710

Ellison, C. G., Acevedo, G. A., & Ramos-Wada, A. I. (2011). Religion and attitudes toward same-sex marriage among U.S. Latinos. *Social Science Quarterly, 92*(1), 35–56. doi:10.1111/j.1540-6237.2011.00756.x

Evangelical Lutheran Church in America (ELCA). (n.d.). One flock. Retrieved from http://www.elca.org/Who-We-Are/Our-Three-Expressions/Churchwide-Organization/Ecumenical-and-Inter-Religious-Relations/Full-Communion/~/media/Files/Who%20We%20Are/Ecumenical%20and%20Inter%20Religious%20Relations/FOS%20document%20FINAL.ashx

Evangelical Lutheran Church in America (ELCA). (1991). Human sexuality/homosexuality. Retrieved from http://www.elca.org/What-We-Believe/Social-Issues/Resolutions/1991/CA91,-p-,07,-p-,51-Human-Sexuality-Homosexuality.aspx

Evangelical Lutheran Church in America (ELCA). (2009a). Human sexuality: Gift and trust. Retrieved from http://www.elca.org/What-We-Believe/Social-Issues/Social-Statements/JTF-Human-Sexuality.aspx

Evangelical Lutheran Church in America (ELCA). (2009b, August 21). ELCA assembly opens ministry to partnered gay and lesbian Lutherans. *ELCA News Service.* Retrieved from http://www.elca.org/Who-We-Are/Our-Three-Expressions/Churchwide-Organization/Communication-Services/News/Releases.aspx?a=4253

Finlay, B., & Walther, C. S. (2003). The relation of religious affiliation, service attendance, and other factors to homophobic attitudes among university students. *Review of Religious Research, 44*(4), 270–393.

Foster, M. L., Arnold, E., Rebchook, G., & Kegeles, S. M. (2011). It's my inner strength: Spirituality, religion and HIV in the lives of young African American men who have sex with men. *Culture, Health & Sexuality, 13*(9), 1103–1117. doi:10.1080/13691058.2011.600460

Garcia, D. I., Gray-Stanley, J., & Ramirez-Valles, J. (2008). "The priest obviously doesn't know that I'm gay": The religious and spiritual journeys of Latino gay men. *Journal of Homosexuality, 55*(3), 411–436. doi:10.1080/00918360802345149

GLAdventist. (2012). About us. Retrieved from http://gladventist.org/blog/category/about/

Griffin, H. (2000). Their own received them not: African American lesbians and gays in Black churches. *Theology & Sexuality, 12,* 88–100. doi:10.1177/135583580000601206

Grocholewski, Z. (2005). Instruction concerning the criteria for the discernment of vocations with regard to persons with homosexual tendencies in view of their admission to the seminary and to Holy Orders. Retrieved from http://www.vatican.va/roman_curia/congregations/ccatheduc/documents/rc_con_ccatheduc_doc_20051104_istruzione_en.html

Guerilus, S. (2011, November 11). Mother Bethel preaches advocacy for the poor. *The Philadelphia Tribune.* Retrieved from http://www.phillytrib.com/religionarticles/item/1460-mother-bethel-preaches-advocacy-for-the-poor.html

Harris, A. C. (2009). Marginalization by the marginalized: Race, homophobia, heterosexism, and "the problem of the 21st century." *Journal of Gay & Lesbian Social Services, 21*(4), 430–448. doi:10.1080/10538720903163171

Heinze, J. E., & Horn, S. S. (2009). Intergroup contact and beliefs about homosexuality in adolescence. *Journal of Youth Adolescence, 38,* 937–951. doi:10.1007/s10964-009-9408-x

Hinckley, G. B. (1999). Why we do some of the things we do. Retrieved from http://www.lds.org/ensign/1999/11/why-we-do-some-of-the-things-we-do?lang=eng&query=homosexual+marriage

Holland, J. R. (2007). Helping those who struggle with same-gender attraction. Retrieved from http://www.lds.org/liahona/2007/10/helping-those-who-struggle-with-same-gender-attraction?lang=eng&query=homosexual+marriage

Human Rights Campaign. (2012). Stances of faiths on LGBT issues: African Methodist Episcopal Church. Retrieved from http://www.hrc.org/resources/entry/stances-of-faiths-on-lgbt-issues-african-methodist-episcopal-church

Hunt, M. E. (2012). Gender and sexuality in the context of religion and social justice. In M. D. Palmer & S. M. Burgess (Eds.), *The Wiley–Blackwell companion to religion and social justice* (pp. 535–546). Malden, MA: Blackwell Publishing.

Integrity USA. (2013). What is Integrity? Retrieved from http://integrityusa.org/about-integrity

Jehovah's Witnesses (JW). (2012). *Questions young people ask: Answers that work* (Vol. 2). Brooklyn, NY: Watchtower Bible and Tract Society of New York. Retrieved from http://download.jw.org/files/media_books/5e/yp2_E.pdf

Jehovah's Witnesses (JW). (2013). The Bible's viewpoint: Does God approve of same-sex marriage? Retrieved from http://wol.jw.org/en/wol/d/r1/lp-e/102005250?q=same-sex+marriage&p=par

Jenkins, L., & Johnston, L. B. (2004). Unethical treatment of gay and lesbian people with conversion therapy. *Families in Society: The Journal of Contemporary Social Services, 85*(4), 557–561. doi:10.1606/1044-3894.1846

Lease, S. H., Horne, S. G., & Noffsinger-Frazier, N. (2005). Affirming faith experiences and psychological health for Caucasian lesbian, gay, and bisexual individuals. *Journal of Counseling Psychology, 52*(3), 378–388. doi:10.1037/0022-0167.52.3.378

Levy, D. L. (2008). Gay, lesbian, and queer individuals with a Christian upbringing: Exploring the process of resolving conflict between sexual identity and religious beliefs. *Dissertation Abstracts International, 69*(08), 282A. (UMI No. AAT 3326661)

Levy, D. L., & Reeves, P. (2011). Resolving identity conflict: Gay, lesbian, and queer individuals with a Christian upbringing. *Journal of Gay & Lesbian Social Services, 23*(1), 53–68. doi:10.1080/10538720.2010.530193

Logie, C., Bridge, T. J., & Bridge, P. D. (2007). Evaluating the phobias, attitudes, and cultural competence of master of social work students toward LGBT populations. *Journal of Homosexuality, 53*(4), 201–221. doi:10.1080/00918360802103472

Lutheran Church Missouri Synod (LCMS). (2011). Marriage/human sexuality. Retrieved from http://lcms.org/page.aspx?pid=726&DocID=550

Mahsman, D. L. (2003, October). God and the gay lifestyle. *The Lutheran Witness.* Retrieved from http://www.lcms.org/Document.fdoc?src=lcm&id=573

Marcum, J. (2009). Go figure. Retrieved from http://www.pcusa.org/media/uploads/research/pdfs/09oct.pdf

Marin, A. (2011). Winner take all? A political and religious assessment of the culture war between the LGBT community and conservatives. *Political Theology, 12,* 501–510. doi:10.1558/poth.v12i4.501

McQueeney, K. (2009). "We are God's children, y'all": Race, gender and sexuality in lesbian- and gay-affirming congregations. *Social Problems, 56*(1), 151–173. doi:10.1525/sp.2009.56.1.151

More Light Presbyterians. (2012a). About More Light Presbyterians (MLP). Retrieved from http://www.mlp.org/index.php?topic=aboutmlp

More Light Presbyterians. (2012b). MLP General Assembly legislative summary, July 3. Retrieved from http://www.ga220.org/2012/07/mlp-general-assembly-legislative_03.html

National Association of Free Will Baptists. (2010). *Treatise of the faith and practices of the National Association of Free Will Baptists, Inc.* Retrieved from http://nafwb.org/site/wp-content/uploads/2012/02/FWB-Treatise.pdf

Newman, B. S., Dannenfelser, P. L., & Benishek, L. (2002). Assessing beginning social work and counseling students' acceptance of lesbians and gay men. *Journal of Social Work Education, 38*(2), 273–288.

Oaks, D. H. (1996, March). Same-gender attraction. *Liahona.* Retrieved from http://www.lds.org/liahona/1996/03/same-gender-attraction?lang=eng

Page, M. J. L. (2011). *Religious and sexual identity in LGB youth: Stressors, identity difficulty, and mental health outcomes.* Master's thesis, University of Miami.

Parks, C. W. (2010). A window illuminating the reservations of black men who have sex with men in fully embracing the institution of same-sex marriage. *Journal of Gay & Lesbian Social Services, 22*(1–2), 132–148. doi:10.1080/10538720903332446

Pew Forum on Religion & Public Life. (2007). U.S. religious landscape survey. Retrieved from http://religions.pewforum.org/

Pew Forum on Religion & Public Life. (2010). Religious groups' official positions on same-sex marriage. Retrieved from http://www.pewforum.org/Gay-Marriage-and-Homosexuality/Religious-Groups-Official-Positions-on-Same-Sex-Marriage.aspx

Phillips, L. (2005). Deconstructing "down low" discourse: The politics of sexuality, gender, race, AIDS, and anxiety. *Journal of African American Studies, 9*(2), 3–15. doi:10.1007/s12111-005-1018-4

Plugge-Foust, C., & Strickland, G. (2000). Homophobia, irrationality, and Christian ideology: Does a relationship exist? *Journal of Sex Education and Therapy, 25*(4), 240–244.

Ratzinger, J. (1986). Letter to the Bishops of the Catholic Church on the pastoral care of homosexual persons. Retrieved from http://www.vatican.va/roman_curia/congregations/cfaith/documents/rc_con_cfaith_doc_19861001_homosexual-persons_en.html

ReconcilingWorks (RW). (2012). ReconcilingWorks! Retrieved from http://www.reconcilingworks.org/

Rodriguez, E. M., & Ouellette, S. C. (2000). Gay and lesbian Christians: Homosexual and religious identity integration in the members and participants of a gay-positive church. *Journal for the Scientific Study of Religion, 39*(3), 333–347. doi:10.1111/0021-8294.00028

Roman Catholic Church (RCC). (1995). The Catechism of the Catholic Church. Retrieved from http://www.vatican.va/archive/ccc_css/archive/catechism/p3s2c2a6.htm

Russell, R. (2008). United Methodists uphold homosexuality stance. Retrieved from http://www.umc.org/site/apps/nlnet/content3.aspx?c=lwL4KnN1LtH&b=2639513&ct=5315905

Schuck, K. D., & Liddle, B. J. (2001). Religious conflicts experienced by lesbian, gay, and bisexual individuals. *Journal of Gay & Lesbian Psychotherapy, 5*(2), 63–82. doi:10.1300/J236v05n02_07

Scruggs, J. R. (2012). The same-sex marriage issue, voting, and Christian responsibility. Retrieved from http://www.nationalbaptist.com/about-us/news—press-releases/the-same-sex-marriage-issue,-voting-and-christian-responsibility.html

Seventh-Day Adventist Church (SDA). (1987). A statement of concern on sexual behavior. Retrieved from http://www.adventist.org/beliefs/statements/main-stat35.html

Seventh-Day Adventist Church (SDA). (1996). An affirmation of marriage. Retrieved from http://adventist.org/beliefs/statements/main-stat16.html

Seventh-Day Adventist Church (SDA). (1999). Seventh-Day Adventist position statement on homosexuality. Retrieved from http://www.adventist.org/beliefs/statements/main-stat46.html

Seventh-Day Adventist Church (SDA). (2004). Seventh-Day Adventist response to same-sex unions: A reaffirmation of Christian marriage. Retrieved from http://adventist.org/beliefs/statements/main-stat53.html

Seventh-Day Adventist Kinship. (2011). About Seventh-Day Adventist Kinship International. Retrieved from http://www.sdakinship.org/en/about.html

Sherkat, D. E., de Vries, K. M., & Creek, S. (2010). Race, religion, and opposition to same-sex marriage. *Social Science Quarterly, 91*(1), 80–98. doi:10.1111/j.1540-6237.2010.00682.x

Shidlo, A., & Schroeder, M. (2002). Changing sexual orientation: A consumer's report. *Professional Psychology: Research and Practice, 33*(3), 249–259. doi:10.1037//0735-7028.33.3.249

Silverstein, E. (2004, July 2). Families paper approved. *News.* Retrieved from http://apps.pcusa.org/ga216/news/ga04112.htm

Solheim, J. (1998, September 3). Sexuality issues test bonds of affection among bishops at Lambeth Conference. *Episcopal News Service.* Retrieved from http://archive.episcopalchurch.org/3577_70963_ENG_HTM.htm

Southern Baptist Convention (SBC). (2003). On same-sex marriage. Retrieved from http://www.sbc.net/resolutions/amResolution.asp?ID=1128

Southern Baptist Convention (SBC). (2008). On the California Supreme Court decision to allow same-sex marriage. Retrieved from http://www.sbc.net /resolutions/amResolution.asp?ID=1190

Southern Baptist Convention (SBC). (2011). On protecting the Defense of Marriage Act (DOMA). Retrieved from http://www.sbc.net/resolutions /amResolution.asp?ID=1212

Southern Baptist Convention (SBC). (2012a). SBC resolutions. Retrieved from http://www.sbc.net/resolutions/default.asp

Southern Baptist Convention (SBC). (2012b). Sexuality. Retrieved from http: //www.sbc.net/aboutus/pssexuality.asp

Steensland, B., Park, J. Z., Regnerus, M. D., Robinson, L. D., Wilcox, W. B., & Woodberry, R. D. (2000). The measure of American religion: Toward improving the state of the art. *Social Forces, 79*(1), 291–318. doi:10.1093 /sf/79.1.291

Summers, A. (2011, October 7). Presbyterian Church USA to ordain first gay minister. *Christian Post.* Retrieved from http://www.christianpost.com /news/presbyterian-church-usa-to-ordain-first-gay-minister-57623/

Thomas, J. N., & Olson, D. V. A. (2012). Evangelical elites' changing responses to homosexuality 1960–2009. *Sociology of Religion, 73*(3), 239–272. doi:10.1093/socrel/srs031

Unitarian Universalist Association of Congregations (UU). (2011). Unitarian Universalist LGBT history timeline. Retrieved from http://www.uua.org /lgbt/history/20962.shtml

Unitarian Universalist Association of Congregations (UU). (2012). Lesbian, gay, bisexual, transgender, and queer welcome & equality. Retrieved from http://www.uua.org/lgbt/

United Church of Christ (UCC). (n.d.). LGBT Ministries. Retrieved from http://www.ucc.org/lgbt/

United Church of Christ (UCC). (1969). Resolution on homosexuals and the law. Retrieved from http://www.ucc.org/assets/pdfs/1969-RESOLUTION-ON -HOMOSEXUALS-AND-THE-LAW.pdf

United Church of Christ (UCC). (1975). Resolution deploring the violation of civil rights of gay and bisexual persons. Retrieved from http://www.ucc.org /assets/pdfs/1977-RESOLUTION-DEPLORING-THE-VIOLATION-OF -CIVIL-RIGHTS-OF-GAY-AND-BISEXUAL-PERSONS.pdf

United Church of Christ (UCC). (1977). Recommendations in regard to the human sexuality study. Retrieved from http://www.ucc.org/assets/pdfs/1977-RECOMMENDATIONS-IN-REGARD-TO-THE-HUMAN-SEXUALITY-STUDY.pdf

United Church of Christ (UCC). (1983a). Resolution in response to the concerns of same-gender oriented persons and their families with the United Church of Christ. Retrieved from http://www.ucc.org/assets/pdfs/1983-RESOLUTION-IN-RESPONSE-TO-THE-CONCERNS-OF-SAME-GENDER-ORIENTED-PERSONS-AND-THEIR-FAMILIES-WITHIN-THE-UNITED-CHURCH-OF-CHRIST.pdf

United Church of Christ (UCC). (1983b). Resolution recommending inclusiveness on association church and ministry committees within the United Church of Christ. Retrieved from http://www.ucc.org/assets/pdfs/1983-RESOLUTION-RECOMMENDING-INCLUSIVENESS-ON-ASSOCIATION-CHURCH-AND-MINISTRY-COMMITTEES.pdf

United Church of Christ (UCC). (1993). Resolution calling on the church for greater leadership to end discrimination against gays and lesbians. Retrieved from http://www.ucc.org/assets/pdfs/1993-RESOLUTION-CALLING-ON-THE-CHURCH-FOR-GREATER-LEADERSHIP-TO-END-DISCRIMINATION-AGAINST-GAYS-AND-LESBIANS.pdf

United Church of Christ (UCC). (1996). Equal marriage rights for same gender couples. Retrieved from http://www.ucc.org/assets/pdfs/1996-EQUAL-MARRIAGE-RIGHTS-FOR-SAME-GENDER-COUPLES.pdf

United Church of Christ (UCC). (1998). Passage of hate crime legislation. Retrieved from http://www.ucc.org/assets/pdfs/1998-PASSAGE-OF-HATE-CRIME-LEGISLATION.pdf

United Church of Christ (UCC). (2009). Affirming diversity/multi-cultural education in the public schools. Retrieved from http://www.ucc.org/lgbt/pdfs/2009-Affirming-Diversity-Education.pdf

United Church of Christ (UCC). (2011). The right of LGBT parents to adopt and raise children. Retrieved from http://www.ucc.org/lgbt/pdfs/2011_THE_RIGHT_OF_LGBT_PARENTS_TO_ADOPT_AND_RAISE_CHILDREN.pdf

United Methodist Church (UMC). (2004). Human sexuality. Retrieved from http://archives.umc.org/interior.asp?ptid=1&mid=1728

United Methodist Church (UMC). (2010). Bishops face challenge on same-sex unions. Retrieved from http://www.umc.org/news-and-media/bishops-face-challenge-on-same-sex-unions

United Methodist Church (UMC). (2011, June 28). Church once more faces homosexuality divide. A UMNS Report. Retrieved from United Presbyterian Church in the United States of America (PCUSA). (1978). The church and homosexuality. Retrieved from http://www.pcusa.org/media/uploads/_resolutions/church-and-homosexuality.pdf

United States Catholic Conference. (2003). Bishops urge constitutional amendment to protect marriage. *Catholic News Service.* Retrieved from http://www.americancatholic.org/News/Homosexuality/default.asp#Background

Universal Fellowship of Metropolitan Community Churches (MCC). (2004). History of MCC. Retrieved from http://mccchurch.org/overview/history-of-mcc/

Universal Fellowship of Metropolitan Community Churches (MCC). (2012). I'm new to MCC. Retrieved from http://mccchurch.org/im-new-to-mcc/

Van Marter, J. (2011, May 11). PC(USA) relaxes constitutional prohibition of gay and lesbian ordination. *Presbyterian News Service.* Retrieved from http://www.pcusa.org/news/2011/5/11/pcusa-relaxes-constitutional-prohibition-gay-and-l/

Wells, M. (2007, February 27). AME Church advocates for voting rights for ex-offenders. *New America Media.* Retrieved from http://news.newamericamedia.org/news/view_article.html?article_id=eeb68bd9dbc5fc9a8cba048bb14abc86

Whitehead, A. L. (2012). Religious organizations and homosexuality: The acceptance of gays and lesbians in American congregations. *Review of Religious Research,* advanced online copy, 1–21. doi:10.1007/s13644-012-0066-1

Woodford, M. R., Walls, N. E., & Levy, D. L. (2012). Religion and endorsement of same-sex marriage: The role of syncretism between denominational teaching about homosexuality and personal religious beliefs. *Interdisciplinary Journal of Research on Religion, 8*(4), 2–29.

Zaimov, S. (2012, May 3). Methodists strike down amendment to "agree to disagree" on homosexuality. *Christian Post.* Retrieved from http://www.christianpost.com/news/methodists-strike-down-amendment-to-agree-to-disagree-on-homosexuality-74312/

CHAPTER 2

Christian Social Work Students' Attitudes Toward Lesbians and Gay Men: Religious Teachings, Religiosity, and Contact

Jill Chonody, PhD, MSW; Michael R. Woodford, PhD; Scott Smith, PhD; and Perry Silverschanz, PhD

The nature of attitudes toward lesbian and gay people is an important topic for social scientists, policy makers, and social work practitioners. Given the current issues associated with bullying and antigay bias as well as highly publicized bullying-related youth suicides in recent years, the National Association of Social Workers (NASW) has encouraged social workers to

> speak out against harassment and bullying, to educate colleagues, students, and institutions about the negative impact of harassing behaviors on the individual and the environment, and to advocate for practice and policies that ensure that students—of all ages—can live and learn in environments free from discrimination and bias. (NASW, 2011, p. 1, ¶3)

This mandate reinforces the importance of addressing sexual prejudice as part of the social work curriculum. The Council on Social Work Education (CSWE) directs programs to train students to engage diversity and difference in practice, including in regard to sexual orientation (CSWE, 2008). Given that social work practitioners work with a wide range of client populations, it is important to understand how those currently being trained for the field perceive same-sex sexuality.

Sexual prejudice remains an ongoing issue among college students, including social work students (Newman, Dannenfelser, & Benishek, 2002; Raiz & Saltzburg, 2007; Sun, 2002), and a number of demographic covariates have been documented in the literature. Knowing someone who is gay, lesbian, or bisexual (GLB) has been associated with less biased attitudes (Bowen & Bourgeois, 2003; Chonody, Siebert, & Rutledge, 2009; Cotton-Huston & Waite, 2000; Swank & Raiz, 2010; Woodford, Silverschanz, Swank, Scherrer, & Raiz, 2012). Contact theory suggests that interaction with individuals of a negatively stereotyped group should decrease negative biases of the group by providing a positive reference point that did not previously exist (Allport, 1954). Support of its influence can be also be found in pedagogical interventions that use intergroup contact, which have had some success in facilitating understanding for heterosexual students (Chonody et al., 2009; Cotton-Huston & Waite, 2000; Dongvillo & Ligon, 2001). Immutable factors such as sex (Chonody et al., 2009; Woodford, Silverschanz et al., 2012) and age (Ellis, Kitzinger, & Wilkinson, 2003; Johnson, Brems, & Alford-Keating, 1997; Woodford, Silverschanz et al., 2012) are also related to sexual prejudice, but they may play a less significant role when religious factors are taken into account (Rosik, Griffith, & Cruz, 2007). Many studies find religiosity to be an influential factor in regard to attitudes toward lesbians and gay men (Schulte & Battle, 2004; Finlay & Walther, 2003; Whitley, 2009), but its contribution may be dependent on the doctrine associated with particular religious affiliations. The vast majority of mainstream Christian religious denominations, especially Evangelical Christian faiths, have specific doctrine and teachings about homosexuality, many taking an unsupportive stance (Rogers, 2009; Subhi et al., 2011).

The intersection of religious beliefs and social work practice has created tension within the profession. Significant debate exists surrounding the issue of epistemological frameworks that may be inconsistent with social work values. Hodge (2005) posits that people of faith are not well-accepted within the social work profession for their beliefs, particularly concerning same-sex attraction/relationships. The premise of his treatise is that most Christians would not condemn gay and lesbian people at a personal level, especially if they were to remain abstinent from sexual behavior (Hodge, 2005). An oft-repeated mantra of "love the sinner, hate the sin" is posited as the mainstream Christian viewpoint. Dessel, Bolen, and Shepardson (2011) counter Hodge's position that the freedom of religious expression within social work practice cannot come at the cost of encouraging those who identify as sexual minorities to suppress their desires for intimate relationships with same-sex partners. Moreover, freedom of speech and religious belief cannot be repackaged in such a way as to support homophobia and institutionalized heterosexism as it has in the past (Dessel et al., 2011).

Although attention has been given to the role of religion in studies about attitudes toward gay and lesbian individuals among social work students, as with studies conducted with the general population, analysis is often limited to religious denomination/tradition and religiosity (Walls, 2010). As a result, these studies have only partially explained the influence of religion. In explaining their findings, some authors theorize about the role of church teachings (e.g., Finlay & Walther, 2003; Schulte & Battle, 2004); yet a dearth of studies in contemporary literature, including social work studies, exists about how specific religious messages about same-sex sexuality influence individuals' attitudes toward gay and lesbian people. Many religious denominations teach that same-sex sexuality is immoral and sinful; however, this is not a universal stance (Rogers, 2009). Some denominations fully embrace sexual minorities by ordaining openly gay and lesbian ministers and performing same-sex marriages. Other denominations take an affirming stance, but do not perform same-sex marriages or ordain "out" gay and lesbian ministers (Rogers, 2009). Even if part of a church that holds antigay views, it is possible that one is not exposed to such messages on the local level (and vice versa).

These factors emphasize the importance of looking beyond religious affiliation and religiosity to examine the role of church messages about same-sex sexuality. To the authors' knowledge, estimates regarding the number of Christian social work students are not available, but this group appears to represent a noteworthy proportion of students entering this major, as evidenced by student organizations on individual campuses (e.g., Christian Social Work Students at Missouri University, Christians in Social Work Association at the University of Michigan) and professional membership organizations such as the North American Association of Christians in Social Work. Therefore, this intersection between social work practice and Christian identification has particular relevance in understanding how attitudes toward lesbians and gay men may be influenced by religious teachings.

The purpose of this study is to explore the role of religious teachings about same-sex sexuality on attitudes toward lesbians and gay men among Christian social work students. Given the consequence of religiosity as well as contact with GLB individuals on attitudinal outcomes in previous studies, we also examine their effects in this study. We hypothesize that the influence of religious teachings about same-sex sexuality on attitudes toward lesbians and gay men is moderated by religiosity and contact with GLB friends.

Method

Sample and Data Collection

This study employed a cross-sectional design using a convenience sample of undergraduate and graduate students enrolled in social work courses at four geographically diverse universities in the United States. All of the universities were secular public institutions. Students were recruited to participate in a study investigating attitudes toward lesbians and gay men (N = 851). For the current study, we limit our analysis to "completely heterosexual" students who identified as either Catholic or Protestant and indicated a specific religious message related to homosexuality (n = 383). Sexual orientation was determined using the Kinsey, Pomeroy, and Martin (1948) continuum (completely heterosexual–completely homosexual). It is recommended that researchers examine sexual prejudice among heterosexuals and sexual minorities separately, because the nature of their attitudes likely differs (Herek, 1988). Although other religious affiliations were represented in the original sample, the number of respondents in each of these affiliations was insufficient for analysis purposes.

Approval from the Institutional Review Board for Human Subjects at each participating university was obtained prior to data collection, which occurred during the 2008–2009 academic year. Students voluntarily completed the anonymous paper-and-pencil survey during class time. Completion of the instrument package was considered consent to participate.

Measures

ATTITUDES TOWARD LESBIANS AND GAY MEN (ATLG)

The short version of the ATLG was used, which contains two separate subscales with 10 total items—5 items to assess attitudes toward lesbian women and the other 5 items for gay men (Herek, 1988). The ATLG is specifically designed for use with heterosexuals (Herek, 1988). The reliability of this scale has been consistently demonstrated with various groups, including social work students (e.g., Krieglstein, 2003; Raiz & Saltzberg, 2007; Rutledge, Siebert, Siebert, & Chonody, 2012). A 6-point Likert scale was used in this study where 1 represented *strongly disagree* and 6 represented *strongly agree.* Items from both subscales were summed to create a global ATLG score. Scores range from 10 to 60, and lower scores indicate a more positive attitude. Reliability for the ATLG in this study was excellent ($\alpha = .93$).

RELIGIOUS VARIABLES

Religious affiliation was reported as *agnostic, Catholic, Jewish, Muslim, Protestant, spiritual, none,* and *other* (again, the analytical sample is limited to Catholic and Protestant). *Religiosity* was determined by: "How important are religious or spiritual beliefs in your daily life?" and used a 10-point Likert scale (1 represented *not at all* and 10 represented *very much*). *Religious message about homosexuality* was assessed by two questions. First a dichotomous question inquired: "Does your religion have a specific message about homosexuality?" If respondents answered yes, then they were instructed to answer: "Which of the following best describes the message about homosexuality?" This item was measured on a 10-point scale where 1 represented *not accepting* and 10 indicated *accepting.* Henceforth, we refer to the latter variable as *religious message.*

SOCIAL CONTACT

Social contact was assessed by a dichotomous (no/yes) survey question that inquired whether the respondent has ever had any friends who are GLB. If respondents indicated yes, they were asked to report the number of GLB friends they have. To provide an adequate sample size for the current analysis, respondents who responded no to the initial question were coded as 0 in the number of *GLB friends* variable.

DEMOGRAPHIC VARIABLES

Age was reported in years. *Sex* was reported as male, female, or intersexed. *Race* was reported as Asian American, Native Hawaiian or Pacific Islander, American Indian or Alaska Native, African American or Black, Caucasian or White, and Other. Because of sample size, race was recoded as White and people of color for regression analysis. *College major* was assessed by an open-ended question. *Year in school* was reported as freshman, sophomore, junior, senior, and graduate. For regression purposes, this was recoded as undergraduate and graduate (referred to as university status).

Data Analysis

Data were inspected to ensure that all statistical assumptions were met prior to analyses, and all assumptions were met. Additionally, continuous variables were assessed for outliers using descriptive statistics. The skewness and kurtosis of the data were examined using a threshold of 2.5 (Kline, 2005). Two interaction items were created to test whether religiosity and the number of GLB friends moderated the relationship between religious message and attitudes toward lesbians and gay men, and hierarchical multiple regression was conducted. The first step evaluated the effect of age, sex, race, religious affiliation, university status, and religiosity on attitudes toward lesbians and gay men. In Step 2 the religious message and the number of GLB friends were added to the model. In Step 3 the two interaction variables were entered: the interaction between religiosity and religious message and the interaction between number of GLB friends and religious message. The insertion of multiple interaction terms or moderators could lead to an inflated Type I error rate, thus, as suggested by Cohen, Cohen, West, and Aiken (2003), we entered all of the moderator terms in a single step to reduce this occurrence. All continuous variables were centered to reduce multicollinearity and improve the interpretation of findings (Pedhazur & Schmelkin, 1991).

Results

Demographics

Participants were largely female (87.5%), Caucasian (62.9%), and on average 25 years of age. The sample was predominately social work majors (78.9%) and undergraduates (61.9%). Other majors were predominantly from other helping professions (e.g., rehabilitation, family science, speech pathology). Results of an independent samples *t*-test indicate no statistically significant differences between social work majors and other majors on the dependent variable, $t(382)=.45$, $p=.65$; therefore, we included non–social work majors in this study because they were taking a social work course.

Slightly more than three-quarters of the sample were affiliated with a Protestant religion. Religiosity was on the higher end of the scale ($M=7.68$), suggesting a fairly religious group. Religious message about homosexuality was on the lower end of the range ($M=2.62$), indicating respondents overall were exposed to antigay messages within their religious affiliations. The scores on the ATLG were normally distributed and indicated a mild amount of antigay bias in the sample ($M=27.86$). Comparisons by university yielded no statistically significant differences in attitudes toward lesbians and gay men, $F(3)=.85$, $p=.50$, nor religiosity, $F(3)=.11$, $p=.96$. Table 1 provides demographic information and distributions for all variables.

Table 1. Demographic Characteristics of the Sample

Variable	*M*	*SD*	%	*n*[a]
Age (range 18–61)	24.70	7.30		379
Sex				
Male			12.3	47
Female			87.5	335
Race				
African American/Black			25.6	98
Asian American			1.6	6
Caucasian/White			62.9	241
Biracial/multiracial			4.2	16
Other (includes Native or Pacific Islander and American Indian or Alaska Native)			5.3	20

(continued)

Table 1 (continued)

Variable		*M*	*SD*	%	*n*[a]
Major					
	Social work			78.9	302
	Other			20.9	80
University status					
	Freshman			6.0	23
	Sophomore			13.5	52
	Junior			24.2	93
	Senior			22.1	85
	Graduate			34.0	131
Know GLB friends (answered yes)				87.7	336
	Number of friends	4.10	4.64		378
Religious affiliation					
	Catholic			22.7	87
	Protestant			77.3	296
Religiosity		7.68	2.36		382
Religious message[b]		2.62	2.12		383
ATLG		27.86	13.36		383

[a] Sample sizes are different on each variable due to missing data.
[b] Refers to the religious message regarding acceptability of homosexuality.
Note. GLB=gay, lesbian, bisexual. ATLG=Attitudes toward lesbians and gay men.

Multiple Regression Results

In the first step of the analysis (Table 2), age, sex, race, religious affiliation, and religiosity were all statistically significant. Specifically, older students held less antigay bias. Male students and students of color were more biased than female students and White students. Catholic students were less biased than Protestant students. The relationship between religiosity and antigay bias was positive, indicating that those who valued religion/spirituality more in their lives tended to hold more negative attitudes toward lesbians and gay men. University status was not statistically significant. This model explained 33% of the variance.

Table 2. Multiple Regression Predicting Attitudes Toward Lesbians and Gay Men Among Catholic and Protestant Social Work Students

Variable	Model 1			Model 2			Model 3		
	B	*SE*	β	*B*	*SE*	β	*B*	*SE*	β
Age	−0.21	0.08	−.12**	−0.17	0.08	−.10**	−0.18	0.08	−.10**
Male	4.95	1.77	.12**	3.15	1.70	.08	2.80	1.68	.07
People of color	2.65	1.20	.10*	1.26	1.17	.05	0.60	1.16	.02
Catholic affiliation	−4.30	1.44	−.14**	−5.03	1.37	−.16***	−4.28	1.37	−.14**
Religiosity[a]	2.64	0.26	.48***	2.57	0.24	.46***	2.62	0.24	.47***
Graduate student	−1.91	1.30	−.07	−1.70	1.24	−.06	−2.08	1.22	−.08
Religious message[a]				−1.22	0.27	−.20***	−1.31	0.27	−.21***
No. GLB friends[a]				−0.48	0.12	−.17***	−0.58	0.13	−.20***
Religiosity × religious message							−0.37	0.11	−.14**
No. GLB friends × religious message							0.07	0.04	.08
R^2			.323			.397			.419
F change in R^2			29.27***			21.56***			7.13**

Note. GLB = gay, lesbian, and bisexual.
[a] Centered.
*$p < .05$. **$p < .01$. ***$p < .001$.

The addition of religious message and the number of GLB friends in the second model increased the explained variance by 7% ($p < .001$). Both of these variables were negatively associated with the outcome, suggesting that the more accepting one's religion's message about same-sex sexuality, the less antigay bias one held. Similarly, the more GLB friends one has the more affirming one's views of lesbians and gay men. With the exception of sex and race, all variables included in Step 1 remained significant in this model.

In the final step the two interaction items were added, and the explained variance increased by 2% (p=.001); however, only the cross-product for religiosity and religious message was statistically significant. A negative association was found between this interaction term and ATLG scores, suggesting that the effect of the level of acceptance of homosexuals conveyed in religious messages on antigay bias changes depending on the level of religiosity in one's life. In other words, the more religious a student is, the greater negative effect of religious message on one's attitudes toward sexual minorities. All variables significant in Model 2 retained their significance in Model 3.

As suggested by Aiken and West (1991), to more closely examine the effects of the interaction on antigay attitudes, we created a graph by plotting religiosity against whether the religious message was not accepting or accepting (Figure 1). The scores on religiosity were divided by using the average of the scores of the highest third of the sample (high religiosity) and the average of the scores of the lowest third of the sample (low religiosity). Religious message was categorized

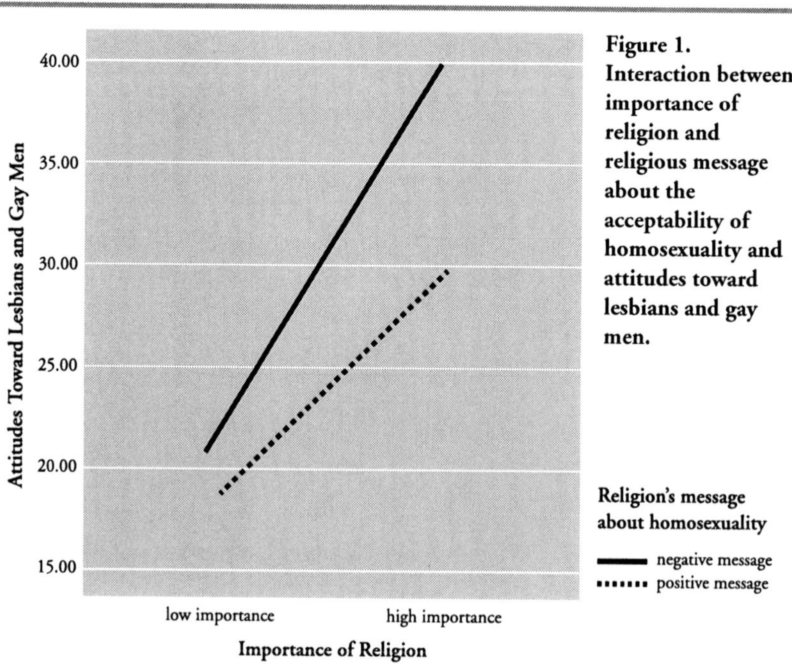

Figure 1. Interaction between importance of religion and religious message about the acceptability of homosexuality and attitudes toward lesbians and gay men.

Note. Lower ATLG score indicates more affirming attitudes.

as nonaccepting message if the respondent selected 1–5 and accepting message if the respondent answered 6–10.

The graph shows the main effect of religious message on attitudes; specifically, if one's religion conveyed a nonaccepting message about lesbians and gay men, respondents had higher antigay bias scores (and if the message was accepting, antigay bias scores were lower). Additionally, in terms of religiosity, we see that individuals in the high religiosity group scored higher on the ATLG than their colleagues in the low religiosity group. The interaction is evident in that those whose religion conveyed a nonaccepting message had considerably higher antigay bias scores if they also rated religion highly important than did those who reported a positive message and also consider religion to be highly important. The graph also shows that when the religious message promotes acceptance, those in the high religiosity category had more bias than those in the low religiosity group. Furthermore, considering the type of religious message, the largest difference for antigay bias occurred between individuals with high religiosity, whereas the differences between those with low religiosity was not as great. Moreover, those individuals whose church has an accepting message scored lower on the ATLG for both categories of religiosity compared to those exposed to a nonaccepting message.

Discussion

This research adds to the literature by examining the role of religious teachings about same-sex sexuality on Christian social work students' antigay bias. We find in adjusted analysis that religious teaching is significantly associated with students' ATLG scores, with those exposed to more accepting messages reporting less antigay bias. Previous studies have found religiosity (Finlay & Walther, 2003; Schulte & Battle, 2004; Whitley, 2009) and contact with GLB people (Bowen & Bourgeois, 2003; Chonody et al., 2009; Cotton-Huston & Waite, 2000; Swank & Raiz, 2010; Woodford, Silverschanz et al., 2012) to be predictors of antigay bias. We hypothesized that the effect of religious message would be moderated by religiosity and the number of GLB friends. Our findings confirm our hypothesis regarding religiosity, but not GLB friends.

Our results highlight the influential role of religiosity in understanding Christian social work students' antigay bias. Based on main effects only (Model 2), the effect size of religiosity (β=.46) was more than double the next largest effect size, which was religious message (β=–.20). Most noteworthy, however, moderation and subanalysis results indicate that religiosity is influential even when students hear religious messages that same-sex sexuality is acceptable. Students who placed high value on religion and received religious messages that homosexuality is unacceptable were the most biased in our sample. Yet, among students who heard accepting messages about same-sex sexuality, religiosity also mattered; that is, those with high religiosity were more biased than those with low religiosity in this particular group. The same pattern was found among those subjected to religious messages that homosexuality is not acceptable. Evidently, both religious message and religiosity matter in students' antigay bias. However, sexual prejudice is greatest among students subjected to antigay religious messages and who place high value on religion in their lives.

We were surprised to find an insignificant result for the interaction effect for the number of GLB friends and religious message, which suggests that religious message has the same effect on ATLG scores regardless of the number of GLB friends in one's life. We did find the main effect for the number of GLB friends to be statistically significant, which is supported by previous research (Allport, 1954; Bowen & Bourgeois, 2003; Brown, 1984; Chonody et al., 2009; Cotton-Huston & Waite, 2000; Deschamps & Brown, 1983; Swank & Raiz, 2010; Woodford, Silverschanz et al., 2012). Although contact with GLB friends influences one's attitudes, it may not influence the role of a religious message on one's attitude because these two variables are qualitatively different, even though they are somewhat correlated (r=.15, p=.005). It is plausible that exposure to religious messages about same-sex sexuality may have occurred over an extended period of time and has thus been reinforced in such a way that it has not been questioned. Finding older students to be less biased than younger students lends some support to this possibility. Perhaps as students are exposed to diversity in the classroom, in their college life, and life in general, some Christian students will develop more acceptance of sexual minorities.

Additional research is needed to explore these possibilities as well as the role that social work education plays in the process of change.

In contrast, religion and religious message about same-sex sexuality are from the domain of religious variables, which may help to explain why their cross-product was significant. We wonder if other factors related to GLB friends, such as the quality of the relationship, might moderate the relationship between religious message and attitudes toward sexual minorities. Simply having GLB friends versus having close GLB friends may lead to different outcomes. The concept of contact and type of contact should be studied further to enhance pedagogical techniques directed at cultural competence and diversity. Similarly, a better understanding of the content of religious messages would shed light on the relationship between each of these variables. For example, if the message is to accept lesbian and gay individuals, but reject the behavior, than no dissonance may be created between having GLB friends and being exposed to a "less accepting" message. Qualitative methods may facilitate increased understanding of the content of these messages and how this relates to attitudes toward lesbians and gay men.

Future research should also seek to further clarify the relationship between religious doctrine and attitudes toward sexual minorities. Using the findings from this study, religious messages about same-sex sexuality could be further explored within the framework of religious fundamentalism and orthodoxy. The extent to which participants are guided by these beliefs and support the infallibility of their particular perspective may further elucidate the complex relationship that exists between religion and attitudes toward gay and lesbian individuals. Additionally, it will be important to examine the degree to which a participant substantiates the particular religious teachings of their affiliation (Moon, 2004; Walls, 2010; Woodford, Levy, & Walls, 2013; Woodford, Walls, & Levy, 2012; Yamane, 2007). Differences between exposure to messages about same-sex sexuality, either positive or negative, and the extent to which this is incorporated into one's personal religious beliefs may further help to untangle this issue. Theories concerning religious identity development (Fowler, 1981) and research concerning the effects of higher education on students highlight the importance of examining this integration process (Pascarella & Terenzini, 2005).

Limitations

A number of limitations are present in this study. First, the participants represent a convenience sample; thus the findings cannot be generalized. The diversity of the sample, both geographically and demographically, is a strength when considering the implications of the findings, but representativeness of the social work student population cannot be assumed. Second, cross-sectional research design prohibits the determination of temporal ordering required to determine causality.

Third, survey methodology is limited. Wording of author-driven questions can create sensitivity issues and influence participant responses. Further research on ways to measure the wide array of religious beliefs, practices, and personal adherence to particular affiliation continues to be refined. It will be important for future research to examine specific religious traditions, including subgroups within the Protestant religions (e.g., evangelicals). It will also be important to examine the degree of conservatism–liberalism within other traditions.

Fourth, our interest was specifically focused on the attitudes of social work students; therefore, our findings may not be applicable to college students majoring in other disciplines. Future research may seek to replicate our study with a more diverse student population to determine the extent to which religious messages, religiosity, and friendships with GLB individuals influence attitudes toward lesbians and gay men.

Implications and Conclusions

Our findings indicate that it will be important for social work educators to purposefully engage Christian students who have been subjected to negative religious messages about same-sex sexuality, especially those who place high value on religion in their lives. In some cases, students who hold antigay biases may not be aware of their attitudes or they may be hesitant to disclose their opinions for fear of judgment or attack. Strategies are needed to help students uncover their biases and explore their personal values. Woodford and Bella's (2003) multifaceted workshop on antiheterosexist practice may be helpful. This model involves providing participants with information about heterosexism using readings and instructor self-disclosure, exploring various ways to address heterosexism in social work practice and policy, and inviting participants to establish a gay–straight alliance (GSA) to advance antiheterosexist practice. In their implementation with social workers, these instructors/researchers found that the invitation to join a GSA provided some participants with the opportunity to recognize the inconsistency between their personal comfort level and the profession's values of advocating with/for sexual minorities. Through dialogue with the instructors, these participants were able to make these differences explicit and begin to address them. Reflection journals could be easily used as part of this model.

Additionally, spaces will need to be created within social work programs for religious students who hold antigay bias to critically examine the potential consequence of religious messages and religiosity on their views about sexual minorities, and the possible tension that may exist between their personal beliefs and social work values (and how that tension may surface in their future practice). Using readings about the social construction of religious teachings regarding same-sex sexuality may be helpful for some students, some of whom may find it useful to discuss their thoughts and reactions with a trusted instructor or mentor. It may also be beneficial to invite guest speakers affiliated with antigay churches but who reject their church's teachings to talk about how they resolve the conflict. The goal of education is not to strip students of their religious beliefs, but rather to create an environment for students to examine the ways in which personal biases can have the potential to harm individual clients.

Perhaps tolerance can be bridged for diversity in religious beliefs alongside sexual orientation spectrum issues, which would ease professional tensions. Although the profession would not support the condemnation of sexual minorities nor encourage practitioners to treat such clients in an oppressive fashion, social workers are often called to suppress their personal beliefs when working with particular clients, and it is possible that those social workers who hold conservative beliefs about same-sex relationships may be able to hold these competing beliefs between the personal and the professional; however, awareness of personal values and how they may play out in practice is a critical first step. Future research may seek to explore how beliefs may be translating into practice behavior, and what, if any, effect this may have on gay affirmative practice.

References

Aiken, L. S., & West, S. G. (1991). *Multiple regression: Testing and interpreting interactions.* Thousand Oaks, CA: Sage.

Allport, G. (1954). *The nature of prejudice.* Boston, MA: Addison-Wesley.

Bowen, A. M., & Bourgeois, M. J. (2003). Attitudes toward lesbian, gay, and bisexual college students: The contribution of pluralistic ignorance, dynamic social impact, and contact theories. *Journal of American College Health, 50,* 91–96.

Brown, R. (1984). The effects of intergroup similarity and cooperative vs. competitive orientation on intergroup discrimination. *British Journal of Social Psychology, 23,* 21–33.

Chonody, J. M., Siebert, D. C., & Rutledge, S. E. (2009). College students' attitudes toward gays and lesbians. *Journal of Social Work Education, 45,* 499–512.

Cohen, J., Cohen, P., West, S. G., & Aiken, L. S. (2003). *Applied multiple regression/correlation analysis for the behavioral sciences* (3rd ed.). Mahwah, NJ: Erlbaum.

Cotton-Huston, A. L., & Waite, B. M. (2000). Anti-homosexual attitudes in college students: Predictors and classroom interventions. *Journal of Homosexuality, 38,* 117–133.

Council on Social Work Education. (2008). *Educational policy and accreditation standards.* Retrieved from http://www.cswe.org/File.aspx?id=13780

Deschamps, J., & Brown, R. (1983). Superordinate goals and intergroup conflict. *British Journal of Social Psychology, 22,* 189–195.

Dessel, A., Bolen, R., & Shepardson, C. (2011). Can religious expression and sexual orientation affirmation coexist in social work? A critique of Hodge's theoretical, theological, and conceptual frameworks. *Journal of Social Work Education, 47,* 213–251.

Dongvillo, J., & Ligon, J. (2001). Exploring the effectiveness of teaching techniques with lesbian and gay content in the social work curriculum. *Journal of Baccalaureate Social Work, 6,* 115–124.

Ellis, S., Kitzinger, C., & Wilkinson, S. (2003). Attitudes towards lesbians and gay men and support for lesbian and gay human rights among psychology students. *Journal of Homosexuality, 44,* 121–138.

Finlay, B., & Walther, C. S. (2003). The relation of religious affiliation, service attendance, and other factors to homophobic attitudes among university students. *Review of Religious Research, 44,* 370–393.

Fowler, J. W. (1981). *Stages of faith: The psychology of human development and the quest for meaning.* San Francisco, CA: Harper & Row.

Herek, G. M. (1988). Heterosexuals' attitudes toward lesbians and gay men: Correlates and gender differences. *The Journal of Sex Research, 25,* 451–477.

Hodge, D. (2005). Epistemological frameworks, homosexuality, and religion: How people of faith understand the intersection between homosexuality and religion. *Social Work, 50,* 207–218.

Johnson, M. E., Brems, C., & Alford-Keating, P. (1997). Personality correlates of homophobia. *Journal of Homosexuality, 34,* 57–69.

Kinsey, A. C., Pomeroy, W. R., & Martin, C. E. (1948). *Sexual behavior in the human male.* Philadelphia, PA: Saunders.

Kline, R. B. (2005). *Principles and practice of structural equation modeling* (2nd ed.). New York, NY: Guilford Press.

Krieglstein, M. (2003). Heterosexism and social work: An ethical issue. *Journal of Human Behavior in the Social Environment, 8,* 75–91.

Moon, D. (2004). *God, sex, and politics: Homosexuality and everyday theologies.* Chicago, IL: University of Chicago Press.

National Association of Social Workers. (2011). *NASW calls upon social work to speak out against bullying.* Retrieved from http://www.naswdc.org/diversity/new/2010/lgbtqbullying.asp

Newman, B. S., Dannenfelser, P. L., & Benishek, L. (2002). Assessing beginning social work and counselling students' acceptance of lesbians and gay men. *Journal of Social Work Education, 38,* 273–288.

Pascarella, E. T., & Terenzini, P. T. (2005). *How college affects students: A third decade of research.* San Francisco, CA: Jossey-Bass.

Pedhazur, E. J., & Schmelkin, L. P. (1991). *Measurement, design, and analysis: An integrated approach.* Hillsdale, NJ: Erlbaum.

Raiz, L., & Saltzburg, S. (2007). Developing awareness of the subtleties of heterosexism and homophobia among undergraduate, heterosexual social work majors. *The Journal of Baccalaureate Social Work, 12,* 53–69.

Rogers, J. (2009). *Jesus, the Bible and homosexuality: Explode the myths, heal the church.* Louisville, KY: Westminster John Knox Press.

Rosik, C. H., Griffith, L. K., & Cruz, Z. (2007). Homophobia and conservative religion: Toward a more nuanced understanding. *American Journal of Orthopsychiatry, 77,* 10–19.

Rutledge, S. E., Siebert, D. C., Siebert, C., & Chonody, J. M. (2012). Attitudes toward gays and lesbians: A latent class analysis of university students. *Journal of Social Service Research, 38,* 18–28.

Schulte, L. J., & Battle, J. (2004). The relative importance of ethnicity and religion in predicting attitudes toward gays and lesbians. *Journal of Homosexuality, 47,* 127–141.

Subhi, N., Geelan, D., McMahon, M., Jusoff, K., Mohamad, S. M., Sarnon, N., . . . Alavi, K. (2011). A better understanding of the potential conflict between Christianity and homosexuality. *World Applied Sciences Journal, 12,* 13–19.

Sun, A. (2002). Homophobia among social work and non-social work students. *Journal of Baccalaureate Social Work, 7,* 15–32.

Swank, E., & Raiz, L. (2010). Attitudes toward gays and lesbians among undergraduate social work students. *Affilia, 25,* 19–29.

Walls, N. E. (2010). Religion and support for same-sex marriage: Implications from the literature. *Journal of Gay & Lesbian Social Services, 22,* 112–131.

Whitley, B. E. (2009). Religiosity and attitudes toward lesbians and gay men: A meta-analysis. *International Journal for the Psychology of Religion, 19,* 21–38.

Woodford, M., & Bella, L. (2003). Are we ready to take a stand? Educating social work students about heterosexism: Fostering anti-oppressive practice. In W. Shera (Ed.), *Emerging perspectives on anti-oppressive practice* (pp. 413–430). Toronto, ON: Canadian Scholars Press.

Woodford, M. R., Levy, D., & Walls, N. E. (2013). Sexual prejudice among Christian college students, denominational teachings, and personal beliefs. *Review of Religious Research, 55,* 105–130.

Woodford, M. R., Silverschanz, P., Swank, E., Scherrer, K., & Raiz, L. (2012). Predictors of U.S. heterosexual university students' attitudes toward lesbian, gay, bisexual, and transgender people. *Journal of LGBT Youth, 9*(4), 297–320.

Woodford, M. R., Walls, N. E., & Levy, D. (2012). Religion and endorsement for same-sex marriage: The role of syncretism between denominational teachings about "homosexuality" and personal religious beliefs. *Interdisciplinary Journal for Research on Religion, 4,* 1–29.

Yamane, D. (2007). Beyond belief: Religion and the sociology of religion in America. *Social Compass, 54,* 33–48.

CHAPTER 3

Religion and Gay Rights Activism Among Social Work Students

Eric Swank, PhD, and Breanne Fahs, PhD

Eliminating heterosexist discrimination is an explicit goal of professional social work organizations. For example, the 2008 revised Code of Ethics for the National Association of Social Workers states, "Social workers should act to prevent and eliminate domination of, exploitation of, and discrimination against any... sexual orientation, gender identity, or expression" (NASW, 2008, section 6.04d). Although ending discrimination has many aspects, a crucial part is the promotion of "social justice and social change with and on the behalf of clients... [through] direct practice, community organizing, social and political activism" (NASW, Code of Ethics preamble).

The empirical literature of how often and why social workers engage in community and political activism for lesbian, gay, and bisexual (LGB) rights is sparse and underdeveloped (see Swank & Fahs, 2013). Instead, studies of social workers have focused mostly on how sexual prejudice is formed (Andrews, 1998; Berkman & Zinberg, 1997; Snively, Krueger, Stretch, Watt, & Chandha, 2004) or how sexual prejudice impedes competent and affirmative practice with sexual minorities (Crisp, 2007; Liddle, 1999; Mullins, 2012; Ryan, 2000). Chapters in the book, and a plethora of other studies, have outlined the links between religiosity and greater homophobia among individuals (Dessel, Woodford, & Gutiérrez, 2012; Swank & Raiz, 2007). Although it seems logical to assume these patterns will spill over into the political behaviors of citizens, studies on LGB activism have mostly overlooked the role of religion in predicting LGB activism in individuals (e.g., Fingerhut, 2011; Friedman & Leaper, 2010; Montgomery & Stewart, 2012; Swank &

Fahs, 2012; Waldner, 2001). Ignoring possible links between religion and LGB activism seems shortsighted and unwise. Some religious traditions lessen the general political participation of their adherents as they tell their followers to abstain from the tainted world of secular politics (Smidt, 1999). Moreover, when religious groups enter the world of sexual and gender politics, they almost always align with the conservative side of the debate (Layman, 1997; Maxwell, 2002; Peterson, 1992; Wald & Calhoun-Brown, 2007). In the realm of LGB politics, religious leaders often proselytize against homosexuality before granting large donations to advocacy groups that oppose "same-sex marriages" or "gays in the military" (Fetner, 2008; Fisher & Tarmakin, 2011; Stone, 2011).

In thinking that religious factors should sway political activism, this quantitative study asks the following question: How do religious factors influence the likelihood of a social work student joining the gay and lesbian rights movement?

Literature Review

Social movements are collective efforts that use both insider and outsider tactics to force change in reluctant opponents. Insider tactics focus on the electoral approaches of voting, campaign contributions, or petition drives, whereas outsider tactics include the direct action means of protesting and various kinds of civil disobedience. New social movements, such as the LGB movement, use both types of tactics when they focus on the "politics of recognition" and "politics of redistribution" (Bernstein, 1997; Fraser, 1995). By prioritizing the politics of recognition, segments of the LGB rights movement want to challenge and eliminate detrimental social customs. When confronting heteronormative thoughts and actions, segments of the LGB rights movement want to break the veil of silence, normalize same-sex relationships, and deconstruct the justifications of heterosexism and compulsory heterosexuality, among other things. The instrumental and redistribution wings of the LGB rights movement center on improving laws, policies, and regulations. This "state-centered" approach emphasizes the expansion of rights, statuary protections, and proper government spending through the use of insider and outsider political tactics.

Political Framing, Individual Consciousness, and LGB activism

Most social customs create and reinforce heterosexual privilege. The superiority of heterosexuals is often deemed normal, natural, or divinely inspired, whereas sexual minorities are routinely dismissed as being weird, perverted, and immoral. This degradation of sexual diversity reifies heterosexual advantages and demeans the efforts of gender rebels. Accordingly, studies have concluded that sexual minorities who hid their sexual identities and criticized homosexuality were less inclined to join political protests (Swank & Fahs, 2011; Taylor, Kimport, Van Dyke, & Andersen, 2009).

Although traditional ideologies often condone heterosexual privilege, other worldviews challenge the fairness of conventional practices. Certain social justice frames motivate liberal activism as they condemn heterosexist biases as being mean or unjust. Previous studies have linked these injustice frames to LGB activism. Heterosexuals who protest for LBT rights often recognize heterosexist discrimination (Goldstein & Davis, 2010; Swank & Fahs, 2012), worry about heterosexual privileges (Montgomery & Stewart, 2012), and have positive attitudes toward sexual minorities (Fingerhut, 2011). Likewise, graduate social work students who doubt the justness of society are more likely to advocate on the behalf of sexual minorities (Morrison Van Voorhis & Hoestetter, 2006; Van Soest, 1996). Political activism also increases when gays and lesbians consider current laws as being heterosexist (Russell & Richards, 2003) or they have personally experienced heterosexist discrimination (Friedman & Leaper, 2010; Hyers, 2007; Jennings & Andersen, 2003; Waldner, 2001).

Religion, Political Framing, and LGBT Activism

Most religious beliefs characterize heteronormativity as righteous, natural, and godly (Layman, 1997; Wood & Bartkowski, 2004). In religious sermons homosexuality is often called a sin or crime against God, the moral standards of homosexuals are questioned, and the Book of Leviticus calls homosexual acts between men an abomination. On top of spreading such messages to their own followers, many religious organizations enter political realms as they support advocacy groups that fight against a so-called gay agenda that threatens the moral fabric of schools, families, the media, the minds of children, and so on (Miceli, 2004; Soule, 2004).

Religiosity, or the degree to which people are involved in religions, is routinely associated with higher levels of sexual prejudice against gays and lesbians (Haider-Markel & Joselyn, 2008). Studies of the general public connect religious fundamentalism to homonegativity (Altemeyer & Hunsberger, 1992; Wood & Bartkowski, 2004) and belonging to a conservative religious denomination (Herek & Glunt, 1993). Studies of employed social workers, as well as social work faculty and students, have also linked many religious factors to negative attitudes toward sexual minorities (Berkman & Zinberg, 1997; Cluse-Tolar, Lambert, Ventura, & Pasupuleti, 2004; Dessel et al., 2012; Newman, Dannenflesr, & Benishek, 2002; Ryan, 2000). Moreover, a recent meta-analysis of 61 studies concluded that opposition to homosexuality is associated with "greater attendance at religious events and the acceptance of fundamentalist or 'orthodox' religious identities" (Whitely, 2009, p. 26).

Religious beliefs can also guide everyday interactions with sexual minorities. Studies of young adults suggest that heterosexual teenagers are more likely to physically assault gays and lesbians when they think their religion condones such actions (Franklin, 2000), and fundamentalist college students are more likely than seculars to make antigay jokes, derisively call someone a fag, and threaten someone because of their sexual orientation (Schope & Eliason, 2000).

Religiosity can also influence the political actions of groups and individuals (Layman, 1997). Aggregated studies on social policies suggest that states with larger percentages of megachurches or religious-based advocacy groups pass antigay referendums more often than states that lack these organizations (Fleischmann & Moyer, 2009; Soule, 2004; Wald, Button, & Rienzo, 1996). Likewise, cities with high percentages of self-identified Mormons and fundamentalist and evangelical Christians are more likely to pass laws that prohibit same-sex marriage (Camp, 2008; Fleischmann & Moyer, 2009) and civil right protections for sexual minorities (McCann, 2011; Wald, Button, & Rienzo, 1996). Studies on individual voting practices echo the same patterns. For example, people who routinely attend religious services and consider themselves fundamentalist or born again are more likely to vote for referendums against same-sex marriage (Barth, Overby, & Huffmon, 2009; Brewer, 2003; Haider-Markel & Joslyn, 2008; Olson, Cadge, & Harrison, 2006).

The absence of strong religious ties seems to increase LGB activism. Two studies noted that AIDS activists in the 1980s rarely attended religious services (Jennings & Andersen, 2003; Rollins & Hirsch, 2003), and LGBT ally groups seem to have a high level of agnostics and atheists among their heterosexual members (Goldstein & Davis, 2010). Likewise the act of leaving the religion of one's parents seems to inspire greater LGB activism among teenagers and adults (Lewis, Rogers, & Sherrill, 2011; Russell & Richards, 2003).

Other Predictors of LGB Activism

Based on prior work, we include a number of potentially important controls. The resource model assumes that class and gender hierarchies are fundamental to political inclinations and activism (Brady, Verba, & Scholzman, 1995). In the simplest terms, a person's class and gender locations grant or impede access to financial resources that make political participation easier. In support of these claims, some studies concluded that educational attainment increases activism among sexual minorities (Elbaz, 1996; Rollins & Hirsch, 2003; Swank & Fahs, 2011) and the tendency to become heterosexual LGBT allies (Fingerhut, 2011). Matters of income and occupational status show inconsistent results for LGB activism, but some studies suggest that higher-income gays and lesbians attended more demonstrations for gay rights (Jennings & Andersen, 2003; Lombardi, 1999; Taylor et al., 2009). The relationship between gender identities and LGB activism is far from settled. Lesbians and gays often report similar levels of political participation (Jennings & Andersen, 2003; Rollins & Hirsch, 2003; Swank & Fahs, 2011; Taylor et al., 2009; Waldner, 2001), but one study argued that gay men attend more protests than lesbians (Herek, Norton, Allen, & Sims, 2010). Finally, gender could have an inverse relationship for heterosexuals because heterosexual women more often joined an LGBT support group than did heterosexual men (Fingerhut, 2011).

These previous studies lead to the main hypothesis of this chapter: Greater religiosity lessens LGB activism among social work students. Although we assume that religion inherently suppresses LGB activism, we also investigate the issue of spurious variables. That is, we investigate whether apparent links between religiosity and LGB activism are actually driven by some crucial third factor (the recognition of heterosexism or the student's income, gender, or educational attainment).

Methods

Sample

This study drew on the impressions of 159 BSW students in the United States. To establish a stratified sample, this study selected respondents through two channels. By seeking a pool of fully engaged student activists, the lead researcher distributed surveys at several college-based protests throughout the Midwest and South (Indiana University, Ohio State University, University of Kentucky). These protests occurred from winter 2001 through spring 2002, and 37 participants suggested that they were undergraduate social work students.

To create a comparison group with fewer activists, this study also distributed surveys to students who attended 12 colleges throughout the United States in the fall of 2000. In doing so, we initially separated all public campuses into research, doctoral, master's, or baccalaureate clusters (using the Carnegie Classification of Institutions of Higher Education). This creation of four clusters enabled access to students from many sorts of colleges, including large research campuses and smaller, state-run commuter colleges. Next, three schools were randomly selected from each of the four clusters.[1]

After selecting these 12 colleges, we contacted faculty from each institution (via e-mail). Professors in the natural sciences, humanities, social sciences, and business were asked to administer surveys in their classrooms, because student attitudes have previously differed between such majors (Astin, 1993). Four of these professors taught in BSW programs, and these four provided surveys of 122 social work students.[2]

In total, 159 BSW students provided fully completed surveys. As expected, this sample had a higher proportion of women (89.3%). The racial breakdown seemed to mirror that of many public institutions, with 85% European

American, 7% African American, 5% Latino(a), and less than 1% Native or Asian American participants. Likewise, the age pyramid conformed to familiar trends, with a mean age of 26.4 years, and 48% of the students were between 18 and 22 years old (standard deviation was 9.5 years, and the mode was 22 years). Finally, the social class composition of the sample was slightly skewed toward lower-middle incomes. Twenty-seven percent of the students reported a family income of less than $20,000 a year, another 28% had incomes between $21,000 and $40,000, 40% had incomes of $41,000 to $80,000, and 15% had family incomes above $81,000.

Measures

LGB ACTIVISM

Measurement of LGB activism was based on a political activities approach. Respondents were given a checklist of many different ways to be politically active (Barnes & Kaase, 1979). Five of the behaviors in this study addressed electoral means of influencing government policies (e.g., making financial contributions to elected officials, writing a letter to a politician, signing a petition, handing out political fliers, and volunteering for a political group), and four items dealt with more unconventional and confrontational tactics (going to a legal demonstration, engaging in civil disobedience, picketing a building, and protesting another group). Students were also asked about the political causes that motivated such actions. If the student indicated engagement in any of these political actions for gay or lesbian rights or AIDS issues, he or she was deemed an LGB rights activist (coded as activist = 1, not activist = 0). In total, 25 of the 159 students indicated that they had engaged in either electoral or protest activities on the behalf of LGB rights or AIDS issues (20 of these 25 LGB activist students came from the sample of political demonstrations, and 5 belonged to the sample of students who were selected through the classroom settings).

RELIGIOUS FACTORS

Different aspects of religiosity were addressed by three independent variables. To test routine involvement in religious ceremonies and religious attendance, we asked, "How often do you attend religious services?" using a four-point scale ranging from 1 (*never*) to 4 (*almost weekly*). Approval of Christian orthodoxy was addressed through biblical literalism. In tracing the notion that the Bible was written by God and contains inerrant truths, we asked, "What is your opinion about the Bible?" (Sherkat & Ellison, 1997). Participants who checked the answer "The Bible is the word of God and should be taken literally word for word" were coded as literalists, and other answers were coded as nonliteralists (other answers were "The Bible was inspired by God, but must be interpreted by humans," "The Bible has some wise ideas, but it was written by humans," or "The Bible was written by humans and does not have important ideas"). Because religious right groups such as Focus on the Family, the Family Research Council, and the Christian Coalition are central to antigay social movements (Camp, 2008; Fisher & Tamarkin, 2011), we crafted a 5-point Likert scale item that claimed, "The actions of the Christian Coalition improve our society." Circling 5 (*strongly agree*) indicated a high degree of liking the Christian Coalition.

CONTROL VARIABLES

The injustice frame dealt with issues of "modern heterosexism" (Morrison & Morrison, 2002), the form of sexual prejudice that fails to recognize discrimination and denies heterosexism: "Too often heterosexuals are unfairly accused of being homophobic" (5=*strongly agree*). For gender, respondents were asked, "What is your sex?" (1=*female,* 0=*male*). Social class was determined through a family income scale (there were 10 categories that started at *under $10,000* and ended with *above $151,000*). For educational attainment, students were asked, "Please indicate your highest level of education." Undergraduates who said they were first-year students received a 1, and seniors were given a 4.

Analytical Plan

To assess the relative strength of the three religious factors, Table 1 displays the results of six logistic regressions. In using a hierarchical approach to hypothesis testing, Models 1, 3, and 5 limit themselves to only one of the religious independent variables (religious attendance, biblical literalism, or liking the

Table 1. Binary Logistic Regressions for Religious Variables, Controls, and Participation in Lesbian, Gay, and Bisexual Rights Activism Among Social Work Students (N=159)

Variable	Model 1			Model 2			Model 3			Model 4			Model 5			Model 6		
	B	*SE*	β	*B*	*SE*	β	*B*	*SE*	β	*B*	*SE*	β	*B*	*SE*	β	*B*	*SE*	β
Religious attendance	–.08	(.02)	–.25**	–.06	(.02)	–.17*												
Biblical literalism							–.11	(.03)	–.24**	–.08	(.03)	–.16*						
Like Christian Coalition controls													–.11	(.02)	–.31***	–.09	(.02)	–.25**
Education				.16	(.04)	.27***				.16	(.04)	.27***				.15	(.04)	.26***
Income				–.02	(.01)	–.11				–.02	(.01)	–.12				–.02	(.01)	–.12
Female				.02	(.09)	.02				.01	(.09)	.01				.01	(.09)	.02
Deny heterosexism				–.08	(.03)	–.20**				–.07	(.03)	–.19*				–.06	(.03)	–.14*

*$p < .05$. **$p < .01$. ***$p < .001$.

Christian Coalition). These three calculations give insights into the bivariate associations between LGB activism and different characteristics of religiosity. Models 2, 4, and 6 test the role of each religious factor after four control variables are held constant (education, income, gender, and perception of heterosexist discrimination). These controls are used to determine whether links between religious predictors and LGB activism remain strong after possible spurious variables are entered into the formulas. As expected, the sample met all the assumptions to run these statistics (a dichotomous outcome variable, constant variance, independence, and normal distributions). With a pairwise treatment of missing data, any person who failed to answer an item was automatically removed from the regressions in this study.

Religious factors worked as expected, as they significantly reduced LGB activism in each regression (see Table 1). In bivariate conditions religious attendance, biblical literalism, and liking the Christian Coalition each displayed significant negative coefficients (β ranged from –.31 to –.25). Moreover, every religious factor remained significant even after the control factors were integrated. Net the effects of the other factors, liking the Christian Coalition provided the strongest multivariate association (β=–.25, $p < .01$), but religious attendance and biblical literalism offered almost identical scores (β=–.16 or –.17, $p < .05$).

The control variables themselves had mixed results. Regardless of religiosity factors, greater educational attainment was related to increased LGB activism (β=.27 or .26, $p<.001$), and the denial of homophobia was related to decreased activism (β=.08 to .06, $p<.05$). Issues of income and gender did not add any significant associations to the regressions.

Discussion

This study offers a unique look into LGB activism among social work students. By exploring possible antecedents to gay rights activism, our analysis focused on religious predictors of LGB activism. In taking a comprehensive approach to religiosity, we explored the relative importance of three religious beliefs and practices (religious attendance, biblical literalism, and respecting the Christian Coalition). After exploring bivariate associations of religious factors with LGB activism, we tried to determine whether the restrictive role of religion resulted from other extraneous variables. To address this issue, we introduced four control variables into a hierarchical regression.

Every facet of religion predicted lesser progay activism. Respecting the Christian Coalitions displayed the strongest inverse relationship with LGB activism, but religious attendance and biblical literalism were also related to lessened LGB activism. Moreover, the adverse effects of each religious variable remained constant after other predictors of LGB activism were accounted for. These findings suggest several key points. First, conservative religious beliefs seem antithetical to LGB activism among social work students (be it embracing fundamentalist religious tenets or respecting the political groups of far-right religious leaders). Second, regular attendance in religion events predicted lesser LGB activism. This suggests that LGB activism may be discouraged when students join many strands of America's major religions. Unfortunately without measures of religious affiliations it is impossible to know which sorts of Christianity, Judaism, or Islam are most antithetical to LGB activism. Third, these findings suggest that religious beliefs and practices are entrenched values that cannot be easily undone by a general social work education. In fact, these religious factors are so potent that they remain significant even after students have completed several social work classes and recognize the existence of heterosexual privilege.

Two of the control variables also showed significant associations. With greater educational attainment being the strongest variable in the regressions, activism was more common among secular and religious students who have completed more classes. Although this bodes well for the general social work curriculum, it is unclear whether the liberalizing effects of education are caused by effective classroom interventions or issues of self-selection and retention (conservative and less politically active students may leave social work at higher rates during their junior or senior years in college). This study also suggests that classes must try to give a reason to do activism. Because the denial of heterosexism was significant, social work classes must help students recognize the sexuality biases that are built into the institutional practices of the United States and elsewhere.

Strengths and Limitations

This study offers some theoretical and methodological contributions to the existing literature. Most research on sexuality issues among social workers has been at the attitudinal level of sexual prejudice, but this study offers unique insights into challenging heterosexism through political behaviors. By having three measures of religiosity, we increased the content validity of the study (e.g., it addresses many domains of the religiosity construct). Moreover, this research design reveals that religion in general stifles LGB activism (rather than simply conservative religious beliefs). Our implementation of a stratified sample allowed us to compare students who did and did not join the LGB rights movement. This juxtaposition of activist and bystander qualities allowed greater specification of the motivations behind LGB rights activism. Finally, our sample of students from different colleges throughout the nation is more representative than the typical choice of studying a single campus.

Research designs can also play havoc with the accuracy and generalizability of research findings. Cross sectional studies lack the necessary conditions of causation, and it is possible that students may leave a religious organization after they become LGBT activists. Several research decisions could have undermined this study's external validity. First, the addition of different control variables could have altered the effect of the religious variables. It is possible that these religious factors could have lost their direct significance if we added different controls into the study, such as a sense of political efficacy (Ritter, 2008; Swank & Fahs, 2011), feeling emotionally closer to sexual minorities (Sturmer & Simon, 2004), being committed to social justice (Fingerhut, 2011; Hyers, 2007), or having greater contact with LGB activists (Lombardi, 1999; Swank & Fahs, 2011; Waldner, 2001). Second, omission of a sexual identity variable can be problematic. It is possible that religious factors could have different effects for heterosexual and sexual minority populations. Third, the small sample size can lead to Type II errors in hypothesis testing. However, even with a small sample every religious factor maintained its statistical significance. Fourth, the small number of men in the sample could have led us to underestimate the importance of gender in LGB activism. Fifth, measurement errors regularly haunt survey items. It is possible that we could have overlooked a dimension of religiosity that does not hinder LGB activism among social work students (perhaps prayer rituals, denominational differences, belonging to gay-affirming congregations, or having a quest or intrinsic orientation). Lastly, the role of education could have been larger if we measured for the type of content and assignments in each college classroom.

Implications for Social Work Education

This chapter can inform social work education in several ways. Faculty must rid themselves of their own homophobia (Dessel et al., 2012) before they recognize that LGB rights activism can lead to less discriminatory laws and ordinances (Kane, 2003; Soule, 2004). After achieving this goal, social work educators should try to motivate activism by revealing the discriminatory and exploitive nature of many U.S. institutions (e.g., systematic sexism, racism, classism, heteronormativity, ageism). This content is important because students are generally more politically active after they are exposed to a class on heterosexism (Stake & Hoffman, 2001), homophobia (van Soest, 1996), intergroup dialogue (Dessel, Woodford, & Warren, 2011), or any form of oppression (Beaumont, Colby, Ehrlich, & Torney-Purta, 2006; Morrison Van Voorhis & Hoestetter, 2006; Rocha, 2000). Moreover, educators should develop assignments and exercises that offer opportunities in advocacy practice. Some of these assignments can be classroom experiences of speaking at a mock congressional hearing, developing an imaginary media campaign, or planning a community meeting (Keller, Whittaker, & Burke, 2001). Equally important, students should be given an opportunity to have firsthand experiences in meeting government officials, attending political meetings, talking with seasoned activists, knocking on doors, chanting at protests, or doing some grassroots fundraising (Haynes & Mickelson, 1997). In fact, some studies argue that political activism among students increases after colleges offer policy practice experiences outside of the classroom (Anderson & Harris, 2005; Rocha, 2000).

Social work educators should also be involved with the LGB rights movement. In their personal and professional lives faculty members should attend gay pride events, write op-eds to newspapers, and make financial contributions to LGB advocacy groups. On campus they should publicize and offer support to student ally groups and try to improve the campus climate for students, faculty, and staff. Social work programs can also augment their policy classes by providing more classes on social action, connecting students to issue-based advocacy groups, and offering greater access to political field practicum placements (Wolk, Pray, Weismiller, & Dempsey, 1996, estimated that less than 20% of BSW programs offer field practice in electoral politics and policy advocacy). Although these suggestions will not convert every student into a full-fledged activist, such efforts will probably lessen the widespread complaint that social work programs inadequately prepare students for policy practice (Ritter, 2008; Wolk et al., 1996).

References

Altemeyer, B., & Hunsberger, B. (1992). Authoritarianism, religious fundamentalism, quest, and prejudice. *International Journal for the Psychology of Religion, 2,* 113–133. doi:10.1207/s15327582ijpr0202_5

Anderson, D. K., & Harris, B. M. (2005). Teaching social welfare policy. *Journal of Social Work Education, 41,* 511–526. doi:10.5175/JSWE.2005.200303120

Andrews, A. B. (1998). An exploratory study of political attitudes and acts among child and family service workers. *Children and Youth Services Review, 20,* 435–461. doi:10.1016/S0190-7409(98)00016-4

Astin, A. (1993). *What matters in college?* San Francisco, CA: Jossey-Bass.

Barnes, S. H., & Kaase, M. (1979). *Political action.* Ann Arbor, MI: Inter-University Consortium for Political and Social Research.

Barth, J., Overby, M., & Huffmon, S. H. (2009). Community context, personal contact, and support for an anti-gay rights referendum. *Political Research Quarterly, 62,* 355–365. doi:10.1177/1065912908317033

Beaumont, E., Colby, A., Ehrlich, T., & Torney-Purta, J. (2006). Promoting political competence and engagement in college students. *Journal of Political Science Education, 2,* 249–270. doi:10.1080/15512160600840467

Berkman, C., & Zinberg, G. (1997). Homophobia and heterosexism in social workers. *Social Work, 42,* 319–331. doi:10.1093/sw/42.4.319

Bernstein, M. (1997). Celebration and suppression: The strategic use of identity by the lesbian and gay movement. *American Journal of Sociology, 103,* 531–565. doi:10.2307/j100067

Brady, H. E., Verba, S., & Scholzman, K. L. (1995). Beyond SES: A resource model of political participation. *American Political Science Review, 89,* 271–294. doi:10.2307/2082425

Brewer, P. R. (2003). The shifting foundations of public opinion about gay rights. *Journal of Politics, 65,* 1208–1220. doi:10.1111/1468-2508.t01-1-00133

Camp, B. (2008). Mobilizing a base and embarrassing the opposition: Defense of marriage referendums and cross-cutting electoral cleavages. *Sociological Perspectives, 51,* 713–733.

Cluse-Tolar, T., Lambert, E., Ventura, L., & Pasupuleti, S. (2004). The views of social work student toward gay and lesbian persons. *Journal of Gay & Lesbian Social Services, 17,* 59–84.

Crisp, C. (2005). Homophobia and use of gay affirmative practice in a sample of social workers and psychologists. *Journal of Gay & Lesbian Social Services, 18,* 51–70. doi:10.1300/J041v18n01_05

Crisp, C. (2007). Correlates of homophobia and use of gay affirmative practice among social workers. *Journal of Human Behavior in the Social Environment, 14,* 119–143. doi:10.1300/J137v14n04_06

Dessel, A. B., Woodford, M. R., & Gutiérrez, L. (2012). Social work faculty's attitudes toward marginalized groups: Exploring the role of religion. *Journal of Religion & Spirituality in Social Work, 31,* 244–262. doi:10.1080/15426432.2012.679841

Dessel, A. B., Woodford, M. R., & Warren, N. (2011). Intergroup dialogue courses on sexual orientation: Lesbian, gay and bisexual student experiences and outcomes. *Journal of Homosexuality, 58,* 1132–1150. doi:10.1080/00918369.2011.598420

Elbaz, G. (1996). Measuring AIDS activism. *Humanity and Society, 20,* 44–60.

Fetner, T. (2008). *How the religious right shaped lesbian and gay activism.* Minneapolis, MN: University of Minnesota Press.

Fingerhut, A. W. (2011). Straight allies: What predicts heterosexual alliance with the LGBT community? *Journal of Applied Social Psychology, 41,* 2230–2248. doi:10.1111/j.1559-1816.2011.00807.x

Fisher, R., & Tamarkin, S. (2011). Right-wing organizers do this too: The case of the Christian Coalition. *Journal of Community Practice, 19,* 403–421. doi:10.1080/10705422.2011.625540

Fleischmann, A., & Moyer, L. (2009). Competing social movements and local political culture: Voting on ballot proposition to ban same-sex marriage in the U.S. states. *Social Science Quarterly, 90,* 134–149. doi:10.1111/j.1540-6237.2008.00607.x

Franklin, K. (2000). Antigay behaviors among young adults. *Journal of Interpersonal Violence, 15,* 339–362. doi:10.1177/088626000015004001

Fraser, N. (1995). From redistribution to recognition: Dilemmas of justice in a post Socialist world. *New Left Review, 212,* 68–92.

Friedman, C., & Leaper, C. (2010). Sexual-minority women's experiences with discrimination: Relations with identity and collective action. *Psychology of Women Quarterly, 34,* 152–164. doi:10.1111/j.1471-6402.2010.01558.x

Goldstein, S., & Davis, D. (2010). Heterosexual allies: A descriptive profile. *Equity & Excellence in Education, 43,* 478–494. doi:10.1080/10665684.2010.505464

Haider-Markel, D. P., & Joslyn, M. R. (2008). Beliefs about the origins of homosexuality and support for gay rights. *Public Opinion Quarterly, 72,* 291–310.

Haynes, K., & Mickelson, J. (1997). *Affecting change: Social workers in the political arena.* New York, NY: Longman.

Herek, G. M., & Glunt, E. K. (1993). Interpersonal contact and heterosexuals' attitudes toward gay men: Results from a national survey. *Journal of Sex Research, 30,* 239–244. doi:10.1080/00224499309551707

Herek, G. M., Norton, A. T., Allen, T. J., & Sims, C. L. (2010). Demographic, psychological, and social characteristics of self-identified lesbian, gay, and bisexual adults in a US probability sample. *Sexuality Research & Social Policy, 7,* 176–200. doi:10.1007/s13178-010-0017-y

Hyers, L. L. (2007). Resisting prejudice every day: Exploring women's assertive responses to anti-black racism, anti-Semitism, heterosexism, and sexism. *Sex Roles, 56,* 1–12. doi:10.1007/s11199-006-9142-8

Jennings, M. K., & Andersen, E. A. (2003). The importance of social and political context: The case of AIDS activism. *Political Behavior, 25,* 177–199. doi:10.1023/A:1023851930080

Kane, M. D. (2003). Social movement policy success: The influence of the gay and lesbian movement on decriminalization of state sodomy laws, 1969–1998. *Mobilization, 8,* 313–334.

Keller, T. E., Whittaker, J. K., & Burke, T. K. (2001). Student debates in policy classes. *Journal of Social Work Education, 37,* 343–355.

Layman, G. C. (1997). Religion and political behavior in the United States: The impact of beliefs, affiliations, and commitment from 1980 to 1994. *Public Opinion Quarterly,* 288–316.

Lewis, G. B., Rogers, M. A., & Sherrill, K. (2011). Lesbian, gay, and bisexual voters in the 2000 US presidential election. *Politics & Policy, 39,* 655–677. doi:10.1111/j.1747-1346.2011.00315.x

Liddle, B. (1999). Gay and lesbian client's ratings of psychiatrist, psychologists, social workers and counselors. *Journal of Gay and Lesbian Psychotherapy, 3,* 81–93. doi:10.1300/J236v03n01_09

Lombardi, E. L. (1999). Integration within a transgendered social network and its effect upon members' social and political activity. *Journal of Homosexuality, 37,* 109–122. doi:10.1300/J082v37n01_08

Maxwell, C. J. (2002). *Pro-life activists in America: Meaning, motivation, and direct action.* Cambridge, England: Cambridge University Press.

McCann, S. (2011). Do state laws concerning homosexuals reflect the preeminence of conservative–liberal individual differences? *Journal of Social Psychology, 151,* 227–239. doi:10.1080/00224540903366792

Miceli, M. (2004). Morality politics vs identity politics: Framing processes and competition among Christian right and gay social movement organizations. *Sociological Forum, 20,* 589–612. doi:10.1007/s11206-005-9059-y

Montgomery, S., & Stewart, A. (2012). Privileged allies in lesbian and gay rights activism: Gender, generation, and resistance to heteronormativity. *Journal of Social Issues, 68,* 162–177. doi:10.1111/j.1540-4560.2012.01742.x

Morrison, M. A., & Morrison, T. G. (2002). Development and validation of a scale measuring modern prejudice toward gay men and lesbian women. *Journal of Homosexuality, 43,* 15–37. doi:10.1300/J082v43n02_02

Morrison Van Voorhis, R., & Hoestetter, C. (2006). The impact of a MSW education on social worker empowerment and commitment to client empowerment through social justice advocacy. *Journal of Social Work Education, 42,* 105–121. doi:10.5175/JSWE.2006.200303147

Mullins, M. H. (2012). The relationship of practice beliefs and practice behaviors among social workers with lesbian and gay clients. *Journal of Human Behavior in the Social Environment, 22,* 1050–1064. doi:10.1080/10911359.2012.707959

National Association of Social Workers. (2008). *Code of ethics.* Washington, DC: Author.

Newman, B., Dannenflesr, P., & Benishek, L. (2002). Assessing beginning social work and counseling student's acceptance of lesbian and gay men. *Journal of Social Work Education, 38,* 273–288.

Olson, L. R., Cadge, W., & Harrison, J. T. (2006). Religion and public opinion about same-sex marriage. *Social Science Quarterly, 87,* 340–360. doi:10.1111/j.1540-6237.2006.00384.x

Peterson, S. A. (1992). Church participation and political participation the spillover effect. *American Politics Research, 20,* 123–139. doi:10.1177/1532673X9202000106

Ritter, J. A. (2008). A national study predicting social workers' political participation: The role of resources, psychological engagement, and recruitment networks. *Social Work, 53,* 347–357. doi:10.1093/sw/53.4.347

Rocha, C. (2000). Evaluating experiential teaching methods in a policy practice course. *Journal of Social Work Education, 36,* 53–63.

Rollins, J., & Hirsch, H. N. (2003). Sexual identities and political engagements. *Social Politics, 10,* 290–312. doi:10.1093/sp.jxg017

Russell, G., & Richards, A. (2003). Stressors and resiliency factors for lesbians, gay men, and bisexuals facing antigay politics. *American Journal of Community Psychology, 31,* 313–328. doi:10.1023/A:1023919022811

Ryan, S. (2000). Examining social workers' placement recommendations of children with gay and lesbian adoptive parents. *Families in Society, 81,* 517–528. doi:10.1606/1044-3894.1053

Schope, R., & Eliason, M. (2000). Thinking vs action: Assessing the relationship between heterosexual attitudes and behaviors toward homosexuals. *Journal of Gay & Lesbian Social Services, 11,* 69–91. doi:10.1300/J041v11n04_04

Sherkat, D. E., & Ellison, C. G. (1997). The cognitive structure of a moral crusade: Conservative Protestantism and opposition to pornography. *Social Forces, 75*(3), 957–980. doi:10.1093/sf/75.3.957

Smidt, C. (1999). Religion and civic engagement: A comparative analysis. *Annals of the American Academy of Political and Social Science, 565,* 176–192. Retrieved from http://www.jstor.org/stable/1049545

Snively, C., Krueger, L., Stretch, J., Watt, J., & Chandha, J. (2004). Understanding homophobia. *Journal of Gay and Lesbian Social Services, 17,* 59–79. doi:10.1300/J041v17n01_05

Soule, S. (2004). Going to the chapel? Same-sex marriage bans in the United States, 1973–2000. *Social Problems, 51,* 453–477.

Stake, J. E., & Hoffman, F. L. (2001). Changes in student social attitudes, activism and personal confidence in higher education. *American Educational Research Journal, 38,* 411–436. doi:10.3102/00028312038002411

Stone, A. L. (2011). Dominant tactics in social movement tactical repertoires: Anti-gay ballot measures, 1974–2008. *Research in Social Movements, Conflicts and Change, 31,* 141–174. doi:10.1108/S0163-786X(2011)0000031008

Sturmer, S., & Simon, B. (2004). The role of collective identification in social movement participation: A panel study in the context of the German gay movement. *Personality and Social Psychology Bulletin, 30,* 263–277. doi:10.1177/0146167203256690

Swank, E., & Fahs, B. (2011). Pathways to political activism among Americans who have same-sex sexual contact. *Sexuality Research & Social Policy, 8,* 126–138. doi:10.1007/s13178-011-0034-5

Swank, E., & Fahs, B. (2012). Resources, social networks, and collective action frames of college sStudents who join the gay and lesbian rights movement. *Journal of Homosexuality, 59,* 67–89.

Swank, E., & Fahs, B. (2013). Why do social work students engage in lesbian and gay rights activism? *Journal of Human Behavior in the Social Environment, 23,* 91–106. doi:10.1080/10911359.2013.740336

Swank, E., & Raiz, L. (2007). Explaining comfort with homosexuality among social work students. *Journal of Social Work Education, 43,* 257–279.

Taylor, V., Kimport, K., Van Dyke, N., & Andersen, E. A. (2009). Culture and mobilization: Tactical repertoires, same-sex weddings, and the impact on gay activism. *American Sociological Review, 74,* 865–890.

Van Soest, D. (1996). The impact of social work education on student attitudes and behavior concerning oppression. *Journal of Social Work Education, 32,* 191–202.

Wald, K., Button, J., & Rienzo, B. (1996). The politics of gay rights in American communities: Explaining antidiscrimination ordinances and policies. *American Journal of Political Science, 40,* 1152–1178.

Wald, K. D., & Calhoun-Brown, A. (2007). *Religion and politics in the United States.* Lanham, MD: Rowman & Littlefield.

Waldner, L. K. (2001). Lesbian and gay political activism: An analysis of variables predicting political participation. *Research in Political Sociology, 9,* 59–81.

Whitely, B. (2009). Religiosity and attitudes toward lesbians and gay men: A meta-analysis. *International Journal of Psychology of Religion, 19,* 21–38. doi:10.1080/10508610802471104

Wolk, J., Pray, J., Weismiller, T., & Dempsey, D. (1996). Political practice. *Journal of Social Work Education, 32,* 91–100.

Wood, P. B., & Bartkowski, J. P. (2004). Attribution style and public policy attitudes toward gay rights. *Social Science Quarterly, 85,* 58–74. doi:10.1111/j.0038-4941.2004.08501005.x

Notes

1 Research schools: University of Delaware, University of Oregon, University of Texas; Doctoral: University of North Carolina–Greensboro, University of Massachusetts–Lowell, Rutgers; Master's: Longwood College, University of Southern Maine, University of Wisconsin–Green Bay; Baccalaureate: Evergreen State College, Mesa State College, Southeast Arkansas College.

2 Clearly this response rate was neither high nor random. Professors who never read e-mail automatically removed themselves from the sample, and the willingness to distribute the surveys was not consistent between schools and disciplines. Of the sample of all professors, about 2% of the research professors distributed surveys, whereas 13% of professors at master's-granting universities did so. Likewise, less than 1% of chemistry, biology, and physics professors assisted in this project, whereas professors in political science, sociology, and social work were most receptive to our requests (11%). Of the social work professors who distributed surveys, all of them taught research or policy classes.

CHAPTER 4

Incongruence With Social Work Values and Culture Among Evangelical Students: The Mediating Role of Group-Based Dominance

N. Eugene Walls, MSSW, PhD, and Kristie Seelman, MSW, PhD

The role of religion is paradoxical. It makes prejudice and it unmakes prejudice. (Allport, 1954, p. 444)

Teaching about religion in social work programs is viewed as a difficult topic fraught with tension and anxiety (Coholic, 2003), but when content about religion is not integrated into the curriculum, social work practitioners have little guidance on how to manage their own personal religious beliefs in the context of social work values in practice (Canda, Nakashima, & Furman, 2004). Given that religious values may influence how one perceives gender, ethnicity, sexuality, and even mental health (Duriez & Hutsebaut, 2000; Wilkinson, 2004) and play a role in the social worker's ability to be authentic with a client and provide positive regard (Laythe, Finkel, Bringle, & Kirkpatrick, 2002), this oversight is problematic.

In this study we examine a number of social psychological constructs related to attitudes about social stratification to determine whether these constructs are associated with higher levels of cultural incongruence, that is, conflict between one's personal values and the perceived culture and values of a profession, in this case social work (Seelman & Walls, 2010). We then test whether, among these same constructs, the ones that are significant actually mediate the relationship between religious identity (evangelical Christian) and cultural incongruence with social work values and the perceived culture of a social work program.

Social Work as a Hierarchy-Attenuating Discipline

Those who endorse egalitarian attitudes often choose and succeed in careers that aim to address social inequality, whereas those who support group-based inequality tend to choose and succeed in careers that justify and replicate social stratification (Sidanius, Liu, Pratto, & Shaw, 1994; Whitehead, 1998). Nursing, social work, and public health are among the disciplines identified as hierarchy attenuating, and students who choose these fields are more likely to support egalitarianism than those who choose hierarchy-enhancing fields such as law and marketing (Sidanius et al., 1994).

Social work is probably perceived by laypersons as hierarchy attenuating (Sidanius, van Laar, Levin, & Sinclair, 2003), which is not surprising given that social work's Code of Ethics (National Association of Social Workers [NASW], 2008) says, "Social workers pursue social change, particularly with and on behalf of vulnerable and oppressed individuals and groups" ("Ethical Principle: Social Workers Challenge Social Injustice," para. 1). Those who work in this field are not expected to advocate for the interests of those who already hold power and privilege; rather, social workers are called to advocate for social change that benefits those who have been exploited, dominated, abused, and disadvantaged by modern and historical systems of social stratification (Barnoff & Moffatt, 2007; NASW, 2008; Pearlmutter, 2002; Sünker, 2005).[1] Both the central theories of social work and the professional literature call for social change that promotes equality and furthering clients' well-being (Abramovitz, 1993, 1998).

Evidence suggests that college students who are in hierarchy-attenuating fields, such as social work, are less likely to endorse attitudes that justify group-based dominance, such as anti-egalitarianism (Sidanius et al., 2003) and prejudicial attitudes such as racism (van Laar, Sidanius, Rabinowitz, & Sinclair, 1999). When social work students first enter the field, they may experience a disconnect between their personal and professional values if they strongly subscribe to beliefs that some groups are inherently better than others or that social change is not needed in today's world. Such value conflicts can arise when a student places a system of personal beliefs as primary above professional ethics, which can be a particular point of conflict for evangelical Christians who may prioritize biblical teachings above the Code of Ethics (Spano & Koenig,

2007). However, one might theorize that it is not the religious identity per se that determines this value conflict but rather the way an evangelical Christian identity is translated into certain sociopolitical values that are at odds with social work ethics and values.

Cultural Incongruence Among Social Work Students

Gatekeeping—the process whereby applicants and current students are evaluated for entry into social work based on their character, knowledge, skills, commitment to social work values, and academic performance (Koerin & Miller, 1995; Moore & Urwin, 1990; Reynolds, 2004)—is generally described as being the responsibility of social work faculty (Currer & Atherton, 2008; Moore, Dietz, & Jenkins, 1998; Moore & Urwin, 1990). Numerous legal decisions have indicated that, for disciplines that involve frequent interaction with vulnerable populations and expect practitioners to adhere to a code of ethics, faculty can act as gatekeepers by determining who is suitable for and who should be denied entrance into the profession (Cobb, 1994).[2] Therefore, the Council on Social Work Education requires that social work programs have procedures for dismissing students, whether for academic or nonacademic reasons (Koerin & Miller, 1995). Nonetheless, scholars disagree about whether and how to analyze student's personal values to assess appropriate fit for the profession (Currer & Atherton, 2008; Gross, 2000; Koerin & Miller, 1995; Ryan, Habibis, & Craft, 1997).

Many social work programs assess applications from students for much more than undergraduate grades and volunteer experience (Fortune, 2003), including a match with social work values (Morrow, 2000; Ryan et al., 1997). Throughout a student's interaction with a school of social work, administrators and faculty can assess whether students demonstrate alignment with the Code of Ethics, including values such as social justice and the dignity and worth of a person (Moore & Urwin, 1990; Morrow, 2000; Reynolds, 2004). Research findings in both the United States and Australia have shown that nonconformity to social work values and related ethical issues is the most common reason for dismissing a student (Koerin & Miller, 1995; Ryan et al., 1997).

Attitudes Toward Social Stratification

Numerous social psychological theories, frameworks, and constructs attempt to explain attitudes toward inequity and social stratification. These include social identity theory (Tajfel, 1981; Tajfel & Turner, 1986), system justification theory (Jost & Banaji, 1994; Jost & Hunyady, 2005), authoritarianism (Altemeyer, 1981, 1988), and social dominance theory (Sidanius & Pratto, 1999). In this study, we examine two constructs that are among the most commonly used in social science research on prejudice: right-wing authoritarianism (RWA) and social dominance orientation (SDO; from social dominance theory).

RWA

The construct of right-wing authoritarianism grew out of early research linking authoritarian personalities, prejudice, and fascism (Adorno, Frenkel-Brunswik, Levinson, & Sanford, 1950). It is defined as the "covariation of three attitudinal clusters: (a) authoritarian submission (a strong tendency to submit to authorities that are perceived to be established and legitimate in the society in which one lives), (b) authoritarian aggression (a general aggressiveness directed against various persons, perceived to be sanctioned by established authorities), and (c) conventionalism (a strong tendency to adhere to the social conventions that are perceived to be endorsed by society and its established authorities" (Altemeyer, 1996, p. 6). As such it is "characterized by a need for clear-cut distinctions between groups and an understanding of the world that is based on group-based hierarchies and an unequal distribution of power" (Seelman & Walls, 2010, p. 106).

RWA positively correlates with prejudice directed toward lesbian women and gay men (Stones, 2006; Whitley & Lee, 2000), people of color (Altemeyer, 1996; Laythe, Finkel, & Kirkpatrick, 2001), feminists (Duncan, Peterson, & Winter, 1997), and immigrants (Quinton, Cowan, & Watson, 1996). It is associated with rigid thinking, ethnocentrism, lack of openness, resistance to change, and aggression toward nonconformity (Altemeyer, 1981, 1988; Butler, 2000; Duckitt, Bizumic, Krauss, & Heled, 2010; Jost, Glaser, Kruglanski, & Sulloway, 2003; McFarland, 1998; McFarland & Adelson, 1996; Sibley &

Duckitt, 2008). High scores on RWA are strongly associated with the dismantling of civil liberty laws in the name of security (Cohrs, Kielmann, Maes, & Moschner, 2005) and with conservative political ideology (Altemeyer, 1998; Lambert & Chasteen, 1997).

A significant amount of research has been conducted on some aspects of religion and RWA. In terms of denominational differences, early work found that Catholics tended to be more authoritarian than Protestants (Rokeach, 1960; Knöpfelmacher & Armstrong, 1963). More recent work has also supported this finding (Dallago, Cima, Roccato, Ricolfi, & Mirisola, 2008; de Regt, 2012). People who score high on RWA also tend to have higher levels of religiosity, whether measured as public (attendance) or private religiosity (prayer and reading scripture) (Altemeyer, 1981, 1988; Altemeyer & Hunsberger, 1992; de Regt, 2012). Finally, aspects of religious beliefs such as fundamentalism (Altemeyer, 1988; Hunsberger, 1995) and Christian orthodoxy (Piazza, 2012) have been found to predict higher levels of RWA. In conflicts between science and religion, right-wing authoritarians tend to believe that science should be subservient to religion (Westman, Willink, & McHoskey, 2000).

SDO

Social dominance orientation is another of the more widely used individual difference measures in the scholarship that examines prejudicial attitudes and behavior (Sidanius & Pratto, 1999). It was originally conceptualized as a unidimensional scale that captured a "general attitudinal orientation toward intergroup relations, reflecting whether one generally prefers relations to be equal, versus hierarchical" and the degree to which "one desires that one's ingroup dominate and be superior to out-groups" (Pratto, Sidanius, Stallworth, & Malle, 1994, p. 742). SDO has been shown to explain much of the variance in prejudicial attitudes toward numerous social outgroups (Altemeyer, 2006; Duckitt, 2001, 2006; Ekehammer, Akrami, Gylje, & Zakrisson, 2004; Sibley & Duckitt, 2008, Whitley, 1999). Those high in SDO are more likely to be opposed to policy that helps those disadvantaged in a society and to hold negative opinions of those who have low status (Pratto et al., 1994; Sidanius

& Pratto, 1999). It has been shown to predict opposition to social welfare policies (Pratto, Stallworth, & Conway-Lanz, 1998), support for harsh punishments for low-status defendants (Kemmelmeier, 2005), and support for wars of dominance (Pratto et al., 1994). Members of high-status groups tend to have higher levels of SDO than members of low-status groups (e.g., race, social class) (Sidanius, Levin, Liu, & Pratto, 2000).

One emerging concern with SDO is whether the measure is one or two constructs. The most recent empirical evidence suggests that SDO combines two related but distinct constructs: opposition to equality and support for group-based dominance (Jost & Thompson, 2000). In the most comprehensive empirical examination of this concern to date, Kugler, Cooper, and Nosek (2010) found significant support for a two-construct conceptualization of SDO. In a series of studies, they found that opposition to equality was more strongly linked than group-based dominance to the rejection of universalism, humanitarianism, and economic redistribution. Therefore, they argue that the opposition to equality domain is motivated primarily by desire to justify the current system of stratification and unwillingness to overturn the current social order. Group-based dominance, on the other hand, was more strongly related than opposition to equality to negative attitudes toward outgroups, hostile competition, and the propensity to stereotype. Group-based dominance, they suggest, reflects social identity motives and support for the dominance of one's own social group.

Although scholarship examining the two constructs of SDO separately is less available, what has been published has found that opposition to equality is closely related to emotional reactions to inequality, including existential and collective guilt, moral outrage, implicit and explicit attitudes toward economic issues and wealth, conservative political orientation (Kugler et al., 2010), and lack of social compassion (Eagly, Diekman, Johannesen-Schmidt, & Koenig, 2004). Group-based dominance has been found to be more predictive than opposition to equality of opposing women's rights, support of anti–gay and lesbian policies (Eagly et al., 2004), endorsement of power distance beliefs (Guimond et al., 2007), intergroup attitudes, competitive world beliefs, RWA, and symbolic racism (Kugler et al., 2010).

For the purposes of this chapter, we are adopting Kugler and colleagues' (2010) two-construct conceptualization of SDO, described as follows:

> *Opposition to [e]quality* is a system justification construct. It is negatively predicted by personality variables related to empathy and universalism and it in turn predicts resistance to changing the status quo, regardless of ingroup involvement. (p. 121)
>
> *Group-[b]ased [d]ominance* captures preference for one's own group compared to those of others. It is driven by negative attitudes toward the outgroup and the belief that the world is a competitive, zero sum, place. It is associated with individual differences in prejudice toward outgroups. Rather than reflecting approval of inequality in general, [group-based dominance] exclusively concerns inequalities that have implications for the ingroup and is most strongly associated with active and aggressive hierarchy promotion. (p. 121)

Theoretically, concern for the disadvantaged and messages of equality and compassion are central to many religious traditions, suggesting that religion might have a hierarchy-attenuating impact (Coward, 1986), leading to predictions of a negative relationship between religiosity and SDO. Conversely, religion can be conceptualized as a hierarchy-enhancing ideology when people believe that their religion is fundamentally better than any other in the world (Altemeyer & Hunsberger, 1997) or when they have an explicit call to convert others to their religious belief system (Walls & Todd, 2014). Rowatt, LaBouff, Johnson, Froese, and Tsang (2009) found that the strength of religious beliefs was related differently to prejudicial attitudes about different groups, providing evidence of this selective intolerance. Thus there is a fundamental paradox in religion whereby some forms of religion that preach brotherly love are actually associated with more prejudice toward specific groups rather than less (Hall, Matz, & Wood, 2010).

The research on religion and SDO has focused almost exclusive on religiosity, the degree of importance of religion in one's life. The findings have been mixed, with some studies finding no relationship between SDO and religiosity (Altemeyer, 2004; Altemeyer & Hunsberger, 1997; Dallago et al., 2008; Heaven & Connors, 2001) and others finding SDO and religiosity to be negatively related (de Regt, 2012; Dru, 2007; Duriez & Van Hiel, 2002; Roccato, 2008). No studies were found that looked specifically at religious tradition (rather than religiosity) and SDO. Given that different religious traditions vary significantly in their conceptualization of humanity (Levy, 2014; Miller & Delaney, 2005), the failure to examine this aspect of religion and SDO seems like an oversight.

Hostile and Modern Heterosexism

There is a substantial body of social psychological research examining attitudes toward lesbian woman and gay men. Much of that scholarship has conceptualized prejudicial attitudes as being negatively valenced and based on moral judgments about same-sex sexuality (which we refer to as *hostile heterosexism*). Although numerous institutions in society manifest and reinforce anti-LGBT intolerance and bias, religion is often viewed as one of the primary underlying sources of such negative attitudes and behaviors (Barret & Logan, 2002). Consistently, findings in the literature have found religious variables (e.g., religious tradition, religiosity, religious orthodoxy) to predict hostile heterosexism (Herek & Capitanio, 1995; Jayakumar, 2009; Rowatt et al., 2009; Whitley, 2009; Wilkinson, 2004).

Recent scholarship on antigay and lesbian prejudicial attitudes has used arguments from modern prejudice theory (Gaertner & Dovidio, 1986) suggesting that, like racism and sexism, justifications for attitudes toward lesbians and gay men have shifted across time as anti-LGBT justifications have become increasingly stigmatized. This more recent manifestation of prejudicial attitudes has fallen under the term *modern heterosexism* or *modern homonegativity* (Morrison & Morrison, 2002; Walls, 2008). Modern heterosexism has numerous subdomains including aversive heterosexism (e.g., "lesbians and gay men are pushing too fast for change"), amnestic heterosexism (e.g., "homophobia is a thing of the past"), paternalistic heterosexism (e.g., "I have nothing against lesbians and gay men, but would not want my son to be gay because it would make his life harder"), and positive stereotypic heterosexism (e.g., "lesbian women are more independent than heterosexual women") (Walls, 2008). Little work has been completed examining modern heterosexism and religious variables.

HETEROSEXISM AND RELIGION

Given that there is no unified view among Christian faith traditions on same-sex sexuality (Levy, 2008, 2014), it seems logical that religious tradition and denomination would be associated with different levels of hostile heterosexism. Among findings from population-based surveys in the United States, more conservative religious traditions are associated with higher levels of hostile heterosexism (Herek & Capitanio, 1995; Rowatt et al., 2009). However, among studies using student samples, results have been inconsistent. Finlay and Walther (2003) found conservative Protestant students to have the most anti-LGBT attitudes, whereas Schulte and Battle (2004) did not find significant differences between Baptist and Catholic students, as they had hypothesized. Woodford, Levy, and Walls (2012) argue that this inconsistency among student samples is an indicator of syncretism whereby people's beliefs about same-sex sexuality may not line up with the official stance of their denomination, an argument that is supported by their findings. In addition to religious tradition, higher levels of religiosity have consistently been shown to predict higher levels of hostile heterosexism (Jayakumar, 2009; Rowat et al., 2009; Whitley, 2009; Wilkinson, 2004).

This study examines cultural incongruence with social work values—that is, discordance between one's own personal beliefs and values and those of the social work discipline—focusing on religious tradition, general attitudes about social stratification (RWA and SDO), and prejudicial attitudes about LGB people (hostile heterosexism and modern sexism). We then examine whether general attitudes about social stratification or prejudicial attitudes mediate the relationship between different religious traditions and cultural incongruence.

Methods

Participants

The sample for the study is made up of incoming graduate students who are enrolled in a 2-year MSW program in the Mountain West region of the United

States. Data were collected during Weeks 3 and 4 of the term in numerous sections of a required foundation year course, allowing new students to acclimate to the school's culture and gain a better understanding of social work values before completing the survey. A total of 143 students were enrolled across the various sections of the course, with 132 (92.3%) agreeing to participate in the survey. Because of missing data on the dependent variable or on more than one question on the mediator scale variables, eight records were dropped. Among the remaining records, no more than 5% had data that were missing on any single question, and multiple imputation by chained equations (van Buuren, Boshuizen, & Knook, 1999) was used to replace those missing values, leaving a usable sample of 124 participants.

The sample was predominantly female (93%, n=116), with 38.7% (n=48) indicating that they grew up in suburban communities, 26.6% (n=33) in small cities and towns, 23.4% (n=29) in cities, and 11.3% (n=14) in rural communities. In terms of religious affiliation, 21.8% (n=27) identified as liberal or mainline Protestant, 21.8% (n=27) as secular, 18.6% (n=23) as conservative or evangelical Protestant, 16.9% (n=21) as other religions, 12.1% (n=15) as Catholic, and 8.9% (n=11) as Jewish.[3]

Procedure

Information on the general purpose of the study was provided to potential participants with assurance that answers from the survey were anonymous and participation was voluntary. Each potential participant was provided with a project information sheet that had been approved by the university's institutional review board. After the project information sheet was reviewed and questions about the study answered, questionnaires were distributed to every student. Filling out a questionnaire was assumed to signal a student's consent to participate in the study. Two envelopes were provided, and students were instructed to return either a completed questionnaire or a blank questionnaire (if they chose not to participate) in the first envelope and a completed lottery form in the second envelope for a lottery drawing for a gift certificate.

Measures

In addition to demographic questions, the survey included a number of social psychological scales, two of which measured general attitudes toward social stratification (SDO and RWA) and two of which measured attitudes toward lesbian women and gay men. In the current sample, Cronbach's alphas for the two general attitude scales were .83[4] for SDO and .88 for RWA.

The two scales that measured attitudes toward lesbian women and gay men were the Attitudes Toward Lesbians and Gay Men Scale (ATLG-S; Herek, 1984, 1988), and the Multidimensional Heterosexism Inventory (MHI; Walls, 2008). The ATLG-S captures hostile heterosexism, traditional negative prejudicial attitudes toward lesbian women and gay men. It is one of the most widely used scales capturing anti-LGBT attitudes and had a Cronbach's alpha of .88 in the current sample.

The MHI captures four subdomains of modern heterosexism: aversive (MHI–aversive), amnestic (MHI–amnestic), paternalistic (MHI–paternalistic), and positive stereotypic (MHI–positive) heterosexism. The subdomains of the MHI had Cronbach's alphas of .93, .91, .97, and .91 respectively, in the current sample. (For more information on the scale, see Walls, 2008.)

All scales used a 7-point Likert scale and were recoded so that higher scores represented greater endorsement of the constructs measured by the scales. In addition, to provide some degree of comparability across scales, we standardized final scores calculated for each scale to a range from 1 to 7 by dividing the total raw score for the summed scale items by the number of items on the scale. To capture cultural incongruence with social work values and the perceived culture of the graduate social work program, a nine-item scale was created to tap into potential areas of dissonance. The response set for the nine items was a 7-point Likert scale ranging from *strongly disagree* to *strongly agree*. All items were coded such that higher levels of agreement indicate greater levels of cultural incongruence. The items can be found in the Appendix. The Cronbach's alpha for the scale in the current sample was slightly lower than desired at .69, but no other scale capturing cultural incongruence with social work values was identified in the existing literature. Clearly, more work on strengthening the measure in future research would be helpful.

Students were asked about their religious affiliation and were initially classified into six religious traditions based on a modified version of Steensland et al.'s (2000) schema: Catholics (*n*=15, 12.1%), evangelical Protestants (*n*=22, 17.7%), mainline and liberal Protestants (*n*=26, 21.0%), Jewish (*n*=11, 8.9%), secular/nonaffiliated (*n*=29, 23.4%), and other (*n*=21, 16.9%). The evangelical Christian group was the only religious tradition that was significantly different from the remaining groups on the social psychological measures of interest to this study. See Table 1 for information on the mean scores for each social psychological measure by religious tradition. Thus, religious tradition was dichotomized so that all students were classified as either evangelical Christians or being from a religious tradition or worldview other than evangelical Christianity.

Table 1. Group Means and Standard Deviations by Religious Traditions

Construct	Evangelical		Secular		Mainline Protestant		Catholic		Jewish		Other	
	Mean	*SD*	Mean	*SD*	Mean	*SD*	Mean	*SD*	Mean	*SD*	Mean	*SD*
Opposition to equality (SDO)	2.27	0.18	2.08	0.16	2.21	0.14	1.95	0.19	2.11	0.27	1.85	0.14
Group-based dominance (SDO)	2.40	0.18	1.81	0.11	2.02	0.11	1.92	0.19	1.92	0.25	1.85	0.18
Right-wing authoritarianism	3.06	0.19	2.11	0.09	2.81	0.12	2.73	0.18	2.51	0.17	2.08	0.11
Hostile heterosexism (ATLG-S)	2.81	0.30	1.63	0.12	2.10	0.14	1.93	0.16	1.62	0.18	1.52	0.09
Aversive heterosexism (MHI)	2.88	0.29	1.72	0.16	2.24	0.19	2.40	0.38	1.63	0.26	1.69	0.14
Amnestic heterosexism (MHI)	1.83	0.19	1.41	0.12	1.52	0.16	1.65	0.13	1.66	0.15	1.45	0.11
Paternalistic heterosexism (MHI)	3.28	0.42	1.07	0.35	2.70	0.46	2.79	0.65	2.39	0.60	0.97	0.36

(continued)

Table 1 (continued)

Construct	Evangelical		Secular		Mainline Protestant		Catholic		Jewish		Other	
	Mean	*SD*	Mean	*SD*	Mean	*SD*	Mean	*SD*	Mean	*SD*	Mean	*SD*
Positive stereotypic heterosexism (MHI)	2.85	0.26	2.09	0.20	2.39	0.21	2.55	0.32	2.45	0.38	2.42	0.24

Note. ATLG-S = Attitudes Toward Lesbians and Gay Men Scale; MHI = Multidimensional Heterosexism Inventory; SDO = social dominance orientation

Analyses

For each mediation test, four ordinary least squares (OLS) regression models were used: the evangelical Christian religious tradition variable (primary independent variable) regressed on the cultural incongruence scale (the same for all four mediation tests), the evangelical Christian religious tradition variable regressed on the mediator variable being examined, the mediator variable regressed on the cultural incongruence scale, and both the evangelical Christian religious tradition variable and mediator variable regressed on the cultural incongruence scale. The coefficients and standard errors were then entered into Preacher and Leonardelli's (2001) interactive calculation tool for the Sobel test[5] to determine whether the change in coefficient was statistically significant (Baron & Kenny, 1986; Goodman, 1960; Sobel, 1982). OLS regression models using multiple imputation were run using Stata 12.0.

Findings

Descriptive Statistics

As reported earlier, evangelical Christians were statistically significantly different from those who were not in the evangelical Christian group on all but one of the social psychological measures of stratification: the opposition to equality construct of SDO. Therefore, opposition to equality is not examined further in the statistical models. Table 2 presents the comparison of means between the two groups.

Table 2. Comparison of Evangelicals and Nonevangelicals

Construct	Group Means				
	Evangelical		Nonevangelical		*t* Test Score
	Mean	*SD*	Mean	*SD*	
Opposition to equality (SDO)	2.27	0.18	2.06	0.08	1.14
Group-based dominance (SDO)	2.40	0.18	1.90	0.07	3.00**
Right-wing authoritarianism	3.06	0.19	2.43	0.06	3.84***
Hostile heterosexism (ATLG-S)	2.81	0.30	1.78	0.06	5.25***
Aversive heterosexism (MHI)	2.88	0.29	1.94	0.10	3.74***
Amnestic heterosexism (MHI)	1.83	0.19	1.51	0.06	1.99*
Paternalistic heterosexism (MHI)	3.28	0.42	1.86	0.22	2.82**
Positive stereotypic heterosexism (MHI)	2.85	0.26	2.35	0.11	1.87*

Note. ATLG-S = Attitudes Toward Lesbians and Gay Men Scale; MHI = Multidimensional Heterosexism Inventory; SDO = social dominance orientation.
*$p < .05$. **$p < .01$. ***$p < .001$.

Mediation Models

For each of the mediation models, the reference group includes everyone who was not an evangelical Christian. Initial bivariate analysis indicates that among religious traditions, only evangelical Christians were significantly different from any other religious tradition or worldview on the cultural incongruence scale (β=.34, *SE*=.15, *t*=2.32, *p*=.02).[6] On average, evangelical Christians were one-third of a point higher on the 7-point cultural incongruence scale than the rest of the sample, a small but statistically significant difference. Each of the mediation models, which examine how the addition of the mediator variable affects this bivariate relationship, is presented in this section. Coefficients are nonstandardized.

SOCIAL DOMINANCE ORIENTATION

The SDO scale consists of two subscales: opposition to equality and group-based dominance. We initially planned to test each subscale separately, but opposition to equality was not significantly different between the two religious groups (evangelical Christians and those who were not evangelical Christians) and was therefore not examined.

As illustrated in Figure 1, group-based dominance fully mediates the relationship between having an evangelical Christian identity and cultural incongruence. Evangelical Christians scored significantly higher on group-based dominance than nonevangelical Christians (B=0.51, *SE*=0.17, *t*=3.02, *p*=.003), and those with higher group-based dominance scores had significantly higher cultural incongruence scores (B=0.29, *SE*=0.08, *t*=3.93, $p < .001$) in the bivariate relationships. In the full model, group-based dominance continues to be a significant predictor of cultural incongruence (B=0.27, *SE*=0.08, *t*=3.43, *p*=.001), while identifying as an evangelical Christian is no longer a significant predictor (B=0.21, *SE*=0.15, *t*=1.41, *p*=.161). In the figure, the first coefficient listed on the path between having an evangelical Christian identity and cultural incongruence (0.34) represents the significant relationship between the two in the bivariate relationship. The second coefficient on that same path, which is listed in the parentheses (0.21), represents the nonsignificant relationship between the two variables once the group-based dominance variable is introduced into the model. Coefficients are nonstandardized and additional information on mediation models is available from the lead author. The Sobel and related test values (Sobel=2.49, *SE*=0.06; Goodman=2.45, *SE*=0.06; Aorian=2.35, *SE*=0.06) are all statistically significant (*p*=.02; *p*=01; *p*=.02, respectively).

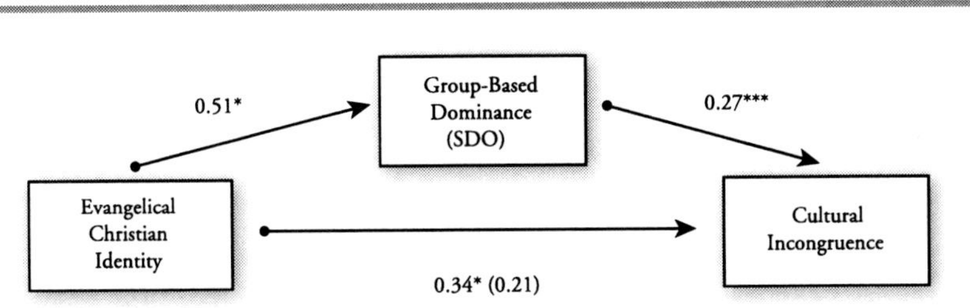

Figure 1. Test of mediation of group-based dominance (SDO).

RWA

The relationship between having an evangelical Christian identity and cultural incongruence is not mediated by RWA (Figure 2). In the bivariate models, evangelical Christians scored significantly higher on RWA than did nonevangelicals (B=0.77, *SE*=0.20, *t*=3.79, $p < .001$), and higher RWA scores predicted higher levels of cultural incongruence (B=0.15, *SE*=0.6, *t*=2.37, *p*=.02; not shown). In the full model, neither RWA nor having an evangelical Christian identity continues to be a significant predictor of cultural incongruence (B=0.11, *SE*=0.07, *t*=1.72, *p*=.09; and B=0.26, *SE*=0.16, *t*=1.64, *p*=.10; respectively). None of the Sobel and related test values (Sobel=1.57, *SE*=0.06; Goodman=1.62, *SE*=0.05; Aorian=1.53, *SE*=0.06) are statistically significant.

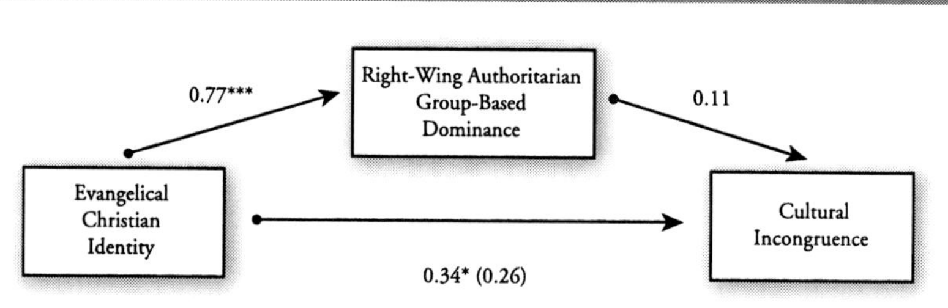

Figure 2. Test of mediation of right-wing authoritarianism.

ATTITUDES TOWARD LESBIANS AND GAY MEN

As illustrated in Figure 3, hostile heterosexism does not mediate the relationship between having an evangelical Christian identity and cultural incongruence. Evangelical Christians scored significantly higher than nonevangelical Christians on levels of hostile heterosexism (B=1.05, *SE*=0.20, *t*=5.34, $p < .001$), and levels of hostile heterosexism significantly predict cultural incongruence in the bivariate relationships (B=0.14, *SE*=0.06, *t*=2.19, *p*=.03; not shown). In the full model, neither hostile heterosexism nor having an evangelical Christian identity continues to be a significant predictor of cultural incongruence (B=0.09, *SE*=0.07, *t*=1.33, *p*=.19; β=0.25, *SE*=0.16, *t*=1.51, *p*=.14; respectively). None of the Sobel and related test values (Sobel=1.29, *SE*=0.07; Goodman=1.31, *SE*=0.07; Aorian=1.27, *SE*=0.08) are statistically significant.

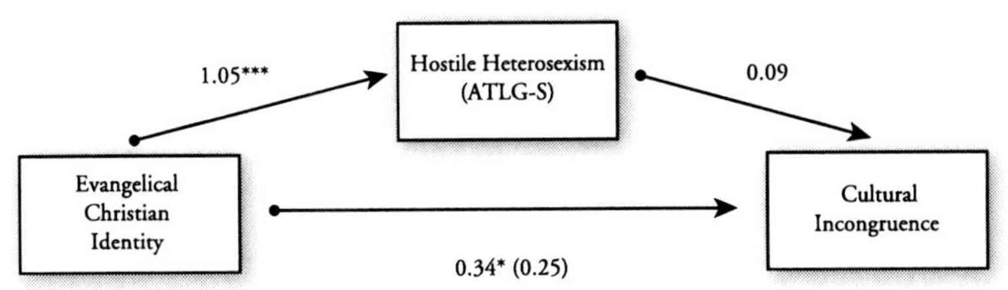

Figure 3. Test of mediation of hostile heterosexism.

MULTIDIMENSIONAL HETEROSEXISM INVENTORY

The MHI scale consists of four subscales: aversive heterosexism, amnestic heterosexism, paternalistic heterosexism, and positive stereotypic heterosexism. The four subdomains are conceptualized as related but independent constructs (Walls, 2008), and therefore we tested each subscale separately.

Aversive heterosexism does not mediate the relationship between having an evangelical Christian identity and cultural incongruence (Figure 4). In the bivariate relationships, evangelical Christians scored significantly higher on aversive heterosexism than other students (β=0.93, *SE*=0.25, *t*=3.74, $p < .001$), and higher scores on aversive heterosexism were significantly related to higher levels of cultural incongruence (β=0.12, *SE*=0.05, *t*=2.26, *p*=.03; not shown). In the full model, neither the independent nor the mediator variable continues to significantly predict cultural incongruence (β=0.09, *SE*=0.05, *t*=1.62, *p*=.11 and β=0.26, *SE*=0.16, *t*=1.67, *p*=.10, respectively). The Sobel and related test values are Sobel=1.49, *SE*=0.06; Goodman=1.54, *SE*=0.05; and Aorian=1.45, *SE*=0.06.

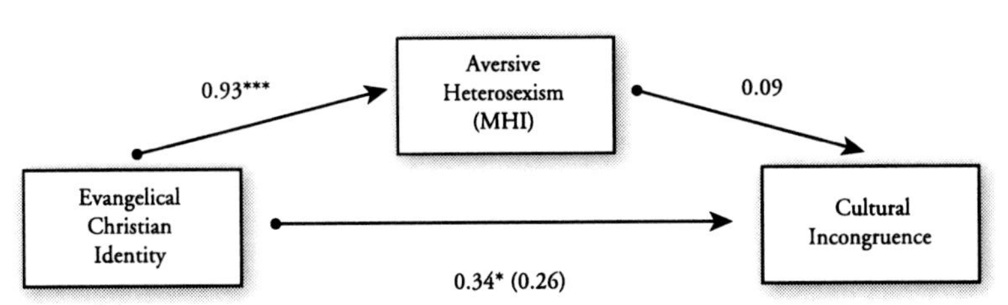

Figure 4. Test of mediation of aversive heterosexism.

Turning now to the remaining subdomains of MHI, we find that neither amnestic heterosexism, paternalistic heterosexism, nor positive stereotypic heterosexism significantly predicts cultural incongruence in the bivariate relationship (β=0.14, *SE*=0.08, *t*=1.69, *p*=.09; β=0.008, *SE*=0.03, *t*=0.30, *p*=.77; β=0.02, *SE*=0.05, *t*=0.41, *p*=.68, respectively). Therefore, we did not proceed further with mediational analyses for these three constructs.

Discussion and Implications

Evangelical Christian graduate social work students were significantly more likely to indicate higher levels of cultural incongruence with social work values and the perceived culture of a social work program than students who identify with some other religion, with other denominational traditions within Christianity, or as unaffiliated. In terms of general attitudes toward social stratification, evangelical Christian students scored significantly higher on the group-based dominance subdomain of social dominance orientation and right-wing authoritarianism but were not significantly different from other students on the opposition to equality subdomain of social dominance orientation. They additionally scored higher on hostile heterosexism, aversive heterosexism, amnestic heterosexism, paternalistic heterosexism, and the endorsement of positive stereotypes of lesbian women and gay men (positive stereotypic heterosexism).

However, among the constructs we tested as potential mediators of the relationship between identification as an evangelical Christian and cultural incongruence with social work values and the perceived culture of a social work program, only one construct fully mediated the relationship. The constructs that were not statistically significant mediators were hostile heterosexism, the four domains of modern heterosexism, right-wing authoritarianism, and the opposition to equality subdomain of social dominance. The only significant mediator was group-based dominance, that is, the "preference for one's own group compared to those of other groups . . . and most strongly associated with active and aggressive hierarchy promotion" (Kugler et al., 2010, p. 121).

Taken together, these findings suggest that although the evangelical Christian social work students in the sample displayed higher levels of most forms of heterosexism and of general attitudes supporting social stratification than social work students who were not evangelical Christians (which is concerning in and of itself), these higher levels—with the exception of group-based dominance—did not significantly mediate the higher levels of cultural incongruence that the evangelical Christian social work students were reporting. Although the sample was restricted to one cohort within one school of social work, it raises questions about what may actually undergird the conflict many evangelical Christian social work students report (Hodge, 2002).

Often, attitudes about same-sex sexuality and attitudes about abortion are the explanations offered in the literature for this dissonance (Ely, Flaherty, Akers, & Noland, 2012; Fram & Miller-Cribbs, 2008; Melendez & LaSala, 2006; Thyer & Myers, 2008). Although this study did not examine abortion attitudes (something future research may want to explore), none of the attitudinal scales capturing prejudice toward same-sex oriented people mediated the relationship between having an evangelical Christian identity and the measure of cultural incongruence. This mirrors Thaller's (2011) findings that devout Christian social workers' "identities and worldviews were more complex than may be assumed" (p. 158). In her qualitative sample of practicing social workers who identified as devout Christians, most reported finding a way in which to negotiate their personal religious beliefs with social work values so as to practice in ethical ways (see also Brice, 2014; Drumm et al., 2014). However, most of the participants in her study also acknowledged a degree of syncretism with the dogma of their faith whereby they did not agree with all the tenets of their denomination, identifying as being "different" from the typical member of their church or denomination. The role of syncretism and the diversity of views across Christian denominations, within Christian denominations, and even within specific congregations is a critical factor for social worker educators to tend to and incorporate into discussions on religion in the classroom (Woodford, Walls, & Levy, 2012).

But what is to be made of the finding about group-based dominance as a mediator of the relationship between reporting an evangelical Christian identity and cultural incongruence with social work values and the perceived culture of a social work program? Given that group-based dominance encompasses a preference for one's own social group, negative attitudes about unpopular outgroups that have implications for one's own social group, and aggressive promotion of hierarchy, social work educators have a number of potential areas in which to intervene to decrease cultural incongruence. Directly addressing issues of Christian privilege (see Walls & Todd, 2014)—including increasing awareness of its existence, its impact on marginalized others, and ways in which to challenge it—as part of social work education seems critical. Failure to name and deconstruct privilege (Christian and other types) leaves unexplored the role of preference for one's own social group in maintaining inequality. Given that privilege is mostly invisible to those who have it (Goodman, 2001; Kendall, 2006), if social workers are not grappling with its role in fostering inequity while in their social work program, it seems unlikely that they will happen upon it as a topic in their continuing education options (Brice, 2014; Drumm et al., 2014; Tan, 2014).

Unpacking perceived threats to a student's evangelical Christian identity, whether they be from other religious traditions, atheism, or pro-LGBT policies (e.g., same-sex marriage, removal of anti-LGBT adoption bans) also seems paramount. The reality that some Christian students feel unable to claim their religious identity in schools of social work seems likely to further heighten these feelings of being under attack, leading to further entrenchment of negative attitudes toward social groups that students deem as leading the attack (e.g., lesbians, gay men, and their allies; atheists; feminists). Work in this arena may entail providing factual information to counter false assumptions and beliefs (e.g., that churches will be forced to marry same-sex couples when same-sex marriage is legal; that one-man, one-woman marriage is the only biblical type of marriage), exploring feelings of self-righteousness and certainty about one's beliefs (whether based on religion, politics, or some other ideology), problematizing attitudes that any one religion's beliefs should be enacted into policy, and supporting students as they wrestle with fear of progressive change, particularly that which decreases the privileging of the Christian faith tradition.

One tool that may be particularly useful in addressing some aspects of these issues is the reflections and narratives of Christian-identified social workers and helping professionals who have successfully navigated the tension between their personally held religious beliefs and social work values (see, for example, Brice, 2014; Drumm et al., 2014; Levy, 2011; Tan, 2014) or who have worked to examine their own Christian privilege (see, for example, Todd, 2010). Another reframing that may be potentially helpful is to broaden the discussion with examples of how conflicts also arise at the liberal end of the political spectrum (e.g., a politically liberal social worker working with a 13-year-old pregnant girl who believes abortion is immoral when the social worker believes that termination of the pregnancy is the most prudent option, or a social worker working with a gay male client who chooses celibacy because of his religious beliefs when the progressive social worker recognizes religiously based internalized homophobia at play).

Finally, intergroup dialogue, which is used frequently in multicultural education, may be another effective tool (Dessel, Woodford, & Gutierrez, 2012; Dessel, Woodford, Routenberg, & Breijak, 2013; Dessel, Woodford, & Warren, 2011; Miles, Henrichs-Beck, & Bourn, 2014). Often the goal of intergroup dialogue is to foster democratic engagement, increase social responsibility, increase students' awareness and critical analysis of group identity processes, and build alliances for collective action (Dessel et al., 2011; Zúñiga, Nagda, Chesler, & Cytron-Walker, 2007). As with most pedagogical tools, intergroup dialogue should be approached so as not to reenact power differences that reflect those that exist in society (Dessel et al., 2011; Walls, Roll, Griffin, & Sprague, 2010). For example, in some situations people who occupy a marginalized identity are vastly outnumbered by those who occupy a corresponding privileged identity or where there may be negative consequences for marginalized others for engaging in dialogue across power differentials. There are the concerns about the ethics of exposing marginalized group members (once again) to the prejudicial attitudes and microaggressions of privileged group members (Miller & Donner, 2000) or placing the burden of educating privileged group members (once again) on members of marginalized groups (Hurtado, 2006).

Regardless of the approach taken and the pedagogical tools used, avoidance of the topic of religion does not move the dialogue forward, nor does it do any favors for marginalized others that the social work student will be working with in the future. Improving cognitive flexibility, deepening humility about one's own beliefs, fostering critical thinking skills, contextualizing clients' lives, enhancing the ability to critique one's beliefs more honestly, and making more nuanced and complex our understanding of the human condition are all aspects of good social work education that can come into play in supporting social work students who experience strong incongruence with social work values and the culture of the discipline. If we attend to these aspects along with the content we are trying to teach, we may be more successful in fulfilling the call to bring about more justice and liberation in the world.

References

Abramovitz, M. (1993). Should all social work students be educated for social change? Pro. *Journal of Social Work Education, 29*, 6–12.

Abramovitz, M. (1998). Social work and social reform: An area of struggle. *Social Work, 43,* 512–526.

Adorno, T. W., Frenkel-Brunswik, E., Levinson, D. J., & Sanford, R. N. (1950). *The authoritarian personality.* New York, NY: Harper & Brothers.

Allport, G. W. (1954). *The nature of prejudice.* Reading, MA: Addison-Wesley.

Altemeyer, B. (2004). Highly dominating, highly authoritarian personalities. *Journal of Social Psychology, 144,* 421–447.

Altemeyer, B. (2006). *The authoritarians.* Morrisville, NC: Lulu.

Altemeyer, B., & Hunsberger, B. (1992). Authoritarianism, religious fundamentalism, quest, and prejudice. *International Journal for the Psychology of Religion, 2,* 113–133.

Altemeyer, R. A. (1981). *Right-wing authoritarianism.* Winnipeg, MB: University of Manitoba Press.

Altemeyer, R. A. (1988). *Enemies of freedom: Understanding right-wing authoritarianism.* San Francisco, CA: Jossey-Bass.

Altemeyer, R. A. (1996). *The authoritarian specter.* Cambridge, MA: Harvard University Press.

Altemeyer, R. A. (1998). The other "authoritarian personality". In L. Berkowitz (Ed.) *Advances in experimental social psychology, 30*, 47–92. Orlando, FL: Academic Press.Altemeyer, R. A., & Hunsberger, B. (1997). *Amazing conversions: Why some turn to faith and other abandon religion.* Amherst, NY: Prometheus Press.

Barnoff, L., & Moffatt, K. (2007). Contradictory tensions in anti-oppression practice in feminist social services. *Affilia, 22,* 56–70.

Baron, R. M., & Kenny, D. A. (1986). The moderator–mediator variable distinction in social psychological research: Conceptual, strategic, and statistical considerations. *Journal of Personality and Social Psychology, 51,* 1173–1182.

Barret, B., & Logan, C. (2002). *Counseling gay men and lesbians: A practice primer.* Pacific Grove, CA: Brooks/Cole Publishing Company.

Brice, T. S. (2014). Is homophobia a conservative Christian value? In A. Dessel & R. Bolen (Eds.), *Conservative Christian beliefs and sexual orientation in social work: Privilege, oppression, and the pursuit of human rights* (pp. 257–272). Alexandria, VA: Council on Social Work Education Press.

Butler, J. C. (2000). Personality and emotional correlates of right-wing authoritarianism. *Social Behavior and Personality, 28,* 1–14.

Canda, E. R., Nakashima, M., & Furman, L. D. (2004). Ethical considerations about spirituality in social work: Insights from a national qualitative survey. *Families in Society, 85,* 27–35.

Cobb, N. H. (1994). Court-recommended guidelines for managing unethical students and working with university lawyers. *Journal of Social Work Education, 30,* 18–31.

Coholic, D. (2003). Incorporating spirituality in feminist social work perspectives. *Affilia: Journal of Women and Social Work, 18,* 49–67.

Cohrs, J. C., Kielmann, S., Maes, J., & Moschner, B. (2005). Effects of right-wing authoritarianism and threat from terrorism on restriction of civil liberties. *Analyses of Social Issues and Public Policy, 5,* 263–276.

Coward, H. (1986). Intolerance in the world's religions. *Studies in Religion, 15,* 419–431.

Currer, C., & Atherton, K. (2008). Suitable to remain a student social worker? Decision making in relation to termination of training. *Social Work Education, 27,* 279–292. doi:10.1080/02615470701381343

Dallago, F., Cima, R., Roccato, M., Ricolfi, L., & Mirisola, A. (2008). The correlation between right-wing authoritarianism and social dominance orientation: The moderating effects of political and religious identity. *Basic and Applied Psychology, 30,* 362–368.

de Regt, S. (2012). Religiosity as a moderator of the relationship between authoritarianism and social dominance orientation: A cross-cultural comparison. *International Journal for the Psychology of Religion, 22,* 31–41. doi: 10.1080/10508619.2012.635045

Dessel, A., Woodford, M., & Gutierrez, L. (2012). Social work faculty's attitudes toward marginalized groups: Exploring the role of religion. *Journal of Religion & Spirituality in Social Work: Social Thought, 31*(3), 244–262.

Dessel, A., Woodford, M., Routenberg, R., & Breijak, D. (2013). Heterosexual students' experiences in sexual orientation intergroup dialogue courses. *Journal of Homosexuality, 60*, 1054–1080.Dessel, A., Woodford, M., & Warren, N. (2011). Intergroup dialogue courses on sexual orientation: Lesbian, gay and bisexual student experiences and outcomes. *Journal of Homosexuality, 58*(8), 1132–1150.

Dru, V. (2007). Authoritarianism, social dominance orientation and prejudice: Effects of various self-categorization conditions. *Journal of Experimental Social Psychology, 43,* 877–883.

Drumm, R., Wilder, K., Baker, E., Souza, L., Burgess-Robinson, Z., & Adams, J. (2014). "Jesus didn't say anything in the Bible about gay people": Understanding pathways to Christian social work LGBT advocacy. In A. Dessel & R. Bolen (Eds.), *Conservative Christian beliefs and sexual orientation in social work: Privilege, oppression, and the pursuit of human rights* (pp. 289–312). Alexandria, VA: Council on Social Work Education Press.

Duckitt, J. (2001). A dual-process cognitive–motivational theory of ideology and prejudice. *Advances in Experimental Social Psychology, 33,* 41–113.

Duckitt, J. (2006). Differential effects of right wing authoritarianism and social dominance orientation on outgroup attitudes and their mediation by threat from and competitiveness to outgroups. *Personality and Social Psychology Bulletin, 32,* 684–696.

Duckitt, J., Bizumic, B., Krauss, S., & Heled, E. (2010). A tripartite approach to right wing authoritarianism: The authoritarianism–conservatism–traditionalism model. *Political Psychology, 31,* 615–815. doi:10.1111/j.1467-9221.2010.00781.x

Duncan, L. E., Peterson, B. E., & Winter, D. G. (1997). Authoritarianism and gender roles: Toward a psychological analysis of hegemonic relationships. *Personality and Social Psychology Bulletin, 23,* 41–49.

Duriez, B., & Hutsebaut, D. (2000). The relation between religion and racism: The role of post critical beliefs. *Mental Health, Religion and Culture, 3,* 85–102.

Duriez, B., & Van Hiel, A. (2002). The march of modern fascism: A comparison of social dominance orientation and authoritarianism. *Personality and Individual Differences, 32,* 1199–1213.

Eagly, A. H., Diekman, A. B., Johannesen-Schmidt, M. C., & Koenig, A. M. (2004). Gender gaps in sociopolitical attitudes: A social psychological analysis. *Journal of Personality and Social Psychology, 87,* 796–816.

Ekehammer, B., Akrami, N., Gylje, M., & Zakrisson, I. (2004). What matters most to prejudice: Big Five personality, social dominance orientation, or right-wing authoritarianism? *European Journal of Personality, 18,* 463–482.

Ely, G. E., Flaherty, C., Akers, L. S., & Noland, T. B. (2012). Social work student attitudes toward the social work perspective on abortion. *Journal of Social Work Values and Ethics, 9,* 34–45.

Finlay, B., & Walther, C. S. (2003). The relation of religious affiliation, service attendance, and other factors to homophobic attitudes among university students. *Review of Religious Research, 44,* 370–393.

Fortune, A. E. (2003). Comparison of faculty ratings of applicants and background characteristics as predictors of performance in an MSW program. *Journal of Teaching in Social Work, 23,* 35–54. doi:10.1300J067v23n01_04

Fram, M. S., & Miller-Cribbs, J. (2008). Liberal and conservative in social work education: Exploring student experiences. *Social Work Education, 27,* 883–897.

Gaertner, S. L., & Dovidio, J. F. (Eds.). (1986). *Prejudice, discrimination and racism: Theory and research.* Orlando, FL: Academic Press.

Goodman, D. J. (2001). *Promoting diversity and social justice: Educating people from privileged groups.* Thousand Oaks, CA: SAGE.

Goodman, L. A. (1960). On the exact variance of products. *Journal of the American Statistical Association, 55,* 708–713.

Gross, G. D. (2000). Gatekeeping for cultural competence: Ready or not? Some post and modernist doubts. *Journal of Baccalaureate Social Work,* 5(2), 47–66.

Guimond, S., Branscombe, N. R., Brunot, S., Buunk, B. P., Chatard, A., Désert, M., . . . Yzerbyt, V. (2007). Culture, gender, and the self: Variations and impact of social comparison processes. *Journal of Personality and Social Psychology, 92,* 1118–1134.

Hall, D. L., Matz, D. C., & Wood, W. (2010). Why don't we practice what we preach? A meta-analytic review of religious racism. *Personality and Social Psychology Review, 14,* 126–139. doi:10.1177/1088868309352179

Heaven, P. C. L., & Connors, J. C. (2001). A note on the value correlates of social dominance orientation and right-wing authoritarianism. *Personality and Individual Differences, 31,* 925–930.

Herek, G. M. (1984). Attitudes toward lesbians and gay men: A factor analytic study. *Journal of Homosexuality, 10,* 39–51.

Herek, G. M. (1988). Heterosexuals' attitudes toward lesbians and gay men: Correlates and gender differences. *Journal of Sex Research, 25,* 451-477.

Herek, G. M., & Capitanio, J. P. (1995). Black heterosexuals' attitudes toward lesbians and gay men in the United States. *Journal of Sex Research, 32,* 95–105.

Hodge, D. (2002). Does social work oppress evangelical Christians? A "new class" analysis of society and social work. *Social Work, 47,* 401–414.

Hunsberger, B. (1995). Religion and prejudice: The role of religious fundamentalism, quest, and right-wing authoritarianism. *Journal of Social Issues, 51,* 113–129.

Hurtado, S. (2006). Diversity and learning for a pluralistic democracy. In W. R. Allen, M. Bonous-Hammarth, & R. Teranishi (Eds.), *Higher education in a global society: Achieving diversity, equity, and excellence* (pp. 249–293). Oxford, England: Elsevier Publishers.

Jayakumar, U. M. (2009). The invisible rainbow in diversity: Factors influencing sexual prejudice among college students. *Journal of Homosexuality, 56,* 675–700.

Jost, J. T., & Banaji, M. R. (1994). The role of stereotyping in system-justification and the production of false consciousness. *British Journal of Social Psychology, 33,* 1–27.

Jost, J. T., Glaser, J., Kruglanski, A. W., & Sulloway, F. (2003). Exceptions that prove the rule: Using a theory of motivated social cognition to account for ideological incongruities and political anomalies. *Psychological Bulletin, 129,* 383–393.

Jost, J. T., & Hunyady, O. (2005). Antecedents and consequences of system-justifying ideologies. *Current Directions in Psychological Science, 14,* 260–265.

Jost, J. T., & Thompson, E. P. (2000). Group-based dominance and opposition to equality as independent predictors of self-esteem, ethnocentrism, and social policy attitudes among African Americans and European Americans. *Journal of Experimental Social Psychology, 36,* 209–232.

Kemmelmeier, M. (2005). The effects of race and social dominance orientation in simulated juror decision making. *Journal of Applied Social Psychology, 35,* 1030–1045. doi:10.1111/j.1559-1816.2005.tb02158.x

Kendall, F. (2006). *Understanding White privilege: Creating pathways to authentic relationships across race.* New York, NY: Routledge.

Kivel, P. (2006). *You call this a democracy? Who benefits, who pays, and who really decides?* New York, NY: Apex Press.

Knöpfelmacher, F., & Armstrong, D. B. (1963). The relation between authoritarianism, ethnocentrism and religious denomination among Australian adolescents. *American Catholic Sociological Review, 24,* 99–114.

Koerin, B., & Miller, J. (1995). Gatekeeping policies: Terminating students for nonacademic reasons. *Journal of Social Work Education, 31,* 247–260.

Kugler, M. B., Cooper, J., & Nosek, B. A. (2010). Group-based dominance and opposition to equality correspond to different psychological motives. *Social Justice Research, 23,* 117–155. doi:10.1007/s11211-010-0112-5

Lambert, A. J., & Chasteen, A. L. (1997). Perceptions of disadvantage vs. conventionality: Political values and attitudes toward the elderly vs. Blacks. *Personality and Social Psychology Bulletin, 23,* 469–481.

Laythe, B., Finkel, D. G., Bringle, R. G., & Kirkpatrick, L. A. (2002). Religious fundamentalism as a predictor of prejudice: A two-component model. *Journal for the Scientific Study of Spirituality, 41,* 623–636.

Laythe, B., Finkel, D. G., & Kirkpatrick, L. A. (2001). Predicting prejudice from religious fundamentalism and right-wing authoritarianism: A multiple regression approach. *Journal for the Scientific Study of Spirituality, 40,* 1–10.

Levy, D. L. (2008). Gay, lesbian, and queer individuals with a Christian upbringing: Exploring the process of resolving conflict between sexual identity and religious beliefs. *Dissertation Abstracts International, 69,* 282A. (UMI No. AAT 3326661)

Levy, D. L. (2011). Journeys of faith: Christian social workers serving gay and lesbian clients. *Social Work and Christianity, 38,* 218–227.

Levy, D. L. (2014). Christian doctrine related to sexual orientation: Current climate and future implications. In A. Dessel & R. Bolen (Eds.), *Conservative Christian beliefs and sexual orientation in social work: Privilege, oppression, and the pursuit of human rights* (pp. 11–42). Alexandria, VA: Council on Social Work Education Press.

McFarland, S. G. (1998, July). *Toward a typology of prejudiced persons.* Paper presented at the annual convention of the International Society for Political Psychology, Montreal, QC.

McFarland, S. G., & Adelson, S. (1996, July). *An omnibus study of personality, values, and prejudice.* Paper presented at the annual convention of the International Society for Political Psychology, Vancouver, BC.

Melendez, M. R., & LaSala, M. C. (2006). Who's oppressing whom? Homosexuality, Christianity, and social work [Points & Viewpoints]. *Social Work, 51,* 371–377.

Miles, J., Henrichs-Beck, C., & Bourn, J. (2014). Intergroup dialogue: A method for engaging students around religion and sexual orientation. In A. Dessel & R. Bolen (Eds.), *Conservative Christian beliefs and sexual orientation in social work: Privilege, oppression, and the pursuit of human rights* (pp. TK). Alexandria, VA: Council on Social Work Education Press.

Miller, W. R., & Delaney, H. D. (Eds.). (2005). *Judeo-Christian perspectives on psychology: Human nature, motivation, and change.* Washington, DC: American Psychological Association.

Miller, J., & Donner, S. (2000). More than just talk: The use of racial dialogues to combat racism. *Social Work with Groups, 23,* 31–53.Moore, L. S., Dietz, T. J., & Jenkins, D. A. (1998). Issues in gatekeeping. *Journal of Baccalaureate Social Work, 4*(1), 37–50.

Moore, L. S., & Urwin, C. A. (1990). Quality control in social work: The gatekeeping role in social work education. *Journal of Teaching in Social Work, 4,* 113–128.

Morrison, M. A., & Morrison, T. G. (2002). Development and validation of a scale measuring modern prejudice toward gay men and lesbian women. *Journal of Homosexuality, 43,* 15–37.

Morrow, D. F. (2000). Gatekeeping for small baccalaureate social work programs. *Journal of Baccalaureate Social Work, 5*(2), 67–80.

National Association of Social Workers (NASW). (2008). *Code of ethics of the National Association of Social Workers.* Retrieved March 25, 2013, from http:// www.socialworkers.org/pubs/code/ code.asp

Okitikpi, T. (Ed.). (2011). *Social control and the use of power in social work with children and families.* Dorset, UK: Russell House Publishing.

Pearlmutter, S. (2002). Achieving political practice: Integrating individual need and social action. *Journal of Progressive Human Services, 13*(1), 31–51.

Piazza, J. (2012). "If you love me keep my commandments": Religiosity increases preference for rule-based moral arguments. *International Journal for the Psychology of Religion, 22,* 285–302.

Pratto, F., Sidanius, J., Stallworth, L. M., & Malle, B. F. (1994). Social dominance orientation: A personality variable predicting social and political attitudes. *Journal of Personality and Social Psychology, 67,* 741–763.

Pratto, F., Stallworth, L. M., & Conway-Lanz, S. (1998). Social dominance orientation and the legitimization of policy. *Journal of Applied Social Psychology, 28,* 1853–1875.

Preacher, K. J., & Leonardelli, G. J. (2001). Calculation for the Sobel test: An interactive calculation tool for mediation tests. Retrieved from http://quantpsy.org/sobel/sobel.htmQuinton, W. J., Cowan, G., & Watson, B. D. (1996). Personality and altitudinal predictors of support of Proposition 187: California's anti-immigrant initiative. *Journal of Applied Social Psychology, 26,* 2204–2223.

Reynolds, L. R. (2004). Gatekeeping prior to point of entry. *Advances in Social Work, 5,* 18–31.

Roccato, M. (2008). Right-wing authoritarianism, social dominance orientation, and attachment: An Italian study. *Swiss Journal of Psychology,* 219–229. doi:10.1024/1421-0185.67.4.219

Rokeach, M. (1960). *The open and closed mind: Investigations into the nature of belief systems and personality systems.* New York, NY: Basic Books.

Rowatt, W. C., LaBouff, J., Johnson, M., Froese, P., & Tsang, J.-A. (2009). Associations among religiousness, social attitudes, and prejudice in a national random sample of American adults. *Psychology of Religion and Spirituality, 1,* 14–24. doi:10.1037/a0014989

Ryan, M., Habibis, D., & Craft, C. (1997). Guarding the gates of the profession: Findings of a survey of gatekeeping mechanisms in Australian bachelor of social work programs. *Australian Social Work, 50,* 5–12.

Schulte, L. J., & Battle, J. (2004). The relative importance of ethnicity and religion in predicting attitudes towards gays and lesbians. *Journal of Homosexuality, 47,* 127–142.

Seelman, K. L., & Walls, N. E. (2010). Person–organization incongruence as a predictor of right-wing authoritarianism, social dominance orientation, and heterosexism. *Journal of Social Work Education, 46,* 103–121.

Sibley, C. G., & Duckitt, J. (2008). Personality and prejudice: A meta-analysis and theoretical review. *Personality and Social Psychology Review, 12,* 248–279.

Sidanius, J., Levin, S., Liu, J., & Pratto, F. (2000). Social dominance orientation, antiegalitarianism, and the political psychology of gender: An extension and cross-cultural replication. *European Journal of Social Psychology, 30,* 41–67.

Sidanius, J., Liu, J., Pratto, F., & Shaw, J. (1994). Social dominance orientation, hierarchy-attenuators and hierarchy-enhancers: Social dominance theory and the criminal justice system. *Journal of Applied Social Psychology, 24,* 338–366.

Sidanius, J., & Pratto, F. (1999). *Social dominance: An intergroup theory of social hierarchy and oppression.* Cambridge, MA: Cambridge University Press.

Sidanius, J., van Laar, C., Levin, S., & Sinclair, S. (2003). Social hierarchy maintenance and assortment into social roles: A social dominance perspective. *Group Processes & Intergroup Relations, 6,* 333–352.

Sobel, M. E. (1982). Asymptotic intervals for indirect effects in structural equations models. In S. Leinhart (Ed.), *Sociological methodology* (pp. 290–312). San Francisco, CA: Jossey-Bass.

Sowbel, L. R. (2012). Gatekeeping: Why shouldn't we be ambivalent. *Journal of Social Work Education, 48,* 27–44.

Spano, R., & Koenig, T. (2007). What is sacred when personal and professional values collide. *Journal of Social Work Values & Ethics, 4*(3). Retrieved from http://www.socialworker.com/jswve/content/view/69/54/

Steensland, B., Robinson, L. D., Wilcox, W. B., Park, J. Z., Regnerus, M. D., & Woodberry, R. D. (2000). The measure of American religion: Toward improving the state of the art. *Social Forces, 79,* 291–318.

Stones, C. R. (2006). Antigay prejudice among heterosexual males: Right-wing authoritarianism as a stronger predictor than social-dominance orientation and heterosexual identity. *Social Behavior and Personality, 34,* 1138.

Sullivan, E., & Johns, R. (2002). Challenging values and inspiring attitude change: Creating an effective learning experience. *Social Work Education, 21,* 217–231. doi:10.1080/02615470220126444

Sünker, H. (2005). Social work, social politics and justice. *Social Work & Society, 3,* 11–29.

Tajfel, H. (1981). *Human groups and social categories. Studies in social psychology.* Cambridge, MA: Cambridge University Press.

Tajfel, H., & Turner, J. C. (1986). The social identity theory of intergroup behaviour. In S. Worchel & W. G. Austin (Eds.), *Psychology of intergroup relations* (pp. 7–24). Chicago, IL: Nelson-Hall.

Tan, A. (2014). Understanding the tension: Christian practitioner perspectives on working with LGBT clients. In A. Dessel & R. Bolen (Eds.), *Conservative Christian beliefs and sexual orientation in social work: Privilege, oppression, and the pursuit of human rights* (pp. TK). Alexandria, VA: Council on Social Work Education Press.

Thaller, J. (2011). Resilience and resistance in professional identity making: Gleanings from the classroom experiences of devout Christian social workers. *Journal of Religion and Spirituality in Social Work, 30,* 144–163.

Thyer, B. A., & Myers, L. L. (2008). Religious discrimination in social work academic programs: Whither social justice? *Journal of Religion and Spirituality in Social Work Thought, 28,* 144–160.

Todd, J. (2010). Confessions of a Christian supremacist. *Reflections, 16,* 140–146.

van Buuren, S., Boshuizen, H. C., & Knook, D. L. (1999). Multiple imputation of missing blood pressure covariates in survival analysis. *Statistics in Medicine, 18,* 681–694.

van Laar, C., Sidanius, J., Rabinowitz, J. L., & Sinclair, S. (1999). The three Rs of academic achievement: Reading, 'riting, and racism. *Personality and Social Psychology Bulletin, 25*(2), 139–151.

Walls, N. E. (2008). Toward a multidimensional understanding of heterosexism: The changing nature of prejudicial attitudes. *Journal of Homosexuality, 55,* 20–70.

Walls, N. E., Roll, S., Griffin, R. A., & Sprague, L. (2010). Teaching about privilege: A model combining intergroup dialogue and single identity caucusing. *Understanding and Dismantling Privilege, 1,* 1–32. Retrieved from http://www.wpcjournal.com/article/viewFile/ 6262/pdf_30

Walls, N. E., & Todd, J. (2014). Defending the faith: Resistance and struggle in recognizing Christian privilege. In A. Dessel & R. Bolen (Eds.), *Conservative Christian beliefs and sexual orientation in social work: Privilege, oppression, and the pursuit of human rights* (pp. TK). Alexandria, VA: Council on Social Work Education Press.

Westman, A. S., Willink, J., & McHoskey, J. W. (2000). On perceived conflicts between religion and science: The role of fundamentalism and right-wing authoritarianism. *Psychological Reports, 86,* 379–385.

Whitehead, J. T. (1998). "Good ol' boys" and the chair: Death penalty attitudes of policymakers in Tennessee. *Crime and Delinquency, 44,* 245–256.

Whitley, B. E. (1999). Right-wing authoritarianism, social dominance orientation, and prejudice. *Journal of Personality and Social Psychology, 77,* 126–134.

Whitley, B. E. (2009). Religiosity and attitudes toward lesbians and gay men: A meta-analysis *International Journal for the Psychology of Religion, 19,* 21–38. doi:10.1080/10508610802471104

Whitley, B. E., & Lee, S. E. (2000). The relationship of authoritarianism and related constructs to attitudes toward homosexuality. *Journal of Applied Social Psychology, 30,* 144–170.

Wilkinson, W. W. (2004). Religiosity, authoritarianism, and homophobia: A multidimensional approach. *International Journal for the Psychology of Religion, 14,* 55–67.

Woodford, M. R., Levy, D., & Walls, N. E. (2012). Sexual prejudice among Christian college students, church teachings, and personal religious beliefs. *Review of Religious Research.* doi:10.1007/s13644-012-0067-0

Woodford, M. R., Walls, N. E., & Levy, D. (2012). Religion and endorsement for same-sex marriage: Role of syncretism between church teaching and personal beliefs. *Interdisciplinary Journal for Research on Religion, 8,* Article 4.

Zúñiga, X., Nagda, B. A., Chesler, M., & Cytron-Walker, A. (2007). Intergroup dialogue in higher education: Meaningful learning about social justice. *ASHE Higher Education Report, 32,* Number 4.

Appendix

Cultural Incongruence Scale

1. I sometimes struggle to accommodate both my personal beliefs and the NASW Code of Ethics.
2. My opinions and values often conflict with the "mainstream" culture of [name of graduate social work program].
3. The majority of students I have met at [graduate social work program] have attitudes and beliefs that are similar to my own.
4. I agree with the statement that "Social workers should act to prevent and eliminate domination of, exploitation of, and discrimination against any person, group, or class on the basis of race, ethnicity, national origin, color, sex, sexual orientation, age, marital status, political belief, religion, or mental or physical disability."
5. The majority of students I have met at [graduate social work program] are intolerant of beliefs with which they disagree.
6. It is better to keep my opinion to myself when I know that most others at [graduate social work program] will disagree with me.
7. There is a lot of support for differences in opinions and beliefs at [graduate social work program].
8. The majority of professors I have met at [graduate social work program] are intolerant of beliefs with which they disagree.
9. Disagreement is encouraged in [graduate social work program] classrooms.

Notes

1 The argument about social work's social control function highlights how power is always relative, and there are clear instances where social workers are perceived as instruments of the state and therefore hierarchy-enhancing (Kivel, 2006; Okitikpi, 2011).

2 Although faculty have accountability for gatekeeping, the task is challenging, and fear of litigation based on various court decisions plays a significant role in faculty ambivalence about this responsibility (Sowbel, 2012).

3 Because of the lack of racial diversity in the sample and concern about identification of participants, race and ethnicity were not queried on the survey. This, in turn, means that one group of Steensland et al.'s (2000) schema, Black Protestants, could not be discerned.

4 All Cronbach's alphas reported were calculated with the data before multiple imputation had been done.

5 The Sobel test examines whether the reduction of the coefficient of the independent variable (religious tradition in this case) on the dependent variable is statistically significant, indicating a statistically significant mediation effect (Sobel, 1982).

6 This is the first bivariate relationship in each of the mediation models and does not change across the models. Therefore, this information is not repeated when we discuss each of the mediation models individually.

CHAPTER 5

The Family, Conservative Christianity, and Lesbian and Gay Youth: A Review of the Literature

Warren J. Blumenfeld, EdD and Elliott N. DeVore, MEd

> *The role of religion is paradoxical. It makes and unmakes prejudice. While the creeds of the great religions are universalistic, all stressing brotherhood, the practices of these creeds are frequently divisive and brutal.* (Allport, 1954, p. 444)

Living on a conservative Christian mission in Florida with his Southern Baptist minister parents, Samuel Brinton lied about his emerging feelings for other boys as a preteen because he feared his parents' reactions. After Samuel acknowledged that he was attracted to his best friend, Dale, when he was 12, Samuel's father told him he had AIDS and repeatedly punched, burned, electroshocked, and inserted needles into his fingers to "cure" him. Eventually, Samuel felt forced to lie by telling his parents that he was actually heterosexual.

His parents sent him to a "religious therapist" who told Samuel, "I want you to know that you're gay, and all gay people have AIDS," and then placed pictures of men dying of AIDS before him (Wareham, 2011). Soon after arriving at Kansas State University, Samuel came out again to his parents, who told him he would not be welcomed home and threatened him if he returned. But he turned his life around. After graduation, he attended the Massachusetts Institute of Technology, and in 2010 Samuel Brinton was chosen as the Top LGBT Activist in the United States by Campus Pride, a national organization working for the rights of LGBT college and university students.

At age 14 Lyn Duff came out to her parents as lesbian. Not being able to accept this revelation, Lyn's mother whisked her immediately and involuntarily to Rivendell Psychiatric Center in West Jordan, Utah, where she was forced to undergo so-called conversion therapy to cure her from what doctors at the facility called gender identity disorder and clinical depression. Although Rivendell was not officially aligned with the Church of Latter-Day Saints, Lyn remembers that on numerous occasions throughout her 6-month incarceration, Mormon missionaries visited her, and that her therapy was highly religious in tone.

This so-called conversion therapy really amounted to aversion techniques including watching same-sex pornography while being forced to smell ammonia and being subjected to hypnosis, psychotropic drugs, and solitary confinement. Staff also imposed so-called behavior modification by requiring Lyn to wear dresses and forced punishments of cutting the lawn with a small pair of scissors and scrubbing floors with a toothbrush. After being locked up for 168 days, Lyn escaped Rivendell and went to San Francisco, where she lived on the streets and in safe houses.

She eventually connected with a local journalist, an attorney, Legal Services for Children, and the National Center for Lesbian Rights, and she fought for and won legal emancipation from her mother. A lesbian couple adopted her when was 15, and today Lyn Duff is a successful activist and journalist for the Pacific News Service and for KPFA radio's *Flashpoints* (Minter, 2012).

Research has shown that the repercussions for youth who come out to their parents as gay or lesbian with no family support can be devastating (see D'Augelli, 1991; D'Augelli, Pilkington, & Hershberger, 2002; Herdt & Boxer, 1993). Family rejection is often more feared than victimization or harassment (D'Augelli, 1991). For example, researchers (Gibson, 1989; Remafedi, Farrow, & Deisher, 1991) found that a significant percentage of LGBT youth are forced to leave home once their sexual or gender identity is questioned by family members, and approximately 20–40% of all homeless youth are lesbian, gay, bisexual, or transgender (National Network of Runaway and Youth Services, 2001). In addition, Ryan, Huebner, Diaz, and Sanchez (2009) reported that 26% of youth who come out to their families are thrown out of their homes because of conflicts with moral and religious values. More than 30% reported suffering physical violence by a family member after coming out. Lesbian, gay, and bisexual young adults who have reported higher levels of family rejection during adolescence were 8.4 times more likely to report having attempted suicide, 5.9 times more likely to report high levels of depression, 3.4 times more likely to use illegal drugs, and 3.4 times more likely to have reported having engaged in unprotected sexual intercourse.

Schools also can be unwelcoming. Gay, Lesbian, and Straight Education Network (GLSEN), in its 2005 National School Climate Survey of 1,732 LGBT students between the ages of 13 and 20, found that both face-to-face and online bullying "remain common in America's schools" (p. 4):

> Homophobic remarks were the most common type of biased language heard at school, with three-quarters of the students (75.4%) hearing remarks such as "faggot" or "dyke" frequently or often at school. ... Nearly a fifth (18.6%) of the survey respondents reported hearing homophobic remarks from their teachers or other school staff. (p. 4, emphasis added)

More than two fifths (41.2%) of respondents reported receiving threatening or harassing text messages or e-mail from other students.

In their subsequent 2009 National School Climate Survey of 7,261 middle and high school students, GLSEN reported that on the basis of sexual identity, 84.6% were verbally harassed, 40.1% physically harassed, and 18.8% physically assaulted, and 61.1% generally felt unsafe on their campuses. In terms of gender identity and expression, 63.7% were verbally harassed, 27.2% physically harassed, and 12.5% physically assaulted, and 39.9% generally felt unsafe. Grade point averages of students more frequently harassed because of sexual or gender identity were almost one half grade point lower than those of students who were less often harassed: 2.7 vs. 3.1. In addition, almost one third of LGBT students skipped at least 1 day of school in the month before the survey because of safety concerns. The report also showed that higher levels of victimization of LGBT youth were related to higher levels of depression and anxiety and lower levels of self-esteem.

For the purposes of our study, we set the contextual basis of the socialization process in the social institutions of the family and religion. Although numerous studies have uncovered the psychological, emotional, and physical effects on young people whose sexual and gender identity and expression transcend established societal norms, the purpose of our study (see Chapter 6, this anthology) was to interview college-aged students who identify as lesbian, gay, or bisexual who grew up in conservative Christian families to understand the meanings they made of and strategies they used while growing up in this environment and how it has affected their sexual identity development and sense of self. Our study looks at the strategies of resiliency used by a selective group of lesbian and gay youth born into conservative Christian households.

The Family

Human beings are a social species. We interact all the time with other people in families, at school, on the job, at home, on the street. We live in society, which comprises a comprehensive social grouping. Every society has culture, which includes the symbols, languages, material items, and set of values, norms, and attitudes that members of the social group share. Culture is the major element that distinguishes humans from other forms of animal life. Unlike human beings, who have to be taught their culture, animals are governed to a much greater extent by fixed, biologically inherited behavior patterns, or instincts. Therefore, human learning occurs in relationship with others.

It makes no difference where a child is born—Atlanta, Paris, New Guinea, China—all children undergo the process of socialization, which can be defined as the lifelong process through which people acquire personality and learn the values, attitudes, norms, and societal expectations of their culture (Blumenfeld & Raymond, 1993). Although the content varies from one culture to the next, the process of socialization varies little. Through this process, people come to understand their culture (and subcultures), begin to develop a sense of who they are, and come to know what is expected of them in terms of their social roles.

A social role is any pattern of behavior that a person in a specific situation is encouraged to perform. The term comes from the language of the theater, being derived from the French *rôle,* referring to the roll of paper containing an actor's part. A role is not the same as the person who is performing it at the moment, just as the role of Macbeth has been played by countless actors over the centuries. Macbeth has certain characteristics that, regardless of the particular actor who plays the part, enable the audience to recognize him as Macbeth. Yet, just as a stage role leaves some room for interpretation, most social roles involve general guidelines but not exact behaviors. Just as an acorn, under the proper conditions, may grow into an oak tree, humans need positive socialization to realize their humanity.

The Family as a Socializing Institution

For infants and young children, the initial and most important agents of socialization include parents or guardians and other members in nuclear and extended families who consciously and unconsciously model behaviors while teaching the social roles youth are to play. When we discuss the units we call "the family," however, we enter into a virtual battlefield of contested and opposing forces arguing for differing definitions and functions.

The sociological theory known as functionalism (or structural functionalism) views each aspect of society as interdependent and contributing to a holistic functioning of society held together by social consensus. A proponent is Coser (1964), who defined *family* as

> a group manifesting the following organizational attributes: It finds its origin in marriage; it consists of husband, wife, and children born in their wedlock, though other relatives may find their place close to this nuclear group, and the group is united by moral, legal, religious and social rights and obligations (including sexual rights and prohibitions as well as such social patterns as love, attraction, piety, and awe). (p. xvi)

Talcott Parsons, also a functionalist, faults some in their claims for the universalization of the "nuclear family," which Parsons argues has not been and is not always the case in all societies.

From the perspective of Marxism, on the other hand, the family, by socializing the young in accepting and following authority and a hierarchal structure within the family unit, prepares their eventual acceptance of authority within the workplace.

> Families are expected to socialize their members into an appropriate set of "family values" that simultaneously reinforce the hierarchy within the assumed unity of interests symbolized by the family and lay the foundation for many social hierarchies. In particular, hierarchies of gender, wealth, age, and sexuality within actual family units correlate with comparable hierarchies in U.S. society. (Collins, 1998, p. 64)

Whereas functionalism views the socialization process as it works within the family unit as promoting conformity to desirable norms and values that increase overall social stability, Marxism argues that the socialization process within the family (and within other social institutions such as schools, religion, and the media) transmits "a ruling class ideology whereby individuals are deceived into accepting the capitalist system and the dominance of the capitalist class more or less without question" (Holborn & Steel, 2012). Friedrich Engels (1884) saw how economic developments encouraging the accumulation of private property required the fortification of the monogamous family to guarantee that men's property would be inherited by their biological heirs. Engels was the one of the first to argue that women's subordination was not the result of any biological dispositions but rather caused by "men's efforts to achieve their demands for control of women's labor and sexual faculties [which] have gradually solidified and become institutionalized in the nuclear family" (Holborn & Steel, n.p.).

Marxist feminists have expanded Engels' and Marx's theoretical foundations to explain the subordination and exploitation of women within the family unit. While acknowledging the problematic nature of the capitalist system, Marxist feminism emphasizes the hierarchal gendered structure socialized and enforced initially within the family and then by other social institutions. In addition, Collins (1998) states, "Predicated on assumptions of heterosexism, the invisibility of gay, lesbian, and bisexual sexualities in the traditional family ideal obscures these sexualities and keeps them hidden" (p. 65).

If a patriarchal social and economic system of male domination can keep women pregnant and taking care of children after birth, it can restrict their entry, or at least their level and time of entry, into the workplace and ensure women's dependence on men economically and emotionally. In addition, the family's incessant reification and promotion of hegemonic binary gender categories

> is now (partially) what drives families in the U.S. to ex-communicate their LGBTQ children, and also provides the fuel for the socially conservative capitalist class to spread trans- and homophobia because of capitalists' direct benefit from traditional gender roles rooted in the family-household system. (Brown, 2012, p. 11)

Thus, when a patriarchal family structure converges with a patriarchal religious system, which itself reinforces and intensifies the enforcement of strictly defined gendered hierarchies of male domination by restricting women's reproductive freedoms and decision making and ordaining requisite sexual and gender matrices, women's oppression and the oppression of those who transgress sexual- and gender-based boundaries became inevitable.

Religion as an Institution of Socialization

For as long as we could articulate such concerns, our species has wondered about the workings of the universe and the significance of our existence. By definition, a religion is a particular system of rites and observances based on faith in and worship of a higher being or beings. Religion emphasizes the sacred and the divine:

> The anxiety of meaninglessness is anxiety about the loss of an ultimate concern, of a meaning which gives meaning to all meanings. This anxiety is aroused by the loss of a spiritual center, or an answer, however symbolic and indirect, to the questions of the meaning of existence. (Tillich, 1952, p. 47)

Many ancient and non-Western cultures—including the Hindu, most Native American, and the pre-Columbian, such as the Mayan and Incan cultures—are based on polytheistic religions. In general, these religious views seem to attribute similar characteristics to their gods. Particularly significant is the belief that the gods are actually created, and they age, give birth, and engage in sex. Some of these gods even have sexual relations with mortals. The universe is seen as continuous, ever-changing, and fluid. These religious views often lack rigid categories, which is particularly true of gender categories, which become mixed and often ambiguous and blurred. For example, some male gods give birth, and some female gods possess great power. At times the gods themselves engage in homosexual sexual relationships (e.g., the ancient Greek god Zeus with the mortal Ganymede, Sun god Apollo and the mortal Hyacinthus) (Andrews, 2002).

In contrast, monotheistic religions generally view the Supreme Being as without origin, for this deity was never born and will never die. This being, viewed as perfect, exists completely independently from human beings and transcends the natural world. In part, such a being has no sexual desire, for sexual desire, as a kind of need, is incompatible with this concept of perfection. This accounts for the strict separation between the creator and the created. Just as the creator is distinct from *his* creation, so too are divisions between the earthly sexes in the form of strictly defined gender roles. This distinction provides adherents to monotheistic religions a clear sense of their designated social roles, the guidelines they need to follow in relation to their god and to other human beings.

Because our study concentrates on orthodox, conservative, and evangelical Christianity specifically, the accompanying sidebars address scriptures and policies from this segment of Christendom.[1]

In general, spirituality is valued and sexuality is viewed as acceptable only in narrowly defined contexts. Therefore, in monotheism generally and specifically Christianity, homosexuality and gender nonconformity are proscribed.

Religion and Bias Toward LGB People

With the variables of religiosity and political affiliations in the research, Walch, Orlosky, Sinkkanen, and Stevens (2010) found a significant correlation between following religious fundamentalist traditions—"rigid belief in one 'true' religion" (Walch et al., p. 313)—or self-defining as religiously conservative and holding more negative attitudes toward homosexuality and homo-

Instructions for Christian Households
On Gender Roles[2]

Ephesians 5:21–24: "Be subject to one another out of reverence for Christ. Wives, be subject to your own husbands as to the Lord. For the man is the head of the woman, just as Christ also is the head of the church. Christ is, indeed, the Saviour of the body, but just as the church is subject to Christ, so must women be subject to their husbands in everything" (p. 241).

Ephesians 5:25–33: "Husbands, love your wives, as Christ also loves the church and gave himself up for it to consecrate it, cleansing it by water and word, so that he might present the church to himself all glorious, with no stain or wrinkle or anything of the sort, but holy and without blemish. In this same way men also are bound to love their wives, as they love their own bodies. In loving his wife a man loves himself. For no one ever hated his own body: on the contrary, he provides and cares for it; and that is how Christ treats the church, because we are members of his body, of which we are living parts. Thus it is that (in the words of Scripture) "a man shall leave his father and mother and shall be joined to his wife, and the two shall become one flesh." It is a great truth that is hidden here, but it applies also individually: each of you must love his wife as his very self; and the woman must see to it that she pays her husband all respect" (pp. 241–242).

1 Timothy 2:8–15: "It is my desire, therefore, that everywhere prayers be said by the men of the congregation, who shall lift up their hands with pure intention, excluding angry or quarrelsome thoughts. Women again must dress in becoming manner, modestly and soberly, not with elaborate hair-styles, not decked out with gold or pearls, or expensive clothes, but with good deeds, as befits women who claim to be religious. A woman must be a learner, listening quietly and with due submission. I do not permit a woman to be a teacher, nor must woman domineer over man; she should be quiet. For Adam was created first, and Eve afterwards, and it was not Adam who was deceived; it was the woman who, yielding to deception, fell into sin. Yet she will be saved through motherhood—if only women continue in faith, love, and holiness, with a sober mind" (pp. 262–263).

1 Corinthians 14:33–35, 37: "It is for prophets to control prophetic inspiration, for the God who inspires them is not a God of disorder but of peace. As in all congregations of God's people, women should not address the meeting. They have no license to speak, but should keep their place as the law directs. . . . If anyone claims to be inspired or a prophet, let him recognize that what I write has the Lord's authority" (p. 214).

sexual people (Henley & Pincus, 1978; Schulte & Battle, 2004; Schwartz & Lindley, 2005; Vanderstoep & Green, 1988). Also, studies found a link between religious and political conservatism and higher levels of homophobic attitudes (Bouton et al., 1989; Henley & Pincus, 1978; Morrison & Morrison, 2002; Young, Gallaher, Belasco, Barr, & Webber, 1991). In addition, "Baptists

Instructions for Christian Households On Same-Sex Sexuality

Romans 1:26: "In consequence, I say God has given them up to shameful passions; Their women have exchanged natural intercourse for unnatural." (p. 184) This passage could be considered the first official religious condemnation against female same-sex sexuality.

Romans 1:27: "And their men in turn, giving up natural relations, with women, burn with lust for one another; males behave indecently with males, and are paid in their own persons the fitting wage of such perversion" (p. 184).

Timothy 1:10: "For whoremonger, for them that defile themselves with mankind, for menstealers, for liars, for perjured persons, and if there be any other thing that is contrary to sound doctrine" (*King James Bible*, 2014).

1 Corinthians 6:9: "Surely you know that the unjust will never come into possession of the kingdom of God. Make no mistake: no fornicator or idolater, none who are guilty either of adultery or of homosexual perversion, no thieves or grabbers or drunkards or slanderers or swindlers, will possess the kingdom of God" (p. 205).

Catholic Catechism: "Basing itself on Sacred Scripture, which presents homosexual acts as acts of grave depravity Cf. *Gen* 191–29; *Rom* 124–27; 1 *Cor* 6:10; 1 *Tim* 1:10., tradition has always declared that 'homosexual acts are intrinsically disordered CDF, *Persona humana* 8.' They are contrary to the natural law. They close the sexual act to the gift of life [reproduction]. They do not proceed from a genuine affective and sexual complementarity. Under no circumstances can they be approved." (*Catechism of the Catholic Church*, 1997).

During his annual Christmas message delivered in December 2012, for example, Pope Benedict XVI asserted that marriage for same-sex couples destroys the "essence of the human creature," and he deemed marriage equality as a "manipulation of nature" that, along with abortion and euthanasia, threatens world peace. "People dispute the idea that they have a nature, given to them by their bodily identity, that serves as a defining element of the human being," he declared. "They deny their nature and decide that it is not something previously given to them, but that they make it for themselves."

In January 2011 Benedict XVI delivered a New Year's speech to diplomats from approximately 180 countries, declaring that marriage for same-sex couples "threatens human dignity and the future of humanity itself," and in 2008, during his end-of-the-year Vatican address, he asserted that humanity needs to "listen to the language of creation" to realize the intended roles of man and woman. He warned of the "blurring" of the natural distinctions between males and females, and he called for humanity to protect itself from self-destruction. The pope compared behavior beyond traditional heterosexual relations as "a destruction of God's work."

(continued)

Southern Baptist Convention, *On Homosexuality and the United States Military*: "RESOLVED, That the messengers to the Southern Baptist Convention … affirm the Bible's declaration that homosexual behavior is intrinsically disordered and sinful, and we also affirm the Bible's promise of forgiveness, change, and eternal life to all sinners (including those engaged in homosexual sin) who repent of sin and trust in the saving power of Jesus Christ (1 Corinthians 6:9–11)" (Southern Baptist Convention, 2010).

Southern Baptist Convention, *On Same-Sex Marriage*: "WHEREAS, Legalizing same-sex 'marriage' would convey a societal approval of a homosexual lifestyle, which the Bible calls sinful and dangerous both to the individuals involved and to society at large (Romans 1:24–27; 1 Corinthians 6:9–10; Leviticus 18:22); now, therefore, be it RESOLVED, That the messengers to the Southern Baptist Convention meeting in Phoenix, Arizona, June 17–18, 2003, affirm that legal and biblical marriage can only occur between one man and one woman; and be it further RESOLVED, That we continue to oppose steadfastly all efforts by any court or state legislature to validate or legalize same-sex marriage or other equivalent unions; and be it further RESOLVED, That we commit ourselves to pray for and support legislative and legal efforts to oppose the legalization of same-sex unions" (Southern Baptist Convention, 2003).

Evangelical Covenant Church, *Human Sexuality*: "We human beings misuse God's creation of sexuality and distort its role in our lives. In I Corinthians 6:9–10 and Romans 1:24–27, Scripture succinctly declares this sin and God's judgment on it. Throughout the Scriptures we see how sin in sexual relationships damages relationship with God and others. We live in a society characterized by imperfect and sinful sexual relationships of many kinds. . . . Evangelical Covenant Church resolution to care for persons involved in sexual sins such as adultery, homosexual behavior, and promiscuity compassionately recognizing the potential of these sins to take the form of addiction" (Evangelical Covenant Church, 1996).

Church of Jesus Christ of Latter-Day Saints, from *Handbook of Instructions* (2010): "Homosexual behavior violates the commandments of God, is contrary to the purposes of human sexuality, and deprives people of the blessings that can be found in family life and in the saving ordinances of the gospel. Those who persist in such behavior or who influence others to do so are subject to Church discipline. Homosexual behavior can be forgiven through sincere repentance."

had greater homophobia," and "Republicans had higher homophobia scores than individuals with other political party affiliations" (Walch et al., p. 320).

To determine whether degrees of religiosity could be linked to levels of racial prejudice, Johnson, Rowatt, and LaBouff (2010) found a direct effect (i.e., a causal relationship) of religion on racial attitudes. They implemented the research technique known as priming. The researchers primed U.S. Christian research participants with religious concepts (e.g., God, religious attendance) to determine whether this would affect participants' racial attitudes. As the researchers noted, historically, priming for religiosity has resulted in both positive and negative changes in attitudes and behaviors. Rowatt and colleagues (2006, 2009) discovered that priming with Christian religious concepts led to substantial increases in negative attitudes toward gay men, Muslims, and atheists.

In their study investigating the relationship between a number of personality and religious dimensions (specifically right-wing authoritarianism, religious fundamentalism, and Christian orthodoxy) with covert or "implicit" assessments of homosexuals relative to heterosexuals, researchers discovered that participants manifested negative attitudes, with the factor of religious fundamentalism, within any world religion, as "the strongest predictor of a negative implicit attitude toward gay men relative to heterosexuals" (Rowatt et al., 2006, p. 397).

Conclusion

Blumenfield states, "We live in a paradoxical society in which loving sameness makes one different while loving difference makes one the same" (2013, pp. 373–374).

Focus on the Family (FOF), a conservative theocratic[3] megamedia Christian ministry, asserted in published accounts (Draper, 2010) that gay rights advocates are forcing their viewpoints (their so-called gay agenda) onto schools in the guise of bullying prevention. In a *Denver Post* article, FOF spokesperson Candi Cushman asserted that gay activists are the real schoolyard bullies, and conservative Christians are the victims. According to Cushman, "We feel more and more that activists are being deceptive in using anti-bullying rhetoric to introduce their viewpoints, while the viewpoint of Christian students and parents are increasingly belittled" (Draper, 2010, para. 3).

On its official website, FOF promotes itself as a global Christian ministry dedicated to helping families thrive. "We provide help and resources for couples to build healthy marriages that reflect God's design, and for parents to raise their children according to morals and values grounded in biblical principles" (Focus on the Family, 2012).

FOF declares that

> ultimately, we believe that the purpose of life is to know and glorify God through an authentic relationship with His Son, Jesus Christ. This purpose is lived out first within our own families then extended, in love, to an increasingly broken world that desperately needs Him. (Focus on the Family, 2012).

We must locate FOF in a wider context, for it certainly does not operate in isolation but is part of a much larger and wider conservative theological, political, and social movement founded and maintained on their interpretation of conservative Christian biblical pronouncements and principles. This informal coalition of conservative Christian groups, often known collectively as the Christian Right, primarily evangelical and Catholic, include the Heritage Foundation (a conservative political think tank founded in 1973), Concerned Women for America, American Coalition on Traditional Values, Coalition for Religious Freedom, Eagle Forum, Moral Majority, American Center for Law and Justice, Christian Coalition, Christian Voice, National Organization for Marriage, and others too numerous to list.

Although the term *Christian Right* has been used to represent this movement, this terminology is inaccurate and misleading. A good number of well-intentioned conservative Christians do not abide by many of the extreme stances taken by movement leaders, leaders who seem to hijack the purpose and intent of Jesus' message. Although a number of leaders and organizations within this movement bristle against the notion of a large centralized government, paradoxically, they seem to be working toward the imposition of a powerful theocracy in their image.

Many of these theocratic right-wing groups and religious ministries push what they call Christian therapy for the purpose of, as they phrase it, removing people from a so-called deviant homosexual lifestyle. It is important that social workers and other mental health professionals know that these so-called therapies go by such names as the X-Gay religious ministries; Exodus International; Homosexual Anonymous (a cynical cooptation of 12-step program methods); Parents, Families, and Friends of X-Gays and Lesbians (PFOX; an obvious rip-off of the LGBT ally support network PFLAG, or Parents, Families, & Friends of Lesbians and Gays); and the so-called Reparative or Conversion Therapies, which promise conversion to heterosexuality if the patient has the necessary motivation to change (Human Rights Campaign, 2014).

Before 1973 the *Diagnostic and Statistical Manual of Mental Disorders* of the American Psychiatric Association characterized homosexuality as a mental disorder. However, a number of members of the psychiatric community along with political activists worked tirelessly to have this designation expunged because they saw no evidence of illness per se. In 1973 the membership of the American Psychiatric Association agreed with their recommendation.

The American Psychological Association passed a resolution (2004) calling on educational, government, business, and funding agencies to address issues of face-to-face and online bullying. In the resolution they particularly addressed acts of harassment "about race, ethnicity, religion, disability, sexual orientation, and gender identity" (p. 1). In addition, the resolution specifically emphasized the high rate of bullying around issues of sexual identity, gender expression, and disability:

> Children and youth with disabilities and children and youth who are lesbian, gay, or transgender, or who are perceived to be so may be at particularly high risk of being bullied by their peers. (American Psychological Association, 2004)

Regardless of social identities, many people have been made to feel "less than" by individuals, by families, by organizations, by social institutions such as religious denominations, and by the systemic nature of the larger society. We do not have to like those identities, but through discussion, interaction, and empathy, we can begin to relax the stereotypes and the possible fear and experience those we previously viewed as the Other and begin to see their humanity and their contributions to our collective society. We have much to share with one another once we can get beyond the divide.

Speaking to a packed audience at the Creating Change Conference, sponsored by the National Gay and Lesbian Task Force in Atlanta, Georgia,

Coretta Scott King (2000) emphasized that LGBT equality is a civil and human rights issue:

> I believe very strongly that all forms of bigotry and discrimination are equally wrong and should be opposed by right-thinking Americans everywhere. Freedom from discrimination based on sexual orientation is surely a fundamental human right in any great democracy, as much as freedom from racial, religious, gender, or ethnic discrimination.

Young people have been and continue to be at the heart of progressive social change movements. In her study of youth participation in social movements, Corrigall-Brown (2005) found that youth who work to improve campus climate and the larger society develop higher levels of self-esteem and self-efficacy, and this is also associated with verification and crystallization of their identity development. In addition, DiFulvio (2011) found that as young people identify with a greater sense of purpose in a larger context, such as engaging in progressive social change by working with and assisting others, they become more personally empowered and more resilient to their victimization.

Although Brown (2012) understands this potential, to facilitate the process of youth engagement, she also suggests,

> In order for queer young people to be able to become social justice activists and ultimately to achieve equality, new structures of family and community must be developed and secured for LGBTQ individuals so they are given equal opportunity and access to education, housing, and other factors that are the foundations of a person's ability to take a leadership role in community organizing. (p. 11)

Brown argues that for the ultimate liberation of sexual and gender minoritized people, as well as members of other oppressed groups, "Both the systems of the family and systems of capitalism must be reconfigured" (p. 25).

References

Allport, G. W. (1954). *The nature of prejudice.* Cambridge, MA: Addison-Wesley.

American Psychological Association. (2004, July). *APA resolution on bullying among children and youth.* Washington, DC: Author.

Andrews, C. (2002). *Lover's legends: The gay Greek myths.* New Rochelle, NY: Haiduk Press.

Blumenfeld, W. J. (2013). Introduction: Heterosexism. In M. Adams, W. J. Blumenfeld, R. Castañeda, H. Hackman, M. Peters, & X. Zúñiga (Eds.) *Readings for diversity and social justice* (3rd ed.). New York, NY: Routledge.

Blumenfeld, W. J., & Raymond, D. (1993). *Looking at gay and lesbian life.* Boston, MA: Beacon.

Bouton, R. A., Gallaher, P. E., Garlinghouse, P. A., Leal, T., Rosenstein, L. D., & Young, R. K. (1989). Demographic variables associated with fear of AIDS and homophobia. *Journal of Applied Social Psychology, 19,* 885–901. doi:10.1111/j.1559-1816.1989.tb01227.x

Brown, A. M. (2012). *Queer youth community organizing: Intents and outcomes of youth mobilization in LGBTQ service programs.* Unpublished master's thesis, St. Cloud State University, St. Cloud, MN.

Catechism of the Catholic Church. (1997, 2nd ed.). Vatican City: Libreria Editrice Vaticana.

Church of Jesus Christ of Latter-Day Saints. (2010). *The handbook of instructions.* Retrieved from http://www.religiondispatches.org/dispatches/joannabrooks /3720/homosexual-thoughts-and-feelings-not-a-sin,-says-new-lds-handbook/

Collins, P. H. (1998). It's all in the family: Intersections of gender, race, and nation. *Hypatia, 13,* 62–68. doi:10.1111/j.1527-2001.1998.tb01370.x

Corrigall-Brown, C. (2005). *Social psychological correlates of social movement participation among youth.* Paper presented at the annual meeting of the American Sociological Association, Philadelphia, PA, August 12. Retrieved from http://www.allacademic.com/meta/p19043_index.html

Coser, L. A. (1964). *The function of social conflict.* New York, NY: Free Press.

D'Augelli, A. R. (1991). Gay men in college: Identity processes and adaptations. *Journal of College Student Development, 32,* 140–146.

D'Augelli, A. R., Pilkington, N. W., & Hershberger, S. L. (2002). Incidence and mental health impact of sexual orientation victimization of lesbian, gay, and bisexual youths in high school. *School Psychology Quarterly, 17,* 148–167. doi:10.1521/scpq.17.2.148.20854

DiFulvio, G. T. (2011). Sexual minority youth, social connection and resilience: From personal struggle to collective identity. *Social Science & Medicine, 72*(10), 1611–1617. doi:10.1016/j.socscimed.2011.02.045

Draper, E. (2010, August 29). Focus on Family says anti-bullying efforts in schools push gay agenda. *The Denver Post.* Retrieved from http://www.denverpost.com/news/ci_15928224

Engels, F. (1884). *The origin of the family, private property, and the state.* Zurich, Switzerland: Hollingen-Zurich.

Evangelical Covenant Church. (1996). *Human sexuality.* Retrieved from http://www.covchurch.org/resolutions/1996-human-sexuality/

Focus on the Family. (2012). About Focus on the Family. Retrieved from http://www.focusonthefamily.com/about_us.aspx retrieved 5/5/12

Gay, Lesbian, and Straight Education Network (GLSEN). (2005). *National School Climate Survey.* New York, NY: Author.

Gay, Lesbian, and Straight Education Network (GLSEN). (2009). *National School Climate Survey.* New York, NY: Author.

Gibson, P. (1989). *Report of the secretary's Task Force on Youth Suicide.* Washington, DC: U.S. Department of Health and Human Services.

Henley, N. M., & Pincus, F. (1978). Interrelationship of sexist, racist, and antihomosexual attitudes. *Psychological Reports, 42,* 83–90. doi:10.2466/pr0.1978.42.1.83

Herdt, G., & Boxer, A. (1993). *Children of horizons: How gay and lesbian teens are leading the way out of the closet.* Boston, MA: Beacon Press.

Holborn, M., & Steel, L. (2012). Marxism and "the" family. *Earlham Sociology Pages.* Retrieved from http://www.earlhamsociologypages.co.uk/marxismfamily.html

Human Rights Campaign. (2014). The lies and dangers of efforts to change sexual orientation or gender identity. Retrieved from http://www.hrc.org/resources/entry/the-lies-and-dangers-of-reparative-therapy

Johnson, M. D., Rowatt, W. C., & LaBouff, J. (2010). Priming Christian religious concepts increases racial prejudice. *Social Psychological and Personality Science, 1*(2), 119–126.

King, C. S. (2000, January). *Plenary address.* Creating Change Conference, National Gay and Lesbian Task Force, Atlanta, GA.

King James Bible. (2014). Retrieved from http://biblehub.com/1_timothy/1-10.htm

Minter, S. (2012). Sharon Minter on NARTH lawsuit against psychological child abuse law. *The Bilerico Project.* Retrieved from http://www.bilerico.com/2012/11/shannon_minter_on_narth_lawsuit_against_psychologi.php

Morrison, M. A., & Morrison, T. G. (2002). Development and validation of a scale measuring modern prejudice toward gay men and lesbian women. *Journal of Homosexuality, 43,* 15–37. doi:10.1300/J082v43n02_02

National Network of Runaway and Youth Services. (2001). *Youth in the margins.* New York, NY: Lambda Legal Education and Defense Fund.

New English Bible. (1976). Osford, UK: Oxford University Press.

Remafedi, G., Farrow, J., & Deisher, R. (1991). Risk factors for attempted suicide in gay and bisexual youth. *Pediatrics, 87*(6), 869–876.

Rowatt, W. C., LaBouff, J. P., Johnson, M., Froese, P., & Tsang, J. (2009). Associations among religiousness, social attitudes, and prejudice in a national sample of American adults. *Psychology of Religion and Spirituality, 1,* 14–24. doi:10.1037/a0014989

Rowatt, W. C., Tsang, J., Kelly, J., LaMartina, B., McCullers, M., & McKinley, A. (2006). Associations between religious personality dimensions and implicit homosexual prejudice. *Journal for the Scientific Study of Religion, 45*(3), 397–406. doi:10.1111/j.1468-5906.2006.00314.x

Ryan, C., Huebner, D., Diaz, R. M., & Sanchez, J. (2009). Family rejection as a predictor of negative health outcomes in white and Latino lesbian, gay and bisexual young adults. *Pediatrics, 123*(1), 346–352. doi:10.1542/peds.2007-3524

Schulte, L. J., & Battle, J. (2004). The relative importance of ethnicity and religion in predicting attitudes towards gays and lesbians. *Journal of Homosexuality, 47,* 127–141. doi:10.1300/J082v47n02_08

Schwartz, J. P., & Lindley, L. D. (2005). Religious fundamentalism and attachment: Prediction of homophobia. *International Journal for the Psychology of Religion, 15,* 145–157. doi:10.1207/s15327582ijpr1502_3

Southern Baptist Convention. (2010). *On homosexuality and the United States military.* Retrieved from http://www.sbc.net/resolutions/1208

Southern Baptist Convention. (2003). *On same-sex marriage.* Retrieved from http://www.sbc.net/resolutions/amresolution.asp?id=1128

Tillich, P. (1952). *The courage to be.* New Haven, CT: Yale University Press.

Vanderstoep, S. W., & Green, C. W. (1988). Religiosity and homonegativism: A path-analytic study. *Basic and Applied Social Psychology, 9,* 135–147. doi:10.1207/s15324834basp0902_5

Walch, S. E., Orlosky, P. M., Sinkkanen, K. A., & Stevens, H. R. (2010). Demographic and social factors associated with homophobia and fear of AIDS in a community sample. *Journal of Homosexuality, 57*(2), 310–324. doi:10.1080/00918360903489135

Wareham, H. C. (2011, August 25). Survivor: MIT grad student Samuel Brinton remembers "ex-gay" therapy. *Bay Windows.* Retrieved from http://www.lgbtqnation.com/2011/08/survivor-mit-grad-student-samuel-brinton-remembers-ex-gay-therapy/

Young, R. K., Gallaher, P., Belasco, J., Barr, A., & Webber, A. W. (1991). Changes in fear of AIDS and homophobia in a university population. *Journal of Applied Social Psychology, 21,* 1848–1858. doi:10.1111/j.1559-1816.1991.tb00508.x

Notes

1 Christianity comprises many sects and denominations in places throughout the world, and therefore Christianity cannot be understood as monolithic, for people adhere to or diverge from a strict interpretation of scriptures depending on their denomination and personal beliefs.

2 Unless otherwise referenced, all biblical quotes in this chapter are drawn from *The New English Bible* (1976).

3 We use the term *theocratic* or *theocratic Right,* as distinguished from *religious Right,* because many of these individuals and groups use their brand of religion as a way to work toward the establishment of a theocracy (a social or government system based on a particular form, denomination, or interpretation of religion). Moreover, many people and groups who practice their forms of religion do not subscribe to the social and political philosophies of many within the theocratic Right. We do not use *religious Right* because we refuse to cede the term *religion* to this exclusionary and reactionary movement.

CHAPTER 6

The Family, Conservative Christianity, and Resiliency of Lesbian and Gay Youth: A Qualitative Study

Elliott N. DeVore, MEd, and Warren J. Blumenfeld, EdD

Some Christian denominations have defended and continue to defend the rights of lesbian, gay, bisexual, and transgender (LGBT) people and are openly welcoming them into congregations (and some into the ranks of their clergy), including the United Church of Christ,[1] Metropolitan Community Church,[2] and some local congregations described as "Welcoming Congregations"[3] in the Baptist, Lutheran, Presbyterian, Methodist, Episcopal, and Brethren/Mennonite denominations. However, a number of the more conservative denominations have released official statements, doctrines, and policies and have delivered sermons in opposition (see Chapter 5, this volume). Some well-intentioned ministers and congregants from conservative and evangelical Christian churches may believe they are offering members of LGBT communities "the gift of Jesus" in their attempts to "bring them out" of the so-called homosexual lifestyle.

For example, Rick Warren, spiritual leader of the Southern Baptist mega-church Saddleback Church and author of the bestselling *The Purpose-Driven Life* (2003), was asked by television host Piers Morgan,

> Can you see a time when not just you but other Christian preachers and indeed the Catholic church and others say, "You know, what actually real equality means [is] everyone has the same right to get married, gay or straight?" Warren responded, "I cannot see that happening in my life. I fear the disapproval of God more than I fear your disapproval or the disapproval of society. And so I can't change what I think God has said." (Chapman, 2014)

In addition, the Billy Graham Evangelical Association (2004), reflecting the views of Billy Graham, the spiritual leader to numerous U.S. presidents, states on the issue of whether the Bible accepts same-sex romantic and sexual relationships,

> The Bible provides God's blueprint for marriage and for His good gift of sex in Genesis 2:24. The gift is only to be enjoyed within a marriage between a man and a woman. There are no exceptions suggested, such as homosexual partnerships. From Genesis on, the Bible praises the marriage of a man and a woman, but it speaks only negatively of homosexual behavior whenever it is mentioned.

What real impact are these and other spiritual leaders having on those around them, particularly LGBT young people who grow up in homes and communities that define them in negative, some say "oppressive," terms? The researchers of this study set out to address this question.[4]

Study Design and Data Collection

The purpose of this study was to interview college-aged students who identify as lesbian, gay, or bisexual who grew up in conservative Christian families to understand the meanings they made of and strategies they used during their growing up experiences in this environment and how it has affected their sexual identity development and sense of self (see Appendix for interview protocol). With official acceptance by our institutional review board, we sent an announcement of the study to the electronic mailing list of LGBTQ campus organizations at a large Midwestern university. In the announcement, we invited potential respondents to pass along the research announcement to others who might qualify for participation in the study. This sampling strategy is called snowball sampling (Glesne, 2006; Groenewald, 2004), one that is advantageous in reaching additional respondents from "invisible" populations or those who may not otherwise be aware of the research announcement (Lichtman, 2006). Our research announcement listed the researchers' e-mail addresses and phone numbers for participants to contact. Once we talked with potential participants and mutually agreed that their participation met the criteria for the study, the five participants signed our informed consent form.

Delimitation

The criteria for selection required that respondents identify along what we called a *queer spectrum* (*lesbian, gay, same-sex loving, bisexual, pansexual,* and other terms indicating sexual identity) and were raised in a conservative Christian household. We limited the study selection to White (European-heritage) lesbian, gay, and bisexual college-age students for a number of reasons. Because this is a small-scale pilot study, we wanted to keep the number of demographic variables limited. We chose White students in an attempt to reduce some of the ethnic variables that would arise in a multiethnic study. In addition, because so few LGB students of color attend the university we used in our study, we did not want to jeopardize their anonymity by including them in this study. We also did not include students who identify along the transgender or transsexual spectrum because issues of religion and sexuality are not necessarily the same as religion and gender identity, and including transgender students might skew the results of this small-scale study.

Qualitative Research Methods: Phenomenological Grounded Theory

We used qualitative research methods, which we found particularly applicable to the present study because this form of research was well suited to the type of in-depth exploratory examination and analysis we were interested in unearthing (Marshall & Rossman, 2006; Patton, 2012; Seidman, 1998). For example, Bogdan and Taylor (1998) support the use of qualitative research methods when the researcher pursues "settings and the individuals within those settings holistically; that is, the subject of the study, be it an organization or an individual, is not reduced to an isolated variable" (p. 4). Marshall and Rossman (2006) emphasize that qualitative methods give the researcher a deeper understanding of respondents' lived experiences and how people define and perceive their situations.

We used the systematic methodological technique of grounded theory, which involves generating theory from the data, rather than other research methods, which begin with a theoretical framework or hypothesis. Within this framework, we used the technique of phenomenology, which seeks to describe "the meaning of the lived experiences for several individuals about a concept or the phenomenon" (Creswell, 1998, p. 51). Some forms of phenomenological inquiry direct the researcher to find the "essence of a phenomenon," that is, the decontextualized meaning that a phenomenon has for all people, regardless of individual characteristics, experiences, or settings (see Barritt, Beekman, Bleeker, & Mulderij, 1985).

From the qualitative data, we marked a series of open coding procedures in the text of respondents' comments. We then grouped or categorized the codes into similar concepts in order to effectively manage data collected. From there, we used the technique of axial coding, defined by Strauss and Corbin (1998) as "a set of procedures whereby data are put back together in new ways after open coding, by making connections between categories" (p. 96). Through this process, we were able to identify a number of emerging themes from which we developed our theoretical framework.

Study Participants

For purposes of our study, to ensure confidentiality, all five participants are listed by pseudonyms chosen by the participants:

- Chad, age 19, is a first-year student whose family's religious background is Church of Christ/evangelical, and who has told his parents he is gay.
- Riley, age 23, is a master's degree student whose family's religious background is Catholic, although her mother grew up Methodist and her father grew up in a Protestant denomination. She has told her family she is lesbian/queer.
- John, age 23, is a senior whose family's religious background is Baptist/evangelical. He defines his sexual identity as gay. Although his parents have known for some time, today John does not speak with them about his sexual identity.
- Mark, age 21, is a junior who attended a Methodist church when he was younger and then changed to a Lutheran church. Although Mark's

mother currently considers herself religious, his father and brothers today identify as atheist. Mark has not told his parents about his sexual orientation.

- Esther, age 23, is a junior whose family's religious background is Christian/Baptist. She has told her parents she is lesbian.

Findings

This section explores emergent themes, which include the church, the family, and the role of community, internalized homophobia, and survival strategies. We begin by detailing participants' experiences with their families.

Family

Faith, family, and church were tied together and inextricable for many of our participants. Although some participants' families did not completely reject them, there was a level of denial of their sexual identities as a way for their families to accept them.

Esther and John both shared stories in which their parents expressed to them that their being gay or lesbian was "a phase" and that they could get over it. John's parents required him to meet with a Christian counselor, demonstrating his parents' beliefs that he could "come out of" being gay. Strong connections can be made between Esther's and John's parents' belief that their children's sexuality is a phase, whereas other parents wanted to ignore their children's sexual identities entirely.

DON'T ASK, DON'T TELL

Esther, Chad, and Mark all experienced their parents ignoring either their or a family member's sexual identity. Ignoring sexuality was either an active decision or something that was enabled by the actions of their child "acting straight" or actively avoiding the topic. Despite Esther being out to her family members, they continue asking her whether she wants to go on dates with boys from church, or they talk about boys in front of Esther and her girlfriend.

> They don't believe that homosexuality is okay. They support me, but they don't support that aspect of my life. They don't ignore it, but we just kind of agree to disagree on it.

Chad's experience is quite different. It seems that his family's ability to ignore his gay identity was a product of him "managing" his image.

> They could ignore it because of their perceptions of what a gay person was, because I was very straight acting. ... I wasn't in their face with my gayness, and so ... it was easy for them to just block it out, I guess.

John also articulated that his parents actively ignored his sexuality and what occurred in the past. Pretending they were straight helped Chad and John maintain what remained of their relationships with their parents.

Although Mark is not currently out to his family about his sexuality, he saw his family ignore his uncle's sexuality his entire life. Mark has been reluctant to come out to his parents, despite his feeling that they might be accepting.

MAKING EXCUSES

The three participants who came out to their parents and experienced resistance all made statements that excused their parents' actions or compared them with the experiences of others who had far worse situations. Gratitude is certainly a component of their assertions of "well, at least my parents didn't. . . ." Esther and Chad repeatedly compared their experiences with those of gay and lesbian youths who were thrown out of their homes, which they believe could have happened to them. Reframing their experiences in this way could be a product of their own healing and strategies for survival. John even said that his parents were "the best parents" at his church:

> My parents were without a doubt the best parents in that church. They did their best to raise the kids. And you know what, textbook says you know, I'm sure Dr. James Dobson [American evangelical Christian author, and

founder in 1977 of the ultraconservative Focus on the Family] would say they did everything right.

Participants used their life experience and worldviews to create a frame of reference that dictated what they were taught was reasonable.

RELATIONSHIP WITH FATHER

All the men who participated in our study struggled with the relationship with their father. In varying degrees, each young man disconnected from his father because of his own sexuality or inability to connect with and perpetuate male gender expectations. It is important to note that the two women in our study did not experience significant struggle with a particular parent because of their sexuality or gender nonconformity. This dichotomy presents us with how demoralizing it is to be perceived as gay among groups of men and within the church. John's interactions with his father were hostile and degrading for him as a gay man. "When I did go to college, that was another really strange car ride because I had to ride with my dad for an hour and a half and 'birds of a feather flock together.'" John's father told him,

> Gay people, you know, they'll find you. They will find you if you want to be with them … and [they will] create scenarios where they're going to pull you in if you don't go to church. … They're just going to swoop down there and they're going to drop you off in some heroin-filled alley. You know you're going to have AIDS and you're going to die by the time you're 24.

Now that John will soon be graduating, he says he wants nothing to do with his family because he does not need them to fill out his financial aid forms. John even decided not to invite them to graduation because he feels they do not deserve to see him.

Chad explained that being gay is not an issue between him and his father. However, Chad's testimony throughout his interview contradicted this statement. After Chad came out on Facebook, his father was very upset and instructed Chad to take it down because his sexuality was no one's business.

Being out and authentic is very important to Chad, because he believes it is imperative for his mental health.

> It's not fair to my mental health, and it's not fair to other people for me to try and live a lie, you know. I just feel like authenticity is more important. And I think secretly he won't admit it, but he is not ashamed, but he's afraid other people will react. . . . He's an insurance salesman now—how his clients will react, how his coworkers will react.

This is clearly in conflict with his father's beliefs. Chad has internalized the "it's no one's business" attitude alongside messages he has received through his church to create the way he presents himself as "straight acting." His father's fear of people knowing he is gay has certainly catalyzed the desire to act as though he is straight.

Mark also struggles with his relationship with his father and feels he cannot connect with him:

> I don't like to talk to my dad as … I guess my [older] brother does. … I can still talk to him, he's my dad, but … I don't know. Sometimes they are just awkward because I think he might know as well. I don't know, I don't want to ask him about it or anything. … With my mom, I can. I don't know. I've always been like a mama's boy, I guess. And that's what I was. My little brother has just been my dad's all-star kid—whatever.

Later in the interview Mark shared that his brothers participate in many of the same sports that his father did, sports that Mark does not enjoy playing. *Mama's boy* is a common playground taunt used against young men who are not very masculine, whose underlying definition is gay. There seems to be some internalization of this ideology in Mark's relationships with his father.

The Church

Varieties of faith traditions were represented among our participants' experiences, including Roman Catholic, Church of Christ, Baptist, Baptist (evangelical), Lutheran, and Methodist. Of the six represented traditions, only one (the evangelical church Chad attended before moving) promoted a message that was remotely supportive of LGBT people. As a cornerstone of community, the church was a location that socialized and molded our participants' concepts of self and identity. Mark was the only participant who was not actively involved in a congregation and whose family was not actively in a congregation.

CHURCH LEADERSHIP

Riley and John were both heavily involved with their churches through leadership positions and through family engagement. For Riley and John, active participation in church was a way to engage and connect with their families. John shared that his father was the president of his church, and his grandfather was the president of the summer Bible camp at which he was a counselor. Summers as a Bible camp counselor were some of his favorite times as a child. His best friend was a fellow camp counselor.

For Riley, Roman Catholic mass was a time for her and her mother to bond. Riley shared,

> She [Riley's mother] was very involved. She also was a liturgical reader and Eucharistic minister, and as I got older I was an altar server, and then I eventually also got trained when I was in high school to be a liturgical reader and altar server. . . . And I did that because, you know, that's what my mom did, and that was kind of a thing we did together, and we would always read together at masses and do the blood and body together.

MESSAGES FROM THE CHURCH ABOUT HOMOSEXUALITY

Four of the five participants expressed hearing negative messages from their church about being gay or lesbian. Images of HIV and AIDS, abusive relationships, and immorality were scare tactics thrust upon our participants from a young age. These messages were often delivered during church youth events or by their parents. The idea that gays and lesbians struggle with mental health concerns or that they are inevitably suicidal was present in stories shared by Riley, Chad, and John.

Riley attended Catholic schools during her entire K–12 career, and she attended confessional and chapel as part of her education. When asked about her education, Riley did not have many positive stories to share about her time in school after she figured out she was a lesbian. During her junior year, Riley wrote a paper about *Dante's Inferno* in which she came out to her teacher. His graded response was less than stellar:

> I remember the whole back was just covered in red pen, and he wrote a whole thing, basically like, "I'll pray for you" and all these things. And how he almost talked about LGBT people as feeling sorry for them, and he told stories of where he worked previously at schools where homosexuals who came out ended up committing suicide, and no one should want to live this, and it's a bad thing. I just really feel sorry for them.

Her teacher's response was not the first or only negative message she received from her Catholic school. The following quote captures her understanding about sexuality in a Catholic context:

> My junior year, being asked to read out of the Catechism the verse or policy on homosexuality, of course I was the one who was asked to read this, right?! Anybody he could have picked in the classroom, he picked me. And no one knew. I was not openly out until pretty much my last week of high school, and more people kind of found out. Basically saying like, "Being a homosexual is a disease like being born without a limb," obviously very much compared to this sickness, a disease, and it's wrong, and it's a sin.

Chad's former minister shared a story of a gay youth group member from his previous church in which he depicted the gay men as feminine and lost from the path of Christ. The former youth group member was said to have been lost and needed to look within to find God again. John talked about his father, the president of his church, who also had terrible things to say about gay men after he suspected John of being gay:

> He [John's father] is crying, and he is telling me that he doesn't want me to get AIDS and he doesn't want me to develop a drug problem; how he doesn't want me to have a giant Black boyfriend who beats me up and puts gerbils up my ass. I'm not kidding, these are all real thoughts that exist in the minds of Christians.

LEAVING THE CHURCH AND CURRENT FAITH

Only one of our participants, Chad, still actively participates in a faith community or even identifies as a Christian. Mark was the only participant who never fully identified as a Christian at any point in his life. His father did not like church and identified as an atheist, although his mother was a Christian and made Mark go to church. Four of the five participants now identify as atheists. Several of our participants began exiting the church during the time they came out because of the internal conflict they experienced and because they felt their churches were hypocritical. Both Riley and Esther stated that it angered them that Christians could pick and choose what to believe and what not to believe in the Bible. Riley said she felt betrayed and that the church had been dishonest her whole life:

> I was having a lot of cognitive dissonance. That was the first time I was challenging anything I had ever thought of before. So it went beyond the sexuality thing and it went to abstinence only, it went to pro-life, it went to all these things where, I'm like, you've lied to me my entire education. And now I'm learning all these other things or a different perspective of it, and it's bullshit!

However, issues of sexuality were not the only reason people left the church. Esther and Riley also shared that they left the church for multiple reasons. Once Riley came out, she started challenging everything she had learned, and she became angry with the church. Esther said that she just knew that God was a fictional thing and that people were talking to their imaginary friend when they prayed. A few participants stopped attending church for other reasons.

Chad was originally from another state, and he shared that his family stopped attending church on a regular basis when they relocated to his current home. Chad attributed his family's level of acceptance of his gay identity in part to their distance from the church. Had they stayed at their old church, Chad felt that his situation would be worse. Mark also shared that he did not attend church during the time he was figuring out his sexuality. His father's open atheism gave him permission not to attend church with his mother.

Counseling

Despite having drastically different experiences, Chad and John both attended psychological counseling during their coming-out process. According to John, his counselor was not accredited by the American Psychological Association. His counselor was, instead, "a Christian Counselor" whose goal was to assist him with his "sin." Knowing the reality of the situation, John said that he quickly learned what he needed to say to get out of the Christian counseling his parents required him to attend:

> I would tell them [the counselor] what they wanted to hear, and that's all they would get. [Playing the role of the counselor]: "John when did you start to feel these feelings?" [John playing himself]: "Well, oh, it was really recently. It was just pure emotion. I couldn't control it." In their mind [the mind of the counselor], that narrative, that idea works. [Playing the role himself]: "Oh, taken over by sin, you know the devil just had his hands." You know, just something like that. Impulse just worked for them. So I would just tell them what they wanted to hear, and that's really just the biggest strategy I had. And not tell them, I guess, the reality of the situation or how big of a scope this was.

Chad never stated that the reason for his depression and attending counseling was his coming to terms with being gay, although it is plausible this had an influence. However, Chad asserted that going to counseling helped him to create a positive self-image as he was growing in his sexual identity.

Wanting to Live in a Bigger Place

When participants were asked what they wish they had had to help them with their emerging sexual identities, Chad and Mark said they wished they had grown up in a bigger place. Chad was born and raised in a major city in another state. When he was about to enter high school, his family moved to their current residence in a small rural town. Chad wanted to live in a larger city to find other gay people of faith:

> I wish that because, see, in living in a large city, I feel like I would have had a better chance of meeting other people who shared my faith but who also shared my sexual orientation. And I really wish I could have had a group like that to help validate me.

Mark wished he had attended a larger high school to have more positive experiences:

> Then in junior high when I figured everything out, I was a little more upset because I wished I was going to a larger school, or a school where it would have been easier.

Mark had been bullied by his older brother and his older brother's friends because they thought he was gay. Had his family not moved, Mark would have attended the high school he felt would have had a more welcoming campus climate.

Community

Community was a major component of the religious experience for our participants in positive and negative ways. The church was the social network in which several of our participants established their first meaningful friendships, for social community was a byproduct of the church. For one of our participants, community was a major component of his religious practices and understanding. The nuanced role of community within religious practice certainly played a role in participants' present faith practices. Chad is the only participant who still practices the faith in which he was raised, and he is the only participant who described creating loving community as a religious practice:

> I mean I guess we had agape meals. "Agape" is a word meaning love and I guess brotherhood as well. And I guess that boils down to more of what the Bible was about from our understanding. And especially, going to church was seen as important, but truly the church is wherever its members are. . . . It's not necessarily about the building so much as it is what we share with each other and how we communicate with each other through prayer.

This depiction of the church is much less hierarchical than John or Riley's experiences in religion that focused more on the church, rules, and their institutionalization. John was raised in a very small church whose membership was composed predominantly of his immediate and extended family. With his father serving as the president of the church, the image of power and control was layered with paternal and religious lenses. John said,

> They would, you know, talk about how churches who accept gay clergy aren't real churches, or churches that allow women to be preachers aren't real churches. Or, you know, churches that are obviously Christian, but to us they weren't Christian because they obviously couldn't follow this fundamental layout that God had presented. And that was what laid out what I could and could not do, and I mean it was just really simple rules like it was black and white. There was no gray area with my church.

After John and Riley came out and left for college, they both stopped attending church and sought out the community elsewhere that they once had within a church. The LGBT community quickly became a space in which they were able to fill that void and find fulfillment. Riley described how she felt betrayed by the church because she was told lies her entire life. These feelings were fraught with confusion because her friendship group was still predominantly Catholic. The camaraderie and support found in the LGBT community quickly became a source of comfort. John described his experience:

> I used to go to that every once in a while, but to me . . . it just wasn't for me, and in a weird way, it kind of did replace church for quite a while, especially back at [my other university]. I have this emptiness, you know.

Riley shared a very similar sentiment:

> But I loved it, and for me it really wasn't, I never really felt this deep connection to Jesus or God, really, or this thing they preached about every Sunday. I just felt a connection to the community. Which I realize is an inherent characteristic of me. I've just found a different community, and that's the gay community. So I just love the sense of community. I loved everyone in it, and it was my family and my friends, right.

Survival Strategies

Interviews with our participants asked about the strategies of resistance and survival they used as crucial components during their developmental process. The responses we received were quite diverse, yet there were several similarities we identified across the board.

MEDIA AND THE INTERNET

Perhaps not surprising, the availability of media and use of the Internet were present in the stories of several of our participants. This is something unique to more recent generations. As time progresses, the role the Internet plays in identity formation will surely expand beyond what we can imagine today. Internet chat rooms, television shows, and the ability to hide Internet search histories were described as being important by the participants. Two participants in particular discussed the role gay pornography played in their exploration.

PORNOGRAPHY

Chad stated that he and his friend were curious, and they had been caught looking at straight pornography (Chad never said during the interview who caught them). Eventually his curiosity extended to gay pornography. This quickly became a habit for him and was something with which he struggled because of his Christian morality. Nonetheless, Chad said it served as a coping strategy for his emerging sexual identity: "I guess one of my coping mechanisms, unfortunately, for most of my adolescence was gay pornography."

Although Mark did not actually say he was looking at pornography, we can deduce this from what he described: "My older brother's friends came over and they found stuff that would make it seem or look like I was gay, and they told people at school. … I think that my brother told my mom." Mark was probably using the Internet to explore his emerging sexual feelings because he was unable to speak about them.

INTERNET SEARCH HISTORIES

John and Chad were very creative in the ways they used various technologies to hide their Internet usage as a coping and identity development strategy. In doing this, not only were they managing their image in day-to-day life, but also they were managing their online presence and the image created through a digital presence. Chad went to incredible lengths to make sure he would still be able to view gay pornography as an outlet.

> I remember myself [going] to such lengths as, when I was on the family computer, I had discovered the program called "c-cleaner," and it would erase the history. … But what I would do was I … would click the arrow and look at all of the websites, and I would write down the URLs letter for letter. And then after I erased everything, I would retype them [his father's favorite websites] in order so that it would [be correct] when they [his favorite websites] would come up. So yeah [laughs], I went to great lengths eventually to hide that fact.

For Chad, monitoring search histories was a reactive strategy because his parents caught him looking at gay porn. His learning to use technology was centered on his usage of the Internet. This was quite the opposite for John.

John learned to monitor his parents' Internet search history in order to stay one step ahead of them:

> It was to always be one step ahead. And by that, whether that meant waiting for my parents to leave, going on their computer and looking up their histories of what they looked. Inversed, you know, let some kids have some power. You know, parents are the only ones who watch their kids. I just changed it up and looked at their websites, and I was like, "Okay. I want to see the crap that you are listening to." I think the thing they wanted me to do in Nashville [earlier in the interview John said his parents were going to send him to a residential facility in Nashville], I brought that up earlier, I think it was Exodus or something. I think that's what they wanted me to do because I've always kind of kept an eye on them.

Monitoring the websites his parents visited allowed John to "play their game" and to give them answers they wanted to hear, which made them believe he was no longer struggling with the "sin" of being gay. John always had to be smarter than his parents in order to outwit them after they found out he was gay. He repeatedly expressed how vital this was for him.

INTERNET CHAT ROOMS AND CABLE TV

Riley was the only person who cited Internet chat rooms and television shows as being an important part of the coming-out process. Early in her process, *The L Word* (a lesbian-themed TV program on Showtime) was a turning point in Riley's coming to understand her feelings. She first watched the show with her friends, and then she fell in love with it and watched every season by herself. She said that this was confusing and overwhelming because it made her question her sexuality. She then experienced the freedom that comes with the Internet:

> I had had those feelings and kind of dove into the Internet. Researching chat groups, online forums, and talking to other people who were struggling with what that meant for them.

Filled with newfound knowledge, Riley was empowered enough to begin her coming-our process.

ACTING STRAIGHT

Acting straight was a theme that emerged in various ways for all the male participants. This ranged from monitoring the way they walked and spoke, to playing sports, to what they wore and being selective about the people with whom they associated. The concept of internalized homophobia undergirds all the experiences explored in this section.

Mark shared many experiences in which he tried to pass as straight to regain credibility at his high school. After his brother told people at their school that he was gay, Mark actively worked to deny it. He felt that many of his friends probably assumed he was gay, so he fabricated lies that he had sex with a woman while he was on vacation.

> I said I went to Mexico. [He told his peers,] "Well I did go to Mexico, but on the trip I met these girls and I slept with them." And they were all like "Whoa!" Just to throw them off the trail or whatever.

Because his brothers all played sports, he also felt the need to emphasize activities considered masculine by competing in sports or talking in jest:

> I don't know, just imitating what everyone else does at school. Just try to be straight I guess, and not talking about chicks ... steering the conversation in another direction because I wouldn't know ... what input I'd have anyway. I could make up stuff, but I don't know.

Chad had many more things to say about the ways in which he monitored others' perceptions of his sexuality. It was obvious that he still struggles with these things today:

> I guess I determined very early that the ways in which I walked, the ways in which I carried myself with my arms and different things that I had to try. And I think it was easy because it was fairly natural. I was never really, in terms of talking, I'm expressive with my hands, but not in a really crazy way. Because I know some people that I've met, who are considered flam-

> boyant, use their hands and are very, just as a stereotype. ... I always made sure that my gait was not flamboyant and wasn't "gay." And I walked very masculinely. I think I became a very stoic individual for a long time. ... But I think for me, personally, I was very blessed in terms of—if you want to say being able to hide it, having that privilege is a blessed thing. It's, call it what you will, I would say it was nice to not have to go through any taunting or teasing once I had kind of constructed this way of being that wasn't [giving] it away. . . . In that sense, my passing privilege made it a lot easier. But I think one thing that really aided in that passing privilege for me personally was that I throughout my early life was an avid reader, and grammar and spelling and language were very important to me. And so, being a more eloquent speaker than most at various stages in my life, at different ages, that coupled with my stoic nature made it very easy to hide. I was seen as just, "Oh, you use big words." . . . I was never inclined to speak flamboyantly. I guess my tone of voice developed to where I would maybe be perceived as gay. There was nothing, there were no mannerisms or speech devices that really led anyone to believe that I might be gay.

FAMILY RELATIONSHIPS WITH LGBT PEOPLE

Surprisingly, family was a factor for our participants, be it through an active or an inactive and passive role. Four of the five participants shared stories about a relationship that their families had with a gay- or lesbian-identified person. Esther has a lesbian cousin, Mark has a gay uncle, Riley had a gay uncle (her mother's best friend), and Chad's father worked with several gay men at his last job. The only person whose family had no previous relationship with a gay or lesbian person was John, and his family relationship was arguably the worst of the five participants.

Two of the participants discussed how they have been involved with the families of people who are close to them. John and his sister have become very close with her boyfriend and chosen family.

> And I actually live with her boyfriend too. We all live together like a happy family, and we really separate ourselves from everything that is our

family. And we like his family, so it kind of fills that familial gap that I'm lacking.

Esther also shared that she has become very close with her girlfriend's family, and she frequently calls her girlfriend's mother "Mom." This seems to have had a positive influence on her because she is able to talk about anything with her girlfriend's mother, who is supportive of Esther's relationship with her daughter.

Unconditional love was another theme that emerged from three of our participants. Esther and Chad said they had received unconditional love from their family, and John said he wished that his parents had given this to him. Overall, Riley and Chad both seem to have fairly positive relationships with their parents and are able to discuss their sexuality with them today. Chad said, "I don't really think I got a whole lot [from my parents] other than unconditional love." Riley shared similarly positive things about her parents' love:

> I remember growing up [and] my mom saying, "You know, we'll love [you] even if you end up being like a lesbian semi-truck driver," which is a ridiculous analogy of we'll love you no matter what.

Although John's parents were not very supportive of him, his older sister Whitney (whom he lives with) was always supportive of him. Like John, she was not religious. In high school, she encouraged him while he still lived at home, telling him that he only had a couple more years until he left home:

> She [said] the things that an older sister should. Like, "John, do you know how ridiculous our parents are?" or "You know what they are telling us is crap, and I'm so sorry. You're going to be out of there in a year. Like just keep doing what you're doing." Yeah, I talked to her pretty much every day. She really was the foundation.

Discussion

Poet and essayist Adrienne Rich (1980) highlights the damage done within our social institutions and within the larger society, which often closes options through the process of silencing and invisibility:

> When those who have the power to name and to socially construct reality choose not to see you or hear you . . . when someone with the authority . . . describes the world and you are not in it, there is a moment of psychic disequilibrium, as if you looked in the mirror and saw nothing. (p. 632)

Those someones "with the authority" include first parents, guardians, and other family members, then our religious leaders, teachers, peers, the media, elected officials, business leaders, and others.

Our research participants were born into and grew up in a diaspora of sorts, within families who exhibited sexual identities and often gender expressions different from their own. In addition, the religious traditions with which they were surrounded often promoted and amplified a conspiracy of silence in their pronouncements reifying heteronormativity.

This patriarchal family structure coupled with deeply patriarchal religious institutions mandated to our participants strict adherence to sexual and gender norms. This compelled them to navigate treacherous developmental waters on their own with few if any positive role models throwing them lifelines.

The participants gained "strength of soul" through their meaning-making processes and by using a number of survival strategies.

"Unconditional Love"

Although most study participants talked about receiving "unconditional love" from their parents, in actuality there is a vast difference between this type of love and authentic support for participants' emerging sexual identity and gender expression. Chad framed the love he received in paradoxical terms when he stated, "I don't really think I got a whole lot [from my parents] other than unconditional love." Although he talked about maintaining a fairly close relationship with his parents, the way he phrased this relationship betrayed the inherent fractures and tensions. In addition, Riley discussed the "ridiculous analogy" in the way her mother expressed her love to her. For these participants, this so-called unconditional (though, in fact, conditional, "don't ask, don't tell") love was better than no love at all.

Exposure to Other Gay and Lesbian People

Four of the five participants in our study shared that their families had exposure to or a preexisting relationship with another person (other than themselves) who identified as gay or lesbian. However, these participants' experiences were not ideal because their parents and family were ambivalent or slightly resistant at best to their children's sexual identities. Their families' prior experiences with gay and lesbian people certainly helped them adjust to or reevaluate prior notions that would have influenced their understandings of their child's experience and identity. Chad specifically stated that his father's experiences working with gay men at his previous job helped positively change his mind about gay people. However, there are interesting layers to be uncovered within his father's movement toward acceptance. Operating under the assumption that the gay men with whom Chad's father worked at the fitness club were masculine, we can understand how he would be more comfortable with Chad's self-constructed straight-acting gay image. Although his father became more comfortable with gay men, it was only within the confines of gender normativity. Through this lens, Chad's pursuit of masculinity is rationalized. His father will love and accept him if he is gay in a certain way.

John was the only participant whose family had no experience building and maintaining a relationship with a gay or lesbian person, and he arguably had the most negative experience with his family about his sexuality. Our findings align with much of the research literature that states that those who personally know a gay or lesbian person generally have more positive attitudes toward them (Berkman & Zinberg, 1997; Hansen, 1982; O'Hare, Williams, & Ezoviski, 1996 as cited in Walch, Orlosky, Sinkkanen, & Stevens, 2010).

Conservative Christian denominations expect that followers will not question the authority of Christ or the institutional power of the church. For example, officials of the United Methodist Church in eastern Pennsylvania defrocked Pastor Frank Schaefer in 2013 for officiating at the wedding of his son to another man (Walton, 2013). By controlling the images and ideas to which people are exposed, systems or structures and power figures are able to manipulate people's ways of knowing and analyzing (Raven, 1999). In many ways, themes of seclusion emerged from the stories of our participants. Two participants expressed a desire to have lived in a larger place because it would have been more diverse and had more LGBT people, which also would have presented their families with a higher level of exposure to LGBT people. John expressed that his parents controlled the people he was around and what media he was allowed to consume as a child. Although this is typical of most households, for John in particular this policing eventually negatively affected his self-esteem and identity development.

Community

Sharon Daloz Parks (2000) explained that young adults rely on their social networks as frames of reference from which they establish social norms, values, and behaviors. She discusses the inevitable tension between one's community and the desire to maintain relationships. Community played such an important role in the development of our participants, and for some it was a place of refuge and survival. Parks's framework can be used to understand the ways in which participants sought out and created new identity networks that mirrored their past faith communities.

The majority of our participants would be described as experiencing Parks's (2000) concept of diffuse community. Parks wrote,

> As one begins to want to know for oneself, however, and moves into a relativized world, often it is precisely the conventional social ordering that one begins to question. Experiencing an other (someone who was previously "them") who contradicts assumptions about who we are and who they are may be a first step in questioning familiar social arrangements. As the social horizon thus expands, the form of community may shift from a well-defined set of assumed associations to a considerably more diffuse form of belonging. (Parks, 2000, para. 1–2)

John experienced a similar effect when he began college.

> I used to go to that [the LGBT student group at his college] every once in a while, but to me ... it just wasn't for me, and in a weird way it kind of did replace church for quite a while, like especially back at my first college [name of university was removed for anonymity]. I have this emptiness, you know.

Although Mark has not engaged in any LGBT activities or organizations, he too has fallen in line with Parks's (2000) model of development by joining the Atheist and Agnostic Society on his campus and breaking away from his obligations to appease his mother's religious traditions. For these three participants, creating a new reference group played a major role in their ability to survive and create meaning within their emerging identities.

Technology

Our participants used technology, specifically the Internet, to open windows to the world. The Internet is creating many avenues through which young people are able to locate others with similar interests, backgrounds, and social identities for the purpose of building community. Chad even acquired new technological skills to circumvent his parents' monitoring his computer activities.

A Foothold on Respectability

Fighting for recognition and respect was a struggle for many of our participants as they worked to reclaim their place that was denied by virtue of their sexuality. It was a race to prove to themselves and to others that they were significant and successful in spite of their sexuality. For Chad, this manifested in his desire to be masculine; for Esther it was her attempts to prove to her parents that she was still going to have a (Christian heteronormative) family and child; and for John it was the "good boy" syndrome. Each worked to overcompensate and prove themselves to others, but in many ways their efforts were rooted in their search for self-worth.

In the article "The Race to Innocence: The Hierarchical Relations Between Women" Fellows and Razack (1998) describe the pursuit of normalization and reclaiming of positions of privilege within power structures. Their article holds powerful precedent as we examine the ways in which our participants engaged in a similar process within their strategies for resilience and survival.

> Feeling only the ways that she is positioned as subordinate, each woman strives to maintain her dominant positions. Paradoxically, each woman asserts her dominance in this way because she feels it is the only way she can win respect for her claim or subordination. We describe this practice as securing a foothold on respectability. (p. 342)

A burning desire to disprove their families' beliefs about them motivated three of our participants in their pursuit of meaning. The fight to disprove was a tangible goal for the participants, and its process was a motivational strategy of coping and resiliency.

This concept could be a motivation for Chad in his purposeful engagement with his faith as he works to educate his family while earning their trust and love. He provided some insight into this experience when he discussed his relationship with his grandmother:

> She has come to the understanding that it's just another way of being. . . . I think she's seen that I'm still a good kid and that I still have a zest for life, and I still love God.

Remaining steadfast in his faith, Chad could also have internalized the pursuit of validation by tirelessly managing himself to be straight-acting. If he is able to maintain his masculine imagine, he may be able to fight against the stereotypical images his preacher used while describing a gay man who had fallen from God. The repudiation of femininity in favor of being masculine or straight-acting is an effort to obtain the full power and privilege patriarchy would have provided him were he not gay. Applying the term *straight-acting* to himself only demonstrates his attempt to reclaim that which has been denied, at least partially, by his sexuality.

John, who arguably had the least healthy family relationship, also experienced this phenomenon as he strove to impress his parents. Success was more than a goal to John, for it seemed that he was competing against other gay people to prove to himself that he was better than what his parents said of gay people. The following exchange in his interview captures this internalization perfectly:

> I talked about, we don't need more gay people, we need better gay people. . . . Well, that's pretty dangerous to say and I know it is. I still kind of latch onto that ideology. That idea that I have to be like them, and I know that post-modernism would say you don't have to! But I still feel compelled to prove to them. … I'm like, "Do you not remember all the awards I won in high school? Do you not remember me coming home with academic trophies or, you know, for being in the newspaper every week or being a great runner? All that doesn't matter, but it should. Because I can still win you over with all the things I can do."

Esther also engaged in this process of bartering for her dignity. Her family had traditional Christian views of marriage and family, which she internalized, perhaps subconsciously. Although she is no longer a Christian and identifies as an atheist, Esther works to convince her mother that her relationship is valid in the same ways a heterosexual relationship would be. She aims to appeal to her mother's Christian heteronormative values:

> "Hey, Mom, I realize that you have this dream for the fact that I'd go find a husband and have kids and blah blah blah blah blah and be successful, have a career, and all that sort of stuff. It's just like, the only thing that is going to change about that is instead of being with a guy, I'm going to be with a girl."

Conclusion

This pilot study investigated the perceptions, experiences, and strategies of research participants in navigating issues of nonheterosexual identity development in primarily conservative Christian family and community contexts. The researchers' objective was to present the ways in which participants made meaning of their lives in their own voices. Because this was a small-scale study, it would be inaccurate to generalize the results beyond this study, although it can set the stage for further research in this area of inquiry.

People hold concurrent and intersecting social identities (consciously or unconsciously) based on socially constructed categories, such as our personal and physical characteristics; our ages, abilities, interests, professions, and class backgrounds; and on our cultural, racial, ethnic, sex, gender, sexual and affectional, and religious identifications, among others. Sometimes these identities are *ascribed* to us by others (sometimes at our birth), and sometimes we self-identify, or these identities are achieved (throughout our lives).

Based on Peggy McIntosh's (1988) pioneering investigations of White and male privilege, by analogy we can understand Christian privilege and heterosexual privilege as constituting a seemingly invisible, unearned, and largely unacknowledged array of benefits accorded to Christians and to heterosexuals, with which they often unconsciously walk through life as if effortlessly carrying a knapsack tossed over their shoulders. This system of benefits confers dominance on Christians and heterosexuals in predominantly Christian majority countries while subordinating members of other faith communities, nonbelievers, and people who do not define themselves or identify as heterosexual. These systemic inequities are pervasive throughout the society. They are encoded in the individual's very being and woven into the fabric of our social institutions, resulting in a stratified social order privileging dominant (agent) groups while restricting and disempowering subordinate (target) groups (Blumenfeld, 2006).

The participants in our study were raised in Christian households, and although they still may maintain the unearned, societally granted privileges accorded to Christians (see Schlosser, 2003) within the nation writ large, by dint of their minoritized sexual identities they may find themselves in a position of "double jeopardy," stigmatized within the larger society and significantly marginalized in many conservative Christian contexts.

Although this study specifically addressed issues of resiliency and resistance, participants in their statements often displayed indicators of internalized oppression, specifically internalized homophobia or internalized heterosexism. According to Blumenfeld (1995),

> Lesbian, gay, and bisexual people themselves often find it difficult not to internalize society's negative notions of homosexuality and bisexuality. Internalized oppression, in this instance heterosexism, can be defined as the internalization, consciously or unconsciously, of external attitudes, myths, and stereotypes of inferiority, inadequacy, self-hatred, and sense of "otherness" by the targets of systematic oppression, here lesbians, gay males, and bisexual people. Internalizing these external negative societal messages is not [the] fault [of lesbian, gay, and bisexual people], for we too have been socialized within the systemic framework of heterosexism. (p. 212)

This internalization becomes further complicated by the number of non-dominant stigmatized and marginalized social identities young people develop that they do not hold in common with parents and guardians, what one of the researchers of this study (Blumenfeld) calls diasporic social identities.

Given that the young people with whom our readers work fall along the broad continuum of social identities, it is difficult to offer any generalizable suggestions. For practitioners, it is vital to acknowledge the context and personal narratives of the young people with whom we work. Social workers and other practitioners must not assume the salience of young adults' identity in the context of oppression; doing so removes the young people's agency in making meaning of their experiences. Acknowledging our wariness of generalizations, however, we would like to name and highlight again the power and influence that finding a positive ideologically based community had in the stories of a few of the participants in our study.

To encourage the healthy integration of young people's sexual and spiritual or faith identities, we suggest supporting young adults in finding a mentoring community.

Although it is not the intention here to give a comprehensive narrative on how to bring about equity in terms of sexual and gender identity in religious congregations—for what might work effectively in one congregation and denomination might not function in another—some foundational guidelines can be considered:

- *Assessment:* Hold public hearings, conduct interviews, or distribute research surveys in your religious community to access the needs, concerns, and life experiences of LGBT and questioning youth and their families.
- *Policies:* Include sexual identity and gender identity and expression as inclusive categories in your welcoming and affirming policies. Also extend equal partner or spousal benefits to employees in your religious organizations inclusive of sexual and gender identities and expressions.
- *Workshops and discussions:* Congregations are encouraged to offer comprehensive trainings and discussion forums to personnel and congregants specifically on the needs and realities of parishioners of all sexual and gender identities and expressions.
- Implement and participate in a Welcoming Congregation program in your congregation.
- *Support and caucus groups:* Religious communities are encouraged to develop support groups for LGBT and questioning congregants—a group for youth, and a group for adults—to meet and share experiences. Also, as in thousands of public schools across the United States and other countries, groups generically called gay–straight alliances bring together people of all sexual and gender identities and expressions to discuss issues of common concern and for educational purposes.
- *Information in religious libraries:* Houses of worship are encouraged to develop and maintain an up-to-date and age-appropriate collections of books, videos, CDs, DVDs, journals, magazines, posters, websites, and other information on issues of sexual and gender identity and expression.
- *Role models:* Congregations are encouraged to select and hire "out" LGBT staff and religious leaders to serve as supportive role models for all petitioners.
- *Continuing education:* Educate yourself about the needs and experiences of LGBT petitioners and their families, attend LGBT cultural and

> community events, wear pro-LGBT buttons and T-shirts and display posters, interrupt derogatory jokes and epithets, and be aware of the generalizations you make. Assume there are LGBT people in your religious community; notice the times you disclose your heterosexuality if you identify as heterosexual as an example of some of the privileges you might have that LGBT people do not have; monitor politicians, the media, and organizations to ensure accurate coverage of LGBT issues in your communities; work and vote for candidates (including school board members) taking pro-LGBT stands; use affirming and gender-inclusive language when referring to sexual and gender identity and expression in human relationships in everyday speech, on written forms, and so on. Say the words *lesbian, gay, bisexual, asexual, transgender,* and *intersex* each day in a positive way.

Parks asserts, "Young adulthood is nurtured into being, and its promise is most powerfully realized through participation in a community that poses a trustworthy alternative to earlier assumed knowing" (Parks, 2000, para. 1). Continuing, she writes, "If a person becomes critically aware and begins to take responsibility for his understanding of faith, then recomposing truth includes recomposing his own sense of trust and power" (Parks, 2000, para. 3). We anticipate that the growing body of studies in this research domain will enhance the knowledge base of youth workers in clinical and nonclinical settings, and also family members, to better serve people in this demographic.

References

Barritt, L., Beekman, T., Bleeker, H., & Mulderij, K. (1985). *Researching educational practice. North Dakota Study Group on Evaluation.* Grand Forks, ND: North Dakota University.

Berkman, C. S., & Zinberg, G. (1997). Homophobia and heterosexism in social workers. *Social Work, 42,* 319–332. doi:10.1093/sw/42.4.319

Billy Graham Evangelistic Association. (2004). *Are homosexuals born that way?* Retrieved from http://billygraham.org/answer/are-homosexuals-born-that-way/

Blumenfeld, W. J. (2006). Christian privilege and the promotion of "secular" and not-so "secular" mainline Christianity in public schooling and the larger society. *Equity and Excellence in Education, 39*(3), 195–210. doi:10.1080/10665680600788024

Blumenfeld, W. J., & DeVore, E. N. (2014). The family, conservative Christianity, and resiliency of lesbian and gay youth: A review of the literature. In A. Dessel & R. Bolen, *Conservative Christian beliefs and sexual orientation in social work: Privilege, oppression, and the pursuit of human rights* (pp. TK). Alexandra, VA: CSWE Press.

Blumenfield, W. (1995). "Gay/straight" alliances: Transforming pain to pride. In G. Unks (Ed.), The gay teen: Educational practice and theory for gay, lesbian, and bisexual adolescents (pp. 211–224). New York, NY: Routledge.

Bogdan, R., & Taylor, S. J. (1998). *Introduction to qualitative research methods: A guidebook and resource* (3rd ed.). Hoboken, NJ: Wiley.

Chapman, M. W. (2013). *Rick Warren to Piers Morgan: 'I fear the disapproval of God' over 'gay marriage.'* CNSnews.com. Retrieved from http://cnsnews.com/news/article/michael-w-chapman/rick-warren-piers-morgan-i-fear-disapproval-god-over-gay-marriage#sthash.2tLmCqSK.dpuf

Creswell, J. W. (1998). *Qualitative inquiry and research design: Choosing among five traditions*. Thousand Oaks, CA: Sage.

Fellows, M., & Razack, S. (1998). The race to innocence: Confronting hierarchical relations among women. *Journal of Gender, Race & Justice, 1*(1), 335–352.

Glesne, C. (2006). *Becoming qualitative researchers: An introduction*. Boston, MA: Pearson.

Groenewald, T. (2004). A phenomenological research design illustrated. *International Journal of Qualitative Methods, 3*(1), 1–26.

Hansen, G. L. (1982). Androgyny, sex-role orientation, and homosexism. *Journal of Psychology, 112,* 39–45. doi:10.1080/00223980.1982.9923532

Lichtman, M. (2006). *Qualitative research in education: A user's guide*. Thousand Oaks, CA: SAGE.

Marshall, C., & Rossman, G. B. (2006). *Designing qualitative research*. Thousand Oaks, CA: SAGE.

McIntosh, P. (1988). *White privilege and male privilege: A personal account of coming to see correspondences through work in women's studies*. Wellesley, MA: Wellesley College Center for Research on Women.

O'Hare, T., Williams, C. L., & Ezoviski, A. (1996). Fear of AIDS and homophobia: Implications for direct practice and advocacy. *Social Work, 41,* 51–58.

Parks, S. D. (2000). *Big questions worthy dreams: Mentoring young adults in their search for meaning, purpose, and faith.* San Francisco, CA: Jossey-Bass.

Patton, M. Q. (2012). *Qualitative research & evaluation methods* (3rd ed.). Thousand Oaks, CA: SAGE.

Raven, B. (1999). Influence, power, religion, and the mechanisms of social control. *Journal of Social Issues, 55*(1), 161–186.

Rich, A. C. (1980). Compulsory heterosexuality and lesbian existence. *Signs, 5*(4), 631–660. doi:10.1086/493756

Schlosser, L. Z. (2003). Christian privilege: Breaking a sacred taboo. *Journal of Multicultural Counseling and Development, 31*(1), 44–51. doi:10.1002/j.2161-1912.2003.tb00530.x

Seidman, I. (1998). *Interviewing as qualitative research: A guide for researchers in education and the social sciences.* New York, NY: Teachers College Press.

Strauss, A., & Corbin, J. (1998). *Basics of qualitative research techniques and procedures for developing grounded theory* (2nd ed.). London, England: SAGE.

Walch, S. E., Orlosky, P. M., Sinkkanen, K. A., & Stevens, H. R. (2010). Demographic and social factors associated with homophobia and fear of AIDS in a community sample. *Journal of Homosexuality, 57*(2), 310–324. doi:10.1080/00918360903489135

Walton, J. (2013). Methodist pastor defrocked following trial for conducting same-sex marriage. *Charisma News,* December 20.

Warren, R. (2003). *The purpose-driven life.* Philadelphia, PA: Running Press.

Appendix

Research Protocol

1. Please tell me about your immediate family's religious denomination and overall values, beliefs, traditions, and observances.
2. Please tell me about the process of your coming to understand your emerging sexual identity including any specific memories, incidents, any problems or difficulties, or joys.
3. Please tell me about your family's religious denomination's understandings, policies, or beliefs on issues of sexuality generally, and specifically on same-sex and/or bisexual sexuality and relationships.

4. Did or do you currently follow your family's religious practices? Why or why not?
5. Tell me something about your relationship with your family members growing up.
6. How is your relationship with your family members today?
7. Does you sexual identity have any effect on your relationship with your family members? If so, how?
8. Do your family's religious values and beliefs have any effect on your relationship with your family members? If so, how?
9. Are you "out" about your sexual identity to your family? Why or why not?
10. What were any strategies or ways of being that you used to live and grow up in your family as lesbian, gay, or bisexual within a conservative Christian family?
11. What did you get from your family that you felt you needed at the time until today to help you in your developing sexual identity?
12. What would you have wanted from your family that they may not have given you in helping you in your emerging sexual identity growing up?
13. Looking back now, is there anything you would have done differently in your relationship with your family regarding your emerging sexual identity in the context of a conservative Christian household?
14. Is there anything else you would like to talk about that I have not already asked you or anything you would like to add to any of my previous questions?

Notes

1 Ordained first gay male minister in 1972; ordained first lesbian minister in 1977; UCC Resolution passed by General Synod: "Calling on United Church of Christ Congregations to Declare Themselves Open and Affirming" to gay, lesbian, and bisexual people in 1985; UCC Resolution passed by General Synod: "Affirming the Participation and Ministry of Transgender People within the United Church of Christ and Supporting Their Civil and Human Rights" in 2003.

2 A network of inclusive churches founded by Rev. Troy Perry, 1968, Huntington Park, California. Today includes congregations in 22 countries.

3 Welcoming Congregations include a network of faith communities, not only Christian, that have worked to ensure a welcoming and supportive religious community for members of all sexual identities and gender identities and expressions.

4 For a review of the research literature setting the background for this chapter, please see Chapter 5, this volume.

SECTION II

Biblical, Methodological, Legal, and Ethical Analyses

CHAPTER 7

Can Conservative Christian Religious Expression and LGB Sexual Orientation Affirmation Coexist in Social Work?

Adrienne B. Dessel, PhD, LMSW, Christine Shepardson, PhD, and Rebecca M. Bolen, PhD

Social work values religious diversity and celebrates people of all religious traditions. To this end, schools of social work are charged with the responsibility of preparing students to work with people of all religious backgrounds (Council on Social Work Education [CSWE], 2001). As part of this educational process, the profession considers the differences between concepts of religion and spirituality. The social work profession also tackles the controversies that have manifested regarding religion and sexual orientation. Finally, social work is obligated by its Code of Ethics to end oppression of all groups (National Association of Social Workers [NASW], 2008).

A significant voice in this discussion is that of David Hodge. This author has been prolific, and his work has provided an important contribution to the understanding of the concepts of religion and spirituality within the practice and teaching of social work. More specifically, his research has promoted a deeper understanding of evangelical Christian views and working with evangelical Christians and those of other religions (Hodge, 2004a, 2004c). Hodge raises important issues germane to the CSWE and schools of social work. First is the issue of how to lift up and celebrate the diversity represented by both sexual orientation and religious identity, especially when belief systems of some religions consider lesbians and gay men to be breaking the laws of God (Hodge, 2005). Another important issue Hodge raises is whether those holding conservative Christian beliefs are marginalized and oppressed by social workers (Hodge, 2002). Within both of these concerns is the issue of whether Christians with a conservative belief system are treated differently in social work education and practice than those students or clients with more mainline or liberal religious orientations.

We address these issues in this chapter. We examine the tensions in social work between the intersection of lesbian, gay, and bisexual (LGB) sexual orientation and conservative Christian religious beliefs that disavow sexual minority people. How does the social work profession value and affirm these two opposing identities? We first examine literature on whether social work discriminates against social workers who identify with more conservative Christian beliefs regarding LGB people. We then provide a critique and analysis of biblical interpretations of lesbians and gay men. Finally, we explore the concept of religious freedom of expression as it relates to social work ethics. We conclude with implications and recommendations for social work professionals.

Does Social Work Discriminate Against Evangelical Christians?

Some evidence suggests that social work does discriminate against some Christians who hold more theologically conservative beliefs. A quantitative survey of 162 Christian social workers who self-identified as theologically very conservative (n=31) or conservative (n=131) found that these workers reported experiencing significantly more discrimination than did social workers who had a liberal or very liberal Christian orientation (Ressler & Hodge, 2000, 2003). A follow-up qualitative study exploring the narratives of 12 conservative-identified Christians in social work indicated the greatest tension was around interpretation of sexual orientation. One participant stated, "It's social justice for gays and lesbians and social justice for HIV victims and social justice for minorities, but no social justice for Christians who are being persecuted and are treated worse than some gays and minorities" (Ressler & Hodge, 2003, p. 134). Thyer and Myers (2009) also used a purposive sample of Christian social work students, practitioners, and faculty. These eight reported religious-based discrimination in their social work settings focused on topics of gay adoption rights and lesbian and gay affirmation, abortion, respecting religious organizations, public prayer, and withholding religious views when practicing social work. These authors pointed out the differing interpretations of discrimination and the importance of defining the term *social justice*. In another study, a stratified random sample of members of Christian churches in three Oklahoma cities found that the 176 Christians professed only a moderate confidence in social workers' competence in working with Christians, with "fundamentalist" Christians having significantly less confidence in social workers than did "traditional" Christians (Pellebon & Caselman, 2008). Streets (2009) indicated that social work education is ambivalent about how to incorporate religion into the curriculum given the importance of both culturally competent practice and the imperative to refrain from engaging personal values in professional practice.

A number of different views have been put forth in the literature with regard to concern about discrimination against and persecution of religious groups, more specifically persecution of evangelical and other conservative Christians. One concern is that evangelical Christians make up "the nation's largest spiritual minority, accounting for perhaps 25% of the U.S. population" (Hodge, 2004a, p. 251) and that they are "keenly aware of the bias fostered by the power differential between the secular and Christian worldviews" (p. 253). Some authors assert that Christians are the "most widely persecuted group in the world" (Hertzke & Philpott, 2000; Hodge, 2007a, p. 258; Marshall, 2000; Shea, 1997).

More specifically, concerns have been raised about whether and how social work practitioners and academics are different from and discriminate against and oppress conservative Christians (Hodge, 2003a, 2003b, 2007c). Hunter (1991) frames these theses by referencing a dichotomy between "culturally liberal" people (i.e., what he calls progressives), including social workers, and "culturally conservative" Christians, whom he probably too narrowly defines as "people of faith" (Hodge, 2003b, p. 286). Such cultural conservatives are said to hold orthodox worldviews in which moral truth is understood to emanate from an external, definable, transcendent source such as the God posited by theistic faith traditions (p. 285). It is believed that social work liberal values may interfere with providing services to "orthodox believers in the U.S. [who] are disproportionately drawn from the very disadvantaged populations that social work has a mandate to serve" (p. 286). Some aspects of conservative worldviews and values, such as antiabortion beliefs, church attendance, recognizing the detrimental effects of day care and the benefits of marriage, and understanding the link between pornography and misogyny, are believed to be absent from social work textbooks.

Concern is expressed that the field of social work is not engaged in a critical analysis of its oppression of conservative Christians, noting that these Christians were formative in the founding of the profession (Hodge, 2002, p. 406). It is suggested that social work should hire more conservative Christian faculty, increase publications by and about conservative Christians, create safe zones for these students, and generally make discourse in the field more welcoming to discussions of spiritual frameworks "in the same manner as gay men, lesbians and feminists" (p. 410).

Finally, there is a fear that social work education settings are hostile environments for students who hold conservative Christian views on LGB people (Hodge, 2002, 2005). Hodge (2002) notes that the social work Code of Ethics does not lay out a hierarchy regarding religion and sexual orientation and that both should be accorded equal respect. For example, it is suggested that conservative Christian values about "sexuality expressed in monogamous male–female dyads" (Hodge, 2005, p. 208) that "reject homosexual practices" (p. 210) as not normal should be affirmed (Hodge, 2004c, p. 33; Hodge & Williams, 2002). Conservative Christian views of "affirming the personhood of gays and lesbians" (p. 208) and denouncing "crimes against homosexuals" (p. 210) should also be given full recognition. In short, there are concerns that progressives hold privilege and power (p. 208), conservative Christian believers are marginalized, and the social work profession is biased in its censorship and denial of freedom of religious expression to Christians holding certain more conservative beliefs.

Not surprisingly, these views have been controversial, especially the articles mentioned earlier (Hodge, 2002, 2005), which have drawn significant critiques. In particular, Melendez and LaSala (2006, p. 375) draw attention to what they consider the problematic description of the oppression of evangelical Christians, as well as the perpetuation of myths about gay men and lesbians and the debilitating effects on LGB people of the "hate the sin and not the sinner" mentality in these articles. Canda (2003) raises concerns about Hodge's false dichotomization of the orthodox people of faith and progressive social workers, his narrow portrayal of the complexity of Christian belief systems, and the need for more rigorous research with regard to oppression of conservative Christians. In reply, Hodge refers to professional practice standards stating that social workers do not have to agree with certain values but do need to understand them to provide culturally competent services (Hodge, 2007b).

It is this ongoing debate in particular that requires further attention from the profession. On one hand, some conservative Christians may feel that their religion and its beliefs, especially those about LGB people, are not affirmed by social work, that social work actively discriminates against them, and that their religion constitutes a cultural minority. On the other hand, LGB people may feel that their identity is not affirmed when social work practice or education allows students or professionals to profess without argument that LGB people do not live a "valid alternative lifestyle" and that same sex attraction is a sin (Southern Baptist Convention, 2012, para. 1). We turn next to a critical analysis of Christian texts and freedom of religious expression to expand the examination of this tension within social work.

Critical Analysis

Biblical Analysis

One of the potential pitfalls of interdisciplinary work stems from the fact that it is difficult for authors and readers to be competent in all relevant fields. Few scholars in social work are likely to have the professional training necessary to write from a religious studies perspective. Those who are not scholars of religion should be given the professional tools to be able to engage with and respond to historical fallacies and misrepresentations. Hodge's (2005) article "Epistemological Frameworks, Homosexuality, and Religion: How People of Faith Understand the Intersection Between Homosexuality and Religion" contains many claims about Christianity that might benefit from further academic study and thus serves as a productive case study. In discussing some of the misrepresentations in this article, however, we set aside other equally valid points of discussion, such as the definition of "people of faith" to exclude many Christians and all LGB people (Hodge, 2005, p. 207), the inaccurate assumption that all LGB people are politically and theologically "progressive" (see Melendez & LaSala, 2006), and the fact that what some call homosexuality today did not exist as such in the contexts in which the biblical texts were written (Foucault, 1980).

The adoption of Hunter's (1991) unconventional use of the term *orthodox*—and the claim that *progressive* represents its opposite—creates misleading categories and oppositions that lead to conclusions that do not hold up to academic scrutiny. The designation *orthodox,* coming from the Greek words for "straight teaching," is a subjective adjective that defines a group's "correct" teachings in contrast to any other groups with whom they disagree. In religious terms, *heresy* is the most common antonym to *orthodoxy,* and the designation itself suggests only that the person applying it is making a judgment about the correctness of a group's teachings.[1] In contrast, Hodge (2005) uses the term to suggest that the Christian group he calls orthodox has a historical validity and priority that other Christian groups do not. Although it is theologically true for many Christians that their own group seems truer than others, historically Hodge's claim is false because the American Protestantism to which he refers developed only in recent history. It is misleading to contrast orthodox and progressive Christians; some people identify with both categories and many with neither. Such linguistic imprecision necessitates the rhetorically convenient but nevertheless illogical conclusion that progressives can by definition never have correct doctrine.

Another problematic claim is that "Because [Christian] values are transcendent, believers do not have the option, at least in principle, of picking and choosing which values they follow based on the prevailing cultural winds" (Hodge, 2005, p. 208). This is contrasted with a "progressive worldview," which Hunter (1991) describes as "an evolving entity informed by the ethos of the current age" (p. 208). Although this is a common claim among certain American Christians, in fact Christian claims such as these are no more and no less culturally and historically contingent than other Christian claims, such as those dismissed as bowing to a "prevailing progressive ethos" (Hodge, 2005, p. 208). Hodge refers to "Traditional Christian views on sexuality" as if the content of those views were stable and clear throughout Christian history (Hodge, 2005, p. 210), but the radical differences in historical Christian interpretations of appropriate sexuality from the first century onward (such as Paul's radical claims advocating celibacy in 1 Corinthians 7) defy this description.[2]

Since the beginning of Christianity, Christians have disagreed with one another about the most accurate interpretation of their scriptural texts (see, for example, Paul's *Epistle to the Galatians;* the *Letter of Peter to James;* Irenaeus, *Against the Heresies;* and Ptolemy, *Letter to Flora*). Interpreters must do at least two things to determine a Christian response to any issue: They must choose which biblical passages they think most closely address the issue, and they must choose how best to interpret those passages. Although there have been Christian leaders since the earliest centuries who have struggled to make their own choices seem inevitable and uniquely correct, history inexorably demonstrates that each claim is contextually contingent and also one among many competing Christian interpretations. Conservative Christian responses to homosexuality are no exception. Some people teach that Christians are scripturally constrained to condemn homosexuality (Hodge, 2005, p. 208), an argument that could be supported by choosing Leviticus 18.22 and Romans 1.26–27 as the most relevant passages and by choosing to interpret those passages as condemning the modern concept of homosexuality. Ironically, the choice to interpret Leviticus 18.22 as an injunction for Christian behavior is unusual because many early Christian texts (e.g., the canonical *Epistle to the Hebrews*) argued that the regulations in Leviticus were superseded by the coming of the Messiah, which is why Christians do not follow kosher food laws, as required in Leviticus 11, and do not avoid wearing "a garment made of two different materials," as forbidden in Leviticus 19.19. Likewise, Romans 1.28 lists envy, strife, deceit, craftiness, gossiping, slandering, insolence, haughtiness, boastfulness, rebelliousness against parents, and foolishness as other results of human disobedience to God, but one rarely sees Christians picketing funerals with "God hates Gossipers" signs or excluding from their church those who are insolent or rebellious against their parents. There can be no question from a critical perspective that Christians who use these passages to condemn the sexual behavior of LGB people are selectively reading certain passages differently from others to support their claims.

These scriptural choices and interpretations ignore other biblical passages that some Christians find more relevant to addressing the sexual behavior of LGB people. Christians' belief that Jesus is the Messiah and Son of God might suggest that statements attributed to Jesus, such as "Do not judge, so that you may not be judged" (Matthew 7.1) or "He has sent me . . . to let the oppressed go free" (Luke 4.19, cf. Isaiah 61.1, 58.6), would take priority over the apostle Paul's letter to the Romans. Many ministers in the United Church of Christ, for example, argue that biblical passages such as these are most relevant to issues of homosexuality, and they interpret them to mean that Christians should struggle against homophobia, not condemn the sexual behavior of LGB people. It is accurate to say that the Christian Bible contains passages that could be interpreted as condemning homosexuality, but it is historically inaccurate to suggest that the Bible requires this Christian response or that such interpretations are not influenced by the cultural context of their interpreters.

Christians have always chosen a variety of biblical passages and interpretations to respond to any issue, and the responses of conservative and liberal Christians can both find support in Christian scripture and tradition, and both are influenced by the political and social expectations of their modern American context. Melendez and LaSala (2006) have already addressed some problems with the misrepresentation of Christianity's history with respect to slavery, an issue that gets to the heart of Christianity's cultural contingency. Early Christianity developed in a context in which slavery was as common and acceptable as was husbands' authority over their wives, as evidenced by Colossians 3.18–22: "Wives, be subject to your husbands, as is fitting in the Lord. ... Slaves, obey your earthly masters in everything" (cf. Ephesians 5.22–6.6). Christians in the Roman Empire and many Christians in the early American South believed that certain interpretations of their Bible allowed slavery, just as some Christians today believe that certain interpretations of their Bible allow the condemnation of the sexual behavior of LGB people. Influenced by modern American culture, some Christians may prioritize certain biblical passages over others to argue that Christians must condemn slavery despite some biblical passages that seem to allow it. Ironically, Christians who similarly prioritize certain biblical passages over others to argue that Christians must condemn homophobia, despite some biblical passages that seem to allow it, are denounced for having a Christianity that is unduly influenced by the culture around it and for falling away from biblical precepts that they "do not have the option . . . of picking and choosing" (Hodge, 2005, p. 208). No such criticism of inappropriate cultural contingency is made for the rejection of biblically sanctioned slavery.

The Bible is a collection of varied texts, and what the Bible says on any given topic depends on which passages are deemed relevant and how those passages are interpreted. The Bible says, "Beat your plowshares into swords" (Joel 3.10), "They shall beat their swords into plowshares" (Isaiah 2.4), "I have not come to bring peace, but a sword" (Matthew 10.34), and "If anyone strikes you on the right cheek, turn the other also" (Matthew 5.39), leaving the reader to determine the appropriate use of each. It is historically accurate to say that Christians who embrace LGB people as fully part of God's community are reading scripture through the lens of their modern world. But it is historically inaccurate to say that other interpretations of scripture have escaped being influenced by their modern context. Hodge presents one modern Christian viewpoint, but his claims should not be mistaken for being required by Christian scripture or for being the only historically defensible Christian response. The points Hodge raises regarding evangelical social workers deserve serious discussion. To be fruitful, however, that discussion must avoid false binaries and historical inaccuracies and must be held to the same professional and methodological rigor expected of other discussions in the field.

Examining Conservative Religious Freedom of Expression

This section explores the complexity of achieving the goal of freedom of religious expression given the struggles delineated in the literature discussed thus far. In another article we address the question of whether social work oppresses evangelical Christian freedom of expression (Bolen & Dessel, 2013; also see Chapter 8, this book). Here we examine the conservative Christian belief regarding same-sex sexuality as sinful behavior and discuss the concept of freedom of speech.

Some authors point out that Christians in social work settings who hold conservative beliefs regarding same-sex sexuality should be permitted to express their views "on the appropriateness of same-sex practice" and that this "speech that some gay men and lesbians disagree with is often censored in public universities" (Hodge, 2005, pp. 208, 209). This censorship could alternatively be characterized as protection from conservative evangelical views that "homosexual behavior is sinful" and "strongly condemned" (Kwon, 2008, para. 12; Oklahoma Baptist University, 2005/2006, [16] Human Sexuality). Indeed, some Christian schools of social work refuse gay men and lesbians entry into their schools (Towns, 2006). The conservative Focus on the Family Christian perspective toward gay and lesbian people is one in which their personhood is affirmed (Hodge, 2005), yet it also calls for the restriction of lesbian and gay sexual fulfillment, marital civil rights, and employment (Canda & Furman, 1999; Jimenez, 2006). These restrictions represent homophobic statements and attitudes. It is critical to recognize that homophobic comments are correlated with, and predict, discrimination and antigay violence (Masser & Moffat, 2006; Parrott, Zeichner, & Hoover, 2006). These comments and practices are experienced as not only oppressive but as dangerous to the LGB community. Such speech has been used by politicians to deny lesbians and gay men equal rights to many activities ranging from adoption to medical access to marriage (Melendez & LaSala, 2006). Some authors (Henrickson, 2009; Jimenez, 2006) suggest that there is no room in the field for views that oppress LGB people and that the profession's standpoint is an "open society" that encourages individuation and difference. Furthermore, NASW standards for cultural competence in social work practice (National Association of Social Workers [NASW], 2001) recommend that social workers develop an understanding of their own personal values and recognize how personal and professional values may conflict. These standards caution social workers not to impose their personal values on clients.

In a discussion of the restriction of conservative Christian youth's freedom of religious speech in public schools, it is noted that "school social workers may be reluctant to support students of faith who experience discrimination for articulating a faith-based perspective on what they perceive to be the moral inappropriateness of homosexual behavior" (Hodge, 2003c, p. 115).

Admittedly, religious freedom and sexual orientation freedom are contentious issues in public schools today (Ciardullo, 2005), and conservative Christian students may experience restrictions on their freedom of religious expression. However, LGB students experience extremely high rates of verbal and physical violence in public schools; LGB students have even been murdered in schools based on their sexual orientation, and this sexual prejudice negatively affects heterosexual students as well (Gay, Lesbian and Straight Education Network, 2008; Poteat & Eslepage, 2007). Furthermore, what may be referred to as freedom of religious speech by some conservative Christian students could be interpreted as harmful speech when that speech suggests that LGB people do not lead moral lives or are sinners. Many LGB people experience such statements as hate speech (Cobb, 2005). In a study of college students, those primed for freedom of speech viewed hate speech as less harmful than those who were primed to recognize the damaging effects of such speech (Cowan, Resendez, Marshall, & Quist, 2002). As Cowan and colleagues so eloquently state, "What is one person's freedom of self-expression can become another person's subordination" (p. 258). To help guide social workers' thinking about freedom of speech, they can use the harm principle, which states that to avoid doing harm social workers should not restrict a person's civil rights (Plant, 2011, p. 19).

It is problematic to construct some social workers' disagreement "with the values of the [gay and lesbian] groups" (Hodge, 2007b, p. 365) as an expression of traditional Christian beliefs, freedom of speech, or culturally competent practice. Furthermore, ascribing common LGB values (Thaller, 2011) is inaccurate because it is unlikely that all gay men and all lesbians hold the same values, except presumably the value of relationships and love that most people hold. It may be more productive to question the portrayal of monolithic evangelical Christian beliefs with regard to LGB people (Hodge, 2007b). Indeed, Maher (2006) has documented the existence of 61 evangelical gay and lesbian religious groups in the western United States. Not only are these two groups not mutually exclusive, but also, more important, there is an inclusive overlap of their communities. Many Christians challenge or reinterpret the beliefs systems of their religious tenets with regard to same-sex sexuality (Adler, 2012; Thaller, 2011; Thomas & Olson, 2012). Other factors, such as essentialist views about marriage, sexual orientation, and sexual contact, may play a stronger role than religion in predicting negative attitudes about same-sex orientation (Baunach, Burgess, & Muse, 2010; Duncan & Kemmelmeier, 2012). Diverse reality constructions of different religions are quite important for social workers to understand in order to provide culturally competent services (Hodge, 2007b). Examples of this competence include refraining from using the term *fundamentalist* unless it is self-ascribed (Hodge, 2004a) and recognizing that social work values related to same-sex sexuality are not inherently anti-Christian (Pellebon & Caselman, 2008).

Educating About Social Work Ethics

The NASW (2008) Code of Ethics equally privileges religion and sexual orientation. Thus, the support of "conservative faith-based constructions of reality" (Hodge, 2002, pg. 406) regarding LGB people is of concern to some social workers. However, the social construction of reality by the dominant White culture in this country has been used to maintain the oppression of African Americans for centuries (Andersen & Collins, 2007). Only two generations ago, it was illegal for African Americans and Whites to marry, and social work education contends with its own racism to this day (Schiele, 2007). It would be unacceptable to affirm White privilege as a construction of reality that needs to be accepted. Might the same standard be applied to those who reject LGB people and their sexuality? If not, what are the arguments for privileging one group's speech that could be considered oppressive and discriminatory? Equal rights for LGB people cannot be construed as inherently oppressing some conservative Christians.

The beliefs of some evangelical Christians and how they construct reality is likened to that of a culture (Hodge, 2002). The sociological literature also addresses the cultures of different churches or denominations (Pattillo-McCoy, 1998; Saroglou, 2011). In fact, the field of social work grapples with the ethical questions of how to respect indigenous cultures while acknowledging the "danger in values and practices ... that may be deemed unjust" (Gray & Fook, 2004, p. 629; Healy, 2007). This struggle encompasses such questions as whether all cultural practices should be universally accepted, even if they violate human rights, and who establishes these cultural norms and "construction of reality" (Hodge, 2002). As scholars in the field of child sexual and physical abuse remark, there is a dangerous tendency to minimize the influence of culture on acceptance of abusive behavior (Fontes, 1995; Gil, 1995). In *Social Work and Human Rights,* Elisabeth Reichert (2003) points out that religion and culture are often elevated over any broader interpretation of the UN Universal Declaration of Human Rights. How, then, is social work to reconcile its commitment to human rights with respect for all cultures?

Hodge (2002) contends that today, social work has an "ideologically inspired drive to control the parameters of the [values] debate by excluding divergent voices" and does not allow "authentic diversity [and] differing constructions of reality or truth" (p. 406). He notes that the NASW Code of Ethics calls on social workers to respect religious diversity and prevent and eliminate domination and discrimination of religious people (Hodge, 2005, p. 213). Reamer (2003), an expert in social work ethics, states in response,

> Social workers who impose their views, for example to oppose . . . homosexuality for religious reasons, on clients who hold different views and exercise different choices—views and choices that clients have a right to hold and exercise and that are consistent with official NASW policies and positions that were enacted through democratic processes—violate the profession's ethical standards. (p. 430)

Most recently, the American Association of Christian Counselors (AACC) put forth their revised code of ethics, which eliminates the promotion of reparative therapy and acknowledges harmful religious beliefs but states, "Christian counselors do not condone or advocate for the pursuit of or active involvement in homosexual, bisexual or transgendered behaviors and lifestyles" (AACC, 2014, p. 15). This will present a continuing challenge for social workers who seek to follow the social work Code of Ethics.

The social work profession has recently been challenged for silencing political and religious freedom of expression in academic settings (Stoesz, 2008; Will, 2007). These charges align with the notion that some conservative

Christians in social work settings believe they are restricted from expressing their beliefs about lesbians and gay men. Although the profession of social work has long been grounded in and embraced faith-based social service provision (Cnaan, Sinha, & McGrew, 2004), the conflicts between religious freedom and LGB human rights can no longer be ignored (Towns, 2006). How does social work education help students reconcile the claim that the "prohibition of sharing religious viewpoints on homosexuality" (Hodge, 2007b) is a "violat[ion] of the human rights of people of faith" (p. 370) with the current violation of equal and human rights for the LGB community?

Conclusion

This critique suggests, first, that the conviction that a specific Christian theological perspective is the only true belief system is problematic. Even though certain conservative Christian belief systems are put forward by their followers as representing transcendent truth, the scholar of early Christianity invited to coauthor this chapter instead states that all interpretations of the Bible are culturally contingent. This scholar further states that the differing Christian belief systems seen across denominations and churches, including those of some conservative Christians, are based on how these different groups selectively interpret passages of the Bible.

In social work education, some conservative Christians desire the freedom of speech to express their religious beliefs that are antagonistic to LGB people (Office of University Communications, 2006). This chapter questions whether this type of freedom of speech violates social work values because it is oppressive of a population of people. There is no doubt that oppression, discrimination, and violence occur based on religion as well as sexual orientation. Sexual orientation freedom, like religious freedom, continues to be restricted internationally. However, although religion is included in the UN Universal Declaration of Human Rights, an amendment to include gays and lesbians has yet to be approved. Furthermore, anti-LGB speech can provoke violence (Masser & Moffat, 2006; Parrott et al., 2006). In an era in which educators are urging students to think critically, this discussion can be brought into the classroom. It is especially appropriate for a discussion of social work ethics and values. Students must consider whether there should be restrictions on freedom of speech and, if so, what they might be.

Social work educators may experience challenges facilitating classroom discussions about the tension between religious beliefs and LGB people (Melcher, 2008; Todd & Coholic, 2007). Faculty and other instructors can use intergroup dialogue pedagogy and the development of critical consciousness to facilitate a more complex and nuanced discussion of this issue (Dessel, 2010; Miller & Donner, 2000; Nagda, 2006; Rozas, 2007; Sakamoto & Pitner, 2005). Intergroup dialogue involves students from different social identity groups who come together to explore the socialization processes involved in social identity development, group-based inequalities, and social action. Intergroup dialogue is a pedagogy used in higher education settings to engage diverse student populations in a critical kind of learning, one that fosters democratic engagement, social responsibility, and ethical decision making with regard to civic action (Nagda, Gurin, Sorensen, & Zuniga, 2009). This method increases perspective taking, appreciation of differences, sense of commonality, communication, and alliance building while also bridging differences, decreasing stereotypes, facilitating trust and relationships, and establishing common ground (DeTurk, 2006; Diez Pinto, 2004; Gurin, Nagda, & Lopez, 2004; LeBaron & Carstarphen, 1997; Nagda, 2006; Pan & Mutchler, 2000; Rodenborg & Huynh, 2006). Social work faculty members use this method to address intergroup conflicts that are based around social identities such as race, ethnicity, and gender (Miller & Donner, 2000; Nagda et al., 2009; Rodenborg & Huynh, 2006; Rozas, 2007).

Intergroup dialogue among social work students could first address various topics such as the wide diversity within Christian religions and belief systems (Smith, 2000) and the recognition of LGB oppression. Such dialogue could include multiple religions other than Christianity. Although some, but not all, conservative Christians may hold belief systems antagonistic to LGB people, many other Christians and members of other religions do not hold these beliefs. A conversation that allows for multiple belief systems, rather than dichotomizing conservative Christians against social workers, allows belief systems other than those of some conservative Christians to be represented as different, nuanced, and equally spiritually fulfilling.

Additionally, there is clearly more than one way to interpret and understand the biblical texts regarding LGB people. Some Christians such as the American Baptists recognize the importance of challenging discrimination and oppression based on sexual prejudice (American Baptists, 2008). Numerous evangelical and other religious scholars have observed, "Christians disagree about God's will for same-sex relationships" (Steen, 1997; Vanderwoerd, 2007, p. 388; Zahniser & Cagle, 2007). Ellens (1997) noted, "homosexual orientation cannot be condemned or proscribed on biblical grounds" (p. 50), and Wolfer and Hodge (2007) have stated that Christian theism affirms human rights as universal (Hertzke, 2003).

Social work educators can also provide an opportunity for students to discuss both normative sexuality and neurophysiologic differences between LGB and heterosexual people. For example, many individuals with same-gender atractions also have other-gender sexual attractions, just as many self-identified heterosexual males and females have same-gender attractions or have had same-gender sexual interactions in the past (see, for example, Rust, 2000, Chap. 3). Even though many are now aware of genetic differences in gay men (Bocklandt, Horvath, Vilain, & Hamer, 2006; Rahman & Wilson, 2003), probably fewer are aware of the different neurophysiologic structures in people with same-sex rather than opposite-sex attraction (Garrett, 2009; Savic & Lindström, 2008). For example, the right side of the brain is larger for heterosexual men and lesbians, whereas heterosexual women and gay men show no cerebral asymmetry. Gay men and heterosexual women share one type of connectivity in the amygdala, whereas lesbians and heterosexual men share another type of connectivity (Savic & Lindström, 2008). Other studies suggest that hormones in the prenatal period may be responsible for traits in lesbians more similar to those of heterosexual men (Littrell, 2014). Becoming more knowledgeable about normative sexuality and genetic, developmental, and neurophysiologic differences provides for a more complex analysis of this debate in the classroom.

Finally, the social work classroom can be considered a laboratory for social work practice. Educators are responsible for preparing students for practice.

Therefore, it is important that religiously conservative students become comfortable working ethically with those who do not share their same beliefs. Conversely, other students need to be comfortable working ethically with those who are religiously conservative and who espouse beliefs with which the students do not agree. All social workers need to be able to work with people even when they find their beliefs offensive. One part of doing so is guiding students in abiding by the NASW Code of Ethics. This means affirming the belief that LGB people should not be discriminated against or oppressed and that regardless of students' personal and religious values or beliefs, they do not impose them on clients.

Facilitating the recommended dialogues can be difficult because students may find it difficult to engage in such sensitive discussions, may fear that their own belief systems will be discounted, or may feel that other students will align against them. Yet Hodge (2007b) calls on social work to engage in an experience of "learn[ing] to hear and understand each other's reality" (p. 371). This learning must take place through carefully planned and facilitated dialogue, where individual stereotypes, assumptions, and ways of knowing can be safely examined and considered. Griffin, D'Errico, Harro, and Schiff (2007) provide a useful heterosexism curriculum design that can be used in such dialogues. Attention to power structures, equality, and human rights is critical (Reichert, 2003). Intergroup dialogue, or similar techniques, on the topic of sexual orientation and religious freedom are a needed pedagogy if the social work profession is to find common ground in this debate and a way to move forward.

References

Adler, G. (2012). An opening in the congregational closet? Boundary-bridging culture and membership privileges for gays and lesbians in Christian religious congregations. *Social Problems, 59*(2), 177–206.

American Association of Christian Counselors (AACC). (2014). AACC Code of Ethics. Retrieved from http://aacc.net/files/AACC%20Code%20of%20Ethics%20-%20Master%20Document.pdf

American Baptists. (2008). *Rainbow Baptists.* Retrieved from http://www.rainbowbaptists.org/abconcerned.htm

Andersen, M. L., & Collins, P. H. (2007). *Race, class & gender: An anthology* (6th ed.). Belmont, CA: Thomson Wadsworth.

Baunach, D., Burgess, E. O., & Muse, C. (2010). Southern (dis)comfort: Sexual prejudice and contact with gay men and lesbians in the south. *Spectrum, 3*(1), 30–64.

Bocklandt, S., Horvath, S., Vilain, E., & Hamer, D. H. (2006). Extreme skewing of X chromosome inactivation in mothers of homosexual men. *Human Genetics, 118*(6), 691–694. doi:10.1007/s00439-005-0119-4

Bolen, R., & Dessel, A. (2013). Is discrimination against evangelical Christians really a problem in social work education? *Journal of Social Work Education, 49,* 528–547.

Canda, E. (2003). Social work and evangelical Christians. *Social Work, 48,* 278–281. doi:10.1093/sw/48.2.278

Canda, E. R., & Furman, L. D. (1999). *Spiritual diversity in social work practice.* New York, NY: Free Press.

Ciardullo, M. (2005). Advocates on both sides are as passionate as ever: SIECUS controversy report 2004–2005 school year. *SIECUS Report, 33*(4), 4–19.

Cnaan, R., Sinha, J., & McGrew, C. (2004). Congregations as social service providers: Services, capacity, culture and organizational behavior. *Administration in Social Work, 28*(3/4), 47–68. doi:10.1300/J147v28n03_03

Cobb, M. (2005). Race, religion, hate and incest in queer politics. *Social Text, 23*(3–4), 251–274.

Council on Social Work Education (CSWE). (2001). *Education policy and accreditation standards.* Retrieved from http://www.cswe.org/File.aspx?id=14115

Cowan, G., Resendez, M., Marshall, E., & Quist, R. (2002). Hate speech and constitutional protection: Priming values of equality and freedom. *Journal of Social Issues, 58,* 247–264. doi:10.1111/1540-4560.00259

Dessel, A. (2010). Effects of intergroup dialogue: Public school teachers and sexual orientation prejudice. *Small Group Research, 41*(5), 556–592. doi:10.1177/1046496410369560

DeTurk, S. (2006). The power of dialogue: Consequences of intergroup dialogue and their implications for agency and alliance building. *Communication Quarterly, 54*(1), 33–51. doi:10.1080/01463370500270355

Diez Pinto, E. (2004). *Vision Guatemala 1998–2000: Building bridges of trust.* New York, NY: United Nations Development Programme. Retrieved from http://democraticdialoguenetwork.org/documents/view.pl?s=13;ss=;t=;f_id=263

Duncan, M., & Kemmelmeier, M. (2012). Attitudes toward same-sex marriage: An essentialist approach. *Analyses of Social Issues and Public Policy, 12*(1), 377–399.

Ellens, J. (1997). Homosexuality in biblical perspective. *Pastoral Psychology, 46*(1), 35–53. doi:10.1023/A:1023071920011

Fontes, L. A. (1995). *Sexual abuse in nine North American cultures.* Thousand Oaks, CA: SAGE.

Foucault, F. (1980). *The history of sexuality.* Volume 1: *An introduction.* Translation of *Histoire de la sexualité* by Robert Hurley. New York, NY: Vintage Books.

Garrett, B. (2009). *Brain & behavior: An introduction to biological psychology* (2nd ed.). Los Angeles, CA: SAGE.

Gay, Lesbian and Straight Education Network (GLSEN). (2008). California middle school student murdered in school because of sexual orientation. Retrieved from http://www.glsen.org/cgi-bin/iowa/all/news/record/2261.html

Gil, E. (1995). Foreword. In L. A. Fontes (Ed.), *Sexual abuse in nine North American cultures* (pp. ix–xii). Thousand Oaks, CA: SAGE.

Gray, M., & Fook, J. (2004). The quest for a universal social work: Some issues and implications. *Social Work Education, 23,* 625–644. Retrieved from http://dx.doi.org/10.1080/0261547042000252334

Griffin, P., D'Errico, K., Harro, B., & Schiff, T. (2007). Heterosexism curriculum design. In M. Adams, L. A. Bell, & P. Griffin (Eds.), *Teaching for diversity and social justice* (pp. 195–218). New York, NY: Routledge.

Gurin, P., Nagda, B., & Lopez, G. (2004). The benefits of diversity in education for democratic citizenship. *Journal of Social Issues, 60*(1), 17–34. doi:10.1111/j.0022-4537.2004.00097.x

Healy, L. (2007). Universalism and cultural relativism in social work ethics. *International Social Work, 50*(1), 11–26. Retrieved from http://dx.doi.org/10.1177/0020872807071479

Henrickson, M. (2009). Sexuality, religion, and authority: Toward reframing estrangement. *Journal of Religion & Spirituality in Social Work: Social Thought, 28*(1), 48–62.

Hertzke, A. D. (2003). Evangelicals and international engagement. In M. Cromartie (Ed.), *A public faith: Evangelicals and civic engagement* (pp. 215–235). Lanham, MD: Rowman & Littlefield.

Hertzke, A. D., & Philpott, D. (2000, Fall). Defending the faiths. *National Interest, 61,* 74–81.

Hodge, D. (2002). Does social work oppress evangelical Christians? A "new class" analysis of society and social work. *Social Work, 47,* 401–414. doi:10.1093/sw/47.4.401

Hodge, D. (2003a). The challenge of spiritual diversity: Can social work facilitate an inclusive environment? *Families in Society, 84,* 348–358. doi:10.1606/1044-3894.117

Hodge, D. (2003b). Differences in worldviews between social workers and people of faith. *Families in Society, 84,* 285–295. doi:10.1606/1044-3894.97

Hodge, D. (2003c). Value differences between social workers and members of the working and middle classes. *Social Work, 48,* 107–119. Retrieved from http://dx.doi.org/10.1093/sw/48.1.107

Hodge, D. (2004a). Developing cultural competency with evangelical Christians. *Families in Society, 85,* 251–260. Retrieved from http://dx.doi.org/10.1606/1044-3894.318

Hodge, D. (2004b). Who we are, where we come from, and some of our perceptions: Comparison of social workers and the general population. *Social Work, 49,* 261–268. doi:10.1093/sw/49.2.261

Hodge, D. (2004c). Working with Hindu clients in a spiritually sensitive manner. *Social Work, 49,* 27–38. doi:10.1093/sw/49.1.27

Hodge, D. (2005). Epistemological frameworks, homosexuality, and religion: How people of faith understand the intersection between homosexuality and religion. *Social Work, 50,* 207–218.

Hodge, D. (2007a). Advocating for persecuted people of faith: A social justice imperative. *Families in Society, 88,* 255–262.

Hodge, D. (2007b). Learning to hear each others' voice: A response to Melendez and LaSala. *Social Work, 52,* 365–374.

Hodge, D. (2007c). Progressing toward inclusion? Exploring the state of religious diversity. *Social Work Research, 31,* 55–63.

Hodge, D., & Williams, T. (2002). Assessing African American spirituality with spiritual ecomaps. *Families in Society, 83,* 585–595.

Holy Bible: New Standard Revised Edition. (1991). Oxford, UK: Oxford University Press.

Hunter, J. D. (1991). *Culture wars.* New York, NY: Basic Books.

Jimenez, J. (2006). Epistemological frameworks, homosexuality, and religion: A response to Hodge. *Social Work, 51,* 185–187.

Kwon, L (2008, June 17). Southern Baptist head: Love the homosexual, hate our sin. *Christian Post.* Retrieved from http://www.christiantoday.com/article/southern.baptist.head.love.the.homosexual.hate.our.sin/19598.htm

LeBaron, M., & Carstarphen, N. (1997). Negotiating intractable conflict: The Common Ground dialogue process and abortion. *Negotiation Journal, 13*(4), 341–361.

Littrell, J. (2014). Incorporating information from neuroscience and endocrinology regarding sexual orientation into social work education. *Journal of Human Behavior in the Social Environment, 18*(2), 101–128. doi:10.1080/10911350802285854

Maher, M. (2006). A voice in the wilderness: Gay and lesbian religious groups in the western United States. *Journal of Homosexuality, 51,* 91–117.

Marshall, P. (2000). *Religious freedom in the world.* Nashville, TN: Broadman and Holman.

Masser, B., & Moffat, K. (2006). With friends like these. . . . The role of prejudice and situational norms on discriminatory helping behavior. *Journal of Homosexuality, 51,* 121–138.

Melcher, J. (2008). Orthodox vs. Progressive: An invitation to transform professional consciousness. *Journal of Religion & Spirituality in Social Work: Social Thought, 27*(1–2), 183–200.

Melendez, M., & LaSala, M. (2006). Who's oppressing whom? Homosexuality, Christianity, and social work. *Social Work, 5,* 371–377.

Miller, J., & Donner, S. (2000). More than just talk: The use of racial dialogues to combat racism. *Social Work With Groups, 23,* 31–53.

Nagda, B. (2006). Breaking barriers, crossing borders, building bridges: Communication processes in intergroup dialogues. *Journal of Social Issues, 62*(3), 553–576.

Nagda, B., Gurin, P., Sorensen, N., & Zuniga, X. (2009). Evaluating intergroup dialogue: Engaging diversity for personal and social responsibility. *Diversity & Democracy, 12*(1), 4–6.

National Association of Social Workers (NASW). (2001). NASW standards for cultural competence in social work practice. Retrieved from http://www.socialworkers.org/practice/standards/naswculturalstandards.pdf

National Association of Social Workers (NASW). (2008). *Code of ethics.* Retrieved from http://www.naswdc.org/pubs/code/code.asp

Office of University Communications. (2006, November 8). *Missouri State settles lawsuit with Emily Brooker*. Retrieved from http://search.gipoco.com/cached/41326/

Oklahoma Baptist University. (2005/2006). Section 17, Human sexuality. Retrieved from http://www.okbu.edu/campuslife/greenbook/section_2.html#2-d-xxii-17

Pan, D., & Mutchler, S. (2000). *Calling the roll: Study Circles for better schools: Policy research report*. Study Circles Resource Center. Retrieved from http://www.studycircles.org/en/Resource.18.aspx

Parrott, D., Zeichner, A., & Hoover, R. (2006). Sexual prejudice and anger network activation: Mediating role of negative affect. *Aggressive Behavior, 32*(1), 7–16.

Pattillo-McCoy, M. (1998). Church culture as a strategy of action in the Black community. *American Sociological Review, 63*(6), 767–784.

Pellebon, D., & Caselman, T. (2008). The perception gap: A study of Christian confidence in social workers. *Social Work and Christianity, 35*(1), 33–47.

Plant, R. (2011). Religion, identity and freedom of expression. *Res Publica, 17*(1), 7–20.

Poteat, V., & Espelage, D. (2007). Predicting psychosocial consequences of homophobic victimization in middle school students. *Journal of Early Adolescence, 27*(2), 175–191.

Rahman, A., & Wilson, G. D. (2003). The neurobiology of human sexual orientation. *Personality and Individual Differences, 34*(8), 1337–1382.

Reamer, F. (2003). Social work, evangelical Christians, and values. *Social Work, 48,* 428–431.

Reichert, E. (2003). *Social work and human rights.* New York, NY: Columbia University Press.

Ressler, L., & Hodge, D. (2000). Religious discrimination in social work: An international survey of Christian social workers. *Social Work and Christianity, 27*(1), 49–70.

Ressler, L., & Hodge, D. (2003). Silence voices: Social work and the oppression of conservative narratives. *Social Thought: Journal of Religion in the Social Services, 22*(1), 125–142.

Rodenborg, N., & Huynh, N. (2006). On overcoming segregation: Social work and intergroup dialogue. *Social Work With Groups, 29,* 27–44.

Rodriguez Rust, P. (2000). *Bisexuality in the United States: A social science reader.* New York, NY: Columbia University Press.

Rozas, L. (2007). Engaging dialogue in our diverse social work student body: A multilevel theoretical process model. *Journal of Social Work Education, 43*(1), 5–29.

Sakamoto, I., & Pitner, R. (2005). Use of critical consciousness in anti-oppressive social work practice: Disentangling power dynamics at personal and structural levels. *British Journal of Social Work, 35,* 435–452.

Saroglou, V. (2011). Believing, bonding, behaving, and belonging: The big four religious dimensions and cultural variation. *Journal of Cross-Cultural Psychology, 42*(8), 1320–1340.

Savic, I., & Lindström, P. (2008). PET and MRI show differences in cerebral asymmetry and functional connectivity between homo- and heterosexual subjects. *Proceedings of the National Academy of Sciences, 105*(27), 9403–9408.

Schiele, J. (2007). Implications of the equality-of-oppressions paradigm for curriculum content on people of color. *Journal of Social Work Education, 43*(1), 83–100.

Shea, N. (1997). *In the lion's den.* Nashville, TN: Broadman and Holman.

Smith, C. (2000). *Christian America? What Evangelicals really want.* Berkeley, CA: University of California Press.

Southern Baptist Convention. (2012). Position statements: Sexuality. Retrieved from http://www.sbc.net/aboutus/pssexuality.asp

Steen, T. (Ed.). (1997). Christianity and homosexuality [Theme issue]. *Christian Scholar's Review, XXVI*(4).

Stoesz, D. (2008). *Reports from the academy: Social work agonistes.* Retrieved from http://www.nas.org/polInitiatives.cfm?Doc_Id=167

Streets, F. (2009). Overcoming a fear of religion in social work education and practice. *Journal of Religion & Spirituality in Social Work: Social Thought, 28*(1), 185–199.

Thaller, J. (2011). Resilience and resistance in professional identity making: Gleanings from the classroom experiences of devout Christian social workers. *Journal of Religion & Spirituality in Social Work: Social Thought, 30*(2), 144–163. doi:10.1080/15426432.2011.567115

Thomas, J. N., & Olson, D. V. (2012). Evangelical elites' changing responses to homosexuality 1960–2009. *Sociology of Religion, 73*(3), 239–272.

Thyer, B., & Myers, L. (2009). Religion discrimination in social work academic programs: Whither social justice? *Journal of Religion & Spirituality in Social Work: Social Thought, 28,* 144–160.

Todd, S., & Coholic, D. (2007). Christian fundamentalism and anti-oppressive social work pedagogy. *Journal of Teaching in Social Work, 27*(3/4), 5–25.

Towns, L. (2006). Ethics and oppression of GLBT citizens: CSWE and NASW involvement. *Journal of Progressive Human Services, 17*(1), 1–4.

Vanderwoerd, J. (2007). Who cares? Social welfare in a diverse society. *Social Work & Christianity, 34*(4), 376–399.

Will, G. (2007, October 14). Code of coercion. *Washington Post.* Retrieved from http://www.washingtonpost.com/wpdyn/content/article/2007/10/12/AR2007101202151.html

Wolfer, T., & Hodge, D. (2007). Epistemology and social work: Toward a Christian critique. *Social Work and Christianity, 34*(4), 356–375.

Zahniser, J., & Cagle, L. (2007). Homosexuality: Toward an informed compassionate response. *Christian Scholar's Review, 36*(3), 323–348.

Notes

1 This definition is complicated somewhat by the historical development of the capitalized use of *Orthodox* to refer to certain forms of Christianity dominant in the eastern Mediterranean (as in Eastern Orthodox), just as the Latin term *catholic,* meaning "universal," over time came to be capitalized in reference to the specific Roman Catholic church that dominated the western Mediterranean world.

2 All biblical quotations are from the New Revised Standard Version of the Christian Bible (*Holy Bible,* 1991).

CHAPTER 8

Is Discrimination Against Evangelical Christians a Problem in Social Work Education? A Methodological Review

Rebecca M. Bolen, PhD, and Adrienne B. Dessel, PhD, LMSW

This chapter reviews the social work literature on national random surveys that compare levels of Christian religiosity among social workers and claims of discrimination by social work educators against evangelical Christian social workers. One of the central reasons for these claims that discrimination occurs is that social work faculty and practitioners are purported to be ideologically different, on average, from the general population (Hodge, 2003a, 2003b). This literature is reviewed also. Embedded in this review is a close examination of the methodological rigor of the national surveys used to support inferences about these differences.

The National Association of Social Workers (NASW) Code of Ethics clearly prohibits discrimination based on religion and calls on social workers to prevent such discrimination (NASW, 2011). A body of literature discusses whether social work educators discriminate against certain faith groups, particularly evangelical Christians (Hodge, 2002a; Ressler & Hodge, 2000). Various reasons for social work discrimination against more conservative faith groups have been advanced. One primary reason suggests that social work is composed of people who are predominantly of more liberal faith and ideological groups (Hodge, 2006a). Furthermore, it is suggested that social work practitioners are part of a knowledge class separate from the working and middle

Parts of this chapter were originally published in Bolen, R. M. (2001). *Child sexual abuse: Its scope and our future* (Chapter 4: Methodology, pp. 41–63). New York, NY: Springer and Kluwer Academic/Plenum Publisher. It is being reproduced here with kind permission from Springer.
Parts of this chapter were originally published in Bolen, R. M., & Dessel, A. B. (2013). Is discrimination against Evangelical Christians a problem in social work education? *Journal of Social Work Education, 49,* 528–547.

classes. According to this theory, people in this knowledge class are more likely to belong to liberal faith groups, to subscribe to a different moral code, and to have more liberal political beliefs than people in middle and working classes. This literature on discrimination against evangelical Christian social workers has direct implications for social work education, because the classroom is the forming ground for professional identity and practice.

A second reason for purported discrimination is the tension in social work education between people who are lesbian, gay, or bisexual (LGB) and certain conservative Christian beliefs held by some social workers (Ressler, 2002; Todd & Coholic, 2007). Hodge's (2005) discussion of evangelical Christian viewpoints toward LGB people and the numerous letters to the editor reacting to the article exemplify this tension (Harrison, 2005; Melendez & LaSala, 2006; Shernoff, 2005). Students who hold evangelical Christian beliefs with regard to LGB people present a particular challenge for faculty to create classroom climates that invite all perspectives while recognizing the differences in power and oppression between these groups (Todd & Coholic, 2007). This literature is addressed within a framework of the different types of methodological validity of the studies used to determine differences between social workers and the general public and those considering whether social workers discriminate against conservative Christians.

The definition of validity differs based on the context in which it is used (Pedhazur & Schmelkin, 1991). Cook and Campbell (1976) recommend a classification scheme using four types of validity: statistical conclusion validity, construct validity, internal validity, and external validity, all of which refer to the validity, or strength, of inferences made from a study. Statistical conclusion validity is the validity of inferences made based on the statistical analyses used, whereas construct validity is the validity of inferences made based on the measures used. Internal validity is the validity of inferences made about the effect of the independent variables on the dependent variable, after methodological features of the study are considered. Finally, external validity is the validity of inferences made to a larger population (i.e., the generalizability of the study).

Each type of validity is critical to the eventual integrity of the study. When any type of validity suffers, the integrity and rigor of the study decrease.

Research constraints sometimes predicate certain weaknesses in the study's design. For example, interpersonal violence cannot be used as a manipulated variable in an experimental design. When constraints do occur, the challenge becomes to design the most rigorous study possible, given the constraints, and then to state clearly not only the methods of the study but also its weaknesses and limitations. The careful reader will then have the information necessary to make an informed decision about the strength of inferences made from the findings.

This chapter discusses types of validity as they relate to research on the potential discrimination against evangelical Christians by social work educators and on differences between social workers and the general public. The different types of validity are somewhat broadly interpreted. For example, all issues of measurement are discussed under construct validity, whereas all issues of research design are discussed within internal validity.

Construct Validity: Measurement Issues

Construct validity is the "appropriateness, meaningfulness, and usefulness of the specific inferences made from test scores" (American Psychological Association, 1985, p. 9). As such, construct validity is concerned not so much with the measure itself but with the ability to infer from the measure (Pedhazur & Schmelkin, 1991). Obviously, poorly constructed measures increase the probability that inferences made from them are not valid.

Whereas construct validity is concerned primarily with the already developed instrument and how well it captures what it was designed to measure, the measure's development is obviously critical to its later validity. For this reason, this section is concerned first with the definition, operationalization, and measurement of the constructs of interest, followed by a discussion of construct validity. Because many issues of construct validity can become extremely technical, this section provides only an overview of the issues.

Issues in Defining, Operationalizing, and Measuring Religion

A construct is a concept that can be uniquely differentiated from another concept. Constructs are embedded in a theoretical framework from which they gain meaning. For example, the construct of depression, which can be differentiated from anxiety, assumes meaning when embedded in a theoretical framework, such as psychodynamic, neuroscience, trauma, or others. The constructs most germane to the discussion in this chapter are religion, political ideology, and discrimination. Our understanding of these constructs gains meaning within the definitions society provides.

Because theory and constructs are inextricably interwoven, the researcher should always formulate a theoretical definition of the construct of interest. Only then can the researcher operationalize the construct by determining how it will be measured. Naturally, the operationalized definition must logically flow from the theoretical definition.

The main construct across the studies to be reviewed is *religion*. On the surface, the construct *religion* seems easily defined. In reality, several definitions could be attached to it. Religion could be conceptualized as the faith to which a person ascribes, such as Buddhism, Christianity, or others; the denomination to which people within the Christian faith belong; or even perhaps the dedication with which a person ascribes to his or her faith. In this chapter, the definition of religion will be the denomination within the Christian belief system to which people hold their allegiance and form their religious beliefs.

Even with such an innocuous definition of religion, there are countless ways to operationalize it. Within Christianity, the different religions are called denominations. Estimates of how many Christian denominations there are in the United States vary, ranging from a few hundred to more than 2,000 denominations (Association of Religion Data Archives, 2013; Djupe & Olson, 2003), so finding a parsimonious method to categorize denominations can be intimidating. Denominations can be grouped by their centralization of authority, historical and theological similarities, and forms of self-government (Sullins, 2004). Denominations can also be grouped based on their location on a continuum from fundamentalism to liberalism (Smith, 1990). Furthermore, within denominations there are different operationalization strategies for evangelical churches, such as by denominational affiliation, self-affiliation, or religious beliefs (Hackett & Lindsay, 2008).

Smith (1990) provides a categorization scheme for denominations based on a continuum from fundamentalism to liberalism, with three primary groups: fundamentalism, "moderatism," and liberalism. In this typology, the fundamentalist group includes conservative Christian and evangelical denominations. Criticisms of this method are that it is crude and imprecise and that more categories are needed (Hackett & Lindsay, 2008). In response, more recent work has created a categorization for denominations that divides them into 18 groups, although it seems that with such a large number it would be difficult to conduct research on them. Another more recent categorization scheme places greater emphasis on religious history and race. In this categorization scheme, conservative Christian groups are categorized within the evangelical Protestant group, whereas African American churches are separated into their own category. Others discuss whether differences between denominations are nominal or ordinal. Thus, it is not at all clear what is the better method of defining and operationalizing religious denominations (Hackett & Lindsay, 2008).

The most significant movement toward allowing self-identification started in 1976 when the Gallup Poll asked respondents whether they were "born again" (Hackett & Lindsay, 2008). If so, they were considered to belong to evangelical traditions. The importance of self-identification is that evangelicalism is not relegated to just Protestants but allows Roman Catholics, Orthodox Christians, and non-Christians to also self-identify as born again. When evangelical individuals are categorized in this manner, more than half of all Protestants identify themselves as born again, or evangelical. Conversely, a study by C. Smith and colleagues (1998, as cited in Hackett & Lindsay, 2008) found that just 7% of the population identify themselves as evangelical, which he operationalized as Protestants who attend church at least two times a month and who state that religion is "extremely important" in their lives. Using this definition, they find that evangelical Christians have more education and greater class mobility and are less likely to come from the South. Contrary to this method of operationalization, Hunter (1983, as cited in Hackett & Lindsay, 2008) determined, using 1979 Gallup Poll data and a different categorization scheme, that evangelicals encompassed 22.5%

of the population and that the typical evangelical Christian was female, poor, and a Democrat living in rural areas in the South. Again, this study excluded non-Protestants. In still another method of categorizing evangelicals, Barna (as cited in Hackett & Lindsay, 2008) defined evangelical individuals as a subset of those considering themselves to be born again. Those born again had to meet additional criteria: that they "have a personal commitment to Jesus Christ that is still important in their life" and that they believe they will go to Heaven because they have "confessed their sins and accepted Jesus Christ as their savior" (Barna, as cited in Hackett & Lindsay, 2008, p. 504). In addition, they must fulfill seven other criteria, such as believing their faith is very important to them, believing in Satan, and believing that Jesus lived a sinless life on Earth, among other criteria. Under this definition, only 7% of the population is evangelical, and the typical person is White, married, and Republican, lives in the South, and is more likely to hold a college degree (Hackett & Lindsay, 2008).

These notably different methods of categorizing denominations and even evangelicals makes for a slippery slope when we are interested in the characteristics of the different groups and their belief systems. Hackett and Lindsay (2008) used the 1998 General Social Survey (GSS) to compare how the different methods of operationalizing evangelicals could lead to vastly different findings. Under different definitions, the percentage of evangelicals in the national sample ranged from 5% to 38%. In other characteristics of evangelicals, those living in the South ranged from 36% to 55% based on the different methods of operationalizing evangelicals, and those voting Republican ranged from 34% to 48% across these different operationalization schemes. Finally, evangelicals who were college graduates ranged from 13% to 24% depending on the definition of evangelicalism. Looking at religious beliefs and based on different types of operationalizations, 50% to 100% of evangelicals believed the Bible was the literal word of God, with most of the others believing the Bible was the inspired word of God. The belief that hell exists ranged from 64% to 100%. Other categories where there were distinct differences were how often evangelicals attended services, how strongly they applied their beliefs in their lives, and whether they had evangelized, or proselytized. Hackett and

Lindsay conclude, "The operationalization of the population under consideration decides the outcome we find" (p. 509). In other words, different definitions and operationalizations of denominations, including evangelicalism, lead to dramatically different results, meaning they all have inherent biases. They conclude, "Research findings are often contingent upon how the subject under investigation is operationalized. We have demonstrated that this is the case when describing basic characteristics of evangelicals in America" (p. 511).

Regrettably, it does not appear that researchers agree as to how to operationalize religion. Until researchers coalesce around its definition and operationalization, it is critical that researchers using a particular definition and type of operationalization provide enough information that readers can identify the biases inherent in that approach. For example, is the definition of evangelicalism more narrow or more broad? Is it self-ascribed? How does its definition influence the religious beliefs and worldviews of people fitting that description?

Such a conversation is especially appropriate in some of the research studying the religious belief systems and worldviews of social workers. For example, Hodge (2003a) uses the method of operationalizing religion done by Smith (1990). At one end of this continuum is fundamentalism, one group of which is evangelicals. At the other end is liberalism. Within this belief system, people are purported to be more concerned about the nature and operation of the world than they are about salvation in the next world, which leads to social action and progressive reform. There is also a greater acceptance of secular change and science as not antireligious. These people do not believe that the Bible is to be understood literally and do not believe in biblical miracles. Moderates are between the poles and tend to reject extreme inerrancy and antiscience leanings while sharing with the liberal and fundamentalist groups some of their beliefs (Smith, 1986).

Smith used five different techniques to categorize the denominations, from which they developed criteria for classifying denominations. An advantage of using this operationalization is that it works well with the GSS (Hackett & Lindsay, 2008), the database that Hodge (2002a, 2002b) used for certain of his studies. The disadvantages are obvious, and this classification scheme has been strongly critiqued (Steensland et al., 2000). How are readers to know that this or any other categorization scheme has construct validity when so many methods of categorizing religions exist and when the method used changes the findings? Can categorization schemes be chosen to advantage the researcher's hypotheses? These concerns weigh heavily on decisions made about the operationalization of religion, especially when these religious categories are then used to consider worldviews and religious beliefs.

For Hodge (2006b), evangelicalism is

> a transdenominational, ecumenical Protestant movement that emphasizes the following historic Protestant tenets: (1) Salvation only through personal trust in Christ's finished atoning work, (2) a spiritually transformed life marked by moral conduct and personal devotion such as scripture reading and missions, and (3) the Bible as authoritative and reliable. (p. 214)

Hodge also defines religious conservatives as those who "derive their value system from an external transcendent source" (Hodge, 2002a, p. 402). The phrase *people of faith* is used to refer to only these evangelical and other conservative Christian groups of worshippers, a practice to which many mainstream and liberal worshippers, as well as some belonging to faiths other than Christian, may take offense. Using these definitions and the operationalization of religion done by Smith (1990), approximately 30% of respondents in the GSS were categorized as fundamentalist, or conservative, whereas 23% were categorized as liberal (Hodge, 2003a). Needless to say, the method of categorization used to operationalize denominations could have a great influence on the findings of the studies.

In this same article, worldviews between social workers and those belonging to a conservative Christian denomination were compared (Hodge, 2003a). Properties Smith (1990) used to operationalize denominations were compared with Hunter's (1983, 1991) characterization of orthodox and progressive worldviews, which were said to "derive their understanding of truth from different sources" (p. 285). For example, in the progressive worldview, "moral truth is viewed as a continually unfolding reality informed by the ethos of the contemporary age" (Hodge, 2003a, p. 285). "Ultimate moral authority is personally constructed within the parameters prescribed by current scientific discourse rationality and the contemporary ethos. ... The moral positions of historic faiths are resymbolized to conform to the prevailing assumptions of societal elites" (p. 286). In this view, truth is an evolving entity. For the orthodox worldview, however, "moral truth is understood to emanate from an external, definable, transcendent source, such as the God posited by theistic faith traditions" (p. 285).

Defining social issues as moral issues, Hodge (2003a) hypothesized that social workers would affirm a progressive worldview similar to that of liberal Christians and that this worldview would differ from that associated with conservative Christians. The three groups of belief systems, or moral issues, hypothesized to emanate from the progressive and liberal worldviews were abortion and euthanasia, family structure and child rearing, and sexual issues.

As would be expected when indicators of worldview are derived from religious differences between conservative and liberal denominations, people from conservative denominations did in fact endorse a more orthodox worldview, whereas those from liberal denominations and social workers endorsed a more progressive worldview. In other words, the analysis simply confirmed what could already be deduced about differences in worldview given that they were derived at least in part from religious beliefs. Furthermore, by having placed a moral value on social issues, one is left to question whether one of these groups is more moral than the other.

Hodge (2003a) also compared political and moral values of social workers with those across socioeconomic classes. He presented values he believed would show differences in orthodox or progressive worldviews. However, the choice of items sometimes appeared to be a bit arcane. Some of the questions included views on euthanasia, abortion, the mother's role in the house (i.e., to sublimate her career to her husband's and take care of the children full time), values to pass on to offspring, the ideal number of children to have, spanking, birth control, and views on sexual relations. He also asked about divorce laws, pornography laws, and whether pornography provides or leads to information on sex, is an outlet for impulses, is a breakdown in morals, or leads people to commit rape. In another article, Hodge (2004) used items from the GSS that questioned respondents about whether they would allow a racist, communist, or homosexual to speak publicly or to teach.

In a final article, Hodge (2003b) compared social workers' views with those of working- and middle-class people regarding spending priorities that included military and defense, welfare, solving problems in big cities, improving conditions of African Americans, dealing with drug addictions, stopping crime, protecting the environment, the nation's health, improving education, space exploration programs, and foreign aid. Views related to social issues were the legalization of marijuana, death penalty for murder, having a gun in the home, requiring a permit to buy a gun, and abortion. Even though differences in views between groups were found, the question is what these differences indicated. In the GSS, were these questions grouped within a larger construct to indicate social and economic issues? If so, knowing the psychometric properties of these groups of variables would be very helpful. This is especially true of the items reflecting social issues, which Hodge described as moral views. For instance, he discussed the "morality of" a married person having an affair and whether the person viewed "homosexual activity as morally appropriate behavior." Again, no psychometrics were provided to determine whether these items held together to capture a larger construct of social issues and which end of the spectrum reflected more liberal views. For example, what are the more moral positions regarding abortion, euthanasia, owning a gun, or improving the conditions of African Americans? Combining a number of items in the GSS does not necessarily mean that the items are measuring what they are intended to measure. Are these items truly indicative of a worldview? Greater information about the items is needed in terms of what they represented in the GSS and whether they held together as a construct (e.g., using exploratory factor analysis). Without this information, it is difficult to attribute importance and meaning to these items.

Summary

The main issue in the construct validity of religion is the different methods of capturing it when it is categorized into smaller, meaningful groups of denominations. As discussed by Hackett and Lindsay (2008), the multiple different methods of measuring denominations leads to the difficult problem of different findings based on different operationalizations. Although this is an issue throughout all research, it appears to be an especially important problem in research of religions, Christian denominations, and even evangelical denominations. The other issue in construct validity is how worldviews are defined, what they are based on (e.g., religious orientation, political orientation), and how to capture them. Needless to say, how they are defined and what they are based on are critical to their operationalization.

Threats to Internal Validity

"Internal validity refers to the validity of assertions regarding the effects of the independent variable(s) on the dependent variable(s)" (Pedhazur & Schmelkin, 1991, p. 224). In other words, is the relationship between the independent variables and dependent variable a result of the independent variables or something else? Obviously, the researcher wants to make the case that the effect on the dependent variable is the result of the influence of the independent variable rather than a flaw in the study.

Internal validity can be improved using a variety of methods. First, certain types of study designs that allow greater control can be used. Second, controls within the research procedures can be used. These are discussed in this section.

A traditional discussion of internal validity usually begins with the stated threats to internal validity, including history, maturation, testing, instrumentation, regression toward the mean, selection, and mortality (Pedhazur & Schmelkin, 1991), only some of which are related to survey designs. Many of these are related to longitudinal designs only. A brief explanation of each of these follows.

- *History* refers to an event that occurs during the study that could affect its outcome, such as a disaster in one of the states in which the study is conducted.
- "*Mortality* refers to attrition of people or other units in the course of the study" (Pedhazur & Schmelkin, 1991, p. 227), such as when respondents drop out of the study.

- *Maturation* refers to changes in respondents that may occur naturally over time. Longitudinal studies are most prone to issues of maturation.
- *Testing* refers to any part of the testing process that may affect the study's outcome. For example, the process of being repeatedly tested on a given measure may affect its outcome.
- *Instrumentation* refers to aspects of the measure itself that may contribute to its outcome, such as a measure that is not culturally sensitive.
- *Regression toward the mean* may occur in a group that has extremely high scores on a given construct (e.g., depression) being measured. The natural inclination, even without treatment, is for improvement to be noted (i.e., for the group to regress toward the mean of a normal population).

Because these issues have the potential to affect the outcome of the study, they can be interpreted as alternative explanations to the hypothesis in question.

The researcher should address all issues of internal validity before the inception of the research. When issues such as maturation and regression toward the mean are expected because of the nature of the study, researchers should have additional methods of ruling out these alternative explanations. Only when researchers can rule out all threats to internal validity can a sufficient case be made that the independent variables are true and significant predictors of the dependent variable. In summary, a properly specified study will use a research design that best answers the research question while using necessary controls to rule out alternative explanations. One way to provide greater controls in a survey is to use a comparison group. For example, if a researcher is interested in following an evangelical religious group over time, a comparison group of other Christian denominations could be used. If the same trend is found across the two groups, the researcher would not be able to make the case that the evangelical Christian group uniquely responded to the variable in question.

External Validity: Sampling Issues

Sampling is the method by which the sample is drawn from a larger population. Two methods—random and nonrandom sampling—exist. The most rigorous method by far, but also the most difficult to obtain, is random sampling.[1] In this type of sampling, every person in the population has an equal chance of being selected (Pedhazur & Schmelkin, 1991). Its advantage lies in the study's ability to generalize from its findings. If a sample is randomly drawn from a larger population, it can then be assumed to be representative, within a calculated margin of error, of the population from which it is drawn. Because it is representative of the larger population, findings can then be generalized to that population within that calculated margin of error, thus increasing the importance of the study. However, the random sampling must be successful, meaning that it is sufficiently large that its findings can be generalized to the larger population and that the method actually did result in a sample that adequately represented the population.

Nonrandom sampling, on the other hand, is sampling of convenience. Because the representativeness of the sample to the larger population cannot be determined, generalizing the findings to the larger population is not appropriate (Pedhazur & Schmelkin, 1991). This section reviews issues that arise in sampling.

Generalizability

The primary goal of sampling procedures is to use a sample that is representative of the larger population so that findings can be generalized to that population. Studies of religiosity, spirituality, and discrimination are best drawn from national populations if possible. Unless the respondents sampled are representative of the larger community, be it a city, state, or nation, the study limits itself because inferences cannot be made beyond the scope of the study sample. Furthermore, any sampling biases will necessarily limit the generalizability of the study. Indeed, only findings from studies using randomly drawn samples can be generalized, and even then the findings can be generalized only to the limits of the sample. For example, studies examining students in a particular school of social work or specific community or state cannot be generalized to other schools, states, or the nation.

Without the ability to generalize to the larger population from which the study is drawn, the replication of findings from nonrandom studies becomes extremely important. If a certain finding is replicated across several studies representing diverse populations, credibility is lent to the finding. Replication of findings is best found in reviews of the literature, including systematic reviews and meta-analyses. The problem with this approach is that it takes time to build such a foundation of knowledge.

Response Rate

Even when samples are randomly drawn, an important issue is the response rate. Specifically, of the individuals contacted, how many actually consent to participate in the study? Lower response rates bring into question the representativeness of the sample. Another concern is how the response rate is defined. Researchers report response rates in different manners and sometimes report more than one response rate based on different methods of calculation. When response rates are low, researchers usually compare demographics of the sample with those of the population as a whole. Significant differences between the drawn sample and population suggest that the sample is not representative of the larger population and that generalization must be done cautiously, if at all. To correct for this problem, researchers sometimes weight the data so that they better reflect the larger population.

For example, to generalize findings to the 9,834 MSW students with a listed phone number in NASW, Hodge (2006a) attempted to randomly survey 352 social work students, 86% of whom agreed to participate. To generalize findings to the 451 social work students with a listed phone number in the National Association of Christian Social Workers (NACSW), Hodge attempted to randomly sample 95 students, 93% of whom agreed to participate. Final sample sizes were 303 for MSW students in NASW and 88 for students in NACSW. The next section discusses whether this sample size is sufficient for generalizing these findings to the larger populations.

Sample Size and Issues of Power

Another concern when drawing a sample is the size of the sample needed to have sufficient power. When a study has sufficient power, it has a large enough sample size, given other constraints, to "detect relationships when they are, in fact, present in the population" (Briere, 1992, p. 201). Although the size of the sample as a whole must be sufficient to test overall hypotheses, it is as important that the sample size of the smallest group also be large enough (Wilson VanVoorhis & Morgan, 2007). For example, a study comparing religious beliefs by denominational groups must have sufficient numbers within each group for findings from these denominational groups to be representative of those in the larger population. Other problems such as unreliable measures, measures without adequate sensitivity, or unsuitable statistical analyses may also affect the power of a study (Briere, 1992). When studies do not have sufficient power, meaningful findings may not reach significance. Because they are not significant, the possibility that they were a result of chance cannot be eliminated.

This remains an issue in research in social work on religious ideology. Although Hodge's work using surveys is some of the best work in this literature base, problems remain. Hodge used two primary random surveys (2002a, 2002b, 2006a) to make inferences to social workers and their intersecting religious beliefs. The first is the GSS, a nationally drawn representative sample of the population of the United States. The population size of this very rigorous survey varies slightly from year to year, but it tends to have about 38,000 respondents. Hodge (2002a, 2002b) used it to compare the views and characteristics of social workers with those of the general population. His hypotheses tended to indicate that social workers would share a perspective closer to those of liberal religious groups than to those of conservative religious groups and working- or middle-class people. However, his sample size was about 65 for baccalaureate social workers and about 32 for graduate social workers, with slight variations by analysis and study. Even when the groups were combined, there was a maximum of only 145 social workers. These he frequently compared with participants grouped by socioeconomic status, which often had 8,000 to 15,000 people in each group. Because of the large number of total respondents, even small differences were often significant. However, effect sizes, that is, the strength or magnitude of the relationship between the two variables under investigation, were often small, and confidence intervals were wide.

Confidence intervals are sensitive to sample size. As sample size increases, confidence intervals narrow and estimates become more precise. Therefore, we are more confident of GSS survey findings for the 16,568 respondents in the working class than we are of findings for the 15 to 145 social work respondents used across Hodge's different studies (2002b, 2003a, 2003b, 2004). Therefore, we would expect confidence intervals for the working class to be narrower and to give more precise estimates than confidence intervals for the social workers. Additional analysis indicates that this is the case.

Table 1 shows confidence intervals computed from Hodge's Table 4 (2002b), which concluded that social workers differed significantly from people in the lower-, working-, and middle-class populations on religious items. What is immediately clear is that confidence intervals are much larger, and therefore far less precise, for social workers than for people in any of the socioeconomic classes. For example, based on these findings, with a 99% level of confidence, we can state that 54% ± 20.8% (or a range of 33.2% to 74.8%) of graduate social workers in the United States believe in life after death. Conversely, 72% ± 0.9% in the middle class and working class and 67% ± 2.8% in the lower class believe in life after death. The differences in range of confidence intervals between the subsamples of social workers, the middle class, and the working class are striking. The same is true for the other questions shown in Table 1. Given the wide confidence intervals for social workers, only very imprecise statements about differences between groups can be made.

In the other set of studies using random sampling, social workers in master's programs belonging to NASW or NACSW were the participants (Hodge, 2006a, 2007a, 2007b). To test the hypothesis that students belonging to a religious affiliation report greater discrimination in social work education than those without a religious affiliation, students were divided into those belonging to a religious affiliation and those not belonging to a religious affiliation. Those NASW members not belonging to a religious affiliation scored experiences they perceived as discrimination as a 2.4 on an 11-point scale (with higher scores reflecting greater perceived discrimination), as compared with those belonging to a religious affiliation, who scored perceived discrimination as a 2.2. This difference was not significant. The second hypothesis—that self-reported evangelical and theologically conservative Protestants report greater religious discrimination than self-reported theologically liberal and

Table 1. Confidence Intervals for Hodge's (2002b) Table 4, Views Regarding Life After Death, Prayer in Public Schools, Organized Religion, and the Bible

	Graduate Social Worker			Bachelor Social Worker			Lower Class		Working Class		Middle Class		Cramer's V
	%	*n*	±CI	%	*n*	±CI	%	±CI	%	±CI	%	±CI	
Life After Death													
Yes	54	21	20.8	66	41	15.5	67	2.8	72	0.9	72	0.9	.027
No	28	11	18.8	19	12	12.8	24	2.5	19	0.8	18	0.7	
Don't know	18	7	16.1	16	10	12.0	10	1.8	9	0.6	9	0.6	
Prayer in Schools													
Approve	56[a]	22	21.0	61	26	19.4	32[a]	2.8	35	1.0	42	1.0	.058
Disapprove	39	15	20.7	35	15	19.0	65	2.8	61	1.0	55	1.0	
Don't know	3	1	5.1	5.1	2	6.8	4	1.2	4	0.4	3	0.3	
Confidence in Organized Religion													
A great deal	8[b]	3	9.7	14[c]	10	10.6	28[bc]	2.7	28[bc]	0.9	30[bc]	0.9	.032
Only some	64	25	20.1	68	49	14.3	44	3.0	48	1.0	49	1.0	
Hardly any	23	9	17.6	17	12	11.5	23	2.5	20	0.8	18	0.7	
Don't know	5	2	7.1	1	1	2.0	6	1.4	4	0.4	3	0.3	
View of the Bible													
Word of God	10[d]	3	12.2	16[e]	6	15.5	51[de]	3.0	38[de]	1.0	27[d]	0.9	.080
Inspired	53	16	23.9	45	17	21.1	32	2.8	47	1.0	53	1.0	
Book of fables	38	11	23.2	40	15	20.7	14	2.1	13	0.7	18	0.7	

Note. All relationships were significant at $p < .001$. The superscripts indicate significant differences between social work students and those in different socioeconomic classes. Confidence intervals were computed for a confidence level of .99 using the sample size calculator at http://www.nss.gov.au/nss/home.NSF/pages/Sample+size+calculator?OpenDocument.

mainline Protestants—was tested for NASW Protestant students and NACSW Protestant students. In both cases, the findings were significant, with evangelical Protestant students scoring significantly higher on perceived discrimination than mainline or theologically liberal members.

From these findings Hodge (2006a) concluded, "Educational programs may not be fostering a learning context that engenders respect for evangelical Christians, and possibly other traditional believers" (p. 259). He recommended changes such as practitioners becoming more familiar with evangelical worldviews, editors soliciting "content from underrepresented traditions," educators ensuring that voices of evangelical Protestants and "other underrepresented faith groups" be represented in course outlines, and administrators considering a candidate's "ability to represent and interpret underrepresented faith groups" when hiring faculty (Hodge, 2007a, p. 61).

Again Hodge did an admirable job of using a random sample, this time of MSW students belonging to NASW or NACSW. Regrettably, however, neither of the sample sizes was sufficient to generalize well to the larger population of MSW students belonging to NASW or NACSW. Analyzing subsamples of only the Protestant MSW students belonging to NASW (n=102) and to NACSW (n=77) simply compounded the problem (Hodge, 2007a). Therefore, the studies using the samples of NACSW and NASW students had the same problem that the GSS studies had—difficulties in generalizing, with great loss of precision, from the findings in the study to the population of NASW and NACSW MSW students. There were simply too few respondents in each group (e.g., four theologically conservative NASW students), and the confidence intervals were too wide, to be able to make meaningful interpretations to the larger population of NACSW and NASW student members. Therefore, although it can be said that these students reported discrimination, until more research with larger sample sizes is conducted, it is difficult to state with any precision that this problem exists in social work practice or education. Furthermore, because a definition of discrimination was not provided to respondents, it can only be said that these students *perceived* discrimination based on their own ideas of what discrimination was. Therefore, inferences drawn from these studies are premature.

Summary

In summary, sampling issues may have a great impact on the ability to generalize findings. The most rigorous method is to use random sampling, which then allows the findings to be generalized to the population from which the sample was drawn. Making inferences beyond the stated population is not indicated. Even then, however, concerns about response rate, sample size, and size of the smallest group may interfere with generalizations that can be made.

Statistical Conclusion Validity: Analytic Issues

Statistical conclusion validity is the validity of inferences made based on the statistical analyses used. To make appropriate inferences, the correct analyses, given the independent and dependent variables, must be used; the assumptions of the analyses must not be violated; and the method must be used properly.

One of the primary issues with statistical conclusion validity in these groups of studies is how the effect size was computed in the GSS. Across studies using the GSS (Hodge, 2002b, 2003a, 2003b, 2004), Hodge used either crosstabs with Cramer's *V* or ANOVA with differences in means as the effect size to assess differences between group membership.[2] Cramer's *V* is a statistical measure of effect size that takes into account sample and group sizes. It ranges from –1.0 to +1.0 and is interpreted somewhat like a correlation, with ±1.0 indicating a perfect relationship between variables and 0.0 indicating no relationship. In Table 1, Cramer's *V* ranges from .027 to .080, indicating very weak relationships, approaching zero, between socioeconomic classes and social worker groups. These extremely small effect sizes, coupled with extremely wide confidence intervals, suggest that the relationships in Table 1 are too small to be meaningful, even if significant. The problem of extremely large confidence intervals and extremely small effect sizes persists in most of Hodge's studies in which the GSS survey was used to capture differences between social workers and the general public.

Summary and Conclusions

The purpose of this chapter was to explicate methodological issues that affect the eventual interpretation of a study's findings. This chapter was intended to leave the reader with the sober recognition that a simple reading of studies is not possible or desirable. There have been only a few studies on religiosity and political views of social workers and how they compare with other groups. It is of utmost importance that the reader consider the methods before interpreting the findings. White and Farmer (1992) state, "Research methods have the potential for shaping one's view of reality" (p. 45). This statement is an exceptionally important point for the reader of literature on social work, religiosity, and claims of discrimination. Research methods profoundly affect these results, and the results shape our view of religion in social work.

The implications for both researchers and readers of the literature are clear. Researchers have an ethical imperative to advance the knowledge base using only the most rigorous methods possible. Study limitations that do exist, and their potential effects on the inferences, must be clearly stated. Readers have an ethical imperative to analyze the literature they read. Taking any study at face value may have important negative consequences for the individuals and families with whom the professional works.

Certain articles reviewed in this chapter put forward the hypothesis that social workers nationwide do not hold values and moral standards similar to those in mainstream America and that they hold significant biases against Christian evangelicals (Hodge, 2002a, 2002b). This chapter reviewed studies that examined the religiosity or political ideology of social workers as compared with the general public. A review of the methods of the studies assessing these hypotheses suggests that it is too early to make that case.

The strikingly small number of social workers in the GSS and in the studies of students in NASW and NACSW (Hodge, 2006a, 2007a, 2007b) suggests that these findings cannot be generalized with any level of confidence or precision to the larger populations of social workers nationwide or of either NASW or NACSW Protestant students. Because of the central interest in these populations, it was essential that the sample sizes for the different groups of Protestant students be large enough for the confidence intervals to be sufficiently narrow. Even if the sample size had been sufficient, however, reliability and validity of certain measures appeared to be weak or lacking, and respondents were not provided with a definition of *discrimination* to reference. The lack of definitions for central constructs was also apparent in studies attempting to determine whether social work discriminates against its conservative religious students (Ressler & Hodge, 2000, 2005). The lack of a definition of discrimination and extremely small sample sizes make it almost impossible to understand the extent and severity of this problem, or even determine whether there is a problem. Thus, the significant methodological limitations in these studies, even when using random samples, require that assertions about the worldviews of social workers nationwide, their religious sensitivity, and potential discrimination against evangelical Christians in social work and social work education be tempered.

A final methodological concern is making conclusions or inferences from data that do not support them. The social work profession is accused of "excluding contradictory narratives" to ensure "that its version of the truth will prevail" (Hodge, 2002a, p. 406) and of superseding its ethical imperatives "by its ideologically inspired drive to control the parameters of . . . debate by excluding divergent views" (p. 406). Hodge calls for social work to acknowledge its oppression of evangelicals both in education and in texts, actively recruit evangelical students and faculty for social work education, provide a climate of support for these social work faculty and students, and increase social work's exposure to conservative believers. However, the methodological limitations of these studies, primarily the sample sizes that are too small to allow generalizations with any accuracy to the larger populations—cannot support such implications. Future research must address the methodological limitations in these studies while attending carefully to conceptual clarity, methodological rigor, and constraint in drawing inferences.

References

American Psychological Association. (1985). *Standards for educational and psychological testing.* Washington, DC: Author.

Association of Religion Data Archives. (2013, July 13). *American denominations: Profiles.* Retrieved from http://www.thearda.com/Denoms/families/index.asp

Briere, J. (1992). Methodological issues in the study of sexual abuse effects. *Journal of Consulting and Clinical Psychology, 60*(2), 196–203. doi:10.1037/0022-006X.60.2.196

Cook, T. D., & Campbell, D. T. (1976). The design and conduct of quasi-experiments and true experiments in field settings. In *Handbook of industrial and organizational psychology* (pp. 223–325). Chicago, IL: Rand McNally.

Djupe, P. A., & Olson, L. R. (Eds.). (2003). *Encyclopedia of American religion & politics* (pp. 134–135). Infobase Publishing. Retrieved from http://books.google.com/ook?id=frt7RDOT1PUC&pg=PA135&lpg=PA135&dq=barrett+1980+denominationalism&source=bl&ots=7hA6UTxCc6&sig=6gHIf_c2QjR7dO_hNbZMyfkYrH4&hl=en&sa=X&ei=boHhUcCL_io4AOkrICABA&ved=0CHMQ6AEwCQ#v =onepage&q=barrett%201980%20denominationalism&f=false

Hackett, C., & Lindsay, D. M. (2008). Measuring evangelicalism: Consequences of different operational strategies. *Journal for the Scientific Study of Religion, 47*(3), 499–514. doi:10.1111/j.1468-5906.2008.00423.x

Harrison, D. (2005). Letter to the editor. *Social Work, 50*(4), 373–374.

Hodge, D. R. (2002a). Does social work oppress evangelical Christians? A new class analysis of society and social work. *Social Work, 47*(4), 401–414. doi: 10.1093/sw/47.4.401

Hodge, D. R. (2002b). Equally devout, but do they speak the same language? Comparing the religious beliefs and practices of social workers and the general public. *Families in Society, 83*(5/6), 573–584. Retrieved from http://dx.doi.org/10.1606/1044-3894.56

Hodge, D. R. (2003a). Differences in worldviews between social workers and people of faith. *Families in Society, 84,* 285–295. doi:10.1606/1044-3894.97

Hodge, D. (2003b). Value differences between social workers and members of the working and middle classes. *Social Work, 48,* 107–119. doi:10.1093/sw/48.1.107

Hodge, D. (2004). Who we are, where we come from, and some of our perceptions: Comparison of social workers and the general population. *Social Work, 49,* 261–268. doi:10.1093/sw/49.2.261

Hodge, D. (2005). Epistemological frameworks, homosexuality, and religion: How people of faith understand the intersection between homosexuality and religion. *Social Work, 50,* 207–218. doi:10.1093/sw/50.3.207

Hodge, D. R. (2006a). Moving toward a more inclusive educational environment? A multi-sample exploration of religious discrimination as seen through the eyes of students from various faith traditions. *Journal of Social Work Education, 42,* 249–267. doi:10.5175/JSWE.2006.200400455

Hodge, D. R. (2006b). Moving toward spiritual competency: Deconstructing spiritual stereotypes and spiritual prejudices in social work literature. *Journal of Social Work Research, 32*(4), 211–232.

Hodge, D. (2007a). Progressing toward inclusion? Exploring the state of religious diversity. *Social Work Research, 31,* 55–63. Retrieved from http://dx.doi.org/10.1093/swr/31.1.55

Hodge, D. (2007b). Religious discrimination and ethical compliance: Exploring perceptions among a professionally affiliated sample of graduate students. *Journal of Spirituality in Social Work, 26*(2), 91–113. doi:10.1300/J377v26n02_05

Hunter, J. D. (1983). *American evangelicalism: Conservative religion and the quandary of modernity.* New Brunswick, NJ: Rutgers University Press.

Hunter, J. D. (1991). *Culture wars.* New York, NY: Basic Books.

Melendez, M., & LaSala, M. (2006). Who's oppressing whom? Homosexuality, Christianity, and social work. *Social Work, 5,* 371–377. doi:10.1093/sw/51.4.371

National Association of Social Workers (NASW). (2011). Code of ethics. Retrieved from http://www.sp2.upenn.edu/docs/resources/nasw_of_ethics.pdf

Pedhazur, E. J., & Schmelkin, L. P. (1991). *Measurement, design, and analysis: An integrated approach.* Hillsdale, NJ: Erlbaum.

Ressler, L. E. (2002). When social work and Christianity conflict. In B. Hugen & T. L. Scales (Eds.), *Christianity and social work: Readings on the integration of Christian faith and social work practice* (2nd ed., pp. 93–117). Botsford, CT: North American Association of Christians in Social Work.

Ressler, L., & Hodge, D. (2000). Religious discrimination in social work: An international survey of Christian social workers. *Social Work and Christianity, 27*(1), 49–70.

Ressler, L., & Hodge, D. (2005). Religious discrimination in social work: Preliminary evidence. *Journal of Religion & Spirituality in Social Work, 24*(4), 55–74. doi:10.1300/J377v24n04_05

Rosenthal, J. A. (1996). Qualitative descriptors of strength of association and effect size. *Journal of Social Service Research, 21*(4), 37–59. doi:10.1300/J079v21n04_02

Shernoff, M. (2005). Letter to the editor. *Social Work, 50,* 373.

Smith, T. W. (1986). *Classifying Protestant denominations.* (GSS Methodological Report No. 43). Chicago, IL: University of Chicago, National Opinion Research Corporation.

Smith, T. W. (1990). Classifying Protestant denominations. *Review of Religious Research, 31*(3), 225–245. doi:10.2307/3511614

Steensland, B., Park, J. Z., Regnerus, M. D., Robinson, L. D., Wilcox, W. B., & Woodberry, R. D. (2000). The measure of American religion: Toward improving the state of the art. *Social Forces,* 79(1), 291–318. doi:10.1093/sf/79.1.291

Sullins, D. P. (2004). An organizational classification of Protestant denominations. *Review of Religious Research, 45*(3), 278–292. doi:10.2307/3512265

Todd, S., & Coholic, D. (2007). Christian fundamentalism and anti-oppressive social work pedagogy. *Journal of Teaching in Social Work, 27*(3/4), 5–25. doi:10.1300/J067v27n03_02

White, J. W., & Farmer, R. (1992). Research methods: How they shape views of sexual violence. *Journal of Social Issues, 48*(1), 45–59. doi:10.1111/j.1540-4560.1992.tb01156.x

Wilson VanVoorhis, C. R., & Morgan, B. L. (2007). Understanding power and rules of thumb for determining sample size. *Tutorials in Quantitative Methods for Psychology, 3*(2), 43–50.

Notes

1 Random sampling, which applies to survey designs, is different from random assignment to groups, which applies to experimental designs.

2 Hodge (2003a) reported another method of determining effect size. This method assumes that a 10-percentile difference between groups is substantive (e.g., if 60% of voters are female and 40% are male, there is a 20-percentile difference). This method does not take into consideration the small sample size for social workers and relies on an assumption that a difference of 10 percentage points between groups is, indeed, substantive. Rosenthal (1996) challenged this assumption, stating that this method might be helpful for laypersons but does not have mathematical properties that allow it to be interpreted exactly. Therefore, we use Cramer's *V* in this chapter to discuss effect sizes.

CHAPTER 9

Freedom of Religion: A Right to Discriminate?

Jay Kaplan, JD

Despite the incredible strides that have been made for lesbian, gay, bisexual, and transgender (LGBT) equality, such as the recent Supreme Court ruling against the Defense of Marriage Act and LGBT-inclusive antidiscrimination laws (Oosting, 2013; Transgender Law and Policy Institute, 2013),[1] opponents remain resistant to the concept that LGBT people should be treated equally under the law. With increasing frequency we are seeing both individuals and institutions claiming a right to discriminate based on religious objections (American Civil Liberties Union, 2013). The discrimination can take many forms, including graduate students planning to be social workers who refuse to counsel gay people; doctors refusing to provide in vitro fertilization services to lesbian women; or bridal salons, photo studios, and reception halls closing their doors to same-sex couples planning their weddings. Although the situations may differ, one thing remains the same: Religion is being used as an excuse to discriminate against and harm others.

Instances of institutions and individuals claiming a right to discriminate in the name of religion are not new. In the 1960s we saw institutions object to laws requiring integration in restaurants because of the owners' beliefs that God wanted the races to be separate. We saw religiously affiliated universities refuse to admit students who engaged in interracial dating (American Civil Liberties Union, 2013). In those cases, both the courts and we as a society recognized that requiring integration was not about violating religious liberty, it was about ensuring fairness. Religious freedom in America means that we all have a right to our religious beliefs, but this does not give us the right to use our religion to discriminate against and impose those beliefs on others who do not share them. And yet we continue to hear the drumbeat of opponents of LGBT rights who claim that having to treat LGBT people fairly under the law undermines their sincerely held religious beliefs (SB 514, 2014). This is reflected in both recent litigation and proposed legislation in Michigan. This chapter provides an overview of recent attempts to use religion to undermine laws and policies that ensure that LGBT people will be treated fairly.

Challenge to Federal Hate Crimes Law

In 2009 Congress passed and President Obama signed into law the Matthew Shepard and James Byrd Jr. Hate Crimes Prevention Act. The statute authorizes federal penalties for cases in which a person

> willfully causes bodily injury to any person or through the use of fire, a firearm, a dangerous weapon, or an explosive or incendiary device, attempts to cause bodily injury to any person, because of the actual or perceived religion, national origin, gender, sexual orientation, gender identity or disability of any person

adding to a list of categories included in previously existing federal hate crime laws (actual or perceived race, color, religion, or national origin). The language of the statute reiterates several times that Congress does not intend to restrict anybody's First Amendment rights, including freedom of speech or the free exercise of religion, focusing on action causing bodily injuries, not on speech.

In February 2010 Gary Glenn, president of the American Family Association of Michigan, joined by three religious ministers as co-plaintiffs, filed a lawsuit in federal court claiming that the law violates their First Amendment right to publicly express their opposition to gay people and the "homosexual agenda" (*Glenn v. Holder*, 2010, 726). They argued that the statute was unconstitutionally vague on "what it means for an offender to cause bodily injury 'because of' the sexual orientation or gender identity of the victim," that the law improperly "criminalizes their constitutional right to express their opinion that homosexual orientation is wrong," and that it "would chill like-minded people from free association" (*Glenn v. Holder,* 728). They also alleged that it "penalizes their religious beliefs about homosexuals and their behavior" (*Glenn v. Holder,* 728).

Judge Ludington concluded that the case should be dismissed, due to lack of standing (*Glenn v. Holder,* 2010, 741). The plaintiffs failed to allege that they had engaged or in the future would engage in behavior that would subject them to prosecution under the statute. (They had not stated any intent to seek out gay people to physically attack and cause bodily injuries.) Their actual fear was that their antigay statements on the airways and in the pulpits might subject them to investigation and possible prosecution if it could somehow be linked with inciting physical attacks on gay people. The plaintiffs even argued that "bodily injury" could include "headaches and stomach aches," which could subject them to prosecution. However, the Justice Department in defending the statute argued that the plaintiffs' conduct (speaking out and against gay people) would not subject them to prosecution (*Glenn v. Holder,* 735). Because there was no credible threat of prosecution, Judge Ludington found the plaintiffs' claim that the law would "chill" their exercise of freedom of speech to be bogus.

Plaintiffs then appealed to the 6th Circuit Court of Appeals, which upheld the district court decision, finding once again that the plaintiffs had failed to allege an intention to violate the act or to facilitate others' violation of the act, through their words. Furthermore, the plaintiffs had failed to demonstrate how publicly denouncing homosexuality would subject them to prosecution (*Glenn v. Holder,* 2012). Plaintiffs then petitioned for certiorari (requesting the U.S. Supreme Court to hear their appeal), which was then denied on March 18, 2013 (*Glenn v. Holder,* 2013).

Julea Ward and Eastern Michigan University

Julea Ward was admitted to the Eastern Michigan University (EMU) graduate program in counseling in 2006, seeking a degree that would enable her to work as a high school counselor. The program includes class work and a clinical practicum where faculty supervise graduate students in counseling actual clients. The curriculum requires that all students comply with the American Counseling Association (ACA) Code of Ethics and the American School Counselor Association's Ethical Standards for School Counselors. Both of these ethical codes prohibit discrimination based on sexual orientation. The accreditation rules for graduate counseling programs require that these ethical codes be incorporated into the program (*Ward v. Wilbanks,* 2010).

As part of her class work, Ward submitted written papers indicating that she could not personally condone homosexuality and that standard texts suggest that counselors who have personal problems dealing with particular topics or clients might refer clients to other counselors (Dial, 2011; Pines, 2011). Ward earned A's in all of her courses, but when she began her practicum, she was presented with a gay client and immediately requested that the client be referred to someone else, because her religious beliefs prevented her from condoning homosexuality in any way, and the gay client was seeking counseling for depression caused by problems in his gay relationship (*Ward v. Wilbanks,* 2010, 3026429).

The faculty expressed concern that Ward could not meet the core curriculum requirement of being able to separate personal views from the needs of clients and that Ward was seeking to exclude an entire class of clients covered by the nondiscrimination policy. The school suggested that Ward participate in a remediation program to help her overcome her resistance to provide nondiscriminatory counseling. She refused and was dismissed from the program (*Ward v. Wilbanks,* 2010, 3026430).

Ward contacted the Alliance Defense Fund (ADF), a conservative legal advocacy organization, which filed a complaint on her behalf in federal court for the Eastern District of Michigan. ADF's complaint alleged that EMU violated Ward's First and Fourteenth Amendment rights to religious freedom and equal protection by singling her out for persecution because of her religious beliefs. The complaint further stated that professional counseling norms permit counselors to refer clients when they are unable to provide appropriate service (*Ward v. Wilbanks,* 2010, 3026434).

District Judge George Caram Steeh sided with EMU, finding that the university had established curriculum requirements that must be followed to meet accreditation standards and that courts have traditionally deferred to educational institutions on curricular matters as long as those curricular standards apply to everyone and are not intended to discriminate on the basis of religion

(*Ward v. Wilbanks*, 2010, 3026442). Steeh found no violation of Ward's First Amendment speech or religious freedom (*Ward v. Wilbanks*, 3026445). She was free to believe what she wanted, but if she wanted to complete EMU's program, which she voluntarily chose to apply to and enroll in, to receive certification to be a high school counselor, she had to comply with the Code of Ethics to deal with a wide range of students who would be seeking her services. Ward was aware that EMU incorporated professional ethical codes in its program and required students to counsel clients without imposing their personal values. This was a core curriculum value of the counseling program. The court found that the requirement to render nonjudgmental counseling services was facially neutral (not aimed at any religion or religious belief) and was justified by the university's legitimate pedagogical concerns. A university can require that students attain skills to provide counseling to all clients, and under the counseling profession's ethical code students may not expect to be certified as counselors when they insist on referring out all clients from a particular protected class (American Counseling Association [ACA], 2005).

Many Christian conservatives decried the federal district court decision, and as a result of this decision legislation was introduced in the Michigan House and Senate that would permit students to "assert conscientious objections" based on moral or religious convictions to providing counseling services and would prohibit punitive actions by colleges against the students for raising those conscientious objections (Senate Bill 0518 of 2011 and House Bill 5040 of 2011). Despite the fact that such legislation could result in the loss of accreditation from the ACA for public universities offering counseling programs, the legislation (supported by Michigan's attorney general Bill Schuette) passed the State House. It did not receive a committee vote in the Senate during the 2011–2012 session.

At the same time, Ward appealed the district court ruling and a unanimous panel of the U.S. 6th Circuit Court of Appeals reversed, holding that the court should not have granted summary judgment in favor of EMU. Circuit Judge Jeffrey Sutton wrote for the 6th Circuit panel that a reasonable jury could conclude, based on the initial record, that Ward was discriminatorily expelled because of her religious beliefs (*Ward v. Wilbanks*, 2012).

The court distinguished the facts in this case from the decision in the federal case of Jennifer Keeton,[2] in which Keeton, a student in Augusta State University's graduate counseling program, had stated that she would try to persuade gay clients to abandon the "gay lifestyle" and refer gay clients for conversion therapy. Ward had stated that she would request that a gay client be assigned to a different counselor so that she would not be in a position to provide counseling that would affirm gay relationships. The court pointed out that both the ACA ethical code and expert testimony supported the proposition that professional counselors whose strongly held beliefs might clash with those of clients can and should refer clients to other counselors (*Ward v. Wilbanks,* 2012, 737).

EMU claimed that the required practicum had a no-referral policy, students were obliged to deal with any client, and that students had to be able to comply with professional standards of rendering nonjudgmental counseling services. However, the court found conflicting evidence as to whether the school actually had such a policy, and in light of the ACA code, which permits professionals to make "value-based" referrals in such circumstances, the court remanded the case back to the district court (*Ward v. Wilbanks,* 2012, 738). The court noted that it was not ruling on the merits of the case, just on whether it was appropriate for the trial judge to grant summary judgment when the record consisted solely of affidavits and depositions and there had been no actual hearing (*Ward v. Wilbanks,* 742).

Subsequent to the 6th Circuit decision, in December 2012 EMU reached a settlement with Ward, paying her $75,000 to resolve the case. EMU vice president for communications Walter Kraft stated that EMU decided to resolve the litigation rather than spend money on a costly trial. Ward's counsel from the ADF, Jeremy Tedesco, stated, "Ward's constitutionally protected rights had been vindicated" (Stafford, 2012).[3]

The Glowackis and Howell Public Schools

The Centers for Disease Control and Prevention (CDC) recognizes school bullying as a public health problem. The CDC explains that "bullying can result in physical injury, social and emotional distress … death … [and] increased risk for poor school adjustment" (CDC, 2012). In addition, "victims and witnesses of bullying can experience mental health problems ... [and] are much less likely to succeed at school or go on to higher education" (CDC, 2012). The CDC has also found that bullying "is bad for the victim, the perpetrator, and even witnesses" (Mental Health America, 2013).

Despite this awareness, bullying in public schools remains prevalent. According to the Department of Justice, almost 30% of students aged 12 to 18 were bullied during the 2008–09 school year (National Center for Education Statistics, 2012). Bullying affects Michigan students as well, with more than 34,000 reported cases of bullying in state public schools during the 2010–11 school year (Higgins, 2012). Bullying may be a heightened risk in cities such as Howell, where there has been a history of discrimination. In 2004, for example, Howell High's Diversity Club hung a rainbow flag, often used as a gay pride symbol, intending it to serve as a symbol of general diversity. This resulted in a furor in which there were "rumors about people wanting to bring in paint balls and fire them at the flag" (Koehn, 2004).

The CDC has also recognized that LGBT youth are more likely than their heterosexual peers to experience violence, including behaviors such as teasing, harassment, and physical assault (CDC, 2013; see also Stopbullying.gov). According to a recent biannual survey with 8,584 student respondents from all 50 states, bullying directed at LGBT students had a damaging effect on their educational opportunities: "LGBT students who reported higher severities of victimization because of their sexual orientation or gender expression were twice as likely as other students to report that they did not plan to pursue post-secondary education" (Kosciw, Greytak, Bartkiewicz, Boesen, & Palmer, 2011, p. 40). The survey also indicated that "students were about three times as likely to have missed school in the past month if they had experienced higher severities of victimization related to their sexual orientation . . . or how they expressed their gender" (Kosciw et al., 2011, p. 40).

In light of data showing that LGBT students face a particularly high risk of educationally disruptive bullying, the CDC (2013) concludes that it is important for schools to recognize that exposure to violence can have harmful effects on the education and health of LGBT youth. The CDC recommends that schools "implement clear policies, procedures, and activities designed to prevent violence" and work to reduce bullying. Indeed, the Gay, Lesbian and Straight Education Network has found that "25.8% of students in schools with comprehensive policies ... always reported incidents of victimization, compared to 13.8% or fewer of students in schools with partially enumerated policies, generic policies, or no policies" (Kosciw et al., 2011, p. 69). Research also found that staff in schools with comprehensive policies were more likely to "intervene when hearing homophobic remarks ... or negative remarks about gender expression" (Kosciw et al., 2011, p. 69).

As demonstrated earlier, empirical studies show that bullying can dramatically interfere with the education of students, particularly LGBT students. That disruption can consist of a "decline in students' test scores [or] an upsurge in truancy" (*Nuxoll ex rel. v. Indian Prairie Sch. Dist.,* 2008, 674). Research also shows that antibullying policies play an important role in counteracting this type of disruption for all students. Public schools have a constitutional obligation to provide all students with a safe environment to learn while protecting students' right to free speech, including the right to participate in discussions of conflicting ideas. Public schools may issue and enforce policies that regulate bullying and harassment in the school environment while bearing in mind that students do not "shed their constitutional rights to freedom of speech or expression at the schoolhouse gate" (*Tinker v. Des Moines Independent County School District,* 1969, 506).

An incident occurred in Howell Public Schools in November 2010 when, as part of School Spirit Day, teacher Jay McDowell led a discussion about bullying against LGBT students. During this classroom discussion, student Daniel Glowacki expressed the belief that he did not support LGBT rights and thought homosexuality was wrong. Glowacki was asked to leave the classroom. When his parents protested that Glowacki's First Amendment rights had been violated, the school district reprimanded McDowell and suspended him for 1 day without pay, ordering him to participate in First Amendment training for violating the actual Howell policy and to apologize to the student and his family. After McDowell filed a grievance, the school district reduced the sanctions and replaced the initial reprimand with a tamer one. The replacement stated, "You are receiving a written reprimand after an investigation into an incident that occurred in your classroom substantiated that you displayed a serious lack of professionalism when you slammed your door, raised your voice and attempted to discipline students for their beliefs. These actions were in violation of District policies and guidelines" (*Glowacki v. Howell Public School District,* 2013, 3148280).

The family then sued the school district over this incident. The Thomas More Law Center, a conservative legal think tank, represented the family. In addition to challenging McDowell's action, the lawsuit alleged that the Howell School District's antibullying policy, by protecting all students from mistreatment, including LGBT students or students who are perceived to be LGBT, violates the religious freedom of the Glowacki children (Daniel Glowacki and his younger brother), who believe that homosexuality is wrong. As in the challenge to the federal Hate Crimes Act, the plaintiffs did not allege that their children intended to bully LGBT students, nor did they indicate how the actual Howell policy would prohibit them from expressing their opinions about homosexuality.[4]

On June 19, 2013, Judge Patrick Duggan issued an Opinion and Order granting summary judgment for the Howell School District against Glowacki, holding that Howell's antibullying policies, which permit the restriction of speech when it pertains to bullying (including the bullying of LGBT students), did not violate the First Amendment rights of the Glowacki children: "Well-crafted anti-bullying policies are constitutionally permissible when they focus on preventing either substantial disruption of school activities or interference with the rights of other students" (*Glowacki v. Howell,* 2013, 3148298). The court found that Howell's antibullying policy, which specifically provides that "this policy is not intended to and should not be interpreted to interfere with the legitimate free speech rights of any individual," did not chill the First Amendment rights of Daniel Glowacki's younger brother to express his religious beliefs about homosexuality. Furthermore, the school district's antibullying policy itself caused no constitutional injury to Daniel Glowacki. By the time this case was decided, Daniel Glowacki had graduated from the Howell School District. However, his younger brother was still a student at the high school. The court found that McDowell's actions in having Daniel Glowacki leave his classroom for stating, "I don't accept gays," was in violation of Daniel's First Amendment rights and awarded Glowacki nominal damages in the amount of $1.00, to be paid by McDowell.

As a result of the Howell controversy and before the filing of the lawsuit, the Michigan legislature took up the issue of passing a law that would require all public school districts to have antibullying policies. Michigan was one of the few remaining states without a comprehensive antibullying law, and a version of the legislation passed out of the Republican-controlled state senate would exempt students from the antibullying policy for "a sincerely held religious belief or moral conviction (SB 514, 2013)." The passage of this language engendered so much controversy and condemnation nationwide that the legislature eventually removed this exemption (Levesque, 2011).

In Michigan we continue to see efforts to create a religious or moral exception to complying with civil rights laws and antidiscrimination policies. Recently the Michigan Senate Health and Policy Committee passed legislation that would allow health care providers to use a "moral objection" or "matter of conscience" standard to refuse to provide services to patients, even if such refusal could endanger the health of the patient and would violate civil rights laws. The current legislation would allow employers and health insurance providers to decline offering other services and medications as well (*USA Today*, 2013). Michigan lawmakers have also introduced legislation that would allow adoption agencies that receive state monies to refuse to place children in homes based on moral and religious convictions, regardless of whether such placement would be in the best interest of the child (Queerty, 2013).

Conclusion

What is most disturbing about the use of religion to discriminate against LGBT people is that these exemptions are being requested for nonreligious activities. Individuals, organizations, and programs are requesting exemptions for nonreligious activities in which they have voluntarily chosen to participate, activities that are often subject to various regulations, laws, and policies. Do we create exemptions for professional standards of medical care, academic standards, and civil rights laws because of individual religious beliefs, and if we do so, will the efficacy of these standards and legal protections against discrimination remain? Fortunately, as reflected by these case decisions, federal courts have served as a safeguard against attempts to erode nondiscrimination and antibullying policies by thoughtfully and accurately applying First Amendment free speech analysis to these constitutional challenges. These decisions can provide guidance to both policy makers and educational institutions in their efforts to ensure fair treatment of LGBT people while acknowledging and protecting the legitimate free speech rights of others who may not support LGBT rights. It is a delicate balance, but we have more than 200 years of jurisprudence and case law precedent that sets forth the parameters regarding the right to have religious beliefs and the right not be discriminated against. Make no mistake, religious liberty is very important and guarantees us the freedom to hold any belief we choose and the right to act on our religious beliefs, but it does allow us to harm or discriminate against others, particularly when we engage in nonreligious activities. As our courts have stated, religious liberty is not a license to use religion to discriminate.

References

American Civil Liberties Union. (2013). Using religion to discriminate. Retrieved from http://www.aclu.org/using-religion-discriminate

American Counseling Association (ACA). (2005). ACA code of ethics. Retrieved from http://www.counseling.org/Resources/aca-code-of-ethics.pdf

Centers for Disease Control and Prevention (CDC). (2012). Understanding bullying fact sheet. Retrieved from http://www.cdc.gov/ViolencePrevention/pdf/BullyingFactsheet2012-a.pdf

Centers for Disease Control and Prevention (CDC). (2013). Lesbian, gay, bisexual and transgender health. Retrieved from http://www.cdc.gov/lgbthealth/youth.htm

Dial, K. (2011). Michigan seeks to protect counselors' rights. Retrieved from http://www.citizenlink.com/2011/10/11/michigan-seeks-to-protect-counselors'-rights/

Glenn v. Holder, 738 F. Supp. 2d 718 (E.D. Mich. 2010).

Glenn v. Holder, 690 F. 3d 417 (6th Cir. 2012).

Glenn v. Holder, 2013 WL 1091774 (U.S. March 18, 2013).

Glowacki v. Howell Public School District, 2013 WL 3148272 (E.D. Mich. June 19, 2013).

Higgins, L. (2012, June 4). Michigan schools face deadline to adopt anti-bullying policies. Retrieved from http://www.freep.com/article/20120604/NEWS05/206040333/Schools-facing-a-deadline-to-adopt-a-bullying-policy

Koehn, S. (2004, December 23). (Rainbow) Flag stirs flap at Howell High. *Ann Arbor News*. Retrieved from http://www.freerepublic.com/focus/f-news/1307475/posts

Kosciw, J., Greytak, E., Bartkiewicz, M., Boesen, M., & Palmer, N. (2011). *The 2011 National School Climate Survey: The experiences of lesbian, gay, bisexual and transgender youth in our nation's schools*. Retrieved from http://www.glsen.org/sites/default/files/2011%20National%20School%20Climate%20Survey%20Full%20Report.pdf

Levesque, B. (2011). Critics blast anti-bullying law for allowing exceptions based on religion, moral beliefs. Retrieved from http://www.lgbtqnation.com/2011/11/critics-blast-anti-bullying-law-for-allowing-exceptions-based-on-religion-moral-beliefs/

Matthew Shepard and James Byrd Jr. Hate Crimes Prevention Act, 18 U.S.C. § 249 *et seq*. (2009).

Mental Health America. (2013). Bullying and what to do about it. Retrieved from http://www.mentalhealthamerica.net/go/bullying

National Center for Education Statistics. *Student victimization in U.S. schools: Results from the 2009 School Crime Supplement to the National Crime Victimization Survey*. Retrieved from http://nces.ed.gov/pubs2012/2012314.pdf

Nuxoll ex rel. v. Indian Prairie Sch. Dist. #204, 523 F. 3d 668 (7th Cir. 2008).

Oosting, J. (2013). Poll: Majority of Michigan voters support gay marriage, anti-discrimination protections. Retrieved from http://www.mlive.com/news/index.ssf/2013/05/poll_majority_of_michigan_vote.html

Pines, J. (2011). Julea Ward Freedom of Conscience Act, like Michigan's amended anti-bullying bill, should not become law. Retrieved from http://www.mlive.com/opinion/kalamazoo/index.ssf/2011/11/julea_ward_freedom_of_conscien.html

Queerty. (2013). MI bill condoning anti-gay adoption discrimination passes committee. Retrieved from http://www.queerty.com/mi-bill-condoning-anti-gay-adoption-discrimination-passes-committee-20121205/#ixzz2XkjLazZP

Stafford, K. (2012). EMU resolves case of Julea Ward, former student kicked out of program for declining to counsel gay client. Retrieved from http://www.annarbor.com/news/ypsilanti/emu-resolves-case-of-julea-ward-former-student-kicked-out-of-program-for-declining-to-counsel-gay-cl/

Tinker v. Des Moines Independent County School District, 393 U.S. 503 (1969).

Transgender Law and Policy Institute. (2013). Retrieved from http://www.transgenderlaw.org/resources/

USA Today. (2013, March 22). Mich. panel OKs "moral objections" health care bill. Retrieved from http://www.usatoday.com/story/news/nation/2013/03/22/michigan-bill-health-care-providers-deny-services-moral-objections/2009539/

Ward v. Wilbanks, 2010 WL 3026428 (E.D. Mich., July 26, 2010).

Ward v. Wilbanks, 667 F. 3d 727 (6th Cir. 2012).

Notes

1 A May 2013 poll by the Glengariff Group found that 56.8% of Michigan residents support the right of same-sex couples to marry and that 54% would repeal Michigan's constitutional ban on same-sex couples marrying and replace it with an amendment to permit gay couples to marry. Furthermore, at least 90% of Michigan voters favor some legal protections for LGBT people, and at least 65% favor changes to laws to allow for civil unions, inheritance rights, adoption, domestic partner benefits, and hate crime protections.

2 Ward's case is in fact very similar to the facts in *Keeton v. Augusta State University,* 773 F. Supp. 2d 1368 (S.D. Ga. 2010), 664 F. 3d 865 (C.A. 11 Ga. 2011). Jennifer Keeton, a student in the university's graduate counseling program, stated that as part of the clinical practicum she would counsel gay clients that homosexuality was wrong (in accordance with her religious beliefs) and that as a high school counselor, she intended to convert students from being homosexual to heterosexual. If she was unable to help a client change his or her behavior, she would then refer him or her to someone practicing conversion behavior. School officials requested that Keeton participate in a remediation plan in order to comply with the standards of the ACA (which accredits Augusta's program) to render nonjudgmental counseling services in order to remain in the program. She refused to do so and filed an action in federal court, alleging that the requirement that she participate in a remediation program violated her First Amendment free speech and free exercise of her religious beliefs. She also requested that the court enjoin the university from dismissing her from the program for failure to participate in a remediation program. The District Court for the Southern District of Georgia denied her request, and the Eleventh Circuit Court of Appeals affirmed that the requirement that she complete a remediation plan in order to participate in the university's clinical counseling practicum did not violate her First Amendment free speech or free exercise rights, for the same reasons articulated in the Ward District Court opinion.

3 Before both the *Ward* and *Keeton* cases, in 2005 Emily Brooker, a social work student at Missouri State University, represented by the conservative advocacy organization the Alliance Defense Fund, sued the university alleging discrimination for her religious beliefs. Brooker claimed that she received a poor grade from her instructor because she refused to participate in a class project supporting the right of gay couples to adopt children. Brooker maintained that such a position violated her Christian beliefs. She was enrolled in a course that had a syllabus that included advocacy in social work. The university settled the lawsuit out of court in 2006, so there is no published case decision or adjudication on Ms. Brooker's allegations. According to an article in the *Washington Post* (March 2007, Alan Cooperman) both the university (Professor Kauffman) and Brooker "insist they were misunderstood." In response to this lawsuit, in April 2007 the Missouri House of Representatives passed the Emily Brooker Intellectual Diversity Act, which has the stated purpose of protecting students from "viewpoint discrimination." The bill would require universities to provide information to the state about the steps they take to ensure the free exchange of ideas in the classroom. The bill did not become law.

4 The Howell policy expressly protects the nondisruptive expression of unpopular opinions. Section 2240 of the Howell administrative guidelines reinforces that "the consideration of controversial issues has a legitimate place in the instructional program of the schools" (*HPSD Administrative Guidelines* § 2240, 2012).

CHAPTER 10

Ethical Issues and Challenges: Managing Moral Dilemmas

Frederic G. Reamer, PhD

In 2005 Frank Kauffman was teaching a course in social work at Missouri State University when he gave his class an assignment concerning adoptions by same-sex couples. Emily Brooker, then a junior majoring in social work, objected that the assignment violated her Christian beliefs. Eventually Brooker was brought before a faculty panel on a charge of discriminating against gays. Brooker sued the university in federal court, claiming she was retaliated against because she refused to support gay adoption as part of a class project. The lawsuit, filed on Brooker's behalf by the Alliance Defense Fund, a Christian legal group, claimed the retaliation against her Christian beliefs violated her First Amendment right to free speech. The lawsuit named the members of the university's Board of Governors, the university president, and four faculty or administrators of the School of Social Work (Cooperman, 2007).

On November 8, 2006, the university settled out of court and agreed to pay Ms. Brooker a sum of $9,000, waive academic fees totaling another $12,000, clear her academic record, and remove her professor from his administrative duties and the classroom. After this settlement, the Missouri State University president commissioned a panel of outside educators to conduct a thorough review of the social work education program. The reviewers' final report, based on extensive meetings with faculty, professional staff, students, alumni, agency field instructors, employers, adjunct faculty, and community representatives, was scathing (Sowers & Patchner, 2007):

> Many students and faculty stated a fear of voicing differing opinions from the instructor or colleague. This was particularly true regarding spiritual and religious matters however, students voiced fears about questioning faculty regarding assignments or expectations. In fact "bullying" was used by both students and faculty to characterize specific faculty. It appears that faculty have no history of intellectual discussion/debate. Rather, differing opinions are taken personally and often result in inappropriate discourse.
>
> Neither of the reviewers have ever witnessed such a negative, hostile and mean work environment. Persons in administrative roles are held in contempt by the faculty; faculty colleagues are disrespectful to one another, and some faculty are disrespectful and demeaning toward students. The consequence is a dysfunctional and hostile work and learning environment.

The troubling Brooker saga is among the best known in social work education regarding management of situations in which social work students question faculty members' teaching approaches, including the complex intersection between pedagogy and students' Christian beliefs. This case raises broad questions about the ethical contours surrounding social work educators' efforts to achieve reasonable balance between social work values, students' rights, and faculty members' academic freedom and teaching approaches, particularly when students' beliefs clash with widely embraced social work values and curriculum content.

Social Work Values

Social work's time-honored ethical traditions and framework clearly embrace the notion that different cultural and social views be handled with respect. Diversity in social work is celebrated, not simply tolerated. The National Association of Social Workers (NASW) Code of Ethics states explicitly that social workers are obligated to learn about and appreciate various forms of cultural and social difference, including sexual orientation and gender identity or expression: "Social workers should obtain education about and seek to understand the nature of social diversity and oppression with respect to race, ethnicity, national origin, color, sex, sexual orientation, gender identity or expression, age, marital status, political belief, religion, immigration status, and mental or physical disability" (Standard 1.05[c]). Thus, it is incumbent on social work educators to explore these issues in the classroom and enhance students' understanding of them by addressing them with intellectual rigor and respectful dialogue. Some students may hold religious beliefs that lead them to be uncomfortable with discussions of sexual orientation and gender identity or expression, and faculty members have a duty to be sensitive to this discomfort. That said, the NASW Code of Ethics clearly supports faculty members' right and duty to broach these issues in the classroom.

The NASW code also prohibits students (and all other social workers) from discriminating against people based on their sexual orientation, gender identity, or gender expression.

> Social workers should not practice, condone, facilitate, or collaborate with any form of discrimination on the basis of race, ethnicity, national origin, color, sex, sexual orientation, gender identity or expression, age, marital status, political belief, religion, immigration status, or mental or physical disability. (Standard 4.02)

Although faculty members have a right and duty to introduce sexual orientation and related diversity issues in the classroom, they do not have a right to impose their personal beliefs on students or require students to engage in activities that violate students' religious beliefs. And here is where the ethical issues become notoriously murky. As Shakespeare says in *Hamlet,* "There's the rub."

Student Free Speech Rights

Students arrive in social work professors' classrooms with wide-ranging beliefs spanning the religious and political spectrum. Some students are politically radical, liberal, moderate, or conservative. Some embrace Christianity, Islam, Buddhism, Hinduism, Judaism, Wicca, or Baha'i, among other faith traditions, and others are atheists or agnostics. Seasoned faculty members expect to hear students' wide-ranging opinions on controversial issues such as immigration reform, abortion, welfare, and sexual orientation. In the United States, students' opinions are protected by free speech rights embodied in the First Amendment of the U.S. Constitution: "Congress shall make no law . . . abridging the freedom of speech."

Daunting challenges arise when students' expressed opinions clash with deeply and widely held social work values (Canda, 2003; Danesi, 2003; Dessel, Bolen, & Shepardson, 2011; Hodge, 2002, 2003, 2004, 2007; Kaufman, 2003; Liechty, 2003; Melendez & LaSala, 2006; Reamer, 2003a). For example, in a widely publicized case, Jacqueline Escobar, an MSW student enrolled at California State University–Long Beach, expressed her faith-based opinions to colleagues during her internship at a public child and family services agency (Price, 2007). Escobar's field placement was terminated because her supervisors believed that she violated ethical standards by failing to separate her personal beliefs from her duties as a social work intern. Escobar's federal lawsuit against the university and field placement agency, in which she claimed that her free speech rights were violated, was unsuccessful. This case clearly showed that there are limits to social workers' free speech rights when they interfere with an employer's mission and duty to assist clients. That is, social workers have a First Amendment right to their personal opinions and beliefs, even when they clash with social work values; however, this right is limited when social workers share these personal opinions and beliefs in the workplace in a way that compromises an employer's ability to carry out its duty to assist clients.

The social work educators in the Escobar case prevailed in part because their behavior in responding educationally to the student was beyond reproach. They extended to the student numerous evenhanded opportunities to accommodate her views and express herself appropriately. In addition, when issues emerged in the Escobar case involving the student's faith-based conduct, the field instructor and school faculty were careful and conscientious with regard to raising these issues in supervision, acquainting the student with NASW Code of Ethics standards, obtaining consultation about how to handle the ethical issues, providing the student with multiple opportunities to change her behavior and conform to school and NASW guidelines, and documenting each step. This is a model of how faculty members should handle these challenges. In these respects, the

Escobar case is in marked contrast to the Brooker case. The different legal outcomes in the two cases resulted in part from the different ways in which the faculty responded. In Escobar, the faculty members' response conformed to guidelines in the NASW Code of Ethics. In the Brooker case they did not.

Academic Freedom

Along with complex issues pertaining to core social work values and social workers' free speech rights, one must also consider prevailing standards concerning academic freedom. In principle, social work educators are free to design and deliver their courses as they see fit. Problems arise when other parties believe that aspects of an instructor's course violate standards in the profession or discipline.

Academic freedom in the United States was formally acknowledged in 1915 when the American Association of University Professors issued its Declaration of Principles on Academic Freedom and Academic Tenure. John Dewey, the first president of the association, had appointed a committee of scholars to draft the declaration, which fundamentally changed conceptions of the nature of the relationship of faculty members from "servants" of the institutional master to independent agents who were autonomous purveyors of knowledge. As O'Neil and colleagues (2009) note,

> The Declaration observed that the functions of the university were to advance the sum of knowledge, to promote inquiry, to provide instruction to students—not to give them "ready-made conclusions" but to "train them to think for themselves"—and to develop experts fit for public service. This required not only disciplinary expertise, gained by years of study and academic apprenticeship, but also independence from regental or administrative control in teaching, research, and publication, save for assurance of adherence to professional standards of care. Where that assurance was questioned, the determination of professional neglect or incompetence, of any departure from professional standards of care, should be placed in the hands of the faculty as the body competent to decide such questions.

Thus, academic freedom is not synonymous with free speech. Faculty members are free to teach as they wish "save for assurance of adherence to professional standards of care." This is a critically important qualification. As O'Neill and colleagues (2009) assert,

> so long as the teacher or researcher has acted in accordance with the applicable standard of professional care, what is taught or endorsed cannot be held to institutional account no matter the resulting disharmony or contentiousness arising from within the institution or instigated by external groups.

The Concept of Standard of Care

Thus, the concept of standard of care is essential to a constructively critical analysis of social work educators' instruction and management of students who have difficulty reconciling their religious beliefs with social work values and course assignments. In any profession, the standard of care is determined by what ordinary, reasonable, and prudent practitioners with the same or similar training would have done under the same or similar circumstances (Johnson, 2011; Madden, 2003; Reamer, 2003b). The concept originated in English common law and is often called the "reasonable person" or "the man on the Clapham omnibus" test that is used when it is necessary to decide whether a party acted in a way that a reasonable person should. (In the 19th century, Clapham, a suburb in south London, was widely regarded as a typical or average community; "the man on the Clapham omnibus" refers to the typical person on a typical bus in a typical community.) The concept of reasonable person also pertains to judgments about how social work faculty members manage ethical challenges in the classroom.

In the United States the Maine Supreme Court introduced the concept of standard of care prominently in its 1896 ruling in the case of *Coombs v. Beede.* This case involved a fee dispute between an architect and his clients. The court ruled that the architect would be held to the standards associated with similarly situated architects:

> The responsibility resting on an architect is essentially the same as that which rests upon a lawyer to his client, or upon a physician to his patient, or which rests upon any one to another, where such person pretends to possess some skill and ability in some special employment, and offers his services to the public on account of his fitness to act in the line of business for which he may be employed.

Over time the notion of holding architects to the standard of ordinary, reasonable, and prudent colleagues was extended to all professions.

In the Missouri State University case, for example, outside experts concluded that the professor's and some of his colleagues' conduct and treatment of the student, Emily Brooker, fell outside standards of care in social work education. The way that faculty members responded to Brooker's objections arising out of her religious beliefs was not ordinary, reasonable, and prudent, in light of prevailing norms in social work and higher education.

Departures from a profession's standards of care, including those in higher education, may result from a practitioner's acts of commission or acts of omission (Johnson, 2011). Commission involves the performance of an action that causes harm. An example involves a social work educator who requires students to engage in activities, such as lobbying or letter writing, that violate the students' rights, without providing these students with reasonable alternatives. Omission involves the failure to perform a duty that one is required to perform. An example is an educator's failure to inform students that they are free to express their personal beliefs as long as they do so in a respectful manner that is consistent with the profession's ethical standards.

Social work educators encounter challenging ethical and related standard-of-care issues at several critically important junctures and settings in the educational stream: admissions, classroom discussions, school hallways and common spaces, faculty offices, and field placements.

Admissions

Social work education programs typically require applicants to submit personal statements as part of the application. Applicants are ordinarily asked to share their reasons for wanting a social work career. Consider the following personal statement excerpt:

> When I was seventeen my older brother committed suicide. We grew up in a devout Christian family that believes that homosexuality is a sin. My brother left a suicide note saying that he was tormented by the fact that he was gay and felt like a family outcast. I was the only one in our family he confided in regarding his homosexuality. I knew that he fought his feelings and wanted in the worst way to be heterosexual. My brother went to counseling, but that didn't seem to help.
>
> Two years ago, six years after my brother's death, I met a local counselor who helps gay and lesbian people become heterosexual. I truly believe that if my brother had seen a skilled counselor he would not have committed suicide. I am eager to assist people like my brother. I want to learn about the best way to help and counsel homosexuals who want to be heterosexual. My current goal is to work in a reparative therapy clinic.

Assuming this applicant met all other standard admission criteria (e.g., undergraduate grade point average, strong recommendations), would an admission committee be obligated to accept this applicant, or do the student's statements violate ethical standards in a way that would warrant rejection? Can an applicant who believes that same sex sexuality is sinful and aspires to be a reparative therapist be an ethical social worker?

The distinction between acts of commission and omission is relevant to this analysis. The applicant has the right to her faith-based beliefs about the sinfulness of same sex sexuality, no matter how unpopular such views may be in social work or elsewhere. However, any behavior that actively discriminates against people based on their sexual orientation, gender identity, or gender expression (acts of commission) violates the NASW Code of Ethics (Standard 4.02). Thus, a social worker who tells lesbian, gay, bisexual, or transgender clients that they are sinful, or treats them harshly, would be unethical.

In contrast, a social worker who believes that she or he cannot be helpful to gay, lesbian, bisexual, or transgender clients because of the social worker's religious beliefs could, in principle, refer such clients to colleagues for assistance. Not assisting these potential clients with a referral would constitute an act of omission. The practical implications of such refusal to treat would vary depending on the social worker's employment setting. A social worker in independent or private practice can decline to work with gay, lesbian, bisexual, or transgender people without adversely affecting colleagues directly. As long as another practitioner in the community is available to assist the potential client, there is no profound harm to colleagues, although there may be harm to the client who is referred. However, if the social worker is employed by a mental health or a family service agency, for example, this could undermine the agency's ability to serve its clients. The agency's resources may be such that it is not practical or feasible to refer clients in every instance when a particular social worker refuses to serve because of her or his religious beliefs. Furthermore, such refusal could harm clients who discover and disclose their gay, lesbian, bisexual, or transgender status after the start of the social worker–client relationship. Social workers who choose to terminate the relationship and refer the client in the midst of an ongoing professional–client relationship may harm clients. Clients whose social workers terminate the relationship unilaterally or against the clients' wishes may feel betrayed, judged, and discriminated against. Even if a referral is not made, the client may be harmed, as the client may sense the worker's negative countertransference.

Other ethical issues arise with regard to the applicant whose goal is to become a reparative therapist (also known in some circles as a gay conversion therapist). The NASW Code of Ethics requires social workers to draw on and apply research findings regarding the effectiveness of interventions, especially when well-established standards do not exist:

> When generally recognized standards do not exist with respect to an emerging area of practice, social workers should exercise careful judgment and take responsible steps (including appropriate education, research, training, consultation, and supervision) to ensure the competence of their work and to protect clients from harm. (Standard 1.04[c])

> Social workers should critically examine and keep current with emerging knowledge relevant to social work and fully use evaluation and research evidence in their professional practice. (Standard 5.02[c])

In this regard, reparative therapy is at best questionable and most certainly controversial, because there are no legitimate research data available to document that it is effective. Following their comprehensive review of research on the efficacy of reparative therapy, Hein and Matthews (2010) conclude that "to date, there is no conclusive evidence that reparative therapy is beneficial to patients" (p. 31). Social workers who use intervention approaches for which there is no empirical support violate ethical standards. Moreover, NASW has taken a strong formal position against the use of reparative therapy and took a leadership role in efforts to pass a California law that prohibits licensed mental health professionals from engaging in sexual orientation change efforts, including "reparative therapy," for minors (Pace, 2013).

Classroom Discussions

On occasion social work students make comments in class that are racist, homophobic, or otherwise insensitive.

> A first-year MSW student enrolled in a required human behavior course. A segment of the course focused on issues related to cultural and social diversity. During one class session the professor asked students to reflect on a time when they felt uncomfortable in the presence of someone who was "different." The professor did not define the term "different"; rather, she asked students to define the term however they wished and to share comments about how they felt in, and managed, those situations. Several students spoke about the first time they met people who were Muslim, Jewish, homeless, and severely disabled.
>
> One student spoke about the first time she met a transgender man, a coworker in a group home for teens who were abused or neglected. The student talked candidly and passionately about her strong "visceral reaction" to her colleague and how, as a Christian, she could not condone the steps

> her colleague took to change his gender identity and expression, including changing his clothing and grooming, adopting a new name, using hormone therapy treatment, and undergoing medical procedures that modified his body to conform to his gender identity. The student cited several passages from Scripture to support her claim that being transgender and taking assertive steps to change gender identity are morally abhorrent.

In these instances faculty members must make spontaneous decisions about whether and how to respond. Options include ignoring the comments; acknowledging them explicitly and inviting class members to respond, without the instructor expressing an opinion about the student's comments; acknowledging the student's comments explicitly and inviting class members to respond, along with the instructor expressing an opinion about the student's comments; and responding directly to the student's comments, which could include helping the student explore the implications of her beliefs and noting their incongruence with social work values. Classroom educators must be mindful of the safety of other students in the classroom, who may, for example, be transgender and hurt and marginalized by other students' comments.

Here, too, standards in the NASW Code of Ethics are relevant. As noted earlier, the code includes explicit standards prohibiting discrimination on the basis of sexual orientation, gender identity, or gender expression (Standard 4.02). In this respect, social work educators have a moral duty to acknowledge and discuss students' discriminatory comments and acquaint them with pertinent social work values and ethical standards. Of course, faculty members should do so constructively and respectfully.

In addition, the code also speaks to the ways in which social workers treat colleagues. The code prohibits a student from treating a colleague disrespectfully; the student's critical, disparaging, and judgmental statements about her coworker's gender identity and expression violated two of the code's mandates:

> Social workers should treat colleagues with respect. (Standard 2.01[a])

> Social workers should avoid unwarranted negative criticism of colleagues in communications ... with other professionals. Unwarranted negative criticism may include demeaning comments that refer to colleagues' ... sex, sexual orientation, gender identity or expression. (2.01[b])

Furthermore, a faculty member's failure to address the student's discriminatory comments—a prime example of an act of omission—would violate the standard in the NASW Code of Ethics that requires social workers to take steps to confront discrimination: "Social workers should act to prevent and eliminate domination of, exploitation of, and discrimination against any person, group, or class on the basis of ... sex, sexual orientation, gender identity or expression" (Standard 6.04[d]). Educators can treat such classroom discussions as teaching moments that include opportunities to explore various ways in which social workers can take steps to challenge discrimination both within and outside the social work profession. Such actions include designing and implementing prevention programs, staff development and continuing education, and policy and legislative advocacy.

Field Placements

Field placements provide students with opportunities to apply social work theories and concepts. In addition, field placements offer students real-life, as opposed to hypothetical, opportunities to adhere to ethical standards in social work and wrestle with any conflicts between students' personal or religious beliefs and social work values. On occasion students find that their faith-based beliefs clash with social work values in ways that interfere with their field placement duties.

> A senior BSW student had a field placement in a community mental health center that provides case management and therapeutic services to people with severe and persistent mental illness. The student served as a case manager for four clients. One of the student's clients, who was diagnosed with depression and cocaine addiction, told the student that after many years of denial, he was finally coming to terms with the fact that he is gay. The client

told the student that he believes that many of his lifelong struggles, including self-medicating with drugs, stem from his unwillingness to acknowledge his sexual orientation. The client told the student that "coming out" as gay felt quite liberating. The client asked the student for advice about how to find resources and support in the local gay community.

During a supervision session, the student told her supervisor that as a devout Christian, she was not comfortable helping this client embrace his homosexuality and find local resources and support in the gay community. The student explained that such activities would "violate church teachings and my conscience—I just can't do it." The field instructor explained that social workers have an obligation to work with all clients, regardless of the practitioner's personal beliefs and values. The field instructor raised issues concerning the student's counter-transference and "use of self." The student was relatively silent during the remainder of the supervision session. The following day, the field instructor contacted his social work department liaison at the student's college to discuss the predicament and how it might be handled.

Social workers' refusal to engage in activities that, they claim, violate their moral conscience raises complex legal and ethical issues. In recent years, various health care professionals, including physicians, nurses, and pharmacists, have asserted their right to refuse to perform services that violate their religious beliefs. For example, various states have enacted laws that permit pharmacists to refuse to dispense emergency contraception drugs, and other states have enacted laws that prohibit pharmacists from refusing to fill prescriptions solely on moral, religious, or ethical grounds (National Conference of State Legislatures, 2012). Clearly, legal guidelines are inconsistent and evolving.

In principle, the rationale behind such diverse legislative policies can be extended to social workers' use of so-called conscience clauses to refuse to serve particular clients on religious grounds. However, to date no legislature in the United States has enacted comparable laws pertaining to social workers. Thus, the social work profession must rely on prevailing ethical standards, which may treat "conscience clauses" differently than do the professions of medicine, nursing, and pharmacy because of social work's unique mission and value base.

On one hand, social workers have a duty to serve people in need, when feasible. Furthermore, social workers have a duty to not discriminate against people based on their sex, sexual orientation, and gender identity or expression. On the other hand, social workers also have an obligation to serve clients only when they believe they have the ability and expertise to meet those clients' needs. When social workers' religious beliefs conflict with clients' needs, social workers encounter a conflict of interests. The NASW Code of Ethics requires social workers to take reasonable steps to resolve such conflicts in a way that best meets clients' needs, including the possibility of service termination and referral. Such termination and referral must be handled in ways that convey deep respect for the client's difference.

> Social workers should be alert to and avoid conflicts of interest that interfere with the exercise of professional discretion and impartial judgment. Social workers should inform clients when a real or potential conflict of interest arises and take reasonable steps to resolve the issue in a manner that makes the clients' interests primary and protects clients' interests to the greatest extent possible. In some cases, protecting clients' interests may require termination of the professional relationship with proper referral of the client. (Standard 1.06[a])

> Social workers should terminate services to clients and professional relationships with them when such services ... no longer serve the clients' needs or interests. (Standard 1.16[a])

These standards suggest that a social work student who believes that working with a particular client would "interfere with the exercise" of the student's "impartial judgment" would be permitted to refuse to work with the client "with proper referral" (Standard 1.06[a]), particularly when working with the client would not "serve the clients' needs or interests" (Standard 1.16[a]). The student might argue that this course of action is in the client's best interests, given the student's religious beliefs: The client deserves assistance from a social worker who can wholeheartedly support the client's sexual orientation and gender identity choice. The NASW Code of Ethics requires social workers to refer clients to colleagues who can meet their needs: "Social workers should refer clients to other professionals when the other professionals' specialized knowledge or expertise is needed to serve clients fully" (Standard 2.06[a]).

It would be unethical for social work students to simply refuse to serve clients without proper referral. Failure to refer—an act of omission—would constitute client abandonment, which is also addressed in the NASW Code of Ethics:

> Social workers should take reasonable steps to avoid abandoning clients who are still in need of services. Social workers should withdraw services precipitously only under unusual circumstances, giving careful consideration to all factors in the situation and taking care to minimize possible adverse effects. Social workers should assist in making appropriate arrangements for continuation of services when necessary. (Standard 1.16[b])

Additional challenges arise when students express their faith-based opinions in ways that compromise and negatively affect their working relationships with colleagues. In the Escobar case in California, for example, colleagues in the child and family services agency at which the student was completing her field placement claimed that Escobar's faith-based comments made it difficult for them to engage in constructive working relationships with her, and this interfered with their ability to perform their professional duties (Price, 2007). Escobar's field instructor and university liaison claimed that her conduct violated ethical standards in the NASW Code of Ethics pertaining to management of her religious beliefs: "Social workers should not permit their private conduct to interfere with their ability to fulfill their professional responsibilities" (Standard 4.03). Thus, social workers must be cognizant of the critically important boundary between their right to their personal beliefs and their duty to manage their personal beliefs in the workplace in a manner that does not compromise their ability or their employer's ability to perform social work duties.

Managing Ethical Challenges

The ways in which social work students manage their religious beliefs with respect to sexual orientation, gender identity, and gender expression have important legal, as well as ethical, implications. Social work students who believe that social work faculty members, college administrators, and field instructors have violated their rights may seek legal remedies in courts of law, as occurred in the Brooker and Escobar cases. Some claims allege educational malpractice (Smith & Fleming, 2007). Disgruntled students may also file formal ethics complaints with licensing boards and professional associations (such as NASW) alleging professional misconduct.

Lawsuits and liability claims that allege malpractice are civil suits, in contrast to criminal proceedings. Ordinarily, civil suits are based on tort or contract law, with plaintiffs (the party bringing the lawsuit) seeking some sort of compensation for injuries they claim to have incurred as a result of the defendant's negligence. These injuries may be economic (e.g., the social work student claims that her graduation was delayed, and earnings diminished, because her field placement was unjustly terminated when she shared her faith-based beliefs with colleagues), physical (e.g., a social work student suffers injuries from a suicide attempt made after the student was expelled from school because she allegedly violated ethical standards), or emotional (e.g., a social work student claims that he became depressed when a faculty member admonished him in front of other students when the student shared his religious beliefs in class).

As in criminal trials, defendants in civil lawsuits (such as social work educators) are presumed to be innocent until proved otherwise. In ordinary civil suits, defendants will be found liable for their actions based on the legal standard of preponderance of the evidence, as opposed to the stricter standard of proof beyond a reasonable doubt used in criminal trials.

In general, malpractice occurs when evidence exists that (1) at the time of the alleged malpractice a legal duty existed between the social worker and the client (e.g., a social work professor or field instructor owes a duty to his or her student); (2) the social worker was derelict in that duty or breached the duty, by either commission or omission (e.g., the social work professor violated the student's rights by requiring the student to engage in activities that the student alleges violated her religious beliefs, or a field instructor improperly terminated a student's field placement because of the student's expression of faith-based opinions); (3) the student suffered some harm or injury (e.g., emotional harm or financial injury caused by delayed graduation and diminished employment prospects and earnings); and (4) the harm or injury was directly and proximately caused by the faculty member's or field instructor's dereliction or breach of duty. Social work education administrators (e.g., department chair, dean, university vice president for academic affairs) can also be sued under the legal doctrines of vicarious liability and *respondeat superior* (Latin: "let the master respond"); that is, even though university administrators did not have a direct relationship with the student, in principle they can be held responsible if their actions or inaction, in their administrative or supervisory roles, harmed the student (Standler, 2003).

In some cases, prevailing standards of care are easy to establish, through citations of the profession's literature, expert testimony, statutory or regulatory language, or relevant code of ethics standards. For example, standards of care in higher education clearly prohibit faculty members from harassing or berating students publicly because of students' religious beliefs. In other cases, however, it is difficult to establish clear, unequivocal standards of care, for example, concerning the appropriate way for faculty members to respond during class discussion when a student makes discriminatory comments related to sexual orientation or gender identity (Austin, Moline, & Williams, 1990; Haas & Malouf, 2005; Reamer, 2006a, 2006b). In these instances, thoughtful, principled, and reasonable faculty members may disagree about the best course of action.

Many social work membership associations throughout the world provide mechanisms for filing ethics complaints. In the United States, ethics complaints filed against NASW members are processed using a peer review model that includes NASW members and, initially, the National Ethics Committee (NASW, 2012). If a student files an ethics complaint against a faculty member and the request for professional review is accepted by the National Ethics Committee, a NASW Chapter Ethics Committee (or the National Ethics

Committee in special circumstances, for example, if there is a conflict of interest at the state level) conducts a hearing during which the complainant (the student filing the complaint), the respondent (the faculty member against whom the complaint is filed), and witnesses have an opportunity to testify. After hearing all parties and discussing the testimony, the committee presents a report to elected chapter officers that summarizes its findings and presents its recommendations. Recommendations may include sanctions (e.g., expulsion from NASW, suspension of NASW membership, notification of findings to a state licensing board and the respondent's malpractice insurer, letter of censure) or various forms of corrective action (e.g., mandated supervision, consultation, continuing education, or restitution; notification of the respondent's supervisor or employer; correction of a student's academic record). In some cases, the sanction may be publicized through local and national NASW publications.

NASW offers mediation in some instances in an effort to avoid formal adjudication and adversarial proceedings, particularly involving matters that do not include allegations of extreme misconduct. If complainants and respondents agree to mediate the dispute, NASW will facilitate the mediation.

Also, in some nations legislative bodies empower social work licensing boards and regulatory bodies to process ethics complaints filed against social workers. A disgruntled student can file a complaint against a faculty member or field instructor who is licensed. Ordinarily licensing boards appoint a panel of colleagues to review the complaint and, when warranted, conduct a formal investigation and hearing; some boards include public members in addition to professional colleagues.

In some jurisdictions formal hearings are conducted by the licensing board itself. In other jurisdictions formal hearings are conducted by administrative law judges. Typically, cases are brought against social workers by prosecuting attorneys representing the licensing body. Social workers are usually represented by legal counsel.

Licensing boards typically have authority to impose sanctions and various forms of corrective actions. Sanctions may include suspension or revocation of a license, a term of probation, and a letter of reprimand. Corrective action may include mandated supervision, consultation, continuing education, restitution, and notification of the respondent's supervisor or employer. Licensing boards may publicize findings on their formal websites or in prominent newspapers and professional publications.

Conclusion

Controversy surrounding the complex relationship between social work ethics and students' Christian beliefs pertaining to sexual orientation, gender identity, and gender expression poses a compelling paradox. Social workers are known for their deep-seated, passionate commitment to diversity and tolerance of difference. The profession's values, ethical principles, and standards are permeated with language that extolls the importance of diversity and tolerance. Yet social work educators sometimes encounter circumstances where this commitment is sorely challenged; true tolerance of some students' faith-based beliefs violates social work's venerable commitment to nondiscrimination and respectful behavior. And this, of course, constitutes an ethical dilemma.

Decades ago, social work educator Dale Hardman (1975) published a provocative and widely circulated essay about the limits of social workers' commitment to the sacred principle of self-determination, especially when honoring self-determination means violating social workers' and the profession's core values. Clearly, this challenge has not gone away, although over time it has assumed new forms, particularly concerning the complex relationship between social work professors', the social work profession's, and students' values and self-determination rights. And the overarching challenge is the same: In cases of conflict, social work educators must hold fast and firm to the profession's bottom-line commitment to social justice, nondiscrimination, and respect. Educators have a duty to respect students' right to form personal beliefs and engage in free speech; however, educators would abrogate their fundamental ethical duty to address and, when necessary, confront students' behavior that promotes injustice, discrimination, and disrespect. Students have a right to believe that certain forms of sexual orientation, gender identity, and gender expression are immoral. They do not have a right to discriminate against or disrespect clients based on these beliefs or to express themselves in the classroom in ways that violate other students or faculty. Students who are not comfortable with social work's values and commitment to diversity and nondiscrimination, particularly concerning sexual orientation, gender identity, and gender expression, are free to enroll in other professions' and disciplines' degree programs that offer more compatible moral and religious frameworks. This is not a matter of political indoctrination, as columnist George Will (2007) suggested when, in his prominent discussion of the Brooker case, he referred to the NASW Code of Ethics as a "code of coercion"; rather, it is a matter of ethics.

Social work educators must take assertive steps to ensure that applicants to social work education programs understand the profession's values, admit students who subscribe to the profession's values, and respond meaningfully when evidence arises that students are violating the profession's values. This is what it means to be an ethical social work educator.

References

Austin, K., Moline, M., & Williams, G. (1990). *Confronting malpractice: Legal and ethical dilemmas in psychotherapy.* Newbury Park, CA: SAGE.

Canda, E. (2003). Social work and evangelical Christians. *Social Work, 48,* 278–281.

Coombs v. Beede, 89 Maine Reports 188, 36 Atlantic Reporter 104 (1896).

Cooperman, A. (2007, May 5). Is there disdain for evangelicals in the classroom? *Washington Post.* Retrieved from http://www.washingtonpost.com/wp-dyn/content/article/2007/05/04/AR2007050401990.html?referrer=emailarticle

Danesi, R. (2003). Does social work oppress Christians? *Social Work, 48,* 273.

Dessel, A., Bolen, R., & Shepardson, C. (2011). Can religious expression and sexual orientation affirmation coexist in social work? A critique of Hodge's theoretical, theological, and conceptual frameworks. *Journal of Social Work Education, 47,* 213–234.

Haas, L., & Malouf, J. (2005). *Keeping up the good work: A practitioner's guide to mental health ethics* (4th ed.). Sarasota, FL: Professional Resources Press.

Hardman, D. (1975). Not with my daughter, you don't. *Social Work, 20,* 278–284.

Hein, L., & Matthews, A. (2010). Reparative therapy: The adolescent, the psych nurse, and the issues. *Journal of Child and Adolescent Psychiatric Nursing, 23,* 29–35.

Hodge, D. (2002). Does social work oppress evangelical Christians? A "new class" analysis of society and social work. *Social Work, 47,* 401–414.

Hodge, D. (2003). The challenge of spiritual diversity: Can social work facilitate an inclusive environment? *Families in Society, 84,* 348–358.

Hodge, D. (2004). Developing cultural competency with evangelical Christians. *Families in Society, 85,* 251–260.

Hodge, D. (2007). Progressing toward inclusion? Exploring the state of religious diversity. *Social Work Research, 31,* 55–63.

Johnson, V. (2011). *Legal malpractice in a nutshell.* St. Paul, MN: Thomson Reuters.

Kaufman, G. (2003). Does social work oppress Christians? *Social Work, 48,* 273.

Liechty, D. (2003). Oppressed evangelicals? *Social Work, 48,* 276–277.

Madden, R. G. (2003). *Essential law for social workers.* New York, NY: Columbia University Press.

Melendez, M., & LaSala, M. (2006). Who's oppressing whom? Homosexuality, Christianity, and social work. *Social Work, 5,* 371–377.

National Association of Social Workers (NASW), (2012). *NASW procedures for professional review* (5th ed.). Washington, DC: Author.

National Conference of State Legislatures. (2012, May). *Pharmacist conscience clauses: Laws and information.* Retrieved from http://www.ncsl.org/issues-research/health/pharmacist-conscience-clauses-laws-and-information.aspx

O'Neil, R., Areen, J., Finkin, M., Gerber, L., Van Alstyne, W., & Nelson, C. (2009). Protecting an independent faculty voice: Academic freedom after *Garcetti v. Ceballos. Academe,* 95(6). Retrieved from http://0-eb.ebscohost.com.helin.uri.edu/ehost/detail?sid=49579aa3-ba2a-4fbe-b755-0aa919c2ed10%40sessionmgr12&vid=15&hid=8&bdata=JnNpdGU9ZWhvc3QtbGl2ZQ%3d%3d#db=a9h&AN=45447259

Pace, P. (2013). Chapter helps to pass state law. *NASW News, 58,* 1, 11.

Price, C. (2007, March 28). Faith under fire: Christian woman fired for "sharing" God. *Digital Journal.* Retrieved from http://www.digitaljournal.com/print/article/151889

Reamer, F. (2003a). Social work, evangelical Christians, and values. *Social Work, 48,* 428–431.

Reamer, F. (2003b). *Social work malpractice and liability: Strategies for prevention* (2nd ed.). New York, NY: Columbia University Press.

Reamer, F. (2006a). *Ethical standards in social work: Review and commentary* (2nd ed.). Washington, DC: NASW Press.

Reamer, F. (2006b). *Social work values and ethics* (3rd ed.). New York, NY: Columbia University Press.

Smith, R., & Fleming, D. (2007). Educational malpractice? *Connection: New England Board of Higher Education, 21*(5), 22–23.

Sowers, K., & Patchner, M. (2007). *School of Social Work site visit report.* Retrieved from http://www.missouristate.edu/provost/socialwork.htm

Standler, R. (2003). Educational malpractice in the USA. Retrieved from http://www.rbs2.com/edumal2.pdf

Will, G. (2007, October 14). Code of coercion. *Washington Post.* Retrieved from http://www.washingtonpost.com/wp-dyn/content/article/2007/10/12/AR2007101202151.html

SECTION III

Transformation

CHAPTER 11

Is Homophobia a Conservative Christian Value?

Tanya Smith Brice, MSW, PhD

> *In a time when "strictness is out of favor," when leniency expressed in relativism, diversity and dialogue is the style of most major denominations, it comes as a shock to be told that faith must not be confused with good causes, that access to church membership must be made difficult, that violations of standards are not to be tolerated, and that accommodation to outsiders is not to be sought. It is in the elaboration of this point of view that the strength of this book lies.* Why Conservative Churches Are Growing *offers a challenge to church people to define those meanings for which they are willing to die.* (Bangs, 1972, p. 852)

This quote is from a review of Dean Kelley's seminal book, *Why Conservative Churches Are Growing* (1972). This book is a manifesto of conservative (also called fundamentalist or evangelical) Christian values in the context of declining church growth among the major Christian denominations. Kelley declares that a move toward conservative values, as summarized by Bangs' review, is the answer to declining church growth.

Although Kelley offers this delineation of conservative Christian values, the literature is unclear as to a definition of conservative Christianity. Scholars of religion generally agree that conservative Christians understand the Bible with a literal framework whose mysteries are accessible to all of its readers. On the other hand, liberal Christians understand the Bible with a contextual framework that requires a view of cultural relevance generally gained from rational study of the text (Bruce, 1983). These opposing views of how to understand the Bible lead to varying views of social issues as informed by the Bible.

When polled, Christian conservatives largely oppose same-sex relationships and marriage. Approximately 59% of conservative Christians report hearing messages from the pulpit that discourage same sex sexuality, compared with 13% of more liberal Protestants and 28% of Catholics. Furthermore, approximately 52% of conservative Christians report their belief that acceptance of same sex sexuality would be bad for our country. Approximately 65% of conservative Christians believe that same sex sexuality can be changed (Kohut, 2003). These findings were results of a Pew Forum survey more than a decade ago, but more recent surveys (Roach, 2012) find that these sentiments continue to hold true, although there is evidence of an increased acceptance of same-sex relationships among Christians (Grant & Bailey, 2012; Pew Research Forum on Religion and Public Life, 2013).

The discourse has moved from "generic homosexuality" to issues of same-sex marriage. In December 2012, the U.S. Supreme Court began reviewing court decisions related to the legality of same-sex marriage. Two of the most conservative Christian groups, White evangelical Protestants and African American Protestants, consistently show disapproval of same sex marriage. Among White conservative Christians, approximately 74% oppose allowing same-sex marriage. Among African American conservative Christians, approximately 62% oppose allowing same-sex marriage (Pew Research Forum, 2013). Figure 1 demonstrates how these two groups consistently report lower approval ratings than other Christian groups. They have remained so over the last decade.

Because conservative Christians use a literal approach to the Bible, their opposition to same sex sexuality is driven largely by literal interpretations of the following scriptures[1]:

- This is the story of the creation of the Earth by God. The emphasis in this narrative is of the creation of Adam (man) and Eve (woman) as procreators. (Genesis 1–2)
- Do not have sex with a man as one does with a woman. That is abhorrent. (Leviticus 18:22)
- If a man has sex with a man as one does with a woman, both of them have done what is abhorrent. They must be put to death; they are responsible for their own deaths. (Leviticus 20:13)

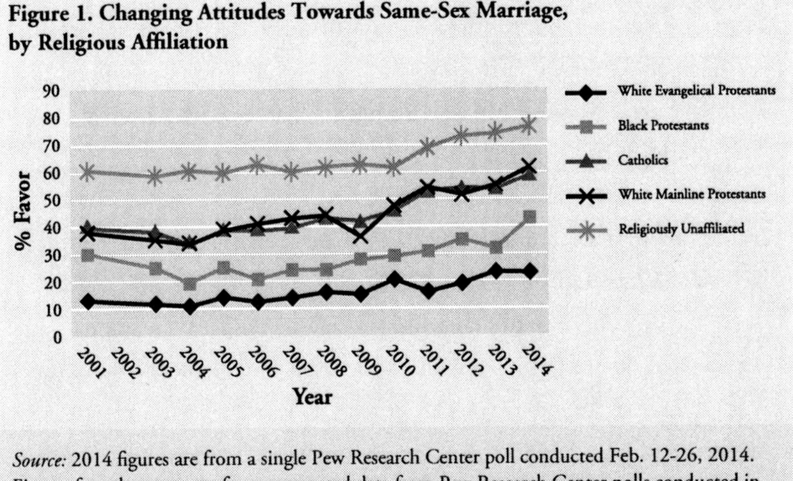

Figure 1. Changing Attitudes Towards Same-Sex Marriage, by Religious Affiliation

Source: 2014 figures are from a single Pew Research Center poll conducted Feb. 12-26, 2014. Figures for other years are from aggregated data from Pew Research Center polls conducted in each year. Question wording is available online (http://www.pewsocialtrends.org/files/2014/03/2014-03-07_generations-appendix-b-Topline-Questionnaire.pdf) (PDF), and information on the Pew Research Center's polling methodology can be found on the Pew website (http://www.pewsocialtrends.org/2014/03/07/millennials-in-adulthood/5/).

- Do you not realize that this is not the way to live? Unjust people who do not care about God will not be joining in his kingdom. Those who use and abuse each other, use and abuse sex, use and abuse the earth and everything in it, do not qualify as citizens in God's kingdom. A number of you know from experience what I'm talking about, for not so long ago you were on that list. Since then, you have been cleaned up and given a fresh start by Jesus, our Master, our Messiah, and by our God present in us, the Spirit. (I Corinthians 6:9–11)
- Worse followed. Refusing to know God, they soon did not know how to be human either—women did not know how to be women, men did not know how to be men. Sexually confused, they abused and defiled one another, women with women, men with men—all lust, no love. And then they paid for it, oh, how they paid for it—emptied of God and love, godless and loveless wretches. (Romans 1:26–27)
- It is true that moral guidance and counsel need to be given, but the way you say it and to whom you say it are as important as what you say. It

> is obvious, is it not, that the law code is not primarily for people who live responsibly, but for the irresponsible, who defy all authority, riding roughshod over God, life, sex, truth, whatever! They are contemptuous of this great Message I have been put in charge of by this great God. (I Timothy 1:10)

In addition to these scriptural references, there is a narrative of the destruction of the cities Sodom and Gomorrah (Genesis 19) as a result of same sex activity. Invoking the name of these two cities elicits a collective agreement among conservative Christians that same sex sexuality is detestable by God. The term *sodomy,* used as a synonym for same sex behavior, comes from the collective agreement, among conservative Christians, that Sodom was a city destroyed because of same sex behaviors. This association is so strong among conservative Christians that rarely are explanations for the destruction of Sodom and Gomorrah, such as those expressed in Ezekiel 16: 49–50, used in the discourse about same sex sexuality. This scripture states the reason for the destruction as follows:

> Now this was the sin of your sister Sodom: She and her daughters were arrogant, overfed and unconcerned; they did not help the poor and needy. They were haughty and did detestable things before me. Therefore I did away with them as you have seen.

According to this scripture, Sodom, and its counterpart, Gomorrah, were destroyed because of their arrogance, abundance of resources, and their unconcern for the poor. This selfish behavior led them to engage in detestable behaviors before God.

Tension Between Social Work and Conservative Christian Values

Studies have shown that conservative Christians view same sex sexuality as sinful behavior (Burdette, Ellison, & Hill, 2005; Fulton, Gorsuch, & Maynard, 1999; Green, 2000; Herman, 1997). The more frequently they attend church, the more intolerant conservative Christians are of same sex sexuality (Chonody,

Woodford, Smith, & Silverschanz, 2013; Petersen & Donnenworth, 1998; Sherkat & Ellison, 1997; Swank & Raiz, 2010). Social workers who identify as conservative Christians may find a conflict between their Christian values and social work values.

The literature highlights some tensions between conservative Christian values and the social work profession. For instance, the literature suggests that the higher the level of religiosity among graduate level social workers, the more likely they are to have perceived homophobic views (Berkman & Zinberg, 1997; Miller, 2007). This applied to those who identified as White evangelicals and African American Protestants.

Most notable is the work of David Hodge and Lawrence Ressler, as they describe this tension in the social work context. Both authors have concluded that conservative Christians experience discrimination in social work, and specifically in social work education (Ressler & Hodge, 2003, 2006; Ressler, 1998. They have found that conservative Christians experience job denial and loss, denial of tenure, denial of admission to graduate school, failing grades, and public ridicule. In addition, they have posited that conservative Christians are negatively portrayed in social work education, social work literature, and service provision (Canda & Hodge, 2003; Hodge, 2005a, 2005b, 2007).

Both authors have been cited extensively by scholars supporting the notion that conservative Christians are discriminated against in the social work context (Berkman & Zinberg, 1997; deRuyter, 2009). However, both Hodges and Ressler dichotomize Christianity as conservative Christians (or Orthodox Christians) and progressives, identified as everyone else. There is little attention to the possibility that there could be conservative Christians who do not hold homophobic views. Furthermore, there is little documented association between the perceived discriminatory actions and the identification as a Christian. There is little distinction made between those who receive pushback for opinions about social issues and those who are discriminated against because they are Christian. For instance, when a conservative Christian expresses homophobic opinions, and when their peers challenge that opinion, is the challenge because of the expressed view, or is it because the view is that of a conservative Christian?

On the other hand, there are those who identify as conservative Christians who do not hold homophobic views. Evangelicals for Social Action, led by Ron Sider, have declared a proposal for evangelicals and those with same-sex attraction (Sider, 2012). It is important to note that there is an admission that evangelical Christians struggle with the need to distinguish between a person with same-sex attraction and same-sex activity. Specifically, Sider writes, "There is nothing sinful in having a gay orientation where one is sexually attracted to a person of the same sex. Gay sexual practice, not gay orientation, is the important issue" (p. 56).

The author goes on to admit that evangelicals have earned the reputation as being homophobic by not condemning "the hateful fringe groups among us or opposed the abuse of the LGBT persons" (p. 56). Sider proposes that evangelical Christians overtly condemn verbal or physical abuse of those with same-sex attraction. Furthermore, evangelical congregations should become welcoming sanctuaries for lesbian, gay, and bisexual (LGB) people who are Christians. Specifically, Sider writes,

> We ought to develop model programs so that evangelical congregations are known as the best place in the world for gay and questioning youth (and adults) to seek God's will in a context that embraces, loves, and listens rather than shames, denounces, and excludes. Surely we can ask the Holy Spirit to show us how to teach and nurture biblical sexual practice without ignoring, marginalizing, and driving away from Christ those who struggle with biblical norms. (p. 56)

This group of evangelical Christians admits that they have not figured out how to reconcile their interpretation of biblical condemnation of same sex activities with the biblical mandate for love and social justice. However, they are attempting to take a step toward reconciliation of the two.

Conservative Christian Social Workers

Historically, conservative Christian values have been defined by politics, not theology, as is evidenced by the pro-slavery stances characteristic of Civil

War–era conservative Christians, the anti–civil rights stances of conservative Christians, and this group's contemporary homophobic stances (Noll, 2004). A social worker who identifies as being a conservative Christian might be tempted to state that his or her intolerance toward those who are homosexual is based on theology. However, it is possible that he or she is more influenced by politics than theology (Malka, Lelkes, Srivastava, Cohen, & Miller, 2012). Although a handful of scriptures (biblical mandates) seem to condemn homosexual behaviors, many more scriptures mandate that Christians pay "particular attention to the needs and empowerment of people who are vulnerable [and] oppressed" (National Association of Social Workers [NASW], 2008).

Social workers who identify as conservative Christians may struggle with providing services to a client who is homosexual. However, as professional social workers, we are guided by a Code of Ethics developed by the NASW. Is there a conflict between the social work code of ethics and biblical mandates? The preamble to the NASW Code of Ethics reads,

> The primary mission of the social work profession is to enhance human well-being and help meet basic human needs of all people, with particular attention to the needs and empowerment of people who are vulnerable, oppressed, and living in poverty. A historic and defining feature of social work is the profession's focus on individual well-being in a social context and the well-being of society. Fundamental to social work is attention to the environmental forces that create, contribute to, and address problems in living. Social workers promote social justice and social change with and on behalf of clients. (NASW, 2008, p. 1)

As a declaration of the beginning of his earthly ministry, Jesus declared the following:

> God's spirit is on me; he's chosen me to preach the Message of good news to the poor, sent me to announce pardon to prisoners and recovery of sight to the blind, to set the burdened and battered free, to announce, "This is God's year to act!" (Luke 4:16–18, The Message, 2002)

In some translations of this text, the words "burdened and battered" are written as "oppressed." There is a biblical mandate "to set the burdened and battered (oppressed) free." Those who identify as LGB are often burdened, battered, and oppressed. Furthermore, another scripture explicitly delineates a mandate:

> But he's already made it plain how to live, what to do, what God is looking for in men and women. It's quite simple: Do what is fair and just to your neighbor, be compassionate and loyal in your love, and don't take yourself too seriously—take God seriously. (Micah 6:8, The Message, 2002)

Again, this text suggests that those who are Christians are mandated to "do what is fair and just to your neighbor." Conservative Christians are characterized as taking the biblical text literally. However, in this particular discourse about same sex sexuality, only the select biblical texts are used to justify homophobic values (Dessel, Bolen, & Shepardson, 2011). The biblical text, viewed as the guiding text for conservative Christians, is replete with scriptures that condemn homophobic values. The biblical mandate viewed as the greatest commandment states,

> Love the Lord your God with all your heart and with all your soul and with all your mind. This is the first and greatest commandment. And the second is like it: Love your neighbor as yourself. All the Law and the Prophets hang on these two commandments. (Matthew 22:37–40, *The Message, 2002*)

This biblical mandate states that after loving God deeply, Christians are to love their neighbor, just as they love themselves. Most importantly, all the stated laws, like those referenced earlier in this chapter used to support heterosexist values, must be supported by this notion of love.

The NASW Code of Ethics is not in conflict with biblical mandates. The Code of Ethics mandates that there be special attention to the vulnerable and oppressed. The way in which social workers address the needs of the vulnerable and oppressed is through service to those in need, by challenging social injustice, respecting the inherent dignity and worth of the client, recognizing the importance of human relationships, behaving with integrity, and exhibiting competence in professional practice (NASW, 2008). There is a biblical mandate to pay special attention to the vulnerable and oppressed. Table 1 provides a sample of the scriptures that support the values exhibited in the NASW Code of Ethics. Conservative Christians, by definition, view the biblical text as the literal word of God. It is difficult to take the biblical text literally and justify intolerance. Intolerance yields oppression, which results in vulnerability. Our clients who are LGB are oppressed and vulnerable. It is difficult to be homophobic and to truly be a conservative Christian.

Table 1. A Comparison of the NASW Code of Ethics and Biblical Mandates

Value	Biblical mandate
Service	Give freely and spontaneously. Don't have a stingy heart. The way you handle matters like this triggers God, your God's, blessing in everything you do, all your work and ventures. There are always going to be poor and needy among you. So, I command you: Always be generous, open purse and hands, give to your neighbors in trouble, your poor and hurting neighbors (Deuteronomy 15:10, 11).
Social justice	Woe to you Pharisees, because you give God a tenth of your mint, rue and all other kinds of garden herbs, but you neglect justice and the love of God. You should have practiced the latter without leaving the former undone (Luke 11:42).
Dignity and worth of person	In Christ's family there can be no division into Jew and non-Jew, slave and free, male and female. Among us you are all equal. That is, we are all in a common relationship with Jesus Christ (Galatians 3:28a).
Importance of human relationships	Get along with each other; don't be stuck-up. Make friends with nobodies; don't be the great somebody. Don't hit back; discover beauty in everyone. If you've got it in you, get along with everybody. Don't insist on getting even; that's not for you to do. "I'll do the judging," says God. "I'll take care of it" (Romans 12:15–19).
Integrity	Anyone who sets himself up as "religious" by talking a good game is self-deceived. This kind of religion is hot air and only hot air. Real religion, the kind that passes muster before God the Father, is this: Reach out to the homeless and loveless in their plight, and guard against corruption from the godless world (James 1:26, 27).
Competence	Learn to do good. Work for justice. Help the down-and-out. Stand up for the homeless. Go to bat for the defenseless (Isaiah 1:17).

Source: The Message (2002). Used by permission of NavPress Publishing Group.

Implications for Social Work Practice

Professional social workers are guided by a code of ethics that can lead to sanctions if there is evidence of violations against this code. According to the NASW Code of Ethics, "the primary mission of the social work profession is to enhance human well-being and help meet basic human needs of all people" (2008, p. 1). Social workers have an ethical responsibility to put their clients' interests before their own (1.01) and to promote self-determination in their clients (1.02). The only exception to this is if the client is in danger of being harmed or in danger of harming others. A client's sexual orientation does not meet this requirement. Social workers must engage in competent practice (1.04), including having an understanding of the nature of oppression and its impact on clients (1.05). This ethical mandate requires that social workers understand the impact of homophobic behaviors on their clients who identify as LGB.

Furthermore, social workers are expected to "engage in social and political action that seeks to ensure that all people have equal access to the resources, employment, services and opportunities they require to meet their basic human needs and to develop fully" (6.04a). This means that even a social worker who identifies as conservative Christian must "ensure that all people," including those who are LGB, "have equal access" to the necessities for their well-being. This ethical mandate goes on to state that social workers "should act to expand choice and opportunity for all people, with special regard for vulnerable, disadvantaged, oppressed, and exploited people and groups" (6.04b). In addition, social workers "should promote conditions that encourage respect for cultural and social diversity within the United States and globally" (6.04c). Regardless of their religion, social workers have an ethical mandate to serve all clients regardless of the client's sexual orientation and to "act to prevent and eliminate domination of, exploitation of, and discrimination against any person, group, or class" (6.04d). These ethical mandates make it difficult to be a social worker and have homophobic values.

Implications for Social Work Education

The Council on Social Work Education (CSWE) is the accrediting body for BSW and MSW programs across the nation. Social work education is currently guided by a set of core competencies, several of which are relevant to the discourse on values about LGB people.

- Identify as a professional social worker and conduct oneself accordingly.
- Apply social work ethical principles to guide professional practice.
- Engage diversity and difference in practice.
- Advance human rights and social and economic justice.
- Engage in policy practice to advance social and economic well-being and to deliver effective social work services.
- Respond to contexts that shape practice.
- Engage, assess, intervene, and evaluate with individuals, families, groups, organizations, and communities.

Social work education programs are mandated by CSWE to ensure that graduates demonstrate competence in these areas, with delineated practice behaviors. Schools of social work should be intentional about providing content related to practice with clients who are LGB. The content should not focus on the practice of same sex sexuality, just as it shouldn't focus on the practice of heterosexuality, but on the context of LGB. Graduates should be aware of their own lens as it relates to this issue and understand why they are mandated by the professional code of ethics to provide high-quality service to all clients, including clients who are LGB. Just as there is no tolerance for denying service to a client because of race or gender, there should be no tolerance for denying service due to sexual orientation. Graduates should work to diminish oppression against all clients regardless of sexual orientation.

The educational mandates set forth by CSWE make it difficult to be a social worker and have homophobic values. Schools of social work should explicitly make this known to their students. Furthermore, schools of social work should be prepared to address oppressive views expressed by students and to help their students understand that as professional social workers, they are to put their clients' needs above the needs of the social worker.

Conclusion

Social workers who identify as conservative Christians often cite heterosexist values due to their religious convictions. And although these social workers can cite scriptures that seem to condemn same sex behaviors, there are biblical mandates that denounce homophobia. Christians are mandated to act justly, with fairness toward others, particularly those who are vulnerable and oppressed. Professional social workers are mandated by the NASW Code of Ethics to act to end oppression, to treat clients fairly, and to act socially just. In addition, CSWE's accreditation standards require that graduates demonstrate competence in acts of justice and fairness toward all clients. Professional social workers are trained to work with people who are in crisis. We often work with people who engage in behaviors that we might not condone or about whom we might hold bias. There is no excuse for a professional social worker to refuse service to a client who identifies as LGB because the social worker does not approve of same sex sexuality. As a profession, we must hold all who enter the profession accountable to our foundational mission:

> to enhance human well-being and help meet basic human needs of all people, with particular attention to the needs and empowerment of people who are vulnerable, oppressed, and living in poverty.

As Christians, we must hold ourselves accountable to the most important commandment that undergirds our faith: to love the Lord God with all of our being, and to love our neighbor as ourselves. According to the scriptures, these are the foundational laws on which all of the other laws stand, including those that seem to condemn same sex sexuality and LGB people. It is possible that social workers who identify as conservative Christians can reclaim the conservative definition of holding a literal view of the biblical text and take the lead to end oppressive acts against those who identify as LGB.

References

Bangs, C. (1972). Deceptive statistics. *The Christian Century, 89*, 852–853.

Berkman, C. S., & Zinberg, G. (1997). Homophobia and heterosexism in social workers. *Social Work, 42*(4), 319–332.

Bruce, S. (1983). Identifying conservative Protestantism. *Sociological Analysis, 44*(1), 65–69.

Burdette, A., Ellison, C., & Hill, T. (2005). Conservative Protestantism and tolerance toward homosexuals: An examination of potential mechanisms. *Sociological Inquiry, 75*(2), 177–196.

Canda, E. R., & Hodge, D. (2003). Social work and evangelical Christians [7] (multiple letters). *Social Work, 48*(2), 278–288.

Chonody, J., Woodford, M., Smith, S., Silverschanz, P. (2013). Christian social work students' attitudes toward lesbians and gay men: Religious teachings, religiosity, and contact. *Journal of Religion and Spirituality in Social Work: Social Thought,* 32(3), 211–226.

deRuyter, M. (2009, October). *Social work ethics in faith based institutions: The interplay of professional, institutional, and spiritual value sets.* Conference presentation presented at the North American Association of Christians in Social Work, Indianapolis, IN.

Dessel, A., Bolen, R., & Shepardson, C. (2011). Can religious expression and sexual orientation affirmation coexist in social work? A critique of Hodge's theoretical, theological, and conceptual frameworks. *Journal of Social Work Education, 47*, 213–234.

Fulton, A. S., Gorsuch, R. L., & Maynard, E. A. (1999). Religious orientation, antihomosexual sentiment, and fundamentalism among Christians. *Journal for the Scientific Study of Religion, 38*(1), 14–22.

Grant, T., & Bailey, S. P. (2012, May 11). How evangelicals have shifted in public opinion on same-sex marriage: And what President Obama's announcement could mean politically and legally. *Christianity Today.* Retrieved from http://www.christianitytoday.com/ct/2012/mayweb-only/evangelicals-shift-same-sex-marriage.html

Green, J. (2000). *Prayers in the precincts: The Christian Right in the 1998 elections.* Washington, DC: Georgetown University Press.

Herman, D. (1997). *The antigay agenda: Orthodox vision and the Christian Right.* Chicago, IL: University of Chicago Press.

Hodge, D. R. (2005a). Epistemological frameworks, homosexuality, and religion: How people of faith understand the intersection between homosexuality and religion. *Social Work, 50*(3), 207–218.

Hodge, D. R. (2005b). Perceptions of compliance with the profession's ethical standards that address religion: A national study. *Journal of Social Work Education, 41*(2), 279–295.

Hodge, D. R. (2007). Religious discrimination and ethical compliance: Exploring perceptions among a professionally affiliated sample of graduate students. *Journal of Religion and Spirituality in Social Work, 26*(2), 91–113.

Kelley, D. (1972). *Why conservative churches are growing: A study of the sociology of religion.* New York, NY: Harper & Row.

Kohut, A. (2003). *Republicans unified, Democrats split on gay marriage: Religious beliefs underpin opposition to homosexuality* (p. 33). Washington, DC: The Pew Research Center.

Malka, A., Lelkes, Y., Srivastava, S., Cohen, A., & Miller, D. (2012). The association of religiosity and political conservatism: The role of political engagement. *Political Psychology, 33*(2), 275–299.

Miller, R. L. (2007). Legacy denied: African American gay men, AIDS, and the Black church. *Social Work, 52*(1), 51–61.

National Association of Social Workers (NASW). (2008). *NASW code of ethics (guide to the everyday professional conduct of social workers).* Washington, DC: NASW.

Noll, M. (2004). The rise of evangelicalism: The age of Edwards, Whitefield and the Wesleys. Downers Grove, IL: Intervarsity Press.

Petersen, L., & Donnenworth, G. (1998). Religion and declining support for traditional beliefs about gender roles and homosexual rights. *Sociology of Religion, 59,* 353–371.

Pew Research Forum on Religion and Public Life. (2013). Changing attitudes on gay marriage. Retrieved from http://features.pewforum.org/same-sex-marriage-attitudes/Ressler, L. (1998). When social work and Christianity conflict. In B. Hugen, & T. L. Scales (Eds.), *Christianity and social work* (2nd ed., pp. 93–117). Botsford, CT: North AmericanAssociation of Christians in Social Work.

Ressler, L. E., & Hodge, D. R. (2003). Silenced voices: Social work and the oppression of conservative narratives. *Social Thought, 22*(1), 125–142.

Ressler, L. E., & Hodge, D. R. (2006). Religious discrimination in social work: Preliminary evidence. *Journal of Religion & Spirituality in Social Work: Social Thought, 24*(4), 55–74.

Roach, D. (2012, May 10). Research: Americans split on whether homosexual behavior is sin. Lifeway Research. Retrieved from http://www.lifeway.com/Article/lifeway-research-homosexual-behavior-survey

Sherkat, D., & Ellison, C. (1997). The cognitive structure of a moral crusade: Conservative Protestantism and opposition to pornography. *Social Forces, 75,* 957–982.

Sider, R. (2012, December). Evangelicals and homosexuality: A proposal. *Prism, 19*(6), 56.

Swank, E., & Raiz, L. (2010). Attitudes toward gays and lesbians among undergraduate social work students. *Affilia, 25*(1), 19–29.

The Message. (2002). Peabody, MA: NavPress Publishing Group.

CHAPTER 12

Understanding the Tension: Christian Practitioner Perspectives on Working With LGBT Clients

Allison M. Tan, PhD

This chapter was thoughtfully titled "Understanding the Tension." It may seem obvious that a tension can, at times, exist between the LGBT community and people of Christian faith; biblical Christianity generally concludes that homosexual activity is sinful, and members of the LGBT community commonly experience judgment and oppression at the hands of Christians and the Christian church. Yet very little has been written or researched that explicitly seeks to understand the implications of those differences. The study presented in this chapter aims to begin this exploratory work. Before proceeding, I want to place the tension in context and offer a few important clarifications. First, although chapters throughout this book address aspects of Christianity and same sex sexuality in a social work context, not every chapter presents the same definitions. Therefore, I find it important to elucidate the ways I conceptualize three main terms: *faith*, *Christian practitioner*, and *LGBT community*.

The research presented in this chapter used a sample of Christian practitioners who are active members of the North American Christians in Social Work (NACSW) organization. Therefore, the terms *faith* and *Christian practitioner* are used herein as they apply to this group. NACSW is a diverse religious group with members representing nearly all denominations of Christianity, ranging from conservative to liberal perspectives. Therefore, *faith* refers to Christian faith of any kind. Throughout this chapter, the findings and discussion refer to implications for Christian practitioners in general, based on the responses from the practitioners included on NACSW's membership roster;

practitioners refers to any member of NACSW currently practicing social work (as opposed to its members in full-time academia).

If those on one side of the tension are represented in this chapter by Christian practitioners, the other side includes members of the LGBT community seeking social work services from those practitioners (although these ends of the spectrum are not mutually exclusive). Much has been written about the challenges of conceptualizing, measuring, and referencing the LGBT community as a whole. The term *LGBT* is used intentionally throughout this chapter because of its commonality in the literature; however, it is fraught with controversy. Some prominent researchers and practitioners in the field argue against this term because it lumps all gay men, lesbian women, and bisexual men and women, along with transgender people, into one category (see Fassinger & Arseneau, 2008). Additionally, much of the research that claims to represent the LGBT population is actually heavily weighted with lesbian and gay men and includes few bisexual and transgender people, if any (Fisher, Easterly, & Lazear, 2008). One of the alternative terms to describe this population is "sexual minority clients" (Dworkin & Gutiérrez, 1992), which also may be seen as controversial. Still, because it is most widely used in American vernacular, the research presented in this chapter simply referred to gay and lesbian people using the acronym *LGBT*. No distinction was made between gays, lesbians, bisexuals, and transgender people in the research or the comments made by survey respondents.

Impetus for the Study

As the title suggests, the impetus for this chapter and the research it cites was a genuine desire to begin to understand the tension between the LGBT and faith communities in a new way. Much has been written, especially in the media and popular literature, from the perspective of LGBT men and women who have experienced discrimination and intolerance from Christians in both personal and professional settings. Less has been written from the perspective of Christians in social work and other helping professions about their occasional discomfort and ethical challenges in working with LGBT clients. However, it is difficult to find any empirical research aimed at understanding the tension from the perspective of Christian social workers, many of whom have developed their own unique strategies in navigating these difficult waters through years of practice wisdom. This chapter is a first exploratory step in that direction.

In the professional literature on religious faith and social work practice (Gotterer, 2001; Hoyt, 2008; Tan, 2011), five scenarios of discordant beliefs between social worker and client are described:

- A nonreligious, nonspiritual social worker who is negative or dismissive toward a client's religion or spirituality
- A nonreligious, nonspiritual social worker who is open to a client's religion or spirituality as a strength in his or her life
- A social worker who is uncertain about his or her own religious beliefs and is therefore wary of discussing religion and spirituality with clients
- A religious or spiritual social worker who is able to acknowledge and respect clients with different beliefs
- A highly religious, spiritual social worker who becomes destructive in working with clients of different beliefs

The research presented in this chapter aimed to capture the experiences, attitudes, and beliefs of social workers in the last two of these discordant belief scenarios. A few years ago, I was commissioned by NACSW to write a book chapter to share with Christian social workers and students some best practices for working with the LGBT population from a faith perspective. That chapter (Tan, 2011) concluded with a section speaking specifically to Christian social workers in these two positions. To the former, there was encouragement to develop affirmative practice models and continue to strengthen their compassion and capacity to understand LGBT clients. To the latter, there was a call to refer LGBT clients elsewhere for services, based on the position that it is more ethical to refer clients whom one's personal beliefs make it difficult to competently serve than to engage in destructive activity and practice. Since its publication, I have corresponded with many Christian social workers eager to share their wisdom and challenges in this area. It is clear that many Christian social workers have successfully navigated this tension and have developed personal and professional practices that allow them to be both Christian and competent social workers for their LGBT clients. As a result, the present research was conducted through an exploratory lens and driven by a nondirectional hypothesis that Christian social work practitioners will report positions of judgment and insurmountable ethical challenges as well as positions of tolerance and thoughtful strategies for integrating faith and practice.

Method

The Sample

A total of 127 people completed the full survey. Table 1 provides a summary of key demographic characteristics of the sample. In general, the respondents reflect the overall practitioner membership of the NACSW. A wide range of Christian denominations were reported, reflecting the full continuum of liberal to conservative perspectives. Although the individual denominations are too many to include in the table, the three most common responses were Catholic (10.2%), Baptist (17.3%), and nondenominational Christian (35.4%). The sample of respondents are all highly religious, with 94.5% of them reporting at least weekly religious service attendance. Respondents work in a range of social work settings. They represent a fairly seasoned group of social work practitioners. The youngest respondent was 27 years old, and 37% of the sample is over 55. More than one third of the sample have been practicing social work for more than 20 years.

Table 1. Demographics of the Sample

	%
Social work practice setting	
Nonprofit organization	30.1
Private practice	19.7
Faith-based organization	15.7
Government or public service	14.0
School	12.5
Hospital	7.9
Gender	
Female	63.0
Male	37.0
Race or ethnicity	
Caucasian	86.6
African American	7.9
Hispanic	3.9
Asian American	1.6
Age	
25–35	24.4
36–45	13.4
46–55	25.2
55+	37.0
Years of social work practice	
Less than 6	18.9
6–15	33.9
16–20	7.9
More than 20	39.4

Procedure

A Web survey was distributed via e-mail to the entire electronic mailing list of NACSW practitioner members; this electronic mailing list included just over 1,100 people. This research was approved by the institutional review board at the University of St. Francis. Each practitioner received an e-mail with an introductory letter from the researcher explaining the impetus for the study and ensuring anonymity of responses. Completion of the survey was taken as an indication of consent to participate. The survey link was open for responses for a period of 6 weeks. The survey included a brief demographic section at the beginning and then asked respondents questions structured around three main areas: attitudes toward LGBT issues, comfort level in practice with LGBT clients, and practice experience and strategies for working with LGBT clients. Attitudes and comfort level were both assessed through a series of 7-point Likert scale questions. Figures 1 and 2 show the items measured. A reliability analysis of the data, discussed later, concluded that these measures can accurately be discussed as cohesive scales, one on Attitudes and the other on Comfort. The data are presented this way in the latter sections.

- Homosexuality is a sin.
- Someone can be both Christian and homosexual.
- People in LGBT relationships can be committed and monogamous.
- LGBT individuals should be able to get married.
- LGBT individuals should be able to adopt children.
- LGBT individuals have chosen to be gay, and can therefore change their sexual orientation.

Figure 1. Items measuring attitudes toward LGBT issues (based on a 7-point Likert scale from *totally disagree* to *totally agree*).

I am comfortable with . . .

- individuals in my family who are gay.
- having friends who are gay.
- interacting with LGBT people in social situations.
- providing social work services to LGBT clients when the presenting problem is not their sexual orientation (i.e., seeking housing assistance, case management, etc.).
- an LGBT client seeking counseling regarding relationship issues.
- an LGBT client seeking counseling regarding coming out, discrimination, and so forth.
- an LGBT client expressing a need for help in finding a religious community to support him/her.

Figure 2. Items measuring comfort level with LGBT people (based on a 7-point Likert scale from *totally uncomfortable* to *totally comfortable*).

The final section of the survey on experience and strategies for working with LGBT clients included questions about how many LGBT family members, close friends, and clients the respondent has had in his or her social work career. During data analysis, these variables were collapsed as grouped variables to allow comparison between those with LGBT family members and those without, those with LGBT friends and those without, and those reporting fewer than five LGBT clients with those reporting more than five. The survey then concluded with the only open-ended question: "Please provide any thoughts or comments you wish to share regarding the strategies you use that help you to provide respectful services to LGBT clients while maintaining your own faith traditions."

Findings

The key findings from this survey are presented in three subsections. First, the respondents' ratings on each of the six statements regarding their attitudes toward and beliefs about LGBT issues are presented. These six statements make up the Attitudes scale. Second, the respondents' ratings on each of the seven statements regarding their level of comfort interacting with LGBT people in a number of different settings are presented. These seven statements make up the Comfort scale. Lastly, we turn our attention to a number of interesting and insightful findings in looking at the relationships between some of the key variables in the study, most notably how both Attitudes and Comfort appear to be correlated with one's personal and professional exposure to the LGBT population.

ATTITUDES

The six statements outlined in Table 2 aimed to assess Christian social work practitioners' personal attitudes, beliefs, and convictions regarding same sex sexuality and LGBT issues. Respondents were asked to rank each statement on a scale from 1 to 7, where 1 was *totally disagree* and 7 was *totally agree*. Mean response values are presented in Table 12.2. Clearly, the majority of respondents lean toward a view of homosexuality as a sin, because the mean (2.84) for this item on the scale ("Homosexuality is not a sin") skews further toward the "disagreement" end of the spectrum than any other item. This is not surprising given the religiosity and biblical or evangelical traditions represented in the sample. However, respondents show a slightly higher level of agreement with statements about LGBT people themselves; the statements about one's ability to be both Christian and gay, one's ability to be in a committed LGBT relationship, and one's lack of control over his or her sexual orientation show higher means. Regarding two major social issues related to gay rights (marriage and adoption), respondents' ratings land in the middle; respondents show slightly less support for same sex marriage than they do for gay adoption.

Table 2. Mean Responses to Attitudes Scale Items

Statement	Mean Response[a]
Homosexuality is not a sin.	2.84
Someone can be both Christian and homosexual.	5.48
People in LGBT relationships can be committed and monogamous.	5.94
LGBT individuals should be able to get married.	3.25
LGBT individuals should be able to adopt children.	4.04
LGBT individuals have not chosen to be gay, and therefore cannot change their sexual orientation.	4.61
Attitudes scale mean	4.38

[a]1 = totally disagree, 7 = totally agree.

In an effort to treat these six items as one aggregate scale, two of the items were recoded in SPSS to account for directionality, because they were originally worded in an opposing direction from the other items. Respondents originally responded to the statements "Homosexuality is a sin" and "LGBT individuals have chosen to be gay, and can therefore change their sexual orientation." The responses were reverse coded during analysis to reflect consistency with the other items. After this recoding, a reliability analysis of the six items in this scale yielded a Cronbach's alpha score of .836, suggesting that one's response to any one item on the scale is likely to be consistent with responses to the other items. With this assurance, much of the remaining data analysis examined the Attitudes scale as a whole. As Table 2 indicates, the overall mean score for the

Attitudes scale of 4.38 is slightly above the mid-range (neutral) response on the 7-point scale, indicating the semantic response closest to *somewhat agree.*

COMFORT LEVEL

The seven statements outlined in Table 3 aimed to assess Christian social work practitioners' comfort level in interacting with LGBT people in a variety of settings, ranging from personal contact to professional practice. Respondents were asked to rank each statement on a scale from 1 to 7, where 1 was *totally uncomfortable* and 7 was *totally comfortable.* Several of the mean response rates presented in Table 3 are particularly notable. Looking at the means in the context of the 7-point scale, responses were all much higher than the midpoint on the scale, which suggests a certain level of comfort with all LGBT people. Yet much variation still exists depending on the setting in which one encounters an LGBT person. Respondents reported the highest level of comfort in interacting with LGBT people in social situations (mean = 6) and in social work practice when the presenting problem is not related to the client's sexual orientation (mean = 6.34). Interestingly, although perhaps not surprisingly given their personal beliefs and convictions, they were less comfortable when the LGBT client was seeking services connected to his or her sexual orientation (means ranging from 4.35 to 4.72). Some suggestions for how Christian social work practitioners have begun to successfully navigate this tension were provided by survey respondents and are included later in this chapter.

Hoping to be able to speak of these seven items as one aggregate scale similar to the Attitudes scale, we conducted a reliability analysis; a Cronbach's alpha score of .885 suggests that, once again, one's response to any one item on the scale is likely to be consistent with responses to the other items. Thus, data analysis continued using the Comfort scale as a whole. As Table 3 indicates, the overall mean score for the Comfort scale of 5.3 is higher than that of the Attitudes scale, which will be discussed further later in this chapter.

RELATIONSHIP BETWEEN VARIABLES

In considering what factors may affect a Christian social work practitioner's attitudes toward or comfort level with LGBT people, a number of correlations

Table 3. Mean Responses to Comfort Scale Items

Statement	Mean Response[a]
I am comfortable with ...	
individuals in my family who are gay.	5.28
having friends who are gay.	5.70
interacting with LGBT people in social situations.	6.00
providing social work services to LGBT clients when the presenting problem is not their sexual orientation (i.e. seeking housing assistance, case management, etc.).	6.34
an LGBT client seeking counseling regarding relationship issues.	4.72
an LGBT client seeking counseling regarding coming out, discrimination, etc.	4.72
an LGBT client expressing a need for help in finding a religious community to support him/her.	4.35
Comfort scale mean	5.30

[a]1 = totally disagree, 7 = totally agree.

were explored through this study's data. I hypothesized early in the process of designing and conducting the survey that age of respondents would be related to attitudes toward and comfort with LGBT men and women, specifically that older people might be more resistant to working with the LGBT population. However, the data proved this hypothesis to be incorrect. In fact, none of the demographic variables in this study were significantly related to either the Attitudes or Comfort scale.

The next hypothesized correlation explored in the data related to whether personal or professional exposure to the LGBT population affects one's attitudes or comfort level. To assess this possible correlation, the three experience-related questions asked in the survey were collapsed into dichotomous variables: family, friends, and clients. The Family variable collapsed respondents who reported any number of LGBT family members together; 54% of respondents reported having at least one gay family member. The Friends variable was collapsed similarly, and 59.1% of those in the sample reported having at least one gay friend. The Clients variable was collapsed slightly differently into two categories: those who reported up to 5 LGBT clients and those who reported more than 5 LGBT clients. Just over 73% of those sampled reported more than 5 LGBT clients in their careers as social workers. With these new variables, correlation analyses yielded very interesting results. Although having LGBT family members was not found to be significantly correlated to either the Attitudes or Comfort scale, Christian social work practitioners reporting exposure to and familiarity with the LGBT population through both personal friendships and professional practice seem to be significantly affected by those experiences.

Table 4 shows the only correlations in the data set found to be significantly correlated with the Attitudes and Comfort scales. Highly significant correlations were found for both scales related to the experience of having personal friendships with LGBT people. Christian social workers who reported having at least one gay friend generally were more favorably positioned attitudinally toward same sex sexuality and LGBT issues than those with no gay friends and also reported higher levels of comfort in interacting with LGBT people in all aspects of life, personal and professional. Although professional exposure to LGBT clients was not found to significantly affect the social worker's attitudes toward and beliefs about LGBT issues, those with five or more LGBT clients expressed a significantly higher comfort level with LGBT people than those with four or fewer LGBT clients. And the Attitudes and Comfort scales were highly correlated with one another (Pearson's $r = .716$, $p < .001$). These findings in particular have tremendous implications for social work practice

Table 4. Correlations Between Attitudes, Comfort, and Experiences

	Having LGBT Friends	Having LGBT Clients
Attitudes scale		
Pearson r	.292**	.148
Significance (2-tailed)	.001	.097
Comfort scale		
Pearson r	.420**	.276**
Significance (2-tailed)	<.001	.002

** indicates $p < .01$

and specifically the ways in which Christian social work practitioners are able to overcome any tension they experience between personal beliefs and professional practice. These implications are discussed further in the final section of this chapter.

Discussion

This chapter, and the research on which it is based, aims to provide a level of understanding about the tension that exists for some Christian social work practitioners who engage in practice with LGBT clients. But, more importantly, it aims to provide a practitioner-focused response to the question of how this type of practice can be done effectively and compassionately. Additional research and publications from this current data set may address questions such as whether one's level of agreement with the "sin" variable affects Attitudes and Comfort. Although the data collected offer even more interesting insights than can be discussed in this one chapter, there are perhaps three overarching implications worthy of discussion: Exposure to LGBT people is related to the social worker's beliefs and actions, there can be a marked difference between a Christian social worker's personal convictions and his or her practice strategies, and that difference is related to the development of competent social work practice skills for working with LGBT clients.

The first implication for social work practice to be gleaned from this research relates to the value of exposure to LGBT people in positively affecting the Christian social worker's attitudes toward and comfort level with LGBT clients. As the data in Table 4 show, respondents with personal friendships with LGBT people held significantly more affirmative attitudes and beliefs about LGBT issues than those who did not have such personal relationships; they were also significantly more likely to report higher levels of comfort in working with LGBT clients on a range of issues. Although there is no way to force personal friendships with LGBT people as a strategy for improving practice skills, this research does seem to support a general recommendation for Christian social work practitioners to seek our diverse experiences in their personal lives, interact with diverse people, and remain open to the LGBT community. Similarly, respondents with more experience working with LGBT clients were more likely to report higher levels of comfort in practice. This suggests a sort of "practice-makes-perfect" implication; that is, if a Christian social worker has a genuine desire to become more comfortable with LGBT clients, he or she should begin by seeking out training in LGBT-affirmative practice models and seeing LGBT clients. Although it is certainly clinically appropriate to offer an LGBT client a referral to a social worker who may specialize in working with the LGBT population, such referral cannot, and need not, be the end of the social worker's response. Several respondents offered suggestions in the open-ended portion of the survey at its conclusion, which stressed the value of improving one's cultural competence and practice skills by intentionally seeking out training and opportunities for continuing education related to LGBT issues.

It is also evident from the data of this study that there is a marked difference for most Christian social work practitioners between their personal convictions and their comfort in providing assistance and support to LGBT clients. In looking at the mean scores for the two scales, it is evident that respondents' personal convictions (Attitudes) about same sex sexuality and LGBT issues were notably lower than their willingness (Comfort) to provide social work services to LGBT clients. From the comments shared by several respondents, this difference can be understood and explained by a professional focus on the call to value the inherent dignity and worth of each client and to maintain a commitment to the client's right to self-determination in the social work Code of Ethics (National Association of Social Workers, 2008). A few quotes from Christian social work practitioners illustrate this separation of personal convictions and professional practice:

> I don't morally approve of becoming transsexual, but I helped a mother accept that her son had become a woman. I knew her disapproval wasn't going to make him a man again but would only hurt the two of them. Realistically thinking of the results of her disapproval versus her approval quickly helped me [determine what I needed to do].

> I focus on healing the traumas, and show acceptance and compassion to them as individuals, respecting their self-determination (free will) to go forward as they choose once healed of the trauma.

> So if I help a gay couple in cultivating Christ-like friendship, brotherly love, and mutuality, I think that Christ is glorified in that, and it makes the world a better place, even if I personally think there is a sinful bent to the erotic part of the relationship.

Without using the term "affirmative practice," this is what most of the respondents are actually doing; affirmative practice is the conscious effort of the social worker to create an environment that fosters comfort, safety, and openness for the client to share and to seek help. Affirmative practice has been widely documented in the literature on best practices for working with the LGBT population (as well as with many other highly stigmatized groups) as an effective and vital strategy for social work practice (see Amadio & Perez, 2008; Bieschke, Perez, & DeBord, 2007; Crisp, 2006; Dworkin & Gutiérrez, 1992; Foreman & Quinlan, 2008; Logan & Barret, 2002; Tan, 2011).

These first two implications taken together lead to the third and final important point for discussion. The research, as well as the comments made by Christian practitioners, suggests that even when faced with personal convictions to the contrary, social workers are able to put aside their personal beliefs in order to provide competent practice to LGBT clients. The comments from respondents overwhelmingly described a number of biblically rooted themes that help the social workers understand and navigate these challenging situations. These themes included remembering the following: It is not their place to judge behavior of others, everyone sins and there are no "worse" sins, all people are God's creation and made in his image, and Christians are called to love. One practitioner stated, "I am not called to hold others to my Scriptural standards. I am a disciple called to love." Still, this is a difficult tension to tread, and listening to the words of a few additional Christian social worker practitioners can help shed light on how it can be done.

> My clients know where I am coming from. I have the same standard for those who are having heterosexual sex outside of marriage. People know where I stand, but, prayerfully, experience me as caring and supporting their journey to a deeper walk with God and a deeper healing in their life.

> I do know that God loves everyone, and that people can come to Him while still dealing with a multitude of issues. If He takes me in while I still struggle with being overweight and selfish, why would there be any reason to doubt that He could love and save someone who has to deal with homosexuality? And if He loves me regardless of how I resolve my struggle (or in my weakness don't resolve it), then He will do the same with others, and I must also do the same.

These are but a few of the pearls of wisdom shared by the seasoned Christian social work practitioners in this study. The task is great. The tension is often palpable. Yet the call is clear to many Christians in social work. As the research suggests, Christian social workers who find themselves wrestling with these questions should seek out ways to increase their exposure to LGBT people personally and professionally, contemplate the ways the Code of Ethics may help them separate personal beliefs from professional practice, and then consult with other Christian social workers to see what words of wisdom they might have to share regarding the call to biblical compassion and competent social work service provision.

References

Amadio, D. M., & Perez, R. M. (2008). Affirmative counseling and psychotherapy with lesbian, gay, bisexual, and transgender clients. In C. Negy (Ed.), *Cross-cultural psychotherapy: Toward a critical understanding of diverse clients* (2nd ed.). Reno, NV: Bent Tree Press.

Bieschke, K. J., Perez, R. M., & DeBord, K. A. (Eds.). (2007). *Handbook of counseling and psychotherapy with lesbian, gay, bisexual, and transgender clients.* Washington, DC: American Psychological Association.

Crisp, C. (2006). The Gay Affirmative Practice scale (GAP): A new measure for assessing cultural competence with gay and lesbian clients. *Social Work, 51*(2), 115–126. doi:10.1093/sw/51.2.115

Dworkin, S. H., & Gutiérrez, F. J. (1992). *Counseling gay men & lesbians: Journey to the end of the rainbow.* Alexandria, VA: American Association of Counseling and Development.

Fassinger, R. E., & Arseneau, J. R. (2008). "I'd rather get wet than be under that umbrella": Differentiating the experiences and identities of lesbian, gay, bisexual, and transgender people. In K. J. Bieschke, R. M. Perez, & K. A. DeBord (Eds.), *Handbook of counseling and psychotherapy with lesbian, gay, bisexual, and transgender clients* (2nd ed.). Washington, DC: American Psychological Association.

Fisher, S. K., Easterly, S., & Lazear, K. J. (2008). Lesbian, gay, bisexual and transgender families and their children. In T. P. Gullotta & G. M. Blau (Eds.), *Family influences on childhood behavior and development: Evidence-based prevention and treatment approaches.* New York, NY: Routledge/Taylor & Francis Group.

Foreman, M., & Quinlan, M. (2008). Increasing social works students' awareness of heterosexism and homophobia: A partnership between a community gay health project and a school of social work. *Social Work Education, 27*(2), 152–158. doi:10.1080/02615470701709485

Gotterer, R. (2001). The spiritual dimension in clinical social work practice: A client perspective. *Families in Society, 82*(2), 187–193. doi:10.1606/1044-3894.209

Hoyt, C. A. (2008). What if the spirit does not move me? A personal reconnaissance and reconciliation. *Social Work, 53*(3), 223–231. doi:10.1093/sw/53.3.223

Logan, C. R., & Barret, R. L. (2002). *Counseling gay men and lesbians: A practice primer.* Pacific Grove, CA: Brooks/Cole Thomson Learning.

National Association of Social Workers (NASW). (2008). *Code of ethics.* Retrieved from: https://www.socialworkers.org/pubs/code/code.asp

Tan, A. (2011). Working with LGBT clients: Promising practices and personal challenges. In T. L. Scales & M. S. Kelly (Eds.), *Christianity and social work: Readings on the integration of Christian faith and social work practice* (4th ed.; pp. 235–254). Botsford, CT: North American Christians in Social Work.

CHAPTER 13

"Jesus Didn't Say Anything in the Bible About Gay People": Understanding Pathways to Christian Social Work LGBT Advocacy

René Drumm PhD, Kristie Wilder JD, Evie Nogales Baker MSW, Lauren Souza MSW, Zaire Burgess-Robinson MSW, and Jennifer Adams MSW

The social work profession demonstrates a long history of advocacy for disenfranchised people (Gibelman, 1999; Krumer-Nevo, Monnickendam, & Weiss-Gal, 2009). From its earliest roots, the social work profession has partnered with religious organizations to promote social justice and protect the vulnerable (Cnaan, Boddie, & Danzig, 2005; Graham & Shier, 2009; Karger & Stoesz, 1998; Magnuson, 1977). Some of the successful initiatives for social work and religion include addressing poverty, challenging substandard living conditions, promoting public health, and fighting against racism (Butler, Elliott, & Stopard, 2003; McDermott, Linahan, & Squires, 2009; Nieman, 2006; Watkins & Hartfield, 2012).

Several religious organizations, including Christian churches, have developed a focus on lesbian, gay, bisexual, and transgender (LGBT) advocacy and acceptance. The United Church of Christ denomination advocates civil rights and has developed welcoming ministries specifically for LGBT people (www.ucc.org/lgbt). The Grace Gospel Chapel in Seattle, Washington, declares their congregation's acceptance of all individuals, "regardless of sexual orientation," as a part of their online statement of faith. Gays in Faith Together is a Christian organization in Grand Rapids, Michigan, with groups, community education, and advocacy campaigns for LGBT people (www.gaysinfaithtogether.org).

In addition, some faith-based, social service organizations also advocate for LGBT equality, such as Christian Social Services of Illinois, which assists both heterosexual and homosexual couples with adoption (www.cssil.org; "Gay Adoptions," 2012). However, to date the social work profession has experienced less overall success in partnering with religious organizations to advocate for civil rights and social justice for LGBT people. One reason for this lack of advocacy may be rooted in traditional religious teachings in the Christian church on sexuality, which predominantly view sexual acts between people of the same gender as sinful (Rodriguez, 2010).

Research on Christians' attitudes toward LGBT people indicates that there is an association between fundamental Christian views and an increased negative perception of LGBT people (Malcomnson, Christopher, Franzen, & Keyes, 2006; Newman, 2002). This negative perception is lessened when people understand the complexity of sexual orientation. People who have a strong affiliation with their religion more often think that sexual orientation is something people choose (Kain, 2006; Malcomnson et al., 2006). In contrast, religious groups that tend to be more accepting of LGBT people are much more likely to think that sexual orientation is something that cannot be changed (Haider-Markel & Joslyn, 2008; Kain, 2006; Wood & Bartkowski, 2004).

Thus, the issue of choice in sexual orientation is clearly important in terms of how it impinges on theological beliefs and how it subsequently influences advocacy behaviors. People who believe that sexual orientation is something that cannot be changed are much more likely to think that homosexuality is "not wrong at all" and to support the civil rights of LGBT people (Kain, 2006, p. 6).

Although these findings pertain primarily to general U.S. populations, to some extent these attitudes and biases are also present in the social work profession. For example, researchers have found an association between people with a Christian affiliation and holding negative biases toward lesbians and gay men (Berkman & Zinberg, 1997; Crisp, 2007; Krieglstein, 2003; Newman, Dannenfelser, & Benishek, 2002; Ryan, 2000).

Yet knowing about the tension and division between Christian beliefs and LGBT advocacy does little to increase understanding of how to work together toward the mutual goals of equality and human rights for all. This chapter presents the findings of a qualitative study about the experiences of Christian social workers in their journey toward LGBT advocacy. The findings highlight advocates' developmental thinking about sexual orientation formation, their educative experiences about sexual orientation, and how those experiences impinged on their theological beliefs. The chapter also highlights advocates' notions about how to bridge the gap between religious beliefs and LGBT advocacy.

Methods

The purpose of this study is to gain an initial understanding of the experiences of and strategies used by Christian social workers in becoming self-identified LGBT advocates. We also identify participants' advocacy strategies on behalf of LGBT populations. Because little is known about how Christian social workers come to identify themselves as LGBT advocates or the types of activities in which they engage in this journey, we chose an inductive, qualitative approach.

Sample Selection and Data Collection

To qualify for an interview, the study participants needed to identify as an LGBT advocate, a Christian, and a social worker. The research team aimed to interview 20 participants and interviewed 21.

All participants self-identified as Christian social work LGBT advocates. The sample contained 11 women and 10 men. The majority of interviewees (14) held an MSW degree, and seven had earned doctoral degrees. The participant's primary social work professional roles varied, with eight identifying as clinical practitioners, three agency administrators, nine social work educators, and two case managers.

All participants were age 18 or older. Participants were recruited through purposive, convenience, and snowball sampling procedures. Researchers used e-mail lists of social workers (university alumni, Christian social work educators, and local NASW members) to contact potential study participants.

Before collecting data, the research team received permission to conduct the study from Southern Adventist University's Human Subjects Institutional Review Board and followed standard guidelines to protect research participants. Participation was voluntary, and no incentives were offered to study participants.

Researchers developed an open-ended interview guide to assist in getting similar information from all participants. All interviewers were trained in the use of the interview guide before conducting the interviews. The interview guide inquired about participants' journeys in understanding sexual orientation, their theological views, their policy and practice advocacy, the etiology of sexual orientation, their advocacy role with the faith community, and the barriers for furthering the dialogue between the Christian community and LGBT people. All interviews were either face-to-face with participants or conducted over the telephone and digitally recorded. The interview times ranged from 20 to 90 minutes.

Analysis

The first step in organizing the raw data was to create verbatim transcriptions of the recorded interviews. The research team members then reviewed the transcripts for completeness and accuracy. Researchers initiated analysis by coding participants' themes throughout the data using the constant comparative method (Charmaz, 2006; Glaser & Strauss, 1967). By examining similar incidents within the data set, researchers constructed initial inductive categories. These general categories were refined through the comparison process across participants and across categories.

As coding continued in the analysis process, researchers examined specific instances of the codes to clarify similarities and differences between the researchers' use of these codes, improving intercoder reliability. Researchers addressed the issues of credibility and trustworthiness of the data by using peer debriefing and conducting negative case analysis (Lincoln & Guba, 1985). Negative case analysis involves searching for incidents in the data set that do not conform to the emerging patterns of the analysis. Interrater reliability was ensured through a modified process suggested by Marques and McCall (2005). The lead researcher for the study drafted initial themes for which the analysis team noted the consistency of use throughout the analysis. The themes and categories were refined to maximize verification of the findings. The research team met immediately after the initial draft of themes and continued to meet weekly to refine the themes and subthemes. This approach provided a way to verify that the study's findings represented a constructive measure in consistency of interpretation rather than an evaluative measure occurring after the analysis.

Results

The findings that follow identify themes and subthemes that emerged from the analysis and offer insights into the journeys of Christian social work LGBT advocates. The findings reveal the collective reflections on how these Christian social workers' conceptualizations of sexual orientation evolved, the participants' developmental thinking about theological issues surrounding sexual orientation, and the various types of advocacy activities in which these participants engage in their social work practice. All participants are identified by a pseudonym to protect their privacy while honoring the participant's experience as a person rather than a research subject.

Learning About Sexual Orientation

To this group of Christian social workers, gaining new understandings about how sexual orientation forms and develops was an important milestone in their journeys toward LGBT advocacy. Many participants recalled not having much, if any, information on sexual orientation other than heterosexuality throughout childhood and adolescence. The following quotes from participants illustrate how absent the topic of sexual orientation was during childhood and adolescence.

> Interestingly enough, it has never really been a subject of conversation at a family level. (Justin)

> When I was growing up, the issue of homosexuality was not spoken about in my churches or in my schools. (Lucy)

> I didn't think much about it [sexual orientation] growing up because it was a pretty tough topic. The only thing that maybe would have surfaced would have been jokes about being gay or something like that, and it wasn't until I

> got to graduate school [that it was] even brought up in discussion . . . because it was never part of the conversation in those days. (Carl)

When the participants did recall early conversations about gay or lesbian sexual orientation, they recalled early negative messages about LGBT people, particularly as they related to religion. The following quotes from participants illustrate the derisive nature of these initial messages.

> I was raised to believe you need to be heterosexual. You are born heterosexual, that is the only way to be, and anyone who's other than that is wrong, bad, evil, and needs to be turned in the right direction. (Felice)

> I remember being very young the first time I . . . asked my parents about it [gays and lesbians]. My parents explained it to me in the terms they wanted to, but I will say I was raised Southern Baptist, so the way my parents explained it to me...was that it was totally wrong and that . . . I shouldn't identify or associate with them. (Natalie)

> When I was really young the message I got clearly was that gay and lesbian people are people you make fun of and shun. (Dennis)

> Besides hearing people use derogatory terms, and probably using them myself, I remember first thinking about this in seventh grade. My teacher was talking about homosexuals, . . . and it was clear in my mind that they had made choices and had degraded and damaged themselves. (Marcus)

Participants received little information or negative messages about lesbian and gay people throughout their adolescence. Later, life circumstances led them to a greater awareness of sexual orientation. There was little consensus among study participants about how sexual orientation differences came to their awareness. For some, it was a matter of having personal encounters with lesbian and gay people. For other participants, the issue of sexual orientation came into their consciousness through extended social relationships, such as friends, relatives, educational settings, or work circumstances.

> I have a dear friend who is a lesbian and a conservative Christian, and she—within the past year—just came out that she's a lesbian. (Kathleen)

> The issue . . . [surfaced] for me when I was about 27, I would suppose, when my younger sister came out as a lesbian. (Justin)

> The first . . . [LGBT awareness I had] is when I was working for an organization and discovered that a few of my coworkers were gay. That's the first time I really started thinking about this. (Stephanie)

> My family and I recently started attending a church that was made up of many homosexuals. And that has really made us look into the issue on a deeper level. We've begun to get to know real people and real situations, and real stories. And it was difficult, it was a struggle—but it has been enriching for me and my family. (James)

Over time, participants became acquainted with lesbian and gay people, and often a new thought occurred—that these people were similar to them, which led to less criticism and disapproval. Instead of seeing lesbian and gay people as "bad," as they had once believed, they saw intelligent and compassionate people with similar life issues.

> When I went to my MSW program at [X] University I had a series of encounters with people that I found out were gay or lesbian, and they were out and comfortable. . . . And they seemed like they were great, intelligent, fun, and interesting people who just happened to be gay. And that was sort of a mental turning point for me because I'd never known anybody who was gay or lesbian up to that point. (Carl)

> I would attend AA meetings, where I experienced love and acceptance for the first time and grace like I had never experienced before in my life. I can remember one lady in particular who was wonderful. She was open and transparent, and we became really good friends, and she was gay. She was helpful to me personally in my recovery journey, and through this I had an experience with someone who was lesbian and a fantastic person. She was comfortable with who she was, and this was just a wonderful experience for me. (Dennis)

> As I got older it was kind of like a realization that they are the same as me... They are people also, [so] there's no reason for me not to want to [associate] with them. Especially...after I got into the social work field...my perspective changed to where I live like we are all the same. We make differ[ent] choices, but we are all equal. (Natalie)

> I think there are unique struggles and challenges to being gay—at work, at home, at church, or in society. But at the end of the day, they're just humans with feelings, and struggles, and insecurities, and fears that go beyond their sexual orientation. (Jack)

Whatever the reason for the issue of sexual orientation surfacing in these participants' lives, some interest was generated that led them to proactively seek out more information on how sexual orientation develops. Some participants read books or articles; others attended workshops or talked to gay and lesbian people about their experiences. The following quotes from participants illustrate how the spark of interest in sexual orientation formation led to a new understanding of a formerly taboo or unexplored subject:

> I started reading a bunch of literature, just trying to read as much as I could about issues of sexual identity and sexual orientation. (Carl)

> I think over time in my practice as a clinical social worker, working with lesbian and gay clients, I wanted to know more about how to provide coun-

> seling to them. I wanted to know more about their culture, more about their community, and so I remember specifically a training I went to where it was a workshop talking specifically about ethics regarding gay and lesbian clients, and the instructor [told us] to just outright ask clients in an assessment, "Are you straight or are you gay?" (Lucy)

To summarize, although their movement was not uniform or linear, participants began their journeys as LGBT advocates from a place of not understanding sexual orientation or understanding differences in sexual orientation as something to be avoided or shunned. Then, participants experienced events or encountered contexts in which their former thinking was challenged. In these cases, the participants actively sought information about sexual orientation to gain a deeper understanding of this issue. This new information, in turn, led participants to evaluate not only their social thinking but also their theological beliefs about sexual orientation.

Integrating Knowledge and Theological Understanding

Nearly all participants had an initial understanding that any sexual orientation apart from heterosexuality came about as a result of a conscious choice and resulted in behavior that was designated as sinful. During their journeys to becoming LGBT advocates, the participants, through various means, came to an understanding that sexual orientation was much more complex than previously believed, which challenged their traditional theological understandings of same-sex interaction. Participants engaged in strategies to accommodate this shift, such as gaining a broader understanding of theology in general or connecting with other Christian LGBT-supportive people.

One issue in particular that helped advocates view sexual orientation as a complex phenomenon centered on the biology of sexuality formation. Before understanding that biological factors that contribute to one's sexual identity play a part in sexual orientation development, participants largely attributed sexual orientation to being a person's choice. The following quotes from participants illustrate coming to understand a role that supersedes choice in sexual orientation development.

> I do not, at any level, believe that this is a choice. The wrestling of every individual I've talked to, their personal struggle, the amount of years that it took to come out, their effort to be with the opposite sex, the suicidal thoughts they've had—I cannot imagine that anyone would choose that. (Kathleen)

> There is a lot of evidence that shows that biology really can lead to or present as lesbian, gay, and transgender. So, for those reasons, I really feel that sexual orientation is not a choice, I really don't. (William)

> I believe that sexual orientation is a part of one's identity. This is who they are, and how do you extract yourself from who you are? I've come to this conclusion because most of the gay people I know would say that if it was a choice, this is not the road they would have chosen because it's hard. It's difficult, wrought with pain and isolation. I've learned it's embedded in their identity and would never want to say to them, or my own kids, "You need to choose to be alone the rest of your life because your sexual orientation does not match the dominant culture." (Sylvia)

> I say that nature gives the range of potential [sexual behaviors], and culture or nurture gives the possible expressions. (Pat)

These participants' theological beliefs had most often initially identified same-sex encounters as sinful. With their new understanding of sexual complexity, these participants set out to reconcile their traditional theological beliefs with this new understanding. Participants' theological and personal beliefs included a full range of views from holding to the traditional conviction that same-sex interaction is sinful, to the belief that same-sex interaction may be sinful but is not worse than another transgression such as pride or gossip, and finally to an attitude that same-sex interaction is not sinful. These positions are illustrated here:

SINFUL

I would say that I believe it's not, like a lot of things, God's will for someone's life. (James)

SINFUL BUT NOT MORE SO

Professionally I spent 5 years as a social work case manager for the local HIV/AIDS service organization. I cared very deeply for my clients and their loved ones who were affected by this dreadful disease. They knew that I loved them, and they also knew that I didn't judge them. Yes, I believe that homosexual behavior is sinful, but so is my pride. Sin is sin. The consequences are not equal. God loves sinners like me. He hates sin. Jesus demonstrated that, and we should follow his example in love. (Rita)

We need to get as a church [that] "they're sinners" out of our thoughts . . . and instead turning the mirror back on ourselves and going, "How are their sins any different from your sins and from my sins?" They're not! We're all in need of a savior. (Elizabeth)

I look at being homosexual as a situation that "no sin is greater than the other sins," so when people kinda don't want to be involved with people who are gay or things like that, I think that's a wrong kind of perception to have. So I've changed over the years in social work. Being a social worker has helped me with that. Has helped me come to grips with my Christianity and accepting people for who they are and where they are regardless of whether I agree with them or not. (Valerie)

NOT SINFUL

I really believe that it is okay for people to be in gay/lesbian relationships with one another theologically and that I would hope and pray and expect for them to function with one another as heterosexual married couples. (Heidi)

I don't believe homosexuality is a sin because I think people are born that way, and I don't think homosexual long-term, committed, loving relationships are a sin either. And I see long-term loving relationships being a pillar in our society, and I think those relationships—if we can sanction them, make them like the relationships that we have already sanctioned that are pillars of our society—it'll just add to the strength of our society and not hurt it. So I feel that way on a religious level as well as on a social level. (Marcus)

I think that nature is the cause, and therefore I feel spiritually that God would not condemn that behavior of what nature created. (William)

Although participants' beliefs about theology specific to same-sex attraction varied, an important cohesive theme emerged concerning beliefs that supported and bolstered these participants' motivation to LGBT advocacy: to love and care about humanity. Participants' theological beliefs that centered on social justice, the value of humanity, and the importance of loving people offset traditional beliefs about same-sex interaction. The following quotes from participants illustrate theological views that proved important to this group of LGBT advocates.

UNIVERSAL RELATIONSHIP RULES THAT SUPERSEDE SEXUAL ORIENTATION

When I hear that homosexuality is a sin, and then I hear the verses like Leviticus 18:22 [that says] something about "mankind should not lie with mankind, Mankind should not lie with womankind, it is an abomination.... And so [I] look at the verses above and it's talking about morals such as do not have sex outside of a relationship. (Lucy)

Jesus didn't say anything in the Bible about gay people. There are other parts of the Bible where it clearly spoke to people of their time. Their behaviors, like ours, were shaped by that place in time. I think this is an area to where our culture and society know more at this point in time about what it means to be a committed gay couple than we did a thousand years ago. I believe the biblical rules about relationships, loyalty, monogamy, and commitment are true for both sets of couples. My concern with the Bible texts that are used to condemn homosexuality is why are we not also concerned that we should be wearing a beard or other conduct about relationships we don't condemn. It doesn't make sense to me to pick things out to fit an argument but ignore others. Maybe I don't have it all figured out, but I do know that the Bible is clear that we are to love God and love our neighbors. And I think that when we enter into personal caring relationships with people who are different from us, we see the world differently. There are things that happen to folks who are gay that are clearly not biblical because they are based in hate. This is a conflict for me. (Sylvia)

CENTRALITY OF LOVING OTHER PEOPLE

I understand what the Bible says [about homosexuality]...but at the same time God also represents love, and you know to me I'd rather see a same-sex relationship than hatred and violence between a man and a woman. (Frieda)

The real question for me is how do we create safe places for people who are different in our churches regardless of what we theologically feel or believe? How can we embrace them? How can we get over our homophobia? How can we love them? I have always come to the conclusion that what is more important to God is that we love people than to be right. (Dennis)

I may be totally wrong. I just figure I'll fall back on what stands the highest to me. If I'm totally wrong on this issue at least I've loved people to the best of my ability. If there's judging to be done, I'm going to work to leave that to God to do in the end. (Marcus)

The theological, spiritual views of love, compassion, caring for another person, you know, "Bring me your weary," trying to help others probably helps my professional practice rather than challenges it, honestly. (Edward)

Beliefs to Action

How did these Christian social workers respond to their theological beliefs and convictions as they relate to LGBT advocacy? Participants in this study moved along several pathways to become Christian social work LGBT advocates. In addition, these participants took various approaches to both their understanding of advocacy and their implementations of advocacy behaviors. Participants for this study self-identified as Christian social workers who were LGBT advocates. For some participants, their initial primary "advocacy" behavior was having a professional policy to not discriminate in offering services to LGBT people.

Although some participants moved toward active advocacy on behalf of LGBT people, for a few participants *advocacy* appeared to be defined as providing appropriate social work services in a nondiscriminatory fashion. None of the interviewees took the stance of simply referring LGBT clients to another social worker. All self-identified advocates provided services directly to LGBT populations or indirectly on their behalf. The following quotes from participants reflect this initial stance of nondiscriminatory service delivery.

> That's part of our job to do things professional and ethical, whether they're gay or transgender. .... My policy is to work with whoever comes in my office and provide appropriate social work care for them. (Valerie)

> I may not necessarily personally agree with their lifestyle choices, and that's okay because my personal preferences and my personal beliefs really don't need to have any kind of bias in how I treat people....My job is to not allow my service delivery to be swayed by my personal beliefs. (Elizabeth)

Many participants offered a full range of advocacy behaviors, from micro to macro, in which they engaged in their personal and professional lives. Micro advocacy behaviors are efforts in which participants engaged to offer assistance directly to individuals. These advocates spent time talking to LGBT students or family members and friends of LGBT people as they grappled with sexual orientation concerns. The advocates became known as safe and reliable sources of information on sexual orientation. It was a goal for the advocates to proactively keep abreast of the latest research on sexual orientation and stay knowledgeable about resources and political issues that might affect LGBT people. This type of self-education and awareness advocacy helped prepare them to be confident in their advocacy roles.

> I had a call a few years ago from one of my former supervisees, "Can you tell me a resource? I'm in this little town in [X state], and I have a 13-year-old who is pretty convinced that she is transsexual. She has a basically male identity and she thinks she's ready to start a transition. Where are the resources?" And I happened to know. (Pat)

> Advocacy for me is just more of a one-on-one interaction with people—or questions that people may have, or if I hear someone say something. You know, I try to just have a dialogue. And so my role, I think, is more just in the moment with individuals, rather than in a larger group or organization. (Jack)

> Since I encounter a lot of younger Christian people, one of my roles is to represent a group that they think doesn't exist. I can represent adults who are Christian who can also be loving, embracing, and provide counsel for the GLBT population. I can represent someone who thinks they have certain civil rights and also represent the face of the church. (Sylvia)

Mezzo-advocacy behaviors include advocacy efforts in small groups and organizations. Participants often took the time to educate their fellow workers, either in educational settings or in agencies, about LGBT issues. In workplaces and educational institutions where LGBT populations were not specified as a protected group, these advocates worked to develop more nondiscriminatory policies that protected LGBT people's rights.

> For me it's just a lot of one-on-one conversations when I'm in a small group. If something is said that is judgmental, hateful, or discriminatory,

I acknowledge that and have a discussion about it; . . . to say nothing is to say something. (Felice)

Advocacy is, I think, hugely important, and I've been engaged in that ever since I came to [X University]. Definitely at the very beginning when we were starting that first [Council on Social Work Education] . . . accreditation [process], one of the first things we needed to do is to make sure that our working policies for the university and our acceptance policies for students included sexual orientation as a protective category.... More recently, advocacy has involved, trying to bring the film *Seventh-Gay Adventists* onto this campus so that people can better understand the journeys of people who are gay or lesbian or bisexual. (Carl)

This summer I went to review some of the books we have in our school library, and it was very interesting. There were definitely some books that said, "How to raise your children so they don't grow up gay." I had a conversation with our librarians, and it was a good conversation in the sense that we have the other side of the conversation also. (Kathleen)

On the macro level, participants engaged in advocacy with communities and political systems. Advocates involved these systems by writing letters to legislators and initiating research efforts to increase knowledge and raise awareness of LGBT issues.

There was a law just passed by legislation by the governor [of California] making it illegal for licensed clinicians to practice reparative therapy with minors. ... If a minor comes to the conclusion that they are LGBTQ, you can't engage in therapy with a minor that is going to try to change that orientation. And I supported that before it was passed by legislation. (Marcus)

I actually do write to my senators and legislators on any issues that come up in this way. (Kathleen)

Limitations of the Study

This study is limited in ways typical of qualitative studies in general. Although the intent of the study was to achieve a broad understanding of the experiences of Christian social work LGBT advocates, it is important to be clear that these findings cannot be generalized to any population. The study is limited by the nature of self-selected participants in the research process, snowball and purposive sampling techniques, and the number of participants.

Conclusions

Although this study offers only an initial understanding of the experiences of Christian social work LGBT advocates, one thing is clear: Becoming advocates for LGBT people was a journey for this group of people. It was a process that unfolded over time and with exposure to new ideas and alongside mentoring people. The process was not linear or uniform, but it contained similar strategies and outcomes that could and should be replicated, in keeping with social work values of social justice for all human beings.

Information about Christian social work LGBT advocates is largely absent from peer-reviewed literature. To many people, the very term "Christian LGBT advocates" is an oxymoron. These participants are often hidden players behind the scenes, providing services that have gone unrecognized. It is important to provide encouragement and support for these advocates in order to multiply their efforts and to note positive outcomes. Although Christian social work practitioner–advocates may be safe in welcoming workplaces and can freely engage in LGBT advocacy, Christian social work educators may not have the same amount of protection. Nontenured faculty may be especially vulnerable if their LGBT advocacy or research is widely known because of the special protections afforded Christian institutions in employment regulation. For example, if an educator in a Christian institution engages in LGBT research or advocacy activities in the public realm and a constituent of the institution makes a complaint to academic administration, the faculty member may be subject to negative employment consequences regardless of tenure status.

These findings lay a foundation for future research and directions for immediate action. For each finding, we will offer some recommendations for action that we hope will result in greater capacity for furthering civil and human rights for all people.

The participants noted the overall absence of the topic of sexual orientation during childhood and adolescence. Social workers can play a part in increasing the availability of information about sexual development and orientation by advocating for accurate and inclusive school curricula beginning at the elementary educational level. Placing information about sexual orientation in the school curricula will bring the conversation to conscious awareness much earlier in people's lives. Resources from Women's Educational Media (http://www.imdb.com/title/tt1139107/), the American Psychological Association (http://www.apa.org/pi/lgbt/resources/just-the-facts.aspx), and the Human Rights Campaign (http://www.welcomingschools.org) provide important videos and informative articles that raise awareness and provide tools for social change.

Although these participants recalled early derisive messages about LGBT people, when advocates encountered LGBT people who were out and approachable, those messages were minimized or discounted. Further growth occurred when the participants recognized similarities and commonly held values in the LGBT people they came to know. We recognize the dilemma of many LGBT people's decisions to not be out because our social climate is hostile and often unsafe. The lack of safety perpetuates the closeted situation, which in turn makes it harder for people to interact openly and find common ground.

Theological beliefs were challenged when participants came to understand the complexities of sexual orientation and the role biology plays in determining sexual orientation development. Though inconclusive and incomplete, research offers mounting evidence of the salience of these biological impacts (Bailey, Dunne, & Martin, 2000; Hamer & Copeland, 1994). This information is helpful for potential straight allies to move toward becoming LGBT advocates. This information is not always easy to find or understand. Even in many human-behavior-in-the-social-environment textbooks, the biological connections with sexual orientation formation are often presented in an inconclusive or unconvincing manner.

One of the most important findings in this study is that these Christian social workers held a range of theological beliefs that did not prohibit them from active advocacy on behalf of LGBT people. These beliefs appeared fluid and were often adjusted and adapted over time. Whatever their beliefs about same-sex activity, these Christian advocates' broader theological beliefs unquestionably played an important part in motivating them to action. The importance of loving people and the centrality of caring for the oppressed stirred an internal response that resulted in social action.

Finally, Christian social workers engaged in a wide variety of advocacy actions on behalf of LGBT people. These actions embraced the expanse of social work intervention systems from micro to macro levels. The advocacy transpired with people they served, within the agencies, organizations, and educational settings, and in the broader political arena. These Christian social workers not only advocated for LGBT people from a commitment to social work values but also from a position of religious or moral conviction. Their adherence to Christian beliefs offered an intrinsic motivation to advocate for a group of people who are often discriminated against, not just in the Christian world but also by the larger society. It is important to acknowledge the work of these advocates and to expand on their efforts to further the dialogue, reduce tensions, and increase the ability to work together toward the same goals. As one participant noted, "The idea that you can't be Christian and a gay-rights advocate is one of the barriers we face in furthering the conversation" (Sylvia).

This chapter offered information about how one group of Christian social workers came to identify as LGBT advocates. Recognizing and emulating the experiences of these people may be an important step in this process, but how can social workers get started on this journey? First, take an inventory of your social and professional networks in terms of diversity. If your networks do not include an array of sexual minorities, be intentional about seeking out opportunities for expanding your network to include LGBT people. Next, as questions arise about sexual orientation issues use your newly expanded network for answers or examine peer-reviewed literature about sexual orientation formation and development. Finally, seek out spiritual and professional mentorship from other Christian social workers on the same journey. They probably will not have all the answers you seek, but they will offer reassurance that you are not alone, and the rewards are worth the investment.

References

Bailey, J. M., Dunne, M. P., & Martin, N. G. (2000). Genetic and environmental influences on sexual orientation and its correlates in an Australian twin sample. *Journal of Personality & Social Psychology, 78*, 524–536.

Berkman, C. S., & Zinberg, G. (1997). Homophobia and heterosexism in social workers. *Social Work, 42*, 319–332.

Butler, A., Elliott, T., & Stopard, N. (2003). Living up to the standards we set: A critical account of the development of anti-racist standards. *Social Work Education, 22*(3), 271–282.

Charmaz, K. (2006). *Constructing grounded theory*. London, UK: SAGE.

Cnaan, R., Boddie, S., & Danzig, R.(2005). Teaching about organized religion in social work. *Journal of Religion & Spirituality in Social Work: Social Thought, 24*(1), 93–110.

Crisp, C. (2007). Correlates of homophobia and use of gay affirmative practice among social workers. *Journal of Human Behavior in the Social Environment, 14*(4), 119–143.

Gay adoptions: "Catholic social services" becomes "Christian social services." (2012). Retrieved from http://www.catholicculture.org/news/headlines/index.cfm?storyid=13159

Gibelman, M. (1999). The search for identity: Defining social work—past, present, future. *Social Work, 44*(4), 298–310.

Glaser, B. G., & Strauss, A. L. (1967). *The discovery of grounded theory: Strategies for qualitative research*. Chicago, IL: Aldine.

Grace Gospel Chapel. (n.d.). Statement of faith. Retrieved from http://www.gracegospelwa.org/about-us/

Graham, J., & Shier, M. (2009). Religion and social work: An analysis of faith traditions, themes, and global north/south authorship. *Journal of Religion & Spirituality in Social Work: Social Thought, 28*(1), 215–233.

Haider-Markel, D., & Joslyn, M. R. (2008). Beliefs about the origins of homosexuality and support for gay rights. *Public Opinion Quarterly, 72*, 291–310.

Hamer, D., & Copeland, P. (1994). *The science of desire: The search for the gay gene and biology of behavior*. New York, NY: Simon & Schuster.

Kain, E. L. (2006, October). *The interconnections between measures of religiosity and attitudes about homosexuality.* Paper presented at the annual meetings of the Society for the Scientific Study of Religion, Portland, OR.

Karger, H. J., & Stoesz, D. (1998). *American social welfare policy* (3rd ed.). New York, NY: Longman.

Krieglstein, M. (2003). Heterosexism and social work: An ethical issue. *Journal of Human Behavior in the Social Environment, 8*(2/3), 75–91.

Krumer-Nevo, M., Monnickendam, M., & Weiss-Gal, I. (2009). Poverty-aware social work practice: A conceptual framework for social work education. *Journal of Social Work Education, 45*, 225–243.

Lincoln, Y., & Guba, E. G. (1985). *Naturalistic inquiry.* Beverly Hills, CA: SAGE.

Magnuson, N. (1977). *Salvation in the slums: Evangelical social work 1865–1920.* Grand Rapids, MI: Baker Book House.

Malcomnson, K. M., Christopher, A. N., Franzen, T., & Keyes, B. J. (2006). The Protestant work ethic, religious beliefs, and homonegative attitudes. *Mental Health, Religion & Culture, 9*, 435–447.

Marques, J. F., & McCall, C. (2005). The application of inter-rater reliability as a solidification instrument in a phenomenological study. *Qualitative Report, 10*, 439–462.

McDermott, S., Linahan, K., & Squires, B. (2009). Older people living in squalor: Ethical and practical dilemmas. *Australian Social Work, 62*(2), 245–257.

Newman, B. S. (2002). Lesbians, gays, and religion: Strategies for challenging belief systems. *Journal of Lesbian Studies, 6*, 87–99.

Newman, B., Dannenfelser, P., & Benishek, L. (2002). Assessing beginning social work and counseling students' acceptance of lesbian and gay men. *Journal of Social Work Education, 38*, 273–288.

Nieman, A. (2006). Churches and social development: A South African perspective. *International Social Work, 49*, 595–604.

Rodriguez, E. M. (2010). At the intersection of church and gay: A review of the psychological research on gay and lesbian Christians. *Journal of Homosexuality, 57*(1), 5–38.

Ryan, S. (2000). Examining social workers' placement recommendations of children with gay and lesbian adoptive parents. *Families in Society, 81*, 517–528.

Watkins, D. C., & Hartfield, J. A. (2012). Health education for social workers: A primer. *Social Work In Health Care, 51*, 680–694.

Wood, P. B., & Bartkowski, J. P. (2004). Attribution style and public policy attitudes toward gay rights. *Social Science Quarterly, 85*(1), 58–74.

SECTION IV

Interventions and Approaches to Resolving the Tensions

CHAPTER 14

Bridging the Conservative Christianity and Sexual Orientation Divide: A Review of Intergroup Dialogue Pedagogy and Practice

Adrienne B. Dessel, PhD, LMSW

Social work pedagogy strives to include discussions of power, privilege, oppression, and social justice. The Council on Social Work Education (CSWE, 2008) Educational Policy and Accreditation Standards specifically identifies social justice, human rights, the dignity and worth of the person, the importance of human relationships, and respect for all people as core values of social work education. Additionally, these standards call on social workers to "practice personal reflection and self-correction to assure continual professional development"; "recognize and manage personal values in a way that allows professional values to guide practice"; "gain sufficient self-awareness to eliminate the influence of personal biases and values in working with diverse groups"; "recognize the extent to which a culture's structures and values may oppress, marginalize, alienate, or create or enhance privilege and power"; and understand the mechanisms of oppression and advocate for human rights and social justice (CSWE, 2008, pp. 3–5).

These are demanding principles, as most people have grown up in a society rife with stereotypes, bias, and prejudice (Adams, Bell, & Griffin, 2007; Spencer, 2008), and leaving these at the door of social work institutions is not easy (Black, Oles, & Moore, 1998; Gross, 2000). Students may be anxious about sharing their biases for fear of offending others or seeming unprofessional (Ferguson, Harding, & Holleran, 2003; Hyde & Ruth, 2002). Multicultural learning, particularly for students from privileged backgrounds, challenges their prior socialization and what they know to be true about the world (Deal & Hyde, 2004; Griffin & Ouellet, 2007). Social work students enter a profession that expects them to adhere to these guidelines and practices, and social work faculty have a responsibility to support students in their learning process (Melville-Wiseman, 2013).

Gatekeeping, or ensuring that only students who are able to adhere to social work ethics and values enter or graduate from accredited degree programs, is one method of meeting these requirements (Gibbs & Blakely, 2000; Reynolds, 2004). Faculty in the United Kingdom developed a model to help incoming students discern conflicts between their personal and professional values with regard to religion and sexual orientation (Melville-Wiseman, 2013). Some faculty suggest that rather than gatekeeping, social work educators should encourage students to reveal their prejudices and examine them in order to achieve more positive attitude changes (Gross, 2000; Todd & Coholic, 2007). Yet many social work educators do not have the comfort and skills to promote this kind of examination (Bracy & Cunningham, 1995; Chinell, 2011; Daniel, 2011; Fleck-Henderson & Melendez, 2009). Faculty concerned about negative student evaluations may be anxious about how to negotiate conflict in the classroom and may be more focused on teaching traditional helping behaviors than critical analysis of social inequalities (Ferguson et al., 2003; Peeler, Snyder, & May, 2008). They may choose safety and avoidance of controversial topics (Fleck-Henderson & Melendez, 2009; Peeler et al., 2008; Wahl, Perez, Deegan, Sanchez, & Applegate, 2000) over critical dialogue (Sakamoto & Pitner, 2005). One study found social work educators were underprepared to engage students with social justice education material, and it illuminated the barriers faculty identified to teaching about social justice, such as limited opportunities to share teaching methods, lack of clarity about accreditation standards regarding social justice pedagogy, and lack of attention in doctoral programs (Funge, 2011). Garcia and Van Soest (2000) note the importance of faculty developing the ability to work with conflict and attend to affect and communication styles when negotiating tense classroom conversations related to social identity prejudice and oppression.

The intersection of sexual orientation and conservative religious beliefs, in particular, creates tension in social work classrooms (Melville-Wiseman, 2013; Streets, 2009; Todd & Coholic, 2007). Melville-Wiseman lays out the assumptions, stereotypes, and complexities that social work students navigate with regard to sexual orientation and religion. As in society, homophobia and heterosexism in social work educational and practice settings are well documented (Brownlee, Sprakes, Saini, O'Hare, Kortes-Miller, & Graham, 2005; Cosis-Brown & Cocker, 2011; Fish, 2007; Jeyasingham, 2008; Weiss, Morehouse, Yeager, & Berry, 2010). Students who identify as lesbian, gay, or bisexual (LGB) are not afforded basic civil, social, political, and economic human rights (Dewees & Roche, 2001; Melendez & LaSala, 2006). LGB people are denied freedom of sexual orientation (Hunter, 2011) and marriage and family equality (Pawelski et al., 2006), are subjected to job discrimination and are at risk of job loss (Badgett, 1996), and are victims of violence because of their sexual orientation (Balsam, Rothblum, & Beauchaine, 2005; Poteat & Espelage, 2007). Social work faculty may be reluctant to examine the heterosexism, homophobia, and structural oppression present in our society, or may lack knowledge and insight, and are in need of specific resources to teach about these issues (Dessel, Woodford, & Gutiérrez, 2012; Fredriksen-Goldsen, Gutiérrez, Luke, & Woodford, 2011). Furthermore, CSWE exempts some religious schools of social work from the nondiscrimination standard with regard to sexual orientation (Eckholm, 2011; George Fox University, 2014; Hunter & Hickerson, 2003; Kriegelstein, 2003), and at least one accredited school includes same-sex attraction in a course on deviant behavior such as murder and alcoholism (Brady, 2012).

On the other hand, some conservative Christian students may feel their views on sexual orientation are not accepted (Grady, Powers, Despard, & Naylor, 2011; Hodge, 2007; Ressler & Hodge, 2003). These students might also experience personal and professional value incongruity, and they might find professional guidelines difficult to follow with regard to LGB people (Hunter, 2010; Osteen, 2011). It is critical that the profession develop methods of teaching about this existing conflict in order to support all students in examining their views and the ethical issues involved.

Whereas there is a plethora of research on teaching about race and racial oppression in social work (Chu et al., 2009; Garcia & Van Soest, 2000; Miller & Donner, 2000; Rozas, 2007), there is very little literature on teaching about the intersection of sexual orientation and religion in the context of social justice education. Absent from much of the discussion about these issues is a critical analysis of power and privilege, of the relationship between bias, discrimination, oppression, and violence (Hyers & Hyers, 2008; Parrott, Zeichner, & Hoover, 2006; Wagner, Christ, & Pettigrew, 2008), and the complicated discussion about sexual orientation as biology or choice (Brookey, 2000; Vanderwoerd, 2002). Currently, interpretations of what social justice means in social work curricula appear to be unclear for some (Hong & Hodge, 2009). The National Association of Social Workers (NASW) Code of Ethics and the Education Policy and Accreditation Standards (EPAS) guidelines are not fully equipped to assist faculty and students in addressing the religion versus sexual orientation values debate in social work, because neither group is privileged above another, yet religious requirements of some accredited schools may be discriminatory toward LGB people (CSWE, 2008; HuffPost College, 2011; Vanderwoerd, 2002). Recognizing the dilemmas presented by the Code of Ethics, Canda and Furman (1999) suggest "constructive dialogue for mutual understanding" (p. 113). Students need an opportunity to engage in critical reflection about their belief systems and how they have developed (Holley & Steiner, 2005; Trotter, Crawley, Duggan, Foster, & Levie, 2009) to fully develop into culturally competent and socially just practitioners.

Given all these challenges, social work education must be intentional about providing explicit opportunities for student learning. Intergroup dialogue is proposed here as one method that can be a resource to faculty, students, and administrators in sorting through the challenging complexity of this conflict between certain conservative Christian beliefs and LGB people. Intergroup dialogue is an important pedagogy that offers faculty the opportunity to engage students in both affective and cognitive learning about social identity conflict and social justice issues (Zúñiga, Nagda, Chesler, & Cytron-Walker, 2007). Knowledge of intergroup dialogue theory and skills is important for social work educators and practitioners (Dessel, 2011; Dessel, Rogge, & Garlington, 2006; Nagda, Kim, & Truelove, 2004; Rodenborg & Bosch, 2008; Spencer, Martineau, & Warren, 2011). This chapter provides an overview of the contributions of intergroup dialogue to teaching about social identity conflicts and the use of this pedagogy in addressing the conflict surrounding sexual orientation and religious identity in social work. The use of intergroup dialogue pedagogy by social work faculty and practitioners is described. Additionally, intergroup dialogue practice by social workers in community settings is discussed to illustrate how the method is used outside the classroom.

Contributions of Intergroup Dialogue Pedagogy to Teaching About Social Identity and Conflict

Intergroup dialogue methods hold great promise for tackling the current conflict in social work with regard to affirmation of LGB sexual orientation and freedom of religious expression. Intergroup dialogue is a face-to-face co-facilitated and sustained group experience involving two (and sometimes more) social identity groups who have a history of conflict (Nagda, Gurin, Sorensen, & Zúñiga, 2009; Zúñiga et al., 2007). Dialogue pedagogy and practice provide a safe, facilitated opportunity for participants to engage in self-reflection, personal sharing, active listening, and perspective taking. This pedagogy allows students to explore attitudes about polarizing social issues, social power, and oppression for the purpose of developing relationships and promoting social change (Dessel et al., 2006; Nagda & Gurin, 2007; Zúñiga et al., 2007). Intergroup dialogue educators, practitioners, and researchers from a wide range of disciplines seek to understand and ameliorate social problems of prejudice, oppression, and intergroup conflict (Dessel & Rogge, 2008). These problems exist on both a micro and macro level, involving psychological, interpersonal, structural, and societal processes (Adams et al., 2007; Dovidio & Gaertner, 1999; Jayaratne et al., 2006; Sibley, Robertson, & Wilson, 2006) (Figure 1). The practice of intergroup dialogue offers social workers the opportunity to combine both the relational and psychological skills of clinical work with macro approaches of community organizing, activism, and structural social change (Dessel et al., 2006; Gutiérrez, Lewis, Dessel, & Spencer, 2012) (see Figure 2). Furthermore, intergroup dialogue bridges individual, group, and structural approaches to analyzing and redressing inequality and oppression in a variety of settings (Peeler et al., 2008; Spencer et al., 2011).

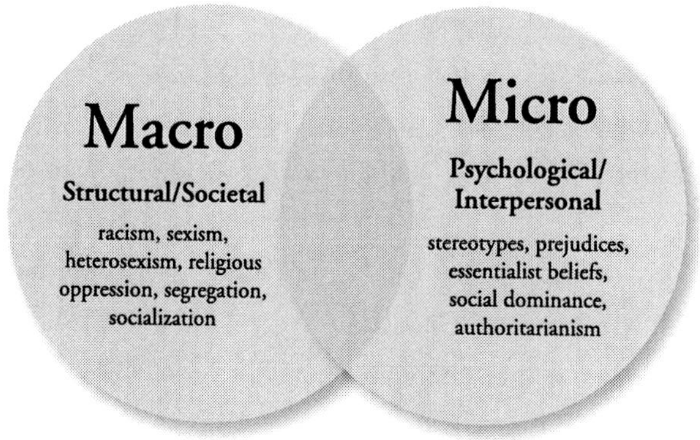

Macro
Structural/Societal
racism, sexism, heterosexism, religious oppression, segregation, socialization
Micro
Psychological/ Interpersonal
stereotypes, prejudices, essentialist beliefs, social dominance, authoritarianism

Figure 1. Processes that interfere with social justice (Source: Adams, Bell, & Griffin, 2007; Dovidio & Gaertner, 1996; Jayaratne et al., 2006; Sibley, Robertson, & Wilson, 2006).

Macro
Social Action
Social Justice Pedagogy
Micro
Perspective Taking
Empathy
Relationships
Knowledge

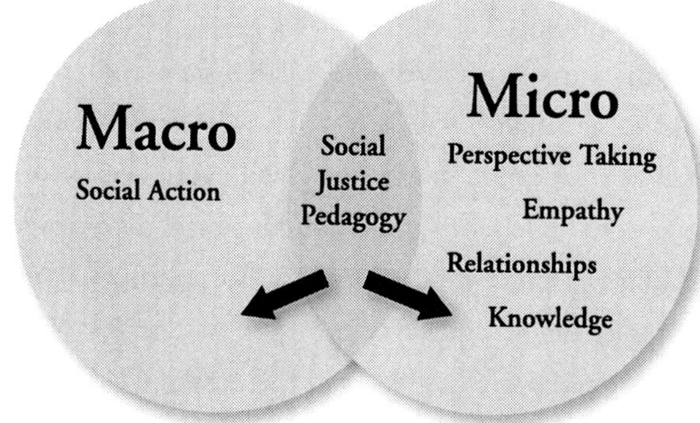

Figure 2. How intergroup dialogue addresses these processes.

There are a number of important theories and processes involved in intergroup dialogue, including contact theory, social identity, attitudes, social constructionism, communication, the relationship between emotions and behavior, and analysis of power (Dessel & Rogge, 2008; Rodenborg & Boisen, 2013). David Bohm, an early theorist, emphasized that the dialogue process explores "closely held values, the nature and intensity of emotions, the patterns of thought processes, the function of memory, the import of inherited cultural myths, and the manner in which neurophysiologic processes structure moment-to-moment experiences" (1996, p. vii). Allport's (1954) contact theory and related social psychological theories provide extensive analyses of intergroup behavior, such as the role of cognitive recategorization of outgroup members and cross-group friendships in facilitating positive intergroup relationships (Pettigrew & Tropp, 2006; Stephan & Stephan, 2001). Emotions play a critical role in intergroup dialogue and bias reduction (Khuri, 2004; Stephan & Finlay, 1999), and the process engages students in affective as well as cognitive learning (Zúñiga et al., 2007). Theories from the field of neuropsychology contribute to an understanding of intergroup relationships with regard to the relationship between prejudice, amygdala activity, and self-regulation (Dovidio, Pearson, & Orr, 2008).

Social identity refers to group-based identities such as race, gender, social class, sexual orientation, and religion (Adams et al., 2007; Sorensen et al., 2009). Intergroup dialogue intentionally engages participants around salient, claimed, and ascribed identities to examine how they interact with power and oppression in society. This method also offers students a needed opportunity to examine multiple and intersecting social identities (Ferguson et al., 2003; Dessel, Massé, & Walker, 2013). Intergroup dialogue facilitators use their own social identity to model sharing of experiences and learning (Garcia & Van Soest, 2000; Nagda & Maxwell, 2011).

Intergroup dialogue offers an important method for communicating across identity and cultural conflict. Early conceptions of dialogue viewed it as a relational mode of communication that was transformative for human relationships (Buber, 1958). Communication theorists contribute to the practice of dialogue by highlighting choice of communication practices, the dynamics of self-expression, and their implications for public deliberation work (Anderson, Baxter, & Cissna, 2004; Anderson & Cissna, 2008). Studies of undergraduate students who take intergroup dialogue courses show that four communication processes contribute to bridge building across social identity conflict (Nagda, 2006). Intergroup dialogue pedagogy in higher education settings uses a critical-dialogic four-stage model: (1) developing relationships and a shared meaning of dialogue (2) analyzing social identity, power, and group-based inequalities, (3) exploring hot topics issues of social justice (4) fostering collaboration and action planning (Nagda & Maxwell, 2011; Sorensen et al., 2009).

Some faculty use social justice education techniques and activities that are part of intergroup dialogue pedagogy to create a safe environment in traditional classrooms to explore conflicting views (Holley & Steiner, 2005; Peeler et al., 2008; Spencer et al., 2011). Creating safe spaces for conflict in the classroom is an imperative goal for social work educators (Fleck-Henderson & Melendez, 2009; Holley & Steiner, 2005). Conflict presents many challenges but can also be a productive catalyst for change (Gundykunst, 2004). Intergroup dialogue facilitators distinguish between safety and comfort, in that it is desirable for all participants to feel safe but not necessarily comfortable, because discomfort can create a learning moment that leads to new knowledge (Hardiman, Jackson, & Griffin, 2007; Peeler et al., 2008). Methods for achieving a safe space to enhance learning include the use of guidelines to reduce anxiety and resistance (Deal & Hyde, 2004), nonviolent communication practices (Love Makes a Family, 1993; Rosenberg, 2003), and sequential lower- to higher-level risk taking in sharing experiences and emotions (Hyde & Ruth, 2002; Zúñiga et al., 2007). Attention to physical space, such as circle seating arrangements, can reduce power imbalances. Use of icebreakers, sharing of personal narratives, and working in dyads and small groups are all techniques used to develop relationships (Adams et al., 2007; Zúñiga et al., 2007). Additional dialogic techniques include use of role plays to examine prejudice (Plous, 2000) and exercises that analyze socialization and power (Adams et al., 2007). Griffin and colleagues (Adams et al., 2007) have developed a specific heterosexism curriculum design that incorporates many of these techniques. These pedagogies are valuable resources for faculty who may not be ready or able to fully establish and offer intergroup dialogue courses.

One study of BSW and MSW students examined students' experiences with "safe" versus "unsafe" classes and found that many intergroup dialogue characteristics, such as instructor comfort with conflict and modeling of participation, use of ground rules, inclusion of cultural content, circular seating, suspension of judgments, and honest sharing led to a safe classroom learning environment (Holley & Steiner, 2005). Intergroup dialogue facilitation builds affective relationships and communication skills (Nagda & Maxwell, 2011), and participation in intergroup dialogue courses has been shown in national studies to increase understanding, relationships, and action across social boundaries (Nagda, Gurin, Sorensen, Gurin-Sands, & Osuna, 2009; Nagda, Gurin, Sorensen, & Zúñiga, 2009).

The method of intergroup dialogue is also a valuable tool in teaching about group work, an area that is defined by a focus on mutually supportive group interactions, transparency, participatory facilitators who are not neutral but contribute their own experiences, and power sharing among group members (Kurland, 2007; Kurland & Salmon, 2006). Dialogue work affords an understanding of social identity and small group process that is critical to promoting positive intergroup relations in society (Hogg, Abrams, Otten, & Hinkle, 2004; Kivlighan & Arseneau, 2009; Spencer et al., 2008). Intergroup dialogue as a small group method promotes social change by supporting empowerment of participants and coalition building across differences (Alvarez & Cabbil, 2001; Gitterman & Schulman, 2005).

Finally, it is imperative to raise social work students' consciousness about power and oppression and support them in making connections across differences in religious beliefs and sexual orientation to ultimately form alliances (Peeler et al., 2008). Analysis of power and privilege is an important component of intergroup dialogue practice (Agbaria & Cohen, 2002; Saguy, Dovidio, & Pratto, 2008; Spencer, Brown, Griffin, & Abdullah, 2008) and is important for social workers to understand as well. For example, examining Christian privilege and the finding that frequent religious attendance for students strongly predicted negative attitudes toward lesbian and gay people (Blumenfield, 2006; Swank & Raiz, 2010). Further, religiosity in Christian social work faculty in one school predicted less accepting attitudes toward lesbian and gay people (Dessel et al., 2012). However, there appears to be little understanding of this oppression in social work by Christians. The field is in dire need of a pedagogy that promotes critical consciousness and social justice around sexual orientation prejudice (Mayhew & Fernández, 2007;

Todd & Coholic, 2007). Intergroup dialogue promotes such critical analysis, which can lead to antioppressive social work practice (Nagda & Gurin, 2007; Sakamoto & Pitner, 2005).

To become culturally competent social workers, all students need to become aware of their own values, biases, and views regarding social identity and justice content, have the opportunity to interact with those different from them in safe and trusting classroom environments, and then be supported to become skilled at working with various populations (Kohli, Huber, & Faul, 2010). Intergroup dialogue methods and pedagogy offer faculty an important and needed resource in social justice education (Deal & Hyde, 2004; Jacobson, 2009). Intergroup dialogue can be facilitated by trained faculty or peer-facilitated by trained graduate or undergraduate students (Dessel & Rogge, 2008; Maxwell, Nagda, & Thompson, 2011). In the next section this method as used by social work educators and practitioners, and others in the field of dialogue, is described in detail.

Intergroup Dialogue Pedagogy in Social Work

A strong and growing contingent of social work faculty recognize the value and effectiveness of intergroup dialogue pedagogy (Boulden, 2006; Dessel, Woodford, & Warren, 2011; Garvin, 2008; Griffin, Brown, & Warren, 2012; Mildred & Zúñiga, 2004; Miller, Donner, & Fraser, 2004; Nagda et al., 2004; Richards-Schuster & Aldana, 2013; Rodenborg & Bosch, 2008; Rozas, 2004, 2007; Sakamoto & Pitner, 2005; Schatz, Furman, & Jenkins, 2003; Scheyett & Kim 2004; Spencer et al., 2008, 2011). To address social inequalities, these faculty members use this method in classrooms and community settings to examine social identity, privilege, power, and oppression, decrease prejudice, communicate across conflict, develop intergroup understanding, foster positive intergroup relationships, and promote intergroup collaboration across differences. This chronology of social work leaders in the field of intergroup dialogue provides examples of the work being done, role models for future work, and resources for social work students and faculty looking to learn more about the practice of intergroup dialogue.

Laura Chasin, Sally Ann Roth, and colleagues cofounded the Public Conversations Project in 1989 as part of an action research project by the

Family Institute of Cambridge that sought to apply family therapy practices to polarized public debates (Chasin et al., 1996). The project's work addresses conflicts such as abortion, environmental sustainability, sexual orientation and religion, and international religious disputes. They aim to shift people who are stuck in debate into dialogic communication and a new type of discourse. They do this through techniques such as collaborative planning, the use of guidelines and crafted questions, and highly structured dialogues that promote genuine inquiry and exploration of gray areas of thinking, or attitudes that may represent ambivalence for some people. Their work is influenced by principles and practices of appreciative inquiry and narrative therapy, and their website (http://www.publicconversations.org) features many useful manuals and videos for practitioners who are interested in learning their methods.

Ratnesh Nagda is a leader in the field of intergroup dialogue, and early on he and his colleagues (1999) pointed out the need for the field of social work to develop pedagogical approaches to teaching about social injustice. Dr. Nagda directs the Intergroup Dialogue, Education and Action (IDEA) Training and Resource Institute in the School of Social Work at the University of Washington, Seattle (http://depts.washington.edu/sswidea/pubs.html) and is part of a national intergroup dialogue project across nine universities and colleges that has examined the processes and outcomes of race or ethnicity and gender intergroup dialogue courses (Nagda, Gurin, Sorensen, & Zúñiga, 2009). His work has focused on racial identity awareness and reconciliation as well as gender, and he engages undergraduate students in intergroup dialogue courses to promote cultural competence and social justice (Nagda et al., 1999; Nagda & Zúñiga, 2003). Dr. Nagda's primarily quantitative research has shown that intergroup dialogue participation increases students' motivation for intergroup learning and their confidence in taking action to reduce prejudice for both White students and students of color (Nagda et al., 2004). Using factor analysis, he delineated four communication processes involved in intergroup dialogue: appreciating difference, engaging self, critical self-reflection, and alliance building (Nagda, 2006). His experimental study found that, for a sample of more than 1,450 students in race and gender dialogues across the country in nine institutions, students developed perspective taking and empathy, learned about structural inequality, and increased their motivation to bridge differences (Gurin, Nagda, & Zúñiga, 2013). Over the years Dr. Nagda has highlighted the important role intergroup dialogue plays in learning about social group–based differences, the development of critical consciousness about social inequality, and the imperative to bridge theory, research, and practice in anti-prejudice work (Nagda & Gurin, 2007; Nagda, Gurin, Sorensen, Gurin-Sands, & Osuna, 2009; Nagda, Tropp, & Paluck, 2006). One community-based example of his work has been his mixed-methods evaluation of Study Circles intergroup dialogues with youth in the Mix-It-Up program, which is designed to support youths in improving relationships across social boundaries (Nagda, McCoy, & Barrett, 2006). Results indicated that students developed relationships and understanding across social barriers and the level of conflict in the school decreased. This was perceived as related to the dialogues, and youths of color in particular increased their feelings of empowerment to create positive change in their schools.

Joshua Miller and social work colleagues at Smith College School for Social Work outline their use of a one-time campus intergroup dialogue on race involving graduate social work students, faculty, and staff (Miller & Donner, 2000). Along with their colleague, Jane Mildred, they recommend dialogic methods for student resistance to conversations about race, gender, sexual orientation, and social class (Mildred & Zúñiga, 2004; Miller et al., 2004). Lisa Werkmeister-Rozas at the School of Social Work, University of Connecticut, offers an analysis of intergroup dialogue pedagogy in connection with Bakhtin's dialogic concepts (Bakhtin, 1934/1981; Dessel, 2011; Rozas, 2004). Dr. Rozas describes a qualitative study of sustained intergroup dialogues focusing on race that were held in residence halls with undergraduate women. Results centered on students' motivations for participating in the dialogue, their experiences in intergroup dialogue, and learning outcomes (Rozas, 2007). Students developed awareness and understanding about social identity, including the complexity of intersectional identities and recategorization of others, and interpersonal action strategies based on the relationships that developed. Dr. Rozas links intergroup dialogue methods to EPAS standards (CSWE, 2008) and highlights their relevancy for both micro and macro social work practice. Rozas and Miller (2009) describe many important social justice education concepts, such as socialization and institutional racism, that are woven into intergroup dialogue pedagogy.

Mona Schatz and colleagues (2003) used intergroup dialogue methods at a multinational conference in Russia and in Washington, DC. They note that dialogue practice is grounded in group work, and is an important skill for global social work practice. To promote greater understanding about people with mental illness, Anna Scheyett and Mimi Kim (2004) also applied dialogue methods in a community setting with consumers of mental health services and MSW students. Pretest, posttest, and qualitative interview data indicated that students lowered their need for social distance and increased their empathy and understanding of the consumer participants, and consumers felt valued and appreciated the dialogue process.

Nancy Rodenborg and Nancy Huynh (2006) examined a 6-year interracial and interethnic community-based dialogue and found that readiness for dialogue engagement, friendship potential, and facilitation strategies all contributed to the sustainability of the group. Participants defined the success of the group in terms of healing interpersonal relationships across racial identity divides, advocacy work, formation of new dialogue groups, and greater interracial awareness and skills. This model offers social workers a method for both community and interpersonal practice work that addresses important issues of social justice. Rodenborg and colleagues at Augsburg College's MSW program recognize the importance of using intergroup dialogue methods in their graduate courses to address segregation, raise awareness about bias and prejudice, and improve cultural competence (Bosch, Rodenborg, & Boisen, 2011; Rodenborg, Boisen, & Bosch, 2011). Their mixed-methods research on these dialogue courses, which are based on intergroup contact theory and the Program on Intergroup Relations model (Maxwell et al., 2011; Pettigrew, 1998), found students showed increased awareness about oppression, privilege, and bias and increased confidence in being an ally for oppressed groups. These researchers recommend quantitative analysis of the data, triangulation of data collection methods, a focus on student skill development, and follow-up data to measure long-terms effects.

Walter Boulden (2006) has implemented intergroup dialogue in a community setting with 223 youth to promote multicultural education and challenge privilege and oppression. A week-long residential session used intergroup dialogue methods, and a mixed-methods analysis of pre and post surveys showed increased awareness and knowledge about racial and ethnic oppression and increased confidence to take action to combat bias and discrimination. Boulden notes that dialogue promotes important discourse about marginalized group experiences, including those of the LGBT community.

My own work with colleagues at the University of Tennessee College of Social Work (Dessel et al., 2006) examined the practice of intergroup dialogue as a method social workers can use in academic and community settings to promote social justice and social change. A subsequent publication offered an in-depth overview and analysis of intergroup dialogue theory, goals, and, most importantly, research methods and outcomes (Dessel & Rogge, 2008).

I also worked with Noor Ali (Dessel & Ali, 2011, 2012) to examine Arab–Jewish intergroup dialogue courses at the University of Michigan, exploring this international conflict that also plays out on U.S. college campuses. We found that students improved their communication skills, perspective taking and empathy, and critical self-reflection about power and oppression, and they developed friendships and commitments to social change efforts. Yet many students remained unchanged in how their identities were attached to the land, and Jewish students resisted acknowledging the social privilege they held. Related community intergroup dialogue work with Arab and Jewish participants over a 2-year period aimed to build bridges in the wake of the terrorist attacks of September 11, 2001 (Gutiérrez et al., 2012).

Michael Spencer and colleagues at the University of Michigan and Washington University St. Louis teach an MSW course that offers experience and training in intergroup dialogue facilitation as a method of multicultural social work practice (Spencer et al., 2011). Dr. Spencer has long advocated for the importance in social work education of examining power, privilege, and oppression related to social identity (Spencer, 2008). This course prepares social work students to critically engage with social identity, power, and oppression, teaches them necessary dialogic communication skills, and prepares them for social action in various settings.

Charles Garvin, Michael Spencer, and colleagues directed a project that facilitates intergroup dialogues in Midwest high school settings, and they note the importance of this intervention for youth who struggle with racial, sexual orientation, and other identity-based conflicts (Garvin, 2008; Griffin et al., 2012; Spencer et al., 2008). They found students improved their relationships across social identities and increased their awareness of intergroup relations. Students increased their desire to improve relationships, learned conflict management skills, and reported changes in behavior such as a reduction in prejudice and bullying. The authors note their valuable partnership with public schools and the particular challenges of integrating dialogue work into these settings.

Katie Richards-Schuster and Adriana Aldana (2013) conducted similar intergroup dialogue work with youth in community settings, focused primarily around race. Their case study assessment of an 8-week summer program found that these youth also strengthened their abilities to communicate across racial differences and developed important leadership skills.

Intergroup dialogue pedagogy as practiced by social work faculty and practitioners has produced important results of learning about privilege and oppression, building relationships across differences, and changing behavior. Studies have used experimental, quasi-experimental, mixed methods, and qualitative designs to evaluate outcomes of this work. Some results indicate the need for further attention within this pedagogy to resistance to learning about privilege. Overall, intergroup dialogue has been demonstrated to be a promising method for engaging social work students, social work faculty, and community members around the tensions that exist with regard to LGB people and conservative Christianity. Studies that have applied dialogue pedagogy and practice to bridge this particular divide will be discussed next.

Intergroup Dialogue and Sexual Orientation Prejudice

A small but growing body of literature specifically examines the use of intergroup dialogue to address homophobia and heterosexism. Wong and Poon (2013) describe a case study of a community-based critical dialogue with 12

Hong Kong Chinese immigrant parents in Toronto that aimed to reduce homophobia and mobilize parents to become active in preventing homophobic bullying. The data collected included observations, parent reflective journals, focus groups, interviews, surveys, and educational materials developed by the parents. Parents increased their awareness of their own heteronormativity and confidence in talking with their children about sexuality, and they challenged homophobia in their communities.

My mixed-methods, experimental design community study examined views and behaviors of heterosexual public school teachers in a highly conservative Christian community in East Tennessee (Scudera, 2013) who engaged in three intergroup dialogue sessions with LGB community members (Dessel, 2010). The majority of the teachers identified as Baptist, Protestant, or Catholic and scored fairly high on a religiosity scale (3.36, range 1–5). Results indicated that after dialogue participation these teachers experienced significant positive changes in their views about LGB civil rights, feelings about gay and lesbian people, perspective taking, and, importantly, affirming and supportive behaviors. Teachers attributed these changes to the participants in the dialogue and the reflective and supportive nature of the dialogue process (Dessel, 2010).

A number of other studies on university campuses examine experiences for college students participating in sexual orientation dialogues. Miles and colleagues (Chapter 15, this volume) examined participation by nine students in a sexual orientation intergroup dialogue course that was one section of an undergraduate multicultural psychology course offered in a counseling psychology program at a university located in a conservative Christian community. This course followed the four-stage critical dialogic pedagogy developed by the Program on Intergroup Relations (Sorensen et al., 2009, Zúñiga et al., 2007) and in particular addressed the intersectionality of religion and sexual orientation. Results indicated students reported a reduction in intergroup prejudice, built relationships across differences, developed awareness of privilege, oppression, and intersectionality, and developed capacities to work for social justice.

Two studies examined undergraduate sexual orientation intergroup dialogue courses offered by the Program on Intergroup Relations at the

University of Michigan. These courses are peer facilitated and balanced with roughly equal numbers of students who identify as either heterosexual or LGB. Religious identity information was not collected. Dessel, Woodford, routenberg, and Breijak (2013) conducted a qualitative study of heterosexual student experiences in these dialogue courses using 46 heterosexual student final papers and interviews of eight heterosexual students. Students learned about the social identity oppression their LGB peers face and also about their own heterosexual privilege. Learning about privilege was enhanced by new awareness of the intersectionality of identity and privilege (Dessel, Massé, & Walker, 2013). With the information learned in this dialogue course they were able to shift their stereotypical views of LGB people. Research on the experiences of LGB undergraduate students in these same dialogue courses explored important questions about the experiences of marginalized groups in intergroup dialogue. Results indicated LGB students learned about their own and other sexual orientation identities and experienced greater critical consciousness and empowerment to create social change. LBG students also faced challenges with regard to their own emotional sharing and the lack of mutual sharing by heterosexual students and recommendations were made for curriculum improvements (Dessel et al., 2011).

Intergroup dialogue is an important pedagogical tool to address the tension often found in social work classrooms with regard to the intersection of sexual orientation and conservative religious beliefs. Dialogue pedagogy builds on intergroup contact theory (Rodenborg & Boisen, 2013) and uses methods that promote reflective learning about social identity and social power, engagement with emotions and conflict management skills, and social action. Intergroup dialogue has the potential to address heterosexist beliefs that some Christian social work students may hold (Walls & Seelman, 2014) and raise awareness about heterosexual privilege (Walls & Todd, 2014) as well as to foster bridge building and collaborative action.

Conclusion

The intersection of freedom of religious expression and freedom of sexual orientation expression poses great challenge and opportunity for social workers.

The field has long embraced the values of self-determination and nondiscrimination (Reamer, 1998), even as it has grappled with prejudices and resistance to self-examination (Black et al., 1998; Bowie, 2003; Rozas & Miller, 2009). As this review indicates, many social work faculty and practitioners use intergroup dialogue pedagogy and practice to address a wide range of conflicts. The method offers tools that are critical to both supporting conservative religious students in exploration of their views and addressing the human rights issues and injustices experienced by LGB members of society. In this way, dialogue bridges the gaps of experience and understanding.

Intergroup dialogue methods take into consideration the strong emotions present in intergroup conflict and offer a supportive way to engage with emotionality in the learning process (Khuri, 2004). Particular attention is paid to power and privilege and the acknowledgment of power differentials based on social identity. Analysis of power in the sexual orientation and religion debate is critical in moving forward with human rights and social justice work (Dover, 2009). Intergroup dialogue also creates opportunity for humanizing the "other" in a way that allows for dignity, personal relationships, and alliance building (Dessel & Ali, 2012). This is important given that this particular conflict between some conservative Christians and lesbian, gay, and bisexual people involves attributions of immorality and shame (American Baptist Churches USA, 2005). Dialogue both acknowledges that there are multiple perspectives present in any particular social identity conflict and also promotes the importance of action and change in redressing social inequities (Zúñiga et al., 2007).

The tension between certain conservative Christian views and antioppressive social work practice cannot be ignored (Todd & Coholic, 2007). The profession is urged to embrace these tensions; conflict is an important learning tool (Pettit, 2006), and dialogue methods can foster greater interpersonal understanding and growth as well as institutional and societal equality. EPAS standards mandate that social work students advance human rights (CSWE, 2008). Christianity likewise has this same commitment (Jimenez, 2006). Yet social work educators still struggle with how to operationalize this goal (Funge, 2011; Hong & Hodge, 2009). Intergroup dialogue offers a method that engages students cognitively and affectively in learning about these issues.

It is a pedagogy that offers faculty the ability to become more proficient in facilitating difficult classroom conversations about sexual orientation and conservative Christian views (Funge, 2011). Finally, intergroup dialogue facilitation methods are valuable skills that social workers can carry out into the community as they implement them in their own practice to promote human rights for vulnerable populations.

References

Adams, M., Bell, L. A., & Griffin, P. (2007). *Teaching for diversity and social justice.* New York, NY: Routledge.

Agbaria, F., & Cohen, C. (2002). *Working with groups in conflict: The impact of power relations on the dynamics of the group.* Waltham, MA: Brandeis University, The International Center for Ethics, Justice and Public Life.

Allport, G.(1954). *The nature of prejudice.* Cambridge, MA: Addison-Wesley.

Alvarez, A. R., & Cabbil, L. (2001). The MELD program: Promoting personal social change and social justice through a year long multicultural group experience. *Social Work With Groups, 24*(1), 3–20. doi:10.1300/J009v24n01_02

American Baptist Churches USA (ABCUSA). (2005). *American Baptist Churches USA: Responses/actions pertaining to homosexuality.* Retrieved from http://www.abc-usa.org/LinkClick.aspx?fileticket=iRGq66AgLAU=&tabid=199

Anderson, R., Baxter, L. A., & Cissna, K. N. (Eds.). (2004). *Dialogue: Theorizing difference in communication studies.* Thousand Oaks, CA: SAGE.

Anderson, R., & Cissna, K. (2008). Fresh perspectives in dialogue theory. *Communication Theory, 18,* 1–4. doi:10.1111/j.1468-2885.2007.00310.x

Badgett, M. L. (1996). Employment and sexual orientation: Disclosure and discrimination in the workplace. *Journal of Gay and Lesbian Social Services, 4*(4), 29–52. doi:10.1300/J041v04n04_03

Bakhtin, M. M. (1981). Discourse in the novel. In M. Holquist (Ed.), *The dialogic imagination: Four essays* (pp. 257–422). Austin, TX: University of Austin Press. (Original work published 1934)

Balsam, K., Rothblum, E., & Beauchaine, T. (2005). Victimization over the life span: A comparison of lesbian, gay, bisexual, and heterosexual siblings. *Journal of Consulting and Clinical Psychology, 73,* 477–487. doi:10.1037/0022-006X.73.3.477

Black, B., Oles, T. P., & Moore, L. (1998). The relationship between attitudes: Homophobia and sexism among social work students. *Affilia, 13*(2), 166–189. doi:10.1177/088610999801300204

Blumenfield, W. J. (2006). Christian privilege and the promotion of "secular" and not so "secular" mainline Christianity in public schooling and in the larger society. *Equity & Excellence in Education, 39*, 195–210.

Bohm, D. (1996). *On dialogue* (Ed. L. Nichol). New York, NY: Routledge.

Bosch, L., Rodenborg, N., & Boisen, L. (2011, October). *Understanding diversity and inequality through intergroup dialogue: Skill development for group facilitation.* Paper presented at the Council for Social Work Education Annual Program Meeting, Atlanta, GA.

Boulden, W. (2006). Youth leadership, racism, and intergroup dialogue. *Journal of Ethnic and Cultural Diversity in Social Work, 15*(1/2), 1–26. doi:10.1300/J051v15n01_01

Bowie, S. (2003). Perceived diversity and multiculturalism content in HBSE courses. *Journal of Human Behavior in the Social Environment, 8*(1), 1–23. doi: 10.1300/J137v08n01_01

Bracy, W., & Cunningham, M. (1995). Factors contributing to the retention of minority students: Implications for incorporating diversity. *Journal of Baccalaureate Social Work, 1*(1), 85–95.

Brady, J. (2012, September 10). College course lumps homosexuality, rape, murder. *NPR.* Retrieved from http://www.npr.org/2012/09/10/160763549/college-course-lumps-homosexuality-rape-murder

Brookey, R. A. (2000). Saints or sinners: Sociobiological theories of male homosexuality. *International Journal of Sexuality and Gender Studies, 5*(1), 37–58. doi:10.1023/A:1010185517893

Brownlee, K., Sprakes, A., Saini, M., O'Hare, R., Kortes-Miller, K., & Graham, J. (2005). Heterosexism among social work students. *Social Work Education, 24*(5), 485–494. doi:10.1080/02615470500132756

Buber, M. (1958). *I and thou.* New York, NY: Charles Scribner.

Canda, E. R., & Furman, L. D. (1999). *Spiritual diversity in social work practice.* New York, NY: The Free Press.

Chasin, R., Herzig, M., Roth, S., Chasin, L., Becker, C., & Stains, R. (1996). From diatribe to dialogue on divisive public issues: Approaches drawn from family therapy. *Mediation Quarterly, 13*(4), 1–19.

Chinell, J. (2011). Three voices: Reflections on homophobia and heterosexism in social work education. *Social Work Education, 30*, 759–773. doi:10.1080/02615479.2010.508088

Chu, M., Jones, T., Phan, P., Vugia, H., Woods, D. R., & Wright, P. (2009). A social work program's experience in teaching about race in the curriculum. *Journal of Social Work Education, 45*, 325–333. Retrieved from http://dx.doi.org/10.5175/JSWE.2009.200700056

Cosis-Brown, H., & C. Cocker, C. (2011). *Social work with lesbians and gay men.* London, England: SAGE.

Council on Social Work Education (CSWE). (2008). Educational policy and accreditation standards. Retrieved from http://www.cswe.org/File.aspx?id=13780

Daniel, C. (2011). Lessons learned: Pedagogical tensions and struggles with instruction on multiculturalism in social work education programs. *Social Work Education, 30*, 250–265. doi:10.1080/02615471003789829

Deal, K., & Hyde, C. (2004). Understanding MSW student anxiety and resistance to multicultural learning, *Journal of Teaching in Social Work, 24*(1–2), 73–86. doi:10.1300/J067v24n01_05

Dessel, A. (2010). Effects of intergroup dialogue: Public school teachers and sexual orientation prejudice. *Small Group Research, 41*, 556–592. doi:10.1177/1046496410369560

Dessel, A. (2011). Dialogue and social change: An interdisciplinary and transformative history. *Smith College Studies in Social Work, 81*(2/3), 167–183.

Dessel, A., & Ali, N. (2011). The Minds of Peace and intergroup dialogue: Two complementary approaches to peace. *Israel Affairs, 18*(1), 123–139. doi: 10.1080/13537121.2012.634276

Dessel, A., & Ali, N. (2012). Arab/Jewish intergroup dialogue courses: Building communication skills, relationships, and social justice. *Small Group Research, 43*, 559–586. doi:10.1177/1046496412453773

Dessel, A., Massé, J., & Walker, L. (2013). Intergroup dialogue pedagogy: Learning about intersectional and unexamined areas of privilege. In K. Case (Ed.), *Pedagogy of privilege: Teaching and learning as allies in the classroom* (pp. 132–148). New York, NY: Routledge Press.

Dessel, A., & Rogge, M. (2008). Evaluation of intergroup dialogue: A review of the empirical Literature. *Conflict Resolution Quarterly, 26*(2), 199–238. doi: 10.1002/crq.230

Dessel, A., Rogge, M., & Garlington, S. (2006). Using intergroup dialogue to promote social justice and change. *Social Work, 51*, 303–315. doi:10.1093/sw/51.4.303

Dessel, A., Woodford, M., & Gutiérrez, L. (2012). Social work faculty's attitudes toward marginalized groups: Exploring the role of religion. *Journal of Religion & Spirituality in Social Work: Social Thought, 31*(3), 244–262. doi:10.1080/15426432.2012.679841

Dessel, A., Woodford, M., routenberg, r., & Breijak, D. (2013). Heterosexual students' experiences in sexual orientation intergroup dialogue courses. *Journal of Homosexuality, 60*, 1054–1080.

Dessel, A., Woodford, M., & Warren, N. (2011). Intergroup dialogue courses on sexual orientation: Lesbian, gay and bisexual student experiences and outcomes *Journal of Homosexuality, 58*, 1132–1150. doi:10.1080/00918369.2011.598420

Dewees, M., & Roche, S. (2001). Teaching about human rights in social work. *Journal of Teaching in Social Work, 21*(1/2), 137–155. Retrieved from http://dx.doi.org/10.1300/J067v21n01_09

Dover, A. (2009). Teaching for social justice and K–12 student outcomes: A conceptual framework and research review. *Equity & Excellence in Education, 42*, 506–524. doi:10.1080/10665680903196339

Dovidio, J., & Gaertner, S. (1999). Reducing prejudice: Combating intergroup biases. *Current Directions in Psychological Science, 8*(4), 101–105. doi:10.1111/1467-8721.00024

Dovidio, J., Pearson, A., & Orr, P. (2008). Social psychology and neuroscience: Strange bedfellows or a healthy marriage? *Group Processes & Intergroup Relations, 11*(2), 247–263. doi:10.1177/1368430207088041

Eckholm, E. (2011, April 18). Even on religious campuses, students fight for gay identity. *The New York Times*. Retrieved from http://www.nytimes.com/2011/04/19/us/19gays.html?_r=2&partner=rssnyt&emc=rss&

Ferguson, M., Harding, S., & Holleran, L. (2003). A dialogue about diversity and pedagogy in the social work classroom. *Reflections, 9*(3), 56–65.

Fish, J. (2007). *Heterosexism in health and social care.* New York, NY: Palgrave Macmillan.

Fleck-Henderson, A., & Melendez, M. (2009). Conversation and conflict: Supporting authentic dialogue in the classroom. *Journal of Teaching in Social Work, 29*, 32–46. doi:10.1080/08841230802212752

Fredriksen-Goldsen, K., Gutiérrez, L., Luke, K., & Woodford, M. (2011). Support of sexual orientation and gender identity content in social work education: Results from national surveys of U.S. and Anglophone Canadian faculty. *Journal of Social Work Education, 47*), 19–35. Retrieved from http://dx.doi.org/10.5175/JSWE.2011.200900018

Funge, S. (2011). Promoting the social justice orientation of students: The role of the educator. *Journal of Social Work Education, 47*(1), 73–90. doi:10.5175/JSWE.2011.200900035

Garcia, B., & Van Soest, D. (2000). Facilitating learning on diversity: Challenges to the professor. *Journal of Ethnic & Cultural Diversity in Social Work, 9*(1/2), 21–39. doi:10.1300/J051v09n01_02

Garvin, C. (2008). Project program development and implementation. *Small Group Research, 39*(1), 60–81. doi:10.1177/1046496407313415

George Fox University. (2014). OneGeorgeFox & LGBTQ Issues. Retrieved from http://www.georgefox.edu/onegeorgefox/

Gibbs, P., & Blakely, E. (Eds.). (2000). *Gatekeeping in BSW programs.* New York, NY: Columbia University Press.

Gitterman, A., & Schulman, L. (2005). *Mutual aid groups, vulnerable and resilient populations, and the life cycle.* New York, NY: Columbia University Press.

Grady, M., Powers, J., Despard, M., & Naylor, S. (2011). Measuring the implicit curriculum: Initial development and results of an MSW survey. *Journal of Social Work Education, 47,* 463–487. Retrieved from http://dx.doi.org/10.5175/JSWE.2011.200900119

Griffin, P., & Ouellet, M. (2007). Facilitating social justice courses. In M. Adams, L. A. Bell, & P. Griffin (Eds.), *Teaching for diversity and social justice* (pp. 89–113). New York, NY: Routledge.

Griffin, S., Brown, M., & Warren, N. (2012). Critical education in high schools: The promise and challenges of intergroup dialogue. *Equity & Excellence in Education, 45*(1), 159–180. doi:10.1080/10665684.2012.641868

Gross, G. (2000). Gatekeeping for cultural competence: Ready or not? Some post and modernist doubts. *Journal of Baccalaureate Social Work, 5*(2), 47–66.

Gundykunst, W. (2004). *Bridging differences: Effective intergroup communication.* Thousand Oaks, CA: SAGE.

Gurin, P., Nagda, B. A., & Zúñiga, X. (2013). *Engaging race and gender: Intergroup dialogues in higher education.* New York, NY: Russell Sage Foundation.

Gutiérrez, L., Dessel, A., Lewis, E., & Spencer, M. (2012). Principles, skills and practice strategies for promoting multicultural communication and collaboration. In M. Weil, M. Reisch, & M. Ohmer (Eds.), *The handbook of community practice* (2nd ed., pp. 445–460). Thousand Oaks, CA: SAGE.

Hardiman, R., Jackson, B. W., & Griffin, P. (2007). Conceptual foundations for social justice courses. In M. Adams, L. A. Bell, & P. Griffin (Eds.), *Teaching for diversity and social justice* (pp. 35–66). New York, NY: Routledge.

Hodge, D. (2007). Religious discrimination and ethical compliance: Exploring perceptions among a professionally affiliated sample of graduate students. *Journal of Religion & Spirituality in Social Work, 26*(2), 91–113. doi:10.1300/J377v26n02_05

Hogg, M., Abrams, D., Otten, S., & Hinkle, S. (2004). The social identity perspective: Intergroup relations, self-conception, and small groups. *Small Group Research, 35*, 246–276. Retrieved from http://dx.doi.org/10.1177/1046496404263424

Holley, L., & Steiner, S. (2005). Safe space: Student perspectives on classroom environment. *Journal of Social Work Education, 41*, 49–64. doi:10.5175/JSWE.2005.200300343

Hong, P., & Hodge, D. (2009). Understanding social justice in social work: A content analysis of course syllabi. *Families in Society, 90*(2), 212–219. doi: 10.1606/1044-3894.3874

HuffPost College. (2011, March 4). State of the gay, queer zine, banned by Harding University. Retrieved from http://www.huffingtonpost.com/2011/03/04/state-of-the-gay_n_830846.html

Hunter, S. (2010). *Effects of conservative religion on lesbian and gay clients and practitioners: Practice implications*. Washington, DC: NASW Press.

Hunter, S., & Hickerson, J. (2003). *Affirmative practice: Understanding and working with lesbian, gay, bisexual, and transgender persons*. Washington, DC: NASW Press.

Hyde, C., & Ruth, B. (2002). Multicultural content and class participation: Do students self censor? *Journal of Social Work Education, 38*, 214–256.

Hyers, L., & Hyers, C. (2008). Everyday discrimination experienced by conservative Christians at the secular university. *Analyses of Social Issues and Public Policy, 8*(1), 113–137. doi:10.1111/j.1530-2415.2008.00162.x

Jacobson, M. (2009). The faculty meeting: Practicing social justice–oriented group work. *Social Work With Groups, 32*(3), 177–192. Retrieved from http://dx.doi.org/10.1080/01609510802527417

Jayaratne, T.-E., Ybarra, O., Sheldon, J., Brown, T., Feldbaum, M., Pfeffer, C., & Petty, E. (2006). White American's genetic lay theories of race differences and sexual orientation: Their relationship with prejudice toward Blacks, and gay men and lesbians. *Group Processes and Intergroup Relations, 9*(1), 77–94. doi: 10.1177/1368430206059863

Jeyasingham, D. (2008). Knowledge/ignorance and the construction of sexuality in social work education. *Social Work Education, 27*(2), 138–151. doi:10.1080/02615470701709469

Jimenez, J. (2006). Epistemological frameworks, homosexuality, and religion: A response to Hodge. *Social Work, 51*, 185–187. Retrieved from http://dx.doi.org/10.1093/sw/51.2.185

Khuri, M. (2004). Facilitating Arab–Jewish intergroup dialogue in the college setting. *Race, Ethnicity and Education, 7*(3), 229–250. Retrieved from http://dx.doi.org/10.1080/1361332042000257056

Kivlighan, D., & Arseneau, J. (2009). A typology of critical incidents in intergroup dialogue groups. *Group Dynamics: Theory, Research, and Practice, 13*(2), 89–102. doi:10.1037/a0014757

Kohli, H., Huber, R., &. Faul, A. (2010). Historical and theoretical development of culturally competent social work practice. *Journal of Teaching in Social Work, 30*(3), 252–271. doi:10.1080/08841233.2010.499091

Kriegelstein, M. (2003). Heterosexism and social work: An ethical issue. *Journal of Human Behavior in the Social Environment, 8*(2/3), 75–91. doi:10.1300/J137v08n02_05

Kurland, R. (2007). Debunking the "blood theory" of social work with groups: Group workers are made and not born. *Social Work With Groups, 30*(1), 11–24. doi:10.1300/J009v30n01_03

Kurland, R., & Salmon, R. (2006). Education for the group worker's reality: The special qualities and world view of those drawn to work with groups. *Social Work with Groups, 29*(2/3), 73–89. doi:10.1300/J009v29n02_06

Love Makes a Family. (1993). Retrieved from http://www.theportlandalliance.org/2006/apr/openhearts.htm

Maxwell, K. E., Nagda, B., & Thompson, M. (Eds.). (2011). *Facilitating intergroup dialogues: Bridging differences, catalyzing change*. Sterling, VA: Stylus Publishing.

Mayhew, M., & Fernández, S. (2007). Pedagogical practices that contribute to social justice outcomes. *Review of Higher Education, 31*(1), 55–80. doi:10.1353/rhe.2007.0055

Melendez, M., & LaSala, M. (2006). Who's oppressing whom? Homosexuality, Christianity, and social work. *Social Work, 5,* 371–377. Retrieved from http://dx.doi.org/10.1093/sw/51.4.371

Melville-Wiseman, J. (2013). Teaching through the tension: Resolving religious and sexuality based schism in social work education. *International Social Work, 56,* 290–309. doi:10.1177/0020872812474485

Mildred, J., & Zúñiga, X. (2004). Working with resistance to diversity issues in the classroom: Lessons from teacher training and multicultural education. *Journal of Social Work Education, 74,* 359–375.

Miller, J., & Donner, S. (2000). More than just talk: The use of racial dialogues to combat racism. *Social Work With Groups, 23*(1), 31–53. Retrieved from http://dx.doi.org/10.1300/J009v23n01_03

Miller, J., Donner, S., & Fraser, E. (2004). Talking when talking is tough: Taking on conversations about race, sexual orientation, gender, class and other aspects of social identity. *Smith College Studies in Social Work, 74,* 377–392. doi: 10.1080/00377310409517722

Nagda, B. A., Spearmon, M., Holley, L. C., Harding, S., Balassone, M. L., Moise-Swanson, D., & De Mello, S. (1999). Intergroup dialogues: An innovative approach to teaching about diversity and justice in social work programs. *Journal of Social Work Education, 35,* 433–449.

Nagda, B. (2006). Breaking barriers, crossing borders, building bridges: Communication processes in intergroup dialogues. *Journal of Social Issues, 62,* 553–576. doi:10.1111/j.1540-4560.2006.00473.x

Nagda, B., & Gurin, P. (2007). Intergroup dialogue: A critical-dialogic approach to learning about difference, inequality, and social justice. *New Directions for Teaching and Learning, 111,* 35–45. doi:10.1002/tl.284

Nagda, B. A., Gurin, P., Sorensen, N., Gurin-Sands, C., & Osuna, S. (2009). From separate corners to dialogue and action. *Race and Social Problems, 1*(1), 45–55.

Nagda, B. A., Gurin, P., Sorensen, N., & Zúñiga, X. (2009). Evaluating intergroup dialogue: Engaging diversity for personal and social responsibility. *Diversity & Democracy, 12*(1), 4–6. doi:10.1007/s12552-009-9002-6

Nagda, B. A., Kim, C. W., & Truelove, Y. (2004). Learning about difference, learning with others, learning to transgress. *Journal of Social Issues, 60*(1), 195–214. doi:10.1111/j.0022-4537.2004.00106.x

Nagda, B. A., & Maxwell, K. E. (2011). Deepening the layers of understanding and connection: A critical-dialogic approach to facilitating intergroup dialogues. In K. E. Maxwell, B. A. Nagda, & M. Thompson (Eds.), *Facilitating intergroup dialogues: Bridging differences, catalyzing change* (pp. 1–22). Sterling, VA: Stylus Publishing.

Nagda, B. A., McCoy, M. L., & Barrett, M. H. (2006). Mix it up: Crossing social boundaries as a pathway to youth civic engagement. *National Civic Review, 95*(1), 47–56. doi:10.1002/ncr.131

Nagda, B. A., Spearmon, M., Holley, L. C., Harding, S., Balassone, M. L., Moise-Swanson, D., & de Mello, S. (1999). Intergroup dialogues: An innovative approach to teaching about diversity and justice in social work programs. *Journal of Social Work Education, 35*(3), 433–449.

Nagda, B. A., Tropp, L. R., & Paluck, E. L. (2006). Looking back as we look ahead: Integrating research, theory, and practice on intergroup relations. *Journal of Social Issues, 62*(3), 439–451. Retrieved from http://dx.doi.org/10.1111/j.1540-4560.2006.00467.x

Nagda, B. A., & Zúñiga, X. (2003). Fostering meaningful racial engagement through intergroup dialogues. *Group Processes and Intergroup Relations, 6*(1), 111–128. doi:10.1177/1368430203006001015

Osteen, P. (2011). Motivations, values, and conflict resolution: Students' integration of personal and professional identities. *Journal of Social Work Education, 47*, 423–444. doi:10.5175/JSWE.2011.200900131

Parrott, D., Zeichner, A., & Hoover, R. (2006). Sexual prejudice and anger network activation: Mediating role of negative affect. *Aggressive Behavior, 32*(1), 7–16. doi:10.1002/ab.20101

Pawelski, J., Perrin, E., Foy, J., Allen, C., Crawford, J., Del Monte, M., . . . Vickers, D. (2006). The effects of marriage, civil union, and domestic partnership laws on the health and well-being of children. *Pediatrics, 118*, 349–364. doi: 10.1542/peds.2006-1279

Peeler, J., Snyder, C., & May, J. D. (2008). Combining human diversity and social justice education: A conceptual framework. *Journal of Social Work Education, 44*, 145–161. doi:10.5175/JSWE.2008.200700052

Pettigrew, T. (1998). Intergroup contact theory. *Annual Review of Psychology, 49*, 65–85. doi:10.1146/annurev.psych.49.1.65

Pettigrew, T., & Tropp, L. (2006). A meta-analytic test of intergroup contact theory. *Journal of Personality and Social Psychology, 90*, 751–783. doi:10.1037/0022-3514.90.5.751

Pettit, R. (2006). Using conflict constructively. In R. McNair (Ed.), *Working for peace: A handbook of practical psychology and other tools* (pp. 137–139). Atascadero, CA: Impact Publishers.

Plous, S. (2000). Responding to overt displays of prejudice: A role-playing. *Teaching of Psychology, 27*(3), 198–200.

Poteat, P., & Espelage, D. (2007). Predicting psychosocial consequences of homophobic victimization in middle school students. *Journal of Early Adolescence, 27*(2), 175–191. doi:10.1177/0272431606294839

Reamer, F. (1998). The evolution of social work ethics. *Social Work, 43*, 488. doi: 10.1093/sw/43.6.488

Ressler, L., & Hodge, D. (2003). Silenced voices: Social work and the oppression of conservative narratives. *Social Thought: Journal of Religion in the Social Services, 22*(1), 125–142.

Reynolds, L. R. (2004). Gatekeeping prior to point of entry. *Advances in Social Work, 5*(1), 18–31.

Richards-Schuster, K., & Aldana, A. (2013). Learning to speak out about racism: Youths' insights on participation in an intergroup dialogues program. *Social Work With Groups, 36*(4), 332–348. doi:10.1080/01609513.2013.763327

Rodenborg, N. A., & Boisen, L. S. (2013). Aversive racism and intergroup contact theories: Cultural competence in a segregated world. *Journal of Social Work Education, 49*, 564–579.

Rodenborg, N., Boisen, L., & Bosch, L. (2011, October). *Understanding diversity and inequality through dialogue and classroom instruction.* Paper presented at the Council for Social Work Education Annual Program Meeting, Atlanta, GA.

Rodenborg, N., & Bosch, L. (2008). Intergroup dialogue: A group work method for diverse groups. In A. Gitterman & R. Salmon (Eds.), *Encyclopedia of social work with groups* (pp. 78–80). Binghamton, NY: Routledge.

Rodenborg, N., & Huynh, N. (2006). On overcoming segregation: Social work and intergroup dialogue. *Social Work With Groups, 29*(1), 27–44. doi:10.1300/J009v29n01_04

Rosenberg, M. (2003). *Nonviolent communication: A language of life.* Encinitas, CA: Puddledancer Press.

Rozas, L. (2004). On translating ourselves: Understanding dialogue and its role in social work education. *Smith College Studies in Social Work, 74*(2), 229–242. doi:10.1080/00377310409517713

Rozas, L. (2007). Engaging dialogue in our diverse social work student body: A multilevel theoretical process model. *Journal of Social Work Education, 43*, 5–29. doi:10.5175/JSWE.2007.200400467

Rozas, L. W., & Miller, J. (2009). Discourses for social justice education: The web of racism and the web of resistance. *Journal of Ethnic and Cultural Diversity in Social Work, 18*(1–2), 24–39. doi:10.1080/15313200902874953

Saguy, T., Dovidio, J., & Pratto, F. (2008). Beyond contact: Intergroup contact in the context of power relations. *Personality and Social Psychology Bulletin, 34*(2), 432–445. doi:10.1177/0146167207311200

Sakamoto, I., & Pitner, R. (2005). Use of critical consciousness in anti-oppressive social work practice: Disentangling power dynamics at personal and structural levels. *British Journal of Social Work, 35,* 435–452. Retrieved from http://dx.doi.org/10.1093/bjsw/bch190

Schatz, M., Furman, R., & Jenkins, L. E. (2003). Space to grow: Using dialogue techniques for multinational, multicultural learning. *International Social Work, 46,* 481–494. doi:10.1177/0020872803464005

Scheyett, A., & Kim, M. (2004). "Can we talk?": Using facilitated dialogue to positively change student attitudes towards persons with mental illness. *Journal of Teaching in Social Work, 24*(1/2), 39–54. Retrieved from http://dx.doi.org/10.1300/J067v24n01_03

Scudera, D. (2013). Don't say it! Retrieved from http://www.huffingtonpost.com/domenick-scudera/dont-say-it_b_2584734.html

Sibley, C., Robertson, A., & Wilson, M. (2006). Social dominance orientation and right-wing authoritarianism: Additive and interactive effects. *Political Psychology, 27*(5), 755–768. doi:10.1111/j.1467-9221.2006.00531.x

Sorensen, N., Nagda, B., Gurin, P., & Maxwell, K. (2009). Taking a "hands on" approach to diversity in higher education: A critical-dialogic model for effective intergroup interaction. *Analyses of Social Issues and Public Policy, 9*(1), 3–35. doi:10.1111/j.1530-2415.2009.01193.x

Spencer, M. (2008). A social worker's reflections on power, privilege, and oppression. *Social Work, 53*(2), 99–101. Retrieved from http://dx.doi.org/10.1093/sw/53.2.99

Spencer, M., Brown, M., Griffin, S., & Abdullah, S. (2008). Outcome evaluation of the intergroup project. *Small Group Research, 39*(1), 82–103. doi:10.1177/1046496407313416

Spencer, M., Martineau, D., & Warren, N. (2011). Extending intergroup dialogue facilitation to multicultural social work practice. In K. E. Maxwell, B. R. Nagda, & M. C. Thompson (Eds.), *Facilitating intergroup dialogues: Bridging differences, catalyzing change* (pp. 147–162). Sterling, VA: Stylus.

Stephan, W., & Finlay, K. (1999). The role of empathy in improving intergroup relations. *Journal of Social Issues, 55*(4), 729–743. Retrieved from http://dx.doi.org/10.1111/0022-4537.00144

Stephan, W., & Stephan, C. (2001). *Improving intergroup relations.* Thousand Oaks, CA: SAGE.

Streets, F. (2009). Overcoming a fear of religion in social work education and practice. *Journal of Religion & Spirituality in Social Work: Social Thought, 28*(1), 185–199. doi:10.1080/15426430802644214

Swank, E., & Raiz, L. (2010). Attitudes toward gays and lesbians among undergraduate social work students. *Affilia: Journal of Women & Social Work, 25*(1), 19–29. doi:10.1177/0886109909356058

Todd, S., & Coholic, D. (2007). Christian fundamentalism and anti-oppressive social work pedagogy. *Journal of Teaching in Social Work, 27*(3/4), 5–25. doi: 10.1300/J067v27n03_02

Trotter, J., Crawley, M., Duggan, L., Foster, E., & Levie, J. (2009). Reflecting on what? Addressing sexuality in social work, *Practice, 21*(1), 5–15. doi:10.1080/09503150902745971

Vanderwoerd, J. (2002). When religion and sexual orientation collide: Ethical dilemmas in curriculum standards for social work education. *Social Work & Christianity, 29*(1), 53––65.

Wagner, U., Christ, O., & Pettigrew, T. (2008). Prejudice and group related behavior in Germany. *Journal of Social Issues, 64*(2), 403–416. doi:10.1111/j.1540-4560.2008.00568.x

Walls, N. E., & Seelman, K. (2014). Incongruence with social work culture among evangelical students: The mediating role of group-based dominance. In A. Dessel & R. Bolen (Eds.), *Conservative Christian beliefs and sexual orientation in social work: Privilege, oppression, and the pursuit of human rights* (pp. 81–114). Alexandria, VA: CSWE Press.

Walls, N. E., & Todd, J. (2014). Defending the faith: Resistance and struggle in recognizing Christian privilege. In A. Dessel & R. Bolen (Eds.), *Conservative Christian beliefs and sexual orientation in social work: Privilege, oppression, and the pursuit of human rights* (pp. 377–406). Alexandria, VA: CSWE Press.

Wahl, A. M., Perez, E. T., Deegan, M. J., Sanchez, T. W., & Applegate, C. (2000). The controversial classroom: Institutional resources and pedagogical strategies for a race relations course. *Teaching Sociology, 28,* 316–332. doi:10.2307/1318582

Weiss, E., Morehouse, J., Yeager, T., & Berry, T. (2010). A qualitative study of ex-gay and ex-ex-gay experiences. *Journal of Gay & Lesbian Mental Health, 14*(4), 291–319. doi:10.1080/19359705.2010.506412

Wong, J. P.-H., & Poon, M. K.-L. (2013). Challenging homophobia and heterosexism through storytelling and critical dialogue among Hong Kong Chinese immigrant parents in Toronto. *Culture, Health & Sexuality, 15*(1), 15–28. doi:10.1080/13691058.2012.738310

Zúñiga, X., Nagda, B. A., Chesler, M., & Cytron-Walker, A. (2007). Intergroup dialogue in higher education: Meaningful learning about social justice. *ASHE Higher Education Report, 32*(4), 1–128.

CHAPTER 15

Intergroup Dialogue: A Method for Engaging Students Around Religion and Sexual Orientation

Joseph R. Miles, PhD, Christine L. Henrichs-Beck, MA, and Jon R. Bourn, MA

Tensions between religious liberties and the rights and well-being of lesbian, gay, and bisexual (LGB) people present unique challenges for educators in the helping professions. This has become especially evident in recent years, as high-profile court cases have sought to determine whether trainees have the right to refuse to learn about or serve LGB clients on the basis of their religious beliefs (e.g., *Keeton v. Anderson-Wiley,* 2010/2011*; Ward v. Polite et al.,* 2012) or whether training programs can mandate that all trainees work toward developing competence in working with all people, regardless of their sexual orientations. Professional guidelines and ethical standards in social work, counseling, and psychology (e.g., American Psychological Association, 2010, 2012; National Association of Social Workers, 2008) are clear, however, that training programs *must* educate multiculturally competent professionals who possess the knowledge, skills, and personal and social awareness necessary to ethically and effectively work with diverse clients, including those with sexual orientations or religions different from one's own (Sue et al., 1982; Sue, Arredondo, & McDavis, 1992).

Furthermore, these helping professions are guided by a belief in social justice. Social justice includes the "full and equal participation of all groups in a society that is mutually shaped to meet their needs"; the equitable distribution of advantages, disadvantages, opportunities, and resources; and the physical and psychological safety of all members of a society (Bell, 2010, p. 21). This means that those in the helping professions must serve as advocates for marginalized and oppressed populations, such as sexual and religious minorities.

Therefore, in order to prepare students to be advocates for social justice, training programs must provide opportunities for students to develop accurate knowledge about social identities, including sexual orientation and religion; to examine their own socialization, biases, and experiences with privilege and oppression; to explore hot topics related to social identities; and to develop the capacities and commitment necessary to work toward social justice. Intergroup dialogue (IGD) has been proposed as one tool to help students engage in this type of learning around religion, sexual orientation, and the complex intersections of these social identities (e.g., Dessel, Bolen, & Shepardson, 2011). However, IGDs on religion and sexual orientation in religiously and socially conservative settings have not been empirically examined. Therefore, in this chapter we describe a study on the use of IGDs on religion and sexual orientation in undergraduate and graduate education in psychology at a large public university in a socially and religiously conservative state.

The Four-Stage Critical Dialogic Model of IGD

IGD is a co-facilitated, small group intervention that creates opportunities for sustained, face-to-face communication between people from social identity groups that have a history of conflict between them (e.g., LGB people and heterosexual people; religious minorities, secular people, and Christians) (Zúñiga, Nagda, Chesler, & Cytron-Walker, 2007; Zúñiga, Nagda, & Sevig, 2002). In higher education, IGD often follows a four-stage critical dialogic model developed by the Program on Intergroup Relations at the University of Michigan in response to racial tensions on their campus in the late 1980s (Thompson, Brett, & Behling, 2001; Zúñiga et al., 2007). Over a period of weeks (typically ranging from 8 to 16 weeks, roughly corresponding to half- and full-semester dialogues), IGD proceeds in four stages: (1) coming together and building relationships, (2) exploring commonalities and differences, (3) exploring hot topics (e.g., same-sex marriage, partner benefits), and (4) alliance building and social action planning (Zúñiga et al., 2002, 2007). As reflected in these stages, IGD shifts over time from lower risk to higher risk as a safe group climate is established and participants feel more comfortable engaging with one another. The goals of IGD typically include the development of relationships across differences and conflict, the development of a critical social consciousness, and the development of capacities and commitment to work toward social justice (Zúñiga et al., 2002, 2007).

IGD differs from other forms of education in three important ways. First, in IGD students learn a specific form of communication, which is distinct from others, such as debate (Bohm, 1996; Flick, 1998). For example, in dialogue the object is not to win or convince others that one's own view is the right view but rather to come to a deeper understanding of one another from the other's point of view (Flick, 1998) and to develop a new, shared meaning about social identities and issues (Bohm, 1996). This involves listening with an open and curious stance for what one might learn from the other and does not require agreement with the other (Flick, 1998). In order to engage in dialogue, participants must develop self-awareness and attend to blocks or assumptions that prevent them from openly listening in order to understand (Bohm, 1996).

Second, IGD is based in part on critical multicultural education (e.g., Adams, Bell, & Griffin, 2007). As Sorensen, Nagda, Gurin, and Maxwell (2009) highlight, in this context *critical* does not mean being critical of one another. Rather, it means that participants "use a critical analysis to better understand the intersection of identity with systems of inequality and its impact on themselves and other students" (Sorensen et al., 2009, p. 14). Included in this process is a "conscientious effort to examine how individual and group life are meaningfully connected to group identity, and how those identities exist in structures of stratification that afford members of different groups privileges and disadvantages, resulting in continued group-based inequalities" (Sorensen et al., 2009, p. 14). That is, a goal of IGD is to help participants develop a "critical consciousness" (Friere, 2008) about the status quo in relation to hierarchical social systems that perpetuate inequality. This effort is fostered through explorations of socialization and the social construction of identities, privilege, power, and oppression, using both structured activities and unstructured dialogue. IGD shifts over time from an examination of identity-based issues on an individual level (e.g., exploring one's own experiences with socialization) to an examination on an institutional or societal level (e.g., exploring systemic inequalities; Zúñiga et al., 2007).

Finally, the sustained, face-to-face communication provided by IGD allows participants to develop relationships with one another, adding an affective learning component not often available in traditional classes. IGD is also based in part on the contact hypothesis (Allport, 1954), which states that intergroup contact, under certain conditions (i.e., equal status in the contact situation, common goals, intergroup cooperation and interdependence, support of some authority, and friendship potential) can reduce prejudice (Pettigrew, 1998). The sustained contact provided by IGD allows the development of cross-group relationships and adds an affective learning component to multicultural and social justice education. A large body of research over more than 50 years has supported the contact hypothesis, even when Allport's optimal conditions are not met (cf. Pettigrew & Tropp, 2006). Similarly, a large and growing body of research on IGDs shows their positive impacts, including stereotype reduction and the development of empathy and understanding, intergroup communication skills, perspective-taking skills, awareness of systemic issues related to power, and cross-group relationships (see Dessel & Rogge, 2006; Gurin, Nagda, & Zúñiga, 2013). More specifically, emerging research on sexual orientation–focused IGD has found positive outcomes, including development of critical knowledge of social identities and social systems, empowerment, and movement toward social action (Dessel, Woodford, Routenberg, & Breijak, 2013; Dessel, Woodford, & Warren, 2011). However, no empirical research has specifically examined IGDs on religion and sexual orientation in religiously conservative settings. Therefore, this was the broad aim of the current study. Specifically, we examined how undergraduate student participants in three IGD groups (two focused on religion and one focused on sexual orientation) experienced the climate of their groups over time and what they thought were the most important things that happened in each session. We also examined the experiences of the co-facilitators of these IGD groups, who were graduate students in counseling psychology enrolled in an advanced course on group interventions. We were especially interested in the questions of whether and how IGD furthered their professional development in terms of group work and their multicultural competence.

Setting of Our IGD Groups

Our IGD groups took place on the campus of a large public university in a religiously conservative southern state. A recent Pew poll of more than 35,000 people found this state ranked among the top five in the United States for percentage of the population that reports that religion is very important in their lives (Pew Forum on Religion and Public Life, 2009). At the time of this writing, the state legislature was considering a bill that would prohibit public colleges and universities from "disciplining or discriminating against" social work, counseling, and psychology students who refuse to "counsel or serve a client as to goals, outcomes, or behaviors that conflict with a sincerely held religious belief of the student, if the student refers the client to a counselor who will provide the counseling or services" (S.B. 514, 2013). In recent years, state legislators have also been working on a bill that would prohibit public school teachers from instructing or providing materials in human sexuality education that are "inconsistent with natural human reproduction" and that would require school nurses, counselors, and administrators who counsel students around issues related to sexuality to report their conversations to the students' parents (S.B. 234, 2013). In 2013, this bill failed to receive support in the House.

The public university where our dialogues were facilitated has made great strides in recent years to address intergroup relations and to promote "civility" on campus (Chancellor's Task Force on Civility and Community, 2010). However, much social justice work still needs to be done related to religion and to sexual orientation. With regard to religion, Christianity still holds a privileged position at the university, evident in continued support for prayer before home football games, Christmas trees that adorn the tops of many campus buildings in December, and the university closure for Good Friday each spring. With regard to sexual orientation, much of the work that has been done to advance social justice for lesbian, gay, bisexual, and transgender (LGBT) students, staff, and faculty has happened only in recent years. For example, through the hard work of LGBT advocates and allies, an advisory group to the administration on LGBT issues, a Safe Zone training program, and an LGBT resource center have all been established within the last 7 years (although the LGBT resource center remains unfunded by the university). The campus also offers an LGBT support group each semester and a Lambda Student Union group. In addition, the university added sexual orientation, and then gender identity, to its equal employment opportunity nondiscrimination statement within the past 6 years. The office of the provost also has a policy that aids in domestic partner hires, and the library and recreational facilities provide partner benefits. However, at the time of this writing, full partner benefits (e.g., health insurance) were not offered outside heterosexual marriage.

A list of courses offered university-wide with LGBT content (published on the LGBT resource center website) includes only four courses, suggesting that LGBT issues are not widely addressed in academic programming at the university. It is with this in mind that we developed IGD groups around both sexual orientation and religion, in the hope of furthering campus interest and critical understanding of these issues, engaging campus community members in cross-group communication, and developing cross-group relationships and alliances to work toward social justice.

The Dialogue Groups

One IGD group focused on sexual orientation (SO) and two IGD groups focused on religion (REL1 and REL2) were the focus of the current study. (Although both religion and spirituality were topics of the REL1 and REL2 dialogues, spirituality tended to be minimally addressed and was addressed only in the early stages as group members explored their identities. Sessions addressing privilege, hot topics, and social action tended to revolve almost exclusively around religion.) The IGD groups were a required component of a larger, advanced undergraduate course in multicultural psychology ($N = 62$ for the larger course). (In addition to these three IGD groups, four other IGD groups were also facilitated as a part of this course: two focused on socioeconomic status, one focused on gender, and one focused on race and ethnicity. These IGD groups are not discussed in this chapter.) IGD groups typically have a single focal social identity (e.g., religion or sexual orientation) in order to allow groups the opportunity to explore this identity (and the associated hot topics) in greater depth, once a safe group climate has been established. However, this does not mean that the intersections of different identities are not explored.

The overall objectives of the multicultural psychology course were designed to help undergraduate students begin developing multicultural competence (i.e., cultural knowledge, awareness and attitudes, and skills), as defined in the multicultural counseling competencies literature (e.g., Sue et al., 1982, 1992). Specific objectives included the development of knowledge about diverse sociocultural groups (e.g., historical background, cultural values, privilege and oppression), awareness of personal and social identities (e.g., awareness of one's own socialization, experiences with privilege and oppression), and critical awareness of hierarchical social systems. The course also sought to develop skills in sustained cross-group communication and in social justice advocacy.

Our IGD groups generally followed the four-stage critical dialogic model established at the University of Michigan and used by a growing number of colleges and universities nationwide (e.g., Sorenson et al., 2009; Zúñiga et al., 2007), with a few modifications based on institutional constraints. For example, students did not register for an IGD about a specific social identity. Rather, they registered for the larger multicultural psychology course, then efforts were made to develop IGD groups that were composed of approximately equal numbers of people from both marginalized social identity groups (i.e., religious and sexual minorities) and privileged social identity groups (i.e., Christians and heterosexual people). To do this, we administered a demographic survey to all students at the beginning of the semester. The students were told that the purpose of the demographic survey was to assign people to IGD groups that included approximately equal representation of people who identified with the marginalized social identity groups and privileged social identity groups and that they did not have to provide any demographic information that they did not want to disclose. Students also listed their top three preferences for dialogue topics (e.g., religion, sexual orientation). Based on the demographics of the class, the instructor and a teaching assistant (who was neither a group member nor a co-facilitator in the current IGDs) assigned students to IGD groups such that they contained approximately equal representation of marginalized and privileged social identity group members, and all students were assigned to one of their top three preferences for IGD topics.

Efforts were also made to create groups that were diverse with regard to other aspects of identity (e.g., gender, race), in order to provide opportunities to explore the intersections of multiple identities with sexual orientation and religion. However, the diversity of the groups in terms of all social identities was limited by the social identities of the students enrolled in the larger course (i.e., students were predominantly Christian, female, heterosexual, and White). Demographics for group members are provided in Table 1. Although all groups followed the four-stage critical dialogic model of IGD, co-facilitators and groups were free to determine specific content of each session.

Table 1. Intergroup Dialogue Group Member and Co-Facilitator Demographics

	SO		REL1		REL2	
	Members (N = 9)	Facilitators (N = 2)	Members (N = 9)	Facilitators (N = 2)	Members (N = 8)	Facilitators (N = 2)
Gender						
Female	5	2	8	1	7	1
Male	4	0	1	1	1	1
Age (years)						
Range	21–25	35 (n = 1)	20–25 (n = 8)	24–26	20–23	31
Year in School						
Junior	4	0	3	0	3	0
Senior	4	0	6	0	5	0
Master's student	1	0	0	0	0	0
PhD student	0	2	0	2	0	2
Race or Ethnicity						
Asian	0	1	0	0	0	1
American Indian	0	0	0	0	0	1
Asian American	0	0	1	0	1	0
Black	4	0	0	0	0	1
Latino/a	1	0	1	1	0	1
White	4	1	7	1	7	0

(continued)

Table 1 (continued)

			Sexual orientation			
Bisexual	1	1	1	0	0	0
Lesbian	1	0	0	0	0	0
Gay	2	0	0	0	0	1
Heterosexual	5	1	8	2	8	1
			Religion			
Agnostic	0	1	1	1	3	0
Atheist	0	0	0	1	1	0
Confucian	0	0	1	0	0	0
Hindu	0	0	1	0	0	0
Sikh	0	0	0	0	0	1
Christian						
Baptist	1	0	0	0	0	0
Catholic	0	0	3	0	2	1
Methodist	0	0	2	0	0	0
Orthodox	1	0	0	0	0	0
Protestant	0	0	0	0	1	0
Unitarian Universalist	1	0	0	0	0	0
Unspecified	2	0	0	0	1	0
Not religious	3	1	1	0	0	0
Unspecified	1	0	0	0	0	0

Note. REL1 and REL2 are 2 separate groups focused on religion; SO is the group focused on sexual orientation.

Participants were able to select all options that apply for the race or ethnicity and gender categories (e.g., 1 co-facilitator for REL2 identified as multiracial and specified American Indian, Black, and Latino). The race or ethnicity, gender, and sexual orientation categories included an "other" category and the option to specify, if none of the categories provided captured participants' self-identification. For religion, participants were asked to specifically indicate whether they identified as Christian or non-Christian and to provide a specific religion or denomination, if applicable. The categories above represent only those used by participants (e.g., no group members or co-facilitators identified as transgender, so transgender is not included as an identity category above)."

All IGD groups were co-facilitated by graduate students in counseling psychology enrolled in an advanced course on group interventions. This course sought to expand on students' introductory knowledge and skill in group facilitation, with a particular focus on multicultural and social justice issues in group work. Although IGD is distinct from therapy or counseling (Bohm, 1996), it is useful in training novice group counselors about group dynamics (e.g., stages of group development, group climate) and basic group facilitation skills (e.g., working with emotion in groups; Khuri, 2004). Additionally, the use of dialogic methods in group counseling has been suggested in the literature on the basis that all groups are multicultural and that all groups represent a social microcosm in which the hierarchical social dynamics of society play out (Chen, Thombs, & Costa, 2003). Thus, students in this course learn the four-stage model of IGD (e.g., Zúñiga et al., 2007), participate in experiential group exercises, and, beginning in the eighth week of the semester, co-facilitate an IGD and participate in group supervision of their work. Demographics for the co-facilitators are also provided in Table 1. Syllabi for both the undergraduate multicultural psychology course and the graduate group intervention course are available from the first author.

Measures

GROUP CLIMATE QUESTIONNAIRE–SHORT FORM (GCQ-S)

In the current study, we were interested in how participants in religion and sexual orientation IGDs in a religiously conservative setting experienced the group climate and what they found to be the most important events in each session. Therefore, participants completed the GCQ-S (MacKenzie, 1983) after each session (Table 2). The GCQ-S is a 12-item scale assessing perceptions of group climate on three subscales: avoiding, conflict, and engaged. The avoiding subscale assesses avoidance of dealing with problems in the group. A sample item is, "The members avoided looking at important issues going on between themselves." The conflict subscale assesses interpersonal conflict and distrust in the group. A sample item is, "There was friction and anger between the members." The engaged subscale assesses the working atmosphere of the group and the importance of the group to the members. A sample item is, "The members felt what was happening was important and there was a sense of participation." All items are answered on a 7-point Likert scale ranging from 1 (*not at all*) to 7 (*extremely*). Previous research on group counseling using the GCQ-S has found it to have good reliability (e.g., Kivlighan & Goldfine, 1991, found Cronbach's alphas of .94, .92, and .88 for the engaged, avoiding, and conflict scales, respectively). Previous research on IGDs using the GCQ-S has found it to have somewhat lower reliability (e.g., Miles & Kivlighan, 2008, found Cronbach's alphas of .76, .50, and .69 for the engaged, avoiding, and conflict scales, respectively). Cronbach's alphas in the current study were similar: .75, .52, and .78 for the engaged, avoiding, and conflict scales, respectively.

The GCQ-S is widely used in research on group psychotherapy, which has found group climate to be related to group member outcomes (e.g., Kivlighan & Lilly, 1997; Ogrodniczuk & Piper, 2003). The GCQ-S has also recently been used in research examining group climate in IGD (e.g., Miles & Kivlighan 2008, 2010). This research has found that perceptions of avoiding tend to significantly decrease over time, perceptions of engagement tend to increase over time, and perceptions of conflict remain stable over time. Miles and Kivlighan (2008, 2010) interpreted this pattern of group climate development as consistent with the four-stage critical dialogic model of IGD (Zúñiga et al., 2002, 2007). Specifically, given that the first stage of IGD is focused on relationship building, it makes sense that engagement would increase over time. In addition, as relationships are formed and a sense of safety develops,

Table 2.
Means and Standard Deviations for Responses to Group Clinate Questionnaire–Short Form

Session	Subscale	*M*	*SD*
1 (*n*=21)	Avoiding	4.58	0.80
	Engaged	4.63	0.81
	Conflict	2.22	0.78
2 (*n*=23)	Avoiding	4.14	1.09
	Engaged	4.91	1.00
	Conflict	1.74	0.64
3 (*n*=24)	Avoiding	4.10	0.84
	Engaged	5.36	0.83
	Conflict	1.86	1.00
4 (*n*=19)	Avoiding	3.46	0.88
	Engaged	5.60	0.90
	Conflict	1.78	0.98
5 (*n*=19)	Avoiding	3.42	1.20
	Engaged	5.60	0.75
	Conflict	1.72	0.63
6 (*n*=20)	Avoiding	3.60	1.26
	Engaged	5.29	1.05
	Conflict	2.16	1.00
7 (*n*=21)	Avoiding	2.75	1.35
	Engaged	5.75	1.20
	Conflict	1.98	0.94
8 (*n*=19)	Avoiding	5.63	1.33
	Engaged	3.19	0.81
	Conflict	1.57	1.15

Note. The scale for the GCQ-S ranged from 1 (*not at all*) to 7 (*extremely*).

group members take greater risks and explore hot topics rather than avoiding the issues between social identity groups. Finally, because the groups are specifically designed to bring together individuals from social identity groups with a history of conflict between them (e.g., Zúñiga et al., 2007), we expect (and hope for) some degree of conflict within a dialogue group. Taken together, this pattern of group development suggests that group members are able to increasingly engage with one another about problems, despite conflict that exists between them. Previous research has not examined the group climate in IGD groups focused on religion and sexual orientation in a religiously conservative setting, however. Therefore, we were interested in whether IGD about these social identities in a religiously conservative setting would show a similar pattern of group climate development.

REFLECTIVE CRITICAL INCIDENT JOURNALS

In addition to the GCQ-S, group members were also asked to write a reflective journal after each IGD session. Specifically, they were asked to respond to the following questions: "What was the most important thing that happened in your intergroup dialogue on [date]? Why was this important to you?" This critical-incident method has been used in group psychotherapy research (e.g., Bloch, Reibstein, Crouch, Holroyd, & Themen, 1979; Kivlighan, 2011) and in research examining change processes in IGD (Kivlighan & Arseneau, 2009).

END-OF-SEMESTER EVALUATIONS

Finally, at the end of the semester, group members completed an evaluation of their IGD experience. This evaluation included 10 questions assessing group members' agreement with statements such as "As a result of my participation in my intergroup dialogue, I have a deeper understanding of the issues related to the individuals and groups involved in my dialogue" and "My intergroup dialogue helped me confront some of my stereotypes and prejudices." Group members responded to these statements indicating the extent to which they agreed with each statement on a 5-point Likert-type scale ranging from 1 (*strongly disagree*) to 5 (*strongly agree*). The questions, and the means and standard deviations for the responses, are listed in Table 3.

Table 3. Means and Standard Deviations for End-of-Semester Evaluation Scores

Item	*M*	*SD*
As a result of my participation in my intergroup dialogue, I have a deeper understanding of the issues related to the individuals and groups involved in my dialogue.	4.35	0.49
My intergroup dialogue helped me confront some of my stereotypes and prejudices.	4.00	0.95
My intergroup dialogue has encouraged me to find opportunities for continued learning and development related to the topic of my dialogue.	4.00	0.60
As the result of participating in my intergroup dialogue, I have a greater appreciation for the diverse life experiences of individuals and groups that are different from me.	4.61	0.58
The facilitators of my intergroup dialogue encouraged participation from all participants.	4.48	0.85
The facilitators created a safe space to talk in my intergroup dialogue.	4.61	0.78
I would be interested in future [university-based] intergroup dialogues.	4.09	1.00
I am interested in participating in future dialogues in the community or elsewhere.	4.17	0.78
I learned things from my intergroup dialogue that I would not have learned in a traditional class.	4.57	0.59
Overall, I am satisfied with my intergroup dialogue experience.	4.78	0.42

Note. The scale for the end-of-semester evaluaiton ranged from 1 (*strongly disagree*) to 5 (*strongly agree*).

Procedure

This study was approved by the university's institutional review board. All participants (group members and group co-facilitators) provided informed consent before participating in the research. The multicultural psychology course met twice per week for 1 hour and 15 minutes. Beginning in the eighth week of the semester, the larger class met together as a full class once per week and in separate IGD groups for the second weekly class meeting through the end of the semester. The groups were based on the four-stage critical dialogic model of IGD (Zúñiga et al., 2002, 2007) and included both experiential activities and unstructured dialogue. The curriculum was designed to shift from an individual focus to a systemic focus over the 8 weeks. Additionally, activities and dialogue topics were planned to gradually increase the level of interpersonal risk over time as a safe group climate was established and relationships were formed. After each session, group members were sent a reminder and a link to an online version of the GCQ-S via e-mail. They also submitted their reflection journals each week via the course website.

After completion of the IGD groups, the co-facilitators of these three groups were invited to participate in a focus group about their experiences. Of the six co-facilitators, three participated: one co-facilitator from the SO dialogue and both facilitators from the REL1 dialogue. The focus group was co-facilitated by the second two authors. Questions were designed to assess how IGD furthered the graduate students' learning about multiculturalism and social justice and how co-facilitating these groups strengthened their group facilitation skills and professional development as counselors. Questions were also asked to specifically investigate whether and how the intersections of religion and sexual orientation were addressed in their IGD groups.

Results

Group Member Experiences

QUANTITATIVE DATA

Participants were 27 students in three intergroup dialogue groups (n = 9, n = 9, and n = 8 for SO, REL1, and REL2, respectively). The response rate for the GCQ-S was 75.96%. GCQ-S data were analyzed using hierarchical linear modeling (HLM; Raudenbush, Bryk, & Congdon, 2005). HLM is appropriate for analyzing longitudinal group data because it takes into account the "nested" nature of the data (i.e., sessions are nested within individual group members, who are nested within different dialogue groups). Because we were interested in group climate as a group phenomenon, we aggregated group climate scores for each subscale (avoiding, engaged, and conflict) by group for each session. Mean group climate scores are included in Table 2. We ran three separate two-level HLM analyses, with each group climate variable serving as the dependent variable in one analysis and session number serving as a predictor variable in each analysis. Consistent with previous research (Miles & Kivlighan, 2008, 2010), we found decreases in avoiding, $\gamma = -.22$, $t(2, 22) = -7.98$, $p < .001$; increases in engagement, $\gamma = .14$, $t(2, 22) = 3.90$, $p = .001$; and stability in the level of conflict over time, $\gamma = -.04$, $t(2, 22) = -1.03$, $p = .32$.

Next we examined means and standard deviations for the quantitative end-of-semester evaluation items (see Table 3). Response rate for this evaluation was 88.46%. Means on this evaluation suggest that group members in these three IGDs felt that they developed a greater understanding of the social issues and groups involved in their dialogue, experienced a reduction in intergroup prejudice, learned things that they would not have in a traditional class, and are motivated to further their learning and participate in future IGDs.

QUALITATIVE DATA

Perhaps more informative than the quantitative data are the qualitative critical incident data provided by the group members after each session in their reflective journals. To examine these data, the authors independently read each of the critical incidents, looking for themes. Through discussion, we then determined that the common goals of IGD (i.e., building relationships across differences, developing a critical social consciousness, and developing capacities to work toward social justice; e.g., Zúñiga et al., 2002, 2007) provided a useful frame for understanding the critical incidents in these IGDs on religion and sexual orientation. We were also particularly interested in how intersectionality (Cole, 2009) was addressed in the IGDs. That is, even though the primary IGD topics were either religion or sexual orientation, we noted that each IGD addressed how these identities intersect and interact with one another. We provide illustrative examples of critical incidents focusing on each of the IGD goals and of dialoguing about intersectional issues in this section.

IGD offers a unique opportunity for participants to connect on a personal and affective level (e.g., Khuri, 2004) in an educational setting. Thus, it creates an interpersonal foundation that confers a space to connect across social identity differences and provides a relational infrastructure for successful dialogue about conflict and challenge.

Group members in the current study identified relationship-building experiences frequently and in detail. Group members discussed the impact and role of relationship building throughout their IGD experiences, most notably in the areas of building trust and safety, increasing openness, connecting across differences, and approaching conflict and challenge.

Relationship-building experiences created a sense of trust and safety for members to begin moving through the IGD experience. As one group member describes,

> I find that getting to know one another was crucial because otherwise we'd be spending an entire semester in a room full of strangers and always be fearful of hurting someone's feelings or offending them. We laid out ground rules to keep ourselves from doing just that and it became a really strong aspect of the discussion. It also let us know how to relate to one another on a personal level because of our differences.

Group members expressed how relationship building played an integral role in fostering an interpersonal environment that felt comfortable and allowed members to be more open in sharing their feelings, thoughts, and experiences. Rather than simply maintaining relationships as classmates, group members evolved from strangers to partners in the IGD processes of disclosing experiences, actively listening, and validating individuals' experiences through hearing and seeing one another without judgment, disregard, or indifference. This sense of openness and sharing was described by one member:

> The most important part of this dialogue was that, while we had our differences among opinions, we could all understand each other's points of view, or at least attempt to. It blew me away! I had an advocate of a different sexual orientation that understood my opinion...This person even stood up for me!

Of all the ways in which building relationships functioned within the IGD experience, facilitating connection across differences was perhaps the most meaningful and profound, as well as one of the primary purposes of IGD. The discovery of differences between group members encouraged members to further explore the differences and similarities between their social identities and related experiences. This exploration involved respectful discourse that catalyzed further openness and curiosity, empathic understanding, and interpersonal and intrapersonal growth, as noted by the following member:

> I found myself siding with someone from an "anti-gay" upbringing, and wanting to help him understand—not strictly as an ally, but as a human being. From one person to another, we learned from each other. We learned to be more accepting of our differing cultures and, in the end, we grew from it.

A similar experience was described by another member:

> We got to experience speaking with each other about a very heated topic whilst holding differing perspectives. I felt that through discussing a topic so sensitive in nature, we were able to gain respect for one another. We kept it very friendly, open, and curious. At the end, I felt as though I gained knowledge of my group members and wisdom about myself.

Lastly, relationship building fashioned an interpersonal environment that allowed members to approach conflict, challenge, and experiential and identity differences within controversial and emotive hot topics without debate, persuasion, or argument. Relational foundations allowed members to listen with nonjudgmental and empathic stances. This aspect of relationship building captures an important goal of the IGD process: increased awareness and knowledge of the self, others, and others' social identity experiences and increased comfort and acceptance of the juxtaposition of differences. This definitive IGD experience was described in the following reflection from a member in the SO IGD group:

> I think the most important aspect of this discussion was the fact that everyone is reaching a more "open minded" consensus. If this topic would've come up on the first day, we would've probably had a brawl, or at the very least a debate about this topic . . . Those that were more . . . "anti-gay" to start with are more open minded and accepting. I didn't realize how much the people in this discussion had grown since the first time that we met…we are bettered for discussing, not for debating, because there is no real right or wrong answer, there is only knowledge and understanding.

For many group members, consciousness raising was a particularly salient outcome of activities designed to create awareness of privilege and oppression based on social identity membership. In one incarnation of such activities, participants each took a clear plastic cup and were asked to add a jelly bean from a communal jelly bean cup in the center of the room to their own cup for each privilege they possessed from a list read by the co-facilitators. For example, in the SO IGD, privileges might include, "I am able to hold hands with my partner without feeling unsafe" or "I never have to worry about making a point of disclosing my sexual orientation to my family." This activity was very impactful for many group members. Remarking on the activity, one group member shared the following:

> By the end of the session, I had several more jelly beans, but they didn't mean the same thing to me that they had before. They were now privileges that I had that the friends I've made in the class didn't have. When we left, we were offered the remaining jelly beans, but I didn't take any. I didn't want any more privileges that someone of a different orientation than mine couldn't have… I couldn't imagine what someone in the LGB community would have to go through just to try to have the basics of healthcare and being able to go out in public with your partner and worry about people staring, or thinking bad of you.

In addition to specific activities, consciousness raising occurred during hot topic discussions, where group members share their thoughts and feelings about controversial topics relevant to religion or sexual orientation. In regard to religion, hot topics included interfaith marriages, the word *God* in the pledge of allegiance, and post-9/11 attitudes toward Muslims. In hot topic sessions in the religion IGDs, members came to realizations about Christian privilege in the United States, as exemplified by the following member's report:

> The most important thing I learned is that even though we may claim we are of a specific religion it is the values and lifestyle of that religion that we hold the closest . . . I think growing up as a Christian in the United States gives you an advantage just like growing up into an Islamic family in Iraq.

In addition, the hot topic sessions helped dialogue participants reflect on the specific experience of Christian privilege in the conservative South, as described by this member after his group had watched a news clip of two congressmen from their state discussing the proposed bill to limit the extent to which teachers can talk about sexual orientations other than heterosexuality:

> I am taken back when I reflect on my personal privileges. I have never considered my skin color, gender, sexual orientation, or religion as a privilege. I have always thought a privilege involved socioeconomic status and education. Now that I am aware of what others struggle with on a daily basis I am more aware of what it means to be a white, Christian living in the "Bible Belt." At the same time I am saddened that I have spent 20 years of my life completely oblivious to the inequalities others suffer. I am even more frustrated with how much we tend to take our personal privileges for granted.

Social action can take a variety of forms at the individual, interpersonal, community, or even societal level. These actions may occur concurrently with or some time after the IGD, once participants have been able to fully internalize their learning.

In the three IGDs in our study, changes ranged from simply being more aware of appropriate and inappropriate language to use to refer to members of different social identity groups, to actively advocating for systemic change of oppressive regulations, policies, and laws. This was a very engaging piece of the IGD experience for the members, allowing them to negotiate what they can and will do to be advocates for religious minorities and LGB people. The IGD also allowed group members to receive feedback about how to best become change advocates and allies. Connecting important themes felt by several group members, one member shared the following:

> The most important part of the dialogue to me was creating an action plan . . . We agreed that [the] best way to share our experience is by setting an example to those around us. I want to personally take it as a challenge to continue to seek opportunities where I can engage in diverse conversations and learn more about others different from myself.

The importance of advocating for change, no matter how difficult it may be, was widely shared by group members. As one member described:

> We discussed different levels of places that might need intervention. We started with ourselves, then our family and friends, then our churches and schools, and finally the community . . . It was easiest to start with ourselves, and got progressively harder as we moved towards the outside of the circle. This helped me realize that the easiest change begins with you, and that while it is much harder [to] influence other people, there are things that can be done.

Intersectionality refers to instances, experiences, and dynamics that relate to the interfacing of various social identities (Cole, 2009). IGD is well suited to illuminate points of intersectionality between religion and sexual orientation and encourage students to explore their identity intersections and those of others. Within our IGD groups, the intersections of religion and sexual orientation became a meaningful and significant focus of discussion.

Within discussions encompassing intersectionality, students gained broader understandings of how multiple social identities interplay with one another to create increasingly idiosyncratic experiences and potentially more complex experiences of privilege or oppression. Through discussions of intersectionality, group members broadened their capacities to understand the complexity of an individual's personal experience as a mural of numerous social identities interplaying in a variety of ways and directions, as one SO IGD member reflected:

> I felt that I had somewhat chosen to be heterosexual, and I wondered why no one else (gay or otherwise) could consider their sexual orientation influenced by choice. Then [another group member] pointed out something important: I had lived a very secluded, Christian, "anti-gay" life, as chosen by my parents. I was raised in a private school where anything apart from heterosexuality was grounds for expulsion. [This group member], a self-identified lesbian, grew up in a similar fashion: she was raised strictly Catholic, and taught from the beginning that homosexual behavior was not acceptable. So it would seem that we had very similar upbringings, and were likely taught many of the same anti-gay sentiments growing up.

Group Co-Facilitator Experiences

The authors each independently read the transcript from the focus group with the co-facilitators, looking for themes. Through discussion, we again determined that the three goals of intergroup dialogue and the theme of intersectionality provided a useful frame in which to understand the co-facilitators' experiences. Although the goals of IGD are typically discussed in relation to the IGD participants, the data provided by the co-facilitators suggested that similar goals might be met for IGD co-facilitators, highlighting the usefulness of IGD in graduate education in the helping professions.

BUILDING RELATIONSHIPS ACROSS DIFFERENCES

For the co-facilitators, relationship building occurred on two levels: building relationships collaboratively with group members through the use of a facilitator–participant model of facilitation (e.g., Nagda, Timbang, Fulmer, & Tran, 2011) and building relationships between co-facilitators themselves. Co-facilitators described their relationships as essential for tracking the group process, handling moments of uncertainty, and conceptualizing the happenings and growth of the group. Like group members, co-facilitators expressed the importance of relationship building as the mechanism behind creating a space that promotes connection between similarities and across differences, using relationship building as a mechanism to maintain openness, listen without judgment or reaction, and fully hearing the experience and identity another person is sharing, as described by one co-facilitator:

> I think it's being able to engage in these conversations, . . . being able to share your differences while also remembering your similarities and being able to connect, even when you disagree on something, being able to go back and connect to that similarity, so that you are not completely tuning out that other person, but they're actually hearing each other.

Unique to the experience of co-facilitators, counseling skills and intervention techniques central to the helping professions became important tools for engaging in the relationship-building process with group members as well as guiding the relationship-building process between group members. Co-facilitators described the importance of being authentic, sharing moments of uncertainty or discomfort, and acknowledging one's learning edges for effectively leading an IGD group. Such efforts helped increase the cohesiveness of the group, model IGD skills and multicultural competence, and increase a sense of positivity in the experience of group members. Such dynamics were summarized by the following co-facilitator:

> For me . . . a lot of it is using the skills that you use in individual therapy and forming a relationship and building a relationship with everybody, just really being . . . authentic, being myself, admitting when I don't know what's going on, because then they felt like there weren't people in the room who knew everything and felt intimidated.

Developing a Critical Social Consciousness

As with the other goals of IGD, consciousness raising also occurs among co-facilitators. This stems largely from co-facilitators being facilitator–participants (Nagda et al., 2011). In our IGD groups, co-facilitators experienced consciousness raising in both similar and unique ways compared with group members. A great deal of consciousness raising was geared toward co-facilitators beginning to see the true power of IGD at work and seeing group members becoming invested in a true dialogue. One co-facilitator remarked,

> There was one young woman who identified as heterosexual just realizing how much privilege she had . . . I get touched by it. It was such a privilege to be able to see her recognize that, to see the light bulb go off. Yeah, it was really great. It felt like I was paying it forward in some way. So that, and then the other young man who was heterosexual, and he came in one day and he just said, "I have questions" and opened up his notebook, and he had written down all these questions that he just wanted to ask them about being gay, lesbian, or bisexual and what that's like, and . . . he just wanted to know and wanted to learn and was frustrated that he had never been exposed to it. It was just so cool to see him take that risk and to see them embrace him and be so happy and excited that he was asking those questions. Yeah, loved it.

Although the preceding quote pertains to an experience that is unique to the co-facilitators, who receive training in the four-stage model of IGD, much of the consciousness raising for co-facilitators reflected similar experiences to the group members. For instance, co-facilitators became more aware of their own experiences with privilege and oppression. One group co-facilitator spoke of what it was like to realize her privilege, in the following statement:

> One of the experiences that stood out for me is [this]: There was one [gay] young man in the group, and he was talking about how . . . [he] and his [gay] friends . . . will talk about straights . . . in a derogatory way. And I noticed myself feeling really bad and like, "But I like you. Why would you not like me, because I'm straight?," and it gave me this whole different perspective of what that's like, you know, really highlighted my privilege that I don't walk around worrying if someone's not going to like me because I'm heterosexual.

DEVELOPING CAPACITIES TO WORK TOWARD SOCIAL JUSTICE

Many of our co-facilitators developed a newfound confidence in their capacity to advocate for social justice. The benefits of IGD for co-facilitators, in terms of increasing social action capacities, reached beyond their duties as co-facilitators of IGD, to the therapy room, interpersonal communication, and the larger communities in which the co-facilitators live, work, and advocate. Particularly moved by her IGD experience, one co-facilitator openly shared how the experience affected her ability to use language proactively and use dialogue in therapy to further empower clients and promote social justice and equality:

> [It gave] me a language to use, it's definitely helped with clients. Like I've said, you're doing therapy on a campus in the South...It definitely comes up with a lot of my clients...When I hear religious issues coming up in therapy, I can think back to my experience in the IGD and use my way of thinking about it and going after it and, you know, using, "Help me understand." You know, ...asking the client to educate me about their religious beliefs and how it affects them, because I can't be the expert on that. And so I feel like that's been a good point of just connecting with clients, and that can definitely, you know, kind of keep moving forward.

Co-facilitators reported that it was helpful, empowering, and invigorating to discuss privilege and oppression, connect with people across areas of difference, engage in healthy dialogue, and plan for social action. Co-facilitators in our study reported being able to connect to the importance of increased social action, regardless of the scale, adding credence to the power of IGD to increase our abilities to promote social action. In summing up her IGD experience, one co-facilitator shared the following:

> Another big aspect that it was a really good reminder in intergroup dialogue is that idea of action in some way, and . . . I felt a lot more compelled after the group to try to do things, even if they're small things to participate in . . . bringing awareness to populations that have less privilege.

INTERSECTIONALITY

Perhaps most poignant and exciting were moments when intersectionality wove into members' discussions and demonstrated the acquisition of new knowledge, increased openness to experience, and broadened understanding on the part of certain group members. Such a moment was recalled by a co-facilitator of one of the RS IGD groups:

> When we talked about religion in regards to sexual minorities and how that differs, you could kind of see them thinking bigger, like "Oh, we're just talking about religion," but then they're seeing how that makes it even more difficult in all these other areas, talking about race and sexual orientation…I like those moments too.

Conclusion and Implications for Practice

IGDs in higher education focusing on religion and sexual orientation have not previously been studied in religiously conservative settings. So, in the current study, we examined the experiences of both undergraduate student group members and graduate student co-facilitators of IGD groups based on religion and sexual orientation in this context. Quantitative data about the group climate showed a similar pattern to group climate development in other settings (e.g., Miles & Kivlighan, 2008, 2010), with avoidance of problems decreasing over time, engagement increasing, and conflict remaining stable. We interpret this pattern of group climate development as consistent with the four-stage model of IGD. That is, the work of building relationships, setting guidelines, and engaging in lower-risk activities and dialogue in the earlier stages seems to have helped the participants to increasingly like and care about each other and to feel that what is happening in the group is important, as reflected in the engaged subscale of the GCQ-S. At the same time, this relationship building and focus on creating a safe atmosphere seems to have allowed group members to engage with one another around real issues, including conflicts that existed between them, rather than avoiding real issues. However, it should be noted that the low Cronbach's alpha for the avoiding scale suggests that the findings about avoidance should be interpreted with caution. This was also reflected in the qualitative data from the group members' reflection journals that highlighted the ways in which group members established relationships with one another, allowing them to engage in the higher-risk dialogue and activities (e.g., the jelly bean activity) that helped them develop a critical consciousness around social issues and a commitment to social justice.

In this study we were particularly interested in whether and how the intersections of religion and sexual orientation were addressed in these IGD groups. The critical incident from the group member cited earlier highlights some of the ways in which intersectionality was essential in these dialogues. Specifically, this group member in the SO dialogue had a point of connection with another group member in terms of their shared Christian upbringing. However, his fellow group member explained to him that she came to hold very different views on LGB identities and issues, and this challenged him to think more deeply about his own socialization.

These findings suggest that the IGD groups helped students achieve the main objective of the course: increasing their multicultural competence (i.e., knowledge, skills, and awareness) around religion and sexual orientation. The value of the IGD as a component of multicultural learning around these issues is reflected in the end-of-semester evaluation where every student except one indicated that they agreed or strongly agreed that they learned things in their dialogue group that they did not think they could learn from a traditional class (the remaining student indicated "neither agree nor disagree" for this item). This suggests that IGD can be an important component of critical multicultural education in the helping professions.

We were also interested in how the facilitation of IGD could be incorporated into graduate education of those in the helping professions. We believed that IGD would allow group members to expand on their knowledge and skills in group work, broadly, and would also contribute to their development of multicultural competence. Group co-facilitators also showed evidence of growth with regard to the three goals of IGD but in ways unique to their role. For example, with regard to relationship building, co-facilitators reported the development of relationships within and between groups with their group members and also with their co-facilitator. The experience of co-facilitating a dialogue additionally helped them develop skills in co-facilitating groups and provided them with additional knowledge, skills, and awareness that they can take to other professional roles (e.g., group and individual therapist). Similarly, the experience challenged co-facilitators to continue to explore their own socialization, privilege, oppression, and biases while increasing their commitment to social justice in their own lives and faith in the dialogue process.

We should note that intergroup dialogue programs can be designed in multiple ways depending on campus needs and resources. For example, the size of the groups was determined by the enrollment of our undergraduate multicultural psychology course and our advanced course on group interventions. Intergroup dialogue programs at other institutions may be similar or larger. In addition, topics of intergroup dialogues need not focus on a primary social identity, as ours did in this study. We realize that not all undergraduate or graduate educators will have the same flexibility or resources to conduct IGD groups, either as stand-alone courses or as part of another course, as we did in the current study. However, we still believe that dialogue pedagogy can be a helpful addition to existing courses. For example, Schoem and Saunders (2001) have written explicitly on the use of dialogue pedagogy in settings outside IGD. One of their suggestions is that instructors or facilitators introduce the LARA (listen, affirm, respond, add information) method in the beginning of a class or intervention as a general way to help encourage an environment characterized by respectful and productive dialogue. We have also used other dialogue exercises in other settings (e.g., the jelly bean activity described earlier; making family trees to explore implicit and explicit socialization messages received about a particular social identity from different family members; the "fishbowl" technique of breaking into two groups, often based on social identity group membership, and having one group sit in a circle in the center of the room to discuss an issue while the rest of the class sits around them and listens attentively, without responding). We have found that the use of these activities in classes or groups outside dialogue can help introduce participants to dialogue as a process and help them to begin to explore social identities and social systems in a deeper and more personal manner than is often possible in more traditional (e.g., lecture-based) settings. However, it is crucial that instructors and facilitators consider the context in which any of these activities occurs and that explicit attention is given to creating a safe environment and adequately discussing and debriefing, given the emotional reactions that these activities may evoke.

Although the intersections of religion and sexual orientation provide unique challenges for educators in the helping professions, these data suggest that IGD can be a useful and effective tool for building relationships across groups, developing a critical consciousness, and developing capacities and commitment to work toward social justice, even in religiously conservative settings in which these issues are especially contentious.

References

Adams, M., Bell, L. A., & Griffin, P. (2007). *Teaching for diversity and social justice* (2nd ed.). New York, NY: Routledge.

Allport, G. W. (1954). *The nature of prejudice.* Reading, MA: Addison Wesley.

American Psychological Association. (2010). *Ethical principles of psychologists and code of conduct: 2010 amendments.* Washington, DC: Author. Retrieved from http://www.apa.org/ethics/code/index.aspx?item=4

American Psychological Association. (2012). Guidelines for psychological practice with lesbian, gay, and bisexual clients. *American Psychologist, 67,* 10–42. doi:10.1037/a0024659

Bell, L. A. (2010). Theoretical foundations. In M. A. Adams, W. J., Blumfeld, C. R. Castañeda, H. W., Hackman, M. L. Peters, & X. Zúñiga. *Readings for diversity and social justice* (2nd ed.; pp. 21–26). New York, NY: Routledge.

Bloch, S., Reibstein, J., Crouch, E., Holroyd, P., & Themen, J. (1979). A method for the study of therapeutic factors in group psychotherapy. *British Journal of Psychiatry, 134,* 257–263. doi:10.1192/bjp.134.3.257

Bohm, D. (1996). *On dialogue.* New York, NY: Routledge.

Chancellor's Task Force on Civility and Community. (August, 2010). *Final report: Chancellor's Task Force on Civility and Community.* Retrieved from http://civility.utk.edu/PDF/FinalReport-ChancellorsTaskForce-CivilityandCommunity_8-23-10.pdf

Chen, E. C., Thombs, B. D., & Costa, C. I. (2003). Building connection through diversity in group counseling: A dialogic perspective. In D. B. Pope-Davis, H. L. K. Coleman, W. M. Liu, & R. L. Toporek (Eds.), *Handbook of multicultural competencies in counseling and psychology* (pp. 456–477). Thousand Oaks, CA: SAGE.

Cole, E. R. (2009). Intersectionality and research in psychology. *American Psychologist, 64*, 170–180. doi:10.1037/a0014564

Dessel, A., Bolen, R., & Shepardson, C. (2011). Can religious expression and sexual orientation affirmation coexist in social work? A critique of Hodge's theoretical, theological, and conceptual frameworks. *Journal of Social Work Education, 47*, 213–234. doi:10.5175/JSWE.2011.200900074

Dessel, A., & Rogge, M. E. (2006). Evaluation of intergroup dialogue: A review of the empirical literature. *Conflict Resolution Quarterly, 26,* 199–238. doi:10.1002/crq.230

Dessel, A., Woodford, M., Routenberg, R., & Breijak, D. (2013). Heterosexual students' experiences in sexual orientation intergroup dialogue courses. *Journal of Homosexuality, 60*, 1054–1080. doi:10.1080/00918369.2013.776413

Dessel, A., Woodford, M., & Warren, N. (2011). Intergroup dialogue courses on sexual orientation: Lesbian, gay and bisexual student experiences and outcomes. *Journal of Homosexuality, 58*(8), 1132–1150. doi:10.1080/00918369.2011.598420

Flick, D. L. (1998). *From debate to dialogue: Using the* understanding process *to transform our conversations.* Boulder, CO: Orchid Publications.

Friere, P. (2008). *Pedagogy of the oppressed* (30th anniversary ed.). New York, NY: Continuum International Publishing.

Gurin, P., Nagda, B. R. A., & Zúñiga, X. (2013). *Dialogue across difference: Practice, theory, and research on intergroup dialogue.* New York, NY: Russell Sage Foundation.

Keeton v. Anderson-Wiley, 733 F. Supp. 2d 1368 (S.D. Ga. 2010), *aff'd,* 664 F. 3d 865 (11th Cir. 2011).

Khuri, M. L. (2004). Working with emotion in educational intergroup dialogue. *International Journal of Intercultural Relations, 28,* 595–612. doi:10.1016/j.ijintrel.2005.01.012

Kivlighan, D. M. (2011). Individual and group perceptions of therapeutic factors and session evaluation: An actor–partner interdependence analysis. *Group Dynamics: Theory, Research, and Practice, 15*(2), 147–160. doi:10.1037/a0022397

Kivlighan, D. M., & Arseneau, J. R. (2009). A typology of critical incidents in intergroup dialogue groups. *Group Dynamics: Theory, Research, and Practice, 13,* 89–102. doi:10.1037/a0014757

Kivlighan, D. M., & Goldfine, D. C. (1991). Endorsement of therapeutic factors as a function of stage of group development and participant interpersonal attitudes. *Journal of Counseling Psychology, 38,* 150–158.

Kivlighan, D. M., Jr., & Lilly, R. L. (1997). Developmental changes in group climate as they relate to therapeutic gain. *Group Dynamics: Theory, Research, and Practice, 1,* 208–211. doi:10.1037/1089-2699.1.3.208

MacKenzie, K. R. (1983). The clinical application of a group climate measure. In R. R. Dies & K. R. MacKenzie (Eds.), *Advances in group psychotherapy* (pp. 159–170). New York, NY: International Universities Press.

Miles, J. R., & Kivlighan, D. M. (2008). Team cognition in group interventions: The relation between co-leaders' shared mental models and group climate. *Group Dynamics: Theory, Research, and Practice, 12,* 191–209. doi:10.1037/1089-2699.12.3.191

Miles, J. R., & Kivlighan, D. M. (2010). Co-leader similarity and group climate in group interventions: Testing the co-leadership team cognition-team diversity model. *Group Dynamics: Theory, Research, and Practice, 14,* 114–122. doi:10.1037/a0017503

Nagda, B. R., Timbang, N., Fulmer, N. G., & Tran, T. H. V. (2011). Not *for* others, but *with* others *for all of us*: Weaving relationships, co-creating spaces of justice. In K. E. Maxwell, B. R. A. Nagda, & M. C. Thompson (Eds.), *Facilitating intergroup dialogues: Bridging differences, catalyzing change* (pp. 179–199). Sterling, VA: Stylus.

National Association of Social Workers (NASW). (2008). *Code of ethics of the National Association of Social Workers.* Washington, DC: Author. Retrieved from http://www.socialworkers.org/pubs/code/code.asp

Ogrodniczuk, J. S., & Piper, W. E. (2003). The effect of group climate on outcome in two forms of short-term group therapy. *Group Dynamics: Theory, Research, and Practice, 7,* 64–76. doi:10.1037/1089-2699.7.1.64

Pettigrew, T. F. (1998). Intergroup contact theory. *Annual Review of Psychology, 49,* 65–85. doi:10.1146/annurev.psych.49.1.65

Pettigrew, T. F., & Tropp, L. R. (2006). A meta-analytic test of intergroup contact theory. *Journal of Personality and Social Psychology, 90,* 751–783. doi:10.1037/0022-3514.90.5.751

Pew Forum on Religion and Public Life. (2009). *How religious is your state?* Retrieved from http://www.pewforum.org/How-Religious-Is-Your-State-.aspx

Raudenbush, S. W., Bryk, A. S., & Congdon, R. (2005). *HLM 6.0: Hierarchical linear modeling.* Lincolnwood, IL: Scientific Software International.

S.B. 514, 108th Cong. (2013). Retrieved from http://www.capitol.tn.gov/Bills/108/Bill/SB0514.pdf

Schoem, D., & Saunders, S. (2001). Adapting intergroup dialogue processes for use in a variety of settings. In D. Schoem & S. Hurtado (Eds.), *Intergroup dialogue: Deliberative democracy in school, college, community, and workplace* (pp. 328–344). Ann Arbor, MI: University of Michigan Press.

Sorensen, N., Nagda, B. R. A., Gurin, P., & Maxwell, K. E. (2009). Taking a "hands on" approach to diversity in higher education: A critical-dialogic model for effective intergroup interaction. *Analyses of Social Issues and Public Policy, 9,* 3–35.

Sue, D. W., Arredondo, P., & McDavis, R. J. (1992). Multicultural counseling competencies and standards: A call to the profession. *Journal of Counseling & Development, 70,* 477–486. doi:10.1002/j.2161-1912.1992.tb00563.x

Sue, D. W., Bernier, J., Durran, M., Feinberg, L., Pedersen, P., Smith, E., & Vasquez-Nuttall, E. (1982). Position paper: Cross-cultural counseling competencies. *Counseling Psychologist, 10,* 45–52. doi:10.1177/0011000082102008

Thompson, M. C., Brett, T. G., & Behling, C. (2001). Educating for social justice: The Program on Intergroup Relations, Conflict, and Community at the University of Michigan. In D. Schoem & S. Hurtado (Eds.), *Intergroup dialogue: Deliberative democracy in school, college, community, and workplace* (pp. 99–114). Ann Arbor, MI: University of Michigan Press.

Ward v. Polite et al., 667 F.3d 727 (2012).

Zúñiga, X., Nagda, B. R. A., Chesler, M., & Cytron-Walker, A. (2007). *Intergroup dialogue in higher education: Definitions, origins, and practices* [Monograph].

Zúñiga, X., Nagda, B. R. A., & Sevig, T. D. (2002). Intergroup dialogues: An educational model for cultivating engagement across differences. *Equity & Excellence in Education, 35,* 7–17.

Chapter 16

Defending the Faith: Resistance and Struggle in Recognizing Christian Privilege

N. Eugene Walls, MSSW, PhD, and Julie Todd, MDiv, PhD

Privilege, "systematically conferred advantages individuals enjoy by virtue of their membership in dominant groups" (Bailey, 1998, p. 109), as a central component of systems of oppression and stratification, has been receiving increasing attention in recent decades among academic researchers and educators (Manglitz, 2003). This has included conceptual and empirical work on issues of White (Pewewardy, 2007; Rodriguez, 2000), male (Anderson & Accomando, 2002; Farough, 2003), and to a lesser extent heterosexual (DiAngelo, 1997; van Every, 1995) and social class (Abramovitz, 2001; Kivel, 2004) privilege. A number of manifestations of privilege have received much less scholarly attention, including able-bodied (McLean, 2008; Pease, 2010a), cisgender[1] (Johnson, 2013; Kurzdorfer, 2012; Walls & Costello, 2010), U.S., American, or Western (Pease, 2010c; Schwalbe, 2005), and Christian (Blumenfeld, 2006; Clark, 2006) privilege. The majority of work on various types of privilege and privilege in general that does exist has centered on defining the manifestations of privilege and outlining how privilege functions as part of systems of inequality. Much less work has been done in the area of teaching about issues of privilege (Curry-Stevens, 2007; Walls et al., 2009).

This study explores themes that emerge as graduate students undertake a course focused on learning about privilege offered in a graduate school of social work. Data are taken from blogs that were written by the students as part of the course requirements and the responses to those entries by co-instructors in the course. All students whose data are used for this study were participating in a caucus focused on Christian privilege. There were additional caucuses around other types of privilege in the course as well. (See Walls, Roll, Griffin, & Sprague, 2010, for a thorough description of the course and its structure.)

In the next section, we examine the literature on teaching about privilege, what is currently known about Christian privilege more specifically, and the study's methods. We then turn our attention to the themes that emerged from the data and end with a discussion of the implications for social work education and future research.

The Inchoate State of Research on Teaching About Privilege

Numerous multicultural and antioppression scholars have argued that dialogue about diversity and traditionally marginalized groups falls short of the educational goal of cultural competence (Allen, 1995; Weiler, 1988) and does not adequately address issues of power, privilege, and oppression and the role they play in maintaining inequalities (Case, 2013; Miller, Donner, & Fraser, 2004; Razack, 2002). Focusing solely on the dynamics of oppression, learning about marginalized groups, and failing to address issues of privilege misses half of the process that maintains systems of inequality (Pease, 2010b) and ignores the rich body of social psychological scholarship that documents the critical role of in-group favoritism in maintenance of stratification and inequality (Brewer, 2002; Efferson, Lalive, & Fehr, 2008).

However, the avoidance of teaching about privilege is not surprising given that classroom discussions on topics of power, oppression, and privilege can be difficult to manage for educators and students (Hyde & Ruth, 2002; Woodford & Bella, 2003). It is not uncommon for students and instructors to end up feeling alienated and attacked (Stone, Patton, & Heen, 1999), with deep misunderstandings emerging between those who are speaking from marginalized identities and those speaking from privileged identities (Miller et al., 2004). Strong feelings of anger, defensiveness, guilt, and pain are not uncommon (Ferber, 2003; Miller et al., 2004; Stone et al., 1999). Because students and instructors alike occupy both marginalized and privileged identities (Miller et al., 2004), the lived reality of intersectionality (Collins, 2000; Crenshaw, 1991) further complicates these discussions. Additionally, students are likely to be at very different stages in their social identity development processes from one another (Goodman, 2001) and are often at very different stages within themselves on different identities they embody (Walls et al., 2010).

To address and manage the many issues that emerge while teaching about privilege, scholars have suggested the use of a number of pedagogical strategies. These include structural and instructional strategies including cross-identity teaching teams (D'Angelo & Flynn, 2010; Walls et al., 2010), intergroup dialogue (Dessel, Rogge, & Garlington, 2006; Dessel, Woodford, Routenberg, & Breijak, 2013; Rozas, 2007), providing students with antioppressive role models (Nichols, 2010), speaker's bureaus (Blackburn, 2004; Delp & Rogers, 2011), single identity caucusing (Walls et al., 2009, 2010), normalizing the intensity and discomfort endemic in learning about these topics (Goodman, 2001), and the development of critical humility (Barlas et al., 2011).

Teaching about Christian privilege has an additional layer of complexity because the topic of religion is frequently seen as taboo in academia (Holden, 2009). It is viewed as a specific topic that is difficult to address in social work classrooms (Coholic, 2003), with little guidance provided to practicing social workers on how to manage their personal beliefs in the context of social work values (Canda, Nakashima, & Furman, 2004). Religious beliefs are by nature considered sacred by many, and as the data from this study will show, the very act of deconstructing and examining religious ideologies may be seen by some as blasphemous. However, the role that religion has historically played and currently plays in justifying violence, discrimination, and oppression situates it as an important topic in multicultural education seeking to foster equality and end oppression across numerous cultural axes. Although many religions have been used as weapons of oppression across history and cultures, the current context of the United States is one in which Christian hegemony is infused throughout politics, cultural norms, and everyday life (Steinberg & Kincheloe, 2009). Christian ideals and values have always been deprivatized to influence policies, laws, and norms, particularly over the last 40 years, with the increased influence of the Christian right in politics (Smith, 1998; Wilcox & Robinson, 2010). Content on religion, and particularly Christianity—both as a source of strength and as a source of oppressive ideology—is sorely lacking in social work education (Furman, Benson, Grimwood, & Canda, 2004; Sheridan & Amato-von Hemert, 1999), with the topic of Christian privilege being even more absent and facing significant resistance and reaction when it is dealt with in the classroom context (Ferber, 2012).

Christian Privilege as an Emerging Frontier

Although some sociologists of religion have argued that the United States is well on its way to being a religiously pluralistic society (Sherkat, 1999; Stark & Finke, 2000), Beaman (2003) eloquently points out that even with the emergence of immigrant religions, the focus of more research on religions at the margins, and the tolerance of more diverse modes of spiritual practice, the overwhelming tone of religion in the United States remains Christian, and Christianity continues to be the predominant reference point for even the variations that exist. She is not denying that there is increasing richness, texture, and diversity in style but rather that those variations dwell solidly within the Christian framework: "They are indeed different, but not so different as to represent a threat to the religious hegemony" (p. 314).

The deep embeddedness of Christian ideals and privilege in U.S. society is well documented (Blumenfeld, 2006; Blumenfeld & Jaekel, 2012; Todd, 2010), dominating the landscape of public debate (Hammond, 1998; Jelen, 2000) and deeply influencing laws, policies, and the cultures of workplaces and schools in the United States (Cole, Avery, Dodson, & Goodman, 2012). Among social workers, there is evidence in bivariate analysis that both Christian affiliation and religiosity are correlated with more negative attitudes toward people of color, women, and LGBT people, and the relationship continues to hold in the multivariate context for attitudes about LGBT people (Dessel, Woodford, & Gutierrez, 2012). Additionally, social work programs in Christian institutions are permitted to ban hiring of LGBT faculty members and admission of students who identify as sexual minorities (Dessel, Bolen, & Shepardson, 2011; Hunter, 2010). In one of the few studies examining education about Christian privilege, Blumenfeld and Jaekel (2012) found that the significant lack of ability to understand issues related to unequal power dynamics in society among preservice teachers resulted in the majority of students being unwilling or unable to "comprehend the privileges society accords them based on their Christian faith" (p. 142). Their findings left them wondering how educators can explore Christian privilege without implying an attack on the Christian faith.

Method

The primary research question guiding this exploratory study is, "What themes emerge as Christian-identified graduate students engage in an educational process that supports and challenges them to explore Christian privilege?" The study uses grounded theory as a paradigm through which to interpret student experiences as a conduit to theorize about what this educational process may entail (Denzin & Lincoln, 1994). The inductive nature of grounded theory provides a structured process for constructing theories that are established from the data collected (Strauss & Corbin, 1990).

After reviewing the data independently, the two co-authors met over a period of months to examine the commonalities in the quotes they identified as representative of emergent themes, cluster them by similarities, synthesize the independent analyses to work out differences in interpretation and understanding of the themes, and finalize themes and their definitions. Then the authors met over a series of meetings to examine the structure of the themes and ended up organizing the themes into the four categories presented herein. No a priori assumptions were made about what themes might emerge.

PARTICIPANTS

Participants in this study include 13 Christian-identified graduate-level students enrolled in a course examining issues of privilege who participated in an in-class caucus that consisted only of Christian-identified students, along with co-instructors for the course who shared that Christian identity and acted as facilitators for the Christian privilege caucus.[2] All but one of the students were enrolled in the graduate school of social work, with the final student enrolled in a joint PhD program housed in a school of theology. Two students were male, and the two caucus facilitators and remaining students were female. Three students identified as people of color, and the remaining students and both caucus facilitators identified as White. All of the students and one of the caucus facilitators identified as heterosexual, and the other caucus facilitator identified as queer.

Primary data for the study were collected from individual blogs of the students and the caucus-level blogs that were kept as part of the course requirements. Course co-instructors who acted as facilitators for the Christian privilege caucus responded to the individual students' blogs with feedback and to the blog to which all students in the caucus had access. Triangulation of data contributes to the soundness of findings in qualitative studies (Denzin & Lincoln, 1994).

Findings

Thirteen themes emerged in the data centering on four overarching categories: contextual factors, relationships with the "Other," emotional reactions and defensiveness, and Christian beliefs as a resource. We discuss the themes in this section, organized by the overarching categories that are the common thread that unite them.

Contextual Factors

Four of the original 13 themes that emerged are contextual factors and previous life experiences that shape the students' struggles of exploring Christian privilege and its manifestation in their lives. Although exploring and unpacking privilege is new to most social work students, many of the students in this course had already done significant work on issues of privilege in their community and activist involvement, but none of them had focused on or given thought to Christian privilege. Thus the newness of the Christian privilege dialogue, both for them as individuals and in the extant scholarship, was jarring to them. As is common with other types of privileges, students were often dismayed at how unaware they were of Christian privilege, much like "the water is to the fish." Similarly, the hegemonic nature of Christianity and Christian beliefs in the world in which they were raised allowed them to be ignorant not only of other religious belief systems but also of differences in belief systems within Christianity. As one student put it, "I have made a gated community of religion." Finally, many of the students had also experienced "victimization at the hands of other Christians" themselves for myriad reasons.

NEWNESS OF THE CHRISTIAN PRIVILEGE DIALOGUE

As part of the manifestation of Christian privilege, students—even those who had done significant work on issues of other types of privilege—reported failure to ever consider Christian privilege as something influencing their lives and the structure of society around them. Similar to many students, one noted, "In the Christian area it's been a whole new world opened up to me. In my life before [this course] I had spent an awful lot of time and energy acting against oppression in all of these other areas but never had the thought of Christian privilege crossed my mind." Another student summed it up, "We all admitted the first day that none of us had heard of Christian privilege before, as was evidenced by our complete lack of understanding of our first group assignment: Identifying the 4 I's (internalized, interpersonal, institutional, and ideological) of our Christian privilege." The dialogue not only was new to the students in the course but is also just emerging in the existing academic scholarship, making even finding readings on Christian privilege a difficult task.

AS THE WATER IS TO THE FISH

Although almost all the students came into the course without having given much thought to Christian privilege and their faith tradition's dominance and role in oppressing other faith traditions and nonreligious worldviews, once they began to look for manifestations they were shocked at the prevalence of Christian privilege in everyday life and their inability to have seen it. They noticed it in the structure of the calendar (e.g., structure of the work week, Christian religious holidays being national holidays) and in the prevalence and normalization of Christian ideology (e.g., the assumptions that being Christian equaled "being normal," the freedom to practice their religion without fear, the allusions to Christian imagery in literature and media, and the assumption that "god" typically meant the Christian God). These very concrete examples of the dominance of the Christian tradition of culture opened up avenues of deeper reflection on the privileging of Christian identity in this country. One student commented to a relative that she had a regular assignment for this course due on a Sunday at noon. The student wrote,

> The first thing my aunt said was, "What?! On Sunday? That's strange . . . won't people be in church?" First, she's assuming that everyone attends church and secondly, it's very customary in Christianity to have Sunday as the day of rest...Many businesses come to a halt on Sunday or have shortened hours at the very least and now I'm wondering how closely that coincides with Christianity. I am struggling with the fact that I did consider myself quite open and aware of the injustices and marginalization that surrounds religion in this country, but I did not and still do not fully comprehend how I am so blind to my own privileges just from being a person who believes in God.

Not only did students notice Christian privilege in cultural norms and mores, but they also consciously linked it to the political arena and how "some policies, values and even views about what it means to be an 'American' have lined up with my personal beliefs and values as Christian." Students listed examples such as the legal definition of marriage, alcohol regulations, restrictions on abortion, and Christian justifications for war.

I HAVE MADE MY OWN GATED COMMUNITY WITH RELIGION

In this theme, students either consciously or unconsciously demonstrate how little they have had to learn about faith traditions other than their own or about nonreligious worldviews and how failure to learn about other's belief systems has had little consequence in their lives. One student noted, "The reading helped me to see that it feels extremely normal to be a Christian even though Christians are only 30% of the world. I realize just how little time I have spent in other [faith] traditions. I can count the times on my hand where I have truly interacted with any other religious tradition different from my own."

Within-group diversity of beliefs in the Christian caucuses also led students to recognize how little they knew about other Christian denominations. One caucus included one Catholic-identified student, with the remainder of students identifying with various Protestant religions. Throughout the course, there were struggles with the Catholic student about whether she even identified as "Christian" or as a "normal Christian" within the group. In relation to the rest of the caucus, this same student commented, "As I've said before the sentiment of 'you are going to hell because you are not Christian' is completely 100% foreign to me. I have never been taught to believe that." Furthermore, she notes, "Proselytizing is a new concept to me and I am still struggling with completely consider[ing] myself Christian."

EXPERIENCE OF BEING VICTIMIZED BY OTHER CHRISTIANS

Many of the students *as Christians* had experienced victimization or marginalization at the hands of other Christians. The victimization or marginalization may have been in the past or current, at times even within the Christian caucus itself. The experiences generally centered around not being the "right kind of Christian" or not living up to others' expectations of what it means to be Christian, but occasionally they were more generic in nature or represented concerns about how one had been raised. This presents a tension for the students as they experience their faith as both a site of privilege and a site from which they had experienced victimization.[3]

> I was the only one in my friend group who had divorced (& remarried & troubled) parents. I was the only one in my friend group who cussed & didn't always have good days & wanted to drink on my 21st bday. I felt "less than" in so many ways & looked down upon in even more ways for my "heathen upbringing" & "imperfect family."

It is common that the recognition of victimization and being judged by others in the Christian faith tradition became a site of connection that helped the students emotionally comprehend how Christian privilege can function to maintain its own hegemony.

Relationship With the Other

The second category of themes that emerged from the data relates to how the Christian students related to others who did not share their religious identity or who are marginalized by the ideology of Christianity as the students understood and practiced it. These three themes address the role of Christian beliefs dominating and marginalizing others and the pain that occurs because of that oppression.

"I AM THE WAY."[4]

In the data underlying this theme, students begin to realize that part of the unique work of challenging Christian privilege has to do with reckoning with the problematic nature of Christian dominance and imperialism over other faiths and literally repairing and reconstructing those relationships. Students recognized concrete instances personally where their theology and practice has dominated others. This is particularly true for evangelical Christians as a result of revisiting their practices of evangelism.

In this quote, one student clearly articulates the role of evangelizing in their understanding of their faith: "At least from the Christian tradition from which I have emerged, Christians are to hope and pray and act in order to 'Christianize' the rest of the world. That is to say, Christian values should be accepted as the norm and any other religious or non-religious beliefs are a direct attack on Christianity." Another student more directly recognized how her own involvement affected those who had different belief systems. She confessed,

> In my search for identity and TRUTH, I discounted everyone else's... who identify with different cultural and/or religious traditions or those who are non-believers. They were all going to hell and I had the TRUTH for their redemption. With this understanding came an urgent sense of responsibility to share the TRUTH. Mission trips, small talk, friendships forged, services given ...all with an agenda. All so I could make my TRUTH your TRUTH.

The certainty and universality of truth claims that were central to some of the students' Christian belief systems created a tension with their desire to live the social work values of self-determination and standing with those most marginalized. One student noted,

Working against my Christian privilege would require a certain degree of tolerance for folks belonging to other religious traditions and who are non-religious. And how much tolerance am I really showing if every time I look at an individual of a different faith than my own and am unwilling to accept their Truth for themselves as valid? If I don't accept that there are perhaps other ways to God—to Truth—then how can I not share my Truth, which I am then assuming is universal truth...holding onto the faith and fighting Christian privilege cause a significant deal of internal dissonance for me . . . because it's so central.

CHRISTIANITY'S ROLE IN REGULATING AND SANCTIONING GENDER AND SEXUALITY

Because most members of the Christian caucus were women, within this theme, tensions about gender were most often focused on women's own experiences of marginalization as women in their churches while occasionally also focusing on the issue of abortion. Around same-sex sexuality, the tensions focused primarily on their disagreement or questioning of their church's prohibitive stance about same-sex marriage, same-sex sexuality in general, or problematizing the idea of "hating the sin, loving the sinner."

One student noted that her experience of being a woman in a church that marginalized women was a place that helped her understand power differences and how they play out in the oppression of the Other: "When I first started thinking about power differentials, I honestly wasn't thinking about all the forms in which hierarchies of power exist...It all started with me feeling icky about being a woman in the church." Another student contextualized the church's control of women in the larger pattern of being the hegemonic definer of what is considered moral. She wrote, "[This exploration] will necessarily lead to issues about the Christian monopoly on morality as well as the firm grip Christianity maintains on defining acceptable expressions of female sexuality and sanctioning expressions that are seen as inappropriate—which all ties together with the issues about who defines 'family.'"

Relatedly, disapproval of same-sex sexuality and relationships was a point of contention for many students in the Christian privilege caucuses. One student stated, "Presently, I feel the need to distance myself from the church because of the outlook on gay people and relationships and my stance on abortion." The deprivatization of faith into political action and influence targeting policy issues affecting LGBT people was also identified. As one student put it,

> Even though this country contains citizens from all different religions and walks of life, many Christians push for legislation, like the banning of gay marriage, that only reflects their religious code. Christians become upset when people who don't subscribe to the same beliefs actively push back against them.

She goes on to label this behavior as "privilege disguised as moral righteousness."

RECOGNIZING THE PAIN OF OTHERS

Whether through hearing painful experiences of non-Christian classmates from other caucuses in the class, taking part in experiential exercises during class, or learning about the violent history of Christianity, some of the students started to more clearly see the pain others experienced because of oppression and religious intolerance. Recognizing and allowing themselves to bear witness to the pain was critical in moving many students through their resistance.

Referring to an in-class exercise, one student noted,

> This very intellectual exercise all of a sudden became very personal and frankly, uncomfortable. Why? I think because it brought to light for the first time the fact that when non-Christians experience fear, are misunderstood, or stereotyped as immoral, unjust or [as] an outside[r] . . . I benefit from these negative experiences. Wow, never realized that before; it doesn't feel too good.

Another student struggled as she watched Christians celebrate the passing of Proposition 8 in California, which aimed to abolish same-sex marriage in that state:

> How they [LGBTQ people] must be feeling after that right was taken back and their family was legally torn apart. There must have been so much grieving going on hidden beneath the celebrations of churches and the religious right who were a driving factor in abolishing gay marriage. But no one around me connected with that pain. They only experienced their privilege being reinforced, and that was worth celebrating.

Emotional Reactions and Defensiveness

As with the process of unpacking oppression and one's role in maintaining systems of stratifications regardless of the type of oppression, students experienced a wide range of emotional reactions and engaged in a number of types of defensive reactions. The themes in this category are clustered around defensive posturing, fears, "yes, but" reactions, self-righteousness, and distancing from other Christians.

DEFENSIVE POSTURING

At times students expressed experiences of defensiveness, that is, psychological stances aimed at protecting themselves, their beliefs, or Christianity itself from criticism. It manifested itself in feelings of being attacked, of wanting to protect oneself from hearing experiences of those who are not Christian, of feeling unsafe, and not wanting to hear the frustration or anger of those marginalized by Christian dominance. One student noted these feelings in relation to the readings on Christian privilege. She recognizes the tension she is experiencing: "I feel like all the Christian privilege articles are repetitive speaking the same words over and over again . . . and I'm trying/searching to feel not scolded or pushed, but [rather be] challenged."

In terms of feeling protective, one student noted,

> I honestly don't feel safe to share my thoughts in the group because I feel like people will jump down my throat saying I'm using my privilege by saying to be strong in the foundation of Christ. I don't see that as my privilege speaking, I see it as a struggling Christian saying to another, I know, without a doubt, that my Lord and Savior is with me . . . I won't be alone in this struggle.

At times students reported that they had felt this lack of safeness, and the resultant defensive protectiveness, throughout their higher education experience:

> My tiredness, as I alluded to last week, also includes the months and months of feeling like I am not allowed to talk about faith or Christianity or ask questions about these things as they relate to social work and practice…so now that we are focusing in on this so intensely, I feel quite hesitant.

In response to questioning and challenge by a non-Christian classmate, one student confesses her reaction of defending the faith: "I shared the urge with several of my caucus colleagues to 'speak up on behalf of Christianity' in relation to [non-Christian student]'s experience."

Included in this theme, students explored their experiences of feeling as if there is little room for their faith in higher education and social work as a discipline more specifically. For evangelicals in particular, this experience resonated with the larger external rhetoric and biblical themes of Christians being victims of persecution. For some this victimization emerged primarily as a defensive emotional response. One student explained,

> I have never really felt privileged to be a Christian in this world. I have felt very much the one that gets a finger pointed at and questioned for the faith that I hold strongly to. It is difficult for me to truly understand this concept… I benefit from what this privilege offers. Yet, at the same time, I see it not as a benefit to be a Christian.

Numerous students noted that being in the Christian privilege caucus "outed" them as Christians for the first time in their graduate program, and this gave rise to fears of being labeled as narrow-minded, irrational, and oppressive. Other students expressed this theme more in analytic and intellectual terms:

> Christianity is unique in that it is a dominant group that often identified itself with persecution. This combination acts to suppress the consciousness of superiority that [is] created when the culture is dominated by Christian

values. It makes it that much more difficult for Christians to step back and question their own oppressive behaviors when their privilege comes into question.

FEARS

The contrary notion to "defending the faith" is "losing the faith." In this theme, students express fears about the effects of "losing their faith" as a result of disrupting Christian privilege. The particular fear, often from an evangelical Christian faith perspective, is that questioning faith is not acceptable in Christian practice. Doing so puts one's very salvation in jeopardy. The fear was at times associated with loss of community and family relationships, loss of self, and loss of faith.

The loss of faith appeared to be connected primarily to the fear of loss of "the faith" as an exclusive "universal truth" in which the superiority of the Christian faith as a historical and theological tradition is grounded. Some students in this category moved from this exclusivist truth perspective toward a willingness to accept that it does not have to be all or nothing, moving into discomfort and ambiguity. Quotes in this theme also seem to dovetail as a tension with the theme of Christian faith as a resource and a shift from viewing disrupting Christian privilege as destroying faith to seeing it as deepening faith.

One student expressed the fear of loss of credibility with their faith community, saying,

> I feel that when I'm confronting Christian privilege, not only do I worry about my actions not paying off, but I fear that I am losing credibility to speak to the issues mixed up with Christianity, my Christianity, because I am that heretic—real believers would never question Christianity.

Similarly, another student reflects on what questioning one's belief system really means: "Too often we are so committed to faith that when someone begins to question even an aspect of our spiritual lives, we see that person as 'stumbling in their walk with God.'" In the following quote, the student is beginning to show movement toward the possibility of living with the ambiguity that would occur if she lets go of her ideological certainty.

> [A] friend felt that she could no longer call herself a Christian because she didn't believe it was the only Way, I don't know that Christian faith and critical realism aren't mutually exclusive. I don't know that I can believe in universal Truth anymore. And while I want to hold onto my faith—it has been a cornerstone of my identity for all my life—I don't know that this [form of] faith allows me to have both.

SELF-RIGHTEOUSNESS

At times students retreated into self-righteousness as a way to defend against acknowledging or understanding the effects of Christian privilege on those who practice other faith traditions or who identify as atheist or agnostic. Self-righteousness manifested itself in patronizing non-Christians, struggles around their belief that they are called to impose their belief system on others, beliefs in the superiority of their own belief system, and discounting those who are not Christian in discussions of Christian privilege. Students often named these feelings and thoughts of self-righteousness as such, recognizing the role of these reactions in defending against new knowledge about Christian privilege.

One student reflects on her experience reading an article on Christian privilege written by someone who does not identify as a Christian. She notes,

> When I began reading the Clark article on Christian privilege, I found myself becoming deeply defensive, criticizing the validity of her statements. I questioned her authority in discuss[ing] Christian privilege, deciding to myself that I would only value the arguments and reflections of someone who was him/herself a Christian.

Another student recognizes the explicit permission and structures that promote a sense of superiority and the "right" to convert others. "I can share about my religion, even proselytize, and be characterized as 'sharing the word' instead of imposing my ideas on others or distributing propaganda." Another notes,

> I know that in my youth group I was conditioned to believe that anyone who wasn't a Christian should be a target for conversion. It makes me so angry thinking about how Christianity polarizes people and reduces complicated humans to a simple category as "saved" or "unsaved."

Finally, a student acknowledges that "one of the thoughts that come up is that Christians think that other people would be so much better off or happier if they only knew Jesus."

"YES, BUT" AMBIVALENCE

Another emotional resistance that emerged in the data occurred when students had clearly recognized the prevalence of the manifestations of Christian privilege in everyday life but were also consciously aware of not wanting to relinquish the conveniences and power of those privileges. This tension was most clearly articulated when a student noted,

> Would I still be a Christian if Christianity didn't have the status, power, privileges attached to it? And that's a little scary to ask...and even more so to discover the answer. My heart wants to say, "Yes, of course...I will still be a Christian and be a believer in Jesus Christ if it was dangerous for me to attend church every week, if I never saw Christian programs on TV, heard Christian songs on the radio, attended a Christian elementary school...But if I'm honest, I do like the comfort of these things.

The centrality of an unchanging and universal truth was at the center of the ambivalence for a number of students with more evangelical backgrounds. A student comments,

> Because if it is a universal truth then a person who believes otherwise is going to hell...How can I believe that and not share the gospel? And which is worse: To proselytize or (assuming a universal truth) allow someone to go to hell?

SEPARATING OR DISTANCING FROM OTHER CHRISTIANS

One defensive strategy used by students was to distance themselves or their type of Christianity from a type of Christianity that they perceived as harmful. This manifested itself in a number of differences including distancing from right-wing political manifestations of Christianity, from evangelical proselytizing, from specific beliefs, from Protestantism, from antiscience attitudes, and from "naïve, do-gooder Christians." It also manifested itself in identification with an "emerging Christian paradigm," "liberation theology radical Christians," a commitment to social justice work, and empathy with those marginalized by Christian ideologies. Finally, another common manifestation was seeing one's faith as individualized and private, distancing from the structural institutions, traditions, practices and history of Christianity as a whole and therefore the role Christianity plays in maintaining its own dominance. Often students acknowledge these feelings and thoughts while recognizing them as part of their resistance,

> But there I go, trying to detach myself from mainstream Christian privilege and culture in the U.S., preferring to take offense and frustration with its manifestation in this country, without recognizing that as a self-identified Christian (no matter the track I prefer to follow), I am myself part of the problem.

Or as another student put it,

> We need to own it all in this work and not just try to say that "we are not that kind of Christian" but really own how we, our ancestors, our friends, our family, oppress non-Christians daily through things as little as that, as Easter candy—because to someone who is not a Christian, it is never going to [feel] little.

At other times, the distance also focused on other students in the Christian privilege caucus. Clearly articulating this resistant stance, one student acknowledges,

> I am also not like "them"—my other caucus members. "They" are not warring, triumphal Christians, but the well-intentioned, naïve, do-gooder

> Christians that don't have a clue...I have more knowledge than they do about oppressive Christian history. I am able to accept more readily that I have Christian privilege than they are. I do not claim that Jesus is unique to salvation . . . I was, I guess, feeling that my faith was better than theirs.

Christian Beliefs as a Resource

The final category emerged primarily in the latter part of the course and represents a shift from the earlier themes of resistance to one where students began to reconceptualize what an antioppressive version of Christianity might look like. Under this theme, students express certain interpretations of their Christian faith as encouraging the work of the course and antioppressive social work practice. From a Christian perspective, doing antioppression work comes to be understood as a means of deepening their spirituality and relationship with God, being more "Christ-like," reflecting the love of God in Christ. Some students see the person of Jesus himself as a model for doing antioppression work.

One student expressed that she felt like she was "re-building my relationship with God in a manner that incorporates how to understand how to disrupt Christian privilege." Another student expressed it in a slightly different way, reporting that she was trying to find "ways in which to continue to move within my belief system and be Christ-like, but not at the expense of others." In terms of viewing Jesus as a model for antioppression work, a student reflected that

> the way in which Christ came to release us from oppression and fight and speak against and live to disrupt and change and free us from that very thing. . . . Christ was not about words but of action and living things out . . . standing up for the oppressed and loving people over any written law.

Summing this category up, a final student asked the question, "How can I be a Christian and NOT do anti-oppression work?"

Discussion and Implications

Although the themes that emerged in this study are not generalizable to Christian social work students in general or even within this particular school of social work, they do provide us with some initial glimpses into some of the issues that are likely to emerge when working with Christian-identified students to acknowledge, see, and challenge Christian privilege as part of their commitment to social work values and ethics. Clearly because of the exploratory nature of this study, future research in understanding students' conceptualization of Christian privilege, fears about addressing the topic, and strategies for being allies with those who identify with other faith traditions or nonreligious worldviews is needed to begin to develop effective educational strategies supported by empirical evidence. Additionally, future qualitative work with different samples of students from other regions, in other schools of social work, and at different educational levels would be helpful to establish the robustness of the findings herein.

Given the dearth of research in this area in the social work (and other scholarly) literature and even with the limitations inherent in qualitative work, we have formulated some initial recommendations to guide educators. Replication of the course from which the data came is one possible avenue to address issues of Christian privilege (see Walls et al., 2010 for information on the course structure), and we offer suggestions for pedagogical approaches that can be incorporated into existing courses to deepen the dialogue on Christian privilege. As with most topics in social work education, incorporation of content across the curriculum is probably the most effective approach. Future research examining these suggestions would be extremely helpful in establishing evidence-based teaching practices around pedagogy of the privileged.

It seems likely that a large number of Christian-identified students might feel as if their ability to discuss their faith and its role in social work has been marginalized. This may entail fears of acknowledging that they are Christian, embracing the "Christians as victims" experience and interpretation of social work education (or higher education or the world), or quick defensive responses to anything they interpret as an attack on their belief system. Patience and support in exploring their fears, particularly facilitated by those who also identify as Christian, may be helpful in moving these students to a less defensive and more open place. In a classroom, the behavioral manifestations of these reactions may trigger other students who have experienced marginalization because of their non-Christian faith tradition or nonreligious worldviews, their gender or gender identity, their sexuality, or some other aspect of their identity. Helping these students manage their triggers (a necessary social work skill in working with client systems) and still stay present and engaged, while not invalidating their experiences of marginalization, is an important skill on the part of the educator (Adams, Bell, & Griffin, 2007). As a strategy, caucusing may be a way to create spaces for exploring reactions on the part of the Christian-identified students, as well as the students who are triggered because of marginalization related to Christian dominance, to help the class manage the differences until there is ability to integrate both experiences. Within the Christian caucus, students can openly express their experiences of marginalization while helping each other understand the difference between the personal experience of prejudice or being stereotyped as Christians in graduate school, for example, and the experience of structural and institutional oppression. Relatedly, having Christian-identified instructors or co-instructors who have done their own work on Christian privilege and can both speak the language of the faith tradition, while challenging Christian students to be accountable, is an invaluable tool for bearing witness to the process for Christian-identified students.

Given the lack of understanding of other faith traditions—or even denominational differences within Christianity itself—that is often the case with Christian students, exploring other faith traditions through cross-cultural or cross-denomination dialogues, cultural immersion experiences, and research can help make students' understanding of worldview differences and their own faith tradition more complex. Although gaining increased knowledge and exposure is not a guarantee that students will be able to see privilege manifested in their internalized superiority, it can at least challenge their notions of their specific understanding of their faith tradition as monolithic or universal.

The frequency with which students in this study identified distancing from other Christians as a strategy to avoid examining their own culpability in supporting Christian dominance suggests that this issue will probably be present among at least some students who undertake this work. Therefore, educators should be cognizant of language, behavior, and emotional reactions that indicate this dynamic as at play (Adams et al., 2007). Manifested in numerous ways, this dynamic had the commonality of students' distancing from some group or type of Christians, labeling them as the "bad Christians" who are responsible for the oppression of others while allowing the students to classify themselves as the "good Christians" who have no responsibility for the oppression of others. This distancing dynamic is common in educational work on power, oppression, and privilege regardless of the type of identity being explored (Govan & Hollins, 2010) and ignores the systemic nature of oppression and how privilege benefits all people in an identity group (Kendall, 2006). Beyond even this common dynamic in privilege work, however, Christian-identified students often credit their faith as motivating their commitment to social justice work generally and social work practice in particular. They are the good Christians who work to alleviate this oppression. A Christian, faith-based calling from God to social justice is part of what makes the work of confronting Christian privilege especially hard for people in social work. Clark (2006) counsels Christians to recognize the obvious historical limits to the liberative nature of Christian theologies and traditions in their effect on social justice. The entanglement of this good Christian faith motivation with the history and practice of the social work tradition in the United States is fertile territory for ongoing reflection and analysis of Christian privilege in this field (Todd, 2010).

Finally, although it began to emerge only toward the end of the course, grappling with how Christian theology and power might also serve as a resource that can be used to challenge religious intolerance and Christian privilege can begin to open new visions of an antioppressive Christian identity. One of the particular challenges of antioppressive revaluing of a Christian identity implies a unique aspect of the work that lies primarily outside the graduate school setting: the matter of biblical interpretation. Students with a more conservative biblical understanding need tools to deconstruct scriptural texts in their relation to historical oppression, theological exclusivism, evangelism, defending the faith, and matters of sin and salvation. Yet even without such tools, simply being able to wrestle with what such an identity might entail in terms of societal shifts, everyday behavioral changes, and changing cultural norms begins to open up avenues for ally behavior, which tends to decrease the despair, defensiveness, and guilt associated with privilege work (Walls et al., 2009).

References

Abramovitz, M. (2001). Everyone is still on welfare: The role of redistribution in social policy. *Social Work, 46,* 297–308. doi:10.1093/sw/46.4.297

Adams, M., Bell, L. A., & Griffin, P. (Eds.). (2007). *Teaching for diversity and social justice* (2nd ed.). New York, NY: Routledge.

Allen, K. R. (1995). Opening the classroom closet: Sexual orientation and self-disclosure. *Family Relations, 44,* 136–141. Retrieved from http://dx.doi.org/10.2307/584799

Anderson, K. J., & Accomando, C. (2002). "Real" boys? Manufacturing masculinity and erasing privilege in popular books on raising boys. *Feminism & Psychology, 12,* 491–516. doi:10.1177/0959353502012004010

Bailey, A. (1998). Privilege: Expanding on Marilyn Fry's oppression. *Journal of Social Philosophy, 29,* 104–119. doi:10.1111/j.1467-9833.1998.tb00124.x

Barlas, C., Kasl, E., MacLeod, A., Paxton, D., Rossenwasser, P., & Sartor, L. (2011). White on White: Communication about race and White privilege with critical humility. *Understanding & Dismantling Privilege, 2*(1). Retrieved from http://www.wpcjournal.com

Beaman, L. G. (2003). The myth of pluralism, diversity, and vigor: The constitutional privilege of Protestantism in the United States and Canada. *Journal for the Scientific Study of Religion, 42,* 311–325. Retrieved from http://dx.doi.org/10.1111/1468-5906.00183

Blackburn, M. V. (2004). Understanding agency beyond school sanctioned-activities. *Theory Into Practice, 43,* 102–110.

Blumenfeld, W. J. (2006). Christian privilege and the promotion of "secular" and not-so "secular" mainline Christianity in public schooling and in the larger society. *Equity & Excellence in Education, 39,* 195–210. Retrieved from http://dx.doi.org/10.1080/10665680600788024

Blumenfeld, W. J., & Jaekel, K. (2012). Exploring levels of Christian privilege awareness among preservice teachers. *Journal of Social Issues, 68,* 128–144. doi: 10.1111/j.1540-4560.2011.01740.x

Brewer, M. B. (2002). The psychology of prejudice: Ingroup love and outgroup hate? *Journal of Social Issues, 44,* 429–444. Retrieved from http://dx.doi.org/10.1111/0022-4537.00126

Canda, E. R., Nakashima, M., & Furman, L. D. (2004). Ethical considerations about spirituality in social work: Insights from a national qualitative survey. *Families in Society, 85,* 27–35. doi:10.1606/1044-3894.256

Case, K. A. (2013). *Deconstructing privilege: Teaching and learning as allies in the classroom.* New York, NY: Routledge.

Clark, C. (2006). Unburning the cross—Lifting the veil on Christian privilege and White supremacy in the United States and abroad: Building multicultural understanding of religion, spirituality, faith, and secularity in educational and workplace settings. In F. Salili & R. Hoosain (Eds.), *Religion in multicultural education* (pp. 167–214). Greenwich, CT: Information Age Publishing.

Coholic, D. (2003). Student and educator viewpoints on incorporating spirituality in social work pedagogy: An overview and discussion of research findings. *Currents: New Scholarship in the Human Services, 2*(2), 1–15.

Cole, E. R., Avery, L. R., Dodson, C., & Goodman, K. D. (2012). Against nature: How arguments about the naturalness of marriage privilege heterosexuality. *Journal of Social Issues, 68,* 46–62. Retrieved from http://dx.doi.org 10.1111/j.1540-4560.2011.01735.x

Collins, P. H. (2000). Gender, black feminism, and black political economy. *Annals of the American Academy of Political and Social Science, 568,* 41–53. doi: 10.1177/000271620056800105

Crenshaw, K. W. (1991). Mapping the margins: Intersectionality, identity politics, and violence against women of color. *Stanford Law Review, 43,* 1241–1299. doi:10.2307/1229039

Curry-Stevens, A. (2007). New forms of transformative education: Pedagogy for the privileged. *Journal of Transformative Education, 5,* 33–58. doi:10.1177/1541344607299394

Delp, C., & Rogers, A. (2011). Inclusivity: Journey of enrichment. *Lifelong Learning Institute Review, 6,* 24–29.

Denzin, N. K., & Lincoln, Y. S. (Eds.). (1994). *Handbook of qualitative research.* Thousand Oaks, CA: SAGE.

Dessel, A., Bolen, R., & Shepardson, T. (2011). Can religion expression and sexual orientation affirmation coexist in social work? A critique of Hodge's theoretical, theological, and conceptual frameworks. *Journal of Social Work Education, 47,* 213–234. doi:10.5175/JSWE.2011.200900074

Dessel, A., Rogge, M., & Garlington, S. (2006). Using intergroup dialogue to promote social justice and change. *Social Work, 51,* 303–315. doi:10.1093/sw/51.4.303

Dessel, A., Woodford, M. R., & Gutierrez, L. (2012). Social work faculty's attitudes toward marginalized groups: Exploring the role of religion. *Journal of Religion & Spirituality in Social Work: Social Thought, 31,* 244–262. doi:10.1080/15426432.2012.679841

Dessel, A., Woodford, M., Routenberg, R., & Breijak, D. (2013). Heterosexual students' experiences in sexual orientation intergroup dialogue courses. *Journal of Homosexuality, 60,* 1054–1080. Retrieved from http://dx.doi.org/10.1080/00918369.2013.776413

DiAngelo, R. (1997). Heterosexism: Addressing internalized dominance. *Journal of Progressive Human Services, 8,* 5–22.

DiAngelo, R., & Flynn, D. (2010). Showing what we tell: Facilitating antiracist education in cross-racial teams. *Understanding & Dismantling Privilege, 1*(1). Retrieved from http://www.wpcjournal.com

Efferson, C., Lalive, R., & Fehr, E. (2008). The coevolution of cultural groups and ingroup favoritism, *Science, 26,* 1844–1849. Retrieved from http://dx.doi.org/10.1126/science.1155805

Farough, S. D. (2003). Structural aporias and white masculinities: White men confront the White male privilege critique. *Race, Gender, & Class, 10,* 38–53.

Ferber, A. L. (2003). Defending the culture of privilege. In M. S. Kimmel & A. L. Ferber (Eds.), *Privilege: A reader* (pp. 319–329). Boulder, CO: Westview Press.

Ferber, A. L. (2012). The culture of privilege: Color-blindness, postfeminism, and Christonormativity. *Journal of Social Issues, 68,* 63–77. doi:10.1111/j.1540-4560.2011.01736.x

Furman, L., D., Benson, P. W., Grimwood, C., & Canda, E. (2004). Religion and spirituality in social work education and direct practice at the millennium: A survey of UK social workers. *British Journal of Social Work, 34,* 767–792. doi:10.1093/bjsw/bch101

Goodman, D. J. (2001). *Promoting diversity and social justice: Educating people from privileged groups.* Thousand Oaks, CA: SAGE.

Govan, I., & Hollins, C. (2010). Common expressions of White privilege and how to counter them. *Understanding & Dismantling Privilege, 1*(1). Retrieved from http://www.wpcjournal.com

Hammond, P. E. (1998). *With liberty for all: Freedom of religion in the United States.* Louisville, KY: Westminster John Knox Press.

Holden, R. (2009). The public university's unbearable defiance of being. *Educational Philosophy and Theory, 41,* 575–591. doi:10.1111/j.1469-5812.2008.00416.x

Hunter, S. (2010). *Effects of conservative religion on lesbian and gay clients and practitioners: Practice implications.* Washington, DC: NASW Press.

Hyde, C., & Ruth, B. J. (2002). Multicultural content and class participation: Do students self-censor? *Journal of Social Work Education, 38,* 241–257.

Jelen, T. G. (2000). *To serve God and mammon: Church-state relations in American politics.* Boulder, CO: Westview Press.

Johnson, J. R. (2013). Cisgender privilege, intersectionality, and the criminalization of CeCe McDonald: Why intercultural communication needs transgender studies. *Journal of International and Intercultural Communications, 6*(2), 135–144. doi:10.1080/17513057.2013.776094

Kendall, F. (2006). *Understanding White privilege: Creating pathways to authentic relationships across race.* New York, NY: Routledge.

Kivel, P. (2004). *You call this a democracy? Who benefits, who pays, and who really decides?* New York, NY: The Apex Press.

Kurzdorfer, M. (2012). Anti-trans hatred in the name of feminism. *Dissenting Voices, 1,* Article 15. Retrieved from http://digitalcommons.brockport.edu/dissentingvoices/vol1/iss1/15

Manglitz, E. (2003). Challenging White privilege in adult education: A critical review of the literature. *Adult Education Quarterly, 53,* 119–134. doi:10.1177/0741713602238907

McLean, M. A. (2008). Teaching about disability: An ethical responsibility? *International Journal of Inclusive Education, 12,* 605–619. doi:10.1080/13603110802377649

Miller, J., Donner, S., & Fraser, E. (2004). Talking when talking is tough: Taking on conversations about race, sexual orientation, gender, class, and other aspects of social identity. *Smith College Studies in Social Work, 74,* 377–392. doi: 10.1080/00377310409517722

Nichols, D. (2010). Teaching critical whiteness theory: What college and university teachers need to know. *Understanding & Dismantling Privilege, 1*(1). Retrieved from http://www.wpcjournal.com

Pease, B. (2010a). Ableist relations and the embodiment of privilege. In B. Pease, *Undoing privilege: Unearned advantage in a divided world* (pp. 149–168). London, England: Zed Books.

Pease, B. (2010b). *Undoing privilege: Unearned advantage in a divided world.* London, England: Zed Books.

Pease, B. (2010c). Western global dominance and Eurocentrism. In B. Pease, *Undoing privilege: Unearned advantage in a divided world* (pp. 39–61). London, England: Zed Books.

Pewewardy, N. (2007). *Challenging White privilege: Critical discourse for social work education.* Alexandria, VA: Council on Social Work Education.

Razack, N. (2002). *Transforming the field: Critical antiracist and antioppressive perspectives for the human services practicum.* Halifax, NS: Fernwood Publishing.

Rodriguez, N. M. (2000). Projects of whiteness in a critical pedagogy. In N. M. Rodriguez & L. E. Villaverde (Eds.), *Dismantling White privilege: Pedagogy, politics, and whiteness* (pp. 1–24). New York, NY: Peter Lang.

Rozas, L. W. (2007). Engaging dialogue in our diverse social work student body: A multilevel theoretical process model. *Journal of Social Work Education, 43,* 5–29. doi:10.5175/JSWE.2007.200400467

Schwalbe, M. (2005). Afterword: The costs of American privilege. In P. Rothenberg, *Beyond borders: Thinking critically about global issues* (pp. 603–605). New York, NY: Worth Publishers.

Sheridan, M. J., & Amato-von Hemert, K. (1999). The role of religion and spirituality in social work education and practice: A survey of student views and experiences. *Journal of Social Work Education, 35,* 125–141.

Sherkat, D. (1999). Tracking the "other": Dynamics and composition of "other" religions in the General Social Survey, 1972–1996. *Journal for the Scientific Study of Religion, 38,* 551–560. doi:10.2307/1387612

Smith, C. (1998). *American evangelicalism: Embattled and thriving.* Chicago, IL: University of Chicago Press.

Stark, R., & Finke, R. (2000). *Acts of faith: Explaining the human side of religion.* Berkeley, CA: University of California Press.

Steinberg, S. R., & Kincheloe, J. L. (2009). *Christotainment: Selling Jesus through popular culture.* Boulder, CO: Westview Press.

Stone, D., Patton, B., & Heen, S. (1999). *Difficult conversations: How to discuss what matters most.* New York, NY: Viking.

Strauss, A. L., & Corbin, J. (1990). *Basics of qualitative research: Grounded theory procedures and techniques.* Newbury Park, CA: SAGE.

Todd, J. (2010). Confessions of a Christian supremacist. *Reflections, 16,* 140–146.

van Every, J. (1995). Heterosexuality, heterosex, and heterosexual privilege. *Feminism & Psychology, 5,* 140–144. doi:10.1177/0959353595051017

Walls, N. E., & Costello, K. (2010). "Head ladies center for teacup chain": Cisgender privilege in a (predominantly) gay male context. In S. Anderson & V. Middleton (Eds.), *Explorations in privilege, oppression, & diversity* (2nd ed., pp. 81–93). Belmont, CA: Brooks/Cole.

Walls, N. E., Griffin, R., Arnold-Renicker, H., Burson, M., Johnston, C., Moorman, N., . . . Schutte, E. C. (2009). Mapping graduate social work students' learning journeys about heterosexual privilege. *Journal of Social Work Education, 45,* 289–307. doi:10.5175/JSWE.2009.200800004

Walls, N. E., Roll, S., Griffin, R., & Sprague, L. (2010). A model for teaching about privilege in graduate social work education. *Understanding and Dismantling Privilege, 1*(1). Retrieved from http://www.wpcjournal.com

Weiler, K. (1988). *Women teaching for change: Gender, class & power.* South Hadley, MA: Bergin & Garvey.

Wilcox, C., & Robinson, C. (2010). *Onward Christian soldiers? The religious right in American politics.* Boulder, CO: Westview Press.

Woodford, M., & Bella, L. (2003). Are we ready to take a stand? Educating social work students about heterosexism: Fostering anti-oppressive practice. In W. Shera (Ed.), *Emerging perspectives on anti-oppressive practice* (pp. 413–430). Toronto, ON: Canadian Scholars Press.

Notes

1 Cisgender people are defined as "individuals who identify as the gender they were assigned at birth" (Walls & Costello, 2010), p. 81). In other words, a cisgender person is one who is not transgender.

2 One co-author of this chapter was the lead instructor for both courses. The other co-author was a student in the Christian privilege caucus in the first class and the caucus facilitator for the Christian privilege caucus in the second class. Although all the quotes emerged from student blogs, we include the caucus facilitators as study participants because they have participated in dialogue through the blogs with the students.

3 However, this theme does not include students' experiences of victimization based on the marginalized identities of gender and sexual orientation, which are discussed in the next section.

4 From John 14:6. "Jesus said to him, 'I am the way, and the truth, and the life; no one comes to the Father but through Me.'" In the evangelical Protestant tradition, this verse is often interpreted as indicating that it is only by salvation through Jesus Christ that one attains eternal life, leading to the idea of Christianity possessing a universal and exclusive truth.

Chapter 17

Heterosexual Students' Experiences in Sexual Orientation Intergroup Dialogue Courses

Adrienne B. Dessel, PhD, LMSW, Michael R. Woodford, PhD, robbie routenberg, MA, and Duane Breijak, LLMSW

The following reprinted article has been included in this book to provide an empirical analysis of a pedagogy that social work educators can use to effectively engage students who hold negative attitudes about sexual minority people. Given heterosexist and hostile campus climates for lesbian, gay, and bisexual (LGB) college students, interventions designed to address bias and discrimination against LGB people and promote their inclusion are needed. The study describes experiences of heterosexual students who participated in a semester-long intergroup dialogue course on sexual orientation designed to reduce prejudice, improve relationships between heterosexual and LGB students, and encourage social justice action.

Intergroup dialogue is a pedagogy that engages students in a co-facilitated and sustained group experience involving two (and sometimes more) social identity groups who have a history of conflict (Nagda, Gurin, Sorensen, & Zúñiga, 2009; Zúñiga, Nagda, Chesler, & Cytron-Walker, 2007). The curriculum involves a four-stage model that teaches students to analyze social identity, power, and group-based inequalities and develops positive relationships, fosters collaboration, and promotes social justice (Nagda & Maxwell, 2011; Sorensen et al., 2009).

The 54 heterosexual students who participated in one of nine sexual orientation intergroup dialogue courses examined in the study reported on their motivations for taking the course, their fears that their peers would not be honest and open, their worries about saying things that would be unintentionally offensive to their LGB classmates, and their concerns about negative stigma if they were perceived as being LGB. They described learning about their LGB peers' experiences, including information that challenged their negative stereotypes of LGB people. They also indicated learning about their own heterosexual privilege, interrupting heterosexism among their peers and family members, and wanting to pursue further learning to become allies.

Although we did not collect data on the religious demographics of the sample, a number of students disclosed having Christian religious backgrounds and holding religious beliefs that challenged their full acceptance and support of LGB people. In our qualitative analysis, we found that one of the areas of conflict in the dialogues centered on religion, Christian teachings, and traditional beliefs about same-sex marriage. Students also learned about intersectionality of identities, specifically heterosexual privilege and religious identity. Heterosexual students who had religious upbringings worried others would view them negatively based on their religious social identities. They also lacked information about LGB students and thus appreciated the learning they gained in the dialogues.

Educators who want to use intergroup dialogue to foster critical thinking and address conflicts between conservative Christians who hold negative beliefs about LGB people and LGB students can use this specific pedagogy. Alternatively, faculty members can incorporate some of the methods into their classrooms, such as use of guidelines to reduce anxiety and resistance during difficult conversations (Deal & Hyde, 2004), paying attention to physical classroom space, use of personal narratives to create safety and develop relationships (Adams, Bell, & Griffin, 2007; Zúñiga et al., 2007), and use of role plays and experiential activities to analyze social power (Adams et al., 2007). Interested faculty members can seek out training in intergroup dialogue methods through consultations with experienced practitioners and attend trainings such as the National Intergroup Dialogue Institute at the University of Michigan (http://igr.umich.edu/about/institute).

Campus climate, or the perceptions and experiences of students in and out of their classrooms, is a critical concept in higher education (Hart & Fellabaum, 2008; Hurtado, Griffin, Arellano, & Cuellar, 2008). College and university communities should be safe places both psychologically and physically for all students. Unfortunately, this is not the case, especially for lesbian, gay, and bisexual (LGB) students. A recent national study on the state of higher education for lesbian, gay, bisexual, and transgender (LGBT) students found that they generally feel unsafe, experience harassment and discrimination, and lack support (Rankin, Weber, Blumenfeld, & Frazer, 2010). Further, LGBT students are more likely than their heterosexual counterparts to consider leaving their institutions (Rankin et al., 2010). Studies conducted at specific institutions have also documented a negative, unwelcoming campus climate for sexual minority students (Evans & Broido, 2002; Silverschanz, Cortina, Konik, & Magley, 2008; Woodford, Howell, Silverschanz, & Yu, 2012; Woodford, Krentzman, & Gattis, 2012; Yost & Gilmore, 2011).

A hostile campus climate can have serious ramifications for students' health and wellbeing (Silverschanz et al., 2008; Woodford, Howell, et al., 2012; Woodford, Krentzman, & Gattis, 2012). Minority stress theory suggests that a hostile social environment, expressed both through overt and subtle acts, can negatively impact the physical and psychological wellbeing of sexual minority students (Meyer, 2003). Students can experience negative climate both through personal experiences of mistreatment and witnessing the mistreatment of others, both of which have been found to be related to negative outcomes for sexual minority students as well as heterosexual students (Silverschanz et al., 2008; Woodford, Krentzman, & Gattis, 2012). In addition, ubiquitous phrases like "that's so gay" that are very common today can threaten LGB students' health and wellbeing (Woodford, Howell, et al., 2012). Collectively, these studies highlight the importance of universities addressing heterosexism and discrimination in order to create safe and accepting places for *all* students.

Institutions often attempt to increase students' awareness and acceptance of LGB people through speakers' bureaus (Blackburn, 2003, 2006; Crawley & Broad, 2004) and ally or safe zone programs (Draughn, Elkins, & Roy, 2002; Evans, 2002; Finkel, Storaasli, Bandele, & Schaefer, 2003; Poynter & Tubbs, 2008; Woodford, Kolb, Radeka, & Javier, in press). One particularly innovative intervention designed to improve relations between sexual minority students and heterosexual students and to contribute to pro-LGB social action is intergroup dialogue. Intergroup dialogue courses generally bring together students from two different, usually conflicting, social identity groups with unequal power. These groups are co-facilitated by peers who identify with each social identity group. Dialogue courses use experiential and didactic learning exercises, including activities outside the classroom, and aim to increase students' awareness and critical analysis of the socialization process related to group identity and individual and institutional privilege and oppression. These interventions also encourage students to develop skills for sustained communication across differences and engagement in individual and collective alliance building and social justice action (Zúñiga, Nagda, Chesler, & Cytron-Walker, 2007). Such awareness, skill building, and action with regard to sexual orientation may help to mitigate the problems of heterosexism and homophobia on college campuses.

Because dialogue groups on race/ethnicity and gender are popular, most research on this method focuses on these topics (Maxwell, Nagda, & Thompson, 2011). Two recent studies examined sexual orientation dialogue groups. Dessel (2010) used a three-session intergroup dialogue intervention with heterosexual public school teachers and adult LGB community members. She found that heterosexual teachers reported significantly more accepting attitudes, feelings, and behaviors toward LGB people after dialogue participation. In an earlier study, we examined campus-based sexual orientation dialogue courses from the perspective of participating LGB students (Dessel, Woodford, & Warren, 2011). Specifically, we explored students' reflections about their motivations and expectations for participating in the courses, the challenges they experienced, and their learning. The results indicated that LGB students took the courses to create a more inclusive environment for LGB people, establish connections and community with other LGB students on campus, and explore their own identities and the LGB community. Concerning challenges, some students reported anxiety about "coming out" within the group (sharing experiences related to one's sexual identity is part of the pedagogy) and experienced frustration with heterosexual students who they believed were not willing to honestly share their experiences and explore their own biases. Despite these challenges, important growth was realized, such as learning about their own and others' identities, including intersecting identities, developing personal empowerment and critical consciousness, and intending to engage in social justice actions to address heterosexism.

Given the privileges that heterosexual individuals enjoy in society and on college campuses (Broido & Reason, 2005), in order to better understand sexual orientation intergroup dialogue courses it is important to explore these courses from the stance of participating heterosexual students. In this study, adopting an exploratory approach we examine heterosexual college students' experiences in and learning from sexual orientation intergroup dialogue courses. Rather than evaluate the effectiveness of these groups, our overall aim is to advance understanding of intergroup dialogue on sexual orientation and to shed light on their potential to meaningfully engage heterosexual students in social justice education concerning heterosexism. Consistent with our previous study (Dessel et al., 2011) we examine students' motivations and expectations, challenges participating in the dialogues, and learning outcomes. We report themes within each of these areas, and discuss implications and recommendations for future interventions and research. To frame the study, we first briefly review the literature on interventions designed to address bias and discrimination against LGB people.

Interventions to Address Heterosexism and Homophobia

Most interventions designed to change heterosexual students' attitudes toward LGB people tend to be educational and rely on speaker panels or similar methods (Tucker & Potocky-Tripodi, 2006). Studies report varying degrees of success in obtaining positive outcomes related to homophobia and anti-gay prejudice. Researchers have examined the effects of college courses on human sexuality and the psychology of prejudice on anti-gay prejudice (Finken, 2002; Pettijohn & Walzer, 2008), and results have been mixed. Using pretest and posttest measures, Finken (2002) found that female students in the course showed decreased prejudice by the end of the semester, while male students did not. Pettijohn and Walzer (2008) found students, generally, showed significantly greater decreases in anti-gay prejudice compared to students in a standard introductory psychology course.

Several studies have examined the effect of one-time workshops on heterosexual bias. Hillman and Martin (2002) designed an active learning activity using a fictional scenario in which students experienced stereotyping and considered social stigma often directed toward gay men and lesbians. Pretest/posttest scores on a Homophobia Scale (Wright, Adams, & Bernat, 1999) suggested that the activity fostered more accepting attitudes toward gay men and lesbians. In 2009, Hodson, Choma, and Costello conducted a follow-up study that examined the psychological mechanisms underlying the active learning activity in Hillman and Martin's (2002) study. Hodson et al. (2009) found that the activity resulted in higher levels of intergroup perspective-taking, empathy, and favorable attitudes towards LGB people and other marginalized groups. This remained true even after controlling for prior attitudes and ideological individual differences predicting anti-gay bias.

Some studies have used control and/or comparison groups to examine the efficacy of their interventions. Rye and Meaney (2009) examined the effectiveness of a homonegativity awareness workshop. The study indicated that workshop participants were significantly less homophobic and erotophobic (fearful of sexual matters) after the workshop compared to a control group of introductory psychology students. Another study compared levels of sexual prejudice and affect for students in rational training, experiential training (affective training), and control groups (Guth, Lopez, Rojas, Clements, & Tyler, 2004). The experiential group ultimately reported more accepting attitudes toward lesbian and gay issues compared to the control group. The experiential group participants also reported more positive affect compared to the other two groups, and more negative affect compared to the rational group.

Although these various interventions generally helped address LGB prejudice among heterosexual students, none of these approaches engaged students in facilitated learning processes over time and few involved both cognitive and affective learning (Nagda, Gurin, Sorensen, & Zúñiga, 2009). Further, the workshops and courses described in these studies were not specifically intended to prepare students to move from learning to action in addressing heterosexism. In addition to engaging students both cognitively and affectively, anti-heterosexist education requires preparing students to address heterosexism through skill building and action (DiAngelo, 1997; Woodford & Bella, 2003).

Intergroup dialogue is an intervention that engages diverse student populations in learning over an extended period that fosters democratic engagement, social responsibility, and ethical decision-making with regard to civic action (Nagda et al., 2009). Various studies demonstrate the effectiveness of this method (Nagda et al., 2009; Sorensen, Nagda, Gurin, & Maxwell, 2009). For instance, a longitudinal study of race and gender intergroup dialogue courses at nine universities, using random assignment and comparison groups, examined outcomes in three areas: intergroup understanding, intergroup relationships, and intergroup collaboration and engagement. The results demonstrate significant increases in awareness of institutional inequality, motivation to bridge differences, and personal responsibility for collaboration and social action (Nagda et al., 2009). Follow-up studies indicate students sustained their gains in learning and commitment to action after the dialogues ended (Gurin, Nagda, & Zúñiga, 2013). These studies suggest a clear connection exists between intergroup dialogue and prejudice reduction among students.

In this article, we explore the experiences of heterosexual identified students who participated in sexual orientation dialogue courses. Specifically, we investigate students' motivations and expectations for joining a dialogue group on sexual orientation. We also report on the challenges they experienced in the courses and their learning outcomes.

Method

A qualitative research design was used for this study. We examined students' participation in nine sexual orientation intergroup dialogue courses held between 2003 and 2011 at the University of Michigan. The data consisted of 46 heterosexual students' final papers from seven dialogue courses held from Fall 2003 through Fall 2007, and post-dialogue semi-structured interviews held with eight heterosexual students who participated in one of two dialogue courses offered in 2011. Sexual orientation was not offered as a dialogue topic during 2008–2010. Interviews were conducted to triangulate findings from the analysis of students' papers from the earlier dialogue groups (Sandelowski, 2003). This study received approval from the University of Michigan's Institutional Review Board.

Table 1. Heterosexual Sexual Orientation Dialogue Participants, Fall 2003 to Fall 2007 Final Papers (*n*=46)

	n	%
Gender		
Female	28	60.87
Male	18	39.13
Race		
White	36	78.25
African American	4	8.70
Latino	2	4.35
Asian	2	4.35
Not indicated	2	4.35

Table 2. Heterosexual Sexual Orientation Dialogue Participants, Fall 2011 Interviews (*n*=8)

	n	%
Gender		
Female	4	50.00
Male	4	50.00
Race		
White	4	50.00
African American	2	25.00
Latino	1	12.50
Asian	1	12.50

Sexual Orientation Intergroup Dialogue Courses

The dialogue courses were offered as undergraduate two-credit courses in psychology and sociology. Students selected the sexual orientation dialogue as one of three choices out of five options and rank ordered their choices. Each sexual orientation group had between 8 and 15 participants, with an average of seven heterosexual identified students, and was co-facilitated by two peers, one of whom identified as heterosexual and one who identified as LGB. Although dialogue courses are traditionally balanced relatively equally between the two participating identity groups (Hardiman, Jackson, & Griffin, 2007), one of the selected groups was less balanced, with six heterosexual students (5 women and 1 man) and two lesbian students.

The pedagogy of these intergroup dialogue courses is constructed in a four-stage model, informed by theories of group dynamics and individual learning (Hogg, Abrams, Otten, & Hinkle, 2004; King & Baxter Magolda, 2005; Zúñiga et al., 2007). In the first stage of the dialogue, which lasts two weeks, groups create guidelines, form relationships, and develop a shared understanding of intergroup dialogue communication practices. The second stage deepens when exploration of differences and commonalities occurs. In this process, students reflect on and articulate their lived experiences as it relates to the dialogue topic and often become vulnerable in the group setting. The third stage is reserved for dialogue on controversial topics (i.e., hot topics) relevant to the dialogue topic and of interest to the participants. This is often when the most conflict occurs. The dialogues close with stage four, which involves building alliances through an intergroup collaboration project and planning for future action outside of the dialogue (Zúñiga et al., 2007). This cumulative pedagogy allows for group members to challenge themselves over the semester while still receiving the support of their group members. Trust and community are developed before risk-taking and vulnerability happens. Experiential activities related to stereotypes, social identity, power and privilege, and heterosexism are designed to foster critical thinking and new learning.

Data Sources and Analysis

The final paper assignment asked the students to reflect on their dialogue experience and what they learned about their social identities and group interaction and communication. Students are also asked to discuss challenges and rewards of dialogue and future social justice engagement. Based on the initial analysis of the students' papers, we developed interview questions that explored students' motivations for taking the course and expectations for the course, experiences both positive and negative during the course, learning about privilege, oppression and heterosexism, attitudinal change, and views on being an ally, including interrupting or challenging sexual prejudice. All students who participated in two groups offered in 2011 (N = 26) were invited to participate in the study and eight agreed. Trained student interviewers conducted the interviews to foster an equal power balance in the interview process (Kvale & Brinkmann, 2009). Interviews ranged from approximately 20 to 40 minutes, and were recorded with permission.

All data were analyzed using QSR NVIVO 8 (QSR International Pty. Ltd, Doncaster, Victoria, Australia). Data analysis began with an initial reading of all the papers. Next, two team members examined 10 randomly selected papers to create salient categories of information, or open codes (Strauss & Corbin, 1990). These open codes consisted of important meaning units (words, phrases, sentences) that emerged from students' writing. Each analyst's open codes were compared and 70 core codes were identified through consensus. The remaining papers were then coded. As needed, additional open codes were created to capture other relevant meaning units not addressed in the initial coding framework. Axial coding was then conducted by interconnecting the previously created codes (Strauss & Corbin, 1990). Some categories were combined or removed depending on the information provided. Throughout the analysis process, the constant comparative method was used to compare and contrast themes identified across papers (Strauss & Corbin, 1990).

The interview recordings were transcribed and coded by two team members using the analytical procedures specified above. Next, comparisons were made between the themes derived from the papers and the interviews. To foster trustworthiness and credibility, throughout the data analysis process methodological and interpretive memos were kept and member checking was conducted with facilitators of a current sexual orientation dialogue course as well as two heterosexual student members, and peer debriefing occurred with two senior colleagues with expertise in dialogue methods (Creswell, 2007; Erlandson, Harris, Skipper, & Allen, 1993).

Results

Sample

As reported in Table 1, of the 54 students in this study, 32 identified as female and 22 as male. Most students (n = 40) identified as White, with six African

American students, three Latino students, three Asian students, and two not indicating race. Participants ranged from 18 to 24 years old, with more than one half being 20 years old. Twelve of the students did not rank the sexual orientation dialogue as their first choice.

Contact with LGB people has been shown to be associated with less sexual prejudice among heterosexual individuals (Engberg, Hurtado, & Smith, 2007; Woodford, Silverschanz, Swank, Scherrer, & Raiz, 2012); therefore, we document reported pre-dialogue known contact. Neither the final assignment nor interviews explicitly inquired about pre-dialogue contact with LGB people; thus, we rely on students' narratives. A total of 12 students (9 from the 2003–2007 groups and 3 from the 2011 groups) indicated having pre-dialogue contact with LGB people, specifically family members and friends. The remaining students (37 from the 2003–2007 groups and 5 from the 2011 groups) did not reference having any direct relationships with LGB people prior to the dialogues. In fact, four students from the earlier dialogues directly reported in their papers no known contact with LGB people.

Motivations and Expectations

All students entered the group wanting to learn more about the LGB community:

> At the beginning of the semester I was very excited to learn that I was going to be taking part in LGB/H dialogue, as this particular group was definitely one I was most interested in and really wanted to broaden my knowledge base about. (White male participant)

Among those with prior LGB contact, they were specifically motivated to learn how they could better support their LGB family members and friends and address heterosexism. Some of these participants reported that they wanted to learn about LGB identity development, coming out, and the needs and strengths of the LGB community so they could better support their family members and friends. Many wanted to learn ways they could become involved with specific issues affecting the LGB community, such as same-sex marriage, in order to become (better) LGB allies. A few of these participants noted that they wanted to learn how to educate others about LGB people and the community's needs, and how to fight heterosexism, such as how to best respond when someone makes a heterosexist comment. Some of these students noted that peers had recommended the dialogue group to them as a safe environment where they could openly acknowledge, explore, and discuss their support for the LGB community.

Concerning expectations about the dialogue group, some students, especially those who did not rank the sexual orientation dialogues as their first choice, raised concerns about participating in the groups. We identified three primary concerns, namely questioning the utility of dialogue method, the possibility of homophobic classmates and the impact on the dialogue process, and the possibility of participants themselves unintentionally offending LGB classmates.

THE UTILITY OF DIALOGUE METHOD

Although students elected to be in the dialogue courses (not always their first choice), a very small number were unsure about how effective a dialogue approach would be in teaching them about heterosexism, the LGB community, and how to address heterosexism. For example, in regard to the last area, one student wrote:

> In the past, I have seen very little use of dialogues in situations where people share different beliefs. Usually, when people are talking and hold opposing viewpoints, they feel the need to defend themselves and view the opposition as a threat or an attack, because of this, debates and arguments are ultimate[ly] the end result a common understanding is hardly almost never reached. (White female participant)

Some students with no prior interactions with LGB individuals were especially worried and were not sure if they would relate to the experiences of LGB individuals, which they understood as being important to the dialogue method. For instance, one student reported concerns about "be[ing] able to understand where the other group was coming from" (African American male participant). As discussed later, important learning was reported in this area.

HOMOPHOBIC CLASSMATES IN THE DIALOGUE GROUPS

Some students from the earlier and later courses raised concerns about having extremely homophobic classmates who would hinder productive discussion: "I feared that there were [*sic*] going to be a handful of people that would be very entrenched in their homophobic ways, and therefore create constant tension within the class" (White male participant). Homophobic and intolerant students were feared to produce non-productive classes, where "constant tension" would polarize the room and discourage open communication. More specifically, some students were concerned that overtly homophobic students would offend LGB group members and create an overall unsafe and hostile learning environment. Such an environment would make it difficult to engage in meaningful dialogue because the trust and other conditions needed for successful dialogue would be absent or threatened, at best. However, it is useful to note that many students commented that once the dialogues began these thoughts diminished as facilitators helped produce a comfortable, safe environment and a lack of extremely homophobic views became apparent (which is related to group challenges; see the following section). Although several of the students still initially felt uncomfortable speaking and opening up the first few weeks of the dialogue, by the end of the course most reported believing their classmates were trustworthy.

UNINTENTIONAL OFFENSE TO LGB CLASSMATES

Some students across the years, including some with LGB family members and friends, were concerned that they themselves might unintentionally offend their classmates. Generally, these students did not wish to come across as biased, "stupid," or "naïve": "I was nervous that my questions might seem naïve, because I knew so little about the LGB community and the difficulties they had to face" (White female participant). Related to this, some students were worried about not being able to express their opinions and views without upsetting someone else in the group. One student raised concerns about not knowing what LGB-related language would be most appropriate to use in the group given LGB students were participating (African American male student). It is interesting to note that a few of the students who reported these concerns noted how asking "naïve" and "stupid" questions was actually helpful in terms of promoting their and some colleagues' learning.

Challenges

Two themes emerged regarding challenging experiences for students: Conflict within themselves, and conflict with other group members. Students reported on intrapersonal conflict, such as when they experienced anxiety around the stigma of association with LGB peers, and they discussed experiences of conflict with other group members. These conflicts centered on a number of topics, such as the concept of allyhood (Edwards, 2006), same-sex marriage, and whether or not same-sex sexuality is biologically determined, as well as concerns about sounding politically correct.

INTRAPERSONAL CONFLICT

Among the students who did not report known pre-dialogue contact with LGB people, many were concerned about the stigma of being mislabeled as LGB at different stages of the course. For some, it was the sheer fact that they were enrolled in this section of intergroup dialogue (focusing on sexual orientation) that was enough to raise concern. Carrying the class books or even telling other people that they were a part of such a dialogue created potential for others to doubt their heterosexual orientation: "I had to field questions about my sexuality when telling my peers my class schedule for the semester. I started to feel like after telling people that I was taking this class they would question my sexual orientation" (White woman participant). For others, the emotional reaction that resulted from the burden of stigma by possibly being perceived to be LGB was prompted by some of the class activities. These reactions to the stigma that LGB people experience daily helped some students learn about heterosexual privilege.

There were two activities during the dialogues that provoked strong reactions in some heterosexual students. It should be noted that these reactions were reported from the final papers between 2003 and 2007, but did not appear in the interviews from 2011. The reaction stemmed from an anxiety of being assumed to be LGB, revealing a stigma that exists in the minds of these heterosexual students. The first is an exercise where students were asked to go to the LGBT student resource center on campus and choose a pin from a sample of ally pins with different styles. These pins varied in terms of the degree to which it would be likely for passersby to assume the wearer was LGB. After choosing their pin, the assignment asks students to wear it on their backpack for two weeks. For some of these students, this time period spanned Thanksgiving break, which had different consequences given its public/family nature. Not all students completed this assignment fully. Many admitted to taking it off at certain times when risk felt higher for them, including in the presence of family.

Each time these pins were referenced in final papers, students discussed the fear of people judging their identity, fearful of being assumed LGB because of the public display of an ally pin. As one White man mentioned, in reference to his decision about wearing the pins:

> I have not reached the point where I am comfortable with the possibility of being mislabeled.... I ultimately chose the second option, the rainbow ALLY pin. This pin, with its rainbow background, stood out as being a pin supporting LGBT rights. However, with the large ALLY printed in the middle of it, I felt comfortable that people who saw the pin would not mislabel my sexual identity. This activity gave me further insight into my own willingness and comfort levels in supporting the LGB cause.

These students were afraid of losing their heterosexual privileges of privacy and safety if someone assumed they had a non-heterosexual sexual orientation, so they instead kept their participation in the dialogue a secret from many people.

The other exercise that was referenced frequently as similarly anxiety producing was not assigned in every section. This exercise asked participants to pair up with someone who shared their gender identity and hold hands for

20 minutes in public. Students were instructed to travel across campus and record observations about reactions they received or perceived to receive. Through reading heterosexual students' reflections on this activity, it is clear that these students were able to relate to and demonstrate empathy for their same-gender-loving peers, some of whom feel this vulnerability in their personal lives. As one White woman wrote, "I had never felt so exposed. I felt that every person was looking at me and judging me without even giving me a chance." Students articulated feelings of discomfort, awkwardness, self-consciousness, and embarrassment. However, many (especially those with no prior known interactions) remarked how eye-opening it was to engage in this level of perspective-taking and saw for the first time what people in same-sex relationships had to experience on a daily basis.

CONFLICT WITH OTHER STUDENTS

Conflict among the students was primarily reported in relation to students striving not to appear unknowledgeable or to say the wrong thing, which led to some silence and frustration. The topics of religion and genetics with regard to sexual minority orientations, and disagreement about how to be an ally, were also areas of conflict. Although most students reflected that the dialogue produced a safe environment for open communication, several felt the need to be politically correct, or socially cautious in their word choices, especially at the start of the course. As one African American man reflected, "For the first few weeks of dialogue, I questioned my words and actions constantly, thinking any and everything I said would be offensive to the people surrounding me." Withholding of complete honesty and openness at times created uncontroversial and "docile" classrooms that made students feel that homophobia was present, but not expressed. Consensus amongst the group, while a great end-goal for the dialogue, was not actually how all individuals felt throughout the course. Students shielded their true feelings periodically to avoid being targeted for criticism in class and to avoid potential class conflict.

Attempts to be politically correct and to hide their true thoughts led several students to believe that a true dialogue was not always met. In discussing the lack of conflict in the dialogues, one White woman noted:

> A lot of people who identify with the heterosexual community began to censor their comments and just agree with people of the queer community, with the hopes of not offending anyone. This was very frustrating, because their [heterosexual students] feelings never came out in front of the people with different sexual orientations, but only came out when they were surrounded by other heterosexuals . . . the lack of opposition and conflict really made our dialogues uninteresting.

The heterosexual students who withheld their true thoughts created an environment where there was false consensus amongst the group. It was not until outside of the dialogue setting that these true thoughts came out, which meant points of disagreement were rarely discussed and opportunities to learn from each other were missed.

When discussing same-sex marriage and the church, the dialogic exchange described during this session helped students to feel like the conversation was constructive and that the differences in opinion were beneficial to everyone's learning. As one student noted, "[M]any of the people in my class started to get emotional and it added a lot to the dialogue." However, during discussions on whether not someone is born lesbian or gay, students moved into debate mode. One student reported: "[A]fter a while people were no longer listening to each other and trying to understand the other's perspective but only were concerned with getting their points across. This eventually led to people primarily being defensive or attacking each other." Facilitators needed to step in and bring the class back to a place where dialogue could again occur. However, students did note that they were not surprised that these conflicts arose as they were discussing politically controversial topics.

On the topic of being an ally, some students reported challenges in embracing the social justice component of being an ally. In one group, when a gay student participant had commented in the dialogue, "[Y]ou're just a good friend, but you are not an ally unless you contact your state representative," a White male heterosexual student reported countering with, "I don't have time to do that." A few students were inclined to believe that as long as they personally were not prejudiced or discriminatory against LGB people, there was no need for activism. Overall, students viewed intergroup conflict as needed in some cases, in that it produced shifts in perspectives.

Learning Outcomes: Awareness, Understanding, and Action

As described earlier, intergroup dialogue aims to foster student learning and growth in intergroup communication, understanding participating groups' social identities and concomitant power, and promotion of social justice for marginalized groups. We focus our attention here on students' learning related to social identities and oppression, and behavioral change related to anti-heterosexism.

SOCIAL IDENTITIES AND OPPRESSION

Cognitive learning is an important component of the dialogue process (Maxwell et al., 2011). Similar to traditional classes, students are assigned readings and other materials that aim to help them understand heterosexual and LGB identities, socialization processes related to group identity and heterosexism and heterosexual privilege, intergroup communication, and social justice and alliance building (Zúñiga et al., 2007). Alongside these readings, the dialogue process itself also aims to facilitate cognitive understanding and learning. Our analysis identified four main learning outcomes related to the dialogue process: affirming perceptions of LGB people and tackling stereotypes, understanding heterosexual privilege, understanding heterosexism, and learning about intersectionality.

Affirming perceptions of LGB people and breaking down stereotypes. Students with LGB family members or friends tended to enter the course with a well-developed sense of their perceptions toward LGB people, which were reportedly very positive. In contrast, among those who did not have such pre-course contacts, they generally reported they were unsure about how perceived LGB people before participating in the course. Some indicated they had never really thought about LGB people or LGB issues in any great depth. Very few students admitted to possessing strong anti-gay biases before entering the group, yet many reported that they endorsed gay stereotypes they had been exposed to by the media and in popular culture. Across the group of students without any pre-group direct LGB contacts, participants unanimously concluded that partaking in the dialogue helped them to accept LGB people and better understand this community (and realize other important outcomes). In one case, a student went from "not liking homosexuals" to becoming friends with many of the LGB participants in the class and recognizing LGB persons as "normal" (White male student). Another student reported the following:

> It is become even more evident after taking this class of how my surroundings and environment have molded my opinions and perceptions of other groupings. I have learned to be more accepting to not only homosexuals and bisexuals, but to the ideas of sexual orientation as being different for everyone. (Hispanic male student)

For many of these students, including some homophobic students, the testimonial exercise played a critical role in helping them to be more accepting and understanding of LGB people. The testimonials, which occur during session four, involve all students, including heterosexual students sharing their personal stories concerning their sexual orientation. Students are asked to disclose their current sexual orientation and to discuss when they first became aware of *their* sexual orientation, how it may have changed, and experiences with family and friends related to their sexual orientation (e.g., disclosing sexual orientation). This exercise brings students' own experiences into the classroom as a legitimate and authentic part of learning and promotes deeper connections and further learning from each other (Zúñiga et al., 2007). As reflected in the following quotation, many students, especially those who had no or very little prior known interactions with LGB individuals, experienced a very meaningful transformation through the testimonials:

> My original thoughts of the other groups [LGB people] were that they were bad people and needed to be taught a lesson. But that all changed when I we had that [*sic*] testimonials and I read the reading "Homosexuality and American society: an overview." This brought me into the light as to where it was started and how they were treated. This changed my whole percep-

tion of the LGBH community. From here on out my views will be forever changed. (African American male participant)

Hearing the stories of others creates a deep sense of trust and openness among group members and promotes perspective taking, empathy, a sense of commonality, and a reduction in judgment of others (Zúñiga et al., 2007). Some students noted how this empathy and perspective taking helped to shift how they perceived the LGB community and personalized the oppression and stereotypes experienced by many target identity classmates.

Not only did dialogue help change students' attitudes, but it helped to break down stereotypes, such as all of their gay male classmates would be flamboyant and attracted to all men, and to assume all lesbians would have short hair and act butch or masculine. From the very first session, students began to realize that these perceptions were not always accurate and that they had stripped all uniqueness and individuality from LGB persons: "It is not as obvious to distinguish between members of the different groups because members of the LGB community do not look any different then members of the heterosexual community" (White male student). With their assumptions challenged, these students began to recognize that every individual, regardless of identity, has a unique persona, and that the stereotypes they had seen in the media were just that, stereotypes. This revelation made students see that judgments based on appearance are not always accurate, and to see that LGB persons are present in every aspect of society.

Heterosexual privilege. To examine social systems, power, privilege, and oppression, participants need to better understand their own identities and roles in society. Scholars of privilege point out that privileged groups are traditionally much more inclined to examine the experiences of marginalized groups than to turn a critical eye toward their own advantages and power (Case, Iuzzini, & Hopkins, 2012; Walls, 2010). The defensiveness and denial present for many privileged groups is both a part of a psychological process and a social function of the invisibility of privilege (Pratto & Stewart, 2012). The analysis indicates that participants were able to explore and recognize heterosexual privilege through engaging in readings, hearing the testimonials, and engaging in dialogue with classmates.

Students with known prior direct interactions with LGB individuals differed slightly in their outcomes than those with no known direct interactions. Heterosexual students with previous interactions tended to indicate that they entered the dialogues with some acknowledgment and recognition of their heterosexual privilege, whereas those without these interactions did not have this same self-awareness. Dialogue helped students with LGB friends and family members to deepen their understanding of their privileges and understand the complexity of the heterosexist society in which they live.

For students without known direct interactions, dialogue played a revelatory role in thinking about their identity and unpacking the rights allocated to them simply by identifying as heterosexual. This student provided powerful illustration of this learning:

> As a heterosexual, I never thought about how much my sexual orientation impacts by life on a daily basis. There has never been a time when I felt discriminated against or was harassed because of my sexual orientation. It never occurred to me how lucky I am that I can display my affection for my boyfriend in public without fear. There is no time when I have to consciously consider the extremely negative consequences that could result from kissing on the sidewalk or holding hands while walking around campus. (White female participant)

Many participants recognized that, prior to the dialogue there was no reason to explore privileged group identities because as an agent group member their identities are part of the social norm. For one White male participant, "recognizing and coming to terms with privilege was easily the greatest challenge, and I'm very grateful that the dialogue curriculum was conducive to this introspection regarding my own role in the system of oppression and privilege."

Participants who recognized their heterosexual privilege were able to describe the tangible privileges of agent group membership. For example, one participant reflected:

> I have never thought twice about how easy it will be for me to get married, how I won't have to think about how to have children, how if I want to adopt children it won't be a difficult issue, and how every day of my life I can walk uninhibited around campus holding my boyfriend's hand without receiving disapproving looks. (White female participant)

Another student acknowledged the experience of benefitting from privilege: "I took advantage of my own privileges and did not actively support the surrounding minority groups because their interests did not seem to affect me" (White female participant). Through the dialogue, these privileges became recognized as part of a system of power, privilege, and oppression that best serves those who are members of the agent groups.

Intergroup dialogue can risk creating imbalanced learning where privileged groups only learn about experiences of marginalized groups (DeTurk, 2010). Through gaining this knowledge and understanding, heterosexual students moved beyond simply learning about marginalized groups to recognize their role and responsibility in dismantling oppression, discrimination, and heterosexual privilege. For many students this movement included engaging or intending to engage in pro-LGB behaviors (discussed later) and for some it involved changing their attitudes on civil rights for LGB persons, such as LGB-bullying protections, open participation of LGB people in the military, and legal recognition of same-sex relationships. For instance, one student who indicated initially "not liking homosexuals" and supporting the federal government's ban on same-sex marriage reflected that he gained a greater consciousness about LGB individuals and issues and began to reevaluate his opinions and biases. By participating in the dialogue process, including the testimonials, this student started to understand all the benefits that come with being able to get married, the importance of these benefits to members of the LGB community, and why it was so important to stop this institutionalized discrimination.

Reflecting on their heterosexual identity, including its concomitant privileges, and being exposed to LGB students was vital to their transformation. Many participants noted that the testimonials were the first time they had ever reflected on or had been invited to reflect on their sexual orientation.

Heterosexism. Participants universally indicated a deeper understanding of heterosexism and how it perpetuates discrimination and oppression of LGB people. Students reported gaining an awareness of how the media and various institutions, such as religious organizations and government, as well as individuals, promote and project heterosexist norms. Heterosexist culture discriminates against the LGB community (Case & Stewart, 2010) and students realized that they live in a heterosexist world. As one student reflected, the dialogues promoted his reflection on "how engrained heterosexuality is with the idea of normalcy in our society" (White male participant). Another student indicated the following:

> Many people consider heterosexuality to be the only "correct" form for relationships because they have been told that their whole lives along with the fact that our society's culture is built so strongly around rigid gender roles. Just the fact that heterosexual unions are the only legally recognizable form of marriage allowed in the United States is one of the countless examples showing how American culture blatantly institutionally discriminates against homosexuals. (White female participant)

Numerous students highlighted the problematic and unjust nature of heterosexist marriage laws.

In terms of how individuals contribute to heterosexism, in addition to acknowledging how heterosexual privilege fosters heterosexism (including their own heterosexual privilege), students discussed the role of individual-level perceptions, behaviors, and attitudes:

> When heterosexual people see two lesbians or gay men kissing they see it as them flaunting the fact that they are members of the LGB. However, it almost sounds absurd when turned around to think that when a man and a woman kiss they're flaunting their heterosexuality. (White male participant)

In terms of understanding how heterosexism operates, a considerable number of students reported gaining rich insights about the challenges their LGB classmates experienced with "coming out." Coming into the dialogue, many of the study participants without pre-group LGB friends and family members did not understand why an individual would hide their sexual orientation and not be honest with their family and friends. Some could not grasp why LGB persons were not "proud of who they were." But hearing the LGB classmates' narratives, most often reporting struggles and fears about their safety and being judgment/rejection by family, conflicts with religious upbringings, and experiences of harassment helped to deepen understanding of the complexity of coming out, including why the LGB community sometimes seems invisible.

Students also reported they learned about LGB harassment and discrimination. In addition to learning from their LGB classmates' experiences, some participants also indicated that exercises helped to develop personal insight about the discrimination. For example, reflecting on the exercise in which students walk through campus holding the hands of a student of the same sex, a participant reported the following:

> After holding hands with another man even for only fifteen minutes, I realized how socially unacceptable it was by the second looks and stares we received. The double standard for heterosexual and homosexual people stuck with me after that day and realized that not only was homosexuality looked down upon but also it can be unsafe. (White male participant)

Identity intersectionality. Intersectionality of social identities speaks to the presence and overlapping or intersectional nature of social identities such as race, gender, class, sexual orientation, nationality, and others. This approach to identity serves to expand the discourse around power and oppression and emphasizes that multiple social identities must be taken into account when seeking to understand an individual's experiences (Case et al., 2012; Cole, 2009). Participants, often connected to understanding heterosexual privilege, noted their learning about the intersections between various identities, especially sexual orientation and race, gender, and religion. Related to learning about their heterosexual privilege, numerous students across the years noted how participation in the dialogues helped them appreciate their privileged identities beyond their heterosexual identity: "I began to think more about how my race, sex, and sexual orientation played such a significant role in shaping me" (White female participant). This mirrors the learning LGB students reported earlier in regard to intergroup dialogue courses (Dessel et al., 2011). Religion and race were particularly salient identities for many participants. For example, students who came from religious backgrounds felt that discussions about LGB issues were absent from their upbringing, and they also felt somewhat defensive or feared being misunderstood on the topic of sexual orientation. Regarding race, students recognized the impact of intersectionality on oppression: "At times I felt I related to the LGB group because of the fact that I am a Latina woman, also a minority in our society by race and gender." An African American woman reflected:

> If I was a lesbian I may be like working class, AA [African American], woman, I would be all kind of screwed. No one ever thinks how each social id [identity] ties into one. Its [sic] funny how they all intersect and can change at any time.

In one group, further highlighting the importance of race, students commented how during the hand-holding exercise (described earlier), they noticed that the interracial male couple received more negative stares than the White couple, and the male couple more than the female couple.

Furthermore, participants were able to recognize connections and relationships between their different identities and the experiences of sexual minority students. In particular, participants were able to identify shared experiences among targeted identity groups, such as similar problems faced by being female or a racial minority.

CHANGES IN BEHAVIOR

Promoting anti-heterosexism. Participants discussed the formation of strong alliances with LGB students, and the various ways in which to disrupt heterosexism in order to avoid maintaining an unjust social system. Students reported changes in behavior they intended to make following the end of the dialogue, as well as reported actual changes they had begun to implement in their lives already. These changes were noted to occur: interpersonally, with changes to relationships with others, intrapersonally, with changes to the individuals' own knowledge and actions, and on a systems, or societal level, with intent to change institutional problems. We report on these levels within the domains of intended and actual behaviors.

Intended behaviors. On the interpersonal level, students left the dialogue feeling as if they could begin to change the behaviors or actions of people in their lives and also have increased relationships with LGB individuals. They planned to do this by interrupting discrimination and offensive language used by peers or family members, providing support to LGB friends, and by simply gaining more friends and acquaintances who are sexual minorities. One disruption mentioned was to no longer be a bystander when acts of discrimination or oppression were seen or heard. Students recognized that they needed to stand up against oppressive behaviors and institutional practices, in order to break the cycles of injustice and let LGB individuals know that they have support systems. Students were no longer going to be passive and dismiss hateful things said, and they gained a sense of agency and power. As one student said, "By taking a class and making friends, I changed without even realizing it. I have become an ally and am no longer afraid or too naive to speak my mind." Intrapersonally, heterosexual students intended to further educate themselves on LGB issues and be more open as an ally by displaying rainbow/pride ribbons or buttons on their personal belongings.

Additionally, some students noted intentions to attempt to change large societal and institutional problems by voting for equal rights measures, attending pro-LGB marches and rallies, and becoming a dialogue facilitator themselves in order to influence the lives of others and perpetuate change. While further follow-up will need to occur to determine to what extent these intended changes took place, many students nonetheless displayed an increase in potential and desire to become active, and left the course "feeling great responsibility" to advocate for social justice.

Actual behaviors. Reports of actual actions taken that were attributed to the dialogue occurred with over half of the participants, many of whom were students who had previously reported no known contact with LGB people. Students had begun to challenge friends and family when hearing negative stereotypes and they promoted dialogic communication in their other classes about LGB issues. As one student reported, "I now confront and/or educate people who use the word gay or fag in a negative way." At the same time, students had begun to understand that words matter and they challenged their own language patterns, and either stopped completely or corrected themselves when they used "fag" or "that's so gay." Some students had also already placed ally and support buttons on their personal belongings and had researched specific LGB issues to better inform themselves, so that they could be better advocates when confronting homophobia.

Discussion

This study examined experiences of undergraduate heterosexual students who participated in sexual orientation intergroup dialogue courses over the span of nine years, during a time in our country's history when public attitudes have been marginally improving with regard to homosexuality and the human rights of sexual minority people (Gallup Politics, 2012; The Pew Forum on Religion and Public Life, 2012). The results of this qualitative analysis offer important insights into this intergroup social justice education method and the outcomes it can produce.

First, participants overall expressed that while they were products of a society that has socialized them with stereotypes, fears, and lack of information about LGB people, they were open to learning about the oppression that LGB people experience, and outcomes about the unearned privileges that heterosexuals, including themselves, are afforded in society were documented. In addition to promoting understanding of heterosexual privilege, dialogue was a useful tool in combating false stereotypes held, and for some students they finally had faces to put with the LGB community. Not only did students without known pre-group contact with LGB people finally get a chance to meet and interact with sexual minority individuals, but dialogue also became a safe place where ideas, questions, and opinions regarding LGB issues could be shared, explored, and cultivated. Despite the challenges noted above, it is clear that heterosexual students developed a sense of empathy and understanding of their LGB peers, and many reported a reduction in bias. These are known outcomes of optimal intergroup contact that is structured and personal (Pettigrew & Tropp, 2008). Participation in these dialogues combated the lack of known prior interactions with LGB individuals that can contribute to a misunderstanding and intolerance toward sexual minority individuals (Engberg et al., 2007). An especially noteworthy positive outcome is the actions that students reported engaging in to cease and prevent verbal harassment among their peers.

Second, participants generally gained a great deal of important knowledge about themselves in terms of their own heterosexual privilege and heterosexist society. They reflected beyond interpersonal relationships on larger unequal societal structures, such as marriage, and how they may be able to challenge them. Critical consciousness has been found to be a key outcome of intergroup dialogue participation for LGB students in sexual orientation dialogues, as well as for both target and agent students in race–ethnicity and Arab–Jewish dialogues (Dessel & Ali, 2011; Dessel et al., 2011; Nagda et al., 2009). Studies on intergroup dialogue show that awareness about structural inequality can lead to commitment to social change actions (Gurin-Sands, Gurin, Nagda, & Osuna, 2012). By the end of the course, students who lacked direct relationships with LGB people before the groups no longer felt confused about their positions on LGB topics and intended to further their education about sexual minority and social justice issues.

Campus climates are still far from ideal for sexual minority students (Rankin et al., 2010; Woodford, Silverchanz, Swank, Scherrer, & Raiz, 2012) and some heterosexual students in the dialogues we examined noted that they or others were reluctant to fully express what might be perceived as biased views. Students with more negative views toward LGB people may have had a very difficult time participating in this dialogue topic, but also may potentially have more to gain. Our specific analysis does not shed light on this; thus, we recommend future research in this area.

Third, conflict can be a positive learning experience when properly facilitated (Pettit, 2006). Students recognized that a lack of conflict may occur when students withhold their true feelings, and that this can lead to lost learning opportunities. In some cases, hot topics, such as conservative religious beliefs and the causes of sexual orientation, may need further exploration in the dialogues.

Recommendations for Pedagogy

In their papers and the interviews, students were asked to offer any suggestions for ways to improve the dialogues. Students noted the need for racial and other sexual identity diversity in some of the groups. This means recruitment from the LGB community needs to focus on underrepresented identities such as people of color, bisexual people, and religious minorities. It also means strategic outreach to minority groups within the heterosexual student population. The lack of diversity may have created a room devoid of much conflict and deep learning in the course. Certain sexual minority viewpoints were not present, so some students thought the course missed important perspectives and did not have the opportunity to become allies to the *full* LGB community. Related, the binary intergroup dialogue model may imply a homogeneous experience for any particular social identity group. We emphasize that within-group diversity needs to be recognized, as lesbian, gay, and bisexual experiences vary greatly. Our participants likely had different experiences and learning based on the identities represented in their specific dialogue group.

Limitations and Future Research

Although producing important insights about sexual orientation dialogues from the perspective of heterosexual students, this study has several noteworthy limitations. Our sample is a convenience sample and students are not randomly assigned to dialogue topic groups. Therefore, it is possible that many of the participants, including those who held homophobic views prior to the group were at least somewhat predisposed to being open to discussing and learning about minority sexual orientation experiences. The use of student final papers can present bias due to the influence of receiving a grade. As well, post-dialogue reflections run the risk of recall bias and make it difficult to be assured of objective reporting of pre-dialogue views. This data also represents the current time period in which it was collected, thus given the growth in public discourse in LGB rights in recent years, some interesting changes may be seen in future studies.

Future research analyzing intergroup dialogue courses can complement the methods used here. Studies that meet the conditions of causality are needed to examine the effectiveness of dialogue. Specifically, the use of random assignment and comparison groups should be considered. As well, quantitative pre/post dialogue surveys will offer another means of determining the change that may have taken place in attitudes and knowledge. Analyzing this data by gender and other social identities would provide a more nuanced picture of the gender differences that may exist in attitudes and experiences.

Sexual orientation prejudice is a persistent societal problem that requires attention at all levels of interaction. Intergroup dialogue courses have much to offer all students who participate (Dessel et al., 2011; Nagda et al., 2009). Higher education provides an opportunity for learning across differences and the development of critical thinking with regard to socialization, power, and social justice. We offer this model as one method to pursue these educational goals in regard to sexual orientation and social inclusion for LGB people.

References

Adams, M., Bell, L. A., & Griffin, P. (2007). *Teaching for diversity and social justice.* New York, NY: Routledge.

Blackburn, M. V. (2003). Exploring literacy performances and power dynamics at The Loft: Queer youth reading the world and the word. *Research in the Teaching of English, 37*(4), 467–490.

Blackburn, M. V. (2006). Risky, generous, gender work. *Research in the Teaching of English, 40*(3), 262–71.

Broido, E. M., & Reason, R. D. (2005). The development of social justice attitudes and actions: An overview of current understandings. *New Directions for Student Services, 2005*(110), 17–28. doi:10.1002/ss.162

Case, K., Iuzzini, J., & Hopkins, M. (2012). Systems of privilege: Intersections, awareness, and applications. *Journal of Social Issues, 68*(1), 1–10. doi:10.1111/j.1540-4560.2011.01732.x

Case, K. A., & Stewart, B. (2010). Changes in diversity course student prejudice and attitudes toward heterosexual privilege and gay marriage. *Teaching of Psychology, 37*(3), 172–177. doi:10.1080/00986283.2010.488555

Cole, E. R. (2009). Intersectionality and research in psychology. *American Psychologist, 64,* 170–180. doi:10.1037/a0014564

Crawley, S. L., & Broad, K. L. (2004). "Be your (real lesbian) self": Mobilizing sexual formula stories through personal (and political) storytelling. *Journal of Contemporary Ethnography, 33,* 39–71. doi:10.1177/0891241603259810

Creswell, J. W. (2007). *Qualitative inquiry and research design: Choosing among five traditions* (2nd ed.). Thousand Oaks, CA: SAGE.

Deal, K., & Hyde, C. (2004). Understanding MSW student anxiety and resistance to multicultural learning, *Journal of Teaching in Social Work, 24*(1–2), 73–86. doi:10.1300/J067v24n01_05

Dessel, A. (2010). Effects of intergroup dialogue: Public school teachers and sexual orientation prejudice. *Small Group Research, 41*(5), 556–592. doi:10.1177/1046496410369560

Dessel, A., & Ali, N. (2011). The Minds of Peace and intergroup dialogue: Two complementary approaches to peace. *Israel Affairs, 18*(1), 123–139. doi:10.1080/13537121.2012.634276

Dessel, A., Woodford, M., & Warren, N. (2011). Intergroup dialogue courses on sexual orientation: Lesbian, gay and bisexual student experiences and outcomes. *Journal of Homosexuality, 58*(8), 1132–1150. doi:10.1080/00918369.2011.598420

DeTurk, S. (2010). "Quit whining and tell me about your experiences!" (In) tolerance, pragmatism, and muting in intergroup dialogue. In T. K. Nakayama & R. T. Halualani (Eds.), *The handbook of critical intercultural communication* (pp. 565–584). Malden, MA: Wiley-Blackwell.

DiAngelo, R. (1997). Heterosexism: Addressing internalized dominance. *Journal of Progressive Human Services, 8*(1), 5–21. doi:10.1300/J059v08n01_02

Draughn, T., Elkins, B., & Roy, R. (2002). Allies in the struggle: Eradicating homophobia and heterosexism on campus. In E. P. Cramer (Ed.), *Addressing homophobia and heterosexism on college campuses* (pp. 9–20). Binghamton, NY: Harrington Park Press.

Edwards, K. E. (2006). Aspiring social justice ally identity development: A conceptual model. *Journal of Student Affairs Research and Practice, 43*(4), 39–60.

Engberg, M., Hurtado, S., & Smith, G. (2007). Developing attitudes of acceptance toward lesbian, gay, and bisexual peers: Enlightenment, contact, and the college experience. *Journal of Gay & Lesbian Issues in Education, 4*(3), 49–77. doi:10.1300/J367v04n03_05

Erlandson, D. A., Harris, E. L., Skipper, B. L., & Allen, S. D. (1993). *Doing naturalistic inquiry: A guide to methods.* Newbury Park, CA: SAGE.

Evans, N. J. (2002). The impact of an LGBT Safe Zone project on campus climate. *Journal of College Student Development, 43*(4), 522–539.

Evans, N. J., & Broido, E. M. (2002). The experiences of lesbian and bisexual women in college residence halls: Implications for addressing homophobia and heterosexism. *Journal of Lesbian Studies, 6*, 29–42. doi:10.1300/J155v06n03_04

Finkel, M. J., Storaasli, R. D., Bandele, A., & Schaefer, V. (2003). Diversity training in graduate school: An exploratory evaluation of the Safe Zone project. *Professional Psychology Research and Practice, 34*, 555–561. doi:10.1037/0735-7028.34.5.555

Finken, L. L. (2002). The impact of a human sexuality course on anti-gay prejudice: The challenge of reaching male students. *Journal of Psychology & Human Sexuality, 14*(1), 37–46. doi:10.1300/J056v14n01_03

Gallup Politics. (2012). *Americans' acceptance of gay relations crosses 50% threshold.* Retrieved from http://www.gallup.com/poll/135764/americans-acceptance-gay-relations-crosses-threshold.aspx

Gurin, P., Nagda, B. A., & Zúñiga, X. (2013). *Engaging race and gender: Intergroup dialogues in higher education.* New York, NY: Russell Sage Foundation.

Gurin-Sands, C., Gurin, P., Nagda, B. R., & Osuna, S. (2012). Fostering a commitment to social action: How talking, thinking, and feeling make a difference in intergroup dialogue. *Equity & Excellence in Education, 45*(1), 60–79. doi:10.1080/10665684.2012.643699

Guth, L. J., Lopez, D. F., Rojas, J., Clements, K. D., & Tyler, J. M. (2004). Experiential versus rational training: A comparison of student attitudes toward homosexuality. *Journal of Homosexuality, 48*(2), 83–102. doi:10.1300/J082v48n02_05

Hardiman, R., Jackson, B., & Griffin, P. (2007). Conceptual foundations for social justice education. In M. Adams, L. A. Bell, & P. Griffin (Eds.), *Teaching for diversity and social justice* (pp. 35–66). New York, NY: Taylor & Francis.

Hart, J., & Fellabaum, J. (2008). Analyzing campus climate studies: Seeking to define and understand. *Journal of Diversity in Higher Education, 1*(4), 222–234. doi:10.1037/a0013627

Hillman, J., & Martin, R. A. (2002). Lessons about gay and lesbian lives: A spaceship exercise. *Teaching of Psychology, 29*(4), 308–311. doi:10.1207/S15328023TOP2904_12

Hodson, G., Choma, B. L., & Costello, K. (2009). Experiencing alien-nation: Effects of a simulation intervention on attitudes toward homosexuals. *Journal of Experimental Social Psychology, 45*(4), 974–978.

Hogg, M., Abrams, D., Otten, S., & Hinkle, S. (2004). The social identity perspective: Intergroup relations, self-conception, and small groups. *Small Group Research, 35* (3), 246–276.

Hurtado, S., Griffin, K., Arellano, L., & Cuellar, M. (2008). Assessing the value of climate assessments: Progress and future directions. *Journal of Diversity in Higher Education, 1*(4), 204–221. doi:10.1037/a0014009

King, P., & Baxter Magolda, M. (2005). A developmental model of intercultural maturity. *Journal of College Student Development, 46*(6), 571–592. doi:10.1353/csd.2005.0060

Kvale, S., & Brinkmann, S. (2009). *InterViews: Learning the craft of qualitative research interviewing*. Thousand Oaks, CA: SAGE.

Maxwell, K. E., Nagda, B., & Thompson, M. (Eds.). (2011). *Facilitating intergroup dialogues: Bridging differences, catalyzing change*. Sterling, VA: Stylus Publishing.

Meyer, I. H. (2003). Prejudice, social stress, and mental health in lesbian, gay, and bisexual populations: Conceptual issues and research evidence. *Psychology Bulletin, 129*(5), 674–697. doi:10.1037/0033-2909.129.5.674

Nagda, B. A., Gurin, P., Sorensen, N., & Zúñiga, X. (2009). Evaluating intergroup dialogues: Engaging diversity for personal and social responsibility. *Diversity & Democracy, 12*, 3–6.

Nagda, B. A., & Maxwell, K. E. (2011). Deepening the layers of understanding and connection: A critical-dialogic approach to facilitating intergroup dialogues. In K. E. Maxwell, B. A. Nagda, & M. Thompson (Eds.), *Facilitating intergroup dialogues: Bridging differences, catalyzing change* (pp. 1–22). Sterling, VA: Stylus Publishing.

Pettigrew, T. F., & Tropp, L. R. (2008). How does intergroup contact reduce prejudice? Meta-analytic tests of three mediators. *European Journal of Social Psychology, 38*(6), 922–934. doi:10.1002/ejsp.504

Pettijohn, T. F. II, & Walzer, A. S. (2008). Reducing racism, sexism, and homophobia in college students by completing a psychology of prejudice course. *College Student Journal, 42*(2), 459–468.

Pettit, R. (2006). Using conflict constructively. In R. MacNair (Ed.), *Working for peace: A handbook of practical psychology and other tools* (pp. 137–139). Atascadero, CA: Impact Publishers.

The Pew Forum on Religion and Public Life. (2012). *Ten years of changing attitudes on gay marriage.* Retrieved from http://features.pewforum.org/gay-marriage-attitudes/

Poynter, K., & Tubbs, X. (2008). Safe Zones: Creating LGBT safe space ally programs. *Journal of LGBT Youth, 5*(1), 121–132. doi:10.1300/J524v05n01_10

Pratto, F., & Stewart, A. L. (2012). Group dominance and the half-blindness of privilege. *Journal of Social Issues, 68*, 28–45. doi:10.1111/j.1540-4560.2011.01734.x

Rankin, S., Weber, G., Blumenfeld, W., & Frazer, S. (2010). *2010 state of higher education for lesbian, gay, bisexual and transgender people.* Charlotte, NC: Campus Pride.

Rye, B. J., & Meaney, G. J. (2009). Impact of a homonegativity awareness workshop on attitudes toward homosexuality. *Journal of Homosexuality, 56*(1), 31–55. doi:10.1080/00918360802551480

Sandelowski, M. (2003). Tables or tableaus?: The challenges of writing and reading mixed methods studies. In A. Tashakkori & C. Teddlie (Eds.), *Handbook of mixed methods in social and behavioral research* (pp. 321–350). Thousand Oaks, CA: SAGE.

Silverschanz, P., Cortina, L., Konik, J., & Magley, V. (2008). Slurs, snubs, and queer jokes: Incidence and impact of heterosexist harassment in academia. *Sex Roles, 58*, 179–191. doi:10.1007/s11199-007-9329-7

Sorensen, N., Nagda, B., Gurin, P., & Maxwell, K. (2009). Taking a "Hands On" approach to diversity in higher education: A critical-dialogic model for effective intergroup interaction. *Analyses of Social Issues and Public Policy, 9*(1), 3–35. doi:10.1111/j.1530-2415.2009.01193.x

Strauss, A., & Corbin, J. (1990). *Basics of qualitative research: Techniques and procedures for developing grounded theory* (2nd ed.). Thousand Oaks, CA: SAGE.

Tucker, E., & Potocky-Tripodi, M. (2006). Changing heterosexuals' attitudes toward homosexuals: A systematic review of the empirical literature. *Research on Social Work Practice, 16*(2), 176–190. doi:10.1177/1049731505281385

Walls, E. (2010). An introduction to the special issue: Issues of privilege in social work and other helping professions. *Reflections, 16*(1), 2–5.

Woodford, M., & Bella, L. (2003). Are we ready to take a stand? Educating social work students about heterosexism—fostering anti-oppressive practice. In W. Shera (Ed.), *Emerging perspectives on anti-oppressive practice* (pp. 413–430). Toronto, ON: Canadian Scholars Press.

Woodford, M. R., Howell, M. L., Silverschanz, P., & Yu, L. (2012). *"That's so gay!"* Examining the covariates of hearing this expression among gay, lesbian, and bisexual college students. *Journal of American College Health, 60*(6), 429–434. doi:10.1080/07448481.2012.673519

Woodford, M. R., Kolb, C., Radeka, G., & Javier, G. (in press). Lesbian, gay, bisexual, and transgender ally training programs on campus: Current variations and future directions. *Journal of College Student Development.*

Woodford, M. R., Krentzman, A., & Gattis, M. (2012). Alcohol and drug use among sexual minority college students and their heterosexual counterparts: The effects of experiencing and witnessing incivility and hostility on campus. *Substance Abuse and Rehabilitation, 3*(1), 11–23. doi:10.2147/SAR.S26347

Woodford, M. R., Silverschanz, P., Swank, E., Scherrer, K., & Raiz, L. (2012). Predictors of U.S. heterosexual university students' attitudes toward lesbian, gay, bisexual, and transgender people. *Journal of LGBT Youth, 9*(4), 297–320. doi:10.1080/19361653.2012.716697

Wright, L. W., Jr., Adams, H. E., & Bernat, J. (1999). Development and validation of the Homophobia Scale. *Journal of Psychopathology and Behavioral Assessment, 21,* 337–347. doi:10.1023/A:1022172816258

Yost, M. R., & Gilmore, S. (2011). Assessing LGBTQ campus climate and creating change. *Journal of Homosexuality, 58*(9), 1330–1354. doi:10.1080/00918369. 2011.605744.

Zúñiga, X., Nagda, B. A., Chesler, M., & Cytron-Walker, A. (2007). Intergroup dialogue in higher education: Meaningful learning about social justice. *ASHE Higher Education Report, 32*(4), 1–128.

CHAPTER 18

Facilitating Dialogue Across Differences: Use of Sociodrama in the Classroom

Patti A. Aldredge, PhD, LCSW

Professional socialization, a purview of social work education, is by definition specific to a chosen career path and involves taking on the standards and values of the profession. One of the historical missions of social work, and therefore social work education, has been to work with clients to achieve social and economic justice. From the Amsterdam Institute for Social Work Training in 1899 to the present, justice has been a primary concern of social work schools across the globe (Kendall, 2000; Van Soest & Garcia, 2003). Teaching knowledge, skills, and behaviors imperative to social and economic justice practice can be an exciting venture. It can also be fraught with potential pitfalls, particularly when it engenders professional dissonance, as in the arena of conservative Christian beliefs and sexual orientation. This chapter examines that tension through a case study and offers specific guidelines for facilitating difficult discussions around the intersection of identity, privilege, and oppression in this arena.

In establishing the critical competencies for student mastery, the Council on Social Work Education (CSWE) identifies the ethical principles of two professional organizations: the National Association of Social Workers (NASW) and the International Federation of Social Workers/International Association of Schools of Social Work (IFSW/IASSW) (CSWE, 2008). NASW's Code of Ethics includes the requirement that social workers "obtain education about and seek to understand social diversity and oppression with respect to race, ethnicity, national origin, color, sex, sexual orientation, gender identity or expression, age, marital status, political belief, religion, immigration status, and mental or physical disability" (NASW, 2008, 1.05); to avoid demeaning remarks about colleagues' individual attributes, particularly as related to the above attributes; to not practice, condone, facilitate, or collaborate with any form of discrimination on the basis of these attributes; and to act to prevent and eliminate domination of, exploitation of, and discrimination against any person, group, or class on the basis of these attributes (NASW, 2008). The IFSW/IASSW Ethics in Social Work Statement of Principles (IFSW, 2012) indicates that social workers have a responsibility to promote social justice by challenging discrimination on the basis of characteristics "such as ability, age, culture, gender or sex, marital status, socio-economic status, political opinions, skin color, racial or other physical characteristics, sexual orientation, or spiritual beliefs." CSWE includes the ability to "recognize and manage personal values in a way that allows professional values to guide practice" in its delineation of core competencies (CSWE, 2008, Educational Policy 2.1.2). A key task of the social work curriculum, then, is to facilitate student ability to recognize and manage personal values as they relate to the NASW and IFSW/IASSW standards (Burgess & Taylor, 2004; Lager & Robbins, 2004; Maidment & Egan 2004).

Background

Tension in the Classroom

This balance of professional standards and personal beliefs can create professional dissonance for both students who hold conservative Christian beliefs and students who identify as lesbian, gay, or bisexual (LGB).[1] Taylor and Bentley (2005) conceptualize professional dissonance in social work as "a feeling of discomfort arising from the conflict between professional values and expected or required job tasks" (p. 470). This sort of professional cognitive dissonance may be experienced by conservative Christian social work students when confronted with inconsistent cognitions of personal beliefs (i.e., homosexuality is a sin) and professional standards (i.e., social workers work to eliminate discrimination based on sexual orientation). Similarly, LGB students may also face dissonance when confronted with inconsistent cognitions regarding the professional responsibility to treat with dignity and respect those whom they experience as devaluing same-sex or bisexual orientation.

Faculty Competence

Faculty competence on issues of diversity is essential to address conflicts related to homosexuality and religion in the classroom. Clearly defined in CSWE's Education Policy are mandates for the inclusion of content on women, people of color, and the LGBT population. Faculties frame the context for this inclusion. However, it is not clear that social work educators have the knowledge, understanding, and skill to teach this content in an effective manner that manages their own worldviews and avoids the stigmatization of individual students (Aldredge, 2007; Dessel, Woodford, & Gutiérrez, 2012; Fredriksen-Goldsen, Woodford, Luke, & Gutiérrez, 2011). Nor is it clear that proper attention is being paid to LGBT issues or religious considerations despite evidence of their importance to competent social work practice. In a 1999 national survey of social work educators regarding diversity content, 78.6% ranked content on people of color or racism as very important, 67% ranked content on women or sexism as very important, but fewer than half ranked content on gays and lesbians or heterosexism or homophobia as very important (Gutiérrez, Fredriksen, & Soifer, 1999). Although recent studies of U.S. and Canadian social work faculty have found more positive attitudes toward LGBT issues (Fredriksen-Goldsen et al., 2011; Woodford, Brennan, Gutiérrez, & Luke, 2013), this has not necessarily translated to inclusion in social work curricula. In a joint CSWE and Lambda Legal study (Martin et al., 2009), 41% of social work program directors thought their programs prepared students to provide services to LGBT people "slightly well" to "not well at all." Only 19% of responding directors reported assessing competence of graduates to provide services to LGBT people. At the same time, content on religious diversity has received little attention. The debate about whether it should be included at all is, at this point, robust among social work scholars (Streets, 2009, p.186; Canda, 1999; Cnaan & Wineburg, 1999). In a 1997 dissertation study of graduate social work students at two universities, Streets (1997) found that highly religious social work students most often choose their personal religious values over professional standards when they are in conflict in practice. Social work scholars continue to explore various models of decision making to address this personal and professional value dissonance (Doyle, Miller, & Mirza, 2009; Spano & Koenig, 2007).

The literature suggests that social work educators, in general, have been remiss in formulating effective responses to such dissonance in the classroom (Ben-Ari, 1998; Fleck-Henderson & Melendez, 2009; Gutiérrez et al., 1999; Hyde & Ruth, 2002; Van Soest & Garcia, 2003), and when they are faced with conflict it is not uncommon for faculty members to rely on a recitation of the professional standards. Solid approaches to such conflict, with clear description and direction, are needed for faculty members to feel confident in formulating effective classroom responses. This chapter describes the author's efforts to address a specific conflict between students holding conservative Christian beliefs and students identifying as gay, lesbian, or bisexual. The approach used and lessons gleaned from the experience are offered as pragmatic suggestions for faculty member facilitation of difficult dialogues on conservative Christian beliefs and sexual orientation in the classroom.

Context

As discussed, a brewing student conflict at one diverse urban university provides a case study of this particularly difficult challenge. In the social work program, students identifying as conservative Christian and students identifying as gay or lesbian reported difficulty in exploring the personal and professional dissonance they were experiencing. As associate director of field education and as faculty advisor for the Gay-Straight Alliance and de facto advisor for the North American Association of Christian Social Workers (NACSW) student chapter, I had opportunity to interact on some level with all students in the program. They dropped by my office, frequently discussing issues related to being gay or lesbian or to being conservative Christian. Sometimes there was a concern about the curriculum from a student who identified as gay or lesbian:

> We actually skipped the chapter. There was [*sic*] developmental issues for kids, then women, suddenly we're talking about old folks and I'm like hey, wait a minute, there was a chapter in there about me. I raised my hand. Soon as I did, everybody, professor included, rolled their eyes. Well, screw 'em all. We are social workers, aren't we?

Sometimes, a gay or lesbian student's concern was more about relationships with peers.

> Sometimes in class I feel anger and dismay when things are said. So many people believe my life to be a sin, I should never be able to marry my partner, even that I am going to hell. In the abstract knowing that there are people out there somewhere who feel that way about me doesn't bother me. But with specific people, people I know, who I've had classes with and knowing that they feel that way about me and my life . . . is hurtful.

Students identifying as conservative Christian were upfront with me about coping strategies:

> I've learned to go under the radar. My first week or two I thought it was okay to just be who I am, to say I was Christian, that this is a calling for me. But after one professor actually told me, in class, in front of everybody, that I should drop the program, without even knowing me, I had to rethink everything. I still want to be a social worker, but I know I can't be myself and make it through. So I fly low.

And conservative Christian students were honest when their personal and professional values were not in consonance:

> I do think homosexuality is wrong. It is against my Christian principles. Why is it okay for others to have values but not me? I'm not saying I'm going to let it interfere with my clients. I think murder is wrong too but if I had to work with a murderer I would. I am a Christian, not God. I am a Christian, and I am a social worker. And yes, I am a Christian social worker.

The conflict brewed in the classroom and spilled out into the hallways. At least one conservative Christian student felt compelled to distribute literature touting reparative therapy, placing written and audio materials in selected student mailboxes. Lesbian and gay students insisted that the student chapter of NACSW be banned as unacceptable in a social work program. Student deficits in intrapersonal and interpersonal reconciliation of differences were abundantly obvious.

Attempts at Resolution

Faculty members faced a difficult task in attempting to teach affirmative practice in accordance with professional guidelines in the context of this simmering conflict. We needed classroom approaches that would respect individual differences, address conflict, and promote development of professional conflict resolution skills. Discussions in faculty meetings were difficult, with responses ranging from acknowledged sense of helplessness and lack of competence to blaming "difficult" students. One particularly painful attempt at assembly discussion between faculty members and students ended with one student in tears as a faculty member declared the meeting adjourned and abruptly stomped out of the meeting hall.

In light of research indicating that despite the tendency by instructors and students alike to avoid conflict—fearing that once started it cannot be controlled—well-managed conflict can be useful in creating the opportunity for discussion and safe exploration of conflict (Steiner, Brzuzy, Gerdes, & Hurdle, 2003), I began to develop an elective course designed to address the conflict while teaching specific practice-relevant interventions to students.

The Agreement

The possibility of a course was discussed with the student leadership for the NACSW student chapter and the Gay–Straight Alliance student group. These leaders offered input in terms of content and agreed to take the course and to encourage members of their respective groups to take the course. Based on this consensus, a draft syllabus was created and presented to the faculty for approval for an elective course offering. The course was approved and scheduled for the winter term.

Course Design

The teaching approach for this course was grounded in transformative learning theory (Mezirow, 2000) and intergroup dialogue (Dessel, Rogge, &

Garlington, 2006; Zúñiga, Nagda, Chesler, & Cytron-Walker, 2007) and organized around a variety of drama-based group methods to facilitate experimental exploration of and dialogue about the conflict. The drama-based activities and techniques came from sociodrama (Moreno, 1972), theater of the oppressed (Boal, 1979), and theater of empowerment perspectives (Boon & Plastow, 2004; Clifford & Herrmann, 1998) and were designed to provide experiential discovery that facilitated intergroup dialogue.

Sociodrama

This term was first coined by Moreno in 1943 and was envisioned as an adjunct to his psychodramatic approach to therapy (Moreno, 1972). Moreno characterized the true subject of a sociodrama as the group and the method as one in which the working tools are representative types within a given culture and not private individuals. A Jewish immigrant himself, Moreno was interested in how cultures intermingle, how prejudices develop, and how to help people overcome intolerance to cultural differences (Sternberg & Garcia, 2000). He used sociodrama to encourage safe dialogue between characters, actors, and audience. He believed that in order for people to experience each other truly, they must both reverse positions and enter into the subjectivity of the other mutually, not unilaterally (Moreno, 1972). One of the outcomes cited by those who use sociodrama is "healing of wounds of stereotyping and stigmatization through the educational and consciousness raising process" (Sternberg & Garcia, 2000; Telesco, 2006).

Sociodrama can be viewed from a system perspective in which the line between oppressed and oppressor is not so clear. Rather, the two live in the same community and are products of the same community; alternatively, one can be the oppressed and the oppressor. Structure is created by patterns of behavior rather than the other way around, and changing structure without changing behaviors that created it is futile (Diamond, 2007). The choice of sociodrama as the teaching method for this course was based on the key features that make it likely to be effective in dealing with intense emotional conflicts when one's personal values and sense of identity are called into question by a group that feels equally devalued. In sociodrama, the "others" are not challenged to confront each other. Rather, they are invited to *become* one another. It is an intervention that gets a person out of her or his head, where the cognitive dissonance foments, and into the other person's shoes, where empathy takes seed. As Moreno himself said, perhaps the greatest value of sociodrama lies in its ability to "cure as well as solve; that it can change attitudes as well as study them" (Moreno, 1972, p. 363).

Theater of the Oppressed

Theater of the oppressed is more specifically focused on exploring the dynamics of group oppression and giving voice to the oppressed. It is a rehearsal theater designed for people who want to learn ways of fighting back against oppression in their daily lives. In theater of the oppressed, oppression is defined, in part, as a power dynamic based on monologue rather than dialogue. It is intended for the voice of the oppressed to be discovered and then presented in a way that it is heard (Boal, 1979).

Accordingly, the theater of the oppressed is a participatory theater that fosters democratic and cooperative forms of interaction between participants. Theater is emphasized not as a spectacle but rather as a language designed to analyze and discuss problems of oppression and power and explore group solutions to these problems (Boal, 1979, 1985).

Theater of Empowerment

Theater of empowerment examines the ability of drama, theater, dance, and performance to empower groups and communities of very different kinds by building on the strength of self in cooperative communication with others (Boon & Plastow, 2004; Clifford & Herrmann, 1998). Theater of empowerment offers not only drama skills but personal development, group work, conflict resolution, and facilitation skills to create a broader experience that is a "tool for social change: a proactive, potentially life-changing experience, that truly empowers the participants to recognize that they have choices in life and to consider these choices from a new perspective" (Clifford & Herrmann, 1998, p. 9). In theater of empowerment, drama engages both the head and heart. Participants take on roles of other characters and experience different situations with an increased understanding of self, others, and the world.

Course Structure

Twenty-seven students enrolled in the course. Twenty-two participants identified as female, five as male, and none as transgender or other gendered. Fourteen of the students identified as White, eight as Black, and five as Latina or Hispanic. Twenty-one indicated they were Christian, ten identified as conservative Christian, one student was Jewish, and five did not identify with any organized religion. Twenty-one of the participants identified as heterosexual, five identified as lesbian, one identified as gay male, and none identified as bisexual or other sexual orientation. The course was offered as an elective and met over two weekends for a total of 30 hours, 15 hours of class time each weekend. Approximately one fourth of the course time was spent on didactic teaching about dramatic techniques and their application in social work. The remainder of the time was spent in experiential exercises related to the specific conflict between conservative Christian and LGB students in the social work program. As indicated, the experiential portion of the course followed a synthesis of techniques from theater of the oppressed, sociodrama, conflict theater, and other models of interactive theater with an ultimate goal of intergroup dialogue. Figure 1 illustrates the transformative learning model within which the experiential exercises were designed to foster affirmative resolution of cognitive dissonance.

The course activities were taken largely from Rohd's work in theater for community, conflict, and dialogue (Rohd, 1998) and Sternberg and Garcia's conceptualization of sociodrama (Sternberg & Garcia, 2000). Rohd focuses more on dialogue than on problem solving. Paterson describes his philosophy as follows:

> If dialogue is essential, then its absence is a violation of the most profound sort. We must be able to signal back, to speak out, especially in situations where we feel we have been wronged. It is so essential that, when dialogue stops and is replaced by the oppression of monologue, we can feel deprived

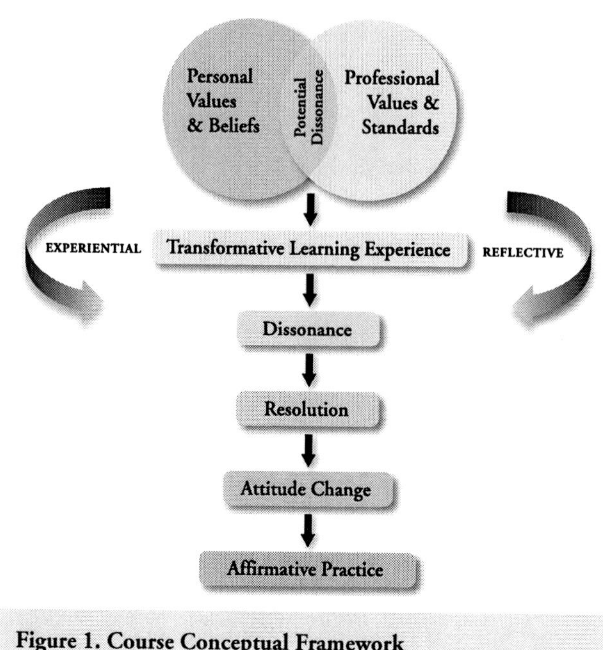

Figure 1. Course Conceptual Framework

of our very humanity...the task then is for the oppressed—whoever feels the object of a monologue—to confront our oppressor and to get on with the ironic task of reestablishing dialogue with the oppressive force. (Paterson in Rohd, 1998, p. xxii)

The structure of each class session followed a synthesized model for creating the dialogue: warm-ups, bridging activities, improvisation, activating material, enactments, and circle sharing, or dialogue as shown in Figure 2.

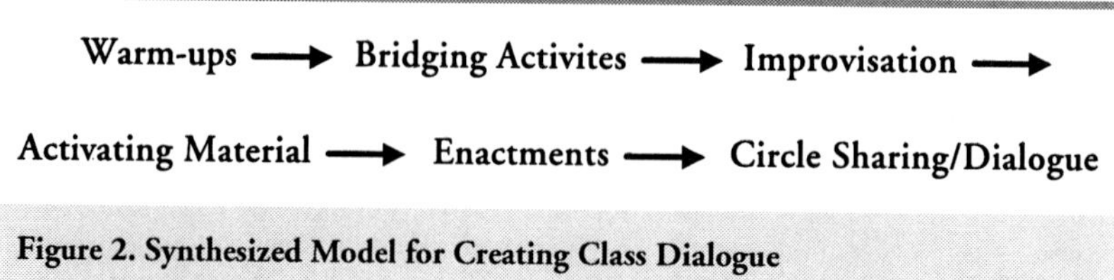

Figure 2. Synthesized Model for Creating Class Dialogue

Warm-ups are exercises conducted to get a group playing together in a safe space, energize the space, and create a sense of comfort in doing structured activities together. Warm-ups have one of two goals: creating energy and focus or creating trust. Bridging activities are exercises and improvisations that theatricalize the space and begin to focus the group on imagination and issues. That is, they introduce the drama-based approach to development of shared group themes (Rohd, 1998). During the warm-ups, the energy and focus increase. As drama-based techniques such as improvisation are introduced, open tension systems—areas of potential conflict—and the shared central issue emerge (Sternberg & Garcia, 2000). Open tension systems are defined as the unresolved issues shared by group members (Sternberg & Garcia, 2000, p. 39). The shared central issue is the one major open tension system that interests participants the most. For the purposes of the course, the open tension system had been identified: the conflict between conservative Christian students and LGB students. Once this shared central issue is identified, the group would engage in enactments. These are simply the scenes that are improvised by participants around the shared central issue. The goal of the enactment is catharsis, insight, and role exploration in an interactive, fictionalized, and spontaneous manner (Sternberg & Garcia, 2000).

Sharing, or discussion, is a critical component of the sociodrama experience. It is used at each juncture of the process to facilitate moving the issue from monologue to dialogue, from oppression to equality. During the sharing, the facilitator guides discussion about exercises or enactments that have just taken place, asking participants to share their own feelings and experiences, with acceptance of all viewpoints required. Sharing facilitates the expression, bonding, and reflection that are critical to the success of sociodrama (Sternberg & Garcia, 2000).

The work of sociodrama follows an arc, the intensity increasing, with exercises designed to move toward the dissonance and then away, toward, and then away, inching closer to the point at which the collision takes place. At the same time, work is done to prepare the actor/student for the moment when thoughts are allowed to merge, emotions are expressed and dispelled, and a new cognition may take hold (Boal, 1979, 2002; Rohd, 1998; Sternberg &

Garcia, 2000). In some cases beliefs will be changed. In others, conflicting personal and professional values may coexist with cognitive compartmentalization, reducing dissonance (Aronson, personal correspondence, 2008).

The Curriculum

Although it is not possible to detail the entire curriculum in one chapter, examples of the activities undertaken in the course are offered here in an effort to make the conceptual model more accessible and to demonstrate how the sequence of activities can lead the class to meaningful dialogue. These exercises are all well known in drama-based pedagogies; the examples used here are exercises adapted by Boal (1992, Sternberg and Garcia (2000), Rohd (1998), and Clifford and Herrmann (1998).

WARM-UPS

Half-hour to 45-minute warm-ups were done at the beginning of each class day. Shorter warm-ups were done after each break, including lunch. The morning warm-ups were designed to energize the space and focus the group on the work to be done. After break warm-ups included those elements as well as trust building. One morning warm-up used was the circle dash. The purpose was primarily to get people moving, although, like most group exercises, it also provided rich material for later discussions. In the exercise, group members stand in a circle around one person who is standing in the middle. Those in the outer circle must switch places with one another at random, reaching the new spot before the person in the middle arrives. If the middle person reaches the spot first, he or she becomes part of the outer circle, and there is a new "middle" person. The exercise is silent; outer group members must find nonverbal ways to communicate their desire to exchange places, reach agreement, and execute the switch. As multiple pairs begin to switch places and the person in the middle attempts to claim a spot, high energy and intense focus are created. The three-act exercise is an example of a trust warm-up. In this activity, the group was asked to move around the room, greeting other group members and revealing three facts about themselves with as many people as possible, varying the facts being told. When time was up they were asked to call out the facts they heard without revealing names. The group attempted to guess to whom the facts belonged. This gentle transition into personal information allowed the group to begin to get to know one another and to trust other group members with their information.

BRIDGING ACTIVITIES

Bridging exercises were designed to move the group into the creative and imaginative space where drama work was introduced. When completed without specific topic instructions, bridging activities spark the imagination and introduce dramatic action. Specific topics can be added to move bridging activities to improvisation and activating material. For example, an exercise known as Tour of the Place was used for the course. For the bridging activity, class members were paired and then instructed to close their eyes and think of an actual place they have been. Once they have a full picture in their mind, down to colors and textures, they open their eyes and take their partner on a 5-minute guided tour of that place, actually walking through the space, describing physical specifics and emotional importance as if the pair were actually in that space.

IMPROVISATION

Improvisation furthers the movement to drama and requires in-the-moment creation of movement—action and reaction—to create a cohesive scene or statement. Building on the bridging exercise a Tour of the Place, students were asked to create a scene in the place they introduced. In the spirit of impromptu creation, they were given parameters at random by the group. For example, the student who took his partner on a tour of a grocery store was instructed to create a scene with a 5-year-old, a bunch of bananas, and announcements over the PA system. As soon as the items were called out, he was required to begin acting with his partner in the exercise. The student created a scene in which the child was running through the store peeling bananas, with the peels thrown on the floor. Soon his store was filled with shoppers slipping on the banana peels as the store manager tried valiantly over the PA system to direct traffic away from the peels. The exercise in isolation may seem silly and hardly worthy of classroom time. However, the energy, focus, trust, and theatricality built to this moment provided the elements necessary for the next phase of the process.

ACTIVATING MATERIAL

When specific material related to the open tension systems is introduced in the dramatic exercises, exploration of the shared central theme is activated. In the bridging and improvisation exercises just described, specific relevant material was introduced after the initial improvisation. Class participants were again paired to imagine a place and give a tour but with specific instructions: The place is a church. Each student was asked to imagine a church where they had actually been and to which they attached some emotional significance. They then took their partner on a tour of that place. Finally, they moved into groups of four and improvised scenes in their churches. One student directed a scene in which she was baptized; another student directed a scene in which she was asked to leave the church because of her sexual orientation.

ENACTMENTS

Enactments were additional scenes improvised by participants around the shared central issue. Given that the goal of the enactments is catharsis, insight, and role exploration, activating material and improvisations were used to move closer to the issues experienced by conservative Christian students and LGBT students. After the activating exercises just described, groups were combined and roles were assigned. The student who acted out the baptism scene was moved to play the part of someone asked to leave the church. Conversely, the student who devised the scene in which she was asked to leave became the baptized person. They were directed by the group in an enactment. This particular pair was assigned the role of mother and daughter in addition to the other parameters of the scene.

CIRCLE SHARING OR DIALOGUE

Throughout this cycle of exercises, the group was periodically asked to circle up and discuss their reactions to the activities. Responses to the circle dash ranged from "it was fun" to "I felt like an outcast when I was in the middle and no one wanted to let me in," leading to a discussion of privilege and "other." Discussion about the improvisations allowed students to talk about their comfort level with acting in general and then more specifically to discuss their responses when required to imagine a church. The dialogue is facilitated with less conflict because it is not about the other students or about what the other student has said. It is about a scene or about a character. This element of removal from the personal created a safer space, allowing more open exploration of the central themes of the course.

Course Outcomes

Students participating in this course immersed themselves in intense warm-ups, bridging, activating, enacting, and dialogue. Over the course of the two marathon weekends, they went beyond differences and discovered commonalities. The outcome of the course was designed to follow a typical sociodrama product. The students were assigned the task of developing a dramatic presentation to be performed for their social work classmates who had not taken the course. The presentation was to address in whatever way they saw fit the overarching conflict of conservative Christian students and LGB students. Those who participated in the class dutifully attempted this assignment. Ultimately they approached the instructor with concerns. They felt they had experienced a profound change that could not be captured in performance. They also felt that a one-time performance would not honor the work they had done. They had a different outcome in mind. Working together they built a rainbow, which they had identified through their work as having deep symbolic meaning both to conservative Christians and to LGB people. On one side of the rainbow they wrote the verse from the Bible about God's promise; on the other side of the rainbow they wrote the meaning of each of the colors of the rainbow in the LGB community. They then individually made clouds. On these clouds they wrote words, phrases, quotes that captured their individual experience of the course. They attached the clouds to the rainbow. Then, as a group, they carried the rainbow down the hall and into the student lounge. There, in the corner where the NACSW student chapter bulletin board and the GSA bulletin board were mounted on adjacent walls, they carefully installed their rainbow. It touched each bulletin board, joining them together. They wanted it there, they said, to let all students, present and future, know that the two groups shared more commonalities than differences and that always there was a way to talk about the differences and build a bridge to the commonalities.

Lessons Learned: Useful Steps in Dialogue Facilitation

The teaching pedagogy and method used in this case study was unique. The course was not a typical hour and a half or three-hour block per week for the course of a semester. Furthermore, the entire focus of the course was on a difficult dialogue topic rather than the more typical controversial module in the context of a larger course or an unexpected "hot moment" in the classroom (Warren, 2000). Finally, the sociodrama approach included extensive drama-based techniques and activities that may not lend themselves to the traditional curriculum. However, use of a drama-based approach in the case study did highlight specific steps and activities that can be helpful in managing and moving forward a difficult dialogue. These include centering yourself, contextualizing the conversation, validating perspectives, neutralizing the dialogue and space, and focusing on takeaways.

CENTER YOURSELF: PLANTING

It is critical that faculty members be ready for difficult dialogues. Faculty competence in leading these discussions is the best predictor of ultimate outcome. In prepping a course for delivery, one can identify the potential hazards and prepare accordingly. When those modules come up on the course schedule, it is important to be ready. On the stage, one learns that planting oneself, and standing still and strong, focuses attention on the words in a monologue and lends power to the performance. In the classroom, psychically planting oneself, and proceeding with certainty, inspires confidence in the ability of the instructor to facilitate dialogue. Planning ahead for this is one thing, of course; a more challenging moment occurs when the dialogue is unanticipated. One student makes a remark, there is a retort, and suddenly the class is embroiled in a hot moment, emotions high, opinions and very often tears flying. Although the instinct may be to duck, defend, or run, planting is critical to a positive dialogue. We duck by changing the subject or immediately suggesting that a topic be abandoned or taken up at a later date; we defend by resorting to recitation of professional standards that trump any discussion; we run by allowing the dialogue to continue with no intervention or facilitation from us.

Preparation for planting in both scenarios is essentially the same. One must engage in self-reflection and in checking one's own biases. Planting in the classroom is not about rigidity or presentation of "truth." Rather, it involves a relaxed approach to the topic and a willingness to allow all voices to be heard, without judgment. Useful activities for planting are as follows.

- When the difficult dialogue is anticipated, it can be helpful to complete the activities that will be required of students. Do the activities and assignments and make note of anything that takes you off center.
- Engage a colleague in discussion of the topic with a goal of providing feedback about untended biases or rigidity that may creep in.
- In all cases, anticipated or unanticipated, deep breathing, active listening, and an unbroken focus in the facilitating moment can provide the instructor with the psychic stance necessary to create a positive exchange of ideas.

CONTEXTUALIZE THE CONVERSATION

Difficult dialogues can devolve into hot moments even with the best faculty preparation if the discussion is not contextualized. Dialogue on the stage has no meaning if it is not connected to the central theme of the play. In this same way, difficult dialogues should relate to the central theme of the discussion or the curriculum in order to be helpful. In the instance of a discussion of conservative Christian beliefs and sexual orientation, for example, what one believes about these is not the critical focus in a classroom dialogue. Rather, whether one can practice following the guidance of professional standards, not personal values, is the central theme. Following are some useful questions for facilitation.

- How is this related to your practice as a social worker?
- How might it affect that practice?
- What professional steps can you take to ensure that you are practicing affirmatively (no matter the belief)?

Useful activities for facilitation include the following:

- In the 1-minute free-write, students write for 1 minute on the questions just listed. The free-write allows them to quickly move from belief defense to focus on professional practice. Students then partner with someone in the course they don't know well and share their free-writes. Students should be instructed not to comment on the free-writes but simply to actively listen.
- Break students into groups. Assign each group to review one of the professional codes or practice guidelines: NASW Code of Ethics, *Social Work Speaks,* CSWE Educational Policy and Accreditation Standards, International Federation of Social Workers' Statement of Ethical Principles, or the North American Christian Social Workers Association website. Groups elect a spokesperson to report their findings back to the larger group.

VALIDATE PERSPECTIVES

Allowing all perspectives to be both voiced and heard is critical to furthering the dialogue. An important responsibility of facilitation is reminding students that no one is right and no one is wrong in the discussion. Taking sides or invoking professional "rules" as an attempt to defuse a heated dialogue simply pushes the discussion underground, either intrapersonally or interpersonally. In teaching affirmative practice related to religion and sexual orientation, individual stories must be told and honored. Again, the important question is not why but how—not why do you feel that way but, given that you feel that way, how will you practice affirmatively? The following are useful responses.

- There is no right or wrong here. You are all offering important perspectives for discussion.

- That is a valid perspective. What can others relate to in what was just said?
- That is an important personal belief. Your awareness of it as you think about your social work practice is to be commended.

NEUTRALIZE THE DIALOGUE AND SPACE

One of the most difficult aspects to navigate in a discussion of conflicting beliefs such as conservative Christian tenets and sexual orientation is the intensely personal nature of the beliefs. When the discussion takes the direction of serial defenses of personal beliefs, a positive outcome is more difficult. A helpful aspect of sociodrama is the ability to place the issue outside individuals. The difficult topic is taken from the individual and placed in a neutral space outside each individual. The effect is akin to taking a malfunctioning engine out of a car and placing it in the center of the room where it can be walked around, examined from all sides, talked about, and subjected to various solutions, all independent of the car in which it belongs. In the same way, sociodrama activities allow individual beliefs to be taken out of the personal context, placed in a neutral space in the center of the group, and examined from all angles and perspectives, once removed from the person holding the belief. The topic, very critically, is the belief and its relationship to affirmative practice, not the person holding it. The following are useful activities.

- Issue Pile: Students jot down their personal perspectives and add them to a pile on a table at the front or center of the room. All are read out one by one. A student volunteer develops, with group input, a visual model of the overarching professional theme informed by the personal perspectives. Discussion is driven by this conceptual model.
- Group Sculpture: This is a silent exercise. Class is broken into groups of five to six people. Each group, without speaking, forms their bodies into a physical sculpture that represents the dialogue theme. Once formed, groups take turns walking around to view the sculptures, again in silence. Once all students have had a chance to review all other groups, discus-

sion of the process of developing a sculpture and of observations of other group sculptures is used as a springboard to discussing the topic.

- Getting to Know You. Each student creates a character who holds the traits they find difficult (i.e., students who hold conservative Christian beliefs create a character who is gay or lesbian; students who identify as gay or lesbian create a character who holds conservative Christian beliefs). The character description should be as detailed as possible, with specific information including family of origin, favorite childhood memory, memories of school, favorite color, type of music listened to, job they hated the most, and so on. The goal of the exercise is for the student to get to know on a different level a person who holds the traits with which they are struggling.
- Who, What, When, Where Improvs: Characters created by students are enacted by them in group improvisations. Two to three students act in each improv. They are given the what, where, and when of the situation by the other students in the class. They are then asked to create the scene in character. Again, the goal is for the students to get to know their character on a deeper level.
- Character Interviews: Students take turns being interviewed by the class, in character. They must consider and respond to questions as they imagine their character would do. The goal of the exercise is further exploration of the lived experience of the person who holds the traits with which they struggle.

FOCUS ON THE TAKEAWAYS

It is imperative that a difficult dialogue end with some sense of the "so what." Students need to gain a sense of movement toward some goal in the dialogue in order to not get stuck in the difference or conflict narrative. Two fundamental takeaways are how this issue affects a student's ability to practice affirmatively and next steps in moving toward a goal of affirmative practice.

A useful activity here is the Circle Share. After any activity, but particularly at the end of a class period in which a difficult dialogue has taken place, it is important to debrief. Students arrange themselves in a circle and review the activities of the day. Although personal reactions should be voiced and listened to, the instructor should continue to focus the discussion on what was learned as it relates to professional standards and affirmative social work practice.

Summary

Development of professional identity is a crucial component of social work mastery. It involves internalizing the essential norms and values of the profession (Berger & Luckmann, 1966). The NASW Code of Ethics and the CSWE Accreditation Standards both require professional competence in diversity, including religion and sexual orientation. It is critical that students who have conservative religious beliefs engage in self-reflection and exploration of content that may produce value dissonance. Likewise, gay and lesbian students who harbor negative beliefs toward those who identify as conservative Christian must explore these beliefs. To accomplish this, it is essential for students to have a safe learning environment that promotes self-reflection and an exploration of personal values juxtaposed against professional values that are central to professional identity development.

The strain within the profession and in the classroom is often palpable. Social work professionals who identify as gay or lesbian, stigmatized in society and covertly stigmatized by some people in the profession, continue to experience overt discrimination. And some social workers who identify as Christian now find themselves stigmatized by people who assign stereotypical attributes to them based on their group membership (Aldredge, 2007; Graff, 2007; Hodge, 2002, 2005a, 2007; Hylton, 2005; Jimenez, 2006; Melendez & LaSala, 2006; Parmet, 2005; Shernoff, 2005; Stulberg, 2006;Thacker, 2006).

As part of the impetus to socialize students to social work's values, schools of social work must be able to recognize and effectively deal with intrapersonal and interpersonal value conflicts that arise during the process of professional socialization. Effective models of teaching are needed that support self-exploration and development of a mature professional identity that includes attitudes and behavior that are consonant with professional standards related to religion and sexual orientation. Despite attempts to find appropriate curricular and effective teaching approaches, academia lags behind in this arena (Black, Oles, & Moore, 1998; Cramer, 1997).

The course described in this chapter yielded important information about a teaching method that can create the safety that is necessary for students to explore and potentially mediate this dissonance. It offers insight not only on how to better prepare students for managing personal and professional dissonance but on how to practice effectively with the "different other." Students who identify as Christian and students who identify as gay and lesbian are suffering in our classrooms because we are not prepared to lead them through a discussion of the tough questions. The drama-based teaching method explored in this course offers implications for development of effective teaching methods and relevant curricular content.

References

Aldredge, P. (2007, October 30). *Can we talk?* Presentation at the Annual Program Meeting, Council on Social Work Education, San Francisco, CA.

Ben-Ari, A. T. (1998). An experiential attitude change. *Journal of Homosexuality, 36*(2), 59–71. doi:10.1300/J082v36n02_05

Berger, P. L., & Luckmann, T. (1966). *The social construction of reality: A treatise in the sociology of knowledge.* London, UK: Penguin UK.

Black, B., Oles, T. P., & Moore, L. (1998). The relationship between attitudes: Homophobia and sexism among social work students. *Affilia, 13*(2), 166–189. doi:10.1177/088610999801300204

Boal, A. (1979). Theatre of the oppressed (translated by Charles A. & Maria-Odilia Leal McBride). New York, NY: Theatre Communications Group. (Originally published in Spanish as *Teatro de Oprimido, Ediciones de la Flor, Buenos Aires,* 1974).

Boal, A. (1992). *Games for actors and non-actors.* New York, NY: Routledge Press.

Boon, R., & Plastow, J. (2004). *Theatre and empowerment: Community drama on the world stage.* Cambridge, UK: Cambridge University Press.Burgess, H., & Taylor, I. (Eds.). (2004). *Effective learning and teaching in social policy and social work.* London, UK: Routledge.

Canda, E. R. (1999). Spiritually sensitive social work: Key concepts and ideals. *Journal of Social Work Theory and Practice, 1*(1), 1–15.

Clifford, S., & Herrmann, A. (1998). *Making a leap: Theatre of empowerment.* London, UK: Kingsley.

Cnaan, R. A., & Wineburg, R. J. (1999). *The newer deal: Social work and religion in partnership.* New York, NY: Columbia University Press.

Council on Social Work Education (CSWE). (2008). 2008 educational policy and accreditation standards. Retrieved from http://www.cswe.org/Accreditation/2008EPASDescription.aspx

Cramer, E. (1997). Effects of an educational unit about lesbian identity development and disclosure in a social work methods course. *Journal of Social Work Education, 33,* 461–472.

Dessel, A., Rogge, M., & Garlington, S. (2006). Using intergroup dialogue to promote social justice. *Social Work, 11,* 303–315. doi:10.1093/sw/51.4.303

Dessel, A., Woodford, M., & Gutiérrez, L. (2012). Social work faculty's attitudes toward marginalized groups: Exploring the role of religion. *Journal of Religion & Spirituality in Social Work: Social Thought, 31*(3), 244–262. doi:10.1080/15426432.2012.679841

Diamond, D. (2007). *Theatre for living. The art and science of community-based dialogue.* Victoria, Australia: Trafford.

Doyle, O., Miller, S., & Mirza, F. (2009). Ethical decision-making in social work: Exploring personal and professional values. *Journal of Social Work Values and Ethics, 6*(1). Retrieved from http://www.socialworker.com/jswve/content/view/113/67/

Fleck-Henderson, A., & Melendez, M. P. (2009). Conversation and conflict: Supporting authentic dialogue in the classroom. *Journal of Teaching in Social Work, 29*(1), 32–46. doi:10.1080/08841230802212752

Fredriksen-Goldsen, K. I., Woodford, M. R., Luke, K. P., & Gutiérrez, L. (2011). Support of sexual orientation and gender identity content in social work education: Results from national surveys of U.S. and Anglophone Canadian faculty. *Journal of Social Work Education, 47,* 19–35. doi:10.5175.JSWE.2011.200900018

Graff, D. L. (2007). A study of baccalaureate social work students' beliefs about the inclusion of religious and spiritual content in social work. *Journal of Social Work Education, 43,* 243–256. doi:10.5175/JSWE.2007.200500526

Gutiérrez, L., Fredriksen, K., & Soifer, S. (1999). Perspectives of social work faculty on diversity and societal oppression: Results from a national survey. *Journal of Social Work Education, 35,* 409–419.

Hodge, D. (2002). Does social work oppress evangelical Christians? A "new class" analysis of society and social work. *Social Work, 47*(4), 401–414. doi:10.1093/sw/47.4.401

Hodge, D. (2005a). Epistemological frameworks, homosexuality, and religion: How people of faith understand the intersection between homosexuality and religion. *Social Work, 50*(3), 207–218. doi:10.1093/sw/50.3.207

Hodge, D. R. (2005b). Perceptions of compliance with the profession's ethical standards that address religion: A national study. *Journal of Social Work Education, 41*, 279–295. doi:10.5175/JSWE.2005.200303134

Hodge, D. (2007). Progressing toward inclusion? Exploring the state of religious diversity. *Social Work Research, 31*(1), 55–63. doi:10.1093/swr/31.1.55

Hyde, C., & Ruth, B. (2002). Multicultural content and class participation: Do students self-censor? *Journal of Social Work Education, 38*, 241–256.

Hylton, M. E. (2005). Heteronormativity and the experiences of lesbian and bisexual women as social work students. *Journal of Social Work Education, 41*, 67–82. doi:10.5175/JSWE.2005.200300350

International Federation of Social Workers (IFSW). (2012, March 3). Statement of ethical principles. Retrieved from http://ifsw.org/policies/statement-of-ethical-principles/

Jimenez, J. (2006). Epistemological frameworks, homosexuality and religion: A response to Hodge. *Social Work, 51*(2), 185–187. doi:10.1093/sw/51.2.185

Kendall, K. A. (2000). *Social work education: Its origins in Europe*. Alexandria, VA: Council on Social Work Education.

Lager, P., & Robbins, V. (2004). Field education: Exploring the future, expanding the vision. *Journal of Social Work Education, 40*, 3–11. doi:10.1080/10437797.2004.10778475

Maidment, J., & Egan, R. (eds) (2004). *Practice skills in social work and welfare: More than just*

common sense. Crow's Nest, NSW: Allen & Unwin.

Martin, J., Messinger, L., Kull, R., Holmes, J., Bermudez, F., & Sommer, S. (2009). Council on Social Work Education–Lambda Legal study of LGBT issues in social work. *Council on Social Work Education*. Retrieved from www.cswe.org/File.aspx?id=25678

Melendez, M., & LaSala, M. (2006). Who's oppressing whom? Homosexuality, Christianity, and social work. *Social Work, 51*(4), 371–377. doi:10.1093/sw/51.4.371

Mezirow, J. (2000). *Learning as transformation*. San Francisco, CA: Jossey Bass.

Moreno, J. (1972). *Psychodrama*. Boston, MA: Beacon.

National Association of Social Workers (NASW). (2008). *Code of ethics*. Retrieved from http://www.socialworkers.org/pubs/code/default.asp

Parmet, B. (2005). Epistemological frameworks, homosexuality and religion: A response to Hodge. *Social Work, 50*(4), 373. doi:10.1093/sw/50.4.373

Rohd, M. (1998). *Theatre for community, conflict & dialogue: The* Hope is Vital *training manual.* Portsmouth, NH: Heinemann.

Shernoff, M. (2005). Epistemological frameworks, homosexuality and religion: A response to Hodge. *Social Work, 50,* 373. doi:10.1093/sw/50.4.373

Spano, R., & Koenig, T. (2007). What is sacred when personal and professional values collide? *Journal of Social Work Values and Ethics, 4*(3), 91–104.

Steiner, S., Brzuzy, S., Gerdes, K., & Hurdle, D. (2003). Using structured controversy to teach diversity content and cultural competence. *Journal of Teaching in Social Work, 23*(1–2), 55–71. doi:10.1300/J067v23n01_05

Sternberg, P., & Garcia, A. (2000). *Sociodrama who's in your shoes?* (2nd ed.). Westport, CT: Praeger.

Streets, F. (1997). Religious values and social work education: Conflicts and outcomes. *blank, 1.* Retrieved from the Yeshiva University, ProQuest, UMI Dissertations Publishing database.

Streets, F. (2009). Overcoming a fear of religion in social work education and practice. *Journal of Religion & Spirituality in Social Work: Social Thought, 28,* 185–199. doi:10.1080/15426430802644214

Stulberg, I. (2006). Epistemological frameworks, homosexuality and religion: A response to Hodge. *Social Work, 51*(2), 189. doi:10.1093/sw/51.2.189-a

Taylor, M. F., & Bentley, K .J. (2005). Professional dissonance among social workers: The collision between values and job tasks in mental health practice. *Community Mental Health Journal, 41*(4), 469–480. doi:10.1007/s10597-005 -5084-9

Telesco, G. (2006). Using sociodrama for radical pedagogy: Methodology for education and change. *Radical Pedagogy, 8*(2), 1–11.

Thacker, D. (2006). Epistemological frameworks, homosexuality, and religion [Letter to the editor]. *Social Work, 51,* 189–190.

Van Soest, D., & Garcia, B. (2003). *Diversity education for social justice: Mastering teaching skills.* Alexandria, VA: Council on Social Work Education.

Warren, L. (2000, October). *Managing hot moments in the classroom.* Retrieved from http://isites.harvard.edu/fs/html/icb.topic58474/hotmoments.html

Woodford, M., Brennan, D., Gutiérrez, L., & Luke, K. (2013). U.S. graduate social work faculty's attitudes toward lesbian, gay, bisexual, and transgender people. *Journal of Social Service Research, 39*(1), 50–62. doi:10.1080/01488376 .2012.666936

Zúñiga, X., Nagda, B. A., Chesler, M., & Cytron-Walker, A. (2007). *Intergroup dialogues in higher education: Meaningful learning about social justice.* ASHE Higher Education Report Series 32(4). San Francisco, CA: Jossey-Bass.

Note

1 In this chapter the term *conservative Christian* is used to identify adherents of Christianity who hold specific ideological views that characterize same-sex attraction as negative (i.e., immoral, sinful, an abomination, in need of repentance).

Conclusion and Recommendations

Where We Started

We began this book as a genuine effort to broaden the discourse in social work with regard to certain conservative Christian beliefs and lesbian, gay, and bisexual orientation. Each of us comes from different religious backgrounds and perspectives and different sexual orientations. Thus, we have different positions related to these topics and tensions. We were each personally and professionally concerned about the state of the social work literature regarding the tensions that existed. We were especially concerned about the tone of some of the literature that we experienced as too confrontational and polarizing. Instead of seeking a position in which religious and sexual orientation diversity could be honored within social work, the literature sometimes felt almost antagonistic, forcing one position over another. We both believed that a conversation was possible in which both positions were understood and reconciled.

At the time we began this journey—when we started writing our first article in 2009—the literature that discussed how the profession of social work oppresses some conservative Christian people did not acknowledge the complexities of this claim. Although the field of social services has a long connected tradition with Christianity, there was little acknowledgment in the literature from the conservative Christian perspective of how conservative Christian beliefs about same-sex sexuality contribute to oppression of LGB people. Furthermore, articles that did discuss the critical role of religion in this oppression suggested to us that a more nuanced examination of the role of Christian religious beliefs was needed (Berkman & Zinberg, 1997; Crisp, 2007; Krieglstein, 2003; Newman, Dannenfelser, & Benishek, 2002; Raiz & Saltzburg, 2007; Ryan, 2000). We thought it was essential to study the implications of this research for Christianity as a whole. Most importantly, we found almost no discussion about how to bridge this divide between Christians holding certain conservative beliefs and sexual minority people that fully supported both groups. Instead, the literature seemed to put forward the position that conservative Christian social work students' religious beliefs could and should be a part of their social work practice either by commission or omission (Hodge, 2005; Ressler & Hodge, 2003; Thyer & Myers, 2009). We strongly believed that social work needed to and could find a way to bridge this divide without the forfeiture or marginalization of either group while also holding to the values of social work. Social work education has examples of how to eliminate racism and sexism (Miller & Donner, 2000; Richards-Schuster & Aldana, 2013; Trolander, 1997). Just as the field has continued to address these prejudices, it needs to address LGB and religious prejudice as part of its process is to sensitize students to different marginalized groups and work for social justice. We also believed that a discussion such as this had to be conceptualized within the context of power and inequality.

In asking authors to contribute to the book, we looked for diversity in perspective and difference in approach. Chapters were written by authors identifying as lesbian, gay, bisexual, and heterosexual, by conservative Christian authors and by more moderate or liberal Christians and non-Christians, and by educators, practitioners, and lawyers. In this book these authors provided overviews of doctrines about same-sex sexuality by different Christian denominations; empirical work that provides a greater understanding of the tension and the participants; policy, theological, methodological, legal, and ethical perspectives; transformative processes; specific interventions that can be used to guide this process of transformation; and a case study in which this transformation occurred among LGB students and Christian students in a social work class. These chapters thus addressed this tension in a new way or were themselves transformative.

What Have We Learned?

Understanding Christian Experiences and Perspectives

A number of themes emerged from the chapters in each section of this book. From the preface and first section, we learned that many churches are still struggling with their doctrine regarding the ordination of LGB clergy and marriage of same-sex couples. A wide range of church doctrine addressing same-sex sexuality exists, and thus there are many opportunities for new thinking concerning these issues, particularly in African American and Latino communities (Levy). Still, most denominations have become more welcoming to LGB people over the years.

Furthermore, as other literature suggests (Jayakumar, 2009; Whitley, 2009; Wilkinson, 2004), Chonody and her colleagues found that greater religiosity was indeed strongly related to a greater antigay bias against LGB people in their sample of heterosexual Christian social work graduate students, whereas negative religious teachings were more weakly related. The number of LGB friends the students had was also directly but weakly related to attitudes toward people whose sexual orientation places them in the minority, with those with more LGB friends having more positive attitudes. However, the number of LGB friends did not act as a moderator with religious messages, whereas the interaction between religiosity and attitudes toward sexual minority people did act as a moderator. More specifically, students with the greatest religiosity and the most negative messages about same-sex sexuality through their churches had disproportionately more negative attitudes toward LGB individuals.

Swank and Fahs had a similar finding in an undergraduate social work sample. They found that greater religious attendance and biblical literalism were weakly related to greater suppression of LGB activism, whereas greater support of the Christian Coalition was more moderately associated. Conversely, greater educational attainment (a moderate association) and the greater recognition of heterosexist discrimination (a weak association) predicted greater activism. They highlighted the overall, although weaker, negative effect of relationship with religion, with a somewhat greater relationship with conservative beliefs, and the promising potential of curriculum that addresses issues of heterosexism and political advocacy (Swank & Fahs).

Walls and Seelman found that self-identified evangelical Christian graduate social work students had significantly higher levels of heterosexism and cultural incongruence, defined as lack of fit with social work culture and values of equality, than did other Christian and non-Christian social work students. Importantly, group-based dominance (i.e., support for the dominance of one's own social group) fully mediated the relationship between evangelical Christian identity and cultural incongruence. Conversely, negative attitudes toward same-sex sexuality and right-wing authoritarianism, the latter of which was "characterized by a need for clear-cut distinctions between groups and an understanding of the world that is based on group-based hierarchies and an unequal distribution of power" (Seelman & Walls, 2010, p. 106), did not act as mediators. That these variables did not mediate the relationship between evangelical Christian identity and cultural incongruence is probably a statistical issue created because of the variables' extremely strong relationships with evangelical Christian identity.[1] The finding that group-based dominance was a full mediator of the relationship between evangelical Christian identity and cultural incongruence in social work suggests that evangelical Christian social work students are far more likely to believe in ingroup dominance over outgroups, even when that dominance is hostile and aggressive, and who are, in turn, less comfortable with the values and norms of a social work culture. Once that mediated relationship was accounted for, the direct relationship between evangelical Christianity and cultural incongruence in social work disappeared. For example, people higher in group-based dominance were more likely to oppose rights of women and LGB people. This study thus suggests that those with a stronger evangelical Christian identity that is bound within the belief sytems of evangelical churches are more likely to aver group-based dominance. Finally, given the statistical issue discussed in the endnote, it can also be said that heterosexist attitudes and right-wing authoritarianism directly predicted cultural incongruity.

DeVore and Blumenfeld described the problematic silencing of LGB youth within the youth's own conservative Christian families and the subsequent internalized homophobia that resulted. These youth strove to create their own welcoming communities, some of which were religious, and depended heavily on technology to locate resources and support. Ultimately, these youth needed validation and support from their families, and lacking that, they needed mentors to empower them.

In summary, this section at times reviewed what is already known, at times advanced that knowledge, and at times offered a window into the struggle of LGB youth. We learned from this section that many indicators of greater religiosity were related to greater heterosexual discrimination and antigay bias. Paired with these findings, we also learned that social work students with the strongest evangelical Christian identity held the most hostile and aggressive heterosexual attitudes, right-wing authoritarianism, and group-based dominance. In opening the window into the struggle of LGB youth brought up in conservative Christian homes, we saw these findings in action. Of course, it is important to recognize the limitations of the different studies and the need for replication in this developing knowledge base.

Biblical, Methodological, Legal, and Ethical Perspectives

In the second section, authors approached the tension between certain conservative Christian beliefs and LGB people from biblical, human rights, methodological, legal, and ethical standpoints. A biblical and human rights analysis indicated that no single, historically factual, scriptural understanding of same-sex attraction exists, that Christian beliefs regarding same-sex sexuality across all faith traditions are culturally contingent, and that conservative Christian beliefs in freedom of expression must take into account social work ethics and human rights mandates, more specifically, the harm their words convey to LGB individuals (Dessel, Shepardson, & Bolen).

Researchers are also struggling with some of the methodological issues inherent in research on religion and its intersection with social work. Research on this tension experienced by some conservative Christians in social work is in its very early stages (Bolen & Dessel), although much progress has been made. One of the most notable features of this research is its use of random national samples. Nonetheless, generalizations remain problematic because of small sample sizes. Another significant issue is construct validity, especially with the constructs of religion, worldviews, and discrimination. With these important methodological problems, it is still too early to determine whether some of the claims this literature has made (e.g., that conservative Christian social workers experience discrimination in social work educational settings [Hodge, 2005; Ressler & Hodge, 2003]) are supported. Clearly, more research on the intersection of religious beliefs and social work values is needed.

In the next two chapters, those from legal and ethical standpoints, the discussion returned to a focus on social work values. Kaplan provided the reader with a review of the most important legal cases involving social work students who have brought charges against their schools of social work and universities, contending that their rights to their religious beliefs and to free speech have been jeopardized. Kaplan further discussed how the Michigan state legislature has attempted, without success to date, to legislate conduct allowed by social work and other students, thus trying to override social work values. This chapter is a sober reflection on just how much work is left to do before certain conservative Christian and LGB students can mutually honor each other in schools of social work.

With regard to ethical dilemmas, Reamer discussed the tension between certain conservative Christian beliefs and LGB students in social work and the importance of social work faculty members supporting student learning about sexual orientation diversity and adherence to social work values (i.e., nondiscrimination, self-determination, detachment of personal beliefs from professional values, use of evidence-based interventions, and commitment to social justice and respect). He also cautioned faculty members to refrain from imposing their own personal views or expecting participation in activities that violate students' religious beliefs, but to expect students to distinguish personal beliefs from professional ethical standards of practice. Examples of how to successfully manage these dilemmas in classroom and field settings provide important guidelines for these conflicts. Reamer further problematized free speech and claims of political indoctrination and emphasized the profession's commitment to social justice, nondiscrimination, and respect.

In summary, this section discussed the travails associated with breaking new ground in areas with long histories and standards: research, the courts, and ethics. Just as the civil rights movement demanded change in all these areas, the current move toward social justice for LGB people in and outside of social work, while allowing Christians holding certain conservative beliefs their identity, also demands change in these systems.

Transformation

From the third section, we may conclude that transformation is possible without sacrificing Christian identity. This section on transformation validates the Christians role models who are welcoming and affirming of LGB people. In her examination of biblical mandates regarding homophobia and social work values, Brice acknowledged the negative attitudes some conservative Christians hold regarding same-sex relationships yet concluded that these conservative Christians need not be homophobic. She also challenged the dichotomization between conservative Christians and progressives as unnecessary and found alignment with biblical directives and the National Association of Social Workers (NASW) Code of Ethics in areas such as combatting oppression, treating others with dignity and respect, and pursuing social justice.

Tan took this standpoint a step further, finding that although highly religious Christian social work practitioners in her sample viewed same-sex sexuality as a sin, they agreed somewhat on LGBT individuals' right to marry and adopt children. Furthermore, they reported varying degrees of comfort in working with LGBT clients. Interestingly, having LGBT family members did not improve their attitude or comfort with LGBT people, whereas having personal friendships and professional experience with LGBT people did improve them. The practitioners in this study shared honestly how they wrestled and came to terms with setting aside their personal views, thus allowing them to offer their best, most affirmative practice to their LGBT clients.

In a groundbreaking study, Drumm and colleagues laid out the pathways to Christian LGBT advocacy. In a qualitative study, 21 self-identified Christian LGBT social work advocates across clinical, administrative, and education arenas talked about the steps for moving toward advocacy of LGB people. These steps were: gaining new information, gaining understanding and awareness about sexual orientation through relationships and personal education, recognizing the complexity of LGB orientation and their previous misperceptions, and developing new views about sexuality choice and biology. Ultimately, these social workers prioritized their theological values of social justice, humanity, and love over their traditional beliefs about same-sex relationships being sinful. Most notably, this prioritization of beliefs translated into challenging discrimination as well as engagement in LGBT advocacy on micro, macro, and mezzo levels. This advocacy was rooted in both social work and Christian value systems.

All chapters in this section offered ways to move forward within social work with regard to conservative Christian views about sexual orientation diversity. Brice found alignment between the NASW Code of Ethics and biblical directives that can help to reduce or eliminate the anti-LGB bias some conservative Christians hold. Both Tan's and Drumm and colleagues' studies then provided examples of how Christian social workers with conservative beliefs regarding LGB people were able to work clinically with LGB clients and also to advocate for LGB people. These powerful chapters show how transformation is possible.

Interventions and Approaches to Resolving the Tensions

The fourth section provided tools for social work educators and practitioners to bridge the tension in the profession. Dessel's chapters provided a literature review of studies of intergroup dialogue and examined outcomes for participants in a variety of dialogue social identity topics, including those of sexual orientation and Christianity. A growing body of research indicates that intergroup dialogue participation leads to positive changes in attitudes and behaviors with regard to prejudice and bias (Griffin, Brown, & Warren, 2012; Gurin, Nagda, & Zúñiga, 2013). In their study, Dessel and colleagues found that undergraduate students reported learning about intersectionality of identities and heterosexual privilege and reported changes in behavior that included building alliances and disrupting heterosexism and bias. Similarly, in Miles and colleagues' study psychology students in a religiously conservative culture discussed in qualitative interviews how the dialogue group climate seemed to improve over time as members' relationship-building skills improved and they became more productive in negotiating conflict. Some also expressed how they felt more multiculturally competent about religion, spirituality, and sexual orientation and provided examples suggesting a heightened critical consciousness about privilege and oppression and the capacity to work for social justice. Co-facilitators of dialogues experienced similar growth while also developing important group facilitation skills. Intergroup dialogue is a key pedagogical resource for social work educators.

Walls and Todd found that in their course "Disrupting Privilege Through Anti-Oppressive Practice," students recognized their own Christian privilege and how this marginalizes others. Some students were defensive and self-righteous, reluctant to relinquish privilege, or sought to distance themselves from "other Christians," a common reaction in privilege education work. By the end of the course, however, many students developed a reconceptualization of antioppressive Christianity, much like what was described in the "Transformation" section of this book.

Last but certainly not least, Aldredge's case study described how social work students in a gay–straight alliance and in a National Association of Christian Social Workers chapter who were engaged in deep conflict with one another chose to work with Aldredge to develop and then take a sociodrama course designed to help them resolve the tensions. Ultimately, these students discovered their commonalities and joined together to create a piece of art that incorporated a rainbow and biblical verses, which they placed in their student lounge as a public representation of their bridge-building.

What Remains to Be Done: Recommendations

The chapters in this book offer the social work profession a number of recommendations and next steps in the areas of education, law, ethics, research, and practice. Many of the authors recommended that faculty members provide religiously conservative Christian students, who may have experienced negative socialization with regard to LGB people, with opportunities for new learning. First and foremost, this educational environment must be safe and one that promotes self-exploration and self-reflection (Dessel, 2014). Possibilities for doing so follow:

- Use of classroom guidelines that can be developed by the group (Deal & Hyde, 2004)
- Communication practices such as the LARA (Listen, Affirm, Add, Respond) method of active listening (Rosenberg, 2003)
- Use of icebreakers, personal narrative sharing, and working in dyads and small groups (Adams, Bell, & Griffin, 2007; Zúñiga, Nagda, Chesler, & Cytron-Walker, 2007)
- Attention to physical space, such as circle seating arrangements, and participation in experiential activities by both students and instructor (Adams et al., 2007; Dessel)

When such an environment is created, this learning should focus on the following areas:

- Tensions between personal values, professional ethics, and social work's emphasis on separating personal values from one's professional self (Chonody et al.; Reamer; Tan; Walls & Seelman).
- Negative consequences of biased belief systems in social work practice (Chonody et al.; DeVore & Blumenfeld; Swank & Fahs; Walls & Seelman).
- Recognition of society's structural inequalities with regard to sexual orientation (Dessel, Shepardson, & Bolen; Swank & Fahs; Walls & Todd).
- Antiheterosexist practices in social work (Chonody et al.).
- Heterosexist privilege (Miles et al.; Swank & Fahs; Walls & Todd).
- Christian privilege (Walls & Seelman; Walls & Todd).
- Exploration of perceived threats to Christian identity in order to counter assumptions and support fears surrounding loss of privilege (Walls & Seelman).
- The role of syncretism, whereby Christians exhibit differing degrees of adherence to religious tenets and to the tenets they recognize as primary. For example, Christians may decide to align their belief system with biblical tenets that are also reflected in social work values, such as combatting oppression, treating others with dignity and respect, and

pursuing social justice (Chonody et al.; Walls & Seelman; Woodford, Walls, & Levy, 2012).

- Deconstruction, redefinition, and reclaiming of biblical interpretations of same-sex sexuality (Walls & Todd).
- Understanding social work ethics of diversity, social justice, and nondiscrimination (Reamer).
- Christian faith and its role in social work (Brice; Drumm et al.; Tan).
- Information about sexual development, sexual orientation (Drumm et al.), and similarities and differences in brain architecture among gay and lesbian individuals and male and female heterosexuals (Garrett, 2009).
- Management of emotional hot buttons (or triggers) (Walls & Todd).
- Cross-religious and denominational dialogues to raise awareness of religious diversity and recognition of Christian dominance (Walls & Todd).

Certain actions can also be initiated in schools of social work to promote safety, support, and understanding, such as the following:

- Use of Christian caucus groups to provide students with greater safety and support in exploring tensions related to LGB affirmation (Walls & Todd)
- Implementation of intergroup dialogue pedagogy (Dessel; Miles et al.) and drama-based teaching methods (Aldredge)
- Implementation of gay–straight alliances in schools of social work (Aldredge)

Additional recommendations for faculty members include the need to critically examine their own homophobia or bias against conservative Christian religions and discomfort with conflict in the classroom around these tensions, and to gain skills in negotiating and teaching about these tensions (Aldredge; Bolen & Dessel; Drumm et al.; Miles et al.; Swank & Fahs). Christian-identified instructors who have done their own work on Christian privilege and can speak the language of the faith tradition while challenging Christian students to be accountable (Walls & Todd) can act as mentors to Christian students who are on their own journey. Faculty members can also provide exposure to Christian LGBT advocates (Drumm et al.).

Additional practice, law, and research recommendations include the following:

- Engaging clergy in this work of bridge building (Levy).
- Leveraging Christian theology and power in antioppression work in order to use Christian privilege and resources to further this work (Drumm et al.; Walls & Todd).
- Not allowing religious legal exemptions for participation in nonreligious activities such as professional service delivery (Kaplan; Reamer).
- Engaging in rigorous research on the experiences of Christian social workers (Bolen & Dessel; Swank & Fahs). For example, future research may seek to explore how beliefs may translate into practice behavior and what effect, if any, this may have on gay-affirmative practice (Chonody et al.).

Concluding Thoughts

The authors of the chapters in this book frequently talked with us about how challenging or transformative the experience of writing their chapter was for them. We experienced these feelings also as we reviewed chapters and wrote our own. One of the most important outcomes was the recognition that we could and should hold LGB social workers, conservative Christian social workers, and those social workers holding a bias against either LGB or conservative Christian people accountable for acting in accordance with the NASW Code of Ethics and social work values of equality and nondiscrimination. When acting professionally, social workers are bound by the Code of Ethics to eschew personal beliefs in favor of professional values. Social workers work with many different populations representing very different beliefs, behaviors, and problems. We are not a profession that cherry picks its clients. Instead, we are mandated to work with all people, with a particular emphasis on those who are oppressed. In this society, and in some schools of social work, LGB people are an oppressed group.

As many of these chapters discussed, change is possible, even for the most conservative Christian social workers, even while still holding onto their strong Christian identities. Therefore, social work educators have a charge to work with these and other social work students with a privileged status in society to facilitate the students' understanding of their privileged status and the effects of such privilege on marginalized groups, including LGB people. Educators also need to provide Christian-identified students with education, support, and role models for how they can change while still retaining a strong Christian identity.

This, then, is the fundamental message of this book: that no social workers are above the NASW Code of Ethics, including certain conservative Christians or others who hold biases against specific marginalized populations. Social workers should respond to conservative Christian clients by recognizing their right to their own belief systems, but social work educators need to respond to conservative Christian social work students or faculty members by expecting them to uphold social work values and ethics in working with clients and pursuing social justice and equality. With social work students, the educator's role is clearly stated in the Council on Social Work Education (CSWE) accreditation standards, in which students are to be exposed to different types of diversity, sensitized to privilege, oppression, and discrimination, and inculcated into the values and ethics of social work.

Finally, faculty members need to seek out their own learning and skill development with regard to these issues. This book provides resources to move this learning forward. Social work faculty members are charged with an important responsibility to create educational climates that challenge the status quo with regard to oppression, discrimination, and equality. Religious and sexual orientation identities need not be in conflict with each other. Resolving these tensions will free up important resources to combat many other serious social problems.

Maya Angelou, whose indelible spirit passed recently from us, was asked many years ago how she hoped to be remembered. The following was her response.

> What I would really like said about me is that I dared to love. By love I mean that condition in the human spirit so profound, it encourages us to

develop courage and build bridges, and then to trust those bridges and cross the bridges in attempts to reach other human beings.

As we and our invited authors have discussed the tension in social work between LGB people and those holding negative religious beliefs about same-sex sexuality, and have offered ways to bring these groups together, we invite you to remember this quotation. The greatest praise this book could receive is that it was part of the initial effort to build bridges between these groups and then to trust the power of dialogue to bring these groups together toward the common goal of eliminating oppression and discrimination of all kind.

References

Adams, M., Bell, L. A., & Griffin, P. (2007). *Teaching for diversity and social justice.* New York, NY: Routledge.

Berkman, C. S., & Zinberg, G. (1997). Homophobia and heterosexism in social workers. *Social Work, 42,* 319–332. doi:10.1093/sw/42.4.319

Crisp, C. (2007). Correlates of homophobia and use of gay affirmative practice among social workers. *Journal of Human Behavior in the Social Environment, 14*(4), 119–143. doi:10.1300/J137v14n04_06

Deal, K., & Hyde, C. (2004). Understanding MSW student anxiety and resistance to multicultural learning, *Journal of Teaching in Social Work, 24*(1–2), 73–86. doi:10.1300/J067v24n01_05

Garrett, B. (2009). *Brain & behavior: An introduction to biological psychology* (2nd ed.). Los Angeles, CA: SAGE.

Griffin, S., Brown, M., & Warren, N. (2012). Critical education in high schools: The promise and challenges of intergroup dialogue. *Equity & Excellence in Education, 45*(1), 159–180. doi:10.1080/10665684.2012.641868

Gurin, P., Nagda, B. A., & Zúñiga, X. (2013). *Engaging race and gender: Intergroup dialogues in higher education.* New York, NY: Russell Sage Foundation. doi:10.1093/sw/50.3.207

Hodge, D. (2005). Epistemological frameworks, homosexuality, and religion: How people of faith understand the intersection between homosexuality and religion. *Social Work, 50,* 207–218. doi:10.1093/sw/50.3.207

Jayakumar, U. M. (2009). The invisible rainbow in diversity: Factors influencing sexual prejudice among college students. *Journal of Homosexuality, 56,* 675–700. doi:10.1080/00918360903054095

Krieglstein, M. (2003). Heterosexism and social work: An ethical issue. *Journal of Human Behavior in the Social Environment, 8*(2/3), 75–91. doi:10.1300/J137v08n02_05

Miller, J., & Donner, S. (2000). More than just talk: The use of racial dialogues to combat racism. *Social Work With Groups, 23,* 31–53. doi:10.1300/J009v23n01_03

Newman, B., Dannenfelser, P., & Benishek, L. (2002). Assessing beginning social work and counseling students' acceptance of lesbian and gay men. *Journal of Social Work Education, 38,* 273–288.

Raiz, L., & Saltzburg, S. (2007). Developing awareness of the subtleties of heterosexism and homophobia among undergraduate, heterosexual social work majors. *Journal of Baccalaureate Social Work, 12*(2), 53–69.

Ressler, L., & Hodge, D. (2003). Silenced voices: Social work and the oppression of conservative narratives. *Social Thought: Journal of Religion in the Social Services, 22*(1), 125–142.

Richards-Schuster, K., & Aldana, A. (2013). Learning to speak out about racism: Youths' insights on participation in an intergroup dialogues program. *Social Work With Groups, 36,* 332–348. doi:10.1080/01609513.2013.763327

Rosenberg, M. (2003). *Nonviolent communication: A language of life.* Encinitas, CA: Puddledancer Press.

Ryan, S. (2000). Examining social workers' placement recommendations of children with gay and lesbian adoptive parents. *Families in Society, 81,* 517–528. doi: 10.1606/1044-3894.1053

Seelman, K. L., & Walls, N. E. (2010). Person–organization incongruence as a predictor of right-wing authoritarianism, social dominance orientation, and heterosexism. *Journal of Social Work Education, 46,* 103–121. doi:10.5175/JSWE.2010.200800082

Thyer, B., & Myers, L. (2009). Religion discrimination in social work academic programs: Whither social justice? *Journal of Religion & Spirituality in Social Work: Social Thought, 28,* 144–160. doi:10.1080/15426430802644172

Trolander, J. (1997). Fighting racism and sexism: The Council on Social Work Education. *Social Service Review, 71,* 110–134. doi:10.1086/604233

Whitley, B. E. (2009). Religiosity and attitudes toward lesbians and gay men: A meta-analysis. *International Journal for the Psychology of Religion, 19,* 21–38. doi:10.1080/10508610802471104

Wilkinson, W. W. (2004). Religiosity, authoritarianism, and homophobia: A multidimensional approach. *International Journal for the Psychology of Religion, 14,* 55–67. doi:10.1207/s15327582ijpr1401_5

Woodford, M. R., Walls, N. E., & Levy, D. (2012). Religion and endorsement for same-sex marriage: Role of syncretism between church teaching and personal beliefs. *Interdisciplinary Journal for Research on Religion, 8,* Article 4.

Zúñiga, X., Nagda, B. A., Chesler, M., & Cytron-Walker, A. (2007). Intergroup dialogue in higher education: Meaningful learning about social justice. *ASHE Higher Education Report, 32*(4), 1–128.

Note

1. The beta coefficients (interpreted like a correlation) between evangelical Christian identity and hostile or aversive heterosexism approached 1.0. Thus, there was no possibility of mediation because the independent variable and potential mediating variable were essentially measuring the same thing (i.e., all or almost all of those with a strong evangelical Christian identity also scored very high on the heterosexism scales). Although the beta coefficient between the right-wing authoritarianism scale and evangelical Christian identity was not quite as strong, it was sufficiently strong that it would have difficulty acting as a mediator between evangelical Christian identity and cultural incongruity.

Index

About the Editors

Adrienne B. Dessel

Adrienne Dessel, PhD, LMSW, is associate director of the Program on Intergroup Relations and lecturer in the School of Social Work at the University of Michigan. She has an MSW from Simmons College and a PhD in social work from the University of Tennessee. She worked for more than 20 years providing clinical and community-based services to diverse client populations and organizations and has worked with school systems in Massachusetts, Pennsylvania, Tennessee, and Michigan. In her current position Dr. Dessel provides administrative and curriculum leadership and consultations to faculty and staff. She also teaches courses on intergroup dialogue facilitation, the social psychology of prejudice and intergroup relations, and global conflict and coexistence. Her community consultations include social justice education for public school teachers and evaluation of LGBT education services. Her research focuses on prejudice reduction, intergroup dialogue processes and outcomes related to topics of Arab–Jewish conflict, religion and sexual orientation and gender, and intergroup dialogue facilitator learning.

Rebecca M. Bolen

Rebecca M. Bolen, PhD, is associate professor at the University of Tennessee College of Social Work. She taught as an assistant professor at Boston University, receiving tenure before moving to the University of Tennessee. Dr. Bolen received her PhD from the University of Texas at Arlington and her MSSW from the University of Tennessee. Her primary research focus is child sexual abuse and female victimization, with a more specific interest in nonoffending parents of sexually abused children. Within these areas she is particularly interested in rectifying oppressive perceptions of female nonoffending caregivers of sexually abused children and the ways in which these caregivers experience discrimination from the powerful and hierarchical institutions that intervene in the abuse. Much of Dr. Bolen's research and writing focuses on a better understanding of the experiences of these caregivers and providing more sensitive measures of assessment. In this area she has conducted several studies, written multiple articles, and given numerous presentations. The similarity in power dynamics between investigations into child sexual abuse, in which the powerful child welfare system often blames the female nonoffending caregiver for the abuse, and the tension between conservative Christian beliefs and LGB people, in which the more powerful conservative Christian religions build into their doctrines the oppression and discrimination of LGB people, led to her interest in the latter.